SELECTED WRITINGS ON RACE AND DIFFERENCE

Stuart Hall: Selected Writings
A series edited by Catherine Hall and Bill Schwarz

SELECTED WRITINGS ON RACE AND DIFFERENCE

Edited by **Paul Gilroy** and **Ruth Wilson Gilmore**

Stuart Hall

DUKE UNIVERSITY PRESS | DURHAM AND LONDON | 2021

All essays © Stuart Hall Estate
All other material © 2021, Duke University Press
Printed in the United States of America on acid-free paper ∞
Designed by Amy Ruth Buchanan
Typeset in Minion Pro by Westchester Publishing Services

Library of Congress Cataloging-in-Publication Data
Names: Hall, Stuart, 1932–2014, author. | Gilroy, Paul, [date] editor. | Gilmore, Ruth Wilson, [date] editor. | Hall, Stuart, 1932–2014. Works. Selections. 2016.
Title: Selected writings on race and difference / Stuart Hall ; edited by Paul Gilroy and Ruth Wilson Gilmore.
Description: Durham : Duke University Press, 2021. | Series: Stuart hall: selected writings | Includes index.
Identifiers: LCCN 2020021829 (print)
LCCN 2020021830 (ebook)
ISBN 9781478010524 (hardcover)
ISBN 9781478011668 (paperback)
ISBN 9781478021223 (ebook)
Subjects: LCSH: Hall, Stuart, 1932–2014—Political and social views. | Race. | Multiculturalism.
Classification: LCC HT1523.H355 2021 (print) | LCC HT1523 (ebook) | DDC 305.8—DC23
LC record available at https://lccn.loc.gov/2020021829
LC ebook record available at https://lccn.loc.gov/2020021830

Cover art: Photo of Stuart Hall by Eamonn McCabe / Popperfoto via Getty Images

CONTENTS

vii   Acknowledgments

1   Introduction: Race Is the Prism
Paul Gilroy

Part I | RIOTS, RACE, AND REPRESENTATION

23   **ONE** Absolute Beginnings: Reflections on the Secondary Modern Generation [1959]

42   **TWO** The Young Englanders [1967]

51   **THREE** Black Men, White Media [1974]

56   **FOUR** Race and "Moral Panics" in Postwar Britain [1978]

71   **FIVE** Summer in the City [1981]

78   **SIX** Drifting into a Law and Order Society: The 1979 Cobden Trust Human Rights Day Lecture [1980]

97   **SEVEN** The Whites of Their Eyes: Racist Ideologies and the Media [1981]

Part II | THE POLITICS OF INTELLECTUAL WORK AGAINST RACISM

123   **EIGHT** Teaching Race [1980]

136   **NINE** Pluralism, Race and Class in Caribbean Society [1977]

161   **TEN** "Africa" Is Alive and Well in the Diaspora: Cultures of Resistance: Slavery, Religious Revival and Political Cultism in Jamaica [1975]

195	ELEVEN	Race, Articulation and Societies Structured in Dominance [1980]
246	TWELVE	New Ethnicities [1988]
257	THIRTEEN	Cultural Identity and Diaspora [1990]
272	FOURTEEN	C. L. R. James: A Portrait [1992]
286	FIFTEEN	Calypso Kings [2002]

Part III | CULTURAL AND MULTICULTURAL QUESTIONS

295	SIXTEEN	Gramsci's Relevance for the Study of Race and Ethnicity [1986]
329	SEVENTEEN	Subjects in History: Making Diasporic Identities [1998]
339	EIGHTEEN	Why Fanon? [1996]
359	NINETEEN	Race, the Floating Signifier: What More Is There to Say about "Race"? [1997]
374	TWENTY	"In but Not of Europe": Europe and Its Myths [2002/2003]
386	TWENTY-ONE	Cosmopolitan Promises, Multicultural Realities [2006]
409	TWENTY-TWO	The Multicultural Question [2000]

435	Index
453	Place of First Publication

ACKNOWLEDGMENTS

I should like to thank a few people. More than thirty years ago, Stuart Hall shared many hours with me in cafés and his kitchen, while we talked at great length about what a book containing some of the pieces in this volume might look like. Two doctoral students—Hilary Wilson and Patrick DeDauw—provided excellent research and editorial assistance. Paul Gilroy invited me to collaborate on this project; I am grateful above all for his friendship. And thank you, Craig Gilmore, for everything else.
 —*Ruth Wilson Gilmore*

INTRODUCTION | Paul Gilroy

Race Is the Prism

The biography of Stuart Hall is well known. It need not be rehearsed again here. His valuable writings have circulated around the world over a very long period of time, drawing responses from all directions and disciplines. The work has been reexamined in detail since his death by readers eager to learn from him and to absorb his many insights into the complexities of our present crisis. Yet I have occasionally overheard very sophisticated academics amusing each other with stories of their surprise at finding out Stuart Hall was a black man who had been born in Jamaica. Those pretended epiphanies unsettled me. It would be unwise to overinterpret casual comments of that sort, but discovering Hall's Caribbean origins or migrant identity could be a shock only in a world where the mission of black intellectuals remains impossible, where being a black intellectual is unimaginable: a freakish possibility. Not only were those silly, shameless remarks premised on an extraordinary ignorance of the breadth of Hall's concerns, commitments, and interests; they were also symptoms of a more widespread and telling failure to understand his political formation and trajectory.

This anthology is intended to encourage an entirely different approach. It begins from the provocative possibility that reckoning with the place of race and racism in Hall's thought is indispensable for coming to terms with the meaning and the politics of his intellectual work as a whole. Since his passing, the resurgence of authoritarian and ultranationalist populisms, to which racism remains integral, confirms that the dynamic, potent effect of appeals to race, and the mobilization of racist discourses, needs to be better understood. Race is, as Hall memorably puts it, a "floating signifier." It is also the highly charged matter of political ontology, located at the epicenter of our volatile environment bounded by nationalism and civilizationism.

The question of how analysis of racial formations might be lodged within the larger architecture of Hall's perspectives on critical and cultural theory has acquired greater importance as his intellectual legacies have congealed. Clarification of the difficult conceptual and interpretative issues raised by racism and the politics of race promises more than just a better grasp of the course of Hall's own thought and the critiques of liberal piety on racial matters that he delivered so inspiringly and energetically from the Left. It can illuminate his shifting relationship with the spectrum of socialist politics, with the New Left, Marxism, and feminism, as well as the international Black Power movement and the ongoing processes of decolonization that were unfolding in Africa, the Caribbean, and elsewhere. These pieces can be read first for the way that they reveal him acquiring a sense of the historical and epistemological significance of racism and race, and then for his eloquent attempts to persuade his readers of their signal political importance.[1]

That way of proceeding affirms the wisdom in not approaching "race" as a separate, freestanding topic but focusing instead on the racism that animates and mobilizes races dynamically, and almost always violently. The problems that converge under those vexed headings can then be used to assemble an apparatus for thinking critically about a number of interrelated issues: culture, power, democracy, and the partial, abbreviated forms of justice and freedom that race-friendly capitalism allows. For Hall, analyzing racism and race in that way helps to identify the seams that separate critical knowledge from traditional knowledge. It can foster an expansive politics of intellectual work, inside and outside universities. Racism is not another layer of misery to be logged and added to the dismal effects of other social processes. It has a constitutive power. It shapes and determines economic and political relations. We can learn to look at history, culture, economic and social relations through the frame it affords us.

Hall discovers and then repeats his enthusiasm for the idea that race has provided "a prism" through which (British) people are "called upon to 'live through' to understand, and then to deal with crisis conditions."[2] The idea of race provides "one of the most important ways of understanding how this society works and how it has arrived at where it is. It is one of the most important keys, not to the margins of society," but offers insight "right into its dynamic centre."³ In conjunction with Hall's scrupulous commitment to historically informed analysis of concrete situations, in other words to commentary produced in tune with the expectation that it will, in time, become intelligible as counterhistory, this approach represents something like a methodological postulate. The distinctive "general syntax" of racisms must, of course, be understood in all its performative complexity.⁴ Their protean capabilities must be scrupulously periodized, but the promiscuous effects of this "scavenger ideology" are laid bare by detailed historical study and should not be brushed aside.⁵

As far as British history is concerned, these texts help to trace the evolution of Hall's concern with racism and the effects of racialized inequality from the era of Suez and the Campaign for Nuclear Disarmament, through Enoch Powell's cataclysmic "Rivers of Blood" and beyond to the righteous riots of the 1980s, into the artistic bloom of Britain's Black Arts movement during the 1990s, the multiculture debates of the Tony Blair years and the crisis of neoliberal culture and society that followed. If that provincial genealogy supplies an immediate context for Hall's serial commentaries and critiques, it should also be clear that his thinking evolved in a transnational, "diasporic" conversation with the work of other black writers drawn from various languages, locations, and generations. Caribbean travelers, "in but not of Europe," like C. L. R. James, Frantz Fanon, George Lamming, Kamau Brathwaite, Sylvia Wynter, Andrew Salkey, Marion O'Callaghan, and John LaRose, are only the most obvious figures whose journeys into, through, and beyond European thought in general and Marxism in particular might now help to illuminate and explain Hall's own path. Their achievements, creative and radical, supply constant points of reference in the dialogical motion of his voice as it drifts in and out of its teacherly register.

This archive also shows how the urgently political aspects of Hall's writing are connected to the more elaborate theoretical positions and concerns that underpinned them and how they can continue to be useful. Their ongoing relevance is less a matter of elevating the interventionist pieces to a theoretical altitude where they were not originally intended to function and more about the slow labor of tacking between the different instances of reflection—concrete, abstract, concrete in abstract—that, when understood in concert, can bring alive his unique perspective and conceptual system. Tracking and reconstructing that shuttling movement reveals all the care and energy that he directed toward the goals of catalyzing and nourishing new cohorts of political intellectuals. They could be brought together by the critical study of racial orders, hierarchies, representations, and signs. As the British Black Arts movement began to flourish and to amplify the emergent political voices and artistic achievements of the children and grandchildren of the 1950s settlers, it became obvious that this mode of education was far from a narrowly academic matter.

Hall's characteristic approach to theoretical matters is set out rigorously in the better-known position papers included here, especially the essays that were aimed primarily at academic debates and remote or cosmopolitan constituencies like UNESCO.[6] Those dispersed readerships, outside the anglosphere, seem to have encouraged him to experiment and take the greater intellectual and political risks that his more usual Left milieux would not so easily accommodate. His engagements with Marxism and post-Marxism are deep, his employment of sociological reasoning fluctuates creatively, and his range of references is exceptionally wide. Disciplinary boundaries are breached with a chuckle. Poets jostle with filmmakers and philosophers to demonstrate the insubordinate agency of culture in the sham stability of formal politics. Colin MacInnes, whose London fiction is discussed in the opening essay here, is cited again when one of his later and more obscure novels, *Westward to Laughter*, pops up in the context of Hall's lucid commentary on Caribbean pluralism.[7] A large number of rhetorical tones are immediately audible: the serious, if decidedly ambivalent intellectual commentator, the cultural translator, the teacher, the unrepentant activist, the insightful critic, and the partisan reporter are a few of them. Hall's writing speaks to all of the discrepant constituencies suggested by those contending labels. Those groupings enjoyed varying appetites for the "jouissance of theory"[8] and the practical political tasks of immediate action, especially in difficult institutional and governmental settings like the broadcast media and the criminal justice system. The attention devoted to lived culture fosters the ability to see not only how those fields overlapped but how they were articulated together, bonded expressively by the iteration of potent racial tropes and symbols. Hall's focus on the role of the media was innovative and influential. Several pieces in this volume show that he was the first academic to identify the systematic construction and structural configuration of racist discourse in Britain's media (mis)representations as well as to highlight the reproduction of racism as common sense. This aspect of his work developed an analysis of the political problems that arose with the stereotyping of black figures beyond the boundaries of news and current affairs television.

By encountering Hall's work in a rough historical sequence and reading these texts as one extended body, we hope that, as his intellectual preoccupations, passions, and symptoms emerge, these essays, articles, and talks will be understood differently. Their primary objects, race and racism, are no longer marginal. They cannot be reduced either to the machinations of capitalist economic life or the melancholy drama of postcolonial psychopolitics. Their mutual assemblage *on the terrain of culture* challenges the reader to adopt a difficult interpretative angle capable of capturing the ceaseless interplay of material interests with racial signs, structures, and systems as well as the trauma of racialized suffering.

These writings readily reveal that the arc of Hall's political imagination did not bend in one direction only, from the properly academic and the authentically militant, down toward the frothily cultural. Instead, his interventions and commentaries seek out moments and problems that convey the urgency, and the value, of taking the neglected fields of culture and representation much more seriously than the dour cults of the British Left would usually permit. The politics of racism and race supplies Hall with trials and tests that can synchronize and sometimes unify his various perspectives and accents. This coordination directs readers to the adjacent problem of how his extensive reflections on racial division may have shaped his analyses of culture, ideology, and discourse or guided his approach to capitalism's mystified kinds of domination and subordination. They are asked to think about how his relentless engagement with the exploitative systems, symbolic dreamscapes, and psychological fantasies on which the racially ordered world relies might have conditioned his innovative approach to what he terms the problem of articulation. How did Hall's analysis of Caribbean and South African social and economic relations inform his observations on multiculture and multiculturalism found elsewhere?[9] These are not entirely abstract inquiries. They remain important for how Britain's "indigenous" racism is to be interpreted, for how it might be undone, and for contemporary debates over exactly how the post-1945 history of Britain's movement for justice and against racism is going to be written.

Apart from his close familiarity with the impossible possibilities raised by the unmapped intellectual heritage of the Caribbean, Stuart Hall was a consistent if irregular participant in the public culture forged by black and antiracist movements in the United Kingdom during more than five decades.[10] These texts help to survey his contribution to those discussions, but they are only a small, indicative selection. Firmly localized concerns with injustice, antiracism, and racialized representation have been braided together with more general conceptual statements. Each dimension enhances and offsets the others to form a whole, but never a final, political interpretation. Here again, the last instance never arrives. In that process of deferral, racism is pluralized and becomes an object worthy of critical investigation rather than some transient, diverting illustration of how ideology can function as a material historical force.

The less familiar pieces gathered here were first printed in a range of ephemeral publications. They stretch from the output of groupings like the Caribbean Artists Movement[11] and the National Association for Multicultural Education to the public outreach organs of the failing Kinnockite Labour Party as it struggled in vain to make itself less doctrinaire and parochial in response to the gains of Thatcherism.[12]

Without reconstructing the debates that were conducted within and around Britain's movement against racism at the time, we may say that these interventions and commentaries tacitly enacted an important change of perspective. They suggest that struggles against racism and racial hierarchy can productively be understood as contributions to the salvaging and consolidation of Europe's ebbing democracies. This was possible even as the looming effects of national democracy's divorce from global capitalism began to be evident. In that dwindling civic light, holding the police to account for the systematic misuse of power revealed in their perennial conflict with Britain's black citizen/settlers was not simply or exclusively a matter of concern to racialized minorities, to blacks and other ethnic groups. Those campaigns offered a precious opportunity to imagine, and sometimes to conduct, justice differently: in proximity to the vital politics of truth and rights. It became possible, for example, to ask what law and legitimacy should be outside of their monochromatic coding in abject black and superior white. Analyzing racism could not be stabilized or formalized as a disinterested academic pastime. It carried with it the onerous abiding obligation to specify how a world unshackled from the cruel constraints of racial hierarchy might actually differ from the present tainted arrangements.

Whether focused acutely on politics or policy, many of the resulting battles sought the extension of democracy. Their demands were enhanced by the images of social transformation that had been pending in racism's repudiation and could be glimpsed in its occasional momentary overcoming. That utopia is not captured in the ideal of colorblindness. It aspired not just to vague reform and reconstruction in the name of enhanced equality of opportunity or what we might now call a corporate McKinsey version of multiculturalism but explicitly to a reconstructed socialism and to what the feminist political culture of forty years ago described as the projection of politics in prefigurative forms.[13] These were political strategies that could identify and thereby hasten alternative ways of living, (inter)acting, and governing. Today, those elusive possibilities can provide encouragement for historical assessments of race and politics that aim to take critical reflection beyond the necessary but insufficient task of repetitively tracing the familiar debilitating outlines of Europe's postcolonial crisis.

Black movements in pursuit of freedom, justice, and independence initially developed from the brutal experience of enslaved, exploited imperial subjects and colonial peoples. Via abolitionism and anti-imperialist struggles, they expanded into a broader pursuit of equality, liberation, and a world purged of capitalist exploitation and racial hierarchy alike. Sometimes those hopes were rooted in religious outlooks, sometimes in communist schemes; at other times, their motivation was entirely profane, practical, or urgently defensive. The social and political movement against racial hierarchy that resulted from those alignments may be muted these days, but the residual glow from these pieces suggests that it might yet be revitalized.

Stuart Hall was, among his other inclinations, a movement intellectual. He was alert to the ways in which the early phases of anticolonial action conditioned later responses to the British Empire's thwarted postimperial settlement. His insistence on culture as a lived relation encouraged examination of how Britain's chronic crisis was played out in and through race. Thus he was able to identify the core dynamics of an authoritarian, populist nationalism in which attachment to the comforting idea of unbridgeable, absolute racial difference has proved both fundamental and enduring. The resulting conflicts have now extended across several generations and been expanded to incorporate settlers, migrants, and refugees from all the corners of what was once Britain's planetary colonial dominion.

Among young activists today there is considerable hostility toward the idea of black as a political color accessible to all nonwhites, especially those who had been victims of Europe's colonial and imperial adventures. In that climate, there is real danger that Hall's apparently old-fashioned view of race politics will be harshly judged because it fails to coincide with the contemporary taste for essentialist self-scrutiny and the accompanying retreat of antiracism into the private interpersonal world beloved of Instagram warriors who dream that racial structures and habits can be overthrown by online gestures alone. Mainstream visibility and inclusion are not the final frontiers of antiracist politics, nor is "self-care" among the ultimate obligations of a black revolution. What Hall calls the "political roof" provided by that open, now anachronistic notion of blackness is an important part of what remains at stake in these proceedings.[14] The idea that black is not a phenotype or a physical description but, rather, an identity and collectivity assembled in adverse circumstances and conditioned by the effects of systematic racism may no longer correspond to the brittle edifice of contemporary black struggle. However, the effort historically to understand how and why black politics in Britain assumed an ecumenical configuration is now a valuable learning opportunity. That act of imagination and solidarity can itself be educative. It can usefully reacquaint us with the combative mentality required if the cause of antiracism is to be redeemed from the twin seductions of narcissism and nihilism that have dominated it of late.

At home, racism, nativism, and xenophobia have been bolstered by learned ignorance of imperial history and a media ecology premised on the idea that blacks are an alien presence that had been foisted on a perennially innocent nation by its duplicitous political leadership. Hostility to the black presence was generated by fantasies of grave injury to national homogeneity and indigenous white pride. Exclusionary violence was answered by a combative outlook wrought, by young blacks in particular, from fragments of the dissident Ethiopianism of the Caribbean diaspora. Drawing on that structure of feeling from the rougher end of the poor educational deal Britain offered to all its working-class youth, the forces that the poet Linton Kwesi Johnson has identified as "the rebel generation" challenged what could count as worthwhile historically rooted knowledge. In the process, they reaffirmed an anticolonial tradition specified in a selection of mostly Jamaican political ancestors: Nanny, Paul Bogle, Marcus Garvey, Norman Manley. In time, that pantheon would be supplemented by additional heroic figures drawn from US Black Power and southern Africa's liberation struggles. Most important, the memory of Atlantic slavery was mobilized to infuse new chapters of dissidence with those bloody modern histories of resistance and rebellion. A second element, which is essential for understanding Hall's particular contribution, communicated the primary importance of policing and criminal justice in the everyday lives of settlers faced with apparently intractable institutional racism. These bold dispositions were animated by a critique of capitalism that, thanks to the cultural accent it gained from Hall's elegant expansion of the Gramscian vocabulary, remains useful today, even as capitalism has evolved and assumed novel, unprecedented psychopolitical and technological patterns that cannot be accessed via the unamended nineteenth-century political language of class exploitation and uniformity.

This selection demonstrates that Hall's work was implicated in several phases of a long conflict that it helps both to chronicle and to explain. That continuing history has produced some small temporary victories in the bitter sequence of defeats that marks out Britain's relentless transformation from a partly social democratic nation to a much less equal society saturated with neoliberal common sense.

Like the other Caribbean incomers of his generation, Hall felt Britain resound to the shocks that followed the discomforting reduction of its global power and reach. The country's postimperial diminution was conveyed by the largely unwelcome appearance of citizen/settlers from the half-known tropical edges of the old empire. They bore the sacred dark blue passports that qualified them officially for belonging, but they were doomed by their unsought immersion in the country's interminable quarrels with itself along the irreparable rifts of class, region, generation, sexuality, and gender.

The incomers had their precious colonial citizenship stripped from them by Left and Right governments alike. Their battles to restore dignity, secure recognition, and transform justice gradually yielded to the malign effects of globalization and were swamped by the austere experiment in virtual and networked social life we see today, triangulated by the imperatives of privatization, militarization, and financialization. However, the warm, active imprint of earlier conflicts can be detected in the damage that is still being done by the characteristically British blend of racism with amnesiac nationalism that Hall saw as the motor for the nation's distinctive pathological racism.

His writing on race and difference now offers a welcome opportunity to re-endow an insurgent history of postcolonial settlement in the regressive order to which we are in danger of becoming resigned. It bears repetition that loud, radical demands for justice recurred at the center of more than half a century of opposition and resistance. Policing and unjust law were important foci for the militant political energy released by Britain's growing black communities. Much of that bleak history has not passed through the filters that determine and fragment the contents of the digital archive. Indeed, that archive may now have been forsaken in favor of more spectacular viral narratives of cruelty, triumph, and uplift sourced from African American culture and experience. However, it can be salvaged and retains the power to deliver an insightful understanding of power and statecraft centered on the contested meaning of racialized difference and the changing political currency of racism, both overt and inferential.

One key mechanism in the metabolism of Britain's indigenous racism was the repatriation of colonial habits to the no-longer-imperial core. Government in the colonies differed markedly from the standard metropolitan arrangements. The colony revealed, as Fanon had seen, distinctive, "exceptional" ways in which power was both spatialized and militarized. We have now learned the hard way that Europe's colonies functioned as laboratories not just for biometric police-craft like fingerprinting but for innovative legal and commercial instruments as well as enhanced varieties of killing technology. We are less well acquainted with the way that the spaces of death emanating from those brutally compartmentalized colonial orders incubated anticolonial demands for a reparative justice that were pitched against the cruel abuses of imperial exploitation made legitimate by racial hierarchy. In the aftermath of conquest, colonial locations were administered through the closest of alignments between police and military powers. Hall saw that intimate association being brought back home and applied organically to management of the principal urban areas of black settlement that were perceived increasingly as repositories of alien social and cultural pathology.

As formal decolonization was transacted in Britain, the Trojan horse of New Commonwealth immigration was thought to have accomplished the invasive task that the Nazis had not been able to complete. The incorrigible patterns of colonial mismanagement appeared again, this time inside the grimy gray fortifications of downwardly mobile overdevelopment. The ranks of London's Metropolitan Police were certainly swollen with ex-military personnel back home from their cold wars against insurgents, communists, and terrorists, but the problems ran deeper still: into a culture of impunity warranted by colonial mentalities that routinely saw blacks as infrahuman and therefore expendable regardless of their formal citizenship status. This was the period in which blackness and immigration were rendered synonymous. That knotted association has had awful consequences that still haunt populist politics in the United Kingdom. So far, the resulting tangle has proved impossible either to cut or undo.

It is important to bear in mind that Hall's sense of politics led him to contribute in different ways to several community-based inquiries into police conduct, institutional racism, and criminal justice. Most notably, these were *Southall 23 April 1979*, the National Council for Civil Liberties (NCCL) report into the west London police riot; *Policing in Hackney 1945–1984*, the Family Support Committee independent inquiry report into the policing of Stoke Newington; and *A Different Reality*, the West Midlands community inquiry into the Handsworth riots of 1986. Those key documents are not, at the time of writing, available online, but they are nonetheless essential for any serious historical analysis of this pivotal period in British political life.

In a sharp contrast to the ambitions of those later publications, the police "Nigger Hunts" of the 1950s and 1960s had been modestly chronicled by respectable campaigning groups like the West Indian Standing Conference and the Colonial Ex-servicemen's and Women's Association.[15] These early organizations were often shaped by a sense of belonging and dignity deriving from the military labor of the "*Windrush* generation" in the Second World War. Like the Indian and Pakistani Workers' Associations, these bodies were imprinted with the trade unions, leftist and communist traditions that incomers had acquired in the formerly colonial zones. The community organizations created by the entitled citizen/settlers were initially content merely to enumerate police wrongdoing and structural bias in the operations of criminal justice, education, and housing, public and private. It took some years for them to adjust their conceptions of belonging and move beyond the task of documenting systematic discrimination. Gradually, they began to define altogether different juridical conceptions of equality that would be dissociated from racial hierarchy and capable of sustaining campaigns for the accountability and transformation of state power in general and police power in particular. It was even longer before those bold dispositions could breach the fiercely defended conventions of British socialism and feminism.

After the Conservatives had flirted with borrowing the neofascist injunction "Keep Britain White" for an electoral slogan, the Labour Party of Harold Wilson's era began to argue that legislation against racial discrimination would be necessary if US-style unrest was to be avoided. That initiative required a specific analysis of the political risks and ethical dangers associated with the institutionalization of racial prejudice. Once again, Hall's critical and imaginative work played a key role. He supplied sophisticated foundations and welcome political orientation for the postcolonial social movement against racism that had emerged from those difficult conditions. That formation was tied to the oppressed social lives of incoming settlers, but it mutated quickly as the bleaker fates of their locally born children and grandchildren gradually came into view. The rising rebel generation was inspired by decolonization, civil rights struggles in the United States, and Cold War conflicts alike. Its cosmopolitical gestures have now been dispersed, but its insurgent contributions were notably present among the struggles that attended the birth of Britain's multicultural and multiethnic society. Today, their echoes endure in ongoing battles to reanimate and sustain it. However, the concept of racism has passed out of favor, displaced by the internet-borne rhetoric of antiblackness and Afropessimism. These essays and talks can be read for their sense of what might be gained politically by racism's reclamation from vacuity and the restoration of its tarnished value.

Hall's perspective is firmly historical. It drew on resources unearthed by the scholarly research of James Walvin, Edward Brathwaite, Folarin Shyllon, and others. That commitment to history came bolstered by the idea that the *narrative* of black life in Britain was unfinished and the related belief that its completion would necessitate an extensive and perhaps painful rewriting of the country's national self-understanding. The classic essay "Race and 'Moral Panics' in Postwar Britain," which sets the creative tempo of this anthology, begins to identify what these adjustments would involve. An initial corrective course was indicated by analysis of the nodal "turning points" that Hall presents as important constituents of Britain's local variant of racialized politics. The first of these moments was marked by the riots of 1958 in Notting Dale and elsewhere.[16] Hall had witnessed them anthropologically from his position as an antiracist activist and secondary school teacher in London. The extended book review essay that begins this anthology explains that "the ins and outs of racial prejudice" were of concern to him from the late 1950s, not least because through them he was able to comprehend the close connections between race and the emergent politics of youth and youth culture in the turbulent aftermath of the war. Racial riots and the complex, ambivalent reactions of the "secondary modern generation" captured the quickening of larger cultural shifts in British social life that would be traced in greater detail in many of his later essays.

The *Young Englanders* pamphlet was published the year before Enoch Powell's epoch-making prophecies had been offered in response to the Labour government's tepid, well-meaning attempts to outlaw racial discrimination in the provision of private dwelling space. It picks up some threads from the late 1950s survey but augments those germs of insight into a richly textured treatment designed to alter the emerging sociological fixations on prejudice and the challenging behavior of dark strangers in Britain's "twilight areas." The nascent sociology of race relations was held firmly at arm's length, but the influence of Richard Hoggart's sensitive, thoughtful work is obvious. His approach gets expanded and enriched as Hall finds his way toward an understanding of how black settlement is changing Britain and demanding new ways of approaching questions of class, urban life, generation, and justice. He outlines an early version of an argument that would evolve and reappear in the succeeding decades. The cultural relationships enacted in fraught encounters between black and white involve systematic misrecognition as well as demands for recognition that were bellowed across the barricades and defensive camps that were being erected in Britain's transitional zones during the era of the Co-ordinating Committee against Racial Discrimination.[17] Those racialized differences, overdetermined by class conflict and accelerated by economic and technological change, were not amenable to any tidy or even any dialectical resolution. The patterns of conflict, contact, and coexistence they effected constituted a politics of identity—defined here as sameness, subjectivity, and solidarity—that required both extensive historical analysis and meticulous anthropological exposition. The significance of racism in shaping the polity and, in particular, in strengthening the hateful but apparently endlessly productive populist strand in its political culture also became harder to overlook.

Thanks to the affirmative efforts of Claudia Jones, Leslie Palmer, and numerous others, the summer carnival in Notting Hill transformed the streets made notorious by the 1958 riots, the murder of Kelso Cochrane, and the fruits of Colin MacInnes's literary imagination. While the likes of V. S. Naipaul, George Lamming, and Andrew Salkey created the West Indian novel in London, the Calypsonians that Hall recalls so fondly were being recorded in Dennis Preston's studio on nearby Lansdowne Road. Their amused and amusing immigrant observations on the city's postwar life fed directly into the bank holiday festivities that would supply an already syncretized precedent for more elaborate patterns of intermixture and recombination. In London, Jamaican culture could mesh with the outflow of Trinidad and the small islands. Persistent demands for dignity emanated from their asymmetrical communion and provided a triple oppositional warrant, for recognition, for healing, and for saturnalia. The ludic disorderly spirit of traditional Mas gradually made room for the brazen rebel modernism of the sound systems. Those public excesses were, as the calypso essay also shows, initially accessible through musical vectors that could speak powerfully to white youth too. That seductive culture spread out through the bombed, decaying postwar streets that the incomers made home. That bleak, cold urban environment had already begun to incubate a great flowering of transplanted creole forms. In turn, that manifestation would contribute to a new moment of black cultural power pulsing out not from Jamaica but from the postcolonial metropolis to the newly wired world. The iconic figure of Bob Marley provides a useful cipher for the whole process he helped to consolidate, to invest with philosophical depth, and to reconcile with the hijacked language of human rights that defined it.

A few years later, during the long, hot summer of 1976, all the pride, disillusion, and resilience that Hall had noted in the pessimistic conclusion to the *Englanders* pamphlet blossomed in the young rioters' angry rejection of continued injustice on the same west London streets. Similarly, worldly demands for transcendent justice and reciprocity, now being imagined outside the grip of racial patterns, were expressed in the many confrontations with White Power skinheads and other organized neofascists which led up to the spring 1979 election that brought Margaret Thatcher's government into power. Thatcher's honeyed mixture of romantic nationalism and free marketeering provided Powellism with a clean uniform, ventriloquizing his old populism to compete politically with the resurgent National Front.

In April that year, Blair Peach, an antifascist demonstrator, was struck with an unauthorized weapon and killed by a police officer from the Special Patrol Group during what came to be known as Southall's police riot. As I have said, Peach's death led to an unofficial tribunal of inquiry established by the NCCL under the chairmanship of Professor Michael Dummett, to which Hall made a significant contribution. That report was followed by several similar publications. They enabled Hall to elaborate further on the arguments about racism, the national state, and the black communities that had been outlined in *Policing the Crisis*, the pathbreaking, collectively authored blend of deviancy theory, history, and Marxian political analysis that he had orchestrated and midwifed in 1978.

The popular tribunals of inquiry into police racism that followed in the 1980s were parajudicial exercises, often organized in association with local trade unions. In some cases, these practical excursions into antiracist politics involved public hearings in which their respected expert panelists received detailed testimony from witnesses and victims. The resulting publications rested on solid academic and political foundations, often inspired by Hall's wieldy formulations.

It bears repetition that these initiatives were typical of a time in which political organizing accommodated the obligation to advocate prefigurative, transitional forms that anticipated, and sometimes even summoned, alternative ways of living and organizing the world. Similar initiatives were adopted in the London boroughs of Islington, Tower Hamlets, and Lambeth, where independent research into local manifestations of police racism and misconduct was undertaken under the auspices of the now-forgotten Trades Councils. The resulting reports—*Under Heavy Manners*, *Blood on the Streets*, and *Final Report of the Working Party into Community/Police*

Relations in Lambeth—repay analysis both for the historical detail they provide and their evident theoretical sophistication.[18]

The spring of 1980 saw an eruption of rioting in Bristol. A year later, it was followed by nationwide violent protests that stretched between April and July. Rechristened "uprisings," those explosive events were the unholy culmination of black communities' bitter reactions against the habitual racism of Britain's police. However, in involving all tribes of hopeless, oppressed, and victimized young people, they opened into wider oppositional gestures based on common poverty, class, and gender. The period leading up to the 1981 disorders and the overall shape of the conjuncture of which they were part had been outlined in *Policing the Crisis*'s arguments about the "moral panic" around black mugging, the country's drifting into a more authoritarian kind of society, and the rise of populist politics. It is significant that in exploring those processes the book had touched gently on the complex theoretical issue of internal or endo-colonialism. That discussion had developed from political analysis of the racially segregated spaces of North America. Hall invoked it in a different setting through his notion of the "colony area," an environment in which policing and law owed something to the modes of administration and enforcement more commonly associated with governing imperial and colonial territory. The book's concluding pages engaged directly with the equally sophisticated but clearly divergent analyses provided by respected organic intellectuals drawn from leading organizations within the black movement.

While recognizing that the rebel generation's desperate young people were fighting to escape the kind of employment their parents had taken on as a "super-exploited stratum" and a "reserve army of labour," Hall insisted that their struggles should not be reduced too swiftly to a mass rejection of the forms of work that were available to them. Youth's battles to be free from that "shit-work" were buoyed by an ill-defined but nonetheless alternative conception of social life. It was the substance of the unruly (sub)culture that they improvised from traces of Garveyism, Black Power, and antiracist sentiment melded with the vernacular appeals to the idea of human rights that had become commonplace in what would be known as the golden age of roots reggae. Again, the idea of nonracial justice strengthened moral foundations of that combative stance.

The race war that Powell prophesied in 1968 appeared more plausible once the scale of antipolice feeling had shifted from smoldering quotidian resentment into more spectacular varieties of violent resistance. Angry reactions from every quarter encompassed a dawning sense of the chronic, intractable character of the economic crisis and the unsavory forces that had been unleashed by accelerating deindustrialization of the urban areas where blacks had provided a replacement population prepared to undertake the work that locals would not do and live in the squalor that they fled. The Conservative government's official records, released some years afterward, revealed that Thatcher's cabinet had quietly debated the likely fate of the riot-torn city of Liverpool if a Detroit-style strategy of "managed decline" was to be adopted.

Hall's interest in urban environments as repositories of cultural relations and political antagonisms continued. Their transformation during the next stage of Britain's chronic crisis is treated at some length in his Amnesty International lecture "Cosmopolitan Promises, Multicultural Realities." It situates the spatial effects of inequality and globalization in the context of the uneven habitable multiculture into which Britain had been able to drift only because the national government had been entirely absent from the process of making it. The history of that creolizing process counterpoints a history of economic change and cultural innovation that saw the ambivalent mainstreaming of black life and style in prestigious as well as vernacular forms. They included the experimental output of the film workshops sponsored and supported by Channel 4 and the invigorating work of the new generation of artists associated with the emergent Black Arts movement that had been enabled by Hall's enthusiastic deconstruction of outmoded aesthetic rules and constraining political recipes. He was extensively involved in the production of the report of the Runnymede Trust's Commission on the Future of Multi-ethnic Britain to the Blair government. It was a book-length document that, like the informal inquiries discussed above, made extensive use of his insights even if it attempted to recast them in the anodyne, think-tanky idiom of the policy-political establishment.[19] Sections of that report covering policing, media, and education reveal the continuity and stability of Hall's critical observations that stretched back at least three decades at the time of its publication. His reactions to its disastrous reception at the hands of the tabloids and subsequent disavowal by its governmental sponsors supply the essential background to the thoughtful Pavis lecture here titled "The Multicultural Question."

I suspect that the mounting frustrations of a blocked national context from which the Left had either evaporated or become complicit in the Blair government's rapprochement with neoliberalism were additional factors in Hall's turn toward the alternative possibilities he saw signposted in the flourishing of Black Art, aesthetics, and their consequent need for institution building. In those less depressing settings, the diasporic subject whose appearance marked the end of political innocence and the acquisition of political maturity was a constant—if not quite a dominant—presence. New energies were released as the ectopic heartbeat of Britain's black communities shifted away from its Caribbean defaults and moved toward Africa. A wider set of sustaining interactions with black European artists, curators, and critics in other countries started to change the parameters of dialogue. In those debates, to which the essay on "New Ethnicities" was central, it was still possible to see, say, and learn new things. There, too, the political pedagogy at which Hall had excelled for so long was able to win new audiences and interlocutors.

His practical recommendations to the antiracist educators of the early 1980s read very much against the grain of current discussion, sounding like a reckless refusal of the signature sensitivities of the anxious "snowflake" generation. However, a number of things remain instructive. Hall's thoughtful advice to the activists and organizers of yesteryear has acquired a new resonance. It turns around a surprising proposition, namely, that the struggle against racism demands a high degree of discipline from its political advocates who must not only reject the disabling simplifications of Manichaeanism and moralism but also learn to create and manage *unsafe* spaces in which the "combustible material" of "commonsense" and working-class racism is allowed to surface and breathe. His position is worth quoting at length:

> I do think you have to create an atmosphere which allows people to say unpopular things. I don't think it is at all valuable to have an atmosphere in the classroom which is so clearly, unmistakeably antiracist that the natural and "commonsense" racism which is part of the ideological air that we all breathe is not allowed to come out and express itself. . . . That experience has to surface in the classroom even if it is pretty horrendous to hear—better to hear it than not to hear it.

These words were spoken almost four decades ago to a group of antiracist secondary school teachers. They do not now translate into some misplaced liberal endorsement of an inviolable, yet utterly banal, right to be offensive. Hall is restating a necessary commitment to the hard, demanding political work of building an innovative movement against racism that is premised on a reckoning with the fundamental importance of culture's political powers and moods. People are not simply either fervently racist or fanatically antiracist. There is substantial ground to be gained among those who have no self-conscious view or may not consider themselves political at all. The alt-right, some of whom have mimicked Gramsci while others transposed his twentieth-century vision into their high-tech, mediatized movement-building, have grasped that possibility. They articulate it in their trademarked insistence that politics is now located "downstream from culture."[20] Perhaps, even among them, the value of that insight has been underscored by understanding the significance of racism's rational irrationality, which generates an intensity of political feeling invulnerable to the flimsy weapons of corrective reason. Looking at that insufficiency from what is left of the Left brings to mind another of Stuart Hall's favorite chuckled phrases: "We are, comrades, in deep trouble."

NOTES

I would like to thank Vron Ware, Angela McRobbie, Les Back, Iain Chambers, and Larry Grossberg for their comments and assistance.

1 On this point see also Hall's interview with Les Back: Stuart Hall and Les Back, "At Home and Not at Home: Stuart Hall in Conversation with Les Back," *Cultural Studies* 23, no. 4 (2009): 658–88, http://research.gold.ac.uk/2321/2/At_Home_and_Not_at_Home-1.pdf.
2 Stuart Hall, "Race and 'Moral Panics' in Postwar Britain" (chapter 4 in this volume).
3 The NAME (National Association for Multicultural Education) journal final page. (chapter 8 in this volume).
4 Stuart Hall, "The Whites of Their Eyes" (chapter 7 in this volume).
5 This idea was first expressed by the historian George L. Mosse in *Toward the Final Solution: A History of European Racism* (New York: Howard Fertig, 1978), 234. The formulation was developed further by George M. Fredrickson and Nancy Leys Stepan, among others.
6 Two of the essays in this volume (chapters 10 and 11) were written for UNESCO publications in which Marion O'Callaghan was extensively involved; they are *Race and Class in Post-colonial Society: A Study of Ethnic Group Relations in the English-Speaking Caribbean, Bolivia, Chile and Mexico* (Paris: UNESCO, 1977) and *Sociological Theories: Race and Colonialism*, introduced by Marion O'Callaghan (Paris: UNESCO, 1980).
7 Colin MacInnes, *Westward to Laughter* (New York: Farrar, Straus and Giroux, 1969).
8 This phrase is taken from Hall's essay on Fanon; chapter 18 of this volume.
9 See, for example, the interview with Hall in the Sussex University student publication "Cultures of Resistance and 'Moral Panics': An Interview with Stuart Hall," *Afras Review*, no. 4 (1979): 2–18.
10 See, for example, *Black People in Britain: The Way Forward: A Report of a Conference Held 17/19 January 1975 Written Up and Edited by Dr. Rajeev Dhavan on Behalf of the Post-conference Constituent Committee* (London: PCCC, 1976). Hall is listed as a "principal participant."
11 See Anne Walmsley, *The Caribbean Artists' Movement, 1966–1972: A Literary and Cultural History* (Finsbury Park, UK: New Beacon Books, 1992). Walmsley reveals

that Stuart Hall had been active in the West Indian Students Society at Oxford and chronicles his participation in the CAM conferences as well as his contribution to the CAM special issue of *Savacou* in 1974 (chapter 3 in this volume).

12 This is a reference to the Labour journal *New Socialist*, from which the essay of the 1981 riots has been reprinted; see chapter 5 in this volume.

13 Sheila Rowbotham, Lynne Segal, and Hilary Wainwright, *Beyond the Fragments: Feminism and the Making of Socialism* (Islington, UK: Islington Community Press, 1979), 71–79.

14 This phrase comes from the intervention "Subjects in History: Making Diasporic Identities" (chapter 17 in this volume).

15 Joseph A. Hunte, *Nigger Hunting in England* (London: West Indian Standing Conference London Region, 1965).

16 Edward Pilkington, *Beyond the Mother Country: West Indians and the Notting Hill White Riots* (London: I. B. Tauris, 1988); Mark Olden, *Murder in Notting Hill* (London: Zero Books, 2011).

17 The Birmingham-based Co-ordinating Committee against Racial Discrimination was formed in the early 1960s.

18 *Under Heavy Manners: Report of the Labour Movement Enquiry into Police Brutality and the Position of Black Youth in Islington Held on Saturday July 23rd 1977* (London: Islington Defence Committee, 1977); *Blood on the Streets: A Report by Bethnal Green and Stepney Trades Council on Racial Attacks in East London* (London: Bethnal Green and Stepney Trades Council, 1978); *Final Report of the Working Party into Community/Police Relations in Lambeth, London* (London: Borough of Lambeth, 1981).

19 Runnymede Trust, *The Future of Multi-ethnic Britain* (London: Profile Books, 2000).

20 This phrase is associated with the right-wing journalist Andrew Breitbart, founder of the Breitbart News Network. See also Hans Georg Betz, "Everything That Is Wrong Is the Fault of '68: Regaining Cultural Hegemony by Trashing the Left," Open Democracy, August 4, 2018, www.opendemocracy.net/can-europe-make-it/hans-georg-betz/everything-that-is-wrong-is-fault-of-68-regaining-cultural-hegemony-by-trashing-left.

PART I | RIOTS, RACE, AND REPRESENTATION

CHAPTER 1

Absolute Beginnings:
Reflections on the Secondary Modern Generation

To Sir, With Love, E. R. Braithwaite. Bodley Head, 13/6.
Journey Into a Fog, Margareta Berger-Hamerschlag. Ace Books, 2/6.
Absolute Beginners, Colin MacInnes. Macgibbon and Kee.
The Teenage Consumer, Dr. Mark Abrams for the London Press Exchange.

I.

Reading the first two of these four books is like reliving the best and worst moments of teaching and working amongst the Secondary Modern generation. They are both well written, sympathetic in their approach to young people, and full of insights. Mr. Braithwaite is a West Indian who went to teach in a Secondary Modern school in the East End. His chronicle is a record of how he managed to win the confidence of his young pupils, with some delicate sidelights (timely in the year of Notting Hill) on the ins and outs of racial prejudice. Mrs. Berger-Hamerschlag taught Art in a youth club in a London slum. Her book (first published with Gollancz in 1955, and reissued, with an appropriately sexy cover, by Ace Books and a blurb about this "savage and sometimes shocking story of teenagers in a London slum") is not, perhaps, so sensational as it looks in its new format. But it must have been quite remarkable when it first appeared, and even now, it has much to add by way of detail and perception.

One cannot help feeling that Mr. Braithwaite was extremely fortunate in his headmaster. He emerges as a figure of extraordinary sympathy and gentleness, with intelligent ideas about his children and their background, about the attitude of staff to pupils, and about the relationship between discipline and freedom in education.

> It is said that here we practice free discipline. That's wrong, quite wrong. It would be more correct to say that we are seeking, as best we can, to establish disciplined freedom, that state in which the child feels free to work, play and express himself without fear of those whose job it is to direct and stimulate his efforts into constructive channels. (Braithwaite 1959, 32)

I don't want to go into the intricacies of the debates about "progressive education," but my experience of young boys' attitudes towards the school suggests that it is disciplined freedom, rather than absolute liberty, which most youngsters want and expect from school. They need, of course, the opportunities for participation and making decisions which the present authoritarian pattern of Secondary Modern schools prevents. But they are neither so self-reliant nor so confident as to expect "free discipline." They would not know what to do with it if they had it. Complete absence of discipline suggests to most Secondary Modern forms that the teacher has no sense of direction, no priorities and no targets. They dislike this drift even when they exploit it. What does matter is the *context* within which discipline is practised, the freedom from fear which Braithwaite's headmaster stressed, the sense of mutual give-and-take, the respect which teachers have for the people they teach. The only discipline worth having is the discipline of *purpose*, in the context of love. It cannot be imposed by fear, formality or the cane. It is the most difficult balance to achieve.

Mr. Braithwaite's headmaster was singular, not in the fact that his relationship with his pupils was good (it very often is): but in the fact that he *cared* what the relationship was between his pupils *and the rest of his staff*, and that he prized directness and outspokenness, even if this appeared as "a form of rudeness at first." So many headmasters pander to the priggish sense of self-importance and prestige which is characteristic of the teaching profession. The teachers stand between the pupils and the head. He is often free to develop a close relationship with his students which is not put to the test of the class-room. In these circumstances, many headmasters "have a way" with the boys and girls which is purely personal, and which makes little or no impact at all upon the relationships which prevail through the rest of the school between staff and pupils.

Mr. Braithwaite was also particularly fortunate in his teaching associates. I do not mean to infer that there are no good, dedicated teachers. There are thousands. But I cannot get rid of the impression that by and large Secondary Modern teachers today suffer an acute lack of morale which has been consciously overlooked because teachers are in such short supply. They consider the Sec Mod to be inferior in status: and they are acutely status-conscious. Often, they despise the areas in which they teach, and the homes from which their students come. They are anxious not to be involved with the personal and informal problems of young people. Often, they have placed a safe distance between themselves and the school—protected from the realities of urban life by the green belt and the suburban line. It is most disturbing to count up the number of young teachers who would like their self-respect and their status to be protected by the agile and relentless use of the headmaster's cane. In many cases, Sec Mod teachers invert their affronted sense of status into an attack upon the supply teachers. How much of this is due to professional jealousy, how much to the fact that supply teachers are often foreigners—Australians, West Indians, Indians, Pakistanis, etc.—is difficult to judge. But the thing is there, and fostered at national level too (witness the disgusting sentiments expressed at a recent conference of the Schoolmasters' Association), in spite of the fact that, without the present numbers of supply teachers, many Secondary Modern schools would fold up tomorrow. This prejudice is merely one of many indications of a deep demoralisation among the shock-troops in the front line of the class struggle in secondary education today. They do not understand what the nature of that struggle is. Many of them are products of the "scholarship boy" revolution in education. They feel all the stresses and tensions of the *parvenu*. Caught themselves between generations, between social allegiances, they find it impossible to project or identify.

Mr. Braithwaite's staff seemed, on the whole, both sympathetic and capable—not beaten down by the irritations of working with bad equipment in crowded classrooms, not disgusted with having to explain about washing and sanitary napkins to the girls, not—with one exception—protected from the immense problems and responsibilities by a cheaply attained cynicism.

But his success, undoubtedly, was with the boys and girls in the top form. Here, he managed what few good teachers in the best Secondary Modern schools seem able to accomplish: making the non-G.C.E. form of school-leavers find something worthwhile in school.

This group of school-leavers is really the alienated generation. Many people who do not view the problems of young people today from the vantage point of the school, see the crucial change in adolescent experience as falling between school and work. But I have little doubt that the most important formative point lies *between* the junior and adolescent phases—roughly at the breaking-point between the second and third years of the Secondary Modern career. Work, of course, adds responsibilities, new skills, a new environment, a wider pattern of movement from the home and its surroundings. But basically, work modifies a pattern of feeling, responses and attitudes already established by the age of fourteen. The next phase begins with marriage.

In spite of cramming for the 11-plus and the consequent neglect of late-starters, the quality of entrants to the Sec Mod from the Primary schools is good. These children have very little sense of how much their future is likely to be affected by having failed at the first jump of the social barrier. They are keen, enthusiastic, childish in their interests and their delights, they possess a high reserve of vitality and enthusiasm, and they are immensely educable. But at the age of thirteen/fourteen, they begin to pass out of the direct influence of home-and-school, and into the wider world of their own groups, the friendships and rivalries of their local gangs, the culture of the youth club and skiffle group, the heady atmosphere of the mass entertainments. However inadequate, the home and school have, until this point, provided some sort of a framework of reference, within which primary experiences are ordered and understood. But in the local gang, the pattern is tribal and self-imposed. Its particular attraction lies in the fact that it draws little upon, and bears only a subterranean relationship with, the adult world. The youth club offers facilities for informal social contact which the school does not: but unless it is an outstanding example of its kind, it provides little "training"—even in the sense of training responses to new adolescent experiences. The youth club is very much the clash of opposing worlds. The pattern of activities, the "rules," the standards and codes of behaviour, the tone, imposed from above: the club drawing its particular vigour and character from the subterranean emotional life of its members, from below.

This is the point at which young people discover the relative irrelevance of the school. And after that, it is difficult to engage their real interests without the spur of academic achievement—(a try at G.C.E.). As Braithwaite says: "It was as if I were trying to reach the children through a thick pane of glass, so remote and uninterested they seemed" (1959, 74). It's not that they long for the more "proper" ethos of the Grammar school. That kind of aspiration is nonexistent—a reflection of how limited the appeal of the Ladder of Success is below a certain educational and social threshold. They consider the Grammar school too strict and too "posh." They prefer the informality which prevails, willy-nilly, in the Secondary Modern. And this in itself throws a certain light on the particular nature of the lacks, the deprivations, which they experience at this point in adolescence. This is the point at which they begin to reflect upon their own sense of failure. They feel their second-class status. They are conscious of the lack of care: and they identify this lack of sympathy and understanding with the school itself. Their range of expectations close up. They are being trained for the semi-skilled positions, and for that limited end, the school has done its job by 13, and they are anxious to get out and get on with it. Much of the aimless frenzy of their leisure life is a displacement of the energies and aspirations which have been trained or drained out of them by school and work. They become in the end what many teachers have always believed they were: unteachable, unclubbable. One of the most disturbing experiences in a Secondary Modern school is the open, callous manner in which many teachers accept the fact that the lively, vital fourth stream class in the First Year will become, inevitably, the blasé, disenchanted, inattentive "shower" in the Fourth—without asking how on earth this transformation ever takes place.

Mr. Braithwaite had to cope with all the external expressions of this state of cultural deprivation: noise (not occasional, but wilful and deliberately indulged as a kind of war of nerves), inattention, persistent clinical use of swear words, a single-track devotion to sex, the irritable and sudden explosions of violence towards authority and towards each other. These things bothered Mrs. Berger-Hamerschlag as well. She is continually reporting the invasion of her Art class by groups of boys, wandering aimlessly about, spilling paint and daubing the desks with a kind of intent, impotent fury.

> Chris's gang appeared this evening. They never walk in, these fifteen- to sixteen-year-old crazies, they rush in vehemently, as if in a commando raid.... They are rebellious because they miss a lot which they think they can never have and their natural longing for love and fun is being twisted through their being beaten, rejected or badly used in other ways. (Berger-Hamerschlag 1956, 92–93)

There are really difficult distinctions to be made here. Working-class children do not have the same respect or value of studious silence that is common among Grammar school children. Frequently, in a classroom of forty, the standard of work and application is high in spite of the continuous undertones of voices and exchanges. This can be irritating, particularly to those teachers who apply Grammar school standards of dress and behaviour to working-class children. But this is a different aspect of their behaviour from the consciously created interruption, which is really a form of inspired violence, and relates more closely to the aimless kicking of dustbins, the scraps and "giggles," the "bashing" and "doing" (including the more organised "doing" of Irish or West Indians) which is so much an integral part of working-class adolescent activity. I think the teenagers who explain all this in terms of boredom and bottled-up energy, rather than consciously thought-out violence directed against any one group, are close to the truth. Particular prejudices about "niggers" or "paddies" or "yids" are inspired: they develop *out of* a deeper level of social frustration against the society and the adult world. They are not, in themselves, the source of violence.

When youngsters, who have been on a giggle to Notting Hill, talk about it afterwards, they are perfectly aware that it is a pointless, and degrading, kind of self-indulgence. But, at the moment, the urge to commit violence is quite clearly overpowering. "There's nothing to do, see, and you're tired of sitting around. They don't want to argue, and if you start an argument they just start swearing to shut you up. And then along comes someone, and there's something about him you don't like, see, he's a coloured man or an Irish or something, and one of the boys gets a thing about him. Let's rush him, he says, and before you know what's going on."

Mrs. Berger-Hamerschlag never managed to surmount this problem with those who came only occasionally to her classes. Those who were interested, either in painting or in the company of the painting class—she found—could easily be involved in creative work: though their staying power was, naturally, limited. Mr. Braithwaite managed to sublimate their energy in the classroom and in work: in one case, he was obliged to take on the most surly of his students in a boxing bout, but I found this episode—even if true to life—an unrepresentative and arbitrary solution to a tough problem. It is interesting that, in their quite different situations, both authors came to much the same conclusions, and adopted the same variety of tactics. Braithwaite realised that, by fourteen, these youngsters were, in many ways, already adult. They had adult interests, and, in many cases, adult experiences. His decision to treat them as such, to honour their sense of importance and seriousness, transformed the relationship between himself and them. I am not sure that many Sec Mod boys would have agreed to call their classmates "Miss," or even that this kind of formality is advisable. Occasionally, when he is on this track, Mr. Braithwaite's tone becomes smug and self-important. But it certainly turned the trick. Mrs. Berger-Hamerschlag discovered that, above all, the kids wanted to be taken seriously.

> They are marvellous and respond easily when an atmosphere of "art college" is being created. It means to them that they are taken seriously and that someone believes in their ability; the hobby idea is poison to them. (Berger-Hamerschlag 1956, 63)

And, more characteristically:

> "Why do they dish out these rotten things to us?" asked Dave. "Why don't we get white paper? Why don't we get decent brushes? These are brooms, wicked! I thought that this was a proper art class!" (Berger-Hamerschlag 1956, 44)

Perhaps we ought to put alongside that Mr. Braithwaite's description of his East End children listening to music:

> They listened, those rough looking, untidy children; every one of them sat still, unmoving and attentive, until the very last echo of the last clear note had died away. Their silence was not the result of boredom or apathy, nor were they quiet because it was expected of them or through fear of the consequences; but they were listening actively, attentively, listening to those records, with the same raptness they had shown in their jiving. (Braithwaite 1959, 53)

II.

We have very little understanding of the roots of cultural deprivation, and of its relation to the pattern of class culture and education in this country. Where does it begin? In the school? In the family? In the give-and-take (or lack of it) between adolescent and adult generations?—and if so, why?

Clearly, the school itself is not wholly to blame, though what happens here is important, for it develops social tendencies which may originate elsewhere. In its own way, the Secondary Modern school—its whole conception as a second-class educational stream, the idea that any kind of modern education can be given in the old school environment—is a careful adjustment to Welfare State Britain. The same double standards which apply elsewhere (see, for example, *Conviction*) can be seen at work in the Secondary Modern. Even where the school is doing its best, the general impression is that in education there is one law for some and another for the rest. The Secondary Modern generation are not only treated as if they are second rate: they *know* they are being treated in this way. The sense of failure, of rejection runs deep in the psychology of this generation: it influences both their attitudes towards the society and their evaluation of themselves.

Streaming takes place at an early stage in the Secondary Modern school, and this is done according to the different class evaluations of "academic" and "vocational" aptitudes, and the differing rewards which these kinds of talents merit in the labour market. There are considerable academic talents going to waste in the Secondary Modern. The top streams receive a poor-man's Grammar school education. By the age of fourteen, in their G.C.E. class, it is clear to everyone in the school that they would have been perfectly capable of coping with a Grammar school curriculum. The effect of the Secondary school upon the more academically advanced is simply that they come to realise, at the school leaving age, what they have missed. They *are* "*Grammar* school boys," with the tell-tale stigma of a Secondary Modern on their progress reports.

For the rest, the level of educational challenge offered is abysmally low. This does not mean that all children deserve an academically biased education—though in my experience the evaluation of their intellectual aptitudes is pitched far below their capacities. That is because most subjects are taught as academic "disciplines" rather than as transmission of social skills. It is possible for both history and geography to be taught as social studies, to a level far in advance of those currently attained in the Sec Mod, provided the subjects are approached within the context of the lives of the students, rather than within the arbitrary framework of the G.C.E. syllabus. Very little work of this kind, which is taking root in the Comprehensives, is attempted in the Secondary Moderns.

Here again, the social valuations established outside the school play a determining role within the school. Thus certain subjects—foreign languages, literature, science, history—are considered suitable for the "academic" streams, and not for the others. This bears little or no relationship to the actual interests or capacities of the pupils concerned. I have yet to meet the average "vocational" or "technical" child who had no interest whatever in any of the so-called "academic" subjects. Every boy in my fifth stream First Year Class for example, wanted to learn French. There is no doubt that, dim-witted as they are considered, they are in fact lively and active, and their imaginative capacities, to judge from their drawings and paintings and essays, are quite equal to it. Any one of these boys would have picked up French inside of six months, had he been living in the country.

But French is an "academic discipline"—the special privilege of the top streams. It is treated not as a linguistic skill but rather as a kind of cultural status-badge. It "belongs" to academic children, preparing for a semiprofessional or white-collar career. I have heard teachers threaten "A" stream classes that "if they did not live up to" their special position, they would be deprived of their French classes! This is only one example of the way in which working-class boys and girls are still adjusted, through the school, to their "proper" cultural and social position. What has been said of French could be equally applied to other subjects—in spite of the fact that in every class it is clear that there is a tremendous range of *combinations* of talents and skills.

The Secondary Modern school is, in essence, an *adaptive* social institution. A level of culture, a certain social status is prescribed from above, and the children are roughly attuned to it. There is, comparatively, little or no breaking through this cultural-social barrier. Therefore, it is not surprising to find that these boys and girls develop early an hostility to intellectual pursuits. They consider a serious interest in art (at which, being uninhibited, they are often very good indeed), or drama, or literature or biology not merely beyond their particular abilities, but outside their social stratosphere. These distinctions, moreover, are social and cultural rather than educational. The children are said to be unequipped to deal with art or literature or biology: yet they adore to paint or to read and perform plays, and they are fascinated by the world of nature and the laboratory. Clearly, the natural aptitudes and interests in the school are at sharp variance with the education provided: why not adjust the education to the interests, rather than squeeze the children into pre-digested categories? At least, the experiment should be tried; though in my view, it would not be successful outside the framework of the Comprehensive school.

Secondary Modern education, then, is not a matter of the extension of the range of experiences and skills beyond the normal level. It is much more a matter of making students familiar, through education, with the social and class barriers to education and culture which the society has already imposed. The cultural frontiers of working-class boys and girls cannot, in the normal way, be expected to broaden out. Whatever the economic position of working-class teenagers today, their cultural status is pretty plain. Here is a deep-rooted dislocation in the society, a social crisis in every way as sharp and as class-bound as economic crises have been in the past. It is ridiculous to talk of economic prosperity working, in the natural course of events, to break down established barriers between social classes. Class distinctions based upon attitudes, taste, education, and rooted in the educational system itself, do not wither away any more quickly than the State Department. A common culture does not "just grow" out of a socially differentiated society, any more than grass roots flourish in stone.

The Secondary Modern pattern of education gives us the most important clue we need for an explanation of the increasing gap between "high" and "popular" culture, and for the degeneration of "popular" culture into "mass culture." Mass culture, of course, is largely a creation by the commercial world for a literate society at an advanced technological stage. But the cultural gap between the "haves" and the "have-nots" of the education world provides the conditions within which the purveyors of mass culture operate. Without this gap, the exploitation and manipulation of tastes, needs and interests by an educated elite would be impossible. Or, to put it differently, a common culture, available to all and modified by the experiences of different social groups, is the only guarantee we possess of a genuinely democratic society. Mass culture is the culture of a mass democracy without democracy. Needless to say, young people are one of the most culturally exposed groups to mass culture. They expend their generous emotional responses in an attachment to its commodities: whilst "high culture" is increasingly taken over by dilettantism, preciosity and narrowness, and marked by that thinness of response and lack of social relevance which characterises so much minority art.

But the Secondary Modern school is, by and large, so well adjusted to the social norms of the society that it cannot afford to recognise the interpenetration of "school" and "leisure" attitudes in young people, or the playback of "teenage" interests in the school and classroom. Needless to say, the School is wholly unequipped to deal critically or responsibly with the "leisure" world, blotting the whole thing out like an unpleasant nightmare. Teachers are to be seen struggling with the symptoms of cynicism, boredom and confusion in the classroom which cannot be explained without reference to the emotional and "personal" interests of young people in the really formative worlds which they inhabit. For the same reason, the "leisure" world of the teenager assumes an importance unrivalled by school or home, an independence of the adult world and a freedom from the constraints of maturity and conformity which constitutes, in itself, its major attraction. In response to the cultural exploitation, which the school assists in, many teenagers erect cultural barriers themselves: so that their leisure world absorbs and consumes all the emotional vitality and the fantasy and imaginative projections of adolescence, and becomes a wholly self-enclosed universe.

The school, then, is constantly competing with the leisure world for the emotional attachments of young people—and losing the battle into the bargain. Neither the family nor the youth club in any sense adequately compensates. Left to themselves, young people develop very much according to the lights and lessons of each other's experiences—a school of life both limited, frustrating and self-enclosed. The gulf between themselves and adult life becomes unbridgeable. The quarrel between the generations becomes a vast, deadly silence of incomprehension.

It is only fair to say that neither Mr. Braithwaite nor Mrs. Berger-Hamerschlag come anywhere within striking distance of this problem. Their books are therefore interesting and humane (which, God knows, is almost enough these days)—but somehow not compelling. There are really crucial connections to be made which never get made. Mrs. Berger-Hamerschlag, for example, finds that her girls are interested "in nothing but their own beauty": but she brings them fashion magazines! She recognises the fantasy element in the cinema—"Hollywood is fairyland . . ."—but she speaks as if she considers their addiction to the cinema as if it were, by definition, a sign of wholesale waste. After all, a few pages later, she makes some very perceptive remarks about her students' passion for "realism" in art. "I can't get any of them to do anything imaginative. . . . Perhaps it's not so strange after all. They are at the age where they change from that introvert period of childhood into the adult stage of realism." Precisely. If that is the case, then the passion for "realism," particularly in the cinema, is a natural and healthy taste: the only problem is *what they are being shown*, what kind of realism are they being fed? Paragraphs of her book which begin with the good sense of this one:

> Relationships, usually fleeting and sensual, can be developed into humane ones in which warmth, comradeship and mutual interests play their part

have a way of ending up in rhapsodies like this:

> Why, wine has been grown in this island in Roman times, so why shouldn't we hope for a freer and happier youth, carried into being on a wave of living art and religion—neither imaginable without the other.

In such passages as these, Mrs. Berger-Hamerschlag seeks a romantic escape from the immense social pressures which are at work in the situation she is describing.

What we have to do is to begin to disentangle what is real and what is phony in the responses of young people today. What is real are the feelings and attitudes involved, the interests aroused: what is phony are the *ways* the feelings are engaged, the trivial and inconsequential directions in which the aroused interests are channelled. The revolt and iconoclasm of youth today arises because of the contradictions between the true and the false elements in their culture: because the wave of postwar prosperity has raised them to cultural thresholds which offer rewards unequal to the expectations aroused. Instead, therefore, most young people compensate for their frustrations by an escape into the womb-world of mass entertainments, by an aggressive revolt against conformist adulthood, by pioneering the frontiers of experience in search of the *feel of living*, or by an aggressive affirmation of the self against the world through violence. This is no temporary, diverting "phenomenon." It is a major social trauma, generalised for a whole generation.

The street or school gang, for example, which is so often criticised because of its antisocial tendencies, must also be understood as the search for a meaningful social group, for real face-to-face relations. As one lad put it, "The gang is always 'us' and 'them.' England against the rest, London against somewhere else, your part of London against another part, your street against the next, you and your mate, even, against the others." His use of the words "us" and "others" represents a serious challenge to the general quality of human relationships in our society. It gives voice to frustration arising from the apparent impossibility to "know other people," from the anonymity of human society and its institutions, and from the lack of care. And these are responses which, if we are honest with ourselves, we know as well, but which we have often consciously shoved to the back of our mind because we have lost the capacity to criticise and understand the working of society *on this human level*, or because we feel it is all somehow "inevitable in the age of mass technology." The truth is that we live in an age in which the very flow between human beings—a truly human and personal thing—has become distorted, part of a total crisis which eats through into the family life, and personal relationships as well. If we are willing to accept this state of affairs for the sake of a high rate of technical and industrial growth, then we are laying in store for our society deep social disturbances, of which racial riots, floating juvenile delinquency and petty crimes are merely unpleasant forerunners. A breakdown in the passage between youth and maturity represents a general condition, and cannot be explained without reference to the social relationships between groups and people in general. What we find in the detail of teenage attitudes today is the distorted moral response to a bureaucratic age. That is why the complex of feelings, pin-pointed, say, in the James Dean portrayal of father-son relationships in *East of Eden* and *Rebel without a Cause*, achieves so immediate a response in England and Western Europe, in Poland and the Soviet Union as well.

III.

It is, therefore, with something of a shock that one turns to this paragraph in the Editorial introduction to Dr. Mark Abrams's recent L.P.E. Pamphlet, *The Teenage Consumer*:

> The teenager is newly enfranchised, in an economic sense. This has given him the chance to be himself and show himself, and has misled a number of people, especially some elderly ones, into the belief that the young of mid-twentieth-century Britain are something new and perhaps ominous. We ourselves see no cause for alarm, and not much for diagnosing novelty except in the new levels of spending power and their commercial effects. There remains the ancient need for the older to understand the younger, and we now confront a business necessity *for* this understanding, as well as the older moral and psychological imperatives. (1959, 3)

The "commercial effects" of the teenage revolution are, of course, staggering—perhaps not quite in the sense that the London Press Exchange (Britain's largest advertising agency) use the words. Every other fact recorded by Dr. Abrams in the pamphlet (which is, in its way, an attractively illustrated job) is not merely "new," but startling in both its "business" and "social" implications. Dr. Abrams reckons that Britain's 5,000,000 unmarried teenagers (up to twenty-five) have a total annual uncommitted spending power of £900,000,000—a rise in *real* earnings over 1938 of 50 percent, and in real "discretionary" spending of over 100 percent. He goes on to point out that this is a market clearly distinguished in its tastes, constantly renewing itself: that it is almost entirely working-class, and predominantly male. Nearly a quarter of teenagers' uncommitted money goes on clothing and footwear, another 14 percent on drink and tobacco, and another 12 percent on sweets, soft drinks and snacks in cafes and restaurants. If we add together the teenage expenditure on records, record-players, books, papers and magazines, "recreational goods," cinema admissions and "other entertainments," we can estimate that the teenage market for "pop" entertainments is about £125,000,000, or about 14 percent of their total uncommitted spending power. The amount spent on clothes, cosmetics, etc., is about £225,000,000.

The pattern of consumption is, of course, extraordinarily specialised. Their spending on "other goods and services"—which includes most adult and "home" consumer goods—is less than 3 percent of the total. Moreover, their expenditure on tobacco and alcohol is comparatively unimportant. "The teenage population visits the cinema much more frequently than do its elders; it watches less television than does the rest of the population, and it tends to concentrate its reading on a few newspapers and magazines with very large circulations." The *Mirror* reaches over two-fifths of them, and the *News of the World* and *Sunday Pictorial* each reach approximately half all teenagers.

In his summing up, Mr. Abrams makes three points of wider interest: that the teenage market depends very heavily upon the one industrial country which has experience of a prosperous working-class adolescent market—the United States; that teenagers are looking for goods and commodities which are "highly charged emotionally": and that, with the rise of the teenage market as a distinctive age group, "ideas, values and experiences" tend to become "superannuated" at an earlier age. The "turn-over" in attitudes and values is just about as rapid as the multiple stores or the advertisers manage on the Charing Cross Road, or the song-writers in Tin Pan Alley.

Prosperity is the backdrop to every other thing which we can say about the Secondary Modern generation today. And while the superficial changes of style and taste ring out successively, there are some important underlying patterns to observe. In London, at any rate, we are witnessing a "quiet" revolution within the teenage revolution itself. The outlines of the Secondary Modern generation in the 1960s are beginning to form. The Teddy Boy era is playing itself out. The LP, Hi-Fi generation is on the way in. The butcher-boy jeans, velvet lapel coats and three-inch crepes are considered coarse and tasteless. They exist but they no longer set the "tone." "Teds" are *almost* square. Here are the very smart, sophisticated young men and women of the metropolitan jazz clubs, the Flamingo Club devotees—the *other* Marquee generation. Suits are dark, sober and casual-formal, severely cut and narrow on the Italian pattern. Hair cuts are "modern"—a brisk, flat-topped French version of the now-juvenile American crewcut, modestly called "College style." Shirts are either white-stiff or solid colour close-knit wool in the Continental manner. Jeans are *de rigueur*, less blue-denim American, striped narrowly or black or khaki. The girls are short-skirted, sleekly groomed, pin-pointed on stiletto heels, with set hair and Paris-boutique dead-pan make-up and mascara. Italian pointed shoes are absolute and universal.

A fast-talking, smooth-running, hustling generation with an ad-lib gift of the gab, quick sensitivities and responses, and an acquired taste for the Modern Jazz Quartet. They are the "prosperity" boys—not in the sense that they have a fortune stashed away, but in that they are familiar with the in-and-out flow of money. In the age of super-inflation, money is a highly volatile thing. They have the spending habit, and the sophisticated tastes to go along with it. They are city birds. They know their way around. They are remarkably self-possessed, though often very inexperienced, and eager beneath the eyes. Their attitude to adults is less resentful than scornful. Adults are simply "square." Mugs. They are not "with it." They don't know "how the wind blows." School has passed through this generation like a dose of salts—but they are by no means intellectually backward. They are, in fact, sharp and self-inclined. Office-boys—even van-boys—by day, they are record-sleeve boys by night. They relish a spontaneous giggle, or a sudden midnight trip to Southend: they are capable of a certain cool violence. The "Teds" are their alter-egos.

They despise "the masses" (the evening-paper lot on the tubes in the evening), "traditionals," "cops" (cowboys), "peasants" and "bohemians." But they know how to talk to journalists and TV "merchants," debs and holiday businessmen. Their experiences are, primarily, personal, urban and sensational: sensational in the sense that the test of beatitude is being able to get so close you feel you are "part of the act, the scene." They know that the teenage market is a racket, but they are subtly adjusted to it nonetheless. They seem culturally exploited rather than socially deprived. They stand at the end of the Teddy Boy era of the Welfare State. They could be the first generation of the Common Market.

The hero of Colin MacInnes's *Absolute Beginners* comes straight at us out of this changing panorama, with a flow and authenticity which marks the book as an excellent and distinguished piece of social documentary. The book asks to be tested against "life"—and this is no mean accomplishment. His social observation is keen, representative, detailed and engaged. He is not afraid of handling the material of teenage life within the framework of his own clearly articulated values. But he has managed, without too many nuances, to embody his attitudes in his hero, and through him, to figure out the contemporary attitudes of a whole range of teenagers. The novel has a backdrop of little deals and rackets which is almost certain to make some distinguished reviewer say, "Mr. MacInnes has overdone it a little. Surely there are too many crooks, prostitutes, perverts and spivs?" I refer to Mr. MacInnes's judgment on this one: this hustling quarter at least of today's teenagers are second-generation spivs. That is one of the things which the War and the floating amoralism of the Welfare State have done for the young. (You have to look at *Ashes and Diamonds* to see what a different kind of War and a different, harsher brand of amoralism have done for the Poles.)

Mr. MacInnes deliberately takes us on a tour of "modern" attitudes. The Teds and the bottle-throwers lurk in the background—and at the end of the novel, which is set graphically in the Notting Hill riots, they emerge to take their proper place in the roll-call of urban violence. If Mr. MacInnes concentrates on the "modern" advance guard I described above, it is not because the cruder, simpler "moral" view of the Ted has ceased to function. In Notting Hill, and elsewhere, their writ runs. I think it is because Mr. MacInnes would have found it impossible to embody his very healthy and humane views about contemporary life in the thwarted, suffocated consciousness of the Teddy Boy. His views need the light and freshness—also the sophistication and sensitivity—of the more "contemporary" article. The Modern Jazz Quartet generation may also be the generation that *could* lift its eyes above the slums of Paddington. Its horizons may be carefully manipulated by Fleet Street and A.R. TV: they are somehow broader, more comprehensive and basically more humane. Are they in any sense "socially" more responsible? No. But they are socially more responsive. They have views which include people other than themselves. And now that the "teenage thing" is a constant source of copy for both the Press and Television, they are both self-conscious about it, and beginning to think and articulate about it. Both things are good, provided the discussion can be made to broaden out and include other subjects besides the inter-generation struggle.

MacInnes "on tour" is, at first reading, a little irritating, and occasionally transparent. But the second reading persuades. He knows where he is going, and he has managed to impose a certain unity on the tale. What is more, he has done it with remarkable personal feeling, and without straining or forcing the sequence of incidents. The novel could easily have degenerated into a series of isolated episodes. In fact, the incidents are related to each other through the hero, and the "plot" provides a kind of loose moral pattern—or at least, the book achieves a unity in its moral tone and attitude towards the different types and points of view portrayed. This makes *Absolute Beginners* more than mere *rapportage*: the hero, in spite of his typicality in many respects, has very strong moral views on certain subjects—coloured people, for example—and an attitude to life and a love for London which is at once sympathetic and at the same time humane and committed. In that sense he is more than a roving camera of the teenage scene: he brings to bear upon it a moral point of view. This makes *Absolute Beginners* a novel rather than a piece of inspired journalism—though, of course, it is a novel in the social documentary genre.

Mr. MacInnes catches the different kinds of "hustling" and petty rackets of the teenagers very well. One lad has adventured into the call-girl business, but most of them are making a fast line with the TV cats who have made a big investment in the "teenage thing," or with journalists who want to know "what young people are thinking today," with ex-debs on the make or sharp business men in the advertising money. He covers, one way or another, most teenage attitudes, without appearing to drag them in by design. Hustling (everybody who is not a square is in some kind of racket), drinking ("either you drink a lot or else you don't drink anything at all"), sex (it really matters: "you can't say 'How's your sex life?' like you say 'How's the weather?'"), jazz ("if anybody doesn't rave about it, all you can feel for them is pity"), traditionals ("here was this trad child, alone among the teenagers, in the days of prosperity, still living like a bum and a bohemian . . ."), Jews ("when the Jewish population have all made enough loot to take off to America, or Israel, then I'm leaving too"), dancing ("your whole damn brain and sex and personality have actually become that dance, *are* it . . ."), ad men's offices ("the joint . . . was like a very expensive tomb . . ."), Notting Hill ("Napoli was like a prison, or a concentration camp; inside, blue murder, outside, buses and evening papers and hurrying home to sausages and mash and tea").

There are some very nice bits. The dialogue all the way through is close to being right—right at least in flow, speed, slickness, cool enough to be offbeat, but still English and cockney in rhythm and idiom. It achieves a kind of mid-Atlantic sophistication. There is one very fine passage, where the hero's queer friend, the Fabulous Hoplite, makes a hit on a TV programme in which he and a retired Admiral make splendid sense together, and defeat the interviewer—an intrepid Aussie called Call-Me-Cobber—on a "challenging" TV series called, suitably, *Junction*! The scene in the studio is memorable:

> The Hop was terrific: boy! If they don't line that cat up for a series, they're no talent-spotters. He hogged the camera—in fact, the damn thing had to keep chasing him about the studio—and spoke up like he was King Henry V in a Shakespearean performance. He told us that what he believed in was the flowering of the human personality, such as his own, and how could a personality flower in the boiler-room of a destroyer. (MacInnes 1959, 158)

Moreover, MacInnes manages to achieve certain moments of real feeling, without strain: the hero and his father at a performance of Gilbert and

Sullivan, with his coloured house-mate, Cool, and on a trip up the river. On the river trip—a scene different from the others because it involves emotional response rather than the portrayal of attitudes—the hero becomes excited by the little row-boats on the Thames:

> A club, it must have been, of athletic juniors each in white vest and pants and brown legs and arms and a red neck—it was cyclists they made me think of, weaving their way at speed through the city traffic—and we, of course, had to slow down almost to zero as they shot by both sides of us in their dozens. And I got up and cheered, and even old Dad did. Wonderful kiddies on that hot-pot cracking day, racing downstream as if only the salt sea would stop them.

Neither so sensitive nor so lyrical as Salinger, *Absolute Beginners* is still the closest we have come to a "British" (Mr. MacInnes is Australian!) *Catcher in the Rye*.

If anything, Mr. MacInnes has made his hero both too sophisticated and too critical. I do not mean that he is merely a vehicle for Mr. MacInnes's values, for we feel him as an authentic character in his own right. But he is, unfortunately, not as typical as we should like. It is characteristic, for example, that he should combine a kind of generous amorality in his attitude to himself and his teenage world, with a more strenuous moral dislike of the fake, the phony, the callous and the inhuman (for example, his attitude to West Indians). But he is altogether more knowing than is, I think, possible for such a "teenage" teenager to be.

Perhaps, on the other hand, Mr. MacInnes has done this generation more justice than others who have written about the same subject. I do not believe that humane attitudes to people and to social justice are bred only in conditions of want and deprivation. If postwar prosperity has lifted this working-class generation up out of poverty, and raised their cultural experiences and their social contacts—that is an unqualified gain. It *is* the sophisticated advance guard of the teenage revolution who are—at universities and training colleges and art schools and in apprenticeships—the most articulate in their protest about social issues, and who feel most strongly about South Africa or the Bomb. If the cool young men of today were to become the social conscience of tomorrow, it would be because they had seen sights in the Twentieth Century closed to many eyes before. It would not be the first revolution which came out of social deprivation, nor the first Utopia with absolute beginnings.

NOTE

This essay first appeared as "Absolute Beginnings: Reflections on the Secondary Modern Generation," *Universities and Left Review*, no. 7 (Autumn 1959): 16–25.

REFERENCES

Abrams, Mark. 1959. *The Teenage Consumer*. London: London Press Exchange.
Braithwaite, E. R. 1959. *To Sir, with Love*. London: Bodley Head.
Berger-Hamerschlag, Margareta. 1956. *Journey into a Fog*. New York: Sheed and Ward.
MacInnes, Colin. 1959. *Absolute Beginners*. London: MacGibbon and Kee.

CHAPTER 2

The Young Englanders

The term "Young Englanders" includes teenagers and young people, both English and "immigrant" (whether West Indian, Pakistani or Indian) who are now growing up as British citizens in this country. They are all members of the community of the young.

We are, however, particularly concerned here with the coloured immirant groups and their special problems. These young people do not in themselves constitute a problem and their problems cannot be understood in isolation. On average, immigrant young people are neither more nor less intelligent, neither better nor worse behaved, than their English counterparts. Problems arise in their interaction with other groups in the society and the solutions can only be formulated when we have understood the nature of this interchange.

Race relations are not—as is commonly believed—simply the relations of the immigrant community to the host community. They are the mutual interrelations of both groups—English-to-immigrant; immigrant-to-English. Race is a collective concept. Essentially, race relations are relations between groups of people rather than individuals; relationships in which the personal exchanges between individuals are mediated through and affected by the whole body of stereotyped attitudes and beliefs which lie between one group and another.

The point at which individuals of one national or racial group treat individuals of a different group as persons, on a wholly individual level, is the point at which "race relations" as such cease to exist. We are not yet at this point. And I believe that there is something confusing about using the language of personal contact to describe and analyse group situations—though I recognise that this tactic is often adopted out of the best liberal intentions.

During the troubles in Notting Hill in 1958, I was teaching at a secondary school in a poor area of London which was also, typically, an area of high migration. Several of the boys in my class had participated in the incidents and we frequently discussed this in the classroom. An interesting fact about the discussions was that the boys held two quite separate and contradictory ideas. On one hand they believed (often repeating the casual conversation of their parents) that West Indians were savages flooding the country, taking jobs, filling up classrooms, stealing women; that they were a lower order of society altogether and should be encouraged to "go home." On the other hand they had the friendliest of attitudes towards me (a teacher who, after all, had "stolen" a job in their school) and their own West Indian classmates (a group clearly "filling up the classrooms").

To these boys, I and the other West Indians they knew were persons, individuals. It was impossible for them to maintain their hostility in the face of personal, day-to-day contact. But the West Indians in Notting Hill were "a group," "them," outsiders, unknowns. There appeared to be very little carry-over from the intimate and personal situation of the classroom to the impersonal situation of the streets of North Kensington.

Insofar as this is a problem, then, it is a problem of and for the whole society. Let us start with the young people of the host community—the teenage "natives." We start here for two reasons: first, it is they who provide the "immediate community" for the immigrant teenager; they who define his situation. Second, it is this group from whom immigrant teenagers most want recognition and confirmation. They are the "significant others" to the immigrant young person. The immigrant wants to grow up a little like his white counterparts, to do some of the things they do, in the same way, because this is one of the important ways in which he makes peace with and comes to terms in his new and alien environment. "Other" (white) teenagers embody, to some extent, one ideal of adjustment and one possible "career" in the new situation.

In the past fifteen years, one of the most important social developments in advanced industrial societies has been the rise of the teenager as a self-conscious generational grouping in the community. In Britain, this group is defined by age and leisure interests, rather than by class or educational background. This does not mean that class and educational background are not important social factors in teenage life. Indeed, social class and education will prove to be the primary determining factors in setting the limits of experience and in defining the "life-chances" of the teenager.

But the aspect we think of as the "youth culture" of the generation is available, to some extent, across class and educational lines (many students, first-generation university people, and young adults of all social classes participate in the youth culture)—although it is essentially the creation of and for the working-class teenager of both sexes. There is no space here to analyse the rise of this youth culture. It clearly exists, it is quite a distinctive patterning of interests and pursuits, and it is available in some form to most young people between the ages of thirteen and twenty-two (or more accurately between puberty and marriage)—though the degree of participation is highly variable.

Let us examine some of the emergent attitudes in this culture—attitudes which make easy intercourse between host and immigrant youth problematical. First, participants in youth culture have a strong sense of group and generation loyalty, which is often accompanied by suspicion and hostility towards those who are not "in." Such groups are not tight groupings or gangs with a firm structure, and they have diverse interests and ways of spending their time. But the inner cohesion, keeping the world of adults at arm's length, is strong.

Second, the main activities are associated with leisure, with informal group life and inter-personal contact. They are not strongly associated with work.

Third, there is a strong sense that the old social barriers have been levelled, that the society is more "open," that it is possible to move through it, that its forms are more fluid and more responsive to choice and selection than would have been the truth for their parents. (We are not concerned here with whether or not British society is more "open" or leisure choices preselected and shaped, our only concern is that the participants believe them to be so.)

Few teenagers are "fully paid-up" members of this culture, but association with it—"fellow travelling, culturally" you could describe it—is widespread. It is a dominant cultural pattern, underpinned by a strong desire to be free of the constraints, disciplines, traditional attitudes, sources of authority of which adult society is composed. This augmented spirit of freedom in the young is, to my mind, a real gain in human and social terms, but it causes multiple points of conflict and tension between this generation and adult society.

The conflict elements should not, however, be over-stressed. For many good reasons the generations are not fundamentally divided, and when the strong, binding elements of youth and group association are loosened by time, experience and family responsibilities, there is a striking recovery of shared interests between young and old. Adolescence, nevertheless, is for many a period of "allowed rebellion," of permissiveness and experiment.

These then are the significant "others" in the mind of the immigrant teenager. His classmates, his workmates, his friends in the neighbourhood or the youth club, are likely to belong, to some degree, to this "tribe." Being a "proper teenager" means taking part in the "going-out," dating, dancing, chatting and other self-programmed routines of teenage life. It means belonging to a group by whom you are immediately recognised and accepted, and where, for a time at least, the necessary veils can be drawn between what you do and what your parents or your schoolteacher or your club leader believe you are doing. It is clearly difficult for a coloured teenager to find recognition in such a situation.

Now we must examine the position of immigrant youngsters when they enter the situation of contact. These newcomers have a wide variety of background. They may have arrived in Britain as teenage or near-teenage children, having spent a good proportion of their school life in the West Indies or Asia. These are first-generation immigrants. Their first contact with British life is as young adults. Their first situation of contact is a place of work (or rather, the Labour Exchange).

Others may be second-generation immigrants—that is to say, they were born in this country of immigrant parents or came at an early age. These spend the major part of their childhood and adolescence in the host community, and their first situation of contact is the school. Still others—a smaller group—are the children of mixed marriages. These are all British citizens—coloured, but British citizens all the same. But it would be a mistake to assume that they are in immediate contact with the whole range of British society.

Their encounters with the British take place, as a rule, in particular parts of Britain and with particular kinds of British people. Typically, the encounter is made in one of the "twilight areas" of large industrial cities, where larger numbers of immigrants live.

These are the deprived urban areas, the subdivided, re-let Victorian houses, badly in need of repair, which have been rapidly vacated since the war by those British tenants able to afford something better. Such areas have suffered swift social decline in recent years. Vacated by the older residents, they have become transition zones for immigrants of all kinds, who are drawn to them by employment opportunities. This group includes people from the North, where relative industrial decline has hit some areas; the Irish and—on the lowest rung of the ladder—West Indians, Pakistanis and Indians.

These "quarters" of the city are falling into disrepair. Many of them are scheduled for demolition. Washing and cooking facilities in these houses are inadequate. Families are in need of care, children of attention. Large numbers of people in these areas are below the poverty line. Even when they manage to make ends meet they are conscious of being relatively far behind in the scramble, perilously close to social disaster and the breakdown of stable patterns of life, and far removed from the main routes of success and self-fulfilment in the society. These are the areas for the socially dispossessed. Coloured immigrants are only one dispossessed social group crowding into these urban ghettoes.

Coloured immigrants in these areas encounter multiple hostilities. They are suspiciously regarded simply because they are coloured and foreign; because they don't fit the mental and cultural landscape and, doubly so, because they are judged from the pressured position of native families already under severe social stress. The British families condemned to the "twilight zones" are only too conscious of others who are doing well. They fear a further decline in their status—already a fragile possession; fear competition for scarce jobs, scarce housing, scarce school places and welfare provision. They believe that the influx of yet another group will bring the few remaining barriers they have erected between themselves and social dislocation crumbling down.

These hostilities are compounded by the alienness, the "otherness" of the coloured strangers, accentuated by differences of background, religious beliefs, family relationships, cultural and dietary habits. It is hardly surprising that native families tend to off-load their social frustrations on to the newcomers. The coloured immigrant and his family have become the personification of the troubles of the twilight zones—troubles which existed long before he arrived. The social problems of the community find in the immigrant a convenient image. So the load is passed from respectable, besieged older residents to the pushing, working-class families settling in as the first group begin their flight to the suburbs, and from the working-class families to the Irish and from them to the West Indians, Pakistanis and Indians—the "blacks," the "spooks," the "nig-nogs." What the older residents say the youngsters repeat and amplify. And at the very end of the line stands the immigrant teenager.

In such situations both the migrant and host families develop defensive, inward-looking attitudes. The schools, clubs, health clinics and hospitals used by immigrants are labelled "black schools," "black clubs" and so on. The "caffs" and street corners and pubs are strips of territory patrolled by white youth. Through these hostile areas coloured youngsters walk in groups and avoid trouble. Our cities are full of young coloured citizens of Britain trying to tiptoe through society.

A whole spectrum of mutual misconceptions and misapprehensions develops. White parents believe that immigrant families are lowering standards, neglecting their homes and families. Paradoxically, immigrant families believe English parents are too lax and indulgent with their children, too slovenly about the house. They feel that they are keeping up standards which "the natives" around them are rapidly abandoning.

Such misconceptions never meet—they coexist. There is no one—except the young immigrant, who is the busiest traveller between the two hostile worlds—to "translate" between the groups. Each stands solidly behind reinforced barricades. And the person most affected by these barricades is the young immigrant. He has to learn to negotiate the hostility of both groups; to cope with the suspicion of his alien environment—neighbours, school friends, workmates, the police. But he also has to negotiate the fears of his own family and the determination of his parents that, at whatever cost, *their* dignity will not be lowered; *their* children will not fraternise too freely lest they be thought "pushing"; *their* girls will not stay out late lest they be thought "loose"; *their* boys will not expose themselves to situations in which they may be rebuffed and rejected.

The young people of immigrant parents pass every day between the two defensive camps and they are held on a very tight rein indeed. This may be due, in part, to a difference of family culture (among some, discipline is in any case more summary, family traditions more patriarchal). But it is due, in large measure, to the immigrant situation itself. Migrants are highly conscious of themselves as a group—a group which is constantly being watched and tested and which is aware that what they do as individuals is accredited to the group as a whole. They and their children are "the conscience of their race." They carry their social identities around with them like packs on their backs.

The lived experience of the immigrant teenager is a little like that of the traveller whose routes in and out of the home take him along extended bridges across deep and dangerous chasms. Already the young immigrant is trying to span the gap between Britain and "home"; trying to make some sense of the striking contrasts in climate, environment, tempo of life and social position. These are not abstract ideas to him; they are two lived identities. There is the identity which belongs to the part of him that is West Indian, or Pakistani or Indian and is continually affirmed in the home and reaffirmed in his relation with his family, in the language he speaks with them, in remembered experiences, in relations he left behind. But there is also the identity of "the young Englander" towards which every new experience beckons him—school, friends, the street, work and England itself.

There may be differences of family background to contend with: mother and younger children still at "home" thousands of miles away, or mother with several children but no father, or a family life cast in a very traditional Victorian (and now, for Britain, increasingly deviant) mould—strong father, indulgent mother, a slightly religious atmosphere in the house, strict hours, rough discipline and justice. There are certainly differences of religious belief, of culture and social custom which the immigrant teenager must bridge. Above all, though the family may be a close unit and emotional supports within the home strong, it is nevertheless a unit trying to find and maintain its equilibrium under the stress of immigration, holding fast to old beliefs and values which are markers in a shifting world, and a unit vulnerable to change and exposed to misunderstanding. The very cohesion of such a family can be claustrophobic and frustrating for the young adventurous immigrant.

Somehow he must learn to reconcile his two identities and make them one. But many of the avenues into the wider society are closed to him. If he ventures into the clubs, he feels as though he is permanently on trial. This he finds especially difficult to bear because the relationship which the youth culture values most is the relaxed relationship in which people are not on trial, in which they simply belong and are accepted.

He might feel happier in "structured situations" in which there is a teacher or youth leader or night-school lecturer to tell the other youngsters to be nice to other people—especially coloured people and dumb animals. But the young immigrant wants recognition and confirmation where there is no one around to organise it for him, where groups form spontaneously, friendships are casual and noninstrumental and activities are unprogrammed. He wants the right to wander and loaf, to pick up friends, to chat the girls up, to dance or listen to records or play cricket, to dress up and move into town on Saturday evenings. This casual rhythm is the essence of teenage life. It mirrors the ebb and flow, the packed moments of activity followed by the prolonged lay-offs; of adolescence itself.

Beside this style of teenage life the young coloured immigrant's existence, for all its gaiety and vitality, is highly structured, careful, purposeful and disciplined. The pressures on him to pick up new skills, to challenge the Youth Employment Officer by having more O Levels than anybody else, to be steady at night-school and evening class, are strong and insistent. By these diligent and strenuous pursuits, the coloured immigrant—like most other immigrant groups—can beat the native at his own game. It is for this reason, then, that such strong emphasis is placed on formal education and the need to acquire industrial skills, to learn the language and the routines of an advanced technological society.

Some migrant families are assimilated to British society through their children. But assimilation has its price. Success in these spheres is the children's only compensation for the rather narrow and constricting range outside of school, work and college. Hard work, a decent job, respectability and self-respect—the young immigrant has to be satisfied with these virtues in his contact with his white counterparts. Yet he can't go "home" again. The route back is closed. But so too is the route forward. He finds the adult community around him hostile, the adolescent world closed against him, he has a sustained sense of unfairness and misrepresentation whenever his activities bring him into contact with authority, he feels that he is, unthinkingly, excluded from the self-selected in-groups of leisure time. He is "them" rather than "us."

I have noticed that the young immigrants I have met in the last year or two are falling back on their own reserves. They are closing-in their lines of contact, rediscovering their own racial and national identities and stereotyping their white counterparts. In itself, this may not be a bad thing—if integration means the enforced loss and rejection of their own identity, then it is too high a price to pay. Most people want recognition by their peers, but it must be recognition on equal and honourable terms.

There is a pride and independence among these youngsters which is a tribute to their resilience, their capacity to survive, their determination to respect and honour not only themselves but also their families, home countries, culture, prowess and achievements. This may be the only platform from which an "assault" on the host community can be made. Nevertheless, it represents lost ground in the struggle for integration.

We are further away from that goal today than we were in the late '50s when heavy immigration began. The lessons of disillusionment are strongly etched in the faces and attitudes of coloured teenagers. The bitterness and resentment of Smethwick have been absorbed. They have taken the place of the shock of Notting Hill, as that shock replaced the brightness and expectancy of the faces of 1956 and 1957. And each new experience of rejection, each new failure to make contact leaves its mark.

The problems of the young immigrants are the problems of the marginal men and women of British society—Britain's new second-class citizens. Few people have begun to understand the stresses placed on them or their complex needs and expectations or their particular vulnerability. Before we try to find "solutions" to their "problems," we must imagine ourselves in their place. We must try to understand what it is like for them, standing at the point of conflict and intersection between two worlds—one world which carries echoes, associations, memories and ideals of the past and another which carries the promise—but also the threat and the danger—of the future.

NOTE

This essay first appeared as *The Young Englanders* (London: National Committee of Commonwealth Immigrants, 1967).

CHAPTER 3

Black Men, White Media

My main thesis is this: there is something radically wrong with the way black immigrants—West Indians, Asians, Africans—are handled by and presented on the mass media. What's more, I don't believe this can be resolved by a few more black faces on the screen, or by an extra documentary or two on immigrant problems. Nor do I think it can be traced to casual discrimination on racial matters within the broadcasting organizations. Its roots lie deep within the broadcasting structures themselves, and good liberal broadcasters, as well as bad racialist ones, are both constrained by these structures.

Broadly speaking, the media exist in a very close, sympathetic relationship to power and established values. They favour a consensus view of any problem: they reflect overwhelmingly middle-class attitudes and experience. Basically, this unfits them for an authentic portrayal of the black community and its problems. The media tend to favour experts, privileged witnesses, middle men—whereas blacks are predominantly an out-group, outside the consensus. The media reflect organized majority and minority viewpoints—whereas blacks are relatively un-organized. The media are sensitive to middle-class ways of life—whereas blacks belong to the skilled and semi-skilled working class. The media favour the articulate—whereas blacks are relatively un-articulate, and their anger and frustration often outruns the terms of polite debate. Above all, the media are defensive about the sacred institutions of society—whereas black people most encounter problems in these sensitive power-areas: employment, public discrimination, housing, parliamentary legislation, local government, law and order, the police.

Now, does this conflict of interest between the media and black people really matter? I believe it does. The mass media play a crucial role in defining the problems and issues of public concern. They are the main channels of public discourse in our segregated society. They transmit stereotypes of one group to other groups. They attach feelings and emotions to problems. They set the terms in which problems are defined as "central" or "marginal."

My own view is that black people have had an invisible presence for centuries in British history: they have been the hidden component in the fate and fortune of Britain as a world-imperial power. In the very moment when that world-historical role is being diminished, blacks have come in large numbers to work and live in what is laughingly called the "host" society. They have always been—and are now *visibly*—central to the society's "quarrel with itself." You exclude them from access at considerable peril to society as a whole.

I ought to be more specific in the charges I am bringing against broadcasting. When blacks appear in the documentary/current affairs part of broadcasting, they are always attached to some "immigrant issue": they have to be involved in some crisis or drama to become visible actors to the media. But problem-centred programmes like these select and process participants in terms of very rigid programme-formulae. Blacks participate, then, in broadcasts defined by the media as "black" problems: and they do so within constraints, given in the very professional definition of what constitutes "good television," by the producers themselves. It is very rare indeed to see a programme where blacks themselves have defined the problem as they see it. Now it matters a great deal whether studio discussions are based on the premise that black people constitute a problem for Mr. Enoch Powell, or that Enoch Powell constitutes a problem for black people.

Further, such programmes are inevitably based on the liberal-consensus assumption that we are all proceeding, slowly but inevitably, towards a racially integrated society. Actually, for blacks, this premise of integration is a highly problematic question. There is much more evidence that Britain is, slowly but inevitably, drifting towards the creation of a permanent black minority of second-class citizens, living in poverty and deprivation, and subject to discrimination as a group. The liberal postulate about "integration" is a politician's and broadcaster's utopia. No black group would, realistically, choose this framework for a discussion of its problems. But, not only is this more realistic view never made the consensual basis of broadcasting, but it is extremely rare to see on television an examination of the real conditions on the ground, in the black/white communities, from which integration or its opposite—permanent conflict—might emerge.

This is because the media, on the whole, naturally gravitate to the liberal middle-ground: they find conflict and oppression—the real conditions of black existence—difficult and awkward. They tend to redefine all problems as failures in communication. But it is also because the media cream their way very thinly indeed through British society. Raymond Williams once remarked that it is hard to believe that there are 56 million people in Britain, since so few of them ever appear on television. The same could be said about the media and working-class people—as Phillip Whitehead pointed out recently in *The Listener*. There has been little attempt either in drama, documentary or features to explore and express the rich, complex, diverse and troubled experience of blacks. There have been few, if any, programmes sufficiently in touch with the grass roots of black opinion to recreate in broadcasting terms how the world looks from that position. The broadcasting formulae seem to inhibit ordinary people talking in their own terms about their own experience to the rest of society. The visible debate, therefore, *about* blacks, conducted in terms primarily set up by the race relations industry, leaves the vast, invisible majority of blacks untouched and unrepresented. They are a repressed part of what—from the viewpoint of the broadcasting studios—is virtually "unknown country." When the debate does surface, it is virtually impossible to hear any but a handful of middle-class blacks—like me—and spokesmen *for* the black community—like most of the people in this studio—speaking for the rest. On the whole, less articulate blacks are mercilessly processed and patronised when they do appear on the screen. What inhibitions, what constraints, what forms of self-censorship, what shallowness of social contacts ensure that the media will be so deeply unrepresentative of the ordinary men and women in this society? Blacks are not puppets attached by strings to some set of issues defined as "black problems." They form a natural minority in *any* cross-section of opinion from a large industrial city in England. They are crucially affected by everything which affects the rest of the society—education, welfare, common market, law and order. They have a right to access when these questions are being discussed.

But they also have problems and viewpoints which are distinctive. In recent years, there has been, within the black communities, a growing sense of identification with black consciousness and culture, with movements for liberation amongst black countries and minorities elsewhere, and a growing impulsion to link informal segregation in Britain with more overt forms of racism elsewhere. Just as there has been a powerful thrust towards defining Britain as naturally and inevitably "white." Now neither of these strands in public opinion are going to disappear because such controversial attitudes and conflicts are difficult for broadcasters to handle. Where such attitudes exist among blacks, and they do—they *must* be allowed clear expression: without the broadcasters silently labelling them "black power" and therefore "extremist" and therefore "wrong" and therefore excluding them, or "cooling them out" in the studio. The thrust towards black consciousness, like the thrust towards more overt racism, are deeply rooted in the real historical situation: they won't disappear because they affront broadcasting's liberal sensibilities.

I have been talking mainly about current affairs. But I hope we won't forget that, in terms of the steady formation of popular attitudes, the maintenance and reinforcement of stereotypes, the drama/series/serial end of broadcasting, and entertainment, exerts a much stronger impact than current affairs. The routine handling of illegal immigrants, with which programmes like *The Saint* and the popular police television series, *Softly Softly*, have recently dealt, helps to confirm the impression, eloquently fostered elsewhere, that Britain is being steadily overrun by Pakistanis on the run.

You can see, from recent speeches on immigrant issues by Mr. Powell and others, what mischief can be worked when such stereotypes are lying around in popular consciousness to be activated in more political and more explosive contexts. We know comparatively little about how early such stereotypes are created, how much the media contribute to them, or whether the media could help to erode them. But we could use broadcasting in a far more positive way here—if we consciously made the choice to do so—than we do at present. Children's television, for example, is still "whiter than white." The affluent thrillers have more stereotyped black villains and problem-families per square footage than they ought to in a society which is confronting an extremely dangerous problem. My impression is that this whole area of drama, serials and entertainment is treated as "routine broadcasting" where the race question is concerned: yet it may be precisely here where the fundamental damage is being done. The important point about television entertainment is that it educates the popular consciousness *informally*; by dealing with real-life problems and situations in fictional terms, it creates images without appearing to do so. And it powerfully attaches feelings and emotions to these images—feelings which can then be triggered off in more explosive situations.

The vast majority of blacks live in the worst housing, in the decaying inner rings of our cities: they do the menial work tasks: they belong to the poorest and most deprived sectors of society. They try to make a life in conditions of deprivation and oppression. This is the heart of the black experience in Britain today. What concerns me is the unwitting biases, the hidden premises, the invisible attitudes and loyalties, the concealed links between broadcasting and power, broadcasting and class which prevent the media from articulating this experience in clear and authentic terms. I doubt whether a little tinkering with the schedules will do here. I believe the constraints are written into broadcasting structures as we presently have them: and I believe that, if the situation does not rapidly change, broadcasters, like politicians, will face a massive withdrawal of confidence from the invisible half—black and white—in the society: a silent revolt of the audience.

NOTE

This essay first appeared as "Black Men, White Media," *Savacou* 9/10 (1974): 97–101.

CHAPTER 4

Race and "Moral Panics" in Postwar Britain

In his book *Black and White: The Negro and English Society, 1555–1945* James Walvin records how, in the last decade of the sixteenth century, England was troubled by an expanding population and a shortage of food. "As hunger swept the land, England was faced by a problem which taxed the resources of government to the limits. Immigrants added to the problem," since "no group was so immediately visible as the Blacks" which, by then, had been distributed in their thousands in English cities as a result of the growing involvement of England in the slave trade. Queen Elizabeth I, accordingly, wrote to the Lord Mayors of the country's major cities, remarking that "there are of late divers blackamoores brought into this realm, of which kinds of people there are alreadie manie, consideryng howe God hath blessed this land with great increase of people." She ordered that "those kinde of people be sent forth of the land." In January 1601, she repeated her advice in a Proclamation: send away "such Negroes and blackamoores which . . . are carried into this realm . . . to the great annoyance of her own liege people" (Walvin 1973, 8). Walvin does not record whether this is the first English "moral panic" about race. But the incident helps to give some historical perspective to the theme of this lecture—the English reaction to race in the postwar period. It suggests also, that the mechanisms involved are not—as we might have supposed—of recent origin: I mean the mechanism by means of which problems *internal* to the society are projected onto, or exported into, an excessive and regressive preoccupation with "race." The 1970s is not the first time that the English official mind, forced to contemplate a "crisis," has turned the conversation in the direction of "the blacks."

This is the first, and perhaps the most important point I want to make. Let me put it more generally. There is an overwhelming tendency to *abstract* questions of race from their *internal* social and political contexts—to deal with "race" as if it had nothing intrinsically to do with the present "condition of England." It is viewed as an "external" problem, foisted on English society from the outside, which has simply been visited on the society from the skies. To hear problems of race discussed in England today, one would believe that relations between Britain and the peoples of the Caribbean or Indian subcontinent began with the first wave of black immigrants in the late 1940s and early 1950s. "The English and race" is debated as if it is a brief and temporary interlude—which will shortly be brought to an end. These poor, benighted people—for reasons which the British now find it hard to bring to mind—picked themselves up out of their villages and plantations and, uninvited, made this long, strange and apparently unpredictable journey to the doors of British industry—which, out of the pure goodness of their hearts, gave them employment. Now the "good times" are over, and the kissing has to stop. The national patience is exhausted, the fund of goodwill used up. It is time the problem "went back home where it came from." The British people require to be assured—so we are told—that a definite and conclusive end to the problem is in sight.

The tendency to abstract race from the internal dynamic of the society, and to repress its history, is not confined to the political "Right." It is also to be found on the "liberal Left." For the "Right," immigration and race are a problem of the control of an external flow—or, as the popular press would say, a "wave," a "tide": stop the flow and racism will subside. The liberal "Left" have long treated immigration and race as a problem in the exercise of "good conscience." Be kind to "our friends from overseas": then racism will disappear. Neither side can bring themselves to refer to Britain's imperial and colonial past, even as a contributory factor to the present situation. The slate has been wiped clean. Racism is not endemic to the structures of British social life, it has nothing intrinsically to do with the dynamic of British politics, or with the economic crisis: it is not part of English culture—it does not belong to the "English Ideology." It is an external virus, injected into the body politic. Its control is a matter of *policy*—but not of *politics*.

I hope to persuade you that this cannot be true. It was not true of the historical past. And it is not true of the decades since the 1950s—the "high" period of black migration to Britain. We cannot account for the emergence of a specifically *indigenous* racism in this way. The latter phase is the main subject of my talk tonight. But something must be said, first, about the historical aspects. Britain's relations with the peoples of the Caribbean and the Indian subcontinent do not begin in the late 1940s. British attitudes to the excolonial subject peoples of a former time cannot be accurately charted from the appearance of a black proletariat in Birmingham or Bradford in the 1950s. These relations are a central feature in the formation of Britain's material dominance, as they are a central theme in English culture and in popular and official ideologies. Britain's rise to mercantile dominance, and the process of "primitive accumulation" which generated the surpluses of wealth that set capitalist development in motion, were founded on the slave trade and the plantation systems of the Americas in the seventeenth century. India provided the material basis for the foundation of Britain's Asian Empire—as well as the basis, in cheap labour and raw materials, for the early industrial revolution—in the eighteenth century. The colonization of Africa and the penetration of the markets of Latin America and the Far East were the centrepiece of Britain's industrial and imperial hegemony in the nineteenth century—the zenith of Empire. In each of those phases, an economic and a cultural chain—the imperialist chain—bound the fate of millions of workers and peasants in the colonial hinterlands to the destiny of those in the Heartland of English society. The wealth—drawn off through conquest, colonization and trade—silently enriched one rising class after another, fed and supported one phase of economic development after another, provided the invisible foundations for the flourishing culture of one English city and seaport after another, across four centuries. It is geography and distance which rendered them "invisible." It is only in the last phase of British imperialism that the labouring classes of the satellites and the labouring classes of the metropolis have confronted one another directly "on native ground." But their fates have long been indelibly intertwined. The very definition of "what it is to be British"—the centrepiece of that culture now to be preserved from racial dilution—has been articulated around this absent/present centre. If their blood has not mingled extensively with yours, their labour-power has long since entered your economic bloodstream. It is in the sugar you stir: it is in the sinews of the infamous British "sweet tooth": it *is* the tea-leaves at the bottom of the "British cuppa."

The indigenous British racism of the postwar period *begins* with this profound historical forgetfulness—the loss of historical memory, the collective amnesia, the ideological repression—which has overtaken the British people since the "end of Empire" in the 1950s. Paradoxically, the homegrown variety of racism begins with this attempt to wipe out and efface every trace of the colonial and imperial past from official and popular recall. Clearly, it is part of the traumatic adjustment to the "end of Empire"—the termination of a long and unrivalled period of world dominance. On the surface, Britain has often appeared to make this adjustment with its customary *sang-froid*. But, undoubtedly, it has left a great reservoir of guilt and a deep, historical resentment. It is not possible to operate so directly and surgically on "popular memory" without leaving deep scars and traces. This reservoir has undoubtedly nourished the springs of an indigenous racism. It may account, in a part, for the resonance of its popular appeal. It has to be reckoned with, in any account of the postwar British reaction to race. But it cannot explain it.

To do this we must turn to the *internal* factors which have made racism a growing and dynamic force in English society since the 1950s. It is not, in my view, helpful to define racism as a "natural" and permanent feature either of all societies or of a universal "human nature." It is not a permanent human or social deposit, waiting to be triggered off when the circumstances are right. It has no natural and universal law of development. It does not always assume the same configuration. There have been many different *racisms*—each historically specific, each articulated in a concrete and specific way with the other structures and relations of the social formations in which they appear. Racism is always historically specific. Though it may draw on the cultural traces deposited by previous historical phases, it always takes on specific forms. It arises out of *present*, not past conditions. Its effects are specific to the present organization of society, to the present unfolding of its dynamic political and cultural processes—not simply to its repressed past. It may matter less than we think that Britain has, over four centuries, been involved in modes of economic exploitation and political domination on a world scale, many of which operated through the mechanisms of race. This only signals the potential—perhaps the propensity—of the society to take that route again. But the indigenous racism of the 1960s and '70s is significantly different—form and effect—from the racism of the "high" colonial period. It is a racism "at home" rather than abroad: the racism, not of a dominant, but of a declining social formation. It is to the social construction of this indigenous racism that we now turn.

First, it is necessary to establish a rough periodization. Here, we must hold two perspectives in mind, at the same time. We must look *sequentially*—at the way racism has been constructed and developed across three decades: at its development as a process: at its connected forms, and its deepening impact, on black and white populations alike. At the same time, we must look *laterally*—sideways, so to speak—at the connections which race contracts with other things in society, at each of its turning points: the relations, structures and events which become harnessed to, or articulated through, race.

The late 1940s to the mid-1950s is the period of initial settlement. Here, we find the buildup of black workers in the labour-hungry centres of production: a period when industry is swinging over from war-time to peace-time production, and into the great productive "boom" of the mid-1950s. The main outlines of the pattern of black settlement are established in this phase: the inner-city black concentrations, multiple occupation, the density of black labour in certain specific occupations. In this period of accommodation and adjustment, blacks and Asians maintain a "low profile": drawing their curtains against the cold and the "outside," effacing themselves as an intrusive presence. It is a period of muted optimism about long-term "assimilation." The real environments where the possibility of racial coexistence is tested out are in the jobs and localities where the black and white working classes meet. There are many problems of adjustment on both sides—but the lines of informal segregation which have come to be the prevailing social pattern in such areas have not yet hardened into place. The whole period—what Sivanandan (1976) has called the "laissez-faire period" in British immigration politics, the period of the "open door," is lubricated by the economic boom. The need for British industry to draw heavily on this new reserve army of labour weakened official resistance to the introduction of a black working class; it also weakened the sharpness of the competition for jobs between black and white workers. The segmentation of black occupations shielded white workers, for a time, from its full impact—in a period of full employment. Above all, rising living standards provided just that economic space—the margin of manoeuvre—in the urban areas, which gave people some room to settle and move. The modest "optimism" about race, in this period, was, if you like, closely dependent on a general climate of economic optimism—the one an expression of the other.

The real history of this early phase remains to be written. But the first signs of an open and emergent racism of a specifically indigenous type appears in the race riots of Notting Hill and Nottingham in 1958. This *cannot* be *directly* attributed to the early warning signs of a developing crisis, of accumulation and balance of payments, in the economy of the late 1950s. Notting Hill was a classic scenario for this emergence: one of those "traditional urban zones" where, for the first time, the incipient "black colony"—and a distinct and different "colony" way of life—begins to flourish and expand. There are three constituent elements in these early riots. The first is the appearance for the first time in real terms since the 1930s of an active fascist political element; the Unionist movement, led by Mosley, and the dissident League of Empire Loyalists. They had seen—quite correctly—that the transitional culture of North Kensington, with its incipient but growing urban problems, provided a more favourable terrain for the construction of a native racism than the more stable traditional structure of an older area of settlement, like Brixton. They introduced the syntax of racism into street-corner politics: but, in effect, they were more symptom than cause. The second element was the more structured antagonism between "colony blacks" and the indigenous white working class and petty-bourgeoisie of this decaying "Royal" borough. Against this fulcrum—which marks the crucial intersection between the politics of race and the politics of the inner city—the wheel of British racism turned. The third, most active element was that which pioneered the open harassment of blacks on the streets: white teenagers. But here—looking laterally—it is important to note that the Notting Hill riots have a double history. They are part of the history of emergent racism: but they are *also* part of the moral panic of the mid-1950s about the antisocial attitudes of youth in an "affluent" and materialist world. If the presence of blacks within the area itself touched the sources of public anxiety about competition over scarce urban resources, the spectacle of black and white youths, locked in confrontation around the tube station and backstreets of North Kensington, fed into those deep and troubled anxieties about the rapid process of postwar social change—a process for which "Youth" had come to stand as a vivid cultural symbol. In a famous editorial, the *Times* mapped the Notting Hill events directly into hooliganism, teenage violence, lawlessness and anarchy. These together with the football spectator and the railway carriage wrecker—"All are manifestations of a strand of our social behavior that an *adult* society can do without" (our emphasis). The editorial was not headed "'Race Riot' in Notting Hill." It was entitled "Hooliganism *Is* Hooliganism." Nevertheless, as the economic downturn began in earnest, Britain introduced—in 1962— the first Commonwealth Immigration Act, imposing controls on the "flow of immigrants."

The second turning point is 1964. By now, the economic boom had tapered off, and the classes which have to be addressed about these growing material problems—which in the 1950s had been defined as never again likely to appear—are no longer runaway Teddy Boys, but adult white workers and their families. The location of the new turning point in the emergence of postwar racism, therefore, takes place, not in the decaying "colony" of a transitional zone like Notting Hill, but in the very heartland of the traditional and conservative nation: Smethwick. Peter Griffiths's successful campaign against black immigration in the 1964 election marks the first moment when racism is appropriated into the official policy and programme of a major political party and legitimated as the basis of an electoral appeal, specifically directed at the popular classes. Here is the beginning of racism as a key element in the official politics of populism—racism in a structured and "legitimate" political form. The defeat of a Labour Minister on the issue proved—if Paul Foot's depressing survey did not—the penetration of racist ideology within the organized working-class and the labour institutions themselves. It revealed the degree to which, as a consequence of all that had happened to the organized labour movement in the period of consensus, the working class was now exposed and vulnerable to the construction of a popular racism. The Smethwick victory—a turning point in the history of postwar racism—was followed by the 1965 *White Paper on Immigration from the Commonwealth*, which, as Robert Moore observed last week, "laid the ideological basis for subsequent policy and as a result the argument that numbers of immigrants was the essence of the problem . . . was defined."

Between 1964 and 1968, the date of our third "turning point," the world itself turned. It turned, specifically, in race relations. The dream of assimilation was laid low, and finally abandoned in the mid-'60s. The black population drew back into its defensive enclaves and, much affected by the rise of black struggles in the US, began to develop a different, distinct and more actively engaged black political ideology. But 1968 is also a cataclysmic year, not only in Britain but elsewhere: in the US, in France, Italy, Germany, Japan. It is the period of the growing protests against the Vietnam War, the year of the student revolutions, of black power and black separatism, of the cultural revolution; of "hot" summers on the streets, followed by "hot" autumns in the factories. It inaugurated a period of profound political, social and cultural *polarization*—when the great consensus, which had uneasily united all classes and strata into the "politics of the centre," backed by an apparently unending boom, definitively came apart, to reveal the contradictions and antagonisms gathering beneath. It is the period in which the state and the governing classes perceive, not simply the erosion of traditional standards and ways of life and belief, which they had identified with the plague of "permissiveness," but the formation of what they construed as an active and organized conspiracy against the social order itself. It is the year in which President Nixon won an infamous victory by summoning up the demons of the "silent majority" in the service of a "law and order" crusade.

"Powellism" is formed in this moment, out of this crucible. By "Powellism" I mean something larger, more significant than the explicit enunciation of new racially defined policies for the black population. I mean the formation of an "official" racist politics at the heart of the political culture itself. Mr. Powell's famous pronouncements on race in 1968 and 1969 have since become justly famous. It is not so often remarked that "Powellism," though it derived its cutting edge from the resonance of its racial themes, was directed, more widely, at the crisis of the social order, at the conspiracy of radical and alien forces threatening "law and order," at what he himself called the "Enemy Within." Nor can the articulation of this talk of "conspiracy" and "order" be laid exclusively at his door. A range of politicians and public spokesmen, the press and the mass media, in this period are mesmerized by the spectacle of a society—Britain is, of course, not the only example—careering through polarization into a deep crisis of social authority, what Gramsci calls a "crisis of hegemony." It is this whole crisis—not race alone—which is the subject and object of law and order crusades, the appeals to "tough measures," the whispers of conspiracy. In one of its principal dimensions, this crisis is *thematized* through race. Race is the prism through which British people are called upon to "live through," to understand, and then to deal with crisis conditions. The Enemy is "within the gates." "He" is nameless: protean: everywhere. He may even be in the Foreign Office, cooking the immigration figures, and fooling the people. But someone will name him. He is "The Other"—L'Autre—the stranger in the midst, the cuckoo in the nest, the excrement in the letter box. "He" is—*the blacks*. This ideology, predicated around this racist "subject," which is formed in response to a crisis, must touch and connect with the lived experiences of the "silent majorities," to become practically effective. It must acquire a concrete purchase on the lives of citizens, on their everyday conditions and circumstances, on their common-sense experiences, if the "threat" to society is to become palpable and real. When the "silent" and beleaguered majorities—the great underclasses, the great, silent, "British Public"—are made to "speak," through the ventriloquism of its public articulators, it is not surprising, then, that it "speaks" with the unmistakable accent of a thoroughly homegrown racism.

"Powellism" may have been kept out of political power, but, in this period, it dominated and defined the ideological terrain. Both the 1968 Act—with its explicit use of racial categories—the infamous "patrial" distinction—and the 1971 Act which succeeded it, bearing down on the "soft underbelly" of the immigration problem—the dependents and families of black and Asian workers—are tributes to its profound success, its popular *mobilizing* appeal.

Through the 1970s, the "backlash" is constructed. It moves on all fronts at once: political, industrial, racial, ideological. As the depth of the British economic recession begins to be revealed, and as the state girds up its loins to confront the hidden materialism of the working class directly, we witness the construction of a "soft law and order" society. The law itself becomes, in part, the engine of this regression. On the industrial front, it is recruited directly into the confrontation with the working class. On the political front, it is mobilized specifically against radicals, political demonstrators and "extremists." The language of extremists versus moderates becomes the everyday syntax of the mass media in this period. The legal harassment of the black colony populations, the overt racist homilies against the whole black population by judges in court, the imposition of tough policing and arrest "on suspicion" in the colony areas, the rising hysteria about black crime, the identification of black crime with "mugging," must be seen in the wider context of this decisive turn into "popular authoritarianism." Here, the panics about race succeed one another with such rapid succession that it is difficult to separate them out. The lulls between them are only temporary: the running warfare between unemployed black youth and the police; the swamping tactics of the Special Patrol Groups; the arrests of black political activists "on sus"; the scare hysteria, fanned by the section of the press which has detached itself into the authoritarian campaign, against Ugandan and Malawi Asians—the great, prophesied "tidal wave"; the pressure on illegal immigrants; the "scandalous" stories of Asian families "living in luxury off the Council"—the black counterpart of that general assault on the welfare state which also produced its repertory of scare stories about white "welfare scroungers" drawing the dole on the Costa Brava; the murder of Asian youths in Southall; the confrontations of Brockwell Park and other scenes of set warfare between youths and the police; above all, the refining and focussing down of the problem into the inner-city zones—the localities where the general nightmares of the "racial threat" to "our way of life" can be made specific and concrete. Here, the programmes of urban aid have failed to stem the tide of urban poverty and decay. Here, the recessive cycles of unemployment, the fears of recession, the competition over dwindling jobs, begin to bite. Young black youths are increasingly unemployed—drifting, as every unemployed section of the working class historically has, into petty pilfering and crime. The colony areas are the incipient basis for an increasingly restless and alienated sector of the population. This is where the crisis intersects. Practically, they have to be *policed*—with increasing strictness. But, also, the crisis has to be explained—ideologically—and dealt with: contained, managed. Blacks become the bearers, the signifiers, of the crisis: racism is its "final solution." The class which is called upon to bear the brunt of the economic crisis is divided and segmented against, and within, itself—along racial lines. If racism had never existed, as a plausible way in which the underclasses of society could be impelled to "live through" the crisis of the social formation, it would surely have had to be invented in the 1970s.

This is not a crisis *of* race. But race periodises and punctuates the crisis. Race is the prism through which the crisis is perceived. It is the justifying scheme by means of which the crisis is analysed and explained. It is the means by which the crisis is to be resolved. It is the operator, the crystallization of the crisis. It is the mechanism through which the movement, at the level of politics and the state, is "pioneered" towards a necessarily exceptional form or moment of the state: a moment which has to rely on law and coercion, since the very foundations of social consensus have been eroded: "more than usual" law and order to deal with a "more than usual" threat to the social order. It is race, above all, which effectively connects the "crisis of the state" above with the state of the streets, and little old ladies hustled off pavements, in the depths, below. Race makes the abstract "crisis of authority" real, concrete, specific. Like hanging, it wonderfully concentrates the popular mind. In his famous speech at Northfield, during the 1970 election, Mr. Powell had warned of the "invisible enemy within"—students "destroying" universities and "terrorising" cities, "bringing down" governments; of the power of the "modern form" of the mob—the demonstration—in making "governments tremble"; the success of disorder, "deliberately fomented for its own sake" in the near-destruction of civil government in Northern Ireland; and the accumulation of "combustible material" of "another kind"—that is, of race. The problem, however, he asserted, had been "miscalled race." Race was being used to mystify and confuse the people. The real problem was the great liberal conspiracy, inside government and the media, which held ordinary people up to ransom, making them fearful to speak the truth for fear of being called "racialist," and "literally made to say black is white." It was race—but now as the pivot of this "process of brain-washing by repetition of manifest absurdities"; race as a "secret weapon," "depriving them of their wits and convincing them that what they thought right was wrong"; in short, race as the conspiracy of silence and blackmail against the silent and long-suffering "majority." This is the syntax of an authentic regressive populism, which is articulated through and around the potent metaphors of race. Its counterpart can be found, extensively, in that period, from many other sources. Its echo lives on, amplified and expanded, in the panic climate of 1978—even if the terms are more polite, the rhetoric less compelling, the accent more "refined." Populist racism is no longer the preserve and prerogative of a minority, prophesying in the wilderness. It has become "naturalized"—normal currency of exchange at the centre of the political culture, and can be read, any day, on the front page of the popular press—the *Daily Mail* for example.

We have said that the emergence of the ideology of indigenous racism has periodically assumed the form of a "moral panic." Moral panics have been defined as follows by Professor Stan Cohen:

> Societies appear every now and then to be subject to periods of moral panic. A condition, episode, person or group of persons emerges to become defined as a threat to societal values and interests; its nature is presented in a stylized and stereo-typical fashion by the mass media; the moral barricades are manned by editors, bishops, politicians and other right-thinking people; socially accredited experts pronounce their diagnoses and solutions; ways of coping are evolved, or (more often) resorted to; the condition then disappears, submerges, or deteriorates and becomes more visible. Sometimes the panic is passed over and forgotten ... at other times it has more serious and long-term repercussions and might produce such changes in legal and social policy or even in the way society conceives itself. (1972, 9)

Professor Cohen was describing the social reaction to the activities of youth in the 1950s and 1960s—the "Teddy Boy" and "Mods and Rockers" phenomena. But his definition can and should be extended to the emergence of indigenous racism. The important features of the "moral panic" as an ideological process are these. It represents a way of dealing with diffuse social fears and anxieties—by projecting or displacing them on to the stigmatized social group. It crystallizes such fears and anxieties—by providing them with a simple and concrete, identifiable social "object." Around these stigmatized groups and events, a powerful, popular groundswell can often be mobilized, calling on the "authorities" to take controlling action. "Moral panics," therefore, frequently serve to pioneer policies and practices by the state which increase social control, which move the apparatuses of the state into a more coercive closure. At the same time, these "panics" give this shift towards coercive closure in the state—the opening up of "exceptional moments" in the postliberal state—a *popular* base and legitimacy. It is one of the forms in which a largely voiceless and powerless section of the community can draw attention and give voice to its concrete problems, and call for remedies and solutions. Thus, the language and stereotypical explanatory terms of a "moral panic" provide a popular vocabulary and discontent which can itself become the ideological vehicle through which "the people" are spoken for, and spoken to. We do not need to have recourse to models of conspiracy here—though the tilt of the pendulum in the state towards the coercive pole is often, itself, supported by conspiratorial nightmares. In formal democracies, where policies—especially if they are tough and constraining—require to be given the legitimacy of popular consent, "moral panics" can sometimes provide the basis by which a popular authoritarianism is actively *constructed*: the means, in short, by which the "consent of the popular classes" is won for the imposition of "more than usual measures" of control.

We have undoubtedly, in the late 1960s and 1970s, seen *both* processes in operation: the "movement towards a closure of control" in the operations of the strong state—which, in crisis conditions, must take the lead, give the semblance of "the smack of firm government"; and the construction of popular authoritarian ideologies. Both have operated within, but are not reducible to, the deepening of the world economic recession, which has bitten particularly hard and sharp in Britain itself. Whichever political Party has been in power, the ideological terrain has undoubtedly been captured, defined and colonized by this shift into popular authoritarianism. We find variants of it in the general assault on the whole concept of social welfare; in the militant advocacy of the virtues of social competition, self-reliant individualism and what are called "social market values." We find it in the concerted assault on "progressive" and "comprehensive" trends in education—the call for a "return" to standards, to the traditional curriculum, to discipline and authority in the classroom—even, if necessary, corporal punishment. We find it in the aggressive defence of traditional moral standards and values—above all, in the defence of the traditional family, and the opposition to every tentative movement in the liberalization of sexual mores or in the position of women.

We find it in the "moral backlash"—the resistance to every vestige of the so-called "permissive society," and the summons to worship and honour the traditional shrines and pieties. Race is only *one* of the elements in this wider ideological crusade to "clean up" Britain, to roll up the map of liberalism, and to turn the clock of history back to the times where the world was "safe for Englishmen." Parties in power, of whatever political complexion, which fondly imagine they are in command of the forces and tendencies moving in popular consciousness, do not remotely appear to understand the degree to which they are not riding, but *ridden*—driven and directed by this authoritarian wave: how the historical stage and the political agenda is set—how the ideological terrain is defined—by forces which they do not control, but with which they, nevertheless, frequently collude.

Race is only one element in this struggle to command and structure the popular ideology: but it has been, over the past two decades, a leading element: perhaps, the *key* element. Since it appears to be grounded in natural and biological "facts," it is a way of drawing distinctions and developing practices which appear, themselves, to be "natural," given and universal. It has, for example, become an "acceptable" explanation for some features of the racism of the British police in their interactions with the black population, to say that, since they are only a cross-section of the "great British public"—there is, "naturally," a due proportion of "racists" amongst them. Race provides the structure of simplifications which make it possible to construct plausible explanations of troubling developments, and which facilitates the application of simplifying remedies. Who now wants to begin to explore the complex of economic and political forces which have perpetuated and multiplied the poverty of the working-class districts of the inner cities? Who will have time for that complicated exercise—which may require us to trace connections between structures of our society which it is more convenient to keep apart: when a simple, obvious, "natural" explanation lies to hand. Of course: they are *"poor"* because *the blacks* are *here*. It is not a logical proposition: but ideologies do not function by that kind of logic—they exhibit a "logic" of their own. Race thus provides, in times of crisis and upheaval, an apparently "natural" and self-justifying circle of explanations.

But it is not this general syntax of racism—which can be found in more than one of the many racisms which have flourished—but a very specific variant form which has become active in the postwar period. Not the racism of a confident class—like the slaveholding plantocracy of the Americas—but a "racism" of a divided ruling class: a racism, not of economic dominance but of economic decline: a racism which, far from expressing—as it does in South Africa—the element of enforced cohesion and imposed unity by a ruling class unified by a racist ideology, is a racism which emerges out of the break-up of social cohesion and consensus. Though no doubt there are active racist elements among the dominant social classes in Britain, British racism has become, specifically, a racism *for* the working classes and the petty-bourgeoisie. Its strident and active *populism* is one of its defining characteristics. In this sense, it has helped to disentangle and *dislocate* the existing ideologies of class—of economic class demands and of the class struggle—and helped to *reconstruct* and recompose them into ideologies of "the nation" and "the people." It has the effect of cementing together the perspectives and interests of groups which may well be, on other grounds, antagonistic or opposed to one another, into the great generic "unities" of nation, people and race. The penetration of working-class ideology and practice by racism thus represents a crisis *for* the working class itself—a crisis of its practice and its institutions as profound as is the problem of race for the society as a whole. The working class now reproduces itself and is socially reproduced—racially structured—in two segments. It is remorselessly divided into two fractions, opposed to one another through race. In this way, the growth of racism has helped to *contain* the representative strategies and struggles of the working class and of the organized labour movement, confining them to struggles which, being race-specific, cannot surmount racism. The class struggle is constantly turned back through its own internal divisions. Consequently, racism in Britain has had the effect of finding, in the very material conditions of this divided class, and in its unreconstructed "common sense," an authentic popular basis.

I hope I will not be misunderstood as attributing an innate and universal "racism" to the working class or indeed to any other class as such in the British social formation. The burden of my remarks has been to resist this universal, psychological attribution of a "racist human nature," and concentrate specifically on the concrete process and circumstances which have produced an indigenous British racism, the real and specific problems to which racism provides a displaced mode of address, the "real" conditions of existence which are misrepresented in the apparently explanatory power of popular racism; how the practices which support it have actually come to constitute a powerful and active social force. Until this *specificity* of British racism has been understood, and practices developed which specifically address the real problems of the British social formation which are *displaced through race*, there isn't in my view a hope of turning the tide. It is the material conditions of the postwar crisis of Britain—economic, political, ideological—which provide the basis, the determining circumstances, which have enabled a popular racism to develop. It is the real conditions of existence of the poorer classes of society—lived, through racism, in a thoroughly ideological and "imaginary" way—which gives reality to its structure, which grounds its appeals and its rhetoric, which supports a racist "common sense." It is to this crisis, in its full economic, political and ideological dimensions—rather than to proscriptions against the grandfathers and daughters of Britain's black working population, waiting to enter in at the pearly gates of Handsworth or Mosside—that we must look, and struggle for a solution. If not, the pace of popular racism is certain to accelerate, step in step with the crisis. And the dynamic and direction of popular racism will be dictated by that infernal dialectic between, on the one hand, the "informal" racism of the streets, which the National Front has been pioneering with some success, working directly at the very base of popular class support of the two major parties; and on the other hand, the "formal" racism which has shaped up partly as a response to this electoral bid, in the major political parties and at the centre of the political culture itself.

NOTE

This essay first appeared as "Race and 'Moral Panics' in Postwar Britain," public lecture, British Sociological Association, London, May 2, 1978; and published in BBC, *Five Views of Multi-racial Britain* (London: Commission for Racial Equality, 1978), 23–35.

REFERENCES

Cohen, Stanley. 1972. *Folk Devils and Moral Panics: The Creation of the Mods and Rockers*. London: MacGibbon and Kee.
Sivanandan, A. 1976. "Race, Class and the State: The Black Experience in Britain." *Race and Class* 17, no. 4 (April): 347–68.
Walvin, James. 1973. *Black and White: The Negro and English Society, 1555–1945*. London: Allen Lane.

CHAPTER 5

Summer in the City

It can't happen here. But of course it can and has. And neither the tolerance of the British people, the flexibility of the constitution, policing by consent, our genius for compromise, nor even a royal summer wedding—none of these great gifts of the Divine to The Nation could save British cities from riots, the petrol bomb, the CS gas canister and rubber bullets.

The spectacle of "decent" working people (many of them, as it happens, out of work) helping themselves to colour TV sets made it seem for all the world as if Liverpool was Watts, Detroit or Harlem.

It can't happen here. But it has been happening here for some time now.

Mrs. Thatcher has spent much of the summer sitting out the H-Block hunger strike, no doubt grateful for the unswerving support of the Labour spokesperson on Northern Ireland. But crises left unattended—like wounds not dressed—fester and infect the body politic. After watching rioting in the Falls Road as a nightly spectacle on television—persisting in believing that it is ten thousand light-years away and nothing to do with us—here we are with Toxteth and Brixton looking like a war-torn Northern Irish city where, for unaccountable reasons, people have risen up against the state.

Can it possibly have happened? It has, and in all likelihood it will happen again. It is not the beginnings of Armageddon—it is not even the birth pangs of St. Petersburg, 1917. Perhaps the most significant, single consequence of the riots is that the police have finally achieved what some of their superior officers and the Police Federation have long been demanding: permission to appear on the streets in full antiurban terrorist regalia, just like the French CRS. It is too early to call anything which has happened a victory—unless it is a victory for the drift into a heavily policed authoritarian democracy. But it is without a shadow of a doubt the grinding noise of a social and political crisis in full swing.

The riots have taken Right and Left alike by surprise. This was only to be expected and is indeed a correct response. We are right to be surprised when the whole tempo of political struggle suddenly and sharply moves into a higher register.

On any other account, we cannot possibly be surprised. Anyone with their ears and eyes half open must know by now that violence between black people and the police has become a way of life in the cities. And when harassment and racism, "move on, gollywog; step this way, nig-nog," become the routine ways in which police and policed relate to each other, sooner or later the situation is certain to blow.

This point has been documented time and time again since the late 1960s. It is the lesson of the black experience in Britain. Not to have learned that lesson is to be guilty of bad faith or social loss of memory on a massive scale. The trouble is, white society—including most of the organised Left and the Labour movement—is so guilty. Accordingly, I so accuse every responsible authority, body or group which claims to offer political leadership in our society and which has nevertheless either: poured scorn on sociologists who predicted trouble; smeared as subversive agents of Trotskyism those social workers, black activists, local councillors or civil rights campaigners who mentioned such a possibility; remained silent when the press has once again floated the conspiracy theory; equated the Anti-Nazi League with the British Movement as extremists of Left and Right; gave comfort to the view that if only the subversive, antipolice element would stay at home, blacks would be happy and content with their lot.

The list is exceedingly long—and growing. It should be headed by almost every chief constable of whatever religious or political persuasion or policing philosophy—men who not only enjoy high office but, it appears, cannot be removed from it by any means yet discovered.

A number of us in the mid-1970s argued that young blacks in their deep alienation from white society were, in effect, being criminalised. We said that, as the recession deepened and things became tougher, blacks would find themselves in the front line of a policy calculated to increase the likelihood of violent counter-resistance. We suggested that this converged with a shift of the political culture; an increase in both respectable and street-fighting racism, and a government of the radical Right which adopted iron policies—a free market, a strong state. Law-and-order measures would, in effect, give the ideological lead to the police to redefine the resultant social and political trouble as being merely a technical matter of more efficient policing. This dismal scenario we called "policing the crisis."

As recession bit deep into both white and black communities and the law increasingly became the means for disciplining wages, the unions, labour and the working class, there was every likelihood that this process would rapidly encompass the white working class and urban unemployed. We take no pride whatsoever in pointing out that this forecast is what has come about. Whether the Left has fully grasped the seriousness and depth of this turn remains in doubt.

One immediate response to the riots has been the fashionable demand to "begin with what is happening on the streets." Another equally pertinent starting point might be to have another look at "monetarism"—not as an economic doctrine, but as a political economy, a regime of social discipline.

Let us, however, start with "the streets"—and with the severe case of social loss of memory. Have those who were "surprised" at trouble in the peaceful St. Pauls district of Bristol not read Ken Pryce's study of that area, *Endless Pressure* (1979), that was published years ago?

(Those fortunate enough to own a pressure cooker will know that the inevitable outcome of applying "endless pressure" is that the lid blows a hole in the roof.)

Is it really a surprise, to those who can cast their minds back, to find that the "docile" Asian community of Southall will not sit at prayer and allow a group of racist-swearing skinheads—imported specially into the area to groove on Oi music and throw bricks through Asian shop windows for an encore?

Those who sign themselves "Surprised, Brixton" might inquire of a local resident for how long, and why, Railton Road has been known as The Front Line. Is it government spending cuts which prevented the Home Secretary from reading the indictment of police-black relations published by the Lambeth Council? The report documents the long list of so-called respectable but bewildered black adults forced by circumstances to remark that respect for the law is one thing, but systematic racist abuse and the failure of senior police officers to prevent physical assault in the local cop shop is another.

This is *not* the voice of street subversives or doped-up rastas. Lord Scarman seemed surprised that events in Brixton might have been triggered off by a police "swamp." But the Lambeth report was itself an inquiry into the earlier disastrous "swamp" of November 1978—one of many such forays by the London SPG. The SPG set up roadblocks, conducted drug swoops and made such free use of the Sus charge that it unwittingly contributed to its eventual repeal. The officer in charge, Assistant Commissioner Kelland, is reported to have declared the operation to be highly successful, leading to a drastic reduction in crime—and, no doubt, a corresponding deepening of the disaffection of the local community. Is it a surprise that such people feel they are policed like a colony population?

In these areas, the black population have long ago been abandoned to tough policing. After all, the Prime Minister, who knows where the backbone of England is, has declared that they are an alien wedge. The police are willing and able, indeed anxious, to impose the neglect of the state on the people who live in such places, and to provide the disciplinary means by which the poor and working people are made to bear the brunt of Mrs. Thatcher's tough medicine.

They take shelter behind scandalous apologetics: We don't make the law, we only apply it; Britain is racist, we recruit a cross section of the population so the police will be racist too. If chief constables are prepared to wear this latter excuse, they must also be prepared to accept its corollary: since some British people are criminals and we recruit a cross-section of the population, a number of the police will be criminals too. The latter, Sir Robert Mark prided himself on doing something about; the former, Sir David McNee feels incapable of remedying.

The overwhelming evidence of police harassment and casual racism is said to lack credibility. It is Manchester Chief Constable James Anderton's considered view that "in the future ... basic crime ... will not be the predominant police feature. What will be the matter of greatest concern will be the covert and ultimately overt attempts to overthrow democracy, to subvert the authority of the state and ... to involve themselves in acts of sedition designed to destroy our parliamentary system."

This not only carries credibility, it is tolerated as evidence of the political impartiality of the police.

Is it surprising that the expendables have taken the message and cast the police in the role they are so anxious to adopt: the thin blue line between the state and the community?

One of the most significant developments brought to light by the riots is that though the repudiation of an oppressive and racist white *society* by blacks is widespread, anti-white *feeling* is neither an automatic nor an unselective response.

Toxteth, a long-standing scandalous example of black-police relations, is a case where white youth and adults were openly involved in both rioting and looting, and the tide of antipolice feeling among the white local population is as high as it is in the black community. Jimmy Kelly, whom readers will remember as the man from neighbouring Huyton, was not black. Nor were those treated by the Whiston hospital casualty in that infamous week of June 1979 when the Knowsley police seemed to go temporarily berserk. These complaints brought the police inspectorate hurrying to Merseyside for one of those many internal and impartial inquiries that always end in exoneration. Chief Constable Kenneth Oxford was convinced that "public regard for our service has never been higher."

The Toxteth tinderbox, like St. Pauls, Brixton and elsewhere, required its spark. In this case it was the pursuit by the police of a black youth riding a motor bike, presumably on the grounds that all black youths on motor bikes must have stolen them (he hadn't). As it happened, Leroy Cooper's father is currently pursuing a civil suit against Mr. Oxford for alleged repeated harassment of himself and his family by the police. This coincidence is telling enough. Though perhaps in the long run not so telling as the fact that in Brixton the mere rumour that an injured black man was being interrogated by the police was enough to trigger off expectations of police harassment and spark serious rioting. Why else, apart from enforcement, would a black person spend more than five minutes in police company?

Toxteth, however, also makes it clear that this is no longer an exclusive black-white or black-police confrontation. The policing strategy in the Merseyside area, coupled with deepening social neglect, growing unemployment, deindustrialisation, hopelessness, frustration and the sense of a whole community being silently consigned to the scrapheap, have combined to *generalise* social disaffection through some white *and* black sections of the community and fuse resistance against the brunt of the crisis being hoisted onto the shoulders of working people of whatever colour.

Comparing Southall—where penetration of organised racism into skinhead culture over the past two years precipitated the conflict along black-white lines—with Brixton—where the lines of black-white cleavage are deep, but the black confrontation with the police overrode all—and Toxteth—where something of a black-white common front began to emerge—obliges us to acknowledge that the patterns revealed by the riots cannot be attributed to a single cause, least of all a pure "economic" one.

The patterns are not simply various; they are uneven, but in a structured way. The multiple social disadvantages suffered by the blacks place them in the front line of the attempt to police the repression. But resistance is by now an historic tradition in black communities; it has been developing for two decades and has behind it a degree of know-how, experience, organisation and leadership—which the authorities wrongly attribute to outside "subversive influences." What is more, it is fed and sustained by a deep and complex *culture* of resistance, with its roots in the black counterculture, reggae, street rastafarianism, etc. It is this—no mere "economic spasm"—which accounts for the depth, intensity and snowballing pattern of black rioting in the cities.

Social deprivation, the profound sense of loss which arises when working men and women are deprived of jobs, and a white working-class political culture equally as complex as, though different from, its black counterpart, also under particular circumstances, bring white people to riot and loot.

Historically, riots of this kind although unpredictable are never without meaning, motive or rationale. They are not mindless eruptions of unconscious violence; they are always precipitated by deep social causes that are complex in their working out; they are rarely sustained through manipulations by subversive demagogues and wilful subversives; and they are almost never without their own forms of organisation and discipline.

One underlying factor is the ways in which—for both communities, though differently in each—rioting, violence and looting follow on from affronts to a sense of social justice: the way a deeply ingrained popular interpretation of "fair treatment" has been callously discarded and the rights and concessions that underpinned a sort of unwritten social contract have been scattered to the four winds.

I do not mean to invoke some ideal period when police relations with working people were "harmonious" and the relations between ethnic groups in poor communities were sweetness and light. But there did emerge as the terms of a wide-ranging social settlement in the postwar period, some rough expectations of a *quid pro quo* between the authorities who regulate and police poor communities and the people in them, an assumption that social justice is a legitimate claim for them to make, even if somewhat harder for them to come by in practice.

This contract—the basis of policing by consent—has been directly assaulted, broken up and destroyed by the political and economic strategies of the radical Right in power. In the absence of such a contract, new forces and strategies appear to fill the vacuum: the populist appeal to accept more law and order; the crusades to create an authoritarian groundswell; the leading role assumed by the ideology and practice of tough, repressive social policing. The latter constitutes not just a means of oppression for black people, but a threat to the roots of popular democracy from within the state. It could not have appeared on its own, without its place being prepared by political and social forces.

The police-black front *is* the front line: policing and the drift into authoritarian social control are front-line issues. Nevertheless, responding to the riots is not a matter of "defending civil liberties" or of "being nice to black people." Rioting and civil disorder grow out of and reflect back on what is happening to the working class as a whole and to society as the crisis cuts into the latter at all levels. The riots are only the outward, if dramatic, symptoms of this inner unravelling of our social, political and community life.

Most frightening of all is that, with notable exceptions, the Labour movement in general and the Labour Party in particular view these events only from the outside as an alternative government, Her Majesty's Loyal Opposition—and cannot articulate a sustained, popular response. It cannot take the side of the people, the oppressed elements in society; it does not seem to have a clue what such a response would require. Indeed, it often takes its lead straight from the mercilessly reactionary headlines of the *Daily Express*. We are, comrades, in deep trouble.

NOTE

This essay first appeared as "Summer in the City," *New Socialist* (September/October 1981): 4–7.

REFERENCE

Pryce, Ken. 1979. *Endless Pressure: A Study of West Indian Lifestyles in Bristol*. London: Penguin Books.

CHAPTER 6

Drifting into a Law and Order Society:
The 1979 Cobden Trust Human Rights Day Lecture

We are now in the middle of a deep and decisive movement towards a more disciplinary, authoritarian kind of society. This shift has been in progress since the 1960s; but it has gathered pace through the 1970s and is heading, given the spate of disciplinary legislation now on the parliamentary agenda, towards some sort of interim climax.

This drift into a "Law and Order" society is no temporary affair. No doubt it is, in part, a response to the deepening economic recession, as well as to the political polarization, social tensions and accumulating class antagonisms which are inevitably accompanying it. In difficult times, it is tempting to avert the gaze from problems whose remedy will require a profound reorganization of social and economic life and to fasten one's eyes, instead, on the promise that the continuity of things as they are can be somehow enforced by the imposition of social order and discipline "from above." Nevertheless, in my view, the drive for "more Law and Order" is no short-term affair; nor is it a mere backlash against the "permissive excesses" of the 1960s. It has its roots in the structural backwardness of the British economy, a fact which has been with us since the closing decades of the last century, only temporarily obscured by a brief period of "affluence" resulting from postwar reconstruction.

It also has its roots in the much augmented power and presence of the State, something which also, and not coincidentally, dates from the imperialist crisis of the 1880s and 1890s, but which has assumed a qualitatively new dimension in postwar British society. At the popular level, it feeds on the social anxieties and tensions generated by the great sea change in Britain's position in the world. And it has been tutored and educated by a new philosophical rationale: that which seeks a restoration of social harmony through the return to a traditionalist morality and the unqualified respect for authority as such.

This regression to a stone-age morality is a theme to which some of the most articulate public spokesmen and women have turned their minds in recent months. Its counterpart, at the popular level, is what can only be described as a blind spasm of control: the feeling that the *only* remedy for a society which is declared to be "ungovernable" is the imposition of order, through a disciplinary use of the Law by the State.

Governments in trouble, it be might be said, always have a strong temptation to reach for discipline and regulation in times of social crisis. These are not times when human freedoms and civil liberties flourish. But the new aspect to this ancient habit is the capacity of those in power to use the augmented means of communication now available to them, in order to *shape* public opinion, constructing a definition of "the crisis" which has, as its inevitable corresponding echo, a popular demand for "more Law and Order."

The construction of this "Law and Order" consensus, the forging of a disciplinary common sense, is one of the most troubling features of the drift. For it draws attention to the ways in which the disciplinarians of the state, and their populist supporters, can couple to them the mass media of communication; those ventriloquists of the popular press, for example, who give voice to the "silent majority," representing it in its most virulently traditionalist and authoritarian disguise, without a single memorandum passing from Whitehall to Fleet Street.

By this means, first, by forming public opinion; then, disingenuously, consulting it, the tendency to "reach for the Law," above, is complemented by a popular demand to be governed more strictly, from below. Thereby, the drift to Law and Order, above, secures a degree of popular support and legitimacy amongst the powerless, who see no other alternative. And this leads to a sharp closure in the whole movement.

Free Economy, Strong State

Against this background, we must speak, not only of the tendency towards authoritarian state, but rather of the production of an *authoritarian populism*. In such a climate of closure, to raise the question of rights and civil liberties is tantamount to declaring oneself a "subversive." We have come to a dangerous pass when the reaction of the Chairman of the Police Federation to the news that the report of the death of a Merseyside man while in the hands of the police has been passed to the DPP is to tell local policemen that critics of the police, who brought this worrying case to public attention, are either "mischievous or misguided." Or when as experienced a senior police officer as the last Metropolitan Police Commissioner, Sir Robert Mark, feels free to put in print his considered opinion that the National Council of Civil Liberties is "a self-appointed political pressure group with a misleading title . . . usually trying to usurp the function of the democratically appointed agencies for the achievement of political change" (Mark 1978, 133).

All this may seem paradoxical in the context of the recent return to power of a populist government of the "radical Right," with a militant hostility to what it describes as the creeping collectivism of an overweening state, and committed to the policy of "rolling the state back." But this is only a seeming paradox. The new *laissez-faire* doctrine, in which social market values are to predominate, many would say, like the old *laissez-faire*, is not at all inconsistent with a strong, disciplinary state. Indeed, if the state is to stop meddling in the fine-tuning of the economy, in order to let "social market values" rip, while containing the inevitable fallout, in terms of social conflict and class polarization, then a strong, disciplinary regime is a necessary corollary.

In "social market doctrine," the state should intervene less in some areas, but more in others. Its preferred slogan is "Free economy: Strong state." There is much talk, within this doctrine, of "Liberty." But here, too, the definition is highly selective. It is the "liberty" of property and contract, of the free movement of capital, of unbridled market forces and of competitive man and "possessive individualism" to which this slogan refers. It is not the "liberty" of those who have nothing to sell but their labour to withdraw it. Make no mistake about it: under this regime, the market is to be Free; the people are to be Disciplined.

Undermining Welfare Rights

We can see how this profound shift in public sentiment has been engineered by looking at an area where the language of "Rights" has gained, at best, little more than a temporary toe-hold: that of the Welfare State and of "Welfare Rights."

The Welfare State was one of the founding principles of the postwar political settlement. It marked the boundaries of a consensus within whose limits both major political parties agreed to contend. True, as the economic storm clouds have gathered, both the consensus about, and the materiality of, the Welfare State have been steadily eroded, by governments of both political stripes. Yet the principle remained, until recently, tattered but intact.

Now, the fact is that the Welfare State entailed a major, substantive redefinition and expansion of social rights. Without this expansion, it is doubtful whether the achievement of universal rights of political representation, accomplished only as the result of a protracted, bitter and deeply divisive political struggle by the unenfranchised, and not concluded until the achievement of women's suffrage in the early years of this century, would have been enough to give the State a substantive basis of popular legitimacy, especially amongst the poor, the powerless and the dominated classes.

"Welfare rights" are *not* a new form of public charity. They are at the core of the "social contract" which has made it possible for the popular classes and the poor to consent to be governed as they are within a class-divided society. They cannot be withdrawn, any more than the franchise can be limited, without eroding that pact of social association which makes democratic class society a viable proposition. The foundation of "welfare rights" gave a new definition and content to the concept of "the citizen."

Nevertheless, we have witnessed in recent months, not merely the savaging of welfare provision, but a steady undermining of the philosophy of "welfare rights," and of the Welfare State itself. It is not difficult to see where this concerted assault on the principle of welfare is primarily coming from. In social market philosophies, "welfare" is one of those so-called "rigidities" from which free-market men and women seek to be "liberated." In the context of such doctrines, it has become acceptable for a paper like the *Daily Telegraph* to describe Britain in the 1970s as a "Land Fit for Scroungers"; to comment not only on the "waste" which welfare represents but on its "damage to the natural character," and to recommend that "supplementary benefit should be what it used to be known as in a less euphemistic era: assistance. It should be a safety net, strictly for emergencies, not a featherbed for every hard luck case around."

Here we see how a popular base is laid for that substantial destruction of the Welfare State which is now on the cards. And nothing has been more effective in coupling this regressive social doctrine with popular anxieties and discontents than the massive investment which the mass media have made in recent months in stories about "Scroungers." Hardly a week passes without another cluster of stories about the Scrounger and Welfare State rip-offs.

These stories have been heavily embroidered with epithets drawn from the stock of populist demonology: the workshy, the feckless poor, the surly rudeness, the feigned infirmities, the mendacity, lack of gratitude, scheming idleness, endless hedonism and "something-for-nothing" qualities of "Britain's army of dole-queue swindlers." So the Welfare State has been constructed in the media as a populist folk-devil: Britain's undeserving poor, the great majority of whom, if the *Mail* and the *Sun* are to be believed, spend most of their days, between signing on, lolling about on the Costa Brava.

The fact is, of course, that proven welfare frauds represent a tiny proportion of those claiming benefits and a very small percentage of the sums expended. Of the 662,000-odd claims for Family Allowance and Child Benefits, proven frauds account for only 0.42 percent of the total; of the 5,548,000 claims for Supplementary Benefits, fraud accounts for only 0.59 percent of the total. By contrast, of the two million people estimated as eligible for Supplementary Benefits, only 60 to 65 percent take them up. In short, the really worrying problem about the Welfare State is not the number of proven fraudulent claims, but the vast numbers who need to exercise welfare rights in order to survive, and the significant number whom the Welfare State, for one reason or another, is not reaching. This is the "problem" which needs public discussion and official action: it is, in fact, the normal problem in democratic class societies, of making the formal rights of the powerless practically and materially effective.

Scroungers as Folk-Devils

But this is not how the media have constructed the "problem of Welfare." They have exploited the Scrounger as a popular folk-devil. They have trawled their lines in the rich and murky pool of popular myth, dredging up the man who wants something for nothing, the Scrounger who lives at the expense of others, who has abandoned the puritan ethic of reward-for-hard-graft and disappeared down the hole of endless protracted pleasure—abroad. What could be more undermining of the national character, the moral fibre of the nation? And, if the Welfare State and welfare rights are principally represented through this composite hate-figure, you can see how the people themselves can be won to consent to, if not actively mobilized behind, the Government, when the cutting and the savaging and the dismantling begins.

Here, a critical area of social rights has become progressively vulnerable, not only to economic erosion and regressive social doctrines, but to what can only be described as ideological subversion. Of course, ordinary people are not simple dupes of the media. They don't believe everything they are told. In an era of racing inflation, a pretty large proportion of the two million people eligible for Supplementary Benefits know how much they need it. But we must not underestimate the critical role of the media in holding the pass between the governing classes and the governed. They provide the inside knowledge, the privileged opinion, the "larger view" on which the definitions of social problems depend. By representing a problem, systematically, in a certain way, for example, by representing the Welfare State in the personification of "The Scrounger," the media can, and do, *construct* public opinion, which they then re-present, in militantly populist and traditionalist accents.

It is not surprising that, when popular opinion is then "consulted," it tends spontaneously to coincide with regressive opinion. It can then be declared to be "what the people want." Thus "the people" also come to be represented, as consenting to the erosion of their own hard-won and barely secured "rights," in a society where massive inequalities of power, property and wealth continue to be secured. This is how a consensus *against* social rights is ideologically constructed. This is one of the mechanisms of "authoritarian populism" at work.

Rights—Outcome of Struggle

I have deliberately used the language of "social rights" in an area somewhat outside that of the litany of more traditional "liberties" so frequently invoked. But the question of terminology deserves a little deeper consideration.

There are at least two problems, as I see it, with the language of "rights." First, it is clear that "rights" can be advanced as enclaves of defined liberties within, or as exceptions to, the dominant and determinate tendencies of a society without necessarily altering the structures, or the basic disposition of wealth, property and power within which those rights have to be exercised.

Social rights to "welfare" intruded the language of "needs" into a system whose dynamic still dominantly depends on the discourses and practices of property, competitive exchange and profit maximization. They were a check against the savage distribution of wealth which the market and private accumulation accomplishes when left to their own devices. It made significant inroads. Its effective establishment represented the countervailing power of the propertyless, the poor and the dependent once, but not until, they had gained, through extended struggle, the right of political representation. They have thus profoundly modified, but not so far transformed, the system within and against which they operate. Certainly, they have helped to humanize and democratize modern capitalism. They have also, as I argued earlier, come to constitute that minimal basis through which the dominated classes secure a measure of economic representation in a society based on private property and thus form a critical element in making democratic class society viable.

The question of whether this countervailing principle and power can profoundly modify, or merely marginally deflect, the driving tendencies of the social system is not, of course, written in to their status as newly won "rights." It depends on the level and character of continuing struggle by which they are defended, maintained and expanded. Society may recuperate these rights to its dominant tendencies and the "welfare state," failing on the whole to transform the private corporate property system, had indeed come to institute, as well as a limit, one of its principal legitimating supports. But that recuperation is *always* a point of contention, conflict and struggle to define.

The state, in that sense, is not a monolithic thing; nor is it a neutral engine, representing the interests of all, equally. It is constantly conformed and conforming relations to the economic system on whose viability the social order ultimately depends. But it is also a space of contending forces. And it is the outcomes of those struggles which define and limit the degree to which "rights" can be expanded into the basis for a new kind of society, a different form of the state, or effectively neutralized.

However, as we shall see in a moment, the "language of rights" is frequently deployed to obscure and mystify this fundamental basis which rights have in the struggle between contending social forces. It constantly *abstracts* rights from their real historical and social context, ascribes them a timeless universality, speaks of them as if they were "given" rather than *won* and as if they were given once-and-for-all, rather than having to be constantly secured.

The second problem is, then, just this sleight-of-hand, this *legerdemain*, by which the historical process through which rights are defined, won or lost is commonly misinterpreted. Of course, they are prized as what makes our society a halfway decent place to live in. They differentiate democratic class societies from more authoritarian and arbitrary regimes. But they do appear in this discourse as if descended from Heaven; bestowed on their grateful recipients through the goodwill and beneficence of their rulers as if this "granting" was unproblematic. But this is to collapse a protracted and bloody series of historical engagements into a Whig myth of inevitable progress.

Rights—Formal and Substantive

This naturalization of the historical process may have something to do with the belief that those rights which we now enjoy are the direct legacy of the doctrine of "natural right." Now "natural rights" were generated in the struggle of the rising commercial classes against arbitrary and absolutist power. They constitute one of the great historic achievements of a rising bourgeoisie. But they were, of course, predicated on a particular form of society: market societies, societies of private property, of "contract" and free exchange and rooted in a "possessive individualist" image of human nature. Not only were the poor, the property-less, the unenfranchised and women not thought fit and proper subjects of this naturalistic universe; the very form in which "liberty" was conceived was *intrinsically hostile* to democracy. Professor Macpherson (1962, 1977) has shown, definitively, that this main liberal tradition was either "undemocratic or anti-democratic."

These natural rights had to be profoundly transformed, and others which were utterly foreign to the universe of natural rights had to be defined and fought for, in order that, in the form of the liberal democratic society we have today, a scheme of democratic government could be fitted on to a class-divided society with some minimal expectation not that antagonisms would disappear, but that they could be largely contained within a framework of legal regulation, on the basis of a measure of popular consent. The so-called right to express opinions and to publish cannot be understood outside of the struggle of the radical and working-class press against the actions of a succession of profoundly illiberal governments; and its "progress" has to be trailed through the prisons and the courts through charges of sedition and imprisonment, as well as through the legislature.

And then, today, this formal freedom to publish, vital as it is, has to be seen in the context of the vast, substantive unfreedom constituted by the size and scale of corporate capital, at the disposal of a very few "citizens," on which the "right" to publish *effectively* substantively depends. Still, more than half a century after the winning of a universal franchise, we have several national newspapers which claim to speak *to* working people, as well as *at* them; none which is *by* them or *for* them. I don't discard this formal right lightly. But it must also be insisted that, here as elsewhere, freedoms precious to our form of society were wrested from vested power and property, not given by them. And they continue to operate within a system of real and substantive power, to which, in the end, every formal right must be referred.

Conquest of Violence?

The paradox is that, nowadays, this real history is not defined as the basis for taking such further measures as would make our formal freedoms practically and substantively more effective, or for the deepening and expansion of their democratic content. Instead, the same history has been rewritten as the legitimating excuse for an increased exercise of regulation and control. The argument runs that, in previous times, when the state was an instrument of government largely at the disposal of the powerful and propertied classes, social conflict and class antagonisms were often legitimately expressed in the form of militant collective action: and the forces of public order, which so frequently appeared on the scene, were, it can now be acknowledged, with convenient hindsight, largely functioning as an extended arm of propertied interests. But, so the argument runs, now that these rights have been "universalized" and "institutionalized," the state has become "fully representative," a state of popular sovereignty; and, for that reason, it not only has the sole, legitimate monopoly of the means of violence, but has itself the right to limit and discipline any further conflict over rights which might arise.

This is the famous thesis of the "conquest of violence" which is supposed to have occurred magically sometime between 1880 and 1920—a period, incidentally, of deep and extensive class conflict in which the so-called rights to combine and to strike were constantly at issue; and where the critical struggle to contain and educate the challenge of organized labour within the framework of representative democracy was conducted with a considerable measure of practical success. The "conquest of violence" is an updated Whig fiction much loved by historians of public order and the police, and a historical thesis to which senior police spokesmen are particularly addicted.

We are arguing, then, that the civil rights and freedoms which make our society what it is are rights which were defined and won in struggle against the dominant interests in society, not bestowed on society by them. These rights, crucial as they are in securing for the powerless and unpropertied classes a measure or representation within the State, are constantly subject, in practice, to the real and substantive dispositions of power, wealth and property, the systems of real relations within which they have to be exercised. Insofar as they can or have been given a substantive *democratic* content, they have run counter to society's main dynamic and therefore have to be constantly secured and defended. And, since the society is both a representative democracy and a class society, such "rights" may be used as a defence against the exercise of arbitrary power: but they *cannot* provide the basis, in themselves, of the dissolution of class antagonisms and social conflict. They hold out no promise of a "harmony of social interests." To abrogate them is tantamount to dismantling the fragile basis on which what can only be the legal regulation of conflict depends.

The Freedom of Organized Labour

One critical test case is the "freedom" of those who have only their labour, mental or manual, to sell, to withdraw that labour under the conditions of a breakdown in the legal regulation of class conflict. Lord Denning, Master of the Rolls, will immediately enter the lists, as he did recently at Birmingham University, to remind us that there is "no such right known to the law." And in the literal sense, of course, he is correct. The French and Italian constitutions define a positive "right to strike." There is no such freedom proclaimed in Britain. Nevertheless, as is so often the case, that freedom *is* positively expressed, as a series of exceptions from the common law; and, as is again so frequently the case, it was established by a protracted struggle, whose progress is staked out by a series of fateful legal decisions (and some remarkable reversals).

The freedom to combine and organize dates back to the repeal of the Combination Acts in 1824; but for another 50 years, until the Conspiracy and Protection of Property Act of 1875, strikers were frequently brought before the law on charges of criminal conspiracy. The Act of 1875 was the direct result of the enfranchisement of the urban working class following the agitations of the 1860s. It was almost immediately replaced by a switch to attack under the charge of civil conspiracy, within the law of tort. This in turn was bitterly contested, through the labour unrest of the 1880s and 1890s, in the period of the unionization of the unskilled, right up to the infamous Taff Vale judgement; and only brought to an end with the Trade Disputes Act of 1906. Those who have followed its subsequent career through *Rookes v Barnard*, the Trade Union and Labour relations legislation of the 1970s, including the attempts of the Heath Government to recruit the law, again, directly into the management of the economic struggle; the intense campaign against the "overweening power of the unions" of recent years; bringing us to the threshold of yet another attempt to deploy the law to limit and contain the power of organized labour, will, no doubt, have some difficulty in recognizing in this sordid progress the clean lines of the "conquest of violence" or the growth to social harmony.

And yet, as Sir Otto Kahn-Freund has argued, "There can be no equilibrium in industrial relations without a freedom to strike. In protecting that freedom, the law protects the legitimate expectation of workers that they can make use of their collective power: it corresponds to the protection of the legitimate expectation of management that it can use the right of property for the same purpose on its side" (quoted in Davies and Freedland 1983, 292). This lucid statement has the considerable advantage of not being bemused by the religion of a "social harmony of interests" or the myths of the "conquest of conflict." It has not allowed itself to fall into the pit of false illusions that, in a capitalist system, the economic class struggle will disappear if only one systematically renames it instead, "industrial relations." "Any approach to the relations between management and labour is fruitless unless the diversity of their interests is plainly recognized and articulated," Sir Otto has also argued. "The conflict between capital and labour is inherent in an industrial society and therefore in the labour relationships. Conflicts of interest are inevitable in all societies. There are rules for their adjustment, there can be no rules for their elimination" (quoted in Davies and Freedland 1983, 28).

The rights to organize, to combine, to withdraw labour and to picket are rights, established only by means of a brutal and extended struggle, which set some minimal exceptions to the rights of property against labour. The "bargain" to contain and regulate the conflicts of interest by negotiation rests, ultimately, on this ultimate freedom to contest the rules of the game themselves. But this inevitable structural conflict continues in and through the rights which organized labour have won. Against this background, the postulation of a "pre-established harmony of management and labour," now the received doctrinal wisdom of Ministers of the Crown, newspaper and television editors, judges and public spokespersons is, as Sir Otto put it, "sheer utopia"— and dangerous nonsense besides (quoted in Davies and Freedland 1983, 28).

The attempts, by Labour and Conservative governments alike, in their efforts to secure particular economic policies, to tamper with and whittle away this freedom, progressively employing the Law and the police as the principal instruments of disciplinary regulation, must be seen as nothing more or less than an attempt to intervene in the economic struggle between the classes, and to do so in a way which settles that inevitable conflict of interest at the expense of working people and to the profit of the dominant classes and their interests.

The Police, Law and Order Front Line

We come, finally, to the most contentious area of all: the role of the Law itself and the police as the hard front, the pioneer corps, the disciplinary arm, the shock troops of the "Law and Order society." This is a tough charge to make and sustain and I am aware of the imminent danger of falling into either Mr. Jardine's "mischievous" or his "misguided" category and, most probably, into both at once. The effort, nevertheless, must be undertaken, for the matter is exceedingly serious.

The problems of exercising the "policing function" in a period of growing social conflict must certainly not be overlooked. Wherever the Law draws the line, the police are required to hold it. Conflicts with the state, with employers, with specific laws and regulations, with policies and conditions, are inevitably displaced on to the police in any serious confrontation. As a society, we lay on them the responsibility for discharging what may be mutually irreconcilable responsibilities: they must enforce the Law impartially, defend the liberties of the citizen, while maintaining public order and the Queen's Peace. These tasks have become more pressing in a period of declining recruitment, when manpower is stretched to the limit. Increasingly, it is the "public order" role which comes to the fore and this brings the police into the public eye in the role which most clearly aligns them with the interests of the state, the powers that be and the *status quo*.

It may be this which, for example, led Sir Robert Mark to itemize the pressures on the Metropolitan police force in 1973 as consisting of "72,750 burglaries, 2,680 robberies and 450 demonstrations" (Mark 1978, 138). All the same, it is a worrying elision where public demonstrations can be associated so easily, and without qualification, with crime. Demonstrations are not yet, so far as we know, a criminal offence. Indeed, from the perspective we have been trying to elaborate, the right of political manifestation is one of those freedoms on which the viability of class democracies fundamentally depends. It is therefore a worrying, tell-tale slide.

The fact is that, increasingly, the police are not only to be seen policing industrial conflict in a tough manner, but actively involved in formulating official views which are publicly hostile to the rights of workers to strike and to picket. Sir Robert did not hesitate to make public his view that the Shrewsbury pickets had "committed the worst of all crimes, worse even than murder, the attempt to achieve an industrial or political objective by criminal violence" (Mark 1978, 325). Mr. George Ward, of Grunwick fame, however, he regarded as someone who "courageously and successfully stood firm against politically motivated violence." He is not alone in this tendency for the police to intervene publicly in a highly contentious area, where the Government intention to legislate is certain to provoke divisive contention within the society. The Chief Constable of Greater Manchester is also on record as holding the view that mass picketting is necessarily intimidatory. "I can't understand the reluctance to make this area of the law precise," he said. The Government has since abandoned any such reluctance.

Sir Robert gave, in his autobiography, *In the Office of Constable* (Mark 1978), the political independence of the police as one of his three conditions for the British tradition of successful "policing with consent." But there has clearly emerged in recent months what one can only call a "police view" in the sensitive matter of policing industrial conflict and picketting: and this viewpoint is not a whit less "political" in its effect because it appears to have been adopted on grounds of technical efficiency. The rights of workers to withdraw their labour, and to make that withdrawal effective through peaceful picketting, is too serious a matter to be discarded as a consequence of convenience to the police.

The second area in which the police have come to play a highly visible and prominent role is in the policing of racial conflict. This is not a matter which requires, at this point, detailed elaboration. Since the late 1960s, a sort of war of attrition has been going on between the police and black people in areas of high urban concentration; and, despite the consistent adverse publicity which this has attracted, those who know these communities at first hand will attest that it shows little sign of abating. The sordid history of these relations runs from the singling out of the Mangrove for special treatment, through the campaigns against black muggers (the two consistently identified as indistinguishable by the police and the media); the saturation tactics of the Special Patrol Group in Lewisham and other parts of London, in Birmingham and Manchester and other cities; all the way through to the revelations, to which both the Runnymede Trust study and Home Office research have given substantiation, of the clear bias against black youth in the pervasive application of "arrest on suspicion"—"sus," to give it its familiar name, under the ancient statutes of the Vagrancy Act of 1824.

I have no wish to repeat here this terrifying tale of the use of police powers to contain and constrain, and in effect to help to criminalize, parts of the black population in our urban colonies. Not all the stories and rumours are, of course, true. Not all of them are traceable to racism within the local police forces. But when all the reasonable allowances have been made, this series of episodes leaves us with no other conclusion than that the police have undertaken, whether willingly or no, to constrain by means which would not long stand up to inspection within the rule of law, an alienated black population and thereby, to police the social crisis of the cities.

What defies explanation, in a police force which prides itself on the practice of policing by consent, is why they seem unable to remedy this situation to any significant degree; if not for the sake of justice to black people then for the more limited reason of securing their own legitimacy. It is now sometimes argued—apparently in mitigation—that, since the police inevitably reflect society, and British society is undeniably racist, the police are bound to have their proportion of racists too. This is an utterly cynical and quite unacceptable proposition. The same thing could be said of the criminal population. And, indeed, the last ten years have revealed the quite appalling degree to which the criminal penetration and corruption of the police has advanced. But no Chief Constable could afford to be so cavalier about the criminalization of his own force. Indeed, Sir Robert Mark's tenure of the office of Chief Constable was distinguished by the lengthy, arduous and by no means as yet completed cleaning up of the Augean stables within major sections of the force and at worryingly senior levels. This was undertaken to "put our own house in order." I know of no evidence that the equally clear evidence of racism within the police forces in sensitive black urban areas is a matter to which similar attention has been given.

The third area which must now be the source of serious concern is the manner in which the technical factors associated with the problems of policing an increasingly restless society have become the legitimate basis for a far-reaching administrative restructuring of the policing function, virtually without reference to the public and certainly without that legislative debate which alone would give substance to Sir Robert's claim to be "the most accountable and therefore the most acceptable police in the world" (Mark 1977, 56).

Both the Home Office Working Party in 1973 and, more recently, the National Security Committee (a title to give most civil libertarians pause), resisted the idea of the creation of a so-called "third force" in the paramilitary style so infamous on the Continent. And yet, it is now clear that, after the substantial revision of riot and public order training and reorganization undertaken in 1972, the Special Patrol Groups have substantially changed their role and function from that of a support anticrime squad to an advanced and highly equipped "responsive or reactive" force of a distinctly public order kind. Its functions are conceived, as the Chief Constable of Devon and Cornwall himself has said, within the framework of a "quasi-military reactive concept" (quoted in Bunyan 1981, 167).

The swamping role of the SPGs in the black areas, their notorious (and exceedingly low-yield) "stop and search" activities, and their highly questionable presence and role at the flashpoints of a whole series of public demonstrations, Red Lion Square, Southall, etc., are well beyond the framework of traditional policing as practised in Britain: activities, as the 1972 Metropolitan Police Commissioner's Report noted, at demonstrations "at which militant elements were thought likely to cause disorder . . . and in protracted industrial disputes involving dockers and building workers"; and without so much as a public by-your-leave.

Since the reformation and equipping of the SPGs and the Spaghetti House disaster, it has become increasingly clear that the claim that the British police remains substantially an unarmed force, the only one in the world, is largely a semantic quibble. The fact that the accessibility to arms and similar equipment is still limited does not undermine the substantive fact that, for good or ill, in all those cases where it matters, the British police are now in effect an armed and fully equipped technical force. I have searched the pages of Hansard in vain for the days when this momentous move was debated by those to whom senior policemen insist they are ultimately accountable. I may have missed it. Otherwise, I feel bound to say that this profound change in the character and exercise of the policing function has been accomplished, as so much else in this society these days, under the apparently neutral sign of technical rationalization and modernization.

Administrative rationale has become one of the principal means by which even formal representative democracy is being short-circuited. The extensive and unchecked amassing and computerization of information, much of which, to judge from the tit-bits which have become available, of a hearsay or otherwise dubious and unreliable character, is another field in which the rights of the public, of democratic accountability and the fundamental exercise of the police function under the civil power, has been subject to technological "updating."

The encroachments on the liberties of the citizen, on civil rights and on democratic control and accountability which stem from these and related developments, hardly need to be more extensively spelled out. It may well be, as we were assured in a recent radio discussion of the Chief Constable of Devon and Cornwall's book, *Policing Freedom* (Alderson 1979), that law-abiding citizens have nothing to fear from these developments. The evidence does not, unfortunately, support this optimistic view. And it is no longer possible and, so far as democratic rights are concerned, no longer advisable, to take these matters on trust. The massive campaign which the police waged against any increase in the independent element in its own complaints investigation procedure is not calculated to inspire confidence.

The plain fact is that these worries and concerns about the arbitrary extension of police powers and the exercise of police discretionary justice in private have been escalating in recent months; much of it on the basis of hard and disturbing evidence, which would never have come to light but for the persistence of some journalists, "crackpot" civil libertarians and the sense of outrage of victims and their relatives and friends. When members of the public come forward with evidence, which has to be taken seriously, of having received physical injury while in the hands or custody of the police, we have gone beyond the moment when civil assurances will do. Frankly, *one such case is one too many*.

These, then, are only some of the ways in which the police forces themselves are being progressively transformed for a wider disciplinary and "Law and Order" role at the present time. But I want to end by drawing to your attention an equally important, but in some ways even more disquieting change: the emergence of the police as what can only be described as an organized ideological force. Sir Robert himself pioneered a substantive shift in the attitude of senior policemen to public opinion, the media and entering directly into public debate. He became, indeed, a relentless and effective publicist. Sir David McNee is less effective at it and has chosen a lower profile. But this has been more than compensated for by the Chief Constable of Greater Manchester, Mr. James Anderton, whom a *Sunday Telegraph* (and favourable) profile describes as "Britain's Toughest Policeman," with, "the gift of feeling the pulse of the public and then making it beat quicker," and "an uncannily successful populist."

As the issues of policing become big news and attract the publicists, so we have come to know more and more about the highly conservative and traditionalist views and values of our most senior policemen: Mr. Anderton's view of his job as "an extension of his Christian mission to raise the moral quality of life," his preoccupation with moral standards, his clean-up pornography crusade, his sombre views of the "over-influence of the libertarian lobby," his commitment to tough sentencing, his militant evangelicalism; Sir David McNee's fundamentalism or Sir Robert's common gauge traditionalism.

Policemen, too, are entitled to their views. We, in turn, are entitled to ask whether it is just by chance that those who get the lion's share of the publicity are *all* committed to such deep social conservatism and whether it is altogether right that there should be so blurred a line between their personal viewpoints and their professional roles. Such publicity has undoubtedly helped to stamp the police indelibly with the inscription of a force of social traditionalism. But that, as they say, is their right.

What cannot be treated so lightly is the constitution of the police as an active "Law and Order" lobby, an ideological force, mobilizing public opinion behind a very special and particular set of "Law and Order" policies. The extensive evidence which the police have submitted to the Royal Commission on Criminal Procedure is, in its sober way, little short of a disciplinary manifesto. The campaigns which Sir Robert initiated when in office, against suspects' rights and the Judges Rules, for majority verdicts and extensive police discretion, have found their way into the philosophy which inspires the evidence.

The same philosophy is to be found in the widely publicized views of the Association of Chief Police Officers; and, with an accession of pungent imagery which was only to be expected from that quarter, from the Police Federation: "If someone had drawn up these rules," their Chairman, Mr. Jardine, told a recent conference, "and sent the idea to the makers of 'Monopoly' as a new board game, Waddingtons would have turned it down because one player, the criminal, was bound to win every time."

These, and similar sentiments now constitute a well-formed and actively publicized "police view." But this is only one throw in what has been, in fact, a substantial public campaign on "Law and Order," launched by the Police Federation in 1975, and culminating in the provocative "Law and Order" advertisement—"an open letter to all General Election candidates from the Police Federation"—which appeared during the General Election of last year. The Police Superintendents' Association has, in fact, expressed its fears that only the police and a small minority of the legal profession will "speak for Law and Order."

Of course, the police are entitled to form views about the best way to carry out the duties with which they are saddled. And certainly, they are, and are bound to be, constantly consulted by senior Ministers of Government on public order questions. But there is a long tradition that, in this area, it is critical that the *making* of law and its *enforcement* be strictly separated. With the ideological mobilization of the police as the best informed, most knowledgeable and now most organized voice, campaigning in a consistently "Law and Order" direction, forming a core element in the Law and Order bloc, that strict separation of powers and functions is becoming seriously blurred. The police themselves are beginning to shape the identity of public opinion on these crucial questions. They are beginning to wield a deep ideological influence and they are consistently exerting that influence in the disciplinary direction.

The Police Federation, to take only one case, now functions in the public domain as a professional association representing the "men in blue" (the body which was constructed out of the debris of the police strikes for the right to unionize, which were routed). But it also functions as expert, neutral witnesses on "policing problems" *and* as an active, militant, "Law and Order" campaigning force. These are, to put it mildly, two functions too many. And the third is the most dubious of all. It blurs a distinction which, if the role of the police under the civil power is to be maintained (and our liberties could come, one day, to depend on its being so maintained), cannot be permitted to be confused. The police cannot both constitute a powerful crusading part of the "Law and Order" lobby and maintain for long the semblance of social and political impartiality. They cannot both claim to "police by consent" and be so actively and publicly involved in constructing public opinion, in shaping consent and producing it, in its most traditionalist and disciplinary form.

If the police now form a sort of vanguard in the drift towards the disciplinary society, they are by no means the only social or political force propelling us along this road. I have singled them out for comment because, in its widest sense, the question of who polices the police is a matter which has been, historically, at the very heart and centre of our civil liberties. But also because they have so successfully cast anyone who raises questions about the police, the law, civil liberties and democratic rights in the role of the "subversive element," the "mischievous and the misguided." And the fears of being so labelled and pricked, marked and damned, has undoubtedly had the effect of rendering the liberal and libertarian public conscience quiescent on these important but controversial matters.

I cannot think of a better occasion than the Human Rights Day Lecture for making the bid to induce those who still regard the "rights of true born Englishmen" and other nonpatrials as the society's most valuable possession, out of their corner. It is time to constitute a force for the expansion, the democratic deepening and extension of the rule of law. I'm afraid that will also mean constituting a social force against the Law and Order brigade. But things are at a pretty pass when Sir Robert Mark can, with impunity, refer, in that derogatory manner, to "the so-called NCCL and those who take it upon themselves to keep a vigilant eye on our civil liberties." He suggests in that statement, despite his great experience, that he does not understand the social and historical nature of that "consent" on which, he claims, English policing is based. Yet without a vigilant eye on our civil liberties, consent is just another empty nod of approval in the general direction of unchecked authority. In that general direction, the civil rights of men and women have passed down a long, winding trail to oblivion before now. It may seem, in our present difficulties, the only and easiest path to take. The road to the disciplinary state, to the Law and Order society, creeping there crablike and sideways, of course by sudden advances and retreats, in that empirical fashion which befits the practical, common-sense English. It is time, citizens, to take a different route.

NOTE

This essay first appeared as *Drifting into a Law and Order Society: The 1979 Cobden Trust Human Rights Day Lecture* (London: Cobden Trust, 1980).

REFERENCES

Alderson, John. 1979. *Policing Freedom: A Commentary on the Dilemmas of Policing in Western Democracies*. Plymouth: Macdonald and Evans.
Bunyan, Tony. 1981. "The Police against the People." *Race and Class* 23, nos. 2–3: 153–70.
Davies, Paul Lyndon, and Mark Robert Freedland. 1983. *Kahn-Freund's Labour and the Law*. 3rd ed. London: Stevens and Sons.
Macpherson, C. B. 1962. *The Political Theory of Possessive Individualism: From Hobbes to Locke*. Oxford: Clarendon.
Macpherson, C. B. 1977. *The Life and Times of Liberal Democracy*. Oxford: Oxford University Press.
Mark, Robert. 1977. *Policing a Perplexed Society*. London: Allen and Unwin.
Mark, Robert. 1978. *In the Office of Constable*. London: Collins.
Metropolitan Police. 1973. Report of the Commissioner of Police of the Metropolis for the Year 1972, HMSO, CMND 5331.

CHAPTER 7

The Whites of Their Eyes:
Racist Ideologies and the Media

In this essay I want to address two, related, issues. The first concerns the way the media—sometimes deliberately, sometimes unconsciously—define and construct the question of race in such a way as to reproduce the ideologies of racism. The second is concerned with the very difficult problems of strategy and tactics which arise when the Left attempts to intervene in the media construction of race, so as to undermine, deconstruct and question the unquestioned racist assumptions on which so much of media practice is grounded.

We need to think about both these questions together: the often complex and subtle ways in which the ideologies of racism are sustained in our culture; and the equally difficult question as to how to challenge them in the practice of ideological struggle. Both form the basis of a wider antiracist strategy which—I argue here—neglects the ideological dimensions at our peril.

For very complex reasons, a sort of racist "common sense" has become pervasive in our society. And the media frequently work from this common sense, taking it as their baseline without questioning it. We need, urgently, to consider ways in which, *in addition* to the urgent and necessary political task of blocking the path to power of the openly organized racist and right-extremist organizations, we can also begin to construct an antiracist common sense. This task of making antiracist ideas popular is and must be part of a wider democratic struggle which engages, not so much the hard-line extremists of the Right, or even the small numbers of the committed and converted, but the great body of common sense, in the population as a whole, and amongst working people especially, on which the struggle to build up an antiracist popular bloc will ultimately depend.

Questions of strategy and tactics are not easy, especially when what is at issue is the winning of popular positions in the struggle against racism. There are few shortcuts or ready-made recipes. It does not follow that, because our hearts are in the right place, we will win the struggle for "hearts and minds." And even the best analysis of the current situation provides few absolute guidelines as to what we should do, in a particular situation. Neither passionate left-wing convictions nor the immutable laws of history can ever replace the difficult questions of political calculation on which the outcome of particular struggles ultimately turns. This essay is written in the firm conviction that we need to be better prepared, both in our analysis of how racist ideologies become "popular," and in what are the appropriate strategies for combatting them. Both, in their turn, depend on a more open, less closed and "finalist" debate of positions among people on the Left committed to the antiracist struggle. In discussing the second aspect, I will draw on some recent experiences of attempts to intervene politically in the area of racism and the mass media.

In 1979, the Campaign Against Racism in the Media (CARM) won the opportunity to make a programme putting its case in the BBC's "access television" slot, *Open Door*. The programme, *It Ain't Half Racist, Mum*, was transmitted twice, in February and March of that year, in the usual corners of the schedule reserved for clearly labelled "minority programmes." The programme produced a significant response. It was widely reviewed; CARM received over 600 letters, the great majority of them favourable; the programme also triggered off an internal storm within the BBC and an appeal by one distinguished programme presenter, Robin Day, to the BBC Appeals Tribunal on the grounds that his performance in a debate on immigration (which he chaired) had been misrepresented in the programme. Since then, the programme has been widely used by a variety of antiracist groups and in schools and colleges, as a way of triggering off a discussion of racism and the media, though the BBC has kept an extremely tight grip on the programme's distribution and has been something less than helpful in promoting it.

The CARM group, composed largely of antiracist media workers, worked for some time preparing and discussing the approach to the programme, viewing extracts and bargaining with the reluctant broadcasters to allow the extracts we wanted to criticize being used in the programme (many, including ITN and BBC News, refused). I was invited, at a fairly late stage in the process, to help prepare a script and to present the programme jointly with Maggie Steed. *It Ain't Half Racist, Mum* has been well received on the whole, by the Left and antiracist groups. It has also been severely criticized, on several occasions, by Carl Gardner and Margaret Henry, original members of the CARM team, who thought the programme seriously misdirected and leaky with missed opportunities (see Gardner 1979a, 1979b; Gardner and Henry 1979). This experience provides us with a useful opportunity to reconsider both the general issue of racism and the media, and the even more serious and knotty problem of strategies of left interventions in mainstream television programming.

In 1980 I was invited by Alan Horrox and his small team in the Thames Television Schools department to help prepare and script a series of four programmes on the media and social problems, to be transmitted for schools as the second "Viewpoint" series in Thames's *English Programme*. The first "Viewpoint" series had also been concerned with representations of social issues on television, and contained the excellent and much-shown double programme on sexual stereotypes, *Superman and the Bride*. It had also proved highly controversial and ran into trouble with the Independent Broadcasting Authority (IBA) who would not agree to repeat the series, despite its highly favourable reception, until a number of changes had been made. The IBA especially required changes to those parts which made the links between programming policy and television company ownership; and to the style of presentation which, in its view, did not sufficiently clearly acknowledge that this was only *one* of many possible "viewpoints" on the subjects treated. (The vast majority of unsigned and unauthored programmes transmitted nightly are, presumably, viewed only through the universal all-seeing, neutral, balanced and impartial "eye" of God.)

The making of the second "Viewpoint" series was, therefore, something of a tricky exercise. One of the programmes we made also covered the handling and presentation of race in the media, though from a different point of view from that adopted in the CARM programme. This programme, *The Whites of Their Eyes*, has also been transmitted twice in the usual ITV School programme schedule, moving up to attract 30 percent of the school viewing audience. This was for a different audience from that which we aimed for in the CARM programme. It was intended for an audience, in a controlled viewing situation, in schools, viewed with a teacher, and allowing for considerable follow-up work in the classroom (a special "project" booklet for the series was produced for classroom use by Andrew Bethel).

The CARM programme, on the other hand, aimed at the general viewing public, or that part of it still able to keep its eyes open late at night or on a sleepy Sunday. Together, these programmes form the background to this article.

Before discussing these programmes in more detail, however, we might usefully begin by defining some of the terms of the argument. "Racism and the media" touches directly the problem of *ideology*, since the media's main sphere of operations is the production and transformation of ideologies. An intervention in the media's construction of race is an intervention in the *ideological* terrain of struggle. Much murky water has flowed under the bridge provided by this concept of ideology in recent years; and this is not the place to develop the theoretical argument. I am using the term to refer to those images, concepts and premises which provide the frameworks through which we represent, interpret, understand and "make sense" of some aspect of social existence. Language and ideology are not the same—since the same linguistic term ("democracy" for example, or "freedom") can be deployed within different ideological discourses. But language, broadly conceived, is by definition the principal medium in which we find different ideological discourses elaborated.

Three important things need to be said about ideology in order to make what follows intelligible. First, ideologies do not consist of isolated and separate concepts, but in the articulation of different elements into a distinctive set or chain of meanings. In liberal ideology, "freedom" is connected (articulated) with individualism and the free market; in socialist ideology, "freedom" is a collective condition, dependent on, not counterposed to, "equality of condition," as it is in liberal ideology. The same concept is differently positioned within the logic of different ideological discourses. One of the ways in which ideological struggle takes place and ideologies are transformed is by articulating the elements differently, thereby producing a different meaning: breaking the chain in which they are currently fixed (e.g., "democratic" = the "Free" West) and establishing a new articulation (e.g., "democratic" = deepening the democratic content of political life). This "breaking of the chain" is not, of course, confined to the head: it takes place through social practice and political struggle.

Second, ideological statements are made by individuals: but ideologies are not the product of individual consciousness or intention. Rather, we formulate our intentions *within ideology*. They predate individuals, and form part of the determinate social formations and conditions into which individuals are born. We have to "speak through" the ideologies which are active in our society and which provide us with the means of "making sense" of social relations and our place in them. The transformation of ideologies is thus a collective process and practice, not an individual one. Largely, the processes work *unconsciously*, rather than by conscious intention. Ideologies produce different forms of social consciousness, rather than being produced by them. They work most effectively when we are not aware that how we formulate and construct a statement about the world is underpinned by ideological premises; when our formations seem to be simply descriptive statements about how things are (i.e., must be), or of what we can "take-for-granted." "Little boys like playing rough games; little girls, however, are full of sugar and spice" is predicated on a whole set of ideological premises, though it seems to be an aphorism which is grounded, not in how masculinity and femininity have been historically and culturally constructed in society, but in Nature itself. Ideologies tend to disappear from view into the taken-for-granted "naturalized" world of common sense. Since (like gender) race appears to be "given" by Nature, racism is one of the most profoundly "naturalized" of existing ideologies.

Third, ideologies "work" by constructing for their subjects (individual and collective) positions of identification and knowledge which allow them to "utter" ideological truths as if they were their authentic authors. This is not because they emanate from our innermost, authentic and unified experience, but because we find ourselves mirrored in the positions at the centre of the discourses from which the statements we formulate "make sense." Thus the same "subjects" (e.g., economic classes or ethnic groups) can be differently constructed in different ideologies. When Mrs. Thatcher says, "We can't afford to pay ourselves higher wages without earning them through higher productivity," she is attempting to construct at the centre of her discourse an identification for workers who will cease to see themselves as opposed or *antagonistic to* the needs of capital, and begin to see themselves in terms of the *identity of interests* between themselves and capital. Again, this is not only in the head. Redundancies are a powerful material way of influencing "hearts and minds."

Ideologies therefore work by the transformation of discourses (the disarticulation and rearticulation of ideological elements) and the transformation (the fracturing and recomposition) of subjects-for-action. How we "see" ourselves and our social relations *matters*, because it enters into and informs our actions and practices. Ideologies are therefore a site of a distinct type of social struggle. This site does not exist on its own, separate from other relations, since ideas are not free-floating in people's heads. The ideological construction of black people as a "problem population" and the police practice of containment in the black communities mutually reinforce and support one another. Nevertheless, ideology is a practice. It has its own specific way of working. And it is generated, produced and reproduced in specific settings (sites)—especially, in the apparatuses of ideological production which "produce" social meanings and distribute them throughout society, like the media. It is therefore the site of a particular kind of struggle, which cannot be simply reduced to or incorporated into some other level of struggle—for example, the economic class struggle, which is sometimes held to govern or determine it. It is the struggle over what Lenin once called "ideological social relations," which have their own tempo and specificity. It is located in specific practices. Ideological struggle, like any other form of struggle, therefore represents an intervention in an existing field of practices and institutions; those which sustain the dominant discourses of meaning of society.

The classic definition of ideology tends to regard it as a dependent sphere, which simply reflects "in ideas" what is happening elsewhere, for example, in the mode of production, without any determinacy or effectivity of its own. This is a reductive and economistic conception. Of course, the formation and distribution of ideologies have determinate conditions, some of which are established outside of ideology itself. Messrs Murdoch and Trafalgar House command (through *The Times, Sunday Times* and the *Express* group) the resources of institutionalized ideological power in ways which no section of the Left could currently aspire to. Nevertheless, ideologies are not fixed forever in the place assigned to them by "the economic": their elements, as Laclau has argued (1977), have "no necessary class belongingness." For instance, "democracy" belongs *both* to ruling-class ideology, where it means the Western system of parliamentary regimes, *and* to the ideologies of the Left, where it means or refers to "popular power," against the ruling power bloc. Of course, though the heads of small shopkeepers are not necessarily filled exclusively with "petty-bourgeois thoughts," certain ideological discourses *do* have or have acquired, historically, well-defined connections with certain class places. (It is easier for a small shopkeeper, than for an assembly-line worker in British Leyland, to think of his or her interests as equivalent to those of an independent self-employed small capitalist.) These "traces," as Gramsci called them, and historical connexions—the terrain of past articulations—are peculiarly resistant to change and transformation:

just as it is exceedingly hard, given the history of imperialism, to disinter the idea of "the British people" from its nationalistic connotation.

New forms of ideological struggle can bring old "traces" to life, thus Thatcherism has revivified liberal political economy. Even in such well-secured cases, transformations *are* possible ("the people" coming to represent, not the "nation, unified under the ruling class," but the *common* people *versus* the ruling class—an antagonistic relation rather than an equivalent and unifying one). The corollary of this is that there is no fixed, given and necessary form of ideological consciousness, dictated exclusively by class position. A third of the British working class has regularly seen itself, in terms of how it votes, as "rightfully subordinate to those who are naturally born to rule over others." The famous working-class deference Tory vote shows they do not necessarily see themselves as their class position would lead us to suppose: e.g., as the "majority exploited class which ought to supplant the class which rules over us."

At the last (1979) election, Mrs. Thatcher clearly had some success in getting skilled and organized workers to *equate* (articulate together) their own opposition to incomes policies, wage control and the demand for a "return to collective bargaining," with her own, very different, conception of "letting market forces decide wage levels." Just as the working class is not impervious to reactionary or social-democratic ideas, so it is not *a priori* impervious to racist ideas. The whole history of Labour socialism and reformism is a refutation of the idealistic hope (rooted in economism) that the economic position of the working class will make it inevitable that it thinks only progressive, antiracist or revolutionary ideas. Instead, what we have seen over the past two decades is the undoubted penetration of racist ideas and practices, not only into sections of the working class, but into the very organizations and institutions of the labour movement itself.

Let us look, then, a little more closely at the apparatuses which generate and circulate ideologies. In modern societies, the different media are especially important sites for the production, reproduction and transformation of ideologies. Ideologies are, of course, worked on in many places in society, and not only in the head. The fact of unemployment, as the Thatcher government knows only too well, is, among other things, an extremely effective ideological instrument for converting or constraining workers to moderate their wage claims. But institutions like the media are peculiarly central to the matter since they are, by definition, part of the dominant means of *ideological* production. What they "produce" is, precisely, representations of the social world, images, descriptions, explanations and frames for understanding how the world is and why it works as it is said and shown to work. And, amongst other kinds of ideological labour, the media construct for us a definition of what *race* is, what meaning the imagery of race carries, and what the "problem of race" is understood to be. They help to classify out the world in terms of the categories of race.

The media are not only a powerful source of ideas about race. They are also one place where these ideas are articulated, worked on, transformed and elaborated. We have said "ideas" and "ideologies" in the plural. For it would be wrong and misleading to see the media as uniformly and conspiratorially harnessed to a single, racist conception of the world. Liberal and humane ideas about "good relations" between the races, based on open-mindedness and tolerance, operate inside the world of the media—among, for example, many television journalists and newspapers like the *Guardian*—alongside the more explicit racism of other journalists and newspapers like the *Express* or the *Mail*. In some respects, the line which separates the latter from the extreme right on policies such as, for example, guided repatriation for blacks, is very thin indeed.

It would be simple and convenient if all the media were simply the ventriloquists of a unified and racist "ruling class" conception of the world. But neither a unifiedly conspiratorial media nor indeed a unified racist "ruling class" exist in anything like that simple way. I don't insist on complexity for its own sake. But if critics of the media subscribe to too simple or reductive a view of their operations, this inevitably lacks credibility and weakens the case they are making because the theories and critiques don't square with reality. They only begin to account for the real operation of racism in society by a process of gross abstraction and simplification.

More important, the task of a critical theory is to produce as accurate a knowledge of complex social processes as the complexity of their functioning requires. It is not its task to console the Left by producing simple but satisfying myths, distinguished only by their super-left-wing credentials. (If the laws and tendencies of the capitalist mode of production can be stated in a simplified form because they are essentially simple and reducible, why on earth did Marx go on about them for so long—three uncompleted volumes, no less?) Most important of all, these differences and complexities have real *effects*, which ought to enter into any serious political calculation about how their tendencies might be resisted or turned. We know, for example, that the broadcasting institutions are not "independent and autonomous" of the state in the way suggested in the official wisdom. But if we neglect to ask why the question of "independence" and the media's "relative autonomy" are so important to their functioning, and simply reduce them to what we think of as their essential nature—pure instruments of ruling-class or racist ideology—we will not be able to deconstruct the credibility and legitimacy which they, in fact, carry (which depends, precisely, on the fact that "autonomy" is not a pure piece of deception). Moreover, we will have an over-incorporated conception of the world, where the state is conceived, not as a necessarily contradictory formation, but as a simple, transparent instrumentality. This view might flatter the super-radical conscience, but it has no place in it for the concept of class struggle, and defines no practical terrain on which such struggles could be conducted. (Why it has passed so long for "Marxism" is a mystery.) So we must attend to the complexities of the ways in which race and racism are constructed in the media in order to be able to bring about change.

Another important distinction is between what we might call "overt" racism and "inferential" racism. By *overt racism*, I mean those many occasions when open and favourable coverage is given to arguments, positions and spokespersons who are in the business of elaborating an openly racist argument or advancing a racist policy or view. Many such occasions exist; they have become more frequent in recent years—more often in the press, which has become openly partisan to extremist right-wing arguments, than in television, where the regulations of "balance," "impartiality and neutrality" operate.

By *inferential racism* I mean those apparently naturalized representations of events and situations relating to race, whether "factual" or "fictional," which have racist premises and propositions inscribed in them as a set of *unquestioned assumptions*. These enable racist statements to be formulated without ever bringing into awareness the racist predicates on which the statements are grounded.

Both types of racism are to be found, in different combinations, in the British media. Open or overt racism is, of course, politically dangerous as well as socially offensive. The open partisanship of sections of the popular press on this front is an extremely serious development. It is not only that they circulate and popularise openly racist policies and ideas, and translate them into the vivid populist vernacular (e.g., in the tabloids, with their large working-class readership); it is the very fact that such things can now be openly said and advocated which *legitimates* their public expression and increases the threshold of the public acceptability of racism. Racism becomes "acceptable"—and thus, not too long after, "true"—just common sense: what everyone knows and is openly saying. But *inferential racism* is more widespread—and in many ways, more insidious, because it is largely *invisible* even to those who formulate the world in its terms.

An example of *this* type of racist ideology is the sort of television programme which deals with some "problem" in race relations. It is probably made by a good and honest liberal broadcaster, who hopes to do some good in the world for "race relations" and who maintains a scrupulous balance and neutrality when questioning people interviewed for the programme. The programme will end with a homily on how, if only the "extremists" on *either side* would go away, "normal blacks and whites" would be better able to get on with learning to live in harmony together. Yet every word and image of such programmes are impregnated with unconscious racism because they are all predicated on the unstated and unrecognized assumption that the *blacks* are the *source of the problem*. Yet virtually the whole of "social problem" television about race and immigration—often made, no doubt, by well-intentioned and liberal-minded broadcasters—is precisely predicated on racist premises of this kind. This was the criticism we made in the CARM programme *It Ain't Half Racist, Mum*, and it was the one which most cut the broadcasters to their professional quick. It undermined their professional credentials by suggesting that they had been partisan where they are supposed to be balanced and impartial. It was an affront to the liberal consensus and self-image which prevails within broadcasting. Both responses were, in fact, founded on the profound misunderstanding that racism is, by definition, mutually exclusive of the liberal consensus—whereas, in inferential racism, the two can quite easily cohabit—and on the assumption that if the television discourse could be shown to be racist, it must be because the individual broadcasters were intentionally and deliberately racist. In fact, an ideological discourse does *not* depend on the conscious intentions of those who formulate statements within it.

How, then, is race and its "problems" constructed on British television? This is a complex topic in its own right, and I can only illustrate its dimensions briefly here by referring to some of the themes developed in the two programmes I was involved in. One of the things we tried to show in *The Whites of Their Eyes* was the rich vocabulary and syntax of race on which the media have to draw. Racism has a long and distinguished history in British culture. It is grounded in the relations of slavery, colonial conquest, economic exploitation and imperialism in which the European races have stood in relation to the "native peoples" of the colonized and exploited periphery.

Three characteristics provided the discursive- and power-coordinates of the discourses in which these relations were historically constructed. (1) Their imagery and themes were polarized around fixed relations of subordination and domination. (2) Their stereotypes were grouped around the poles of "superior" and "inferior" natural species. (3) Both were displaced from the "language" of history into the language of Nature. Natural physical signs and racial characteristics became the unalterable signifiers of inferiority. Subordinate ethnic groups and classes appeared, not as the objects of particular historical relations (the slave trade, European colonization, the active underdevelopment of the "underdeveloped" societies), but as the given qualities of an inferior *breed*. Relations secured by economic, social, political and military domination were transformed and "naturalized" into an order of *rank*, ascribed by Nature. Thus, Edward Long, an acute English observer of Jamaica in the period of slavery, wrote (in his *History of Jamaica*, 1774)—much in the way the Elizabethans might have spoken of "the Great Chain Of Being"—of "Three ranks of men [sic], (white, mulatto and black), dependent on each other, and rising in a proper climax of subordination, in which the whites hold the highest place."

One thing we wanted to illustrate in the programme was the "forgotten" degree to which, in the period of slavery and imperialism, popular literature is saturated with these fixed, negative attributes of the colonized races. We find them in the diaries, observations and accounts, the notebooks, ethnographic records and commentaries, of visitors, explorers, missionaries and administrators in Africa, India, the Far East and the Americas. And also something else: the "absent" but imperializing "white eye"; the unmarked position from which all these "observations" are made and from which, alone, they make sense. This is the history of slavery and conquest, written, seen, drawn and photographed by The Winners. They cannot be *read* and made sense of from any other position. The "white eye" is always outside the frame but seeing and positioning everything within it.

Some of the most telling sequences we used was from early film of the British Raj in India—the source of endless radio "reminiscences" and television historical show-pieces today. The assumption of effortless superiority structures every image—even the portioning in the frame: the foregrounding of colonial life (tea-time on the plantation), the background of native bearers. . . . In the later stages of High Imperialism, this discourse proliferates through the new media of popular culture and information—newspapers and journals, cartoons, drawings and advertisements and the popular novel. Recent critics of the literature of imperialism have argued that, if we simply extend our definition of nineteenth-century fiction from one branch of "serious fiction" to embrace popular literature, we will find a second, powerful strand of the English literary imagination to set beside the *domestic* novel: the male-dominated world of imperial adventure, which takes *empire*, rather than *Middlemarch*, as its microcosm. I remember a graduate student, working on the construction of race in popular literature and culture at the end of the nineteenth century, coming to me in despair—racism was so *ubiquitous*, and at the same time, so *unconscious*—simply assumed to be the case—that it was impossible to get any critical purchase on it. In this period, the very idea of *adventure* became synonymous with the demonstration of the moral, social and physical mastery of the colonizers over the colonized.

Later, this concept of "adventure"—one of the principal categories of modern *entertainment*—moved straight off the printed page into the literature of crime and espionage, children's books, the great Hollywood extravaganzas and comics. There, with recurring persistence, they still remain. Many of these older versions have had their edge somewhat blunted by time. They have been distanced from us, apparently, by our superior wisdom and liberalism. But they still reappear on the television screen, especially in the form of "old movies" (some "old movies," of course, continue to be made). But we can grasp their recurring resonance better if we identify some of the base-images of the "grammar of race."

There is, for example, the familiar *slave-figure*: dependable, loving in a simple, childlike way—the devoted "Mammy" with the rolling eyes, or the faithful field-hand or retainer, attached and devoted to "his" Master. The best-known extravaganza of all—*Gone with the Wind*—contains rich variants of both. The "slave-figure" is by no means limited to films and programmes *about* slavery. Some "Injuns" and many Asians have come on to the screen in this disguise. A deep and unconscious ambivalence pervades this stereotype. Devoted and childlike, the "slave" is also unreliable, unpredictable and undependable—capable of "turning nasty," or of plotting in a treacherous way, secretive, cunning, cutthroat once his or her Master's or Mistress's back is turned: and inexplicably given to running way into the bush at the slightest opportunity. The whites can never be sure that this childish simpleton—"Sambo"—is not mocking his master's white manners behind his hand, even when giving an exaggerated caricature of white refinement.

Another base-image is that of the "native." The good side of this figure is portrayed in a certain primitive nobility and simple dignity. The bad side is portrayed in terms of cheating and cunning, and, further out, savagery and barbarism. Popular culture is still full today of countless savage and restless "natives," and soundtracks constantly repeat the threatening sound of drumming in the night, the hint of primitive rites and cults. Cannibals, whirling dervishes, Indian tribesmen, garishly got up, are constantly threatening to overrun the screen. They are likely to appear at any moment out of the darkness to decapitate the beautiful heroine, kidnap the children, burn the encampment or threatening to boil, cook and eat the innocent explorer or colonial administrator and his lady-wife. These "natives" always move as an anonymous collective mass—in tribes or hordes. And against them is always counterposed the isolated white figure, alone "out there," confronting his Destiny or shouldering his Burden in the "heart of darkness," displaying coolness under fire and an unshakeable authority—exerting mastery over the rebellious natives or quelling the threatened uprising with a single glance of his steel-blue eyes.

A third variant is that of the "clown" or "entertainer." This captures the "innate" humour, as well as the physical grace of the licensed entertainer—putting on a show for The Others. It is never quite clear whether we are laughing with or at this figure: admiring the physical and rhythmic grace, the open expressivity and emotionality of the "entertainer," or put off by the "clown's" stupidity.

One noticeable fact about all these images is their deep *ambivalence*—the double vision of the white eye through which they are seen. The primitive nobility of the ageing tribesman or chief, and the native's rhythmic grace always contain both a nostalgia for an innocence lost forever to the civilized, and the threat of civilization being overrun or undermined by the recurrence of savagery, which is always lurking just below the surface; or by an untutored sexuality, threatening to "break out." Both are aspects—the good and the bad sides—of *primitivism*. In these images, "primitivism" is defined by the fixed proximity of such people to Nature.

Is all this so far away as we sometimes suppose from the representations of race which fill the screens today? These *particular* versions may have faded. But their *traces* are still to be observed, reworked in many of the modern and updated images. And though they may appear to carry a different meaning, they are often still constructed on a very ancient grammar. Today's restless native hordes are still alive and well and living as guerrilla armies and freedom fighters in the Angola, Zimbabwe or Namibian "bush." Blacks are still the most frightening, cunning and glamorous crooks (and policemen) in New York cop series. They are the fleet-footed, crazy-talking under-men who connect Starsky and Hutch to the drug-saturated ghetto. The scheming villains and their giant-sized bully boys in the world of James Bond and his progeny are still, unusually, recruited from "out there" in Jamaica, where savagery lingers on. The sexually available "slave-girl" is alive and kicking, smouldering away on some exotic TV set or on the covers of paperbacks, though she is now the centre of a special admiration, covered in a sequinned gown and supported by a white chorus line. Primitivism, savagery, guile and unreliability—all "just below the surface"—can still be identified in the faces of black political leaders around the world, cunningly plotting the overthrow of "civilization": Mr. Mugabe, for example, up to the point where he happened to win both a war and an election and became, temporarily at any rate, the best (because the most politically credible) friend Britain had left in that last outpost of the Edwardian dream.

The "Old Country"—white version—is still often the subject of nostalgic documentaries: "Old Rhodesia," whose reliable servants, as was only to be expected, plotted treason in the outhouse and silently stole away to join ZAPU in the bush.... Tribal Man in green khaki. Black stand-up comics still ape their ambiguous incorporation into British entertainment by being the first to tell a racist joke. No Royal Tour is complete without its troupe of swaying bodies, or its mounted tribesmen, paying homage. Blacks are such "good movers," so *rhythmic*, so *natural*. And the dependent peoples, who couldn't manage for a day without the protection and know-how of their white masters, reappear as the starving victims of the Third World, passive and waiting for the technology or the Aid to arrive, objects of our pity or of a *Blue Peter* appeal. They are not represented as the subjects of a continuing exploitation or dependency, or the global division of wealth and labour. They are the Victims of Fate.

These modern, glossed and updated images seem to have put the old world of Sambo behind them. Many of them, indeed, are the focus of a secret, illicit, pleasurable-but-taboo admiration. Many have a more active and energetic quality—some black athletes, for example, and of course the entertainers. But the connotations and echoes which they carry reverberate back a very long way. They continue to shape the ways whites see blacks today—even when the white adventurer sailing up the jungle stream is not *Sanders of the River*, but historical-drama reconstructions of Stanley and Livingstone; and the intention is to show, not the savagery, but the serenity of African village life—ways of an ancient people "unchanged even down to modern times" (in other words, still preserved in economic backwardness and frozen in history for our anthropological eye by forces unknown to them and, apparently, unshowable on the screen).

"Adventure" is one way in which we *encounter* race without having to *confront* the racism of the perspectives in use. Another, even more complex one is "entertainment." In television, there is a strong counter-position between "serious," informational television, which we watch because it is good for us, and "entertainment," which we watch because it is pleasurable. And the purest form of pleasure in entertainment television is *comedy*. By definition, comedy is a licensed zone, disconnected from the serious. It's all "good, clean fun." In the area of fun and pleasure it is forbidden to pose a serious question, partly because it seems so puritanical and destroys the pleasure by switching registers. Yet race is one of the most significant themes in situation comedies—from the early Alf Garnett to *Mind Your Language, On the Buses, Love Thy Neighbour* and *It Ain't Half Hot, Mum*. These are defended on good "antiracist" grounds: the appearance of blacks, alongside whites, in situation comedies, it is argued, will help to naturalize and normalize their presence in British society. And no doubt, in some examples, it does function in this way. But, if you examine these fun occasions more closely, you will often find, as we did in our two programmes, that the comedies do not simply include blacks: they are *about race*. That is, the same old categories of racially defined characteristics and qualities, and the same relations of superior and inferior, provide the pivots on which the jokes actually turn, the tension-points which move and motivate the situations in situation comedies. The comic register in which they are set, however, protects and defends viewers from acknowledging their incipient racism. It creates disavowal.

This is even more so with the television stand-up comics, whose repertoire in recent years has come to be dominated, in about equal parts, by sexist and racist jokes. It's sometimes said, again in their defence, that this must be a sign of black acceptability. But it *may* just be that racism has become more normal: it's hard to tell. It's also said that the best tellers of anti-Jewish jokes are Jews themselves, just as blacks tell the best "white" jokes against themselves. But this is to argue as if jokes exist in a vacuum separate from the contexts and situations of their telling. Jewish jokes told by Jews among themselves are part of the self-awareness of the community. They are unlikely to function by "putting down" the race, because both teller and audience belong on equal terms to the same group. Telling racist jokes across the racial line, in conditions where relations of racial inferiority and superiority prevail, reinforces *the difference* and reproduces the unequal relations because, in those situations, the point of the joke depends on the existence of racism. Thus they reproduce the categories and relations of racism, even while normalizing them through laughter. The stated good intentions of the joke-makers do not resolve the problem here, because they are not in control of the circumstances—conditions of continuing racism—in which their joke discourse will be read and heard. The time *may* come when blacks and whites can tell jokes about each other in ways which do not reproduce the racial categories of the world in which they are told. The time, in Britain, is certainly *not yet arrived*.

Two other arenas which we tried to illustrate in both programmes related to the "harder" end of television production—news and current affairs. This is where race is constructed as *problem* and the site of *conflict* and debate. There have been good examples of programmes where blacks have not exclusively appeared as the source of the "problem" (ATV's *Breaking Point* is one example) and where they have not been exclusively saddled with being the aggressive agent in conflict (the London Weekend Television *London Programme* and the Southall Defence Committee's *Open Door* programme on the Southall events are examples). But the general tendency of the run of programmes in this area is to see blacks—especially the mere fact of their existence (their "numbers")—as constituting a problem for English white society. They appear as law-breakers, prone to crime; as "trouble"; as the collective agent of civil disorder.

In the numerous incidents where black communities have reacted to racist provocation (as at Southall) or to police harassment and provocation (as in Bristol), the media have tended to assume that "right" lay on the side of the law, and have fallen into the language of "riot" and "race warfare" which simply feeds existing stereotypes and prejudices. The precipitating conditions of conflict are usually *absent*—the scandalous provocation of a National Front march through one of the biggest black areas, Southall, and the saturation police raiding of the last refuge for black youth which triggered off Bristol—to take only two recent examples. They are either missing, or introduced so late in the process of signification that they fail to dislodge the dominant definition of these events. So they testify, once again, to the disruptive nature of black and Asian people *as such*.

The analysis of the media coverage of Southall contained in the National Council of Civil Liberties Unofficial Committee of Inquiry Report (1980), for example, shows how rapidly, in both the television and press, the official definitions of the police—Sir David McNee's statement on the evening of 23 April, and the ubiquitous James Jardine, speaking for the Police Federation on the succeeding day—provided the media with the authoritative definition of the event. These, in turn, shaped and focused what the media reported and how it explained what transpired. In taking their cue from these authoritative sources, the media reproduced an account of the event which, with certain significant exceptions, translated the conflict between racism and antiracism into (a) a contest between Asians and the police, and (b) a contest between two kinds of extremism—the so-called *fascism* of Left and Right alike.

This had the effect of downgrading the two problems at the centre of the Southall affair—the growth of and growing legitimacy of the extreme Right and its blatantly provocative antiblack politics of the street; and the racism and brutality of the police. Both issues had to be *forced* on to the agenda of the media by a militant and organized protest. Most press reports of Southall were so obsessed by embroidering the lurid details of "roaming hordes of coloured youths" chasing young whites "with a carving knife"—a touch straight out of *Sanders of the River*, though so far uncorroborated—that they failed even to mention the death of Blair Peach. This is selective or tunnel vision with a vengeance.

A good example of how the real causes of racial conflict can be absorbed and transformed by the framework which the media employ can be found in the *Nationwide* coverage of Southall on the day following the events. Two interlocking frameworks of explanation governed this programme. In the first, conflict is seen in the conspiratorial terms of far-Left against extreme-Right—the Anti-Nazi League against the National Front. This is the classic logic of television, where the medium identifies itself with the moderate, consensual, middle-road, Average viewer, and sets off, in contrast, extremism on both sides, which it then equates with each other. In this particular exercise in "balance," fascism and antifascism are represented as *the same—*both equally *bad*, because the Middle Way enshrines the Common Good under all circumstances. This balancing exercise provided an opportunity for Martin Webster of the National Front to gain access to the screen, to help set the terms of the debate, and to spread his smears across the screen under the freedom of the airwaves: "Well," he said, "let's talk about Trotskyists, extreme Communists of various sorts, raving Marxists and other assorted left-wing cranks." Good knockabout stuff. Then, after a linking passage—"Southall, the day after"—to the second framework: rioting Asians *vs* the police. "I watched television as well last night," Mr. Jardine argued, "and I certainly didn't see any police throwing bricks.... So don't start making those arguments." The growth of organized political racism and the circumstances which have precipitated it were simply not visible to *Nationwide* as an alternative way of setting up the problem.

In the CARM programme *It Ain't Half Racist, Mum*, we tried to illustrate the inferential logic at work in another area of programming: the BBC's "Great Debate" on Immigration. It was not necessary here to start with any preconceived notions, least of all speculation as to the personal views on race by the broadcasters involved—though one can't expect either the BBC hierarchy or Robin Day to believe that. You have simply to look at the programme with one set of questions in mind: Here is a problem, defined as "the problem of immigration." What is it? How is it defined and constructed through the programme? What logic governs its definition? And where does that logic derive from? I believe the answers are clear. The problem of immigration is that "there are too many blacks over here," to put it crudely. It is *defined* in terms of *numbers of blacks* and what to do about them. The *logic* of the argument is "immigrants = blacks = too many of them = send them home." That is a racist logic. And it comes from a chain of reasoning whose representative, in respectable public debate and in person, on this occasion, was Enoch Powell. Powellism set the agenda for the media. Every time (and on many more occasions than the five or six we show in the programme) the presenter wanted to define the baseline of the programme which others should address, Mr. Powell's views were indicated as representing it. And every time anyone strayed from the "logic" to question the underlying premiss, it was back to "as Mr. Powell would say . . ." that they were drawn.

It certainly does not follow (and I know of no evidence to suggest) that Robin Day subscribes to this line or agrees with Mr. Powell on anything to do with race. I know absolutely nothing about his views on race and immigration. And we made no judgement on his views, which are irrelevant to the argument. If the media function in a systematically racist manner, it is not because they are run and organized exclusively by active racists; this is a category mistake. This would be equivalent to saying that you could change the character of the capitalist state by replacing its personnel, whereas the media, like the state, have a *structure*, a set of *practices* which are *not* reducible to the individuals who staff them. What defines how the media function is the result of a set of complex, often contradictory, social relations; not the personal inclinations of its members. What is significant is not that they produce a racist ideology, from some single-minded and unified conception of the world, but that they are so powerfully constrained—"spoken by"—a particular set of ideological discourses. The power of this discourse is its capacity to constrain a very great variety of individuals: racist, antiracist, liberals, radicals, conservatives, anarchists, know-nothings and silent majoritarians.

What we said, however, about the *discourse* of problem television was true, despite the hurt feelings of particular individuals: and demonstrably so. The premiss on which the Great Immigration Debate was built and the chain of reasoning it predicated was a racist one. The evidence for this is in what was said and how it was formulated—how the argument unfolded. If you establish the topic as "the numbers of blacks are too high" or "*they* are breeding too fast," the opposition is obliged or constrained to argue that "the numbers are not as high as they are represented to be." This view is opposed to the first two: but it is also imprisoned by the same logic—the logic of the "numbers game." Liberals, antiracists, indeed raging revolutionaries can contribute "freely" to this debate, and indeed are often obliged to do so, so as not to let the case go by default: without breaking for a moment the chain of assumptions which holds the racist proposition in place. However, changing the terms of the argument, questioning the assumptions and starting points, breaking the logic—this is a quite different, longer, more difficult task.

One element of the struggle, then, is to try to start the debate about race somewhere else. But this depends on making visible what is usually invisible: the assumptions on which current practices depend. You have to expose, in order to deconstruct. This is certainly not the *only* kind of intervention—and one of the problems with the discussion of strategy on the Left is exactly the Left's inflexibility: the assumption that there is only one key to the door. That, at any rate, was the main (though not the only) reason why the group involved in making the final version of the CARM programme decided not to go for the all-out, overarching résumé of the antiracist case, in twenty-five minutes, but instead to adapt to the given terrain (we don't choose our own battlegrounds), and take a very specific target. In short, to do a programme *about* the media and racism, *on* the media, *against* the media.

This, however, is one of the main criticisms levelled at the CARM programme by its critics: that it was too confined to and preoccupied with exposing the media, and didn't make the general antiracist case. About this opinions can and do genuinely differ, though the critics—I'm afraid—preferred to attribute these differences, not to the genuine problems of political calculation, but to "bad faith" on our part (see, for example, Gardner and Henry 1979). I did think that the limited opportunity provided by *Open Door*, with all its problems (out-of-prime-viewing scheduling, low budgets, little time in the studio, restricted access to equipment, etc.) should best be used to hammer a particular target: to make the media, for once, speak "against" the media's dominant practice, and thus reveal something about how they normally function. This means limiting the topics covered, going for a narrow-gauge approach rather than a scatter-fire programme covering the history and causes of racism *in general*. It may have been the wrong choice. It wasn't necessarily because we lost our "left-wing" nerve—as I think is the main, and familiar, imputation.

A second line of criticism is about the audience aimed for. Gardner and Henry, for example, criticize CARM for going for the "general audience," which, they argue, is to adopt the traditional media view of the audience as an undifferentiated, passive mass. They would have preferred the programme to "equip the black, left-wing and antiracist movements with the tools and knowledge about the workings of television racism" (1979, 75). Again, a genuine matter of disagreement. Another view (the one I took) is that black, left-wing and antiracist groups, already active in the antiracist struggle, are the last people who need to be instructed about how media racism works—least of all in a twenty-five minute programme on a public TV channel. Such organized activists have far more effective, internal channels for such purposes. What such groups face is the stark fact of a growing racist common sense and the lack of "access" to the means to engage with this type of popular consciousness. But I'm afraid that, to enter the struggle on this *popular* level is a quite different order of political task from that of confirming the already-confirmed views of the converted. It means struggling over the muddy and confused middle-ground: the ground where Powellism, Thatcherism and the National Front have, in recent years, made such remarkable headway.

I suspect that behind this criticism lies a much deeper debate about political strategy which these critics did not openly engage: the Left confronts very sharp alternatives now between the broadening and deepening of democratic struggle, pressing on with "class-against-class" confrontations as if nothing had happened to left-vanguardism since the heroic days of May 1968—although the whole terrain of popular struggle has shifted decisively against the left offensive. Ultimately, then, the debates about strategies turn on the analysis of political conjunctures. And it is *this* which should be openly debated—rather than caricatured into an eternal conflict between the "true" and the "false" Left.

Not only the "middle ground" but liberal consciousness itself must be an object of struggle—if what we intend is the winning of positions in a protracted war of position. Indeed, if the CARM programme had a "target audience," I would unhesitatingly define it, not as the casual or confirmed racist (who are unlikely to be converted by twenty-five minutes on BBC 2) but precisely the *liberal consensus*. For the "liberal consensus" is the linchpin of what I called "inferential racism." It is what keeps active and organized racism in place. So this was one, at least, of the targets we aimed for. And recognizing, from our analysis, that one kind of common sense is not displaced in an evening, we deliberately tried to think realistically about what the programme could and *could not* do. "Pessimism of the intellect, optimism of the will": there is nothing worse, for the Left, than mistaking a tiny skirmish for the final showdown. For, if optimistic voluntarism raises hearts and hopes for a little while, it is followed, as day follows night, by a corresponding gloom and pessimism. (Gramsci is excellent on the oscillations of high optimism and deep pessimism on the Left in periods of rapidly shifting fortunes.) CARM's intervention could not be anything but a tiny movement in a long war of position, on the stony ground which television, regularly, delivers to the wrong side. Political calculation begins with defining the target of action, the limits of the terrain, an accurate assessment of the balance of forces and a correct estimation of the enemy's strength. Horses for courses.

The third major criticism was that the programme's style and form reproduced that of the standard formats of dominant television practice—trying to beat the professionals at their own game, rather than consciously breaking those frames. In fact, this is predicated on a much more complex, though largely unstated, argument that it is the forms rather than the content and premises of ideological discourses which constitute their effectivity. Therefore, the main task is to "deconstruct the forms of the television discourse." "We wanted the programme to be *offensive* . . ." Gardner and Henry argued. This is a complicated issue, and a contentious one: by no means the simple either/or alternative in which it is presented. I myself thought we should go further in the direction of "deconstruction" than the material constraints on programme production eventually allowed. So that is to concede one major weakness in the programme's conception. But after that, argument, not assertion, needs to take over.

Is it true that ideologies work exclusively by their forms? This position depends on an antirealist aesthetic—a fashionable position in debates about ideology in the early 1970s. In its absolute form, it needed to be, and has been, quite effectively challenged and qualified. It represented at the time a certain justified "formalist" reaction to the over-preoccupation with "content" and "realism" on the traditional Left. But it was and is open to very serious criticism. For one thing it was founded on a rather loony and quite ahistorical view of the narrative and presentational forms in television. They were said *all* to belong to the same type of "realism"—*the* realism of *the* realist text, was the phrase—which, apparently, was introduced in the fourteenth century and had persisted, more or less, right up to *Man Alive*. This highly specious account was sealed—quite incorrectly—with the signature of Brecht. In this absolutist form, the thesis has proved quite impossible to defend, and many of those who first proposed it have since either backed away from its excesses or fallen into an eloquent silence.

The view that lumps together the latest, banal, TV documentary and the TV drama documentary on the General Strike of 1926, *Days of Hope*, is so historically naive and simplistic, and so crude politically, as to give it the status of a blunderbuss in a war conducted by missile computer. This is not to deny the importance of form in the discussion of ideology. Nor is it to deny that programmes which simply reproduce the existing dominant forms of television do not sufficiently break the frames through which audiences locate and position themselves in relation to the knowledge which such programmes claim to provide. But the argument that *only* "deconstructivist" texts are truly revolutionary is as one-sided a view as that which suggests that forms have no effect. Besides, it is to adopt a very formalistic conception of form, which, in fact, accepts the false dichotomy between "form" and "content"; only, where the Left has traditionally been concerned exclusively with the latter, this view was concerned only with the former. There were other calculations to be made. For example, that using the existing format of the typical programme which viewers are accustomed to identify with one kind of truth, one could undermine, precisely, the credibility of the media by showing that even this form could be used to state a different kind of truth.

A second consideration is this: if all the dominant television forms are "realist" and realist narratives are bad, does it follow that all avantgarde or "deconstructivist" narratives are good? This is also a rather loony position to take. The history of culture is littered with nonrevolutionary "avantgardes": with "avantgardes" which are revolutionary in form only; even more, with "avantgardes" which are rapidly absorbed and incorporated into the dominant discourse, becoming the standard orthodoxies of the next generation. So, "breaking and interrupting" the forms is no guarantee, in itself, that the dominant ideology cannot continue to be reproduced. This is the false trail along which some of the French theorists, like Julia Kristeva and the *Tel Quel* group, tried to drive us, by a species of polite intellectual terrorism, in the 1970s. In hindsight, the Left was quite right to resist being hustled and blackmailed by these arguments.

This is no abstract debate, restricted to intellectuals of the left bank exclusively. It relates to political choices—harsh ones, to which there are no simple solutions, but which confront us every day. In any left bookshop today, one will find the imaginatively designed, style-conscious, frame-breaking, interrogative avantgarde "little journals" of the Left: interrupting the "dominant ideologies" in their form at every turn—and remorselessly restricted to a small, middle-class, progressive audience. One will also find the traditionally designed, ancient looking, crude aesthetics of the "labour movement" journals (*Tribune*, the *Morning Star*, *Socialist Challenge*, for example)—remorselessly restricted to an equally small and committed audience. Neither appears to have resolved the extremely difficult problem of a truly revolutionary form *and* content: or the problem of political effectiveness—by which I mean the breakthrough to a mass audience. This is not simply a problem of the politics of popular communication on the Left: a burning issue which no simple appeal to stylistic aggressiveness has yet been able to solve. If only the social division of labour could be overcome by a few new typographical or stylistic devices!

Actually, however, it would be wrong to end this piece with a simple defence of what was done, which simply mirrors by reversal the criticisms levelled. We knew we had an exceedingly rare opportunity, not something the Left can afford to squander. We knew the programme could have been better, more effective—including using more effectively ideas we did or had to jettison. These are genuinely matters of debate and properly the subject of criticism. I want, instead, to draw a different lesson from this episode. It is the degree to which the Left is unable to confront and argue through constructively the genuine problems of tactics and strategy of a popular antiracist struggle. To be honest, what we know collectively about this would not fill the back of a postage stamp. Yet, we continue to conduct tactical debates and political calculation as if the answers were already fully inscribed in some new version of Lenin's *What Is to Be Done?*. Our mode of political calculation is that of the taking of absolutist positions, the attribution of bad faith to those genuinely convinced otherwise—and, thereby, the steady advance of the deathwatch beetle of sectarian self-righteousness and fragmentation.

It somehow enhances our left-wing credentials to argue and debate as if there is some *theory* of political struggle, enshrined in the tablets of stone somewhere, which can be instantly translated into the one true "correct" strategy. The fact that we continue to lose the key strategic engagements and, in the present period, have lost very decisive terrain indeed, does not dent, even for a moment, our total certainty that we are on the "correct line." My own view is that we hardly begin to know how to conduct a popular antiracist struggle or how to bend the twig of racist common sense which currently dominates popular thinking. It is a lesson we had better learn pretty rapidly. The early interventions of the Anti-Nazi League in this area, at a very strategic, touch-and-go moment in the antiracist struggle, was one of the most effective and imaginative political interventions made in this period by groups other than the already-engaged groups of black activists. It is an experience we can and must build on—not by imitating and repeating it, but by matching it in imaginativeness. But even that leaves no room for complacency—as we watch the racist slogans raised on the soccer stands and listen to racist slogans inflect and infect the chanting of young working-class people on the terraces. Face to face with this struggle for popular advantage, to fight on only one front, with only one weapon, to deploy only one strategy and to put all one's eggs into a single tactic is to set about winning the odd dramatic skirmish at the risk of losing the war.

NOTE

This essay first appeared as "The Whites of Their Eyes: Racist Ideologies and the Media," in *Silver Linings: Some Strategies for the Eighties*, edited by George Bridges and Rosalind Brunt (London: Lawrence and Wishart, 1981), 28–52.

REFERENCES

Gardner, Carl. 1979a. "Limited Access." *Time Out*, 23 February.
Gardner, Carl. 1979b. "It Ain't Half a Hot Potato, Mum." *Time Out*, 23 February.
Gardner, Carl, and Margaret Henry. 1979. "Racism, Anti-racism and Access Television." *Screen Education* 31 (Summer).
Laclau, Ernesto. 1977. *Politics and Ideology in Marxist Theory*. London: New Left Books.
Long, Edward. 1774. *History of Jamaica*. London: T. Lowndes.
National Council for Civil Liberties. 1980. *Southall, 23 April 1979: Report of the Unofficial Committee of Inquiry*. London: National Council for Civil Liberties.

PART II | THE POLITICS OF

INTELLECTUAL WORK

AGAINST RACISM

CHAPTER 8

Teaching Race

[EDITORS' NOTE: *This is an edited transcript of an informal talk given to the London Branch of the Association of Teachers of Social Science on Wednesday, 30 April 1980, at Isledon Teachers' Centre, Highbury, London N1.*]

What I broadly want to do is to address four sets of problems. First of all, I want to identify what seem to be some of the difficulties with teaching about race and then I want to say something about the economic, political and ideological aspects of race. These remarks are not directly addressed to the kinds of specific curriculum interests that might arise in schools or indeed the kinds of questions that might be posed in examinations—but instead I have tried to organise them to address the issues with which one needs to engage when teaching in this area.

I.

First of all, there are pedagogical difficulties which are especially important because it is an area about which people feel very strongly indeed. One of the strategies which some teachers adopt is to try to sidestep the explosive nature of the subject itself and walk around it, to catch it unawares (except that it usually catches you unawares rather than the other way round). It is not possible to do very much with the area at a steadily high classroom temperature but several points are important. You have to recognise the strong emotional ideological commitments people have to positions about race—this isn't an area where people simply think they know things but it is very strongly charged emotionally and this fact has to be recognised and be brought out. Whatever your own commitments and feelings are about the area (and all of us have feelings about it) they have to be made clear in the way in which we handle the topic and the kinds of things we say about it. It's not a topic where an academic or intellectual neutrality is of much value. Nevertheless, I do think you have to create an atmosphere which allows people to say unpopular things. I don't think it is at all valuable to have an atmosphere in the classroom which is so clearly, unmistakably antiracist that the natural and "commonsense" racism which is part of the ideological air that we all breathe is not allowed to come out and express itself. What I am talking about here are the problems of handling the timebomb and doing so adequately so that it connects with our students' experience. That experience has to surface in the classroom even if it is pretty horrendous to hear—better to hear it than not to hear it, because what you don't hear you don't engage with, and this is after all part of the very material about which we are teaching. We are not talking here about an abstract topic with which we are entertaining ourselves or over which we are stretching our minds. We are talking about very real concrete social, political and economic issues which touch the students' lives, which they experience. So we have to consider the problem of how to create an atmosphere in which those questions can be openly and honestly discussed—one in which your own position can emerge without people feeling over-weighted by its authority (although that authority is always exerted whether you are at the front or back of the class).

Now to move on more substantively to the empirical, conceptual and theoretical problems which are involved when teaching in this area. Because the subject is so exceedingly complex it is very difficult to teach about it clearly. One of the curious paradoxes about the area is that people know very simply what they feel and where they stand but when it comes to explaining the phenomena—i.e., relations between different ethnic groups, racist practices, racist beliefs, racial prejudice, however you want to put it—it becomes a great deal more complex because it requires putting together explanations from different areas of knowledge. All the attempts at a simple explanation must fail. There are two obvious examples; one is to argue that racism has to do with race which actually is not quite as obvious as it sounds. Here the statement is taken in its own right in an attempt to explain social phenomena in this area of concern by applying single-mindedly the categorical criteria of relations between races, but it does not provide an adequate explanation. The other, which is a mirror reflection of it, is to say that the whole question of race is an epiphenomenon of more classical traditional kinds of structures and practices, especially economic and class ones, and that one can on the whole dissolve questions of race by looking at them in terms of economic relations and social and economic structures, etc., of a more familiar kind. This will take you some of the way, but it certainly won't take you all the way. It does involve a greater theoretical argument (which I won't engage in here) but I certainly don't think that in a general theoretical sense racism is attributable in a simple way to capitalism, although it would be impossible to study racism in isolation from the economic and social structures in which it functions and operates.

Now if you take those two examples on the basis of their double-negatives, you begin to see that to try to explain phenomena in this area, one has to look at the relations or articulations between two things which appear in our world closely linked (and are linked in important ways) but are not dissolvable one into the other. Whichever way round you try to do it—to dissolve class relations into race relations or vice-versa—there are so many things you still can't explain. We are concerned here with handling quite complex social phenomena which are produced by different sets of determinations and which, though linked, have different and in some ways distinct histories. It is, though, not always possible to separate or isolate out ethnic relations from the other social relations and the social structures in which you find them. I am very much opposed to constituting this as a kind of specialist area of social science—the "race relations" problem as it were. This is by definition a phenomenon which one only begins to understand when one sees it in terms of the different institutions, processes and practices of whole societies in their full complexity in which race becomes a pertinent aspect of the social structure, the way in which its relations work and the way in which the social relations in institutions are linked and connected with one another. These relations will always exist differently in different social formations.

I suppose the first point that I'm making is that there is something really intrinsically difficult and complicated about the area. The questions of explanation are ones which we all hope will inform our ability to transform racist societies and racist situations—whether you are handling them at a simple or sophisticated level. We have a kind of wager or bet that if we understand things better we might be able to unlock or shift them. One does have to recognise the complexity of the analytic and explanatory problems we have in dealing with these phenomena, while at the same time trying to use them to connect back to questions of politics and practice. It is not possible in the end to deal with this issue in a wholly analytic way—that is to say, in a way which does not raise the questions of changing the existing structures that we are examining.

I might have implied a moment ago that it doesn't matter how you set up the teaching situation, whether in terms of racism or ethnic relations or racial prejudice or discriminatory attitudes and actions or whatever. I do however think it matters crucially. There is a kind of liberal common-sense way of approaching the topic which fastens on to questions of discriminatory attitudes between people from different ethnic populations, prejudicial actions, beliefs and opinions, etc. One tendency in teaching is to take these immediate surface manifestations of the problem at face value and to look at how these prejudices arise through a kind of attitudinal or social psychological explanation of what the phenomenon is. There is a second strategy which says that all of that is just the surface and we should rather go to the structures which generate particular kinds of relations, which generate particular kinds of racial structures, etc., and on the whole I tend to go for the second of these alternatives.

We have to uncover for ourselves in our own understanding, as well as for the students we are teaching, the often deep structural factors which have a tendency to persistently not only generate racial practices and structures, but reproduce them through time, which account for their extraordinarily immovable character. One of the things I want to come back to when I talk about racism and ideology is the deeply based way in which racism in a particular society manifests itself and its deeply resistant character to attempts of amelioration, good feeling, gentle reform and so on. For that reason I turn to the structural questions, although it would be a mistake not to bring whatever explanations you are dealing with back to what I just a moment ago called the surface phenomena. One has after all to explain what students will be most sensitive to, i.e., the interplay of feelings between the groups which are structured around the awareness of racial difference. No matter how deep you go into structural factors, you need to show that they do generate particular interactions between groups of people, but you have to be able to show that you can get a deeper understanding of those surface relations.

Teaching strategies which engage people's most obvious, uncomplicated, unreflexive apprehension of the problem are important, but if having engaged them at that level you try to change attitudes and prejudices by putting good attitudes and good prejudices against them, what you get is a kind of "ding-dong" of: "Well you believe that and I believe this, you see it that way and I see it this way," and it becomes extremely difficult to move on in any sort of productive way. Social science is about deconstructing the obvious, it is about showing people that the things they immediately feel to be "just like that" aren't quite "just like that." The really crucial question is how do you begin to make that move away from the level of prejudice and belief? One needs to undermine the obvious. One has to show that these are social and historical processes and that they are not written in the stars, they are not handed down. They are deep conditions which are not going to change if we start tinkering around with them. We must not give our students that kind of illusion. We can however begin the process of questioning what the structures are and how they work.

II.

Having said that, let me say a bit more about economic and industrial factors. Here again I issue a kind of warning or qualification. There is a tendency in this area either to think that the structural economic features explain pretty much all that one needs to know. Or, on the other hand, that to deal with the structural economic features is to collapse into a kind of economistic account of a phenomenon which is more complex than that. I don't think that any structural or generative account of racism could afford to leave out the crucial determinations which emerge from the economic relations of a society like this one. Although it is not a sufficient explanation of the phenomena, it will take us a good deal further than antieconomistic or antireductionist sociologists would like to think. This is one area where the economic dimensions do explain a good deal, particularly if you think of the kinds of questions which systematically appear on examination papers—questions about the tendency of racial groups to cluster or concentrate, whether it is in the occupational or industrial sectors, or in terms of class structures more generally, or in terms of housing, or of differential relations in education, etc. There is a long history to the British situation which happened overseas, but what you are trying to explain is the identifiable growth, at a certain stage in the postwar period, of the black commonwealth migrant workforce. One can of course find black enclave populations in Britain centuries before that, but what we are trying to explain from the early fifties onwards is a qualitatively new phenomenon. It undoubtedly had a very close relationship to the kind of labour demands of British industry at that particular period. It would be impossible to try to explain the full factors—those which opened the doors for working people from the Asian subcontinents, the Caribbean and parts of Africa—without looking at the particular labour needs of British industry at that stage. Only if you go back to the debates about whether in fact the black overseas population should be recruited in that way—there was an interesting debate which was kept under wraps for a long time before the decision was taken to encourage black migration on any substantial scale—will you see that paramount in people's minds at that time was a relative shortage of labour. This provides a starting point not only to explain the internal movements in terms of the economic—the need for certain kinds of surplus labour. This will explain the particular clustering of the black working population in specific areas. It enables one to look at the way recruitment into particular industries, particular occupations and at particular occupational levels clearly have a very strong economic substratum to them.

The real question is how much you are going to try and explain that way. You can attempt to match up in a very fine-tuned way either the rise in indigenous racism or the shifts in particular legislative policies with particular economic movements. For instance, what are the correlations between economic movements and, say, the introduction of the very early race legislation? How much was it due to the fact that at that stage already the demand for that kind of labour was beginning to tail off in the British economy? How much did it have to do with the fact that already the first wave of black migration, certainly from the Caribbean, was beginning to tail off before those economic dips became manifest? How much does it have to do with the fact that, already from the late fifties, certainly from fifty-seven and fifty-eight onwards, there was beginning to be an explicit political and social problem around race which must have had its bearing on both the decision to legislate in the area, the making of it into a manifest political topic about which politicians were going to conduct a debate on how to legislate their policies, etc., this obviously affecting the way in which those issues would be debated in the society as a whole?

I am not convinced that the question of economic determination can provide either adequate explanations or the sort of fine-tuned intermesh that I was talking about a minute ago. If, for instance, you try to explain the movements of black populations and their settlement and position in the British social structure by kinds of functional explanation, it won't do. If you constitute the devilish collective mind of capital—if only you could tell me where the committee meets sometime, if you could just imagine it meeting occasionally and saying, as it were, "What do we need next, chaps, and where do we need them from?"—your understanding will not progress. If you look at what is happening in detail you will see that the relationships between functional and dysfunctional features, that is to say the contradictions which are sometimes built into what is happening economically and what is being legislated and discussed politically, are too divergent to constitute anything like a neat functional fit. The important questions are concerned with the ways in which one begins to conceptualise the relationship between surplus populations of this kind and the dynamic movements of the economy. The questions of surplus populations and the notions of the surplus labour force or reserve labour force are both generative and productive ideas, which move the relationship between the patterning of race and the dynamic of the economy into a somewhat deeper and more adequate theoretical or explanatory level. The moment you do that you are beginning to shift away from any sort of explanation which would identify race exclusively as the element which you have to consider. At that point you do, for matters of teaching strategy as well as for reasons of explanation, have to identify other surplus or reserve populations including the native unemployed and women and the Irish, all three of whom in British history constituted and played something of the same functional role in relation to the expelling needs and the sucking-in needs of different developments within capitalist industry. Nothing in this area is assisted by identifying the racial question, either negatively or positively, as in some way abstractable from the other dynamic and historical processes of the society.

One should be attentive to the important ways in which one can speak of an Irish racism in Britain, and one should be attentive to the ways in which racism and sexism as ideologies are more comparable in some ways than either racism or sexism and class because there are ways in which both racism and sexism as ideologies depend on the processes of naturalisation and tend more easily than class relations in terms of their ideological syntax to refer themselves to what "mother nature" did. There is, of course, that tendency in class relations too, to think that they were really born that way, but a social structure is harder to find in the early books of the Bible than either of the other two—the other two are really right there from quite early on and can be ascribed to nature. It is part of that naturalisation that gives those two ideologies their deep-seated structuration, which makes them very hard to remove. "Use the evidence of your eyes, don't you see they are different?" I am not attempting to privilege race and sex over class, I am trying to account for certain differences one can make in the functioning of different kinds of ideology. One of the ways in which ideologies function is to naturalise themselves. They disguise the fact that they are historic and symbolic constructions by appearing to be part of what nature is. Some ideological formations find it easier to make that move of naturalisation giving them a long and deep persistence although that is not the only mechanism of ideology. There are other ideologies and other ideological forms which function in ways which give them a greater kind of efficacy. I am only comparing race and class ideologies in terms of their power to disappear behind nature and I am drawing the similarity between sex and race which is very often appealed to in terms of "You can see the difference" and if you looked at the syntax of class in that kind of obvious sense the cues and signs would be more complicated. They are not so immediately and manifestly obvious, although it is a very fine distinction as people do not use exactly natural and symbolic and material cues to try and place people and locate them socially.

It is not only correct to connect race with other dimensions in terms of what it can explain, but also in terms of the underlying politics of your teaching in this area, because, unless one can show those correspondences and differences and be sensitive to them, one can't deal with the question which a good student trained in your hands is going to ask you. "Yes, I now understand it, what do we do about it?"

III.

Now let me say something about the more political aspects. Having tried to take questions of economic structure and the relation of the needs of labour and types of labour force, you can see why it is that particular forms of migrant labour form a specially flexible reserve army especially in the early phases when that black labour force came more or less fully reproduced. It was ready for work, to put it crudely—whereas in the next generation, what is happening right now is that you have to reproduce them, I mean reproduce them socially. You have to born them, and then grow them, and teach them, and educate them, and train them, and discipline them before you get them in at all, and by then there are actually no jobs for them to go to. So then you have to look after them in unemployment, reproduce them through enforced leisure, and police them quite hard, and then, unfortunately like other people they faintly resemble, they are going to get old and go on living—they live quite a long time, West Indian women particularly are strong and long survivors. So the reproduction costs of this labour force look particularly attractive in 1951 and look particularly unattractive and expensive in 1971, when in any case you have less money in your pocket and fewer schools to reproduce them through and less plots in the cemeteries and so on—you are short of everything, as it were. The reproduction costs begin to turn back on you.

There is an argument that says that one of the ways to understand the legislative policies of race in Britain is that as the cost of reproducing the black part of the labour force has grown, as Britain had to take the fact seriously that they are here to stay and to settle throughout the full life cycle, so the legislation has tended to try to reconstitute that black population more as a really authentic migrant force, like Southern Italian labour whom you send back home for Christmas and deny the right to vote and so on. If you have tried to travel on the train from South to North Italy during the Swiss industrial holiday you will know what keeps those clocks going. They travel up and down. The reproduction costs are in Calabria, and they are in the North Coast of Africa, and they are in the interior of Turkey behind the NATO line. They have managed to maintain that system of backwards and forwards movement partly because of geographical factors but partly also by making it difficult to bring families and making it unattractive for them to stay. This backwards and forwards movement was quite common in a previous period of migration, i.e., that between the Caribbean and North America, until it was limited by legislation during the latter part of the war. In the early part of the 1950s, there was a constant movement of migrant labour moving backwards and forwards to the Southern states, and if they were able to stay for the whole part of a year, they took very substantial earnings to the family back home. Part of that argument says that what is happing here is a retrospective political enforcement of migrant status on a settled black population. This involves discouraging anybody else from coming and especially discouraging the formation of extended black families, curtailing the nonlabouring part of the population—the aged—and then encouraging repatriation—"After you've worked it out, shove off back where you came from!"—leaving the black population here not exactly like, but very much more like, a long-term "guest worker." It is more sensitive not only to economic dimensions but also to the political climate in a period when there is not a shortage of labour, but a growing unemployment coupled with the economic problems of welfare, reproduction and social reproduction and so on, when far from the need for such a force there is the need to expand the areas for employment opportunities for the white population, tending to generate much higher levels of unemployment among blacks in general and especially among black school-leavers. In this situation, you are politically making the black population into a more flexible and responsive labour force. This is the more sophisticated way of trying to extend what is basically an economic argument to account for political developments. One of the best statements of this argument, which is worth looking at, is Sivanandan's short pamphlet *From Immigration Control to "Induced Repatriation"* published by the Institute of Race Relations (1978). I think however that, although it provides part of the explanation, it doesn't adequately deal with the dynamic political and ideological factors attached to questions of race and racism in Britain which have to be introduced into the explanations that you are dealing with.

I don't want to say a great deal, but I do want to say something, about the political level. I want to point, on the one hand, to the lurchy rise to visibility of the question of race as an indigenous theme of British political life and political relations. We have to examine how it happens, when it happens, in response to what factors and how it is brought about—and it cannot be exclusively explained in terms of the early clashes in North Kensington or Enoch Powell himself as an individual, etc. When attempting to explain the politics of race in Britain we do have to give some attention to the institutional basis in which that politics has developed. We have to look at those particular sections of political leadership which have chosen to make statements about race and which have made a deep political investment in the topic of race, which have, with Powellism as a phenomenon, actually used race to open up quite a wide range of political themes, some of which had very little to do with race at all. We have to look at the very real and growing importance of the media and especially of the press and above all the popular press in a quite specific campaigning role around issues of race, around very primitive appeals to the notions of a "British way of life," of "British and alien cultures," etc. This is a very complicated operation particularly in the functioning of the media, and I don't have time to go into that in detail, but I don't think we should talk as if the politics of race fell out of the sky. It does have its institutional implications.

IV.

Ideological questions are one of the ways in which we return to what we previously spoke of as attitudes, prejudices and beliefs. The difficulty with focussing on attitude and beliefs is that you eventually come back to a notion that these are individual emanations of good and bad, that they are to do with the differential perceptions of other people. Before long you can fall into the position of "Well, don't we all like to hang about among our own, and don't we all make differences and jokes about people who are different from ourselves?" You begin to sketch out a world which ought to have eaten itself from end to end because of multiple racism, brown and black hair, green and pink eyes, etc.—any difference. One really has to stop that runaway rout into difference and ask why some of those differences have consistently become historically pertinent. It's along *that* channel that populations divide, that societies structure themselves, that perceptions crystallise and that people bring out truncheons. We must beware of dissolving the question of race into an infinite scatter, an inventory of all the possible differences that people can make, and show that it has served a very powerful social and historical function in various societies at different stages in history.

As far as questions of race are concerned, what matters much more than the differences are the already available languages which surround us from birth in this society—powerfully charged, well-developed languages which have consistently tried to come to understand the historical relation between the people of this nation and other nations, this economy and other economies, in ways connected with race which made those relations work, made them pertinent and which have been in existence for a very long time. The way in which we begin to think racially and to perceive racially has a great deal to do with the languages of racism available in societies like ours. The elements of those languages can be used to put together ideological explanations of phenomena which are really quite different. It isn't that anybody confuses in their head old-style imperialism with the indigenous racism of the '70s and '80s, but this language of racism has been used to explain the sorts of structural differences which were implied in plantation society; then the sorts of structural differences which were implied in the gap between a rapidly developing, primarily industrialising capitalist society and the rest of the globe; and then to explain a set of relations between a truly imperial power and its imperial relations. It's a well-minted, well-developed language which is around and which people draw on in order to explain to themselves new situations.

There is no sense in which you could try to explain the distribution of racist ideologies in a simply class-structured way. There is no way in which relations between Britain, either as a slave-owning or as an imperial economic and political power, and the rest of the world could have been lived out over long periods of time, leaving one whole class sector of the population saturated with those ideas and the rest of the population totally free of them. It's an inconceivable notion, not only in terms of how ideologies penetrate societies but also when you look at actual ideological and political practices. Racism in our society is in part sustained by the defensive institutions of the working class as much as the rampant and offensive institutions of the capitalist class. The fact that certain forms of working-class and trade-union racism differ in their extent, in their modality, in their grip on people's imaginations from other types—say, National Front racism—the fact that it is quite significantly different in its articulation, is not the same thing as saying that it would be possible to make a cut through the British population and come out with goodies on the one hand and baddies on the other. Those differences have to be confronted because, if you go back to the politics of race and to the resistance to racism, they have been one of the most pertinent factors which have consistently divided the working class politically within itself and throughout the whole of the period that I am talking about. It has prevented the emergence of anything that even remotely resembled a mass nonracial political organisation or struggle, whose principal kind of thrust was the internal unity of classes across the divide constituted by race. In fact, the history of the period is the history of the continued internal segmentation of the labouring force, and one of the principal ways in which that segmentation has expressed itself politically and ideologically is around questions of race. That has been one of its crucial political and ideological effects, and in an increasingly non-expanding economic and political climate, racism of a virulent kind has been able to provide a kind of adequate explanation, not so much for people at the top of the society but more for people at the bottom of the society, as to what it is they are experiencing and why it is that a kind of racist politics makes sense.

This is not safe but combustible material that you are dealing with, and if you try to stop the story about racial politics, racial divisions, racist ideologies short of confronting some of these difficult issues, if you present a kind of idealized picture which doesn't look at the way in which racism has combined with, for example, sexism working back within the black population itself, if you try to tell the story as if somewhere around the corner some whole constituted class is waiting for a green light to advance and displace the racist enemy and constitute a nonracist society, you will have done absolutely nothing whatsoever for the political understanding of your students. You can also tell the story I have just been trying to sketch out in a way which so undermines the possibility of building and developing social and political movements around those issues, that it doesn't do them any good either. One has to walk a very fine line here, and not tell a story which is really nice for the fireside, makes you glow inside, which lines up the goodies and baddies, for that will not explain the real world which you and I live in, a world which is not unified around those ideological symbols in the way which we would like. We want to change or transform the world as it is so that it begins to approximate more to that, but that is something which has to be done: it isn't something which is written into the conditions which we inherit. If on the other hand you tell the story so that the students come out saying, "Well, everybody is racist, we all are and we have been from ever since, there is nothing you can do about it and it has disabled us, we have been able to develop politically around this, the forms of resistance which develop in the black community are containable, etc.," you are simply preventing the possibility of acting on the situation.

Somehow one has to steer that difficult line whilst not selling short the complexity of the issues with which you are dealing. Instead of thinking that the questions of race are some sort of moral duty, moral intellectual academic duty which white people with good feelings do for blacks, one has to remember that the issue of race provides one of the most important ways of understanding how this society actually works and how it has arrived where it is. It is one of the most important keys, not into the margins of the society, but right into its dynamic centre. It is a very good way of getting into the political and social issues of contemporary British society because it touches and connects with so many facets. That does make it a difficult problem to handle and to explain adequately, and one mustn't try to go for simple explanations, because one does want to create a dynamic which involves people in the problems of trying to build antiracist politics.

NOTE

This essay first appeared as "Teaching Race," *Multiracial Education* 9, no. 1 (1980): 3–14.

REFERENCE

Sivanandan, A. 1978. *From Immigration Control to "Induced Repatriation."* London: Institute of Race Relations.

CHAPTER 9

Pluralism, Race and Class in Caribbean Society

I.

This paper deals exclusively with the non-Hispanic Caribbean. I have résuméd here a more detailed and extended argument. Its basic aim is to complement the fuller and more detailed papers by Henriques and Manyoni (1977) and A. Kuper (1977) with a cruder, more "typological" look at the role which "race" and "its symbol, colour" (M. G. Smith 1965) plays in the structuring of group relations across Caribbean society. As has been universally noted, these societies present a picture of complex (and changing) social structures with varying degrees of cultural pluralism and ethnic diversity.

In terms of a broad breakdown along stratification patterns, Lowenthal (1972) has proposed the following rough descriptive scheme:

1. Homogeneous societies without distinctions of class/colour, e.g., Carriacou, Barbuda, Caicos.
2. Societies differentiated by colour not class, e.g., Saba, Anguilla, Desirade.
3. Societies stratified by class/colour; this includes most of the territories, all those of any size, e.g., Jamaica, Trinidad, Barbados, St. Vincent, Grenada, St. Kitts, Martinique, etc.
4. Societies lacking white Creole elites, e.g., Grenada, St. Lucia, Dominica.
5. Stratified societies containing additional ethnic groupings of some size, e.g., Trinidad, Guyana, Surinam, Honduras.

The islands in groups 1 and 2 are very small in size, with virtually homogeneous class and ethnic composition. Those in group 4 vary from those in group 3 by not having a white Creole elite; they are, however, like group 3 stratified by class/colour. Singham (1968) notes that "a white minority need not be present to produce this pattern; [as in Grenada] the brown middle class maintain their links with the metropolitan power as well as their own Creole society. However the black mass find it difficult if not impossible to cross the class-colour barrier." Those in group 5 are distinct in that they contain substantial and distinct ethnic segments different from those, but in addition to those, found elsewhere in the dominant class/colour systems. Trinidad and Guyana, which contain large East Indian groups, are also fully stratified on class/colour lines.

We assume, then, that we are dealing with a stratification system complexly composed of class and colour elements which is modally appropriate to all but the tiniest of the island societies. In colour terms, this mode is composed of the graded differentiation by class plus the graded differentiation between white and "African" in some combination. All Caribbean societies, with the exception of the very small ones, belong to this "modal type." Societies in group 4 fundamentally belong to this type, though they represent truncated versions of it: the white element at the very top of the spectrum is literally absent, though, in another sense, it remains symbolically "present," so to speak, by extrapolation and projection. Societies of the fifth kind also belong to the type, but have the significant variation of sizeable ethnic segments. Let us note, however, that societies, like Jamaica, which belong clearly to the modal type, also contain small ethnic enclaves other than those ranged on the black–white continuum: so that it may be essentially the size and historical role of the ethnic segments in Trinidad, Surinam, Guyana and Honduras which constitute their difference. In essence, the pivotal contrast, then, is between "societies stratified by colour/class" and "societies which, being stratified by colour/class" also contain ethnic groups with what may possibly be described as a "segmental" relation to the dominant class/colour mode of stratification.

The questions are: What fundamentally distributes the populations of these societies into this kind of relation between groups? What, especially, is the role of race/colour in the distribution of groups and the maintenance of the social order? How have these structures evolved and what role has the race/colour element played in this transformation? Finally, how are we to understand the relation to these factors of the societies with large ethnic segments? Overall, the aim is to try to comprehend what the specific role of the race/colour element is in relation to class in the stratification matrix. How, then, is this matrix affected by what here, as distinct from race/colour, we would call, for our purposes, the *ethnic* element?

II.

In the English context, this debate has, in recent years, been dominated by the concept of "plural societies." This concept, stemming from the work of Furnivall (1948) has been considerably expanded and developed, most notably by M. G. Smith (1955, 1962a, 1965), with extensive reference to the Caribbean and, more recently, some extrapolation to African societies (Kuper and Smith 1969). Some brief consideration of the "plural society" concept is, therefore, obligatory. To what extent can the modal type of stratification in the Caribbean be described as generating "plural societies"?

L. Kuper, among others, has recently noted that, from its inception, the "plural society" concept has suffered from its confusion with the theories of the "American pluralist" school (L. Kuper 1971, 1972). While the concept of "pluralism" assumes extensive consensus and social cohesion, adaptation and accommodation between the different groups, and the emergence of an integrative "central value system," the notion of "plural society" stresses differentiation and separateness, the maintenance of parallel but not overlapping institutions, assumes the role of conflict between the segments, and notes that social order is maintained by the monopoly of political power by one of the segments and its superimposition over all other segments by the exercise of control and coercion. Still, the sense of "unity in differentiation" continues to haunt the "plural society" idea, even in its later forms.

In his classic statement, Smith (1965) remarks on the racial, colour and ecological complexity of Jamaican society. He notes that four-fifths of Jamaican society is "black," nine-tenths of the rest is coloured, "of mixed ancestry," and tiny minorities are white, Chinese, East Indian, Syrian, Jewish and Portuguese. This presents considerable racial complexity. But, arguing that "race concepts are cultural facts and their significance varies with social conditions," Smith goes on to select "institutions" as the basic focus for his analysis: "The basic institutions of a given population are the core of the people's culture." It is, then, to the culturally varied institutional structure of Jamaican society that he turns. His argument is that, with respect to each institutional subsystem in Jamaican society—kinship, family, magico-religious systems, education and occupation, etc.—there are "diverse alternatives," and the three main "cultural sections," white, brown and black, exhibit very distinct patterns of behaviour. This institutional arrangement is part of a class society that is transposed, without very extensive argument, into a cultural pattern: "Although usually described as a social class, the population which practices a distinctive set of institutions is best described as a cultural or social section."

The great strength of this "plural society" framework is the attention it focuses on the extraordinary complexity and differentiation of Caribbean society. It has, however, certain crucial weaknesses. For our purposes, three criticisms are relevant.

(1) The patterns of race/colour stratification, cultural stratification and class-occupational stratification overlap. This is the absolutely distinctive feature of Caribbean society. Its stratification systems and the relations between social groups are massively overdetermined. It is this overdetermined complexity which constitutes the specificity of the problem requiring analysis. It does not help, here, to depress some factors of this matrix, e.g., race/colour, class, in favour of others, e.g., culture, and then, analytically, to subsume the former into the latter, since it is precisely the generative specificity of each, plus the overdetermined complexity of the whole, which is the problem. Thus all class societies exhibit enormous cultural complexity as between the class segments and fractions: they may not be as sharp as the distinction to be found in Caribbean society, but there is certainly no cultural one-dimensionality as between, say, working-class, middle-class, and aristocratic "segments" in English society. So the Caribbean example is distinct, not because there is class-cultural differentiation, but because (a) this class-cultural differentiation is peculiarly sharp, and because (b) it is coincident to a high degree with race/colour stratification.

(2) Second, the "plural society" model blurs the distinction between parallel or horizontal, and vertical or hierarchical segmentation. Societies where substantial cultural differentiation exists, perhaps along ethnic lines, between segments which are parallel (but where power in the political sphere is monopolized by one segment) are radically different from societies which are culturally and racially differentiated, but where the segments are hierarchically arranged, within—so to speak—a single pyramid of domination. In the former case, there might be two forms of, say, institutional marriage, each with equal status in the overall value structure, and exhibiting some genuine parallelism. Societies of this type, if they can be found, could be said to conform to the plural type. But societies of the latter case are not

"plural" in this sense. True, the three classes or groups—say, white, brown, and black—may exhibit a cultural preference for three variants of the marital institution. But, just as the groups are ranked hierarchically, in terms of economic and political power and status, so the marital institutions will be "ranked" hierarchically in terms of the structure of legitimation. This consideration forces us to attend to the pivotal feature of Caribbean societies which is otherwise repressed and deflected by the "plural" model: namely, what it is which maintains the dominant structure of legitimations through this apparent complexity, what produces the structures of these societies as "structures in dominance" (Althusser 1969; Althusser and Balibar 1970).

A closely related point is how, given this structure of domination and legitimation, did the "culturally variant" patterns emerge? For the "plural society" model also tends to displace the historicity of the structure (even when, in its detail, it is attentive to historical variation).

We may put this point in the following form. "Hindu marriage," which persists in some of the East Indian ethnic communities of Trinidad and Guyana, is an inherited cultural form. The indentured East Indians brought this marital form from their homeland, where it is widespread, indigenous, and preferred: and to some extent the pattern has been preserved (though no longer as the exclusive marriage form of this ethnic group) into and through the period of indenture and after. Hindu marriage thus exists, by virtue of its antecedent forms, its importation and preservation, as the mark of distinct cultural continuities alongside and parallel with the dominant marriage of the "western" type, and other variants (i.e., whether or not sanctified by religious observance or by the law). Provided this "Hindu marriage" was conceived in the folk systems of the society as equal in standing—though different—to marriage of the western type, we would call this form of Hindu marriage a "plural" cultural form.

In fact, most writers on the subject seem to acknowledge that it is only in the case of the East Indians that "plural" cultural institutions can be said to exist, in this strong sense, in the Caribbean: i.e., where the ethnic minority is (a) large, distinct, ethnically identifiable, (b) comes from a well-articulated, strong cultural tradition, which (c) has not been broken or destroyed, as African cultural traditions were destroyed under slavery, and where the ethnic minority (d) enters the socioeconomic system late, after its basic structures have been formed, and (e) has not been obliged, by law or coercion, to conform or acculturate to the dominant forms, but (f) lives and works under conditions where ethnic homogeneity and cultural continuity enable inherited cultural patterns to be preserved, transmitted, honoured and actively practised (Crowley 1960; Klass 1961; Despres 1967; M. G. Smith 1962a, 1965). Where East Indians exist in small numbers (e.g., in Jamaica) the institutions and patterns of "cultural pluralism" are nowhere as distinct. Moreover, many would argue (e.g., Crowley) that substantial numbers of the East Indian population have assimilated to the Creole patterns; that, where Indian institutions separately exist, they are no longer "pure Hindu" but are themselves "Creolized" versions of the Indian-Hindu institution; and that, from the point of view of the major value system (i.e., that defined by the interaction of "white," "brown," and "black" groups along the Creole spectrum), a great deal of actual difference is perceived as nonexistent or "disappearing," despite East Indian resistance to "Creolization" (Klass 1961). There are strong pressures to assimilate the "plural cultural pattern" into the overall "Creole" value system and accord it a status within it. And, of course, even where cultural pluralism is strong and intense, and has found active expression even in the political domain (e.g., Guyana), many social relations between the different ethnic segments are articulated by "broker" institutions (such as the communications media, trade unions, labour organizations, agencies of public service, religious and ethnic associations, and political parties) (Despres 1967).

In societies which are "culturally plural" in the "weaker" sense—that is, where social relations between white, brown, and black are differentiated, and stratified, but belong within one socioeconomic and political system—it has been widely noted that there are widely differing "sectional differences of family organization and . . . mating pattern."

> The small, dominant section [white] observes contemporary West European norms of marriage. . . . The intermediate section [brown] practises a creolized version of Victorian marriage. . . . The third section [black] typically mates outside the context of marriage. (M. G. Smith 1965)

But the marital variant of the "intermediate section" (brown), for example, is not a distinct, *preserved*, differentiated form (as it is in East Indian communities) but a modified version of the dominant pattern, as Smith himself acknowledges: a "creolized version of Victorian marriage." It is different from, but also a transformation of, the "dominant" pattern, whereas, in "societies with large ethnic segments," the Hindu marriage form would be both different, and distinct in its root and origin, from any of the variants on the "dominant" type. The "typical form" of mating and marital arrangement in the third (black) section is, of course, radically distinct. It is, predominantly and typically, the preferred mating pattern of the most numerous, black, "African" group. But few historians would make the case that this is a mating form preserved and transmitted, with little or no modification, from the African tribal past. It is clearly the product and legacy of the slave period and the subsequent history of this group within plantation society. Thus, though the "black" variant is highly distinctive, it has been formed and shaped in relation to the dominant (white) institutions: its persistence cannot be accounted for outside the complex and differentiated "unity" of the society as a whole, as a historical formation. It is not, in the sense in which we said above that "Hindu marriage" was, a "plural" institution: though, of course, the fact that three, highly different mating and marital forms exist within the same so-called society, and the fact that these are distributed, like most other cultural forms, through the society in a pattern which almost perfectly matches the three broad colour-race and class groupings, *is* of the highest interest, and requires further clarification.

In a curious way, then, some "taint" of the pluralist model has, after all—even if negatively, in its absence—lingered on within the "plural" model. For it seems to be assumed as a tacit premise of the "plural" model that, indeed, societies are either highly homogeneous and "unified" in their cultural and institutional forms, mores, attitudes and belief systems; or they are culturally segmented and "plural." In fact very few societies, if any, are culturally homogeneous in this way. Most societies with complex social structures achieve their "unity" via the relations of domination/subordination between culturally different and class-differential strata. What we are required to "think" is the nature of the difference which constitutes the specific "unity" and complexity of any social formation. The "unity" of a social formation is never a simple, undifferentiated unity. Once we grasp the two ends, so to speak, of this chain—differentiated specificity/complex unity—we see that we are required to account, not simply for the existence of culturally distinct institutions and patterns, but also for that which secures the unity, cohesion and stability of this social order in and through (not despite) its "differences." Whereas the focus on plural differentiations requires us to concentrate on plural institutions, complexity-and-unity requires us to concentrate on the mechanisms of power, legitimation and domination: of *hegemony* (Gramsci 1972).

(3) Our third argument is, then, closely related to our second. It is that the concept, in the "plural society" model, which suggests that the overall cohesion of the society is achieved via the domination of one segment, by coercion, in the political institutional order, though correct in acknowledging the centrality of questions of power and conflict, conceives these questions in too limited and segmentary a fashion. Imperative coordination is not achieved in such societies exclusively via the means of political institutionalization. It is achieved via the hegemonic domination of one sector over all the others in every feature of organized social life. The "plural model" concentrates our attention on plural cultural values, but not on the structure of legitimation. In the period when white settler groups predominated in the political sphere, their values, customs, language, social patterns, etc. also monopolized the sphere of legitimation: an "order of current and historical dominance ... the exact reverse of their relative numerical strength" (M. G. Smith 1965). Indeed, since in some respects these groups continue to exercise profound economic power long after they have been politically displaced, it is questionable whether, even now, after decolonization and independence, the political institutions, as a distinct segment, can be said to exercise anything like the "leading" role reserved for them in the "plural society" model. Our specific criticism here is that the whole conception of "cultural power," of legitimation, of domination and hegemony in its enlarged sense, is badly foreshortened by the manner in which it is conceptualized in the "plural society" model.

Nothing which we have said so far should be taken to imply that the widely differing degree of social and cultural pluralism which characterizes Caribbean societies of the "modal type" does not represent significant features of these societies. But a model which accounts for and takes account of this diversity, but which cannot account for its structure in dominance, has, in some fundamental sense, missed the point. As Lowenthal (1972) observes,

> The shape and structure of West Indian societies depend on three basic elements: class hierarchy, social pluralism and cultural pluralism. The rigidity of stratification varies from place to place, but the social pyramid is almost everywhere identical: a small upper class controls access to power and rewards; successively larger middle and lower classes have less and less status, wealth and self-esteem.

It is to the intersection of class, race, colour and ethnicity in the generation, maintenance and modification of this "pyramid" that we must turn our attention.

III.

History has been absolutely decisive in constructing the "modal type" of Caribbean social structure in its most rigid, simplified and dichotomous form. Though all these societies have a long, and largely undiscovered, preconquest history, preconquest society is everywhere virtually extinct within a century of European colonization. There is, in some islands, a period when economic production is largely sustained by white indentured labour, but the need for labour on the cotton and sugar plantations led almost immediately to the slave trade. It is in slave society or, to put it more precisely, in "slave plantation society" that the paradigm of Caribbean social structures is first laid down. Every subsequent development or stage represents, in our view, a modification and transformation, but not a structural break, with this generative model. The structures of Caribbean slave societies need not be rehearsed here. Fundamentally, they distribute the populations into two broad and dichotomous groups along rigidly racial, colour and status lines: white owners and managers, black "unfree" slave labour. Since the line between slave and "masters" was dictated by law, physical and social coercion and separation, there was absolutely no social mobility between these caste-like groups. We have said that the formative context for this social structure is "slave plantation society" because its most typical features are to be seen in the "separate worlds" of the plantations, which both laid down the prevailing pattern of social relations for the rest of the society and served to maintain and preserve—and ultimately to modify—it.

Fundamentally, it is economic production which draws these two social groups into a relation of domination/subordination, conquest and the institutions of slavery which define the relations, and the "extrinsic" composition of the two groups (neither belong ethnically to the region) and the decimation of preconquest populations and preconquest society which give to this structure such clearly delineated "origins." No single society quite conforms, for long, to this "typological schema," but virtually all the societies of any size and social complexity approximate closely to it. Instead of a detailed description of this slave-plantation-dominated social structure (Beckford 1972; E. Brathwaite 1968, 1971; Curtin 1969; Goveia 1965; D. Hall 1962, 1964; Patterson 1967), let us abstract a number of points which directly relate to our immediate concern.

(1) It is in this crucible period that the absolute identification between race, colour and "caste-status" is established. It is important to observe that

this is also true of the structure of legitimations. The slave caste is, from the viewpoint of dominant white plantation society, "unfree," chattels and goods not people, black, African and powerless. The whole idiomatic framework of "normative degradations" is cast by the syntax of slave society. When all that has been said about "white bias" (black towards white-European society) has been said, we need to remark the widespread evidence of "black bias" (negative, white towards slave society). Insofar as direct coercion was not employed to maintain this "internal caste system" (R. T. Smith 1967), the authority structure was massively framed by the legitimations derived from this overdetermination of "secondariness" of the slave population in white eyes.

(2) Slave-plantation society transforms and ruptures the inherited African cultural forms. What of the inherited pattern is retained persists only through its accommodation to the conditions of slave society. The exact degree of African preservation is still in dispute, but most commentators quarrel about the "degree" to which Africanisms were retained within emergent sociocultural forms of slave society, not about their absolute preservation. Thus, the culture and institutions of the slave population are rigidly differentiated from that of the "master" class; and African "traces" enter into the structure of these institutions. These cannot, however, be called "plural" in the strong sense, since their formative context is the adaptation to and emergence within the slave society context. These are the institutions, the culturally differentiated patterns of the dispossessed, the enslaved: they are not the institutions of a racially and culturally distinct segment. We might say that, though both white European owners and overseers and black African field-hands derive from inherited, and distinct, cultures, the differentiation between the cultural institutions which arise within slave society is a differentiation of slave society itself. The adaptation and "Creolization" of both cultures, European and African, is a prominent and persistent feature of these societies since slavery.

> Of course whites and blacks in the West Indies were at first ethnically and culturally as well as socially distinct, but the African slaves were stripped of their ethnic identities, were left with only scattered remnants of their cultural heritage, and were forced to undergo creolization. Slave culture became in large measure a creolized form of European culture. (Lowenthal 1972)

To put it crudely, the "world" of the slave house and the village and the "world" of the plantation great house are two sociocultural "worlds" which form differentiated parts of a single socioeconomic system: they are not plural segments of parallel but distinct cultures. To put it another way, the "unity" of slave-plantation society required the differentiation between the world of slave and master. What matters is not simply the plurality of their internal structures, but the articulated relation between their differences. In the socioeconomic system of Caribbean slavery, the slave is "unfree" because (as well as in order that) the masters are "free": the one is the condition for the realization of the other. The two sides of a socioeconomic system based on the exploitation of labour, as Marx convincingly showed, depends, not on the "immediate identity" between the terms, but on the articulation of the differences which make them a "differentiated unity": a complexly structured social formation, rather than a simple, unitary, expressive totality (S. Hall 1974). In slave society, as in "colonial" society which followed, and to some degree in "decolonizing society" today, the relation between the terms of this "couple" is always articulated in the form *domination/subordination*.

We can see this clearly if we revert to our example of kinship and mating patterns.

> Among themselves slaves lacked any generally acceptable mode of establishing permanent mating relationships.... In the areas of their origin, permanent mating relationships were established for spouses by their kinship or lineage groups, which vary in type and constitution from one tribe to another.... It is obvious that such heterogeneous collections of individuals, shipped to slavery in the West Indies, would be unable to develop common procedures for establishing marriage since they would lack the lineage and kinship groupings....
>
> Marriage as a legal institution had no place in slave society ... since slaves were prohibited from forming legal relationships of marriage which would interfere with and restrict their owner's property rights....

Hence

> mating of slaves was typically unstable.... Polygamous mating associations were widely practised.... Absence of any formal procedure for establishing unions ... was paralleled by the informality with which unions were dissolved.... Half-siblingship predominated.... The woman normally acted as the sole permanent element in the slave family whether or not her male partner was polygamous. (M. G. Smith 1965)

Now we can understand how this pattern may be defined as "culturally pluralistic," in the sense that "it contained sections which practised different forms of the same institution." It is much more in doubt, however, whether this can be extended (as Smith does extend it in the next sentence) to mean that this was "a plural society," i.e., "a society divided into sections, each of which *practised different cultures*": for this formulation disguises the connexion between the different institutional forms, it disguises the determinant role which "master" society played in the development of "slave" variants, and it identifies different institutional forms with different cultures.

(3) There is some occupational and status differentiation in white "master" society, as between, say, plantation owners, white overseers, attorneys and skilled workers: white society, during slavery, produces stratification on class lines. There are parallel distinctions in the "slave" society, as between, say, domestic slaves, field-hands, carpenters, masons, boilermen, gang slaves, etc. (*inter alios*, Patterson 1967), but, in relation to white society, slaves as a group are closer to a caste than a class. These distinctions of rank and position highlight the hierarchical framework into which the social and cultural relations between the different groups in slave-plantation society were inserted; and thus the connexions which linked these differentiated statuses and cultural forms into what we would describe as one sociocultural economic system. The two major factors which modify the strict internal caste lines of this rigidly unified, rigidly stratified society are (a) the ending of slavery and the shift from "unfree" to "free labour," and (b) the growth of an intermediary "coloured" social group, whether from freed slaves or the progeny of mixed liaisons between white masters and black slave women. This intermediary group is, characteristically, half-way in status as it is typically "half-way" in racial composition and in colour (both, in some islands, carefully marked and graded); and its mechanisms of adaptation, modification and acculturation to the white-dominant forms and values makes it very dubious indeed as to whether it can be defined as in any sense constituting a distinct cultural segment "practising its own culture," even in the early period of its formation.

(4) The most profound alternative cultural process to cultural domination, which begins as slave-plantation society develops, and which continues into the period of "colony" society, is creolization. Insofar as cultural cross-ties develop which to some degree cut into the hierarchical disposition of groups, and institutional patterns, their most authentic form is Creole culture. The term itself is hard to define, its ambiguity being, itself, an index of its complex articulation with the structured form of the cultures and some groups with which it intersects. A Spanish word, originally designating African slaves born in the New World, it was extended to

anyone, black or white, born in the West Indies. It was then extended to things, habits and ideas; plants grown, goods manufactured, and opinions expressed.... Recently the term has reverted to its earlier association, and in some areas "Creole" is now a euphemism for coloured or black. But its meaning varies locally. In Jamaica "Creole" designates anyone of Jamaican parentage except East Indians, Chinese and Maroons.... In Trinidad and Guyana it excludes Amerindians and East Indians; in Surinam it denotes the "civilized" coloured population as apart from tribes of rebel-slave descent.... In the French Antilles "Creole" refers more to local-born whites than to coloured or black persons; in French Guiana, by contrast, it is used exclusively for whites. (Lowenthal 1972; see also E. Brathwaite 1971; Nègre 1966)

The restriction, everywhere, of the term "Creole" to some combination or other of the white–black spectrum, plus nativization, and the exclusion of preconquest or large-scale indentured groups within its range of meanings is an additional reason for assuming that the white–black, European–African scale constitutes the dominant cultural scale, and that its parts are not, simply, distinct cultural segments.

IV.

The major "typological" shift comes with the ending of slavery and the birth of "colony" society, often but not always based on the plantation economy, almost universally, in the case of the "British" West Indies, on some form of Crown colony government. The ending of slavery is also the ending of legally enforced caste barriers between "slave" and "master" society. It marks the end of "unfree" labour and the beginning of a rudimentary market society and of a peasant class in the countryside (especially where ex-slaves formed "free villages" in large numbers; cf. D. Hall 1959) and of the exploitation of "free labour." Thus we may think of this as the transition point between caste and class society in the Caribbean. The indenture of East Indian labour, however, forms a distinct intermediary stage between slavery and "free labour" and, where the development of the sugar-plantation economy is relatively late, and East Indians rather than black slaves form a sizeable proportion of its labour base (as in Trinidad, Guyana and Surinam), indenture provides a watershed between caste and class which has shaped social structures profoundly since.

Some significant variations must be noted. In the West Indian territories the white slave-owners tolerated and recruited to their side free people of colour much more easily and willingly than in North American slave society. This no doubt reflects the great imbalance, in the Caribbean, between the small number of whites and the great majority of black slaves, the relative absence of white women. In every Caribbean society the emergence during and after slavery of strata of people of "free colour" is of critical significance. But since colour, race and status remain pivotal to the stability of postslave "colony society," the mediation of the "free coloured" group, while opening up intercourse between white and black groups, also institutionalizes, in a customary if not in an official way, the symbolism of race, colour and status as the idiom of social stratification and mobility. As "colony" society develops, there is movement along its more diverse occupational structure, and what Lloyd Braithwaite has described as a *tilting* of the ethnic composition of class and status groups. Some people of colour appear in menial occupations or in peasant areas; some blacks penetrate into middle-ranking occupations. These are the marks of a degree of social mobility across the race-colour frontiers. It remains true, however, that the numbers of each are not large, compared with those left behind. Typically and overwhelmingly, whites (Europeans) and those able to assimilate closest to the white plantocracy in looks, colour, manners, language, dress, education and values rank highest on every social cultural and economic dimension, and are legitimated as such; the coloureds (mixed) again, typically and overwhelmingly, occupy intermediary occupations and statuses, and are graded within the legitimation system in terms of their approximation to the dominant group; overwhelmingly and typically, the poorer classes (Africans) are in the lower and more menial occupations in town and countryside, and the positions with least rank are occupied by blacks, even where their ethnic inheritance is no longer "pure." The persistence of this pattern, through the tumultuous historic changes which transform slave society into colony society and "unfree" slaves into "free labour," is remarkable.

It testifies to the profound stability of a system of stratification where race, colour, status, occupation, power and wealth overlap and are ideologically mutually reinforcing.

This is not to deny the enormous territorial variation which this basic paradigm society permits. In islands where the plantation dominates, a substantial white-minority plantocracy is present, with considerable local political, economic and cultural power, and the system is peculiarly inflexible; and though the free coloureds form a distinct, intermediary group, the

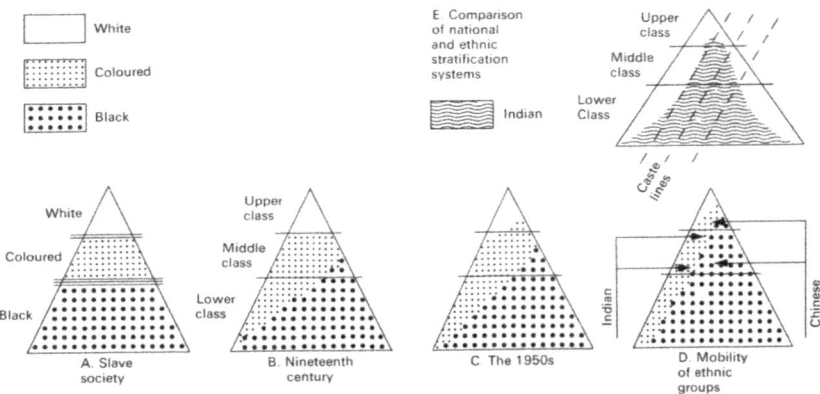

Figure 1. Stratification in Trinidad (B, C, and D adapted from Braithwaite 1953)

barriers between them and "white settler society" remain high. One consequence is that this intermediary coloured stratum tries even harder to assimilate and to distinguish itself from those poor blacks beneath (Barbados). In other islands, where the plantation economy dominates, but where there is also a peasantry, an independent agricultural sector and urbanization, and where the white plantocracy is powerful but small, the free coloured group win an independent role for themselves, and are more easily assimilated to elite society, though never identified with it. Occupational diversity is greater, and so the movement of coloureds up the scale into previously dominated white social enclaves, and of blacks into middle-class, "coloured" statuses, is greater (Jamaica). In others, where the white settler group is small or nonexistent, and the economy is not wholly dominated by the plantation, coloureds are considerably "evolved" culturally, and gain a prominent role in political society, since, as Colin MacInnes recorded of Trinidad, "Planter no bother, sailor and soldier not stay long, white trash too stupid, black slave is chained. That leave we" (MacInnes 1969).

The classic description of stratification in a colony-class society is L. Braithwaite's study of Trinidad (1953), and some of its features relevant to our purposes are probably best summarized by adapting some of his diagrams (see figure 1).

The stratification system which Braithwaite describes is, of course, a "late" variant of what we have called here "colony society." Its stages can best be marked by the changing political status of Caribbean societies in relation to the metropolitan power: the early phase when a good deal of political power goes, locally, to the "Assemblies," in which the white plantocracy and (in some islands) "free coloured" planters are strongly represented; the "Crown colony" period, when Whitehall and London govern in a more direct sense, but with local "Legislative Councils," on limited franchise, with powerful planter and elite (white and coloured) interests; the period "towards independence," when the franchise is widened and a good deal of power is devolved to the local political elites. It is in this third phase of "colony society" that the classic institutions of class society are formed and emerge in the political domain: trade unions, political parties, the full parliamentary system, the civil service and government administrative apparatus. Again, there are variations on this basic pattern in the different islands and territories: where English colonization is early and the white planter class strong, local assemblies are powerful, early, and the plantocracy retains a good deal of political influence in the legislative councils (Barbados); where large numbers of coloured men have been assimilated into the local elite, the ethnic composition of the legislatures is more mixed (Jamaica). In both cases, however, the political representatives are more mixed, ethnically and in terms of colour, than the planter class: members of the coloured elite preponderate over the white planters in the political domain, though the latter retain economic and social power.

As in all class societies, the character, composition and trajectory of the most powerful classes cannot be deduced directly from the character and composition of the political elite which governs. This is a crucial point, which has often been missed. And it should warn us against "reading" too much into the role of the political segment, in terms of the overall structure of power, authority and hegemony in the societies as a whole. L. Braithwaite's models refer to the latest stages of "colony society," to societies in the transition to independence. Once again it is noticeable that, though he is dealing with Trinidad, and therefore gives a great deal of attention to the position of the Indian group in the stratification system, he assumes (we believe correctly) that a dominant, "national" stratification system exists and that, here, race, colour and class strongly and powerfully overlap. In his diagrams for example, taking the white–coloured–black spectrum, the lines of ethnic mobility are an exact representation of social-class mobility.

We have argued that, in this period, Caribbean societies move from caste to class societies. This question is more usefully discussed in relation to the third (and present) stage, the postindependence stage, or what we are calling "decolonizing" society. The main point to underline with respect to "colony society," however, is the means by which stratification is registered and publicly accomplished. In this period, race, colour and status form a basic stratification matrix. Race and colour have, here, to be taken together. Since no legal boundaries exist which prevent blacks from rising in the social hierarchy, and the population is already ethnically mixed, the mechanisms of social mobility are largely "informal." Race is not a "pure" category in the Caribbean as it is, say, in South Africa, where it is legally defined and defined "genetically" rather than socially. In the Caribbean, even where a strong white local elite is present, race is defined socially. Thus it enters into the mechanisms of social mobility and stratification via its visible registrations: physical characteristics, pigmentation, in some more indeterminate way, "culture."

Of these, colour is the most visible, the most manifest and hence the handiest way of identifying the different social groups. But colour itself is, also, defined socially: and it, too, is a composite term. Black men with "good" (i.e., straight, European) hair or features would rank higher in the ethnic scale than coloured men with clearly Negroid features. "Colour," then, includes physical characteristics, associated with race, other than skin pigmentation. However, in the trading of stratification "insignia"—in the symbolism of social mobility—factors other than race-colour, however defined, are taken into account. Thus, black men with clearly Negroid features and hair who are either wealthy or educated or in middle-class occupations rank higher in the stratification scale than the coloured poor and uneducated. So that the race-colour element combines with the usual elements of nonethnic stratification systems (education, wealth, occupation, income, lifestyle, values) to compose the stratification matrix.

We would argue that this is not, usefully, considered as an ethnic or race-based or even race-colour-based social system, but a social-class stratification system in which the race-colour elements in the stratification matrix constitute the visible index of a more complex structure. Of course, where class, status, race and colour so strongly coincide, the stratification system is "overdetermined": its public signification is more explicit than in societies (e.g., European class societies) where no "ethnic" index exists; it is a more rigid system, since any member of the society rising in status has to negotiate more than one system of status symbolism. The calculus of social mobility is far more complex. "Passing" from one status position to another means negotiating the public signification of the social structure along several dimensions; the society as a whole—both those "passing" and those who are static in it—is preoccupied with this activity of status signification. It is the double or triple articulation of the systems of status symbolization which makes

Caribbean society one of the most complex social systems on earth. But this complexity—and, especially, the role of the race-colour or "ethnic" signifier within this complex—should not permit us to reinterpret this as a system of cultural pluralism. For the positions between black and white form a single spectrum: the complex cultural notations of "African" and "European" and "Creole" are hidden composites of this system of social notation. Once again, these concealed "cultural" elements are not "pure." "African" does not mean African, but the highly modified, adapted and transformed cultural patterns, relations and institutions of New World blacks.

We have suggested that the formative context for these institutions is not Africa but slavery (even where African "survivals" and influences remain profound). The "African" elements have been transformed and reworked—nativized and naturalized—as essentially black, "folk," Caribbean cultural forms. The nature and complexity of this cultural syncretism can be observed, not only in institutions like kinship, the family and marital arrangements, but in the practice of religion and in music. Similarly—and more rarely observed—the "European" element is no longer "pure." Local white society represents, culturally, the absent paradigm: its representatives are, so to speak, "stand-ins" for the invisible and ideal culture which validates the whole graded structure *by its very absence*: Europe, more particularly, the metropolitan culture, as an ideal value-system. A great deal of European culture has been "nativized," naturalized and creolized in local planter or settler society, a fact which is observable, once again, not simply in institutional terms, but in terms of customs and language. In short, though in the status signification system "African" refers to Africa, "Europe" to Europe and (in terms of colour, the symbol for race), "black" connotes African/slave and "white" refers to and connotes European/plantocracy—terms, so to speak, outside or extrinsic to Caribbean society—the operational value of the terms "black, coloured, white" refers directly and dominantly to the internal status system. They connote the internal social dynamics of Caribbean society, not the societies (with their complex ethnic and cultural meanings) external to it. This "internalization" of external forces, influences and conditions is, in many ways, the paradigm Caribbean cultural experience, and marks its deeply structured cultural dependency.

In what sense, then, is "decolonizing society"—the phase of national independence—a class society, in which ethnic, racial and cultural elements play a crucial role; and in what sense is it a society of a significantly different type?

This requires a rapid sketch of the social structure of the Caribbean variant of societies of this type. Independence is relatively recent. Further, it has been accomplished under the reigning ideology of "nationalism," which has the effect of obscuring some of its most significant features. Since the function of a "nationalist" ideology is to weld all the social groups together and to distinguish "society as a whole" from metropolitan dependency, the nature and mechanisms of internal division and conflict are often unsignified, the "unity" of classes and groups in the struggle for independence is oversignified. The work required to describe this "decolonizing" national society therefore remains to be done, and few models which find general acceptance, and which refer to the specificity of Caribbean conditions, have been generated.

Broadly speaking (with Jamaica here as the paradigm example), the old white plantocracy still exists, but its economic and political role has substantively declined. This is often attributed to the decline of sugar in the world market, with which its fortunes were closely tied. But it also has to do with the changing structure of sugar itself as an economic domain. Sugar has long since ceased to be an economic domain in which the plantation represented a sort of semi-independent microcosm, and where the individual planter and his family dominated. The production of sugar is organized, on a world market level, by the multinational incorporated companies; family plantations have been forced to combine and to integrate and subordinate their own production to their relation with these global units: and sugar has had to negotiate its sale and market price as a "national" entity on a global scale. In short, the white planter class has long since lost its real independent economic base. In sugar and other cash crops, this class remains as an older, near-"feudal" class, anachronistic to the modern mode of production. This is not to deny its pivotal, and continuing, social role: it remains the repository of many social values and ideals, the "great house" and the values and way of life associated with its culture exert a powerful influence on the ritualization of social values in the society. Its role is not unlike that of the British "feudal" aristocracy. It has been noted that, in England, the bourgeois classes seal their hegemony by assimilating themselves to feudal-aristocratic values and ways of life. The summit of a successful business career is still to disappear into the gentry or "country-house" life. This is no mere surface phenomenon or social snobbery. It marks the deep and profound coalescence of the class fractions and, beneath that, the combination of more than one mode of production under which, in fact, the industrialization of English society was accomplished (Anderson 1966; Gramsci 1972; Marx, passim).

Where "planter society" remains, it is the bearer of profound social symbolism and the source of legitimation not accounted for simply by looking at its economic base and role. To survive the death of sugar as "King," however, many of the sons of this group have thrown their fortunes into business and forged alliances with the emergent political elite. If their style of life remains "plantation-feudal," they have become, economically, a "bourgeois-aristocracy," if the term is not too far-fetched. In keeping with the shift of economic gravity from the plantation to business, commercial activities and trade, the most visible parts of "white" society are expatriate or "local" whites in business, in commerce or in tourism.

The growth of commercial society and of government and administration has also transformed the middle classes. As in other modern capitalist class societies, one can distinguish here a range of lower-middle-class status occupations: service industries, teachers, the secretariat and salariat, considerably expanded; a "traditional" middle class, very much stemming from the older "free coloured" intermediary group, and subscribing to the values of Victorian respectability, "white bias," and the preservation of distinctions between "brown people of good colour" and the peasantry or black masses. This is a declining social group, in power, authority and status, if not in actual numbers.

The most startling change is in the emergence of the new commercial and administrative classes, connected with business and government, of the new professionals alongside the older professions (medicine, the law) and of a university-trained native "intelligentsia." This is the national bourgeoisie, a confident, thrusting free-enterprise social stratum, much more ethnically mixed because it subscribes more to a "national" and less to an "ethnic" ideology, with its commitments to the nation-state, cosmopolitan and consumption-oriented in outlook. This is the class which underpinned and now inherits the thrust towards national independence, which has gained most financially and socially out of the diversification of the economy and "development," and which is most identified with a national bourgeois revolution. Here, the older symbolism and matrix of stratification and mobility counts for far less than education, income, status and style-of-life. In ethnic composition, though it is an "emergent" class as compared with the "traditional" and declining middle classes, it is widely constituted in ethnic, racial and colour terms. Blacks, more than "coloureds," have advanced farthest under its banner. Below this class, the working classes and the peasantry are also, relatively, diversified. In addition to small farmers on peasant and other holdings, the rural proletariat on the plantations or in mining, and in domestic service, there are those in service occupations, in small-scale factory work, the urban and rural poor and the urban "lumpen" class, all still overwhelmingly black or near black in terms of their ethnic composition, though in some of the smaller islands there is a higher proportion of coloureds and the ethnic distribution is, in any event, historically different (e.g., Dominica).

This is not a "class society" in any simple dichotomous sense: there are precious few actual societies which are. The social structure briefly and "modally" outlined here is complex, but no more so—though in a different way—than modern industrial social structures. The difficulty with applying a "class analysis" to societies of this type lies, we believe, not so much in the empirical reality to which the class concepts would apply, but in the nature and crudity of the conceptual scheme itself. M. G. Smith long ago argued (1965) for the "plural society" model against the crude application of "economic determinism" to Caribbean society by the economic historians. L. Kuper, more recently (Kuper 1971, 1972), has argued for the lack of "fit" between Marxist concepts of class as applied to "plural societies." But it may be that the whole conceptualization of the nature and complexity of class concepts, and their application to specific historical formations, has been inadequately applied. Kuper, for example, argues that in "plural" societies the predicted class solidarity across ethnic and culturally segmented lines does not appear. But there has never been, in sophisticated Marxist analysis, any simple and predetermined necessity that class solidarity always does and must appear, for this would be to make "consciousness" automatically coincident with objective economic position, and structure-superstructural relations simple and transparent. The distinction between "classes in themselves" and "classes for themselves" is pivotal to the analysis: and the whole domain of ideology and of political-class practices (not to mention the more difficult concept of "false consciousness") intervenes to effect crucial and massive displacements. The theory of automatic class solidarities and of transparency of structure-superstructure relations is mechanistic in the extreme. If there is no predictable "class solidarity," then there are certainly no "ethnic" or "cultural" solidarities either.

A great deal of political mobilization in recent years in the Caribbean has been conducted under the slogans of "Black Power," and the mediation of "ethnic" concepts like this one, in the formation and mobilization of consciousness, is profound, specific and not to be dissolved. However, since, in the adopted "black" rhetoric of independence-nationalism, "black" includes "coloureds" (it has, so to speak, been socially and politically redefined), to take this at its face value would imply the solidarity of interests (however defined) between the black rural proletariat or the black urban lumpen-classes of the cities and the "black bourgeoisie."

It has often been said that the more strictly Marxian analysis of class (as opposed to social-class/occupational/income stratification models) does not cohere with the actual complexity of Caribbean class systems. But, once again, there has always been a distinction drawn, in all but the most mechanistic models, between the "modal" distribution of classes and the distribution of means of production by the "mode of production" (productive forces plus social relations of production), and the actual historical distribution of classes and class fractions into empirical groups in specific societies (the difference, say, between Marx's analysis in *Capital* and of French society in *Civil War in France* or *The Eighteenth Brumaire*). In any event, we cannot, here or elsewhere, speak properly of a single-subject ruling class, but of class fractions and coalitions (ruling "blocs"—Caribbean society has few instances of the first, many of the second): just as we cannot speak of "mode of production" but of "modes of production" in some specific combination. Further, where the mechanistic model applies a straight alignment between economic power/position and class composition of the ruling political elite, modern applications of the theory acknowledge the major displacements between these two domains. Finally, the role of ethnic and other "complexifying" factors in the formation of self-images, social symbolism, identity and culture presents an insuperable difficulty only to a reductionist model, in which "consciousness" is taken to proceed directly and unmediately from "social being." Such an idea would not survive for long in any sophisticated contemporary application of a Marxist class analysis. While no such analysis, using these sophisticated variants, has been employed, it is not clear that the undertaking is impossible.

This task cannot be undertaken here: it remains as a pivotal next stage. Such an analysis would have to pay considerable attention to the ethnic, cultural and ideological factors which are at play in modern Caribbean societies in their "national-bourgeois" stage, but it would not abandon a class analysis of such societies in favour of a less powerful "plural" or a more loosely defined "ethnic" analysis. The comparison between Caribbean societies, where cultural-ethnic factors are significant, with other "modernizing" societies at the same "national-bourgeois" phase of their development is at least as important, now, in refining comparatively the model of Caribbean society as comparisons between similar societies within the area. In this respect, for example, Beckford's comparative analysis of Caribbean with other "plantation economies/societies" is extremely illuminating, not least with respect to the incomplete insertion of ethnic segments into the "national" patterns, though this is not in fact his major concern (Beckford 1972). Since the UNESCO programme of which this is a part has very wide bases for comparative analysis, in Latin America, Africa and the Far East, it may be that work of this "comparative" kind, based on cross-regional comparisons, might prove of considerable interest and value. Such cross-comparisons would have to be based on similar "regional" modal-type models, but such work would prevent the generalization of models of the "plural society" type on the basis of too rapid a process of conceptualization.

NOTE

This essay first appeared as "Pluralism, Race and Class in Caribbean Society," in *Race and Class in Post-colonial Society: A Study of Ethnic Group Relations in the English-Speaking Caribbean, Bolivia, Chile and Mexico* (Paris: UNESCO, 1977), 150–84.

REFERENCES

Althusser, Louis. 1969. *For Marx*. London: Allen Lane; Penguin Press.
Althusser, Louis, and Étienne Balibar. 1970. *Reading Capital*. London: New Left Books.
Anderson, Perry. 1966. "Origins of the Present Crisis." In *Towards Socialism*. Ithaca, NY: Cornell University Press.
Beckford, George. 1972. *Persistent Poverty: Underdevelopment in Plantation Economies of the Third World*. Oxford: Oxford University Press.
Braithwaite, Lloyd. 1953. "Social Stratification in Trinidad." *Social and Economic Studies* 2, nos. 2/3: 5–175.
Braithwaite, Lloyd. 1960. "Social Stratification and Cultural Pluralism." *Annals of the New York Academy of Sciences* 83: 816–36.
Brathwaite, Edward. 1968. "Jamaican Slave Society: A Review." *Race and Class* 9, no. 3: 331–42.
Brathwaite, Edward. 1971. *The Development of Creole Society in Jamaica: 1770–1820*. Oxford: Clarendon.
Crowley, Daniel J. 1960. "Plural and Differential Acculturation in Trinidad." *American Anthropologist* 59, no. 5: 817–24.
Curtin, Philip D. 1969. *The Atlantic Slave Trade: A Census*. Madison: University of Wisconsin Press.

Despres, Leo A. 1967. *Cultural Pluralism and Nationalist Politics in Guyana*. Chicago: Rand McNally.
Furnivall, John Sydenham. 1948. *Colonial Policy and Practice: A Comparative Study of Burma and Netherlands India*. Cambridge: Cambridge University Press.
Goveia, Elsa V. 1965. *Slave Society in the British Leeward Islands to the End of the Nineteenth Century*. New Haven, CT: Yale University Press.
Gramsci, Antonio. 1972. *Prison Notebooks*. London: Lawrence and Wishart.
Hall, Douglas. 1959. *Free Jamaica, 1838–65*. New Haven, CT: Yale University Press.
Hall, Douglas. 1962. "Slaves and Slavery in the British West Indies." *Social and Economic Studies* 11, no. 4: 305–18.
Hall, Douglas. 1964. "Absentee Proprietorship in the British West Indies." *Jamaican Historical Review* 4: 15–35.
Hall, Stuart. 1974. "Marx's Notes on Method: A 'Reading' of the 1857 Introduction to the *Grundrisse*." *Working Papers in Cultural Studies* 6. Birmingham: Centre for Contemporary Cultural Studies, University of Birmingham.
Henriques, Fernando, and Joseph Manyoni. 1977. "Ethnic Group Relations in Barbados and Grenada." In *Race and Class in Post-colonial Society: A Study of Ethnic Group Relations in the English-Speaking Caribbean, Bolivia, Chile and Mexico*, edited by John Rex. Paris: UNESCO.
Klass, Morton. 1961. *East Indians in Trinidad: A Study of Cultural Persistence*. New York: Columbia University Press.
Kuper, Adam. 1977. "Race and Class Structure in Jamaica." In *Race and Class in Post-colonial Society: A Study of Ethnic Group Relations in the English-Speaking Caribbean, Bolivia, Chile and Mexico*, edited by John Rex. Paris: UNESCO.
Kuper, Leo. 1971. *Pluralism, Part I*. Paris: UNESCO.
Kuper, Leo. 1972. *Pluralism, Part II: Theories of Race Relations*. Paris: UNESCO.
Kuper, Leo, and M. G. Smith, eds. 1969. *Pluralism in Africa*. Berkeley: University of California Press.
Lowenthal, David. 1972. *West Indian Societies*. Oxford: Oxford University Press.
MacInnes, Colin. 1969. *Westward to Laughter*. London: MacGibbon and Kee.
Nègre, André. 1966. "Origines et signification du mot 'creole.'" *Bulletin de la Société d'histoire de la Guadeloupe* 5–6: 38–41.
Oxaal, Ivar. 1968. *Black Intellectuals Come to Power*. Cambridge, MA: Schenkman.
Patterson, Orlando. 1967. *The Sociology of Slavery: An Analysis of the Origins, Development and Structure of Negro Slave Society in Jamaica*. London: MacGibbon and Kee.
Singham, A. W. 1968. *The Hero and the Crowd in a Colonial Polity*. New Haven, CT: Yale University Press.
Smith, Michael G. 1955. *A Framework for Caribbean Studies*. Mona: Extra-Mural Department, University College of the West Indies.
Smith, Michael G. 1962a. *Kinship and Community in Carriacou*. New Haven, CT: Yale University Press.
Smith, Michael G. 1962b. *West Indian Family Structure*. Seattle: University of Washington Press.

Smith, Michael G. 1965. *The Plural Society in the British West Indies*. Berkeley: University of California Press.

Smith, R. T. 1956. *The Negro Family in British Guiana*. London: Routledge and Kegan Paul.

Smith, R. T. 1967. "Social Stratification, Cultural Pluralism and Integration in West Indian Societies." In *Caribbean Integration: Papers on Social, Political and Economic Integration*, edited by Sybil Lewis and Thomas G. Mathews. Rio Piedras: Institute of Caribbean Studies.

CHAPTER 10

"Africa" Is Alive and Well in the Diaspora:
Cultures of Resistance: Slavery, Religious Revival
and Political Cultism in Jamaica

By the rivers of Babylon, there we sat down, yea we wept, when we remembered Zion. For there, they that carried us away captive required of us a song; and they that wasted us requires of us mirth, saying sing us one of the songs of Zion. How shall we sing in the Lord's song in such a strange land?
—Psalms 137, quoted by the Ras Tafari Brethren

I do not have the knowledge of or familiarity with Southern Africa such as would enable me to write usefully about it. I have therefore chosen to express my solidarity with the aspirations of the peoples of Southern Africa and the Liberation Movements leading their struggle for freedom by more indirect means. My references are to the Caribbean; specifically to Jamaica and the experiences and struggles of the Afro-Caribbean masses. I hope that something useful and important can be learned about the role of *culture* in practical struggle, both from the parallels and from the differences between our two situations. Against this Afro-Caribbean history and context, I have addressed myself to some of the principal themes signalled for your deliberation. I have tried to look at the question of traditional culture and its survival, tracing both its tenacity and its fluidity of forms. I have tried to suggest how essential culture is in providing the ground base to the historical and political actions of an oppressed class: but also, how profound are the modifications, the cultural transformations and contradictions which arise as conditions change, as the logic of history *imposes itself* upon cultural forms. I look at the complicated interplay, the "cultural dialectic," between the "cultures of domination" and the "cultures of resistance." I examine, in passing, the difficult issues of cultural preservation and survival, cultural syncretism, cultural hierarchies and cultural polarization. Above all, I am concerned with "cultures of resistance": the extent to which they preserve, borrow, alter and transpose elements in order that the historically developing and emergent trajectory of the masses and classes in struggle can find articulation.

I have two themes principally in view in this paper. The first is the extraordinary variety of *forms* which, from one historical conjuncture to another, the "cultures of resistance" assume. The second is the complex historical and contemporary relation between the struggles of the black masses in Africa, and the struggles of the masses of the "African" *diaspora*. Both these themes are touched on in the magisterial contribution made to the 1972 UNESCO meeting on the theme "Race, Identity and Dignity" by Amilcar Cabral—from which this meeting, quite properly, takes its point of departure. I salute the richness and the clarity of Cabral's contribution on this topic, and would be more than satisfied for my contribution to stand as a footnote to his.

Since I have, of necessity, to refer to a history and to details of another part of the world, with which participants will not necessarily be familiar, I have adopted the procedure of argument and illustration via a selective historical narrative. This allows me to exemplify my arguments at the same time as I make them. I have chosen to structure this narrative, principally though not exclusively, around the theme of *religion*. Religion, in its many forms, has played a crucial role in the history of the Afro-Caribbean people. It links them both with their African and their European contexts. I have treated religion here *not* as revealed truth but as a historical and cultural form. I am concerned with religion—religion*s* is more accurate—as a material and practico-social force, as a powerful ideological domain. I am concerned with its appropriation, its modification, its transformation, as it is inflected by the actions of the masses. I do not resolve the extremely complicated issue of its *adequacy* as a form of knowledge, either about the spiritual realities to which it claims to refer, nor to the secular realities upon which it manifestly works and which it refracts. I analyse religious cultures as bearers of the collective aspirations of collective historical actors, and thus as parts or aspects of cultures of resistance. It follows from the argument (though it is not argued through) that, as circumstances change, so developing struggles discover new and more appropriate cultural forms in which their aspirations can be framed and expressed. As Cabral (1971, 19) remarked, "To be sure, the exercise of imperialist domination demands cultural oppression, and the attempt at direct or indirect liquidation of what is essential in the subject people's culture. But this people is able to create and develop a liberation movement only because it keeps its culture alive in the teeth of permanent and organized repression of its cultural life—only because, its politico-military resistance being destroyed, it continues to resist culturally. And it is cultural resistance which, at any given moment, may take on new forms." My aim has been to expand and amplify on this profound observation about the nature and forms of resistance: and to explore how necessary, but also how complex and contradictory is that "return to the sources" among the black descendants of "old" Africa in the *diaspora* of the New World.

The indigenous culture of the Carib and Arawak peoples in the Indies was destroyed during the period of Spanish tutelage, long before the British established their hegemony over Jamaica (1655). The growth of the slave trade (early 1700s onwards until abolition in 1807) and the establishment of a slave plantation economy under British colonization thus provided the essential conditions in which Jamaican culture coalesced and developed: it set the pattern for the succeeding three centuries. There were, principally, two major cultural forces brought together under the conditions of slave plantation society. The "culture" of the European colonizers—plantation owners, some white estate workers, overseers, merchants and lawyers and the colonial administrators; and the "cultures" of the enslaved and colonized—first, those transported directly through the "Middle Passage" from the West African kingdoms and sold into slavery in the New World, and, subsequently, the slave populations born and bred in the New World—"creole" slaves. These constituted two internally differentiated, but mutually exclusive cultural "castes"—the basis of what Curtin (1955) calls the "Two Jamaicas." Gradually, the number of the offspring of white-black unions grew—the basis of the intermediary "coloured" strata, ranked between black and white according to a complicated ladder graded by colour and blood (Sambo, Mulatto, Quadroon, Mustee, Mustiphini, Quintroon, Octoroon). Legally, all "coloureds" counted as "Mulattoes." Many of them remained slaves, though many were freed (remaining, however, without civil rights as such): those with the least "stain" of Negro blood—Octoroons—were automatically "free coloureds" (Cohen and Greene 1972). On very rough estimates, there were about 59,800 "coloureds" in Jamaica in 1830, of which about 15,000 were still slaves (Duncker 1960, Brathwaite 1971). Gradually many of these "free coloureds" assimilated to the intermediary positions in slave society—artisans, clerks, tradesmen, wharfingers, schoolmasters, etc.: they were to become the basis of the more fully assimilated Jamaican "creole" culture and the backbone and basis of the modern Jamaican middle class.

The vast majority of Africans taken into Jamaica were drawn from the West African kingdoms: the Coromanti, from the Ashanti region of the Gold Coast; Ibos from the Niger delta; the Mandingo, from the area between the Niger and Gambia; and slaves from the Dahomey kingdom. These people bore an African cultural heritage with them into slavery in the New World. They formed the basis of that gigantic "African" *diaspora* half-way across the globe. But how much of this African culture survived the conditions of enslavement? Clearly, the conditions were not propitious for the survival of African cultures as coherent entities. Slaves were transported from all the catchment kingdoms with scant regard for their tribes or kingdoms of origin. Peoples of different languages and religions were herded together in the slave ships of the "Middle Passage." On arrival, they were bought and sold on the basis of physical stamina, not of culture—though a racist "folk-system" did arise among the plantation owners as to the stereotyped characteristics of the different slave peoples, ranked of course, exclusively in relation to their economic potential for the slave system (the Ashanti were reputed physically strong but rebellious; the Ibo as more "docile" but cunning and deceitful [Curtin 1955]). Once purchased, slaves were "apprenticed" into the productive social relations of plantation forced labour and into the "social world" of slave society—conditions different in almost every respect from those which had sustained their distinctive ways of life. There was a lively inter-Island trade in slaves which helped further to fragment each shipment. Though there was less of a consistent effort to "diseducate" the African of his cultural heritage and "retrain" him for plantation life than might be imagined, the very severe conditions of slave plantations served, objectively, to perform this "work" of progressive destabilization of the cultural heritage of the African slaves. The driving motive of slave society was the economic one of production under conditions of forced labour: yet these conditions of economic necessity created the "world" of the plantation; and this was a world in which, as a matter of conscious slave-owning policy, the African character of the slave population played a purely contingent role. The slave economy imposed its own internal differentiations within and between the tribal groups, marking out field hands and drivers from skilled slaves and "house niggers." The successive waves of importation introduced a further differentiation between newly arrived "African" slaves and "creole" slaves born into slavery in the New World. Slaves themselves re-marked these differences in their daily lives—and plantation owners and overseers exploited them. Finally, the very condition of forced labour produced a never-ending problem of controlling the slave population, controlling rebellion, preventing escape, maintaining the discipline of whip and reward. Plantation owners quickly recognized the "African" element as a key factor in this matter. The more slaves preserved something of their heritage or renewed it through contact with recent arrivals, the stronger the memory of Africa, the greater was their hunger for freedom, the more rebellious and recalcitrant to hard labour they became. Africans, though regarded as something less than human, had nevertheless to be *broken* to slavery; and one of the most effective instruments at the slaveowners' command was the destruction of what remained of their indigenous culture and way of life.

It is therefore all the more remarkable how much of "Africa" survived the slave experience: and even more remarkable how—in what forms, and by what means—those culture "survivals" were sustained. No single African cultural tradition survived in slavery intact. But the tribal cultures were all West African in origin and constituted regional variants of what was in fact, a common culture area (Herskovits 1941). If this factor of diversity "helped to make Jamaican Negro culture American rather than African" (Curtin 1955), it also enabled more of Africa to persist in the New World than would have been the case had each tribal group been thoroughly distinct. Of course, it also had the effect of exposing African slaves to European "colonial" influences: and it is this process of "cumulative adaptation" which produced that cultural amalgam—the "native" New World culture of African and European elements, adapted to native and local conditions, which constituted the extraordinary cultural complex known as *creole*. For the purpose of this exposition, I select *three* key areas where, in transposed forms, Africa survived into and through slavery and *one* where a process of massive adaptation, not only preserves something, but also bears witness to the fluid and adaptive nature of culture itself. The three "survival" themes are language, religion and music: the adaptation theme is that of the so-called "slave personality."

Since slaves were not legally "human" they were not understood by their white masters to need—or to be capable of developing, under plantation conditions—anything approaching a human "way of life." Thus, for long periods, white colonizers did not push forward the process of acculturation and "Europeanization" any further than was necessary for plantation work. In Jamaica, there was no conscious effort, until the end of the eighteenth century, to Christianize the slaves: the official Church of England remained the "white" church of the colonizer. In rough and ready ways, slaves were left to educate their children. They had to speak with one another—but also to address and understand the commands of their English-speaking masters. Frequently, slaves used English amongst themselves but they spoke a dialect their African bondsmen could not understand. Language, that major bearer of culture, is perhaps the best, because the most succinct and convenient, way of suggesting *how* and *in what form* the African elements persisted and were sustained, and at the same time transformed, in the folk-culture of slavery. Curtin puts it neatly. Slaves needed English in the dominant master-slave relationship. But in West Africa they shared common grammatical forms, though not the same language. They adopted the vocabulary and basic forms of ruling-class speech but persistently *inflected it* with African forms and constructions; and, in many crucial instances, they preserved African terms for classifying out important sectors of their daily life under slavery. The outcome is that peculiar form of Jamaican dialect which the majority of native people now speak (to some degree or the other) and understand (cf. Jahn 1968; Cassidy 1961; LePage 1960). Brathwaite suggests that "it was in language that the slave was perhaps most successfully imprisoned by his master, and it was in his (mis-)use of it that he perhaps most effectively rebelled" (1971). The forms of this process of cultural imprisonment and subversion in language are worth noting. Slave dialect speakers appropriated those English words and grammatical forms necessary for their daily existence and their enforced labour. They inflected English grammatically for common convenience and use. They retained certain key African terms, for things and relationships which found no equivalent in their masters' world. They adapted it tonally and rhythmically. They preserved within it certain distinctively African *genres*—proverbs and sayings; songs; elaborate modes of polite address and courtesies of greeting; respectful kinship terms; folk tales (like the wholesale tradition of the West African *Akan* folk stories)—stories of deep cunning and survival—into the Jamaican *Anancy* folk-tale cycle. They also, crucially, learned—in all their languages—to flatter and to deceive. They neither kept alive African languages, for all purposes in the New World, now "dead" forever; nor did they quite begin entirely to speak their condition in the words and phrases of their dominators: instead, they slowly evolved and constructed something both *new*, and at the same time, *built up*, bricolage-fashion, out of the cultural elements "to hand"—*creole speech*.

Something similar is to be observed in the crucial arena of religion. In West Africa, the worship of the gods had been organized in cult groups, based on the fetish and on the magical control of Nature, on a complex religious universe of good and bad spirits. Religious practice was ceremonial, accompanied by dancing, feasting, drumming and possession. Religion, magic, witchcraft and ceremonial celebration were thus deeply and integrally intertwined, pervading social life as a whole. Once again, none of these religious practices or cosmologies were preserved intact. Witchcraft and magic were formally outlawed in slave society. But there is a good deal of evidence that the slaveowners did not comprehend the religion of the slave, missed the degree to which religious practices were preserved in what they took to be secular entertainment, and underestimated the immensely powerful cultural resonance which religion—again of a *transformed* kind—continued to play in the daily life of the enslaved. Monk Lewis noted in his *Journal* (1834) that it was difficult to know whether the slaves had any real religious beliefs or practices at all. Yet, from the very earliest days, the *obeah-man* was a constant and key figure on any plantation—a magical practitioner able to summon up and set off against one another good and bad spirits on behalf of his clients, through the mediation of detailed, intricate and secret potions and practices. He was not only a priest, magician, healer and philosopher (keeper of ancient wisdoms) but came to play a key role as unofficial organizer and go-between amongst the plantation's slave populations. Keeper of the mediations between man and the gods, men and the spirit world, the dead and the living, he also, in the network of everyday relations in plantation life, mediated between groups and individuals, and even between estates. The *obeah-man* was a secret practitioner; and this may have assisted in the long preservation of residual African religious beliefs and practices through slavery and into "abolition." His counterpart—the leader of organized religious cults, the *myal-man*—preserved more the rituals and customs surrounding worship, birth and death; but he was more visible and thus easier, from time to time, to discipline and forbid (though his position was somewhat more favourably regarded, as compared with the obeah-man, since myal was thought of by the slaveowners as "white magic," whereas obeah was clearly "black magic"). Thus the customs of religious practice—dancing, drumming, feasting, spirit-possession—were preserved to a degree in *myal*; and when, finally, the Christianizing onslaught was launched towards the end of the eighteenth century, African religions came through with a vengeance; from half-submerged sources, they inflected every form and aspect of the

"Christianity" adopted by the black population with parallel forms of "folk religious" enthusiasm, its evangelical and revivalist spirit, its focus on baptism as "rebirth," and its intense superstition. If, finally, the European gods won out officially they were spiritually infused and emotionally re-thought in African terms from beneath. When the Christian missions to slaves were introduced in the nineteenth century, it was with this folk religious base that it fused to form a distinctive Afro-Christianity that persists in twentieth-century Jamaica.

The area in which the complex "continuity" of Africa is to be observed is in music, singing and dancing. As in Africa itself, Brathwaite notes, slaves "sang and danced at work, at play, at worship, from fear, from sorrow, from joy" (1971). Slave dancing and singing the Europeans, on the whole, considered harmless, indeed—sometimes even quaint, "picturesque." They were aware that some kinds of singing and dancing had deeper religious meaning, but they could not clearly distinguish the religious from the secular, and after a time—much to their own good—neither could many slaves. So both persisted, the one form frequently hidden inside the other. The political meaning of drumming *was* understood for what it was—a rich and dynamic language as well as the natural, basic rhythm of African ritual. There were frequent efforts to suppress it and the occasions associated with it. But the John Canoe (Jonkunnu) dance, for example, performed in Jamaica with elaborate headdress, accompanied by dancers and supporters in processions which took place at the permitted three-day holiday at Christmas, was tolerantly observed as a suspension of "real time" (though later the missionaries expressed concern at the rum-drinking and debauchery involved). Undoubtedly it had deep African religious connotations. So, of course, did the singing, drumming and dancing which accompanied funerals and burial wakes. Many of the songs and dances connected with them, communally performed, were, of course, authentically secular. As time went on, these African chants and songs, half-remembered from the past, were interlarded with English words and contemporary slave references. Many were work songs, built on African chant-and-response choruses, but adapted in musical form and content to slave-work conditions and employed to lighten heavy field work, to raise the depressed spirit (in the degrading conditions of transportation and the early months following purchase, slave suicide constituted a significant source of loss to the slave-owner); to communicate between groups permitted no other form of inter-relationship during work hours and to "carry" messages of hope—whether real ones, about escape routes, or spiritualised ones, about "escape" from "bondage" to a "promised land"—between slaves in a coded language their masters could not comprehend. Many chants were religious in origin, even if denuded of their setting of ceremony and practice (for example, invocations from the *Kumina* ceremonies used for calling down ancestral spirits and deities). But others were deeply secular and contemporary, with both general and particular comment on, and often ridicule of, the strange ways of the white "backra" and *his* folkways (cf. Van Dam 1954, quoted in Brathwaite 1971). Missionaries found the dancing of slave entertainments "most licentious," the music "rude and monotonous": they noted the instruments were African, "the singers and dancers observing the exactest precision as to time and measure" with "stamping of the feet, accompanied by various contortions of the body, with strange and indecent attitudes." "Making the head and limbs fixed points, they writhed and turned the body upon its own axis, slowly advancing toward each other, or retreating to the outer parts of the circumference. Their approaches to each other ... were highly indecent." What is being observed is clearly a pattern of African dancing; however, by this time its precise connection to ritual and ceremonial had been attenuated: the eye which is observing it is, of course, unremittingly European. The instruments were improvised, recapitulating African instruments: flutes, mouth violins, gourds or boxes filled with stones to rattle, scrapers across corrugated sticks; a range of goat skin drums, from treble to bass. At the same time, the slaves began to listen, to imitate and copy, and to reproduce European songs, music and dancing: adapting them back to a more "native" beat and instrumentation. On Christmas Eve, 1612, a Moravian missionary noted, with pride, that evening-service was well attended. But "scarcely was our worship closed, before the heathen negroes on the estate began to beat their drums, to dance and sing, in a most outrageous manner" (quoted from John Becker's Diary, in Brathwaite 1971).

There has been an important debate, in recent years, about the nature of the social personalities which slaves typically developed in response to the domination of slave society: and though it principally related to the experience of North American slavery, it bears significantly, if indirectly, upon the Jamaican situation. In its most extreme form, the thesis was proposed by Stanley Elkins in his controversial study *Slavery: A Problem in American Institutional Life* (1959). Elkins advanced the proposition that slavery was a "total society of domination," like the Nazi concentration camps: that its impact upon the culture of slaves was to actively "deculturalise" them—to destroy and denude them of the last vestiges of this African cultural heritage. In the North American context—where Elkins suggests there were comparatively few slave rebellions—the slave was positively *infantilized*—reduced to the personality of the dependent child. Slave-owning society developed a characteristic stereotype for this docile and helpless creature: Sambo—"the perpetual child incapable of maturity."

There seems little doubt that the stereotype of "the African" as simple, primitive, excitable and "childlike," as well as submissive, already existed from the earliest contacts between Arabs and Europeans, and the African continent: and that it long *predates* the opening of the Atlantic slave trade. Religion (Christianity, that is, with its metaphorical-liturgical syntax of "darkness" and "light") and European attitudes toward Nature, the natural and the "primitive" accounts for some aspect of this (cf. Walvin 1973), but cannot explain it all. Even so sophisticated a figure as the deeply learned Arab historian of the fourteenth century, Ibn Khaldun, could write of African negroes as characterized by "levity, excitability and great emotionalism . . . eager to dance whenever they hear a melody, stupid and submissive . . ." (quoted in Genovese 1973). But then Khaldun was already looking at the African in the context of Arab enslavement: Mandeville's travel (1360 circa), plagiarising every available source, transmitted this medley of fact and fiction about the African to a credulous and uninformed English public. The stereotype was actively revived and embellished in one version or another throughout the New World during the period of slavery. If "Sambo" seems, retrospectively, peculiarly well adapted to North American slavery, he was not peculiar to the period of modern slavery. The convergence of despised stereotype characteristics into a popular "typology," and its convenient availability as a stigmatised image wherever and whenever slave-owning peoples had, mentally, to conjure up or describe an image of the black peoples they were enslaving, cannot be coincidence. Certainly, as Genovese and others show, the "Sambo" stereotype and its peculiar cultural traits existed "wherever slavery has existed"—Genovese quotes Brazilian, Haitian and Puerto Rican evidence, and there is plenty of further material of a similar kind in journals and observations from both French and British Antillean slavery. North American commentators thought Sambo "lazy, irresponsible, cunning, rebellious, untrustworthy and sexually promiscuous" (Davis 1966): a retarded "man-child." Brathwaite's list for Jamaica is similar: "lazy, lying, profligate, promiscuous, cowardly, savage, debased, tyrannical, ugly and . . . demonstrably inferior to whites" (1971). Though it sometimes appears as if the slaveowners enslaved millions of Africans in a fit of collective amnesia or forgetfulness, the fact is that—appropriately—this forbidden and despised area of slave society was thoroughly filled out and elaborated in the "folk-ideology" of the culture of domination. Edward Long, whose *History of Jamaica* (1774) is one of the major, classical sources, proclaimed upon "the beautiful graduation, order and harmony, which pervade the whole series of created beings on this globe." Submissive, dependent "Sambo" was one element in this segmented ideological figure.

What Genovese has suggested is that, though "Sambo" undoubtedly existed, it would be quite incorrect to collapse the reality of it as lived by the slaves into the stereotype of the role as it appeared to slave-owning eyes. If "Sambo" was "childish" he or she was also sly: slavish, cunning, deceitful, untrustworthy: dependent like a lap-dog but given the frequency of acts of rebellion, sabotage, etc., also vicious like a wild animal. The stereotypes are resonant in their ambivalence. They betray the fact that, though the adapted slave could produce—present—those forms of dependency, submission and fawning flattery which the slaveowner class constantly required, as a symptom that "all was well in the world of slavery," the slave's complex socialization into the dependent role, total adaptation to unfreedom, could *never* be depended on. Though personal bonds did develop between slaves of the household and their owners (cf. Genovese 1971b), the evidence is overwhelming that the latter were never absolutely certain of the devoted loyalty of the former, and lived constantly with the lurking fear of well-earned reprisal. What is even clearer is that slaveowners did not know *how to decode* the exaggerated flattery and submissiveness which "Sambo" frequently presented: there was always *something* too calculated, something too transparent, too falsely innocent about it. And certainly, if a slave wanted to laugh at and ridicule the master, he or she had better know how to make a joke with a straight face or produce one so ambiguous as to be capable of being "read" two ways, or covering one kind of laughter (the laughter of fear, ridicule and contempt) with another. It is hardly surprising that plantation overseers and drivers found their slaves to be "lazy." But if slaves, who laboured in the harshest of conditions from sun-up to sun-down . . . and beyond, really mastered the art of "being lazy," then it can hardly have been simply an expression of innate natural character: since it required intricate skill and profound mastery. In short, if in the character of "Sambo" we see, undoubtedly, some of the results on enslaved human beings of the prolonged and infinite habituation to life-long servitude, we can also immediately recognize it as deeply contradictory—an aspect of what George Rawick (whose monumental volumes *From Sundown to Sunup* have done so much to recapture the "world the slaves made for themselves") calls the "contradictory nature of the human personality in class societies," without which, as he says, "we can never portray reality" (Rawick 1968). "Sambo" is also clearly recognizable as a crucial part of the way slaves reshaped slavery—that is, as part of the complex master/slave dialectic of slave society: and thus, an aspect of the *cultures of survival*, and so, in their own way, also of the *cultures of resistance*.

"Survival" and "resistance" may seem odd terms to use, since the debate about "Sambo" originally turned precisely on docility and submissiveness in the North American context: on the slave's assumed "failure to resist"; traced, in turn, to the cultural infantilization endemic to the condition of servitude. Three points, briefly, must be made about this, which connect to our earlier argument. The first is that, characteristically, in the history of slavery written "from the top downwards" the extent and degree of slave resistance has been systematically underplayed. This systematic historical distortion—comparable to the "history of mankind" we have, until recently, had, which was a history of man *without women*—is only now, belatedly being repaired: and that has come about, not as a consequence of a scholarly revolution—the fact is that the scholarly revolution has been precipitated by the renewal of black resistance, and the new movement of black people is on the historical stage of the New World. Only when this "history of below" reaches the degree of detail and comprehensiveness of the history of the slave-owning class can an adequate assessment of the extent and nature of slave resistance, the pattern and causes of its ebbs and flows, and the differences between the successes and failures of slave rebellions in the different slave plantation economies, be made. The second point, is, however, to note how limited and impoverished—how deeply unhistorical have been the terms in which this argument has been conducted. It seems to have been assumed that, if there were not regular, massive, concerted and successful slave rebellions of the openly organized and violent kind, *then there is no history of slave resistance*. (Undoubtedly, the European polarity between "revolution" and "reform," conceived not as a historical dialectic, but as a static interchange between two opposite and discontinuous poles, has set its fatal, and fatalistic, mark upon the history of slavery *too*.) In fact, aside from the Haitian revolution, there *were*, almost continuously throughout the slave societies of the New World, open and smothered rebellions and revolts: some of them, of course, devastating in extent; more frequently localized—and consequently, easily crushed and dismembered. Given the conditions of slavery, the nature of its regime, the armed presence of plantation staff and the militia, as against the unarmed condition of the slaves and relatively high rates of whites to blacks in some places, especially in the North American case, where the numbers often, in the Deep South, favoured the whites, the patterns of success characteristic of open slave rebellions are not difficult to understand. But much more important is the massive evidence of daily resistance, like the runaways to freedom—a more or less continuous, daily plantation drama—which in Jamaica led to a series of successful Maroon wars and the formation in the hinterland of an independent Maroon kingdom of runaway slaves in the 1740s. In North America, similar patterns constructed the Underground Railroad to "the North" and freedom which is what most slaves mean when, in true "Sambo" fashion, they sang of "going across the river to the Promised Land!" There were continuous slave strikes over one aspect of slave labour or another—leading to the frequent selection of hostages and the administration of the branding iron and the whip. Above all, there were the day-to-day struggles of the slave to *avoid* the impact of the daily routines and the conditions of slavery—the systematic avoidance which, through adept lying, cunning, irresponsibility, phoney incomprehension, assumed stupidity, violent twists of temperament and unpredictability, sheer bloody-minded *mulishness*, enabled slaves temporarily to *hold slavery at bay*. Here, every stereotype of the much abused "Sambo"—but now registered on an inverted scale—comes back to haunt those of the slave-owning class who fondly imagined that because they owned a man or a woman, lock, stock and barrel, they had captured and conquered their spirits. Genovese (1971a), relying on C. L. R. James's magnificent early history of the Haitian revolution of 1791 in Saint-Domingue led by the black leader Toussaint L'Ouverture, in the wake of French Jacobinism (cf. James 1963), argues that, before Toussaint set the whole island aflame, the efforts of the escaped Jamaican slave Mackandal was "the only hint of an organized attempt at revolt during the hundred years preceding the French Revolution." Rawick charges Genovese—properly—with underplaying the extent of slave resistance in Saint-Domingue in the years preceding Toussaint; but here he does appear to miss Genovese's point, since the argument is, precisely, that if it was our old friend "Sambo" who lay behind the revolt of the "Black Jacobins," then he can't have been quite the docile, submissive figure he is made out to be. Rawick's—and James's—overall argument is unchallengeable—that behind Toussaint there was the continuous, day-to-day struggle and resistance of the oppressed slave population "in forms of their own choosing" (Rawick 1968). The plurality of *forms of resistance* is the critical issue. It is only when we understand this "culture of daily resistance" that the paradox of a "weak tradition of rebellion" being not incompatible with a strong and unbroken "culture of resistance" (and thus the possibility of its construction, in the right conditions, into open rebellion) becomes intelligible. But—and this is the third strand in the argument—such a "culture of resistance" is inseparable, and unthinkable, without the maintenance, construction and stubborn defence of an African adapted *slave culture* at the heart of slave society itself. This brings us back to the ineradicable continuity, but also the variety and versatility of *forms*, in which the culture of the slaves kept something of Africa alive, made an enforced adaption to the "culture of domination" which enclosed them from dawn to dusk, and, above all, built up from below the New World "culture" of slave society. It is here that we must begin to redefine what earlier we had described in the more inert, "culturalist" language of African survivals. What is critical, historically, is not *how much* of Africa survived, but how the African and other elements were welded into a "culture of the oppressed" that under slavery *enabled the slaves to survive culturally*. It is the historical dynamic of culture that must engage us, not the retrospective perspective of ethnographic purism. Of course, as we have already suggested, the two were inseparable; the "culture of survival" *was*, in critical ways, massively dependent on, and drawing extensively on, the African trace. But, historically, the question of *survivals* is less significant than the *uses* to which the class of the oppressed put them, and the *forms* in which the past was made historically active for and by the present. And that returns us—but by a necessarily devious route—to themes already signalled: to the *impure* nature of the New World African cults; to the administration of religion and folk-custom and singing and dancing and drumming, in short to the *double-articulation of languages* (here, "Sambo" begins to smile and dance for us again . . .). To survive, African and creole slaves, as best they could, kept alive and preserved their African roots, customs, traditions, traces and culture. But "cultural preservation" was not the only name of the game they were engaged in. What is of infinitely more historical significance is that slaves found ways of erecting cultural defences against the brutal culture of domination; and this enabled them to fashion something like an independent slave community for themselves which, however, and whatever it was in its deep impoverishment, gave slaves, their daily lives, and their collective forms of action and resistance, an independent slave base, a *slave community* of their own, in the whites' own back yard.

Religion has already played an important part in this truncated historical narrative, and it can provide the necessary, single, all-important thread allowing us to connect the construction of the "folk-culture of slavery" with the present.

Alongside the transposed forms of African "cult" practices, preserved in *obeah* and myalism, we must not overlook the opening up of the Afro-Christian sects. These date from the American Revolution, when fleeing Loyalists often brought converted slaves with them to the Indies, and the latter became almost at once the first black unofficial Christian missionaries to the slaves and "freed" black populations (Curtin 1955). The most renowned was George Leile (or Lisle), a free slave from North America, who became an itinerant black preacher in the 1780s, established his own church and attracted a great number of followers until he was put away in prison for "uttering dangerous and seditious words." A variety of split-off sect churches were established in Leile's wake, and these formed the basis of the black Native Baptist movement. Though the spectacle of his and his followers' success triggered a revival of white missionary proselytising (the first Baptist missionaries arrived in 1814, though a small, rather unsuccessful Moravian mission existed as early as the 1750s and a Methodist mission in the 1780s), to all intents and purposes, "Native Baptism" had indelibly imprinted itself, for evermore, on the patterns and character of the black "folk religion." This black Christianity was syncretic and *unorthodox* from beginning to end: and the roots and forms of its unorthodoxy should, by now, not be hard to discern. Native Baptists borrowed the form of congregational organization, including the class-leader system—but transformed it into a system of collective organization and mobilization. Typically, the class-leaders became "real spiritual guides, taking a position equivalent to leadership of a myal cult group, and their power over their classes was authoritarian to the point of tyranny" (Curtin 1955). More important, the Christian pantheon was elided with the remnants of the African pantheon; Christianity was deeply infused with an emphasis on the *spirit world*, and spirit possession became a common feature; as a practice, baptism and immersion were raised to the status of cult ceremonies. Once again, the outer forms of religious Christianization may have been distantly European, but the underlying rhythm, the hidden, internal content, the ethos and practice was indelibly "native," if not positively

"African." When, stimulated by the significant growth of "leaders" to positions of social and political authority amongst slaves and freed blacks and the successful synthesis of Afro-Christianity, the European missionaries arrived, they sometimes sought to graft their work and teaching on to "native roots." That they succeeded in spreading a general spirit of intense religious fervour in the black population is evidence from the depth and intensity of religious practice in the Jamaican country population to this day: but as to who was grafting what on to what, the story remains considerably more open ended. The Dissenting and Non-Conformist missionaries, who—rather than the Established Church—made headway in the period just before and after the Abolition of the Slave Trade (which, of course, predated the Emancipation of the Slaves by thirty years) were in an ambiguous position, since, in England, they were part of the growing metropolitan movement for the Abolition of slavery. Hence, they regarded the slaves as proper material for Christian conversion and salvation in the world hereafter (even if not yet fully human beings), and they positioned themselves in some senses as the "enemies" of the local planter ruling class. Their position was thus an ambiguous one. And this deep ambiguity comes out clearly in the immediate history. Many slaves and freedmen were genuinely converted. Many others, in Brathwaite's words, "found the missionaries a convenience" (1971). This "conversion" and "conveniencing" were complex. Since Christianity was official, and thus tolerated though not positively encouraged by the slave-owning society, it provided a public and officially sanctioned *space* in which slaves could come out, get together, develop new interests, learn new things, above all learn to read and write—if only to read more intensely the Bible. But the spread of the white missionary churches had at least three other "conveniences." It permitted and forwarded the *syncretism* between African religious survivals and Christianity. It allowed Native Baptism and Afro-Christianity to survive, flourish and develop, so to speak, in Christianity's "official" shadow. But, third, it provided a *religious* framework and language within which black men began to develop, enunciate and mobilize, *politically*, around the growing movement for Emancipation. Thus, not inconsequentially, the growing tide of black and white "Christianisation" in this period *coincided with* a rising tide of slave rebellion and rebellious activity and with the birth of a black political movement pushing forward the Abolitionist movement from below. Rawick (1968) has pointed up the significant contribution which black slaves and freedmen in North America made to the Abolitionist Movement, normally interpreted as an exclusively white "humanitarian" movement. Williams (1944) was among the first to unmask the economic foundations of "humanitarianism." In the period after Emancipation—the period in which Jamaica became a "crown colony," in which the slave population was transferred into a "free labour" force of small peasants and rural proletariat, when the falling plantocracy made their last bid to establish and buttress its independent political power in an unsuccessful thrust towards a Jamaican "UDI"—this intertwining of religious and political movements *proceeded together*. Even before Emancipation, the plantation class had come to conceive of black religion, white missionaries, the Haitian revolt and humanitarian pressure from England as locked together into a single, hydra-headed conspiracy against their power base. Their fears were confirmed in 1831 when, as the tempo of the Abolitionist movement gathered pace, slaves in the west end of the island revolted and estate houses were burned to the ground. The rebellion was not coordinated; but some loose organization undoubtedly lay behind it. One of the key figures was Samuel Sharp, a slave and class-leader in a Native Baptist congregation. Sharp worked through the network of plantation drivers, cult-leaders and class-leaders. The slaves called the uprising "the Baptist War." Between this uprising and the Morant Bay Rebellion of 1865, the consequences for Jamaica of the ending of the slave economy and the constitution of a "free labour" system were worked through to their conclusion. It involved the final shift of power from the declining plantocracy, with their dreams of independence and separatism founded in the preservation of slavery, and the reconstitution and recomposition of the new Jamaican ruling class, under the direct hegemony of the English metropolitan government. We cannot trace this story through in detail. But the Morant Bay uprising was, again, preceded by an enormous and intense religious revival—the so-called "Great Revival" of 1860–61 (following the great evangelical upsurge overseas, both in England and the United States). The island was once again suffused with an intense religious fervour. But what began as a Christian success story ended with the triumph of Afro-Christianity. In Curtin's words, "The Great Revival had turned African." In this intense and extraordinary period, the fusion of "African," native and Christian elements was driven to a new point. Myal became in this period fully syncretic—Christian hymn-singing, Bible reading and "prophesying" fusing indistinguishably with spirit possession, dancing, confessions, sacrifice and collective trances, as the day when God would "come to Jamaica" approached. As the missionary movement declined, "native" revivalism triumphed. In the Morant Bay Rebellion, which, three years later, concluded this transitional phase in the history of Jamaican society, the two leading political figures were both also religious figures in an important sense. Gordon, a wealthy coloured lawyer, fierce nationalist and elected representative of the small farming class which emerged as a strong political force in this period, was both a radical opponent of the ruling planter class and "an evangelical religious fanatic." Governor Eyre hanged him for his pains. Paul Bogle who led a group of black settlers to the Morant Bay courthouse to protest against a decision made by the local magistrates, ended by burning the building and raising the cry of a full popular rebellion. He was an ex-slave and a Native Baptist preacher; and he was hanged off the yardarm of the HMS *Wolverine*. The era of direct colonial rule had arrived.

In the period between Emancipation and the 1920s, Jamaican society underwent a profound transformation which transposed a slave society into a dependent "colony society." There was a considerable diversification of the social structure of the society: the old slave populations gradually formed the basis of an independent small peasantry in domestic, small-scale cultivation; the landless plantation proletariat and the urban unskilled and semi-skilled sub-proletariat; the coloured middle strata evolving into the professional administrative classes less successfully, until later, when they reemerged as a native commercial national-bourgeoisie. A slowly declining plantocracy (cf. Ragatz 1928) was replaced by a more complex ruling class, composed principally of "creole" and coloureds and expatriate whites, the recruits alongside these dominant positions of men of "high colour" with education and breeding, and the growing number of white people in commerce, representing the penetration of foreign capital into the native economy. The massive and impenetrable caste-like divisions of slave society do not persist in their full form. But the society remains socially graded through complicated mechanisms of a class-caste colour system—the capitalist class divisions of a dependent "free" economy over-ridden and over-determined by the legacy of caste and colour (cf. Hall 1977). What concerns us principally here is, what were the main elements of the culture, under the impact of this profound historical adaption of a slave economy into a plantation-based "colony" society? As social organization, education, literacy and urbanisation develop, one cultural *pole* of this society becomes "Europeanized" *in the creole sense*. Patterns of life, attitudes, values, *mores* and outlooks are adopted as the cultural basis of life among the better-off, better-educated, "better-coloured," higher-statused strata of the population. This embraced, in differing degrees, the remnants of the plantocracy, the newer commercial and administrative classes, professional people and the "respectable" lower-middle classes: whether white or "brown," the *backbone* of elite "creole" Jamaican society. That it was a "creole" version of European culture indexes the degree of distance between the life of "colony" society and its metropolitan base: that it was "European"—however modified by native and Jamaican traditions—indexes the degree of cultural dependency. When slavery finally drew to a close and the slave populations moved into their "independent" and "free market" forms, there was no longer the fixed and impenetrable line of caste separating them from the life of the rest of the island. Hence *to some degree* all the Jamaican people, rich, poor and middling, white, black and brown, were touched by, penetrated to some extent by and to some degree assimilated within this "creolized" culture and way of life. When respectable middle-class Jamaican society came, in the 1930s, to dream of and to ponder on the promise of "national independence," it was the legitimation of *this* "creole culture" (including its intrinsic, though frequently invisible "white bias"—a cultural system with its real apex *somewhere else*, over the ocean) which they imagined would follow and be hegemonized in the independence process. At the other cultural pole, was what for general purposes, we might call "lower-class Jamaica"—whether the lumpen poor of the cities and towns, the small hill-top cultivators of the countryside or the landless rural plantation proletariat and the "country-people"—remained partially enclosed within this creolised version of a European-Caribbean colony culture. But they also deeply and massively retained much of another folk-cultural base, deriving and developing from what we have called the "folk-culture of slavery," which had taken root in "the Other Jamaica," and which thrived and prospered largely unpenetrated (though not untouched) by the culture of "respectable" colony society.

In this period, so far as respectable Jamaica was concerned, these "folk survivals" were largely unnoticed and invisible: remnants of a by-gone past, preservations and survivals for ethnographers like Beckwith and Herskovits, but, principally because they spoke so eloquently of the slave past which respectable Jamaica expended enormous cultural energy to forget, they tended to be massively repressed. Though it lay almost beyond recall in the folk-memory of respectable colonists, it preserved its cultural identity and material base in the teeming enclaves where the "Other Jamaica" lived and had its existence: in the country-parts and the mountainous interior; in the small towns and villages; in the barrack-room culture of the sugar estates; in the shanty-towns and settlements and yards of the towns and, above all, of the capital city, Kingston. For "respectable colony society," to be Jamaican was, of course, to relish, from time to time, certain of these cultural survivals—to enjoy "raw patois"; to savour "folk cooking"; to retell folk stories to their children and to relish "bush life." But they were treated, essentially, as "survivals" of the past: not—as indeed they were—elements only in a continuing way of life for the rural and urban poor (who were also, nearly universally, the progeny of the slave plantation system, and thus, nearly universally, black—"Africans"; what, in the inimitable folk-lineage of respectable Jamaican talk was—like "Sambo" further North—now referred to, with a mixture of wonder and contempt, as "Quashee").

In this "Other Jamaica"—to pick up the continuing thread—the enormous variety and intensity of religious life and practice (among many other cultural strands we cannot examine here) survived—changing, but flourishing. The *obeah-man* took up residence and hung out his sign in the tenement yards. At night, the sleep of respectable Jamaica would—like that of the plantation owners before them—awaken disturbed by drumming and singing, burial "wakes" and "nine night" celebrations. In the yards and settlements of the *barrios* around Kingston, women domestic servants on their way home from their coloured masters' residences, the small traders and hustlers of the shops and streets, and the great mass of the black unemployed, the semi-employed and the lumpen would be attracted into "yard" religious services: conducted in the home of rival revivalist sects, each with its own "preacher" and attendants, celebrating some black deity of infinitely mixed lineage in a medley of practices and observances rooted in Afro-Christianity. Here the "religion of the oppressed" assumed the complex forms of Christian, "native," and African rituals, fused, and was raised into an intense spiritualized *millenarianism*. If the preaching and the harangue was of sin, hell-fire and punishment, the testimonies were of the "suffering" of the people; the singing was pure "Moody and Sankey" but dragged and elongated by dark and deeper rhythms, accompanied by tambourines, hand-clapping and drums. The forms of the "service" were ecstatic, exalted and transporting—lifting men and women whose eyes were dazed with hard work and the sheer struggle for survival into a spiritual transport; and the prophesying was of fulfilment to come, the redemption, *the deliverance*. Where, in this spectrum of obeah, cultism, myalism, Pocomania, Revivalism and baptismal fervour (the baptism both of "fire" and of "water") "Africa" ended and "Europe" began, it would have been impossible even for believers and practitioners to say. Respectable Jamaicans—intensely religious in their own, more Orthodox way—would have been mystified, had they strayed so far. Few did. From this period we want to note only two developments, along our chosen spectrum of concern. Largely under North American inspiration (and often black North American rather than white), there was another enormous burst of Revivalism: this time taking the form of the founding of a rich and diverse set of *sect* Churches (each, then, almost at once splitting into further sectarian fractions), many of them called after the "Churches of God." The history of Jamaican Pentecostalism is too complex and intricate in its sectarian unfolding to enter into here (cf., inter alia, Calley 1965). Its range and variety, as well as its syncretism, is demonstrated in Simpson's pioneering 1956 study, based on fieldwork in the 1940s and early 1950s. Of the fifteen sections of West Kingston—the urban heartland of this culture—which Simpson studied, eleven had no churches of an established kind. But there were from 60 to 80 revivalist churches in the area, in addition to the "established sect" churches—the Churches of God, City and Pentecostal Missions, Jehovah's Witnesses and the Churches of Christ the Redeemer. And that list did not include the continuing "cult" religions of Pocomania, Cumina and the massively popular and extensive congregations of Revival Zion.

But the early years of this enormous and intensified millenarian revivalist upsurge, beginning in the 1920s (and lasting into the 1940s and 1950s) was also distinguished by the appearance within it of the first forms of an explicitly black quasi-political movement based on the dream of returning the children of the enslaved "Back to Africa." One of the great revivalist figures of this period was Alexander Bedward, an uneducated worker, mesmeric preacher, healer and baptiser, who finally declared himself the Son of God, promised he would ascend to Heaven in a chariot of fire, bearing up the elect with him, after which he would destroy the "unheathen" remnants below. He was obliged to postpone his ascension, and his prophesied "flight" in 1921 took him only as far as the Kingston Asylum, where he was committed for lunacy. But those who are familiar with millenarian preaching and prophecy will not miss either the potency nor the popular appeal of this "promise" to lift "the oppressed" out of struggle and suffering directly into the Promised Land. By that time, slaves and the sons and daughters of slaves had been singing, praying, and hoping for *some* kind of deliverance, *some* return of promise, *some* compensation for a life-time in "bondage," for nearly two hundred years. "Bedwardism" was only one of a myriad of religious and millenarian forms in which this secular dream of the oppressed crystallised. Better known, and predating Bedward, was the Jamaican evangelic preacher

Marcus Garvey, who in 1914 founded the Universal Negro Improvement Association and emigrated to North America, where he began to preach a heady mixture of black nationalism and evangelical revivalism, attracting, by the 1920s, two million members in what was certainly the largest mass black movement ever seen in the United States before the 1970s. Garvey was a formidable orator, a messianic preacher in the cause of black emancipation as well as a demagogue and a suspected conman. His doctrine seemed confused: attacking imperialism, yet recommending the Negro's loyalty to all national flags under which he lived; passionately against the system of white oppression of blacks, yet militantly anti-Communist. His actual schemes came to naught. And yet, undoubtedly, in his mystical and mystified way, he forged the first modern black nationalist movement in the New World. And what—apart from his charismatic personality—most contributed to his temporary success between 1917 and the early 1920s was his ability to connect with the powerhouse of native religious ideas and symbolism rather than the logic and cogency of his message. Blacks, he said, were born free but were everywhere in chains. They would not be free until they returned to their "homeland"—Africa. His slogan was "Back to Africa." In fact, Garvey never proposed to return *all* blacks to Africa. But he believed black men would not be free until there was a strong African nation, peopled with blacks from the New World, which could extend its protective arm to black men and women everywhere (cf. Cronon 1964; Weinstein 1964, referred to in Genovese 1971a, 155n) Where, precisely, in Africa and how this "nation" was to be established were not spelled out. However, this message together with his "Black Jesus," the African Orthodox Church he tried to found, the parades, titles, offices and uniforms electrified his black audiences. But, by now, as we have tried to show, the reality that was "Africa" in the minds and practices of New World blacks had more to do with what it had *become* rather than what, in some "real" past, it had once been. Black nationalism in the New World in its modern form began here: black men and women of the diaspora continue to live, today, in its shadow. The fusion of politics and religion, of nationalism and millenarianism, of the themes of revival and redemption, and the transmogrification of spiritual and secular release which Garveyism represented were also—again, as we have tried to show—deeply rooted in the very communities from which Garvey came and drew his followers; and, in its syncretic form, typical—utterly characteristic of its energising "politics."

Garvey was deported from the United States back to Jamaica in 1927, preached and proselytised for eight years until his final emigration to

England. He did not win as many followers as he had further north. But his message touched a popular nerve in that "Other Jamaica," and from his final mission and message there arose the latent form in this unfolding dialectic of which we treat: the foundation of the Ras Tafari brethren, in the immediate wake of Garvey's decline.

III.

Garvey sent his black brothers back to the Bible: and out of that intensified search in the Sacred Book for a millenarian message, a token, a sign, there emerged the doctrine and movement of the Ras Tafari. The Ras Tafari began as a millenarian cult; but the fusion of Africa and "black" Christianity within it was direct and immediate. The Book of Revelation spoke of "the Lion of Judah" who loosed the seven spirits of God. The brethren inspired by Garvey discovered God in the person of the first modern King of an independent African nation—Emperor Haile Selassie I of Ethiopia, whom they at once declared The Living God. He was the King of Kings, Messiah, Redeemer. His mission was to "deliver" black men from Babylon. The origins of those who first, in the early 1930s, began to preach the Lion of Judah's divinity are diverse and indistinct, spread by various preachers—Howell, Hibbert, Dunkley. But the movement's roots were laid in the heartland of black life found in the West Kingston area. The soil from which this early preaching developed had much to do with the deposit left behind by Garveyism. Here, Ras Tafarianism at once revealed its other face—as a black nationalist political movement, with its emphasis on the disciplining of the brethren, on the reform of social conditions, its militant hostility to white Babylon—and its dream of "going back home to Africa," now to Ethiopia rather than to West Africa. The invasion of Ethiopia by Mussolini in the 1930s fulfilled another prophecy of the Book of Revelation—that "the Beast and the kings of the earth and their armies" would gather together "to make war against him." (For the early history, see Smith, Augier and Nettleford 1960; Barrett 1968; Nettleford 1970.)

Where much of Revivalism had simply turned its eyes upward and away from white and respectable society, the Ras Tafari adopted from the beginning a militantly hostile attitude towards the society and culture of domination around them. And though, for many years, they remained—like so many other cult sects—a relatively small and self-contained brotherhood, their anti-white attitudes, their quasi-political consciousness and their militancy constantly brought them into confrontation with official society. Howell was imprisoned for two years on charges of sedition in 1934. In the context of the invasion of Ethiopia, some of the Rastamen had identified themselves as Nyabinghi, after the Ethiopian Order devoted to the overthrow of white domination by racial war. They declared "Death to black and white oppressors." Other Rasta preachers—Dunkley and Hibbert—were also frequently arrested. On his release, Howell purchased an abandoned estate at Pinnacle and established it as a Rasta settlement. In 1941, it was razed time and again and broken up by the police, often on the charge that Rastamen were growing and smoking *ganja*—which in their code of beliefs is a sacred plant, facilitating meditation and "peace." Pinnacle has sometimes been described as "rather more like an old Maroon settlement than part of Jamaica" (Smith, Augier and Nettleford 1960). It was irrevocably broken up in 1954. In the years just before and preceding this, Rastamen, with their beards and long uncut, plaited hair—known, therefore, as "locksmen"—began drifting once again into the city, where they were regarded as an exotic, strange and separate cult. The breakup of Pinnacle was related to the appearance of these marching bands of locksmen in Kingston and elsewhere. Not all the Rastamen of this period belonged to the more warrior-like part of the movement.

In 1937 Haile Selassie had licensed the foundation of his own organization in the New World—the Ethiopian World Federation—which established local branches in Jamaica: and, typically, this permitted a fusion of Rasta teaching with the more conventional revival churches, like the Ethiopian Coptic Church and the United Afro-West Indian Brotherhood, which helped to diffuse its doctrines. In 1955, as migration from Jamaica to Britain of the great surplus unemployed populations began in earnest, Haile Selassie granted 500 acres of fertile land in Ethiopia to "the Black Peoples of the West" and the idea of black repatriation to Ethiopia, until then a relatively minor theme in Rasta doctrine, assumed enormous and tangible proportions. In 1959 a dispute involving a bearded Rastaman and a policeman triggered a major confrontation in West Kingston near the Coronation Market, followed by a riot between followers and the police. The more than 60 sentences passed on Rastamen strengthened the view of the more religious Rastamen that they were the objects of an organized religious purge, and the views of the more "political" Rastamen that the white system of repression was determined to wipe the sect out. Their hostility—and the dream of "going back to Africa"— grew apace, and together. In the same period, in 1959, the Reverend Claudius Henry, founder of the African Reform Church, who organized a Jubilee to celebrate, once again, the imminent return to Africa, was arrested for feloniuous treason. Links with black American communism and Castroist Cuba were alleged, and an arsenal of guns, explosives and machetes discovered. The coalescence, in the minds of official, respectable Jamaica, between Rastafarianism, back-to-Africa movements, millenarianism, black militancy, communism and armed insurrection was complete.

In June 1960, there was another bloody and violent confrontation at Red Hills between the police, the army and a number of "bearded men" (cf. Hebdige 1974). Other such confrontations followed in the 1960s, and in 1960 three sociologists were invited to report on the grievances of the sect and to relay something of its aspirations to the government (Smith, Augier and Nettleford 1960). The context of that report, and its consequences, are discussed in detail in Nettleford 1970, chapter 2.

The doctrines of the Ras Tafari, like similar millenarian sects, are based in a detailed exegetic decoding of the Sacred Book and are too complex to be entered into here. In any event, as we shall see, they have been powerfully modified and inflected by the historical conjuncture in which they subsequently developed, and are more relevant, for us, in terms of their practico-social effect than for their doctrinal coherence (but cf. Hebdige 1974; Owens 1975; Garrison 1976; Dalrymple 1976). In the early days, Rastamen presented a fearsome spectacle to respectable Jamaicans, since they were enjoined neither to shave nor to cut their hair; and they used a vivid and violently apocalyptic language. In fact, the doctrines of the majority were peaceful (though the Nyabinghi always presented a more warrior-like aspect). They were strict vegetarians and if employed often worked as self-employed and self-sufficient small cultivators, living or scraping a living communally. As much as possible, they tried to do without money, which they considered a token of their wider withdrawal from involvement in an alien society which oppressed them and to which they neither belonged nor subscribed. They preached a gospel of brotherhood, of "peace and love"; they were bound to one another by strong ties of loyalty, charity, solidarity and support. Some (not all) used *ganja* to facilitate this withdrawal into the world of the spirit; though respectable Jamaican society steadfastly, against all the pharmacological evidence, asserted that smoking "the weed" drove Rastas to frenzy and violence. They referred to God in the Old Testament form of *Jah*; to themselves and to other men only in the first person, since all men possessed the centre of life within themselves—"I and I"; they called their women-folk "queens"; and they insisted on the divinity of Emperor Haile

Selassie. But even in earlier and quieter times, there were aspects of the Ras Tafari which made them socially and politically a potent force—aspects which make nonsense of Lanternari's mistaken judgement that they were "typically an escapist movement rather than a revolutionary force" (1965). Their political potential arose from three aspects of the cult. The first was their place and social context of origin. Ras Tafari gained at once a strong base in the enclaves of the dispossessed in West Kingston. The second was their consistent orientation to Africa and Ethiopia, and their cry of repatriation. Not only did this put a question mark over the commitment to the emerging, independent Jamaican state; it awakened one of the deepest of radical themes amongst the black poor—the African connection. It reawakened the trauma of enslavement, the "sojourn" in Babylon and the promise of deliverance, return, reunion, with the lost and repressed past. But third— and somewhat at odds with the second—was their analysis of social conditions in Jamaica itself. For they insisted that black men had not only been oppressed but were *continuing to be oppressed* in "modern" Jamaica. The black dispossessed classes were *still* "in bondage" to the white masters and their black supporters, and would remain so until "delivered." What they made active was the continuing domination of the ruling classes in Jamaica over the black masses. It was not enough to suggest (as Smith, Augier and Nettleford 1960 did) that it was simply Rasta language—the language of the Old Testament, of prophecy and revelation—that was violent and radical. The thrust of their analysis of contemporary Jamaican society was intrinsically radical, objectively revolutionary, in the context of a divided and class-exploited society. And, insofar as they took their beliefs literally, and conceived their oppressors as manifestations of Satan himself, their actions were bound to have a militant, politically mobilizing and confrontationist effect in practice, no matter how much their doctrines enjoined "peace and love."

We conclude this narrative simply by tracing the complex and profound reconfiguration of Rastafarianism as a cultural force which has marked the movement's subsequent history. Of the many possible strands which could be treated here, we choose briefly to refer only to some.

The expansion of Ras Tafarianism from a small, obscure cult to its present position must be referred to the wider social, economic and political context. The Rasta man came to symbolize for and in these culture practices and languages to articulate the mass economic, political, social and cultural alienation of the black poor and the dispossessed from respectable and official Jamaica life. The details need not be rehearsed here. West Kingston, where the cult had its origin, is typical of those shanty-towns of deep and persistent poverty which have grown up around the peripheries of all the tropical colonial cities. If others in the countryside were less systematically depressed and oppressed than the inhabitants of the West Kingston *barrios*, they were only marginally so. This has also to be seen in the context of the political conjuncture of the 1960s. For Jamaica was entering the final phase in a long and relatively stately progression to a well-managed "transition to independence": an independence which, ideologically, held out the hope of the harmony and unity of "all Jamaicans," while in fact, economically and socially, it provided the basis exclusively for the "independence" of the national colonial classes, the professorial and administrative middle classes, and the new native commercial bourgeoisie, often the local agents of the commercial penetration of her dependent economy by foreign interests. The alienated masses and the rural and urban poor had little or no central place in this "new Jamaica," even when both the major political parties mobilized them at election times for political advantage. The presence of the Rastas, and their power to symbolize the great masses who, though they were not in the strict sense "brethren," stood behind them, tore the veil from this "independence dream." The unrest, mobilization, the high rates of crime and the routine and sporadic violence which characterized the daily existence of the enclaves in which these dispossessed masses lived reinforced, symbolically, a political identity grounded on the African connection, blackness and the vernacular culture. This was ironic given that the Rasta movement had, paradoxically but deliberately, *withdrawn* from a society which the local elites held out to them as "theirs." For Rastas insisted that they remained, like the slaves in slave Jamaica or the Israelites in exile and bondage in Egypt, *strangers*. The Rastas then emerged as a political force—and received at once the full brunt of state repression and public obloquy—the same moment as the economic and social reality of neo-colonial dependency and the stark lineaments of Jamaican modern class society detached themselves from the ideological cover over which, for a time, the rhetoric of Nationalism had been cast, like a cloak. The Rastas preached the message of repatriation to Africa: but concretely, the thrust of their appearance on the historical stage pointed right at the heart of Jamaican society itself.

That is more than sufficient to explain how it came about that, in the early 1960s, a substantial number of the dispossessed, hitherto untouched by the details of Rasta cult practice, became members of the "dreadlocks" movement: and an even larger number, including sections of the radical middle class, students and the intelligentsia, detached themselves from their traditional loyalties to "respectable Jamaica" and became Rasta "fellow-travellers"—*political Rastas*. That they then adopted some aspects of Rasta doctrine, belief, life-style, dress and attitude is significant, not in terms of their passing over from a quasi-political to a fully religious attachment, but rather—the reverse—a token of the rapid *generalization* of the inner core and the social content of the movement to the wider society. Whether they knew it or not, the symbolic interpretations of social conditions which the Rasta doctrines offered could be immediately transposed into secular terms, offering a pertinent and thoroughly radical analysis of Jamaica's very secular present plight. This political transformation was indeed made. Here, we need only note the different sectors which made this spiritual affiliation. The adoption of Rasta attitudes to the smoking of *ganja* undoubtedly attracted a fringe of what can only be called "counter-culture" and drop-out black youths in the middle classes. But its impact was perhaps most profound on lower-class youth—to be seen in the adoption of Rasta symbols, slogans, and beliefs by Kingston's "rude boys"—"rudies" being a Jamaican term for anyone who "is openly defiant of constituted authority." (For an analysis of "rude boy" culture, see Hebdige 1974.)

The forms of these affiliations may now be briefly treated. This is the period of the great awakening of the black nationalist and black power movements in North America. It is also the period of the renewal of anti-colonial, nationalist, and independence struggles in the Third World. Respectable Jamaica had long, as we have suggested, repressed the depth of its black-African connection: it was also militantly anti-communist, anti-Marxist, anti-revolutionary—a deeply conventional and traditionally minded elite, formed in deference to white authority and white cultural symbols. The birth of a native radical movement like that of the Rastas was, in the 1960s, the *form* in which both a native, indigenous *black nationalism*, and, to a lesser extent, an indigenous "native" *black Marxism* appeared, and took root in Jamaican politics. No wonder the University Report went so far out of its way to assure the government of its day that Rasta "has no links with Marxism, either of analysis or prognosis," while at the same time issuing the teasing warning that "the Marxist vanguard wears a Nyabinghi cloak."

The fourth strand is the most complex of all. Here we must return to the paradox that, in the very moment when the Rasta movement as doctrine asserted that blacks were "strangers" in an "alien" land, and would only be released from "suffering" when repatriated to the African homeland, they were becoming, not just Jamaican, but the *essence of Jamaican-ness*. The alienation, which doctrinal Rastas thought of in terms of the Israelites, and more secular interpreters referred to as slavery, was appropriated as the statement of a radical but common truth about Jamaican society itself. It was *here*, day-to-day, in the concrete experience of everyday life as well as in the concrete structures of "modern" Jamaican society, that men were "suffering," that they were "alienated": it was to a "Promised Land" *in Kingston* that those who responded to the Rasta call wanted, in the long run, to be "repatriated." It was from their material, social, cultural and economic expropriation and oppression that they looked for "redemption." But this essence of the message, the repressed revolutionary social content at the heart of the doctrine, Rastamen insisted, referred to "Africa." So that what Rasta posed for Jamaican society as a whole was *how Africa could be liberated*—not the spiritual Africa over the ocean, but *the concrete "Africa" here at home*, so long hidden, repressed, forgotten, for which the Rastamen now only openly stood.

In doctrinal terms, Rastamen were "the lost tribes." But *culturally*, they became the symbol and focus for everything of Africa and slavery and the exploitation of black people over the centuries which had left a trace. What political independence—and then the failure of that independence to deliver the goods for the great masses of the dispossessed—posed was the urgent political question as to where, if anywhere, the cultural centre of gravity of the new society lay. From whence, culturally, could an authentic rather than a spurious and manufactured Jamaican "cultural unity" arise? What were the cultural sources from which its energies, dissipated in the great bonanza of wealth for the foreign companies and the middle-class elites of the 1950s and 1960s "development programmes," could be renewed? Clearly, the culture of respectable Jamaica possessed neither the historical relevance, nor the reach, nor the concrete immediacy to provide the symbols of a cultural national identity into which *all* Jamaicans could enter and "find themselves." In that moment, for the first time in its entire history, and decisively—in a fashion which can never be over-turned or reversed however difficult and dangerous will be its final resolution—*the cultural centre of gravity of Jamaican society shifted unalterably to the cultural pole of "the Other Jamaica."* And the figure which most articulately and resonantly embodied, culturally, that "other culture" was the image and idea of the Ras Tafari.

In one way or another, the political and administrative elites of Jamaican society understood the message—and set about expropriating and appropriating the newly revealed spiritual centre of black culture as best they could. Lacking the means to *realize* this cultural potential economically and politically—for that involves nothing short of the upturning and revolutionizing of Jamaican society from end to end—the political elites have attempted to *appropriate* it culturally and ideologically as other "cultures of domination" have done before. Though they do not and cannot fully represent the black masses politically, they are the same time fully aware that without roots in this massive black cultural awakening at the base of the black society they have neither power nor legitimacy: they lack the means to mobilize the society. There is no need to follow the twists and turns of this appropriation of the "power of the black masses" by the political elite in detail. In a critical election in the early 1960s, a rising young politician appropriated a new form of African-based music which had appeared in the shanty-towns—the *ska*—and tried to erect it into a "national music." In a critical election in the 1970s, the leader of the opposing party appeared, clasping an African headman's staff, referred to, in classic Rasta terms, as a "Rod of Correction." In the last five years, Rasta terms have infused and suffused all middle-class and political language. So have the symbols and rituals of the sect. In short, every effort has been made, as the Rastas themselves would say, to "ground" national politics in the cultural roots of the people. So far, this attempted cultural appropriation has been, largely, unsuccessful. It is true that, in a quite unexpected manner, Rasta has captured and revivified the life and culture of the black poor and the lumpen. It has given a new spiritual centre, a coherence, an outlook, a language, above all—in music and dancing—a new rhythm to the culture of the dispossessed. Its pervasive penetration of every feature of contemporary Jamaican life is astonishing, when its small beginnings and its exclusivity and arcane character are considered. But the heart of the movement, and the hearts of those who respond in depth to its currents remain—as the folk-culture of slavery remained—outside, beyond, below either civil society or the state apparatus. The latter can appropriate its symbols but they cannot as yet create the political, economic, and social conditions which would, materially, bring "Africa"—the Africa of Trench Town—home to its historical fulfilment. The "Other Jamaica" remains untouched. And yet *from this source*—only from this source (for there is, authentically, no other)—the renewal, the "Repatriation," has in fact already begun. The explosion of Rasta art, poetry, language and song, coupled with the return to African models and to the historical roots of the slave culture of the Jamaican blacks, has already triggered a cultural explosion, the beginnings of that cultural revolution, which, in all societies, has always pre-heralded momentous historical transformations.

We end with one further twist of the cultural wheel. The predominant form in which the narrow doctrines and sect-life of Ras Tafari has entered the mainstream of Jamaican cultural life and threatened altogether to colonize it from within is music. Already, in the 1950s, the renaissance of Jamaican music began drawing on African and black North American models and influences, but with a characteristic native inflection, leading to a succession of new musical forms—from *ska* and Blue Beat to contemporary Reggae. The trend has been steadily back towards a simpler, less "harmonic" music and orchestration—a music overtly and authentically "Afro-Jamaican" in form and inspiration. Though in recent years much of this new music has been recorded and exported, the social basis of its developments lies deep in the infrastructure of black shanty-town life: in the blues parties, the dances, the bands, the competitions between "Sound Systems," and the native Dee-Jays characteristic of lower-class life and entertainment (cf. Kallyndyr and Dalrymple 1974; Dalrymple 1976; Johnson 1976). By far the most popular of these new indigenous musical forms is the music called *Reggae*: and the music and lyrics, as well as the rituals surrounding the performances of these Reggae bands—that of Bob Marley and the Wailers—combines direct social comment on the life and conditions of the dispossessed in the Kingston ghettoes, political commentary on Jamaican society and statements of Rasta philosophy. It is a throbbing, steadily driving militant music: its themes are the themes of pressure, suffering, struggle, redemption and release. The titles of his songs are significant within themselves, without the lyrics, which are saturated with biblical and Rasta references: *Soul Rebel, African Herbsman, Rasta Revolution, Rude Boy, Simmer Down, Duppy Conqueror, Trenchtown Rock, Keep on Moving, No Woman No Cry, Rebel Music, Positive Vibration, Rastaman Vibration, Get Up, Stand Up* . . . Marley is a committed Ras Tafarian, a man from Trench Town, rebel, militant figure with a capacity to articulate in the new language of suffering and rebellion what his audience is thinking and feeling and hoping for. He has remarkable gifts, both as performer and songwriter; but he is only one of hundreds of small bands, playing new and modified versions of Reggae, sounding out over the land out of the urban depths.

That music, and the wider message which it bears, has nowhere taken such profound roots as amongst the alienated black youth in English cities—the children of those thousands of Jamaican unemployeds who came to Britain as immigrant labour in the 1950s and 1960s, who have become in their turn alienated from white society and from the polite racism of the "home country," and who, in their search for an authentic cultural roots and an alternative identity, have, in recent months, adopted not only Reggae music but the whole "rude-boy" style and the emblems of the Ras Tafarian sect. Both Hebdige and Kallyndyr and Dalrymple have examined the roots of this response by metropolitan blacks of the music and beliefs of a sect which they have never encountered at first hand; the basis of this cultural diffusion in the "colony life" of the black ghettoes in British cities; and the manner in which the closed vocabularies and abstruse references to doctrine and scripture as well as to native Jamaican everyday life are used by young black men and women as a collective language and mode of communication whose difficulty of penetration serves both to keep the alien white cultures (who are nevertheless responding to Reggae music, at least in its commercially distributed forms) out and to intensify the solidarity within. This is only the last—not by any means the final—twist in the long cultural dialectic we have been tracing.

NOTE

This essay first appeared as "'Africa' Is Alive and Well in the Diaspora: Cultures of Resistance: Slavery, Religious Revival and Political Cultism in Jamaica," paper presented at UNESCO Seminar on Social Structure, Revolutionary Change and Culture in Southern Africa, Maputo, Mozambique, July 1976.

REFERENCES

Barrett, L. 1968. *The Rastafarians: A Study in Messianic Cultism in Jamaica*. Río Piedras: Institute of Caribbean Studies, University of Puerto Rico.
Beckwith, M. W. 1929. *Black Roadways: Jamaican Folk Life*. Chapel Hill: University of North Carolina Press.
Beltran, C. 1959. "African Influence in the Development of Negro Culture in the New World." In Rubin 1959.
Brathwaite, E. 1971. *The Development of Creole Society in Jamaica, 1770–1820*. Oxford: Clarendon.
Burridge, K. O. 1971. *New Heaven, New Earth*. Oxford: Blackwell.
Cabral, A. 1971. *Role of Culture in the Struggle for Independence*. Paris: UNESCO.
Calley, M. 1965. *God's People*. Oxford: Oxford University Press.
Cassidy, F. 1961. *Jamaica Talk*. London: Macmillan.
Cohen, D., and J. P. Greene, eds. 1972. *Neither Slave nor Free*. Baltimore: Johns Hopkins University Press.

Cronon, E. D. 1964. *Black Moses: The Story of Marcus Garvey and the Universal Negro*. Madison: University of Wisconsin Press.
Curtin, P. 1955. *Two Jamaicas 1830–1865*. Cambridge, MA: Harvard University Press.
Dalrymple, H. 1976. *Marley: Music, Myth and the Rastas*. Middlesex, UK: Carib-Arawak.
Davis, D. E. 1966. *The Problem of Slavery in Western Culture*. Ithaca, NY: Cornell University Press.
Duncker, S. 1960. "The Free Coloured and Their Fight for Civil Rights, in Jamaica, 1800–1830." Master's thesis, University of London.
Elkins, S. 1959. *Slavery: A Problem in American Institutional Life*. Chicago: University of Chicago Press.
Garrison, L. 1976. "Rastafarians: Journey out of Exile." *Afras Review* 2, Sussex University.
Genovese, E. 1971a. *In Red and Black*. London: Allen Lane.
Genovese, E. 1971b. *The World the Slaveholders Made*. New York: Vintage Books.
Genovese, E. 1976. *Roll, Jordan, Roll*. New York: Vintage.
Hall, Stuart. 1977. "Pluralism, Race and Class in Caribbean Society." In *Race and Class in Post-colonial Society: A Study of Ethnic Group Relations in the English-Speaking Caribbean, Bolivia, Chile and Mexico*, 150–84. Paris: UNESCO, 1977.
Hebdige, D. 1974. "Reggae, Rastas and Rudies." Centre for Cultural Studies, Stencilled Papers, Birmingham University.
Herskovits, M. 1941. *The Myth of the Negro Past*. New York: Harper and Brothers.
Hodgkin, T. 1962. "Mahdism, Messianism and Marxism in the African Setting." Conference paper, Khartoum University.
Jahn, J. 1968. *A History of Neo-African Literature*. London: Faber and Faber.
James, C. L. R. 1963. *Black Jacobins*. New York: Vintage Books.
Johnson, K. 1976. "The Reggae Rebellion." *New Society*, 10 June.
Kallyndyr, R., and H. Dalrymple. 1974. *Reggae, a People's Music*. Middlesex, UK: Carib-Arawak.
Lanternari, V. 1965. *Religion of the Oppressed*. London: McGibbon.
LePage, R. 1960. *Jamaican Creole: An Historical Introduction to Jamaican Creole*. London: Macmillan.
Lewis, Matthew Gregory "Monk." 1834. *Journal of a West Indian Proprietor Kept during a Residence in the Island of Jamaica*. 3 vols. London: John Murray.
Long, E. 1774. *History of Jamaica*. 3 vols. London.
Nettleford, R. 1970. *Mirror, Mirror*. London: Collins-Pangster.
Owens, J. 1975. "Literature on the Rastafarians 1955–74." *Savacou* 11/12.
Ragatz, L. 1928. *Fall of the Planter Class in the British Caribbean, 1763–1833*. New York: Octagon Books.
Rawick, G. 1968. "Historical Voices of Black Liberation." *Radical America* 11, no. 4 (July–August).
Rubin, V., ed. 1959. *Plantation Systems of the New World*. Washington, DC: Pan American Union.

Simpson, G. 1956. *Jamaican Revivalist Cults*. Vol. 5 of *Social and Economic Studies*. Kingston: University of the Virgin Islands.

Smith, M., R. Augier, and R. Nettleford. 1960. *The Rastafarian Movement in Kingston, Jamaica*. Jamaica: University of the West Indies.

Sundkler, B. G. M. 1948. *Bantu Prophets in South Africa*. London: Lutterworth.

Van Dam, T. 1954. "The Influence of West African Songs of Derision in the New World." *African Music* 1, no. 1: 53–56.

Walvin, J. 1973. *Black and White: The Negro and English Society, 1555–1945*. London: Allen Lane.

Williams, E. 1944. *Capitalism and Slavery*. Chapel Hill: University of North Carolina Press.

Worsley, P. 1957. *The Trumpet Shall Sound*. London: McGibbon.

CHAPTER 11

Race, Articulation and Societies Structured in Dominance

The aim of this paper is to mark out a set of emergent questions and problems in the study of racially structured social formations, and to indicate where some new and important initiatives are developing. In order to do this, it is necessary to situate the breaks which these studies represent from the established field of study; this, in turn, requires a crude characterization of the field. I begin with a crude sketch, at a very general level of abstraction—offering only passing apologies for the necessary simplification involved. The attempts to deal with the question of "race" directly or to analyse those social formations where race is a salient feature constitute, by now, a formidable, immense and varied literature, which is impossible to summarize at all adequately. No justice can be done to this complexity and achievement here.

Something important about this field of inquiry can nevertheless be grasped by dividing many of the varied tendencies represented within it into two broad dominant tendencies. Each has generated a great variety of different studies and approaches. But the selection of these two tendencies is not wholly arbitrary. In many ways, they have come to be understood as opposed to one another. As is often the case with such theoretical oppositions, they can also be understood, in many respects, as inverted mirror images of one another. Each tries to supplement the weakness of the opposing paradigm by stressing the so-called "neglected element." In doing so, each points to real weaknesses of conceptualization and indicates, symptomatically, important points of departure for more adequate theorizations. Each, however, I suggest, is inadequate within the operative terms of its present theorization. The break thus constitutes a theoretical rupture, in part or in whole, with each of these dominant tendencies, and a possible restructuring of the theoretical field such as might enable important work of a new kind to begin.

For simplification sake, the two tendencies may be called the "economic" and the "sociological." Let us begin with the first—the economic. A great range and variety of studies must, for convenience, be bundled together under this crude heading. These include both differences of emphasis and differences of conceptualization. Thus, some studies within this tendency concentrate on internal economic structures, within specific social formations (analyses of the economic and racial structures of South Africa would be a good example). Others are more concerned with relations between internal and external economic features, however these are characterized (developed/underdeveloped; imperialist/colonized; metropolitan/satellite, etc.). Or very different ways of conceptualizing the "economic" are involved, based on radically different economic premises or frameworks. For the purposes of this paper, I shall group together within this tendency—the pertinent differences will be dealt with later—those which are framed by neoclassical "development" economics (e.g., a dual sector analysis: capitalist and subsistence sectors); those which adopt a modernization or industrialization model (e.g., based on something like Walt Rostow's theory of "stages of growth"); those, like the "dependency" theorists associated with the Economic Commission for Latin America, utilizing a radical theory of the economics of world underdevelopment; or those like Paul Baran or Andre Gunder Frank, who have employed a Marxist orientation (how classical it remains, as shall be seen, is a matter of continuing controversy). What allows for a characterization of these very different approaches as belonging to a single tendency is simply this: they take economic relations and structures to have an overwhelmingly determining effect on the social structures of such formations. Specifically, those social divisions which assume a distinctively racial or ethnic character can be attributed or explained principally with reference to economic structures and processes.

The second approach I have called sociological. Here again—rather tendentiously—a great variety of approaches are placed under a single rubric. Some concentrate on social relations between different racial or ethnic strata. Some deal more exclusively with cultural differences (ethnicity), of which race is only one, extreme case. Some pursue a more rigorously plural theory, derived from J. S. Furnivall and M. G. Smith and others of that school. Some are exclusively concerned with forms of political domination or disadvantage, based on the exploitation of racial distinctions. In the vast majority of these studies, race is treated as a social category. Biological conceptions of race have greatly receded in importance, though they have by no means wholly disappeared (for example: the revival of bio-sociology, and the reintroduction of biologically based theories, through the genetic principle, in the recent work of Jensen and Eysenck). The principal stress in this second tendency is on race or ethnicity as specifically social or cultural features of the social formations under discussion. Again, what distinguishes the contributors to this school as belonging—for the purposes here alone—to a single tendency, is this: however they differ internally, the contributors to the sociological tendency agree on the autonomy, the nonreductiveness, of race and ethnicity as social features. These exhibit, they argue, their own forms of structuration, have their own specific effects, which cannot be explained away as mere surface forms of appearance of economic relations, nor adequately theorized by reducing them to the economic level of determination.

Here it can be seen how the two paradigms have been counterposed to one another, each correcting the weakness of its opposite. The first tendency, whether Marxist or not, gives an overall determinacy to the economic level. This, it is said, imparts a hard centre—a materialist basis—to the otherwise soft-centredness or culturalism of ethnic studies. The stress on the sociological aspects, in the second tendency, is then a sort of direct reply to this first emphasis. It aims to introduce a necessary complexity into the simplifying schemas of an economic explanation, and to correct against the tendency of the first towards economic reductionism. Social formations, the second tendency argues, are complex ensembles, composed of several different structures, none of which is reducible to the other. Thus, whereas the former tends to be monocausal in form, the latter tends to be pluralist in emphasis, even if it is not explicitly plural in the theoretical sense.

It will be seen that this debate reproduces, in micro, the larger, strategic debates which have marked out the field of social science in general in recent years. Consequently, developments in the latter, larger, field—whether they take racially structured social formations as their specific objects of inquiry or not—are bound to have theoretical effects for that region of study. Hence, the consequences of such breaks in the paradigms for the "sociological theories of race." The debate is not, however, exclusively a theoretical one. Differences of theoretical analysis and approach have real effects for the strategies of political transformation in such societies. If the first tendency is broadly correct, then what is often experienced and analyzed as ethnic or racial conflicts are really manifestations of deeper, economic contradictions. It is, therefore, to the latter that the politics of transformations must essentially be addressed. The second tendency draws attention to the actual forms and dynamic of political conflict and social tension in such societies—which frequently assume a racial or ethnic character. It points to the empirical difficulty of subsuming these directly into more classical economic conflicts. But if ethnic relations are not reducible to economic relations, then the former will not necessarily change if and when the latter do. Hence, in a political struggle, the former must be given their due specificity and weight as autonomous factors. Theory here, as always, has direct or indirect practical consequences.

Political circumstances—while not sufficient to account for the scientific value of these theories—also provide one of the conditions of existence for theory, and have effects for its implementation and appropriation. This has clearly been the case, even if restricted (as is done for a good section of this paper) primarily to Latin America and the Caribbean. The dual sector model—based on an export-led, import-substitution, foreign investment supported type of economic development—sponsored a long and disastrous period of national economic development, which further undermined the economic position of one country after another in the region. The theory of modernization was for long the economic cutting-edge of alliance-for-progress strategies in the continent.

Versions of the "dependency" school have been harnessed, under different conditions, to the promotion of anti-imperialist, national-capitalist development of a radical type. The metropolitan/satellite theories of Frank and others were specifically developed in the context of the Cuban Revolution and the strategies of Latin American revolution elaborated, for example, in the resolutions to the 1962 Second Declaration of Havana. The whole field, indeed, provides an excellent case study of the necessary interconnections between theory, politics and ideology in social science.

Each tendency exhibits something of its own rational core. Thus, it may not be possible to explain away race by reference to the economic relations exclusively. But the first tendency is surely correct when it insists that racial structures cannot be understood adequately outside the framework of quite specific sets of economic relations. Unless one attributes to race a single, unitary transhistorical character—such that wherever and whenever it appears it always assumes the same autonomous features, which can be theoretically explained, perhaps, by some general theory of prejudice in human nature (an essentialist argument of a classic type)—then one must deal with the historical specificity of race in the modern world. Here one is then obliged to agree that race relations are directly linked with economic processes: historically, with the epochs of conquest, colonization and mercantilist domination, and currently, with the "unequal exchanges" which characterize the economic relations between developed metropolitical and "underdeveloped" satellite economic regions of the world economy. The problem here is not whether economic structures are relevant to racial divisions but how the two are theoretically connected. Can the economic level provide an adequate and sufficient level of explanation of the racial feature, of these social formations? Here, the second tendency enters its caveat. Similarly, the second tendency is surely correct to draw attention to the specificity of those social formations which exhibit distinctive racial or ethnic characteristics. The critique of economic reductionism is also, certainly, to the point. The problem here is to account for the appearance of this "something else"—these extra economic factors and their place in the dynamic reproduction of such social formations. But these "real problems" also help us to identify what weaknesses are obscured by the inversions which each paradigm practices on the other. If the dominant tendency of the first paradigm is to attempt to command all differences and specificities within the framework of a simplifying economic logic then that of the second is to stop short with a set of plural explanations which lack an adequate theorization, and which in the end are descriptive rather than analytic. This, of course, is to state the differences in their sharpest and most oversimplified form. It is worthwhile, now, exploring some of the complex terrain and arguments which are contained by this simple binarism.

The first aspect can be pinpointed by looking at some features of the recent controversies which have arisen in the analysis of the South African social formation. South Africa is clearly a "limit case" in the theoretical sense, as well as a "test case" in the political sense. It is perhaps the social formation in which the salience of racial features cannot for a moment be denied. Clearly, also the racial structures of South African society cannot be attributed to cultural or ethnic differences alone: they are deeply implicated with the forms of political and economic domination which structure the whole social formation. Moreover, there can be little argument that this is a social formation in which the capitalist mode of production is the dominant economic mode. Indeed, South Africa is the "exceptional" (?) case of an industrial capitalist social formation, where race is an articulating principle of the social, political and ideological structures, and where the capitalist mode is sustained by drawing, simultaneously, on what have been defined as both "free" and "forced" labour.

Now substantial parts of the literature on the South African social formation deal with the racial aspects of the society as accounted for, essentially, by the governing economic relations. These relations are characterized as, for all practical purposes, class relations in the classical sense. The structuring of the South African labour force into black and white strata is therefore analysed as similar to the "fracturing" of the working class, which one finds in all capitalist social formations—with the single exception that, here, race is the mechanism by which this stratification of the class is accomplished. As Harold Wolpe has observed, these analyses assume that white and black working classes stand in essentially the same relation to capital. Hence, the dynamic of social relations will fall within the basic logic of class struggle which capitalist relations or production classically assume. The racial divisions amount to "nothing more than the specific form which the fractionalization of the working class, common to all capitalist modes of production, has taken in the South African social formations" (Wolpe 1976). Such analyses—Wolpe refers to several sources—thus tend to fall into what we have defined as our "first" paradigm: the subsumption of racial structures under the "logic" of capitalist economic relations. This approach can then be easily matched by its immediate, and inverted, opposite. These alternative analyses treat economic class formations as largely irrelevant to the analysis of the social and political structures, where race, rather than class, is treated as the pertinent factor, through which the society is socially structured and around which social conflicts are generated. Such a "sociological" approach can be found in, for example, Kuper (1974) and van den Berghe (1965).

Much more important—and more difficult to slot easily into either of the two approaches—is the work of John Rex, himself a South African and a distinguished sociologist. Rex has not worked extensively on South African materials. But his writing, though often necessarily programmatic, represents the "sociological" approach at one of its richest and most complex points. Rex's first essay on the subject, "South African Society in Comparative Perspective" (Rex 1973), opens with a critique of the failure of both structural-functionalist and Marxist perspectives to deal effectively with race and ethnicity in South African society. He is equally critical of, though he gives more attention to, the "plural" theory of Furnivall and Smith. Smith argued that the different ethnic segments of Caribbean society were "plurally" distinct, held together only through the monopoly, by one of the segments, of political power: "The monopoly of power by one cultural section is the essential precondition for the maintenance of the total society in its current form" (Smith 1965). Against this, Rex correctly argues that "the dynamics of the society turn upon the involvement of men of differing ethnic backgrounds in the same social institutions, viz., the slave plantation" (Rex 1973, 261). The same could be said of the attempts to extend the "plural society" paradigm, with its primacy of attention to cultural segmentation, and its ascription of the factor of cohesion to the instance of political monopoly, to South Africa. However, he is equally critical of any attempt to explain the racial forms in which social conflict appears in such societies as a species of "false consciousness."

Rex bases his own approach on a significant historical fact of difference. Whereas, "classically," capitalism has been installed through the expansion of market relations, production for which is based on "free labour," capitalism in South Africa arose on the basis of conquest (of the Bantu peoples) and their incorporation into the economic relations on the basis of "unfree labour," "as part of an efficient capitalist system of production." This inaugurates the capitalist mode on very different historic "presuppositions" from those derived from the general account said to be offered by Marx—presuppositions, however, more typical of "colonial" formations, where conquest and colonization have been central features, and thus pertinent to the appearance, in such societies, of "not simply the class struggle engendered by capitalist development, but the 'race war' engendered by colonial conquest" (Rex 1973, 262). Rex makes a great deal of these differentiating features: the "capacity of the employers to command the use of coercive violence during and after colonial conquest," and the fact that the "central labour institution" is not classical free labour but "migrant labour in its unfree form."

Taking as the central feature of his analysis this quite atypical "central labour institution," Rex is able to delineate more precisely the specific economic mechanisms which have served to "incorporate" the African working class into the capitalist system in ways which preserve rather than liquidate its segmentary racial character. The racial structure of the South African social formation is thereby given concrete economic conditions of existence—the link being traceable, precisely, through its "peculiarity," its deviation from the "classical" capitalist path. Rex traces historically the various economic forms of this "unfreedom": the rural reserves, the labour compound, the emergence of the third element of the migrant labour system, the "urban native location." "Nearly all African labour partake, in some measure of the characteristics of the compound worker and the domestic worker's status. All are liable to masters and servants legislation, and none are completely free, even though the development of secondary manufacturing industry may lead to greater flexibility of wages, greater permanence of the labour force and hence greater recognition of the needs of the worker for kinship and community" (Rex 1973, 278). These "differences," both in the mode of entry and in the status of African labour, are seen by Rex as operating principally through the means by which African labour supply is recruited to capitalist industry. The economic relations are thus the necessary but not the sufficient condition of the racial structure of the South African social formation. For this is also preserved by a "nonnormative" element—for example, political and legal factors—which stems from the political domination of the state by the white settler capitalist class, and the "workable compromise" between this class and the white working class, which leads both to reap the advantages of confining native labour to its subordinate status in the labour market. In the context of the "classical" line of capitalist development, a capitalism which preserves rather than abolishes such "irrational" features must be, to say the least, a "deviant" case.

There is certainly no simple counterposing of "social" as against "economic" factors here. Rex cannot be accused of neglecting the level of economic relations, as many "culturalists" can. Indeed, it is his concern with the specificity of the forms of economic relations peculiar to the South African case which enables him to grasp some of the fundamental features of a social formation which is both identifiably "capitalist," and yet different in structure from "the capitalist type" of social development—as the latter has been derived from one reading of the Marxist literature. The attention to the "central labour institutions" of this formation enables him to bring forward what Marx in another context called the "differentia specifica"—the basis, as he put it, of an adequate historically specific abstraction: "Just those things which determine their development, i.e., the elements which are not general and common, must be separated out . . . so that in their unity . . . their essential difference is not forgotten" (Marx 1973, 85).

Nor is there a neglect of class relations and the class struggle. The segmentary approach of "pluralism" is specifically refused. "If there is division, the divisions can be seen as functionally integrated within an over-all pattern of political conflict generated by the capitalist development of the country since the mineral discoveries of 1867 and 1886." The "revision" involved is rather the refusal of any attempt to subsume these into a universal and univocal form—"capitalist class relations" in general.

> Clearly what we have here is not something which can be adequately interpreted in terms of some universal Marxist law of class struggle but a specific kind of class struggle there undoubtedly is, namely one in which the classes are groups of varying rights and degrees of rightlessness, according to the kind of conquest or unfreedom which was imposed on them in an earlier period. The history, the structure and the forms of social differentiation which South Africa presents [i.e., its "racial" aspect] are, as in the case of any former colonial society, the product of such conquest and unfreedom.

These two criteria—conquest and "unfree" labour—are the critical conceptual mechanisms through which Rex's analysis is organized. The "origin" of the capitalist mode in conditions of conquest, coupled with the "peculiar institutions" of unfree labour, thus preserve, at the economic level, and secure its continuing racially ascriptive features. This is a capitalism of a very specific and distinctive kind: "There are a number of different relationships to the means of production more subtle than can be comprehended in terms of distinction between owners and non-owners," each of which "gives rise to specific class situations . . . a whole range of class situations." The analysis therefore begins with the economic level but differentiates it from the classical type.

In addition, however, there are other relations which are not ascribable within the "social relations of production." These include distinctions at the level of culture and values—maintained, for example, by such institutional structures as the system of Bantu education and forms of political power—established through the separation of political and economic power, such as the control of political power by the whites. These generate conflicts between groups distinct from "control of the means of production." Here the analysis encompasses the position of social groups—the African "middle class," the Cape Coloureds, the Indian traders—which cannot be easily assimilated to the earlier analysis of economic relations. From them many ascriptive features of South Africa's "closed" structure of social relations also arise.

This analysis, while predicated on the "peculiarity" of the South African system, is not limited to it. Rex (1977) has recently proposed a similar sketch as the basis for analyzing ethnic relations in Latin America and the Caribbean.

Here, too, the analysis begins with delineating "the basic forms of economic exploitation which can arise in colonial conditions," including "other possible types of capitalist and non-capitalist exploitation and accumulation." In this instance, the range includes forms of "unfree" or "partly-free" labour—the economy of slavery and the plantation system, the formation of a "dependent peasant." It includes a similar range of social strata—the "settlers," pariah trader groups, middlemen, caciques, missionaries, administrators. The general form of the argument is very similar to that employed in the South African case.

> Some of these groups are opposed to one another as classes in a Marxian sense. All of them, however, form relatively close groups with their own distinctive cultural traits and social organization. The overall effect is of too much overlap and inter-penetration to justify us in calling it a caste system, but too much closure of avenues of mobility for us to call it a system of social stratification. It is much too complex, involving overlapping modes of production, for it to be described as a situation of class struggle in the Marxian sense. All of these aspects need to be kept in mind when we speak of a colonial system of social stratification. (Rex 1977, 30)

On the broad theoretical plane, we must see this as a model founded on a very specific theoretical revision. Without undue simplification, it combines elements of a Marxist and a Weberian approach. The synthesis is, however, secured on essentially Weberian terrain. I say this, not because Rex constantly counterposes his own approach to what he sees as an inadequate and simplifying application of the "Marxist law of class struggle"—though he does. Rather, this characterization refers to the conceptual structure of Rex's revisions. The synthesis is accomplished, theoretically, in two different, complementary ways. The first is the distancing of the analysis from what is conceptualized as a "classical" Marxist approach. Much depends on how this definition is established. "Classical" Marxism is characterized as a mode of explanation which assumes that all the various instances of conflict are subsumable within and dominated by the class struggle. Classes are defined by economic position—loosely, in terms of the distinction between "owners and nonowners" of the means of production. They are economic groups "in themselves" which can be organized, through the pursuit of their distinct class interests in competing market situations, by means of the class struggle, to become "classes-for-themselves." The Marxist approach is also identified, here, with a set of propositions as to the form, the path and the logic of capitalist development. The classical form is that in which free labour confronts the capitalist in the labour market. Capitalism "can spring to life only when the owner of the means of production and subsistence meets in the market with the free labourer selling his labour-power. And this one historical condition comprises a world's history" (Marx 1961, 170). The classical path is that which makes this struggle between owners and nonowners the typical, dominant and determining set of relations in all social formations in which the capitalist mode is dominant. The classical logic is that the "economic rationality" of capitalist market relations sooner or later prevail over and transform those relations stemming from previous, now displaced, modes of production, so that capitalist relations "net" the latter within their sway. Rex distances himself from this "classical" account, in terms of the pertinent differences between it and the actual social formations it is required to explain. True, he concedes that where there is capitalism, there will be economic struggles of a capitalist type—class struggles. However, social formations of a colonial type exhibit different forms which take a different path and obey a different logic. In addition, there are in such social formations other structural relations which are not attributable to class relations of a classical capitalist type.

The second feature is a recuperation of these problems within the framework of a "classical" Weberianism. By this we mean that, contrary to those who have adopted Weber against Marx, as a way of moving decisively from economic-structural to more "superstructural" features, Rex always works from that often-forgotten side of Weber's work which treats extensively of economic relations including, of course, economic class conflict of a capitalist type, as one among a range of possible types of such relations. This is a distinctive stress, which allows Rex to encompass Marxian analysis of class relations as one, limited case within a more inclusive range of economic relations, defined as a set of "ideal types." This "one among a range" approach thus also permits the elaboration of other economic relations to explain peculiar features of social formations which do not exhibit Marx's hypostasized classical capitalist structure. For Weber, economic class conflicts were conceptualized as one among a range of possible market situations, in relation to which groups, differently composed, struggled in competition. For Weber, these different market relations do not overlap into anything which can be called the general form of the class struggle. Groups competing in the struggle over prestige or status may not be the same as groups competing over the power over scarce resources. Thus, in his work on immigration and housing, Rex distinguishes between and within economic groups in terms of the stratification of the housing market—in relation to which he identifies a set of distinct "housing classes." It follows that the groups dominant in each market situation do not cohere into anything so singular as a single ruling class in the Marxian sense. Instead, one must generate, according to each empirical case, a range of ideal-typical market situations, the sum of these plural structures constituting the social formation. This does not mean that the analysis excludes questions of exploitation. This is not, however, a general feature but one which remains to be specified in each individual case. It is, thus, Weber in this "harder" form—Weber, so to speak, "corrected for" by Marx—which is the theoretical basis of the synthesis Rex proposes. The solution to a limited, one-sided form of Marxian explanation is the adoption of a powerful and distinctive "left Weberianism." It should be pointed out here that this "solution" is not restricted exclusively to those who are opposed to the "totalism" of Marxian forms of explanation. It has been noted recently (see McLennan 1976; Schwarz 1978) that some Marxist theorists, when required to integrate political and ideological structures into an economic analysis of a Marxist kind, sometimes also attempt to deal with these levels by a somewhat untheorized appropriation of Weberianism. (This, it has been suggested, is sometimes the case with the work of so distinguished a Marxist economic historian as Maurice Dobb.) So what has been pinpointed here is something like a "theoretical convergence," operated at one time or another from arguments which begin from either the Marxist or the Weberian pole of the debate.

Significantly, there is one point where Rex challenges both Marx and Weber—a point where, incidentally, they both appear to agree. This is the contention that "free labour was the only form of labour compatible in the long run with the logic of rational capitalism" (Rex 1973, 273). This argument—founded, in Weber, by his particular ideal-type definition of "capitalist rationality," and in Marx, by his historical analysis of the "typical" path of capitalist development, based on the English case—is contested by Rex on both fronts. Instead, Rex argues that historical deviations from this "modal" type can often be found in social formations of a "specifically colonial type." Here, in contrast, conquest, and a variety of forms of "unfree labour" (based on apparently irrational forms of ascriptive relations, such as those founded on racial differences) can be possible conditions of existence for the emergence and development of an "effective" capitalist mode of production. Lying behind this analytic distinction is, undoubtedly, a theoretical-political point: namely a refusal of the "Euro-centredness" of Marxism, based as it is on extrapolating to other social formations forms of development, paths and logics peculiar to, and illegitimately generalized from, European cases (especially, of course, the English case, which forms the basis for the analysis in Marx's *Capital*).

With this important qualification, we can now identify the dominant tendency of this synthesis (the following passage may stand for many other instances in Rex's work):

> Of course, one problem in adopting terms like "caste" and "estate" . . . is that all of them seem to omit what is essential to the Marxist definition of class, i.e., relationships to the means of production. What we wish to suggest here, however, departs from simple Marxism in a twofold sense. First it recognizes that at the level of relationships to the means of production there are more possible positions and potentialities for class formation than simple European Marxism seems to allow; and second, that over and above the actual means of production, there are a number of social functions and positions and that these functions are appropriated by closed groups which, thereafter, have their own interests and their own power position vis-à-vis society as a whole.

When this "Marx plus Weber" theoretical position is then translated to the domain of politics, it yields a "Marx plus Fanon" sort of argument (see Rex 1977, 23–24, 45).

The position, the synthesis of which has been outlined here, has of course been criticized in the context of its application to South Africa. For example, Wolpe in a recent article (1976) points out that the distinction between "free" and "forced" labour is not an adequate way of conceptualizing the relations of production of a capitalist social formation, since, for Marx, even in its classical form, "free labour" is "free" only in a very specific and formal sense: it is, after all, subject to economic compulsions to sell its labour-power as a commodity. Thus, in the South African case, the free/unfree couple, while effective in distinguishing the different constraints which structure the availability of black and white labour in the market, is not theoretically powerful enough to establish, for black labour, a relation to capitalist production of a conceptually distinct kind: "All labour-power is in some way and in some degree unfree, the type, gradation or continuum of degrees of unfreedom 'merely' affect the intensity of exploitation but not its mode" (Wolpe 1975, 203). Secondly, this distinction does not encompass what for Marx was central to "relations of production"; namely, the mode of appropriation of surplus labour. Thirdly, such an approach abstracts the labour market and its constraints from the system of production relations proper, which are in fact the central preoccupation of a Marxian analysis. Fourth, the absence of an adequate theorization at the mode of production level leaves us with a political and ideological definition of "classes" which are then too easily homogenized with the main racial groupings. However, a detailed analysis of the position of the black and white working class in South Africa, in terms of both their complex relations to capitalist production and their internal stratifications, does not allow us to "treat racial groups" as "homogeneous in their class composition." Wolpe, indeed, uses Guglielmo Carchedi's recent work (1977) on the identification of social classes to say that the "functions" of even the white working class with respect to capital are not homogeneous. Fifth, Wolpe argues that political and ideological positions cannot be ascribed as a bloc to classes defined at the economic level: "A social class, or fraction or stratum of a class, may take up a class position that does not correspond to its interests, which are defined by the class determination that fixes the horizon of the class struggle" (Carchedi 1977). The example taken is that of the "labour aristocracy." This leads on to a more general argument, that the analysis of classes and class struggle must begin from the level of the relations of production, rather than from political and ideological criteria; but that the latter have their specific forms of "relative autonomy" which cannot be ascribed to the place of a class or class fraction in the relations of production.

I am not concerned to assess in detail the merits of these arguments as they relate to the South African case. Instead, I want to use the example of this exchange to establish the basis of a more general argument. Rex's arguments may not be entirely satisfactory in themselves, but undoubtedly they win effective ground from what he calls "simple Marxism"—as Wolpe is obliged to concede. These represent real theoretical gains, against some of the weaknesses and lacunae in what has become the dominant form in which the classical Marxist paradigm has been applied. These gains are not wholly offset by pointing, correctly, to the ways in which Rex sometimes misrepresents Marx, and distorts Marx's real theoretical effectivity. Secondly, Wolpe's response shows that these weaknesses can only be "corrected for," while retaining the broad outline of a Marxist approach, by significantly modifying the dominant form in which the Marxist paradigm has been applied: either by means of a more scrupulous or rigorous application of Marx's protocols (which have often, over time, been subject to severe theoretical simplification and impoverishment); and/or by bringing to the fore aspects and arguments which, though they can be shown not to contradict Marx, have not tended to play a very significant part when applied to the peculiar features of postconquest or postcolonial social formations. This paper's interest in certain new approaches to these problems, from within a substantially new application of Marxist protocols of analysis, arises precisely from a concern to indicate where and how these new emphases are beginning to develop.

Wolpe himself concedes some of the points, at least. He acknowledges that Rex "was right to insist upon the need for a more comprehensive and more refined conceptualization of class than was encompassed by the bare reference to property relations." This however, he suggests, means moving away from the attention which Rex gives to market relations and constraints on the labour supply, into a fuller analysis of the relations of production and "modes of production" analysis. He acknowledges that Rex was correct to draw attention to pertinent differences in the conditions affecting the entry into the labour market of "black" and "white" labour: though he would add that the distinction between free/unfree labour is then too sharply and simply applied. Wolpe also recognizes that Rex brings forward a point of great theoretical interest by his reference to the form of the "political compromise" between the white capitalist and the white working classes, and the consequent "supervising and policing" functions which white labour exerts over black. It follows from this that some of the more simplistic political recipes based on the call for "black" and "white" labour to sink their differences in a common and general class struggle against capital—the famous call to "unite and fight"—are abstract political demands, based on theoretically unsound foundations, since they do not adequately grasp the structurally different relations in which "white" and "black" labour stand in relation to capital.

Indeed, on this point, Wolpe may not have gone far enough. For a larger argument is involved here, even if only implicitly. Rex is arguing that the South African social system shows no strong or "inevitable" tendencies to be gradually assimilated to the more "rational" forms of "free" labour, which Marx suggested was a necessary precondition for the establishment and reproduction of the capitalist mode of production. Hence, he would argue, the racial fractioning of the South African working classes has a real and substantial basis, with pertinent effects at the economic, as well as at the political and ideological level. Rex thus points to the need for a definition of "the capitalist mode" which is able to deal with "other types of capitalist and non-capitalist exploitation and accumulation"—that is, to a "capitalist" system founded quite securely on forms of labour other than traditionally free and mobile labour. This formulation may be criticized as being, finally, too plurally descriptive. It avoids the necessity to specify the articulating mechanisms, and the modes of dominance, between these different "types." But Rex has clearly succeeded, once again, in putting into question an analysis predicated unquestioningly on a general and necessary classical path of capitalist development, with a classical and irreversible sequence of evolutionary stages. To put this more broadly: he opens up the crucial theoretical question of the teleological and evolutionary form in which Marx's work on the necessary preconditions and optimal line of development of the capitalist mode has been interpreted—from the famous assertion, in *The Communist Manifesto*, that "the bourgeoisie . . . compels all nations on pain of extinction, to adopt the bourgeois mode of production. . . . It creates a world after its own image" (Marx and Engels 1967) through to the legendary discussion on the "sequence of stages" which is often derived from the section on "Pre-capitalist forms" in the *Grundrisse* (Marx 1964). Against this teleological extrapolation, it must be said that the fact of conquest, and thus the very different conditions in which preconquest social strata have been inserted into the capitalist mode, have not on the whole played a central role in the versions of Marxist theory usually applied to such postconquest societies. (The difficulty of deciding precisely what was the nature of the American slave systems—clearly inaugurated within yet separate from the expanding mercantile capitalist phase—is an aspect of the same theoretical problem [Genovese 1965; Hindess and Hirst 1975.])

These, then, represent some of the gains which Rex's critique makes against a too-simple Marxism. What I am concerned to show, now, is how current Marxist theorizings on these questions have begun, through their own internal critique of what earlier passed as "classical" or orthodox Marxism, to rectify some of the weaknesses correctly pinpointed by the critics of reductionism. These departures are, at once, rich and complex, often only at a rudimentary stage of formulation, and—as is often the case at a critical moment of paradigm shift—locked in an intricate internal debate. Only certain indications of some of the main directions in this work can be provided in this review.

We might begin, here, by looking at one, very distinctive formulation with respect to the development of the social formations of Latin America, which not only defines itself within "classical" Marxism, but which develops, in what is held to be a Marxist direction, one of the lines of argument which the critique by Rex and others has put in question: namely, the work of Frank, and recent critiques of Frank's work from within a transformed Marxist perspective.

One distinctive but seminal application of what is taken to be the Marxist paradigm is to be found in Frank. His work was itself counterposed to the dominant and formative school of "dependency" theorists, grouped around the United Nations Economic Commission for Latin America (ECLA) which was established in 1948. This school adopted a more rigorously structural analysis to explain the "underdevelopment" of the underdeveloped countries of the region. As against earlier developmentalist models, the ECLA "school" insisted that development and underdevelopment had to be treated within the single framework of a world economic system. The "underdeveloped" countries were the dependent sectors of such a world economy: as Celso Furtado put it, "The theory of underdevelopment turns out to be essentially a theory of dependence" (Furtado 1971, cited in O'Brien 1975). This starting point within a global economic framework had much in common, in a "broadly" Marxist way, with those writers who had attempted to deal with modern aspects of capitalist development on a world scale in terms of a "theory of imperialism" (e.g., Lenin, Luxembourg, Hilferding and Bukharin). The ECLA theorists accepted some such general framework of imperialism, giving of course greater attention than the classical theorists did to the effects of this world system at its peripheries. They were not necessarily Marxist in any other sense. These general relations of dependency, they argued, had created internal structures promoting a form of what they called "dependent capitalist development" in those sectors, and among those classes, closely linked with the imperialist chain, whilst marginalizing other sectors, including the great mass of the population, especially the peasantry. "The differences between the internationalized sector and the non-industrialized or marginal sector are the direct result of capitalist expansion, and become a form of structural dualism" (O'Brien 1975). However, the "school" promulgated a variety of different strategies for overcoming this externally induced sectoral imbalance—often of a technical-economic, rather than of a political kind.

Frank certainly shares with the dependency theorists the necessity to begin from a world capitalist system in which development and underdevelopment were structurally related. However, he explicitly argued against the possibility of a genuine, indigenous programme of economic development, of, say, a national-bourgeois type, as a possible path for Latin America out of its phase of dependent development. And this argument was supported by a startling thesis, which takes us back to the problems posed earlier. Frank argued that Latin America had been thoroughly incorporated into capitalist world relations since the period of the conquest by the European powers in the sixteenth century. Its underdevelopment stemmed from this dependent nature of its early insertion into the world capitalist market. Implicit in this thesis was the view that no structural differences remained between the more and the less developed sectors of these dependent social formations. "Dependency," he argued, was no recent phenomenon in the region. It was only the latest form of the long-standing "satellitization" of the Latin American economies within the framework of imperialist economic relations. The "expansion of the capitalist system over the past centuries effectively and entirely penetrated even the most isolated sectors of the under-developed world" (Frank 1969). The fundamental term for understanding this penetration and subversion by capitalist relations which had brought about the structural coupling of development and underdevelopment was that of a single continuum—the "metropolis-satellite polarization ... one and the same historical process of the expansion and development of capitalism" which continues to generate "both economic development and structural underdevelopment." This was the imperialist chain, which "extends the capitalist link between the capitalist world and the national metropolises to the regional centres ... and from these local centres and so on to the large landowners or merchants who expropriate surplus from small peasants or tenants, and sometimes even from these latter to the landless labourers exploited by them in turn" (Frank 1969).

The most telling critique of Frank's work is offered in Ernesto Laclau's review essay, "Feudalism and Capitalism in Latin America," republished in a recent volume of essays (Laclau 1977). Laclau's specific criticisms are easily résuméd. The object of his critique is Frank's assertion that Latin America has "been capitalist from the beginning"—a single process, which must, for Frank, be "identical in all its aspects from the sixteenth to the twentieth century" (Laclau 1977). Laclau, first, criticizes Frank's conception of "capitalism." Frank defines this as a system of production for the market, of which profit forms the driving motive. This, Laclau argues, differs fundamentally from Marx's conception of mode of production insofar as it dispenses with Marx's principal criteria for defining a "mode"—the relations of production. This "error" leads Frank to assume that, wherever there is capital accumulation, then Marx's "law"—the rapid and inevitable transformation of the social formation by capitalist relations—must follow. However, as Laclau shows, for Marx, the accumulation of commercial capital is perfectly compatible with the most varied modes of production and does not by any means presuppose the existence of a capitalist mode of production: e.g., "However, not commerce alone, but also merchant's capital is older than the capitalist mode of production, is in fact historically the oldest free state of existence of capital" (Marx 1974, 319-21). This leads Laclau to mount a further critique of Frank's lack of historical specificity—exploitative situations as different as the Chilean inquilinos, the Ecuadorian huasipungeros, West Indian plantation slaves and Manchester textile workers being, for all practical purposes, subsumed into a single relation, declared "capitalist." The same can be said in more detail of the troublesome case of plantation slavery in the New World. This is, of course, the site of a protracted, and still unresolved debate. Ulrich B. Phillips—whom, despite his offensive antislave viewpoint, Eugene Genovese correctly praises for a seminal analysis of the political economy of slavery—argued, long ago, that plantation slavery was a form of capitalism. That was, indeed, the basis of his objection to it (Genovese 1971). Genovese himself argues that slavery had a distinct set of exploitative relations—a "seigneurial society . . . [which] created a unique society, neither feudal . . . nor capitalist" (1971). Barry Hindess and Paul Hirst constitute plantation slavery as its own distinctive "mode," using primarily formal criteria. Eric Williams, early on, and subsequently Genovese, and Janius Banaji among others, have concentrated on the relationship between plantation slavery—whatever its characteristic "mode"—and the global capitalist economy. Robert Fogel and Stanley Engerman have recently described slavery as a profitable form of "capitalist agriculture" (Hindess and Hirst 1977; Williams 1944; Genovese 1971; Banaji 1977; Fogel and Engerman 1974.)

Frank quotes Marx's observation which describes the plantations as "commercial speculations, centres of production for the world market" as proof that Marx regarded them, too, as "capitalist." Laclau reminds us that Marx, pertinently, added, "if only in a formal way." Actually, Marx seemed to be arguing the opposite to Frank; for he insists the plantation slavery could only be "formally capitalist," "since slavery among the Negroes excludes free wage-labour, which is the base on which capital production rests. However, those who deal in slave-trading are capitalists." As Beechey (1978) has recently argued, slavery certainly presupposed private property, a class of owners and a propertyless class. However, whereas under capitalism the worker owns his own labour-power which he sells as a commodity to the capitalist, slaveholders owned both the labour-power and the slave. "The slaveholder considers a Negro, whom he has purchased, as his property, not because the institution of slavery as such entitles him to that Negro, but because he has acquired him like any other commodity through sale and purchase" (Marx 1974, 776). However, both the slave trade itself, and the extraction of the commodities so produced, were funded by mercantile capital and circulated within the global circuits of capital. As Beechey (1978) puts it, with great clarity: "Slaveholders were both merchants, dealing with the purchase and sale of commodities on the world market, and slaveholders exploiting their slaves within the plantation system, which emerged as a specialized agricultural region, a kind of internal colony within the expanded world market."

What Marx was describing, then, was something radically different from Frank's interpretation: namely, an articulation between two modes of production, the one "capitalist" in the true sense, the other only "formally" so: the two combined through an articulating principle, mechanism or set of relations, because, as Marx observed, "its beneficiaries participate in a world market in which the dominant productive sectors are already capitalist." That is, the object of inquiry must be treated as a complex articulated structure which is, itself, "structured in dominance." Slave plantation owners thus participated in a general movement of the world capitalist system: but on the basis of an internal mode of production—slavery in its modern, plantation form—not itself "capitalist" in character. This is a revolutionary proposition in the theoretical sense, since it departs from that very teleological reading of Marx which produced, in Frank, the indefensible thesis that Latin America has been "capitalist" since the Conquest. What we have now, in opposition to the thesis of "inevitable transformation" of precapitalist modes and their dissolution by capitalist relations, is the emergent theoretical problem of an articulation between different modes of production, structured in some relation of dominance. This leads on to the definition of a social formation which, at its economic level, may be composed of several modes of production, "structured in dominance" (Althusser and Balibar 1970; Hindess and Hirst 1975, 1977; Poulantzas 1973). This has provided the basis for an immense amount of formative work, especially on "precapitalist modes of production," offering a more rigorous approach to that reading of Marx, rightly criticized—on this very point—by Rex, whilst retaining the systematic terms of a Marxist analysis. This work is, of course, pitched principally at the level of economic relations. Though it has clear consequences for other levels of the structure of social formations (class formations, alliances, political and ideological structures, etc.), these have not been spelled out (for example in Laclau's essay quoted here: though for related developments pertaining to these levels, see Laclau, and others referred to more extensively below). It has, for example, pertinent effects for any analysis of the way this articulated combination of modes inserts economic agents drawn from different ethnic groups into sets of economic relations which, while articulated into a complex unity, need not be conceptualized as either necessarily the same or inevitably destined to become so.

This emergent problematic constitutes perhaps the most generative new theoretical development in the field, affecting the analysis of racially structured social formations. The emergent theoretical position is grounded by its proponents in a certain "re-reading" of the classical Marxist literature. It is part of that immense theoretical revolution constituted by the sophisticated return to the "reading" of Marx's *Capital* which has had such a formative intellectual impact over the past decade. It is also being currently developed in a range of different theoretical fields. Laclau puts the essential argument in a strong form: "The precapitalist character of the dominant relations of production in Latin America was not only not incompatible with production for the world market, but was actually intensified by the expansion of the latter." Marx, in a passage less well known than the *Communist Manifesto* "scenario" quoted earlier, spoke of the fact that

> the circuit of industrial capital ... crosses the commodity circulation of the most diverse modes of social production. ... No matter whether commodities are the output of production based on slavery, of peasants ... of state enterprise ... or of half-savage hunting tribes ... they come face to face with the monies and commodities in which industrial capital presents itself. ... The character of the process of production from which they originate is immaterial. ... They must be reproduced and to this extent the capitalist mode of production is conditional on modes of production lying outside of its own stage of development. (Marx 1956, 109)

Charles Bettelheim, who may appear to take a more "classical" view, argues that the dominant tendency is towards the dissolution of other modes by the capitalist one. But this is often combined with a secondary tendency— that of "conservation-dissolution": where noncapitalist modes "before they disappear are 'restructured' (partly dissolved) and thus subordinated to the predominant capitalist relations (and so conserved)" (Bettelheim 1972).

Using this schema, Wolpe shows that certain problems of the South African social formation, referred to earlier, which could not be satisfactorily explained within the older reading, and which Rex among others correctly criticized, begin to be resolvable through the use of these new theoretical instruments and in a manner which throws significant light on the racial fracturing of class relations in South Africa. While the detailed outlines of this attempted "solution" cannot be entered into here (Wolpe 1975), its broader consequences are worth quoting. Wolpe suggests, for example, that the reliance of the capitalist sector in South Africa on the noncapitalist sectors in the African areas for both cheap labour supply and subsistence reproduction enables capital to pay for labour-power below the cost of its reproduction, whilst having always available a plentiful labour supply whose costs of subsistence it does not fully bear (Wolpe 1972). He employs both the "articulation" and the "dissolution-conservation" variants of the thesis. In South Africa, the tendency of capital accumulation to dissolve other modes is cross-cut and blocked by the counteracting tendencies to conserve the noncapitalist economies—on the basis that the latter are articulated in a subordinate position to the former. Where capitalism develops by means, in part, of its articulation with noncapitalist modes, "the mode of political domination and the content of legitimating ideologies assume racial, ethnic and cultural forms and for the same reasons as in the case of imperialism . . . political domination takes on a colonial form" (Wolpe 1975). He adds: "The conservation of non-capitalist modes of production necessarily requires the development of ideologies and political policies which revolve around the segregation and preservation and control of African 'tribal' societies"— that is, the relation assumes the forms of ideologies constructed around ethnic, racial, national and cultural ideological elements.

In short, the emergent theory of the "articulation of different modes of production" begins to deliver certain pertinent theoretical effects for an analysis of racism at the social, political and ideological levels. It begins to deliver such effects—and this is the crucial point—not by deserting the level of analysis of economic relations (i.e., mode of production) but by posing it in its correct, necessarily complex, form. Of course, this may be a necessary but not a sufficient starting point. In this respect, Wolpe's term "requires" may go too far, suggesting a necessary correspondence, of a too functionalist kind, between the structure of modes of production and the specific forms of political domination and ideological legitimation. The level of economic analysis, so redefined, may not supply sufficient conditions in itself for an explanation of the emergence and operation of racism. But, at least, it provides a better, sounder point of departure than those approaches which are obliged to desert the economic level, in order to produce "additional factors" which explain the origin and appearance of racial structuring at other levels of the social formation. In this respect, at least, the theoretical advances briefly outlined here have the merit of respecting what we would call two cardinal premises of Marx's "method": the materialist premise—that the analysis of political and ideological structures must be grounded in their material conditions of existence; and the historical premise—that the specific forms of these relations cannot be deduced, a priori, from this level but must be made historically specific "by supplying those further delineations" which explain their specificity. Both premises are well expressed in one of the most justly famous passages from *Capital*: "The specific economic form, in which unpaid labour-surplus is pumped out of direct producers, determines the relationship of rulers and ruled, as it grows directly out of production itself and, in turn, reacts upon it as a determining element. Upon this, however, is founded the entire formation of the economic community which grows up out of the production relations themselves, thereby simultaneously its specific political form" (the materialist premise). But "this does not prevent the same economic basis—the same from the standpoint of its main conditions due to innumerable different empirical circumstances, natural environments, racial relations, external historical influences, etc.—from showing infinite variations and gradations in appearance, which can be ascertained only by analysis of the empirically given circumstances" (the historical premise) (Marx 1974, 791–92). Both premises are indeed required, if the conditions of theoretical adequacy are to be met: each, on its own, is not sufficient. The first, without the second, may lead us straight back into the impasse of economic reductionism; the second, without the first, snares us in the toils of historical relativism. Marx's method, properly understood and applied, provides us with the conditions—though not, of course, the guarantee—of a theoretical adequacy which avoids both. (For a further elaboration of the "basic premises" of Marx's method, see Johnson, McLennan and Schwarz 1978; Johnson 1978; for a condensed version of the argument outlined by Wolpe, as applied to Latin American and Caribbean social formations, see Hall 1977.)

The application of the "articulation" thesis, briefly outlined here, has had revolutionary theoretical consequences in other fields of inquiry, which can only be shortly noted here since they fall outside of our principal concern. They can be found, in the English context, in the work on "precapitalist modes" and social formations, by Hindess and Hirst (1975, 1977); in Banaji

(1977); in the recent work on "colonial modes of production" (e.g., Alavi 1975); in recent issues of the *Review of African Political Economy*, *Critique of Anthropology* and *Economy and Society*; also, in a related form, in the renewed debate about "transition," sparked off by the reissue of the formative set of essays *The Transition from Feudalism to Capitalism* (Hilton 1976); and in the forthcoming work on Jamaica by Ken Post (1978). In France, it is most noteworthy in the context of the revived interest in the new "economic anthropology" to which such writers as Maurice Godelier, Claude Meillassoux, Emmanuel Terray, Pierre-Philippe Rey and Georges Dupré have made outstanding contributions (see the selection by Seddon 1978). (For interpretive overviews and critiques in English, see, *inter alia*, Clammer 1975; Bradby 1975; Foster-Carter 1978; Seddon 1978; Wolpe 1980.) Meillassoux principally deals with "self-sustaining" agricultural social formations, and their dissolution-transformation, when they have grafted onto them production for external "capitalist" markets. This has certain theoretical consequences for those articulated social formations where the noncapitalist sector is "able to fulfil functions that capitalism prefers not to assume in the under-developed countries" (see Wolpe's development of this argument, above)—and thus for such societies as the South African one, where (as John Clammer [1975] extrapolates) "people who are obliged to become wage-labourers in a neo- and quasi-colonial situation are forced back on the 'traditional' sector to obtain precisely those services which the capitalist does not provide." Clammer correctly points out that this revives the "dual sector" analysis—though in a radically new form since, as Meillassoux argues, it is precisely the ideological function of "dual sector" theories to "conceal the exploitation of the rural community, integrated as an organic component of capitalist production" (Meillassoux 1972, 1974; for a more extended critique, see Clammer 1975).

Rey's work deals principally with "lineage" societies and, like Meillassoux, derives from African fieldwork: but wider extrapolations of a theoretical nature have been made from this terrain (Rey 1971, 1973, 1975; Rey and Dupré 1973). It differs from other work in the French "economic anthropology" tradition by being concerned, in part, with problems of extending the "articulation" argument—as the title of his second book indicates—to the question of class alliances, and thus to the political level. Rey also departs somewhat from the problematic of "articulation." He is concerned with the "homoficence" of capitalism—what Aidan Foster-Carter (1978) calls the problem of the "parallelism of action" of capitalism, delivering also a more substantive review/critique both of Rey and of the "articulation" literature. A major distinction in Rey's work is, however, the attempt to periodize this "parallelism of action" as a process, into three principal stages, marked by the character of the articulation in each. These are: (1) the period of the slave trade, where the European market acquires supplies, through relations of exchange, "essentially by playing on the internal contradictions of the lineage social formations"; (2) a transitional phase—colonialism in the full sense—where capitalism takes root, grounding itself in the precapitalist mode and gradually subordinating it; (3) a new type of social formation, with the capitalist mode of production internally dominant; frequently, then, dependent on a metropolitan capitalism (neocolonialism). To each phase a different set of class alliances corresponds. Rey is also much concerned with the way the lineage societies are interrupted and disarticulated by the exterior force of capital—often through violence and what Marx called the "fact of conquest" (Foster-Carter 1978). Rey sees the "rooting" of capitalism in these precapitalist modes as possible only with the implantation of "transitional modes"—precisely the function of the colonial period. While giving to this phase a seminal role not normally accorded to it, or even distinctly remarked, Rey's approach leaves the history of capital and the mechanism of transition as one largely "written outside such social formations" and he tends to treat the relations of exchange as the central articulating feature (for a wider critique, see Clammer 1975; Foster-Carter 1978; Terray 1972; Bradby 1975).

The term "articulation" is a complex one, variously employed and defined in the literature here referred to. No clear consensus of conceptual definition can be said to have emerged so far. Yet it remains the site of a significant theoretical rupture (*coupure*) and intervention. This is the intervention principally associated with the work of Althusser and the "school" of structuralist Marxism. The term is widely employed, in a range of contexts, especially in the *For Marx* essays (Althusser 1969), and in the succeeding volume, with Étienne Balibar, in *Reading Capital* (Althusser and Balibar 1970). At least two different applications are particularly relevant to our concerns here (though, interestingly, the term is not defined in the "Glossary," prepared by Ben Brewster and sanctioned by Althusser himself, which appeared in the English editions of both books). Aside from these particular usages, the term has a wider reference of both a theoretical and a methodological nature.

Foster-Carter correctly suggests that articulation is a metaphor used "to indicate relations of linkage and effectivity between different levels of all sorts of things"—though he might have added that these things require to be linked because, though connected, they are not the same. The unity which they form is thus not that of an identity, where one structure perfectly recapitulates or reproduces or even "expresses" another; or where each is reducible to the other; or where each is defined by the same determinations or have exactly the same conditions of existence; or even where each develops according to the effectivity of the same conditions of existence; or even where each develops according to the effectivity of the same contradiction (e.g., the "principal contradiction" so beloved, as the warrant and guarantee of all arguments, by so-called "orthodox" Marxists). The unity formed by this combination or articulation, is always, necessarily, a "complex structure": a structure in which things are related, as much through their differences as through their similarities. This requires that the mechanisms which connect dissimilar features must be shown—since no "necessary correspondence" or expressive homology can be assumed as given. It also means—since the combination is a structure (an articulated combination) and not a random association—that there will be structured relations between its parts, i.e., relations of dominance and subordination. Hence, in Althusser's cryptic phrase, a "complex unity, structured in dominance."

Many of the classic themes of the Althusserian intervention are résuméd in and through his various uses of this term: for example, his argument that Marx's "unity" is not the essentialist "expressive unity" to be found in Hegel, and that, therefore, Marx's dialectic is not merely an inversion, but a theoretical advance over Hegel. This is the critique against conceiving Marx's "totality" as an "expressive totality," which grounds Althusser's early critique of the attempts to rescue Marx's work from "vulgar materialism" by way of a detour through Hegelianism (see Althusser's *For Marx* [1969], especially the chapter "On the Marxian Dialectic"). It also founds Althusser's critique of the attempt to read Marx as if he meant that all the structures of a social formation could be reduced to an "expression" of the economic base; or as if all the instances of any historical conjuncture moved in a relation of direct correspondence with the terms of the "principal contradiction" (that of the "base," between forces and relations of production)—this is Althusser's critique (the opposite of that against Hegelian idealism) against "economic reductionism." Marx's "complex unity," Althusser argues, is neither that in which everything perfectly expresses or corresponds to everything else; nor that in which everything is reducible to an expression of "the Economic." It operates, instead, on the terrain of articulation. What we find, in any particular historical conjuncture (his example, in "Contradiction and Overdetermination" in *For Marx*, is Russia in 1917) is not the unrolling of the "principal contradiction," evenly, throughout all the other levels of the social formation, but, in Lenin's terms, the "merger," "rupture," condensation of contradictions, each with its own specificity and periodization—"absolutely dissimilar currents, absolutely heterogeneous class interests, absolutely contrary political and social strivings"—which have "merged . . . in a strikingly 'harmonious' manner" (Lenin 1932). Such conjunctures are not so much "determined" as overdetermined, i.e., they are the product of an articulation of contradictions, not directly reduced to one another.

Althusser and Balibar, then, employ this general theoretical concept in a variety of different contexts. They conceive of a social formation as composed of a number of instances—each with a degree of "relative autonomy" from one another—articulated into a (contradictory) unity. The economic instance or level, itself, is the result of such a "combination": the articulation between forces and relations of production. Particular social formations, especially in periods of "transition," may be an "articulated combination" of different modes with specified, shifting terms of hierarchical ordering between them. The term also figures in Althusserian epistemology, which insists that knowledge and the production of knowledge are not directly produced, as an empiricist reflection of the real "in thought," but have a specificity and autonomy of their own—thought "established on and articulated to the real world of a given historical society" (Althusser and Balibar 1970, 42). The scientific analysis of any specific social formation depends on the correct grasping of its principle of articulation: the "fits" between different instances, different periods and epochs, indeed different periodicities, e.g., times, histories. The same principle is applied, not only synchronically, between instances and periodizations within any "moment" of a structure, but also diachronically, between different "moments." This connects with Althusser's objections to the notion of a given and necessary sequence of stages, with a necessary progression built into them. He insists on the nonteleological reading of Marx, on the notion of "a discontinuous succession of modes of production" (Althusser and Balibar 1970, 204), whose combined succession—i.e., articulation through time—requires to be demonstrated. Indeed, "scientificity" itself is associated with "the problem of the forms of variation of the articulation" of the instances in every social structure (Althusser and Balibar 1970, 207). The same is said of the relations between the economic and the political and ideological forms of their appearance. This, too, is thought on the analogy of an articulation between structures which do not directly express or mirror each other. Hence, the classical problem for Marxism—the problem of determinacy of the structure, the "determination in the last instance by the economic" (which distinguishes Marxism from other types of social scientific explanation)—is itself redefined as a problem of "articulation." What is "determined" is not the inner form and appearance of each level, but the mode of combination and the placing of each instance in an articulated relation to the other elements. It is this "articulation of the structure" as the global effect of the structure itself—or what has been called, by Balibar, "the matrix role of the mode of production"—which defines the Althusserian concept of determination as a structural causality (Althusser and Balibar 1970, 220). It is this conception, on the other hand, which has provided the basis for the critique by Hindess and Hirst (1975) of Althusser's "determinacy of articulation by the structure" as, itself, an "expressive totality"—a Spinozian eternity. Dealing with the example of the relation between feudal ground rent and the feudal relation of lordship and servitude, Balibar treats it as a reduced instance of the articulation of two different instances, an "economic" instance and a "political" instance. Likewise, Balibar defines the concept of mode of production as, itself, the result of a variant combination of elements (object of labour, means of labour, labour-power). What changes, in each epoch, are not the elements, which are invariant (in the definitional sense), but the way they are combined: their articulation. While it is not possible to "tell" the whole of the Althusserian intervention through the terms of a single concept, like articulation, it must be by now apparent that the concept has a wide and extensive reference in the works of the structuralist Marxists.

Though we cannot go into the theoretical and methodological background to the emergence of the concept, we can at least note, in passing, two pertinent provenances. The first is that of structuralist linguistics, which provided the master-model of a substantial part of the whole "structuralist" venture. Saussure, the "founder" of this school, who argued that language is not a reflection of the world but produces meaning through the articulation of linguistic systems upon real relations, insists that meaning is no mere "correlation between signifier and signified, but perhaps more essentially an act of simultaneously cutting out two amorphous masses, two 'floating kingdoms' . . . language is the domain of articulations" (Barthes 1967). More pertinent, perhaps, is the warrant which Althusser and others have found, in Marx's most extensive "methodological" text—his "1857 Introduction" to the *Grundrisse*—for a theory of the social formation as what Marx himself calls an "articulated hierarchy" (*Gliederung*)—or, as Althusser translates him, "an organic hierarchized whole." "In all forms of society," Marx wrote, "it is a determinate production and its relations which assign every other production and its relations their rank and influence" (Marx 1973). If this represents a slender warrant for the construction of the whole structuralist edifice, it is certainly clear that, in that text, Marx was decisively opposing himself to any notion of a simple identity between the different relations of capital (production, circulation, exchange, consumption). He spoke, at length, of the complexity of determinations between these relations, the sum of whose articulations, nevertheless, provided him (in this text) with the object of his inquiry (adequately constructed in a theoretical sense); and, in *Capital*, with the key to the unravelling of the necessarily complex nature of the relations between the different circuits operating within the capitalist mode (see Hall 1973). This is the real burden of Marx's extensive criticisms in the "1857 Introduction" against treating the different relations which compose the capitalist mode as a "regular syllogism"—an "immediate identity." "To regard society as one single subject is . . . to look at it wrongly; speculatively." "The conclusion we reach is not that production, distribution, exchange and consumption are identical, but that they all form the members of a totality of distinctions within a unity" (Marx 1973). In the same way, there seems to be a clear warning issued against any simple notion of an evolutionary sequence or succession of stages in that development: "Their sequence is determined, rather, by their relation to one another in modern bourgeois society, which is precisely the opposite of that which seems to be their natural order or which corresponds to historical development. The point is not the historic position of the economic relations in the succession of different forms of society." This last point indicates what we would want to call (in addition to those already signalled) the third premise of Marx's method: the structural premise. It is, above all, the employment of the structural premise in the later, mature work of Marx, and the manner in which this has been appropriated and developed by Althusser and the structuralists, which produces, as one of its theoretical results, the extensive-intensive concept of articulation.

The term itself is by no means unproblematic, indicating here a certain approach, rather than providing in itself a theoretical resolution to the problems it indexes. It has been subjected to a searching critique. In itself, the term has an ambiguous meaning, for, in English, it can mean both "joining up" (as in the limbs of the body, or an anatomical structure) and "giving expression to" (Foster-Carter 1978). In Althusserian usage, it is primarily the first sense which is intended. There are, in any case, theoretical objections to the notion that one structure "gives expression to" another: since this would be tantamount to seeing the second structure as an epiphenomenon of the first (i.e., a reductionist conception), and would involve treating a social formation as an "expressive totality," precisely the object of Althusser's initial critique of Hegelianism. Some notion of an "expressive" link—say, between the economic and political structures of a society—remains, even in Althusserian usage, but this is elaborated by other terms which break up or break into any residual sense of a perfect and necessary "correspondence." Thus, in addition to insisting on the specificity, the nonreductiveness, the "relative autonomy," of each level of the society, Althusser always uses such terms as "displacement," "dislocation," "condensation," in order to demonstrate that the "unity" which these different relations form are not univocal, but mislead through "over-determination." Another criticism, then, is that the concept of "articulation" may simply leave two dissimilar things yoked together by a mere external or arbitrary connexion: what Marx once called "independent, autonomous neighbours... not grasped in their unity" (Marx 1973, 90). Althusser attempts to overcome this "mere juxtaposition" by using the concept of "overdetermination," and by always speaking of "articulation" as involving hierarchical as well as lateral relations, i.e., relations of dominance and subordination. (Relevant in this regard is Marx's discussion of money in different historical epochs, which does not "wade its way through all economic relations" but is defined by where it plays a "dominant" or a "subordinate" role.) This, however, leads on to other criticisms. The schema, constructed around articulation has, often with justice, been described as too "formalist." Thus, in the full-blown "structural causality" of Althusser and Balibar's *Reading Capital* (1970), the "economic" determines "in the last instance" not substantively but principally by "giving the index of effectivity" in the structure to one or another level: i.e., in a formal way—even though Althusser retreats from some of these more formalist excesses (Althusser 1976). While the whole attempt to develop such an analysis is predicated on the need for an approach which is not reductive, it has been criticized as giving rise to a conception of "structure" which—since it contains within itself all the conditions of its own functioning—is itself that "expressive totality" which Althusser seeks to avoid (Hindess and Hirst 1975; Hirst 1976). The framework is also open to the criticism that it leaves the internal elements of any "structural combination" unchanged, with change or transition being limited to the variations (different articulations) through which the "invariant elements" are combined. This weakens the historicity of the approach—contravening what we have called the historical premise of Marx's work (although again see Althusser 1976). This notion of the variation between invariant elements has resulted in a formalist way of defining a "mode of production" (following, especially, Balibar): so that some of the real advances made in attempting to ground analysis in a more developed and sophisticated understanding of modes of production and their combination can easily be vitiated by a sort of formalist hunt for one, separate "mode of production" after another. Nevertheless, we would continue to insist on the potentially generative value of the term and its cognate concepts, which give us a start in thinking the complex unity and differentiae specificae of social formations, without falling back on a naive or "vulgar materialist" reductionism, on the one hand, or a form of sociological pluralism, on the other.

So far, I have been speaking, exclusively, of the application of the term "articulation" to the economic structure of complex social formations. But I have also said that the social formation itself can be analyzed as an "articulated hierarchy." At the economic level, this may involve the articulation of a social formation around more than one mode of production. Some of the political and ideological features of such societies can then be explained with reference to this particular combination. But it is also possible to conceptualize the different levels of a social formation as an articulated hierarchy. Since we must assume no "necessary correspondence"—no perfect replication, homology of structures, expressive connection—between these different levels, but are nevertheless required to "think" the relations between them as an "ensemble of relations" (marked by what Marx in his "1857 Introduction," when dealing with these issues, defined as the "law of uneven development")—then it is, once more, to the nature of the articulations between them to which we must turn. The attention—of a more detailed and analytic kind—to the nature of modes of production helps to ground these other aspects of the social formation more adequately at the level of the economic structures (the materialist premise). However, we cannot thereby deduce a priori the relations and mechanisms of the political and ideological structures (where such features as racism make a decisive reappearance) exclusively from the level of the economic. The economic level is the necessary but not sufficient condition for explaining the operations at other levels of the society (the premise of nonreductionism). We cannot assume an express relation of "necessary correspondence" between them (the premise of historical specificity).

These are, as Marx put it, "a product of historical relations and possess their full validity only for and within these relations." This is an important, indeed a critical qualification. It requires us to demonstrate—rather than to assume, a priori—what the nature and degree of "correspondence" is, in any specific historical case. Thus, through this opening, some of the criticisms which, as was noted earlier, are made from the perspective of "sociological" explanations—for example the requirement to be historically specific— begin to be met within the framework of this seminal revision.

Here, however, different positions within the general problematic of "articulation" can be identified. Some theorists argue that all we can do is to deal with each level, in terms of its own specificity, and of the "conditions of existence" which must be fulfilled for it to function (e.g., the economic relations of the capitalist mode require, as a condition of existence, some extraeconomic, juridical framework, which secures the "contract" between buyer and seller of labour-power). But, it is argued, the internal forms and specificities of the extraeconomic levels can neither be prescribed nor identified from the economic level which "requires it," as a formal necessity of its functioning. This is tantamount to a theory of the "autonomy" (not "relative autonomy") of the different levels (Hirst 1976; Cutler et al. 1977). This, however, fails to deal with social formations as a "complex unity": Marx's "unity of many determinations."

Other approaches recognize that there may well be "tendential combinations": combinations which, while not prescribed in the fully determinist sense, are the "preferred" combinations, sedimented and solidified by real historical development over time. Thus, as is clear from, say, the Latin American case, there is no "necessary correspondence" between the development of a form of capitalism and the political forms of parliamentary democracy. Capitalism can arise on very different political foundations. Engels himself showed how capitalism can also harness and adapt very different legal systems to its functions. This does not prevent us from arguing that the advent of capitalism has frequently (tendentially) been accompanied by the formation of bourgeois parliamentary democratic regimes: or even from accepting Lenin's percipient observation that parliamentary democracy provides "the 'best possible' political shell for capitalism." We must, however, see these "combinations" as historically specific, rather than specified a priori: as "laws of tendency"—which can be countermanded by "counteracting tendencies." To take a pertinent example: in Europe, the rise of capitalism is consequent upon the destruction of feudal ties and the formation of "free labour"—of labour-power as a commodity. It is hard to think of a capitalist formation in which there would be no form of labour-power available to capital in its "free" form. This, in turn, means that, whatever is the specific legal form with which capitalist development "corresponds," it must be one in which the concept of the juridical "contract" between "free persons" appears, which can legally regulate the forms of contract which "free labour" require. This "requirement" is something more than a mere, empty, or formal "condition of existence." However, this does not mean that the tendency to combine capitalism with "free labour" cannot, under specific historical conditions, be cross-cut or countermanded by a counteracting tendency: namely, the possibility of certain of the conditions of existence of capitalism being effectively secured by combining "free labour" with certain forms of "unfree" or "forced" labour. Once we move away from European to post-Conquest or postcolonial societies, this combination—free and "unfree" labour, on the basis of a combination of different modes of production—becomes more and more the paradigm case. This leaves almost everything of importance, still, to be done in developing a better understanding of the "laws of motion" of capitalist formations which are structured in this alternative manner. Naturally, it has consequences, then, for political and legal structures. In such "deviant" social formations (deviant only in the sense of departing from the European paradigm-case), there will be political structures which combine (or may combine) forms of parliamentary democracy with other forms of political representation—or legal structures which elaborate more than one form of citizen status. The "articulation" of "free" and "forced" labour, the combination of "equal" and "restricted" franchises, the position of the chiefs and the Bantustan "internal colonies," and the different legal statuses of "white" and "black" citizens, in the South African social formation, perfectly represent the elements of such a "variant" case—one which is in no sense "noncapitalist"; provided, that is, we read Marx's "laws of development and motion" as laws of tendency (and countertendency) rather than as a priori laws of necessity.

Where, then, the relations between the different levels of a social formation are concerned, one needs additional concepts, i.e., to supply further determinations, to those which have been mobilized for the analysis of the economic "mode of production" levels. And one needs to acknowledge that the economic level, alone, cannot prescribe what those levels will be like and how they will operate—even if their mechanisms are not fully specifiable without attending to the level of the economic. Here, the work of Althusser, and of the Althusserians—for example, Poulantzas's work on the state—requires to be supplemented by the work of another Marxist theorist whose elaboration, at this level, constitutes a contribution to the development of a rigorously nonreductionist Marxism of the very first importance. This is the work of Gramsci. Gramsci's work is more fragmentary (much of it written in prison, under the eyes of the censor, in one of Mussolini's jails), far less "theorized" than that of Althusser. Gramsci has been formative for the development of Althusser's problematic: though, since in certain respects Gramsci remained a "historicist," the relationship between Althusser and Gramsci is a complex one. In a recent review of this relationship, we have expressed it in terms of Gramsci providing the "limit case" of historicity for Marxist structuralism (Hall, Lumley and McLennan 1977).

We cannot elaborate in any depth, here, on Gramsci's concepts (for a review, see Hall, Lumley and McLennan 1977; Anderson 1976; Mouffe 1979). The central concept in his work is that of hegemony. Hegemony is that state of "total social authority" which, at certain specific conjunctures, a specific class alliance wins, by a combination of "coercion" and "consent," over the whole social formation, and its dominated classes: not only at the economic level, but also at the level of political and ideological leadership, in civil, intellectual and moral life as well as at the material level: and over the terrain of civil society as well as in and through the condensed relations of the state. This "authority and leadership" is, for Gramsci, not a given a priori but a specific historical "moment"—one of unusual social authority. It represents the product of a certain mastery of the class struggle, certainly, but it is still subject to the class struggle and the "relations of social forces" in society, of which its "unstable equilibrium" is only one, provisional, outcome or result. Hegemony is a state of play in the class struggle which has, therefore, to be continually worked on and reconstructed in order to be maintained, and which remains a contradictory conjuncture. The important point, for Gramsci, is that, under hegemonic conditions, the organization of consent (by the dominated classes to the "leadership" of the dominant class alliance) takes precedence (though it does not obliterate) the exercise of domination through coercion. In such conditions, the class struggle tends to assume the form, not of a "frontal assault" on the bastions of the state ("war of manoeuvre") but of a more protracted, strategic and tactical struggle, exploiting and working on a number of different contradictions (Gramsci's "war of position"). A state of hegemony enables the ruling class alliance to undertake the enormous task of modifying, harnessing, securing and elaborating the "superstructure" of society in line with the long-term requirements of the development of the mode of production—e.g., capital accumulation on an expanded scale. It enables such a class alliance to undertake the educative and formative tasks of raising the whole social formation to what he calls a "new level of civilization," favouring the expanded regime of capital. This is no immediate and direct imposition of the narrow, short-term, "corporate" class interests of a single class on society. It forges that unity between economic, political and ideological objectives such that it can place "all the questions around which the struggle rages on a 'universal' not a corporative level, thereby creating a hegemony of a fundamental social group over a series of subordinate groups." This is what Gramsci calls the "educative and formative role of the State. . . . Its aim is always that of creating new and higher types of civilization; of adapting the 'civilization' and the morality of the broadest popular masses to the necessities of the continuous development of the economic apparatus of production"—the formation of a "national-popular will," based on a particular relationship between the dominant and dominated classes. This, then, depends, not on a presumed, necessary or a priori correspondence between (economic) structure and (political and ideological) superstructures, but precisely on those historically specific mechanisms—and the concrete analysis of those historical "moments"—through which such a normative relationship between structure and superstructures comes to be forged. For Gramsci, the object of analysis is always the specificity of this "structure-superstructure" complex—though as a historically concrete articulation. "It is the problem of the relations between structure and superstructure which must be accurately posed and resolved if the forces which are active in history . . . are to be correctly analysed." This is a rigorously nonreductionist conception: "How then could the whole system of superstructures be understood as distinctions within politics, and the introduction of the concept of distinction into a philosophy of praxis hence be justified? But can one really speak of a dialectic of distincts, and how is the concept of a circle joining the levels of the superstructure to be understood? Concept of 'historical bloc,' i.e., . . . unity of opposites and distincts? Can one introduce the criterion of distinction into the structure too?" Gramsci, clearly, answers these questions in the affirmative. He is especially sharp against any form of vulgar economism: "It is therefore necessary to combat economism not only in the theory of historiography, but also and especially in the theory and practice of politics. In this field, the struggle can and must be carried on by developing the concept of hegemony." (All the quotes are from two essays in Gramsci 1971.)

Gramsci's theoretical contribution has only begun, recently, to be recognized—though his role as an outstanding militant in Italian politics in the 1920s and 1930s has long been acknowledged. His analysis bears, in a specially rich and productive way, on the analysis of the great bourgeois social formations of a developed capitalist type in Europe—Western Europe, where a reductionist economistic analysis, clearly, will not suffice to account for the depth of the transformations involved. Perhaps for this very reason, he has been thought of as, par excellence, the Marxist theorist of "Western capitalism." His work has, therefore, hardly been applied or employed in the analysis of non-European formations. There are, however, very strong grounds for thinking that it may have particular relevance for non-European social formations, for three, separate reasons. First, Gramsci may help to counteract the overwhelming weight of economism (Marxist and non-Marxist) which has characterized the analysis of post-Conquest and "colonial" societies. Perhaps because the weight of imperialist economic relations has been so powerfully visible, these formations have virtually been held to be explainable by an application of "imperialism" as essentially a purely "economic" process. Second, these societies present problems as to the relation in the "structure-superstructure complex" equal in complexity to those about which Gramsci wrote. Naturally, no simple transfer of concepts would be advisable here: Gramsci would be the first to insist on historical specificity, on difference. Third, Gramsci viewed the problem of "hegemony" from within the specific history of the Italian social formation. This gave him a particular, and highly relevant, perspective on the problem. For long periods Italy was marked precisely by the absence of "hegemony": by an alliance of ruling classes governing through domination rather than through hegemonic class leadership (direction). So his work is equally relevant for societies in which, according to the rhythm and punctuation of the class struggle, there have been significant movements into and out of a phase of "hegemonic direction." Moreover, Italy was/is a society brutally marked by the law of uneven development: with massive industrial capitalist development to the North, massive underdevelopment to the South. This raises the question of how the contradictions of the Italian social formation are articulated through different modes of production (capitalist and feudal), and through class alliances which combine elements from different social orders. The problem of the state, and the question of strategic alliances between the industrial proletariat and the peasantry, the "play" of traditional and advanced ideologies, and the difficulties these provide in the formation of a "national-popular will" all make his analysis of Italy specially relevant to colonial societies.

Gramsci's work has recently been taken up and developed in a structuralist manner—especially in Althusser's essay "Ideological State Apparatuses" (Althusser 1971). This seminal essay differs from Gramsci's work, specifically, in posing the problem in terms of "reproduction." But the concerns which underlie this approach are not all that distant from those of Gramsci. The economic relations of production must themselves be "reproduced." This reproduction is not simply economic, but social, technical and, above all, ideological. This is another way of putting Gramsci's observation that, to achieve its full development, capitalist social relations require to be coupled with an elaborate development and elaboration at the "noneconomic" levels of politics, civil society and culture, through moral, intellectual and ideological leadership. Althusser then shares with Gramsci a classical concern for the manner in which the "hegemony" of a ruling class alliance is secured, at these other levels, through a formative and educative class leadership or authority over the social formation as a whole. Both of them argue that this enlarged or expanded hegemony is specific to the institutions, apparatuses and relations of the so-called "superstructures" of the state and civil society. Both Althusser and Gramsci, then, insist that ideology, while itself a contradictory site and stake in the class struggle, has a specific function in securing the conditions for the expanded reproduction of capital. It is, therefore, a pertinent, and distinctive level of struggle, where leadership is secured and contested: with mechanisms and sites of struggle "relatively autonomous." Both also maintain that "ideology" is not a simple form of false consciousness, to be explained as a set of myths or simple false constructions in the head. All societies require specific ideologies, which provide those systems of meaning, concepts, categories and representations which make sense of the world, and through which men come to "live" (albeit unconsciously, and through a series of "misrecognitions"), in an imaginary way, their relation to the real, material conditions of their existence (which are only representable to them, as modes of consciousness, in and through ideology). Althusser sometimes tends to represent ideology as rather too functionally secured to the rule of the dominant classes: as if all ideology is, by definition, operative within the horizon of the "dominance ideas" of the ruling class. For Gramsci, ideologies are thought of in a more contradictory way—really, as sites and stakes in the class struggle. What interests Gramsci is how the existing ideologies—the "common sense" of the fundamental classes—which are themselves the complex result of previous moments and resolutions in the ideological class struggle, can be actively worked upon so as to transform them into the basis of a more conscious struggle, and form of intervention in the historical process. Both insist, however, that ideologies are not simply "in the head," but are material relations—what Lenin called "ideological social relations"—which shape social actions, function through concrete institutions and apparatuses, and are materialized through practices. Gramsci insists on the process which transforms these great "practical ideologies" of fundamental social classes. Althusser, for his part, adds that ideologies operate by constituting concrete individuals as the "social subjects" of ideological discourses—the process of what he calls "interpellating subjects."

These propositions have recently been taken forward in a seminal intervention by Laclau (1977). In the essays on "Populism" and "Fascism," he argues that the individual elements of these ideologies (e.g., nationalism, militarism, racism, "the people," etc.) have, in themselves, no necessary class-belonging, "no necessary class connotation." We cannot assume, a priori, that these elements necessarily "belong" to any specific class, or indeed that a class, as a single homogeneous entity, has a single unitary and uncontradictory "world view" which, as Poulantzas says, it carries around with it, through history, "like a number plate on its back" (Poulantzas 1973). Ideologies, as concrete discursive formations, do exhibit a peculiar "unity" of their own. This unity arises, first, through what Laclau calls "condensation": where each element "fulfils a role of condensation with respect to others. When a familial interpellation, for example, evokes a political interpellation, or an aesthetic interpellation, and when each of these isolated interpellations operates as a symbol of the others, we have a relatively unified ideological discourse." (This has been defined as "ideological unity" through a process of connotative condensation. See O'Shea 1978.) Secondly, unity is secured through "the specific interpellation which forms the axis and organizing principle of all ideology. In trying to analyse the ideological level of a determinate social formation, our first task must be to reconstruct the interpellative structures which constitute it" (Laclau 1977). If separate ideological elements have no necessary class belonging, and classes do not have paradigmatic ideologies assigned or ascribed to them, what then is the relationship between classes and ideologies? As might be assumed, this relation is understood in terms of the way the class struggle articulates the various ideological discourses. "Articulation requires ... the existence of non-class contents—interpellations and contradictions—which constitute the raw materials on which class ideological practices operate. The ideology of the dominant class, precisely because it is dominant, interpellates not only the members of that class but also members of the dominated class" (Laclau 1977). It succeeds to the extent that it articulates "different ideologies to its hegemonic project by an elimination of their antagonistic character." Ideologies are therefore transformed "through the class struggle, which is carried out through the production of subjects and the articulation/disarticulation of discourses." This follows Gramsci, who argued that ideologies cannot be reduced to the transparent, coherent "class interests" of their class-subjects, and that ideologies are transformed, not by one class imposing a unitary "world vision" upon all other classes, but by "a process of distinction and of change in the relative weight possessed by the elements of the old ideology. . . . What was secondary or subordinate or even incidental becomes of primary importance, it becomes the nucleus of a new doctrinal and ideological ensemble" (Gramsci quoted in Mouffe 1979; see also Mouffe 1979 for an important elaboration of this argument in relation to Gramsci).

There are problems with Laclau's tentative formulations: for example, what are "class practices" which can operate to transform ideologies but which are, themselves, presumably, without any specific ideological elements which "belong" to them? Despite these difficulties, these theorists begin to give us the tentative elements by means of which we can attempt to construct a nonreductionist theory of the superstructural or extraeconomic aspects of social formations—once again, powered through the use of the concept of articulation.

What I have tried to do in this paper is to document the emergence of a new theoretical paradigm, which takes its fundamental orientation from the problematic of Marx, but which seeks, by various theoretical means, to overcome certain of the limitations—economism, reductionism, "a priorism," a lack of historical specificity—which have beset certain traditional appropriations of Marxism and which still disfigure the contributions to this field by otherwise distinguished writers, leaving Marxism vulnerable and exposed to effective criticism by many different variants of economistic monism and sociological pluralism. This is a survey of an emergent field, not a comprehensive critical account. It must in no sense be assumed that the solutions attempted have been fully demonstrated, or that they are as yet adequately developed or without serious weaknesses and lacunae. With respect to those racially structured social formations, which form the principal objects of inquiry in this collection, the problematic has hardly begun to be applied.

Thus all that I have been able to do is to indicate certain strategic points of departure in such a potential field of application, certain protocols of theoretical procedure. Specifically, there is as yet no adequate theory of racism which is capable of dealing with both the economic and the superstructural features of such societies, while at the same time giving a historically concrete and sociologically specific account of distinctive racial aspects. Such an account, sufficient to substitute those inadequate versions which continue to dominate the field, remains to be provided. Nevertheless, in the hope of sponsoring and promoting such a development, it might be useful to conclude with a brief outline of some of the theoretical protocols which—in my view, of necessity—must govern any such proposed investigation.

This would have to begin from a rigorous application of what I have called the premise of historical specificity. Racism is not dealt with as a general feature of human societies, but with historically specific racisms, beginning with an assumption of difference, of specificity rather than of a unitary, transhistorical universal "structure." This is not to deny that there might well be discovered to be certain common features to all those social systems to which one would wish to attribute the designation "racially structured." But—as Marx remarked about the "chaotic" nature of all abstractions which proceed at the level of the "in-general" exclusively—such a general theory of racism is not the most favourable source for theoretical development and investigation: "Even though the most developed languages have laws and characteristics in common with the least developed, nevertheless, just those things which determine their development, i.e., the elements which are not general and common, must be separated out ... so that in their unity ... their essential difference is not forgotten" (Marx 1973). Racism in general is a "rational abstraction" insofar as "it really brings out and fixes the common element and saves us repetition" (Marx 1973). Thus it may help to distinguish those social features which fix the different positions of social groups and classes on the basis of racial ascription (biologically or socially defined) from other systems which have a similar social function. However, "some determinations belong to all epochs, others only to a few. Some will be shared by the most modern epoch and the most ancient." This is a warning against extrapolating a common and universal structure to racism, which remains essentially the same, outside of its specific historical location. It is only as the different racisms are historically specified—in their difference— that they can be properly understood as "a product of historical relations and possess ... full validity only for and within those relations." It follows that there might be more to be learned from distinguishing what, in common sense, appear to be variants of the same thing: for example, the racism of the slave South from the racism of the insertion of blacks into the "free forms" of industrial-capitalist development in the postbellum North; or the racism of Caribbean slave societies from that of the metropolitan societies like Britain, which have had to absorb black workers into industrial production in the twentieth century.

In part, this must be because one cannot explain racism in abstraction from other social relations—even if, alternatively, one cannot explain it by reducing it to those relations. It has been said that there are flourishing racisms in precapitalist social formations. This only means that, when dealing with more recent social formations, one is required to show how thoroughly racism is reorganized and rearticulated with the relations of new modes of production. Racism within plantation slave societies in the mercantilist phase of world capitalist development has a place and function, means and mechanisms of its specific effectivity, which are only superficially explained by translating it out from these specific historical contexts into totally different ones (Finley 1969; Davis 1969, 1966). Others have argued that, though slavery in the Ancient World was articulated through derogatory classifications which distinguished between the enslaved and enslaving peoples, it did not necessarily entail the use of specifically racial categories, whilst plantation slavery almost everywhere did. Thus, there can be no assumed, necessary coincidence between racism and slavery as such. Precisely the differences in the roles which slavery played in these very different epochs and social formations may point us to the necessary ground for specifying what this specific coincidence between slavery and racism might secure. Where this coincidence does in fact appear, the mechanisms and effectivity of its functioning—including its articulation with other relations—need to be demonstrated, not assumed.

Again, the common assumption that it was attitudes of racial superiority which precipitated the introduction of plantation slavery needs to be challenged. It might be better to start from the opposite end: by seeing how slavery (the product of specific problems of labour shortage and the organization of plantation agriculture, supplied, in the first instance, by nonblack, indigenous labour, and then by white indentured labour) produced those forms of juridical racism which distinguish the epoch of plantation slavery. The elaboration of the juridical and property forms of slavery, as a set of enclaves within societies predicated on other legal and property forms, required specific and elaborate ideological work—as the history of slavery, and of its abolition, eloquently testifies. The same point may be made, in extenso, for all those explanations which ascribe racism-in-general to some universal functioning of individual psychology—the "racial itch," the "race instinct"—or explain its appearance in terms of a general psychology of prejudice. The question is not whether men-in-general make perceptual distinctions between groups with different racial or ethnic characteristics, but rather, what are the specific conditions which make this form of distinction socially pertinent, historically active? What gives this abstract human potentiality its effectivity, as a concrete material force? It could be said, for example, that Britain's long imperial hegemony, and the intimacy of the relationship between capitalist development at home and colonial conquest overseas, laid the trace of an active racism in British popular consciousness. Nevertheless, this alone cannot explain either the form and function which racism assumed, in the period of popular imperialism at the height of the imperialist rivalry towards the end of the nineteenth century, or the very different forms of indigenous racism, penetrating deep into the working class itself, which has been an emergent feature of the contact between black and white workers in the conditions of postwar migration. The histories of these different racisms cannot be written as a "general history" (Hall et al. 1978). Appeals to "human nature" are not explanations, they are an alibi.

One must start, then, from the concrete historical "work" which racism accomplishes under specific historical conditions—as a set of economic, political and ideological practices, of a distinctive kind, concretely articulated with other practices in a social formation. These practices ascribe the positioning of different social groups in relation to one another with respect to the elementary structures of society; they fix and ascribe those positionings in ongoing social practices; they legitimate the positions so ascribed. In short, they are practices which secure the hegemony of a dominant group over a series of subordinate ones, in such a way as to dominate the whole social formation in a form favourable to the long-term development of the economic productive base. Though the economic aspects are critical, as a way of beginning, this form of hegemony cannot be understood as operating purely through economic coercion. Racism, so active at the level—"the economic nucleus"—where Gramsci insists hegemony must first be secured, will have to contract elaborate relations at other instances, in the political, cultural and ideological levels. Yet even put in this way, the assertion is still too a priori. How specifically do these mechanisms operate? What further determinations need to be supplied? Racism is not present, in the same form or degree, in all capitalist formations: it is not necessary to the concrete functioning of all capitalisms. It needs to be shown how and why racism has been specifically overdetermined by and articulated with certain capitalisms at different stages of their development. Nor can it be assumed that this must take one, single form or follow one necessary path or logic, through a series of necessary stages.

This requires us, in turn, to show its articulation with the different structures of the social formation. For example, the position of the slave in pre-emancipation plantation society was not secured exclusively through race. It was predominantly secured by the quite specific and distinctive productive relations of slave-based agriculture, and through the distinctive property status of the slave (as a commodity) and of slave labour-power (as united with its exerciser, who was not however its "owner"), coupled with legal, political and ideological systems which anchored this relation by racial ascription. This coupling may have provided the ready-made rationale and framework for those structures of "informal racism" which became operative when "freed" black labour migrated northwards in the United States or into the "free village" system in the postemancipation Caribbean. Yet the "coupling" operated in new ways, and required their own ideological work—as in the Jim Crow legislation of the 1880s and 1890s (Woodward 1957). The reproduction of the low and ascribed status of black labour, as a specific fraction of the "free labouring" classes of industrial capitalism, was secured with the assistance of a transformed racism, to be sure: but also through other mechanisms, which accomplished their structured positioning with respect to new forms of capital in new ways. In the latter case, pertinent struggles have developed which exploited the gaps, or worked directly on the contradictions between racial ascription and the official ideologies of "equal opportunity" which were simply not available to black slaves under a plantation system (Myrdal 1962). We treat these differences as "essentially the same" at our peril. On the other hand, it does not follow that because developed capitalism here functions predominantly on the basis of "free labour" that the racial aspects of social relations can be assimilated, for all practical purposes, to its typical class relations—as does Cox (1970), despite his many pertinent observations. Race continues to differentiate between the different fractions of the working classes with respect to capital, creating specific forms of fracturing and fractioning which are as important for the ways in which they intersect class relations (and divide the class struggle, internally) as they are mere "expressions" of some general form of the class struggle. Politically and culturally, these combined and uneven relations between class and race are historically more pertinent than their simple correspondence. At the economic level, it is clear that race must be given its distinctive and "relatively autonomous" effectivity, as a distinctive feature. This does not mean that the economic is sufficient to found an explanation of how these relations concretely function. One needs to know how different racial and ethnic groups were inserted historically, and the relations which have tended to erode and transform, or to preserve these distinctions through time—not simply as residues and traces of previous modes, but as active structuring principles of the present organization of society. Racial categories alone will not provide or explain these. What are the different forms and relations in which these racial fractions were combined under capital? Do they stand in significantly different relations to capital? Do they stand within an articulation of different modes of production? What are the relations of dissolution/conservation between them? How has race functioned to preserve and develop these articulations? What are the functions which the dominated modes of production perform in the reproduction of the dominant mode? Are these linked to it through the domestic reproduction of labour-power "below its value," the supply of cheap labour, the regulation of the "reserve army of labour," the supply of raw materials, of subsistence agriculture, the hidden costs of social reproduction? The indigenous "natural economies" of Latin America and the forms of semidomestic production characteristic of the Caribbean societies differ significantly, among and between them, in this respect. The same is true even where different ethnic fractions stand in the same sets of relations to capital. For example, the position of black labour in the industrial North of the United States and of black migration to postwar Britain show highly distinctive patternings along racial lines: yet these situations are not explicable without the concept of the "reserve army of labour." Yet it is clear that blacks are not the only division within the "reserve army": hence race is not the only mechanism through which its size and composition is regulated. In the United States, both white immigrants (e.g., European and Central American) and women, and in Britain, both women and the Irish, have provided a significant alternative element (see Braverman 1975; Castles and Kosack 1973).

The either/or alternatives, surveyed in the opening parts of this paper, are therefore seriously disabling, at a theoretical level, whether it is "metropolitan" or "satellite" formations which are under discussion; and whether it is historical or contemporary forms which are under scrutiny. As I have recently argued (Hall et al. 1978), the structures through which black labour is reproduced—structures which may be general to capital at a certain stage of development, whatever the racial composition of labour—are not simply "coloured" by race: they work through race. The relations of capitalism can be thought of as articulating classes in distinct ways at each of the levels or instances of the social formation—economic, political, ideological. These levels are the "effects" of the structures of modern capitalist production, with the necessary displacement of relative autonomy operating between them. Each level of the social formation requires its own independent "means of representation"—the means by which the class-structured mode of production appears, and acquires effectivity at the level of the economic, the political, the ideological class struggle. Race is intrinsic to the manner in which the black labouring classes are complexly constituted at each of these levels. It enters into the way black labour, male and female, is distributed as economic agents at the level of economic practices, and the class struggles which result from it; and into the way the fractions of the black labouring classes are reconstituted, through the means of political representation (parties, organizations, community action centres, publications and campaigns) as political forces in the "theatre of politics"—and the political struggles which result; and the manner in which the working class is articulated as the collective and individual "subjects" of emergent ideologies—and the struggles over ideology, culture and consciousness which result. This gives the matter or dimension of race, and racism, a practical as well as theoretical centrality to all the relations which affect black labour. The constitution of this fraction as a class, and the class relations which ascribe it, function as race relations. Race is thus, also, the modality in which class is "lived," the medium through which class relations are experienced, the form in which it is appropriated and "fought through." This has consequences for the whole class, not specifically for its "racially defined" segment. It has consequences in terms of the internal fractioning and division within the working class which, among other ways, are articulated in part through race. This is no mere racist conspiracy from above. For racism is also one of the dominant means of ideological representation through which the white fractions of the class come to "live" their relations to other fractions, and through them to capital itself. Those who seek, with effect, to disarticulate some of the existing syntaxes of class struggle (albeit of a corporatist or social-reformist kind) and to rearticulate class experience through the condensed interpellations of a racist ideological syntax are, of course, key agents in this work of ideological transformation. This is the ideological class struggle, pursued, precisely, through harnessing the dominated classes to capital by means of the articulation of the internal contradictions of class experience with racism. In Britain, this process has recently attained a rare and general pitch. But they succeed, to the measure that they do, because they are practising on real contradictions within and inside the class, working on real effects of the structure (however these may be "misrecognized" through racism)—not because they are clever at conjuring demons, or because they brandish swastikas and read *Mein Kampf*. Racism is, thus, not only a problem for blacks who are obliged to suffer it. Nor is it a problem only for those sections of the white working class and those organizations infected by its stain. Nor can it be overcome, as a general virus in the social body, by a heavy dose of liberal inoculation. Capital reproduces class relations, including their internal contradictions, as a whole, structured by race. It dominates the divided class, in part, through those internal divisions which have racism as one of its effects. It contains and disables representative class institutions, by neutralizing them, confining them to strategies and struggles which are race-specific, which do not surmount its limits, its barrier. Through racism, it is able to defeat the attempts to construct alternative means of representation which could more adequately represent the class as a whole, or which are capable of effecting the unity of the class as a result: that is, those alternatives which would adequately represent the class as a whole—against capitalism, against racism. The sectional struggles, articulated through race, instead, continue to appear as the necessary defensive strategies of a class divided against itself, face-to-face with capital. They are, therefore, also the site of capital's continuing hegemony over it. This is certainly not to treat racism as, in any simple sense, the product of an ideological trick.

Nevertheless, such an analysis would need to be complemented by an analysis of the specific forms which racism assumes in its ideological functioning. Here, we would have to begin by investigating the different ways in which racist ideologies have been constructed and made operative under different historical conditions: the racisms of mercantilist theory and of chattel slavery; of conquest and colonialism; of trade and "high imperialism"; of popular imperialism and of so-called "postimperialism." In each case, in specific social formations, racism as an ideological configuration has been reconstituted by the dominant class relations, and thoroughly reworked. If it has performed the function of that cementing ideology which secures a whole social formation under a dominant class, its pertinent differences from other such hegemonic ideologies require to be registered in detail.

Here, racism is particularly powerful and its imprint on popular consciousness especially deep, because in such racial characteristics as colour, ethnic origin, geographical position, etc., racism discovers what other ideologies have to construct: an apparently "natural" and universal basis in nature itself. Yet, despite this apparent grounding in biological givens outside history, racism, when it appears, has an effect on other ideological formations within the same society, and its development promotes a transformation of the whole ideological field in which it becomes operative. It can, in this way, harness other ideological discourses to itself—for example, it articulates securely with the us/them structure of corporate class consciousness—through the mechanism previously discussed of connotative condensation. Its effects are similar to other ideologies from which, on other grounds, it must be distinguished: racisms also dehistoricize—translating historically specific structures into the timeless language of nature; decomposing classes into individuals and recomposing those disaggregated individuals into the reconstructed unities, the great coherences, of new ideological "subjects": it translates "classes" into "blacks" and "whites," economic groups into "peoples," solid forces into "races." This is the process of constituting new "historical subjects" for ideological discourses—the mechanism we encountered earlier, of forming new interpellative structures. It produces, as the natural and given "authors" of a spontaneous form of racial perception, the naturalized "racist subject." This is not an external function, operative only against those whom it disposes or disarticulates (renders silent). It is also pertinent for the dominated subjects—those subordinated ethnic groups or "races" which live their relation to their real conditions of existence, and to the domination of the dominant classes, in and through the imaginary representations of a racist interpellation, and who come to experience themselves as "the inferiors," *les autres*. And yet these processes are themselves never exempted from the ideological class struggle. The racist interpellations can become themselves the sites and stake in the ideological struggle, occupied and redefined to become the elementary forms of an oppositional formation—as where "white racism" is vigorously contested through the symbolic inversions of "black power." The ideologies of racism remain contradictory structures, which can function both as the vehicles for the imposition of dominant ideologies, and as the elementary forms for the cultures of resistance. Any attempt to delineate the politics and ideologies of racism which omit these continuing features of struggle and contradiction win an apparent adequacy of explanation only by operating a disabling reductionism.

In this field of inquiry, "sociological theory" has still to find its way, by a difficult effort of theoretical clarification, through the Scylla of a reductionism which must deny almost everything in order to explain something, and the Charybdis of a pluralism which is so mesmerized by "everything" that it cannot explain anything. To those willing to labour on, the vocation remains an open one.

NOTE

This essay first appeared as "Race, Articulation and Societies Structured in Dominance," in *Sociological Theories: Race and Colonialism* (Paris: UNESCO, 1980), 305–45.

REFERENCES

Alavi, Hamza. 1975. "India and the Colonial Mode of Production." *Socialist Register* 12.
Althusser, Louis. 1969. *For Marx*. London: Allen Lane.
Althusser, Louis. 1971. *Lenin and Philosophy and Other Essays*. London: New Left Books.
Althusser, Louis. 1976. *Essays in Self-Criticism*. London: New Left Books.
Althusser, Louis, and Étienne Balibar. 1970. *Reading Capital*. London: New Left Books.
Anderson, Perry. 1976. "The Antinomies of Antonio Gramsci." *New Left Review*, no. 100.
Banaji, Jarius. 1977. "Modes of Production in a Materialist Conception of History." *Capital and Class* 1, no. 3 (October): 1–44.
Barthes, Roland. 1967. *Elements of Semiology*. London: Cape Editions.
Beechey, Veronica. 1978. "The Ideology of Racism." DPhil diss., Oxford University.
Bettelheim, Charles. 1972. "Theoretical Comments." In *Unequal Exchange: A Study of the Imperialism of Trade*, by Arghiri Emmanuel, 271–322. New York: Monthly Review Books.
Bradby, Barbara. 1975. "The Destruction of the Natural Economy." *Economy and Society* 4, no. 2: 127–61.
Braverman, Harry. 1975. *Labor and Monopoly Capital*. New York: Monthly Review Books.
Carchedi, Guglielmo. 1977. *On the Economic Identification of Social Classes*. London: Routledge and Kegan Paul.
Castles, Stephen, and Godula Kosack. 1973. *Immigrant Workers and Class Structure in Western Europe*. London: Oxford University Press.
Clammer, John. 1975. "Economic Anthropology and the Sociology of Development." In *Beyond the Sociology of Development: Economy and Society in Latin America and Africa*, edited by Ivar Oxall, Tony Barnett, and David Booth, 208–28. London: Routledge and Kegan Paul.
Cox, Oliver. 1970. *Caste, Class and Race: A Study in Social Dynamics*. New York: Monthly Review Books.

Cutler, Antony, et al. 1977. *Marx's "Capital" and Capitalism Today*. Vol. 1. London: Routledge and Kegan Paul.

Davis, David Brion. 1966. *The Problem of Slavery in Western Culture*. Ithaca, NY: Cornell University Press.

Davis, David Brion. 1969. "The Comparative Approach to American History: Slavery." In *Slavery in the New World*, edited by Eugene Genovese and Laura Foner. Englewood Cliffs, NJ: Prentice Hall.

Finley, Moses. 1969. "The Idea of Slavery." In *Slavery in the New World*, edited by Eugene Genovese and Laura Foner. Englewood Cliffs, NJ: Prentice Hall.

Fogel, Robert, and Stanley Engerman. 1974. *Time on the Cross: The Economics of American Negro Slavery*. Boston: Little, Brown and Company.

Foster-Carter, Aidan. 1978. "The Modes of Production Controversy." *New Left Review*, no. 107: 47–77.

Frank, Andre Gunder. 1969. *Capitalism and Underdevelopment in Latin America*. New York: Monthly Review Books.

Genovese, Eugene. 1965. *The Political Economy of Slavery: Studies in the Economy and Society of the Slave South*. New York: Vintage.

Genovese, Eugene. 1969. *The World the Slaveholders Made: Two Essays in Interpretation*. New York: Pantheon.

Genovese, Eugene. 1971. *In Red and Black: Marxian Explorations in Southern and Afro-American History*. Knoxville: University of Tennessee Press.

Gramsci, Antonio. 1971. *Selections from the Prison Notebooks*. Edited by Geoffrey Nowell-Smith and Quintin Hoare. London: Lawrence and Wishart.

Hall, Stuart. 1974. "Marx's Notes on Method: A 'Reading' of the 1857 Introduction to the *Grundrisse*." *Working Papers in Cultural Studies* 6. Birmingham: Centre for Contemporary Cultural Studies, University of Birmingham.

Hall, Stuart. 1977. "Pluralism, Race and Class in Caribbean Society." In *Race and Class in Post-colonial Society: A Study of Ethnic Group Relations in the English-Speaking Caribbean, Bolivia, Chile and Mexico*. Paris: UNESCO.

Hall, Stuart, Chas Critcher, Tony Jefferson, John Clarke, and Brian Roberts. 1978. *Policing the Crisis: "Mugging," the State and Law and Order*. London: Macmillan.

Hall, Stuart, Bob Lumley, and Gregor McLennan. 1977. "Politics and Ideology: Gramsci." *Working Papers in Cultural Studies* 10.

Hilton, Rodney, ed. 1976. *The Transition from Feudalism to Capitalism*. London: New Left Books.

Hindess, Barry, and Paul Hirst. 1975. *Pre-capitalist Modes of Production*. London: Routledge and Kegan Paul.

Hindess, Barry, and Paul Hirst. 1977. *Modes of Production and Social Formation: An Autocritique of "Pre-capitalist Modes of Production"*. London: Macmillan.

Hirst, Paul. 1976. "Althusser and the Theory of Ideology." *Economy and Society* 5, no. 4: 385–412.

Johnson, Richard. 1978. Unpublished mimeographed papers, Centre for Contemporary Cultural Studies, University of Birmingham.

Johnson, Richard, Gregor McLennan, and Bill Schwarz. 1978. "Three Approaches to Marxist History." Occasional Paper 50. Centre for Contemporary Cultural Studies, University of Birmingham.

Kuper, Leo. 1974. *Race, Class and Power*. London: Duckworth.

Laclau, Ernesto. 1977. *Politics and Ideology in Marxist Theory*. London: New Left Books.

Lenin, V. I. 1932. *Letters from Afar*. New York: International Publishers.

Marx, Karl. 1956. *Capital*. Vol. 2. London: Lawrence and Wishart.

Marx, Karl. 1961. *Capital*. Vol. 1. Moscow: Foreign Languages Publishing House.

Marx, Karl. 1964. *Precapitalist Economic Formations*. Edited by Eric Hobsbawm. London: Lawrence and Wishart.

Marx, Karl. 1973. "1857 Introduction to the *Grundrisse*." London: Penguin.

Marx, Karl. 1974. *Capital*. Vol. 3. London: Lawrence and Wishart.

Marx, Karl, and Friedrich Engels. 1967. *The Communist Manifesto*. New York: Penguin Books.

McLennan, Gregor. 1976. "Some Problems in British Marxist Historiography." Centre for Contemporary Cultural Studies, University of Birmingham.

Meillassoux, Claude. 1960. "Essai d'interpretation du phénomène economique dans les sociétés traditionnelles d'auto-subsistence." *Cahiers d'études africaines* 4.

Meillassoux, Claude. 1972. "From Production to Reproduction." *Economy and Society* 1, no. 1: 93–105.

Meillassoux, Claude. 1974. "Imperialism as a Mode of Reproduction of Labour Power." Unpublished seminar paper.

Mouffe, Chantal. 1979. "Introduction: Gramsci Today." In *Gramsci and Marxist Theory*, edited by Chantal Mouffe, 1–18. London: Routledge and Kegan Paul.

Myrdal, Gunnar. 1962. *An American Dilemma: The Negro Problem and Modern Democracy*. New York: Harper and Row.

O'Brien, Philip J. 1975. "A Critique of Latin-American Dependency Theories." In *Beyond the Sociology of Development: Economy and Society in Latin America and Africa*, edited by Ivar Oxall, Tony Barnett, and David Booth, 7–27. London: Routledge and Kegan Paul.

O'Shea, Alan. 1978. "A Critique of Laclau's Theory of Interpellation." Mimeograph. Centre for Contemporary Cultural Studies, University of Birmingham.

Post, Ken. 1978. *Arise, Ye Starvelings: The Jamaican Labour Rebellion of 1938 and Its Aftermath*. New York: Springer.

Poulantzas, Nicos. 1973. *Political Power and Social Classes*. London: New Left Books.

Rex, John. 1970. *Race Relations in Sociological Theory*. London: Weidenfeld and Nicolson.

Rex, John. 1973. *Race, Colonialism and the City*. London: Routledge and Kegan Paul.

Rex, John. 1977. "New Nations and Ethnic Minorities." In *Race and Class in Postcolonial Society: A Study of Ethnic Group Relations in the English-Speaking Caribbean, Bolivia, Chile and Mexico*. Paris: UNESCO.

Rey, Pierre-Philippe. 1971. *Colonialisme, néo-colonialisme, et transition au capitalisme*. Paris: Maspero.

Rey, Pierre-Philippe. 1973. *Les alliances de classes*. Paris: Maspero.

Rey, Pierre-Philippe. 1975. "Power, Descent and Reproduction: Reflections on the 'Lineage Mode of Production' in Chinese Society." *Critique of Anthropology* 1, no. 3.

Rey, Pierre-Philippe, and Georges Dupré. 1973. "Reflections on the Pertinence of a Theory of Exchange." *Economy and Society* 2, no. 2: 131–63.

Rose, Stephen, John Hambley, and Jeff Haywood. 1973. "Science, Racism and Ideology." *Socialist Register* 10.

Schwarz, Bill. 1978. "On Maurice Dobb." In *Economy, History, Concept*, by Richard Johnson, Gregor McLennan, and Bill Schwarz. Centre for Contemporary Cultural Studies, University of Birmingham, Occasional Paper 50.

Seddon, J. D., ed. 1978. "Introduction." *Relations of Production*. London: Cass.

Smith, M. G. 1965. *The Plural Society in the British West Indies*. Berkeley: University of California Press.

Terray, Emmanuel. 1972. *Marxism and "Primitive Societies"*. New York: Monthly Review Books.

van den Berghe, P. L. 1965. *South Africa: A Study in Conflict*. Middletown, CT: Wesleyan University Press.

Williams, Eric. 1944. *Capitalism and Slavery*. Chapel Hill: University of North Carolina Press.

Wolpe, Harold. 1972. "Capitalism and Cheap Labour in South Africa." *Economy and Society* 1, no. 4: 425–56.

Wolpe, Harold. 1975. "The Theory of Internal Colonialism." In *Beyond the Sociology of Development: Economy and Society in Latin America and Africa*, edited by Ivar Oxall, Tony Barnett, and David Booth, 229–52. London: Routledge and Kegan Paul.

Wolpe, Harold. 1976. "The White Working Class in South Africa." *Economy and Society* 5, no. 2: 197–240.

Wolpe, Harold, ed. 1980. *The Articulation of Modes of Production: Essays from Economy and Society*. London: Routledge and Kegan Paul.

Woodward, C. Vann. 1957. *The Strange Career of Jim Crow*. New York: Oxford University Press.

CHAPTER 12

New Ethnicities

I have centred my remarks on an attempt to identify and characterise a significant shift that has been going on (and is still going on) in black cultural politics. This shift is not definitive, in the sense that there are two clearly discernible phases—one in the past which is now over and the new one which is beginning—which we can neatly counterpose to one another. Rather, they are two phases of the same movement, which constantly overlap and interweave. Both are framed by the same historical conjuncture and both are rooted in the politics of antiracism and the postwar black experience in Britain. Nevertheless, I think we can identify two different "moments" and that the difference between them is significant.

It is difficult to characterise these precisely, but I would say that the first moment was grounded in a particular political and cultural analysis. Politically, this is the moment when the term "black" was coined as a way of referencing the common experience of racism and marginalization in Britain and came to provide the organizing category of a new politics of resistance, amongst groups and communities with, in fact, very different histories, traditions and ethnic identities. In this moment, politically speaking, "the black experience," as a singular and unifying framework based on the building up of identity across ethnic and cultural difference between the different communities, became "hegemonic" over other ethnic/racial identities—though the latter did not, of course, disappear. Culturally, this analysis formulated itself in terms of a critique of the way blacks were positioned as the unspoken and invisible "other" of predominantly white aesthetic and cultural discourses.

This analysis was predicated on the marginalisation of the black experience in British culture; not fortuitously occurring at the margins, but placed, positioned at the margins, as the consequence of a set of quite specific political and cultural practices which regulated, governed and "normalized" the representational and discursive spaces of English society. These formed the conditions of existence of a cultural politics designed to challenge, resist and, where possible, to transform the dominant regimes of representation—first in music and style, later in literary, visual and cinematic forms. In these spaces blacks have typically been the objects, but rarely the subjects, of the practices of representation. The struggle to come into representation was predicated on a critique of the degree of fetishisation, objectification and negative figuration which are so much a feature of the representation of the black subject. There was a concern not simply with the absence or marginality of the black experience but with its simplification and its stereotypical character.

The cultural politics and strategies which developed around this critique had many facets, but its two principal objects were: first the question of *access* to the rights to representation by black artists and black cultural workers themselves. Secondly, the contestation of the marginality, the stereotypical quality and the fetishised nature of images of blacks, by the counter-position of a "positive" black imagery. These strategies were principally addressed to changing what I would call the "relations of representation."

I have a distinct sense that in the recent period we are entering a new phase. But we need to be absolutely clear what we mean by a "new" phase because, as soon as you talk of a new phase, people instantly imagine that what is entailed is the *substitution* of one kind of politics for another. I am quite distinctly not talking about a shift in those terms. Politics does not necessarily proceed by way of a set of oppositions and reversals of this kind, though some groups and individuals are anxious to "stage" the question in this way. The original critique of the predominant relations of race and representation and the politics which have developed around it have not disappeared and cannot possibly disappear while the conditions which gave rise to it—cultural racism in its Dewesbury form—not only persists but positively flourishes under Thatcherism.[1] There is no sense in which a new phase in black cultural politics could replace the earlier one. Nevertheless, it is true that as the struggle moves forward and assumes new forms, it does to some degree *displace*, reorganise and reposition the different cultural strategies in relation to one another. If this can be conceived in terms of the "burden of representation," I would put the point in this form: that black artists and cultural workers now have to struggle, not on one, but on *two* fronts. The problem is, how to characterize this shift—if indeed, we agree that such a shift has taken or is taking place—and if the language of binary oppositions and substitutions will no longer suffice. The characterization that I would offer is tentative, proposed in the context of this essay mainly to try and clarify some of the issues involved, rather than to preempt them.

This shift is best thought of in terms of change from a struggle over the relations of representation to a politics of representation itself. It would be useful to separate out such a "politics of representation" into its different elements. We all now use the word "representation," but, as we know, it is an extremely slippery customer. It can be used, on the one hand, simply as another way of talking about how one imagines a reality that exists "outside" the means by which things are represented: a conception grounded in a mimetic theory of representation. On the other hand the term can also stand for a very radical displacement of that unproblematic notion of the concept of representation. My own view is that events, relations, structures do have conditions of existence and real effects, outside the sphere of the discursive; but that only within the discursive, and subject to its specific conditions, limits and modalities, do they have or can they be constructed within meaning. Thus, while not wanting to expand the territorial claims of the discursive infinitely, how things are represented and the "machineries" and regimes of representation in a culture do play a *constitutive* and not merely a reflexive, after-the-event role. This gives questions of culture and ideology, and the scenarios of representation—subjectivity, identity, politics—a formative, not merely an expressive, place in the constitution of social and political life. I think it is the move towards this second sense of representation which is taking place and which is transforming the politics of representation in black culture.

This is a complex issue. First, it is the effect of a theoretical encounter between black cultural politics and the discourses of a Eurocentric, largely white, critical cultural theory which, in recent years, has focussed so much analysis of the politics of representation. This is always an extremely difficult, if not dangerous, encounter. (I think particularly of black people encountering the discourses of poststructuralism, postmodernism, psychoanalysis and feminism). Secondly, it marks what I can only call "the end of innocence," or the end of the innocent notion of the essential black subject. Here again, the end of the essential black subject is something which people are increasingly debating, but they may not have fully reckoned with its political consequences. What is at issue here is the recognition of the extraordinary diversity of subjective positions, social experiences and cultural identities which compose the category "black"; that is, the recognition that "black" is essentially a politically and culturally *constructed* category, which cannot be grounded in a set of fixed transcultural or transcendental racial categories and which therefore has no guarantees in Nature. What this brings into play is the recognition of the immense diversity and differentiation of the historical and cultural experience of black subjects. This inevitably entails a weakening or fading of the notion that "race" or some composite notion of race around the term "black" will either guarantee the effectivity of any cultural practice or determine in any final sense its aesthetic value.

We should put this as plainly as possible. Films are not necessarily good because black people make them. They are not necessarily "right-on" by virtue of the fact that they deal with the black experience. Once you enter the politics of the end of the essential black subject you are plunged headlong into the maelstrom of a continuously contingent, unguaranteed political argument and debate: a critical politics, a politics of criticism. You can no longer conduct black politics through the strategy of a simple set of reversals, putting in the place of the bad old essential white subject, the new essentially good black subject. Now, that formulation may seem to threaten the collapse of an entire political world. Alternatively, it may be greeted with extraordinary relief at the passing away of what at one time seemed to be a necessary fiction: namely, either that all black people are good or indeed that all black people are *the same*. After all, it is one of the predicates of racism that "you can't tell the difference because they all look the same." This does not make it any easier to conceive of how a politics can be constructed which works with and through difference, which is able to build those forms of solidarity and identification which make common struggle and resistance possible but without suppressing the real heterogeneity of interests and identities, and which can effectively draw the political boundary lines without which political contestation is impossible, without fixing those boundaries for eternity. It entails the movement in black politics, from what Gramsci called the "war of manoeuvre" to the "war of position"—the struggle around positionalities. But the difficulty of conceptualizing such a politics (and the temptation to slip into a sort of endlessly sliding discursive liberal-pluralism) does not absolve us of the task of developing such a politics.

The end of the essential black subject also entails a recognition that the central issues of race always appear historically in articulation, in a formation, with other categories and divisions and are constantly crossed and recrossed by the categories of class, gender and ethnicity. (I make a distinction here between race and ethnicity to which I shall return.) To me, films like *Territories, Passion of Remembrance, My Beautiful Laundrette* and *Sammy and Rosie Get Laid*, for example, make it perfectly clear that this shift has been engaged; and that the question of the black subject cannot be represented without reference to the dimensions of class, gender, sexuality and ethnicity.

Difference and Contestation

A further consequence of this politics of representation is the slow recognition of the deep ambivalence of identification and desire. We think about identification usually as a simple process, structured around fixed "selves" which we either are or are not. The play of identity and difference which constructs racism is powered not only by the positioning of blacks as the inferior species but also, and at the same time, by an inexpressible envy and desire; and this is something the recognition of which fundamentally *displaces* many of our hitherto stable political categories, since it implies a process of identification and otherness which is more complex than we had hitherto imagined.

Racism, of course, operates by constructing impassable symbolic boundaries between racially constituted categories, and its typically binary system of representation constantly marks and attempts to fix and naturalize the difference between belongingness and otherness. Along this frontier there arises what Gayatri Spivak (1987) calls the "epistemic violence" of the discourses of the Other—of imperialism, the colonized, orientalism, the exotic, the primitive, the anthropological and the folklore. Consequently the discourse of antiracism had often been founded on a strategy of reversal and inversion, turning the "Manichean aesthetic" of colonial discourse upside down. However, as Fanon constantly reminded us, the epistemic violence is both outside and inside, and operates by a process of splitting on both sides of the division—in here as well as out here. That is why it is a question, not only of "black-skin, white-skin," but of "black skin, white masks"—the internalisation of the self-as-other. Just as masculinity always constructs femininity as double—simultaneously Madonna and Whore—so racism constructs the black subject: noble savage and violent avenger. And in the doubling, fear and desire double for one another and play across the structure of otherness, complicating its politics.

Recently I've read several articles about the photographic text of Robert Mapplethorpe—especially his inscription of the nude, black male—all written by black critics or cultural practitioners (Mercer 1987; Bailey 1986). These essays properly begin by identifying in Mapplethorpe's work the tropes of fetishisation, the fragmentation of the black image and its objectification, as the forms of their appropriation within the white, gay gaze. But, as I read, I know that something else is going on as well in both the production and the reading of those texts. The continuous circling around Mapplethorpe's work is not exhausted by being able to place him as the white fetishistic gay photographer; and this is because it is also marked by the surreptitious return of desire—that deep ambivalence of identification which makes the categories in which we have previously thought and argued about black cultural politics and the black cultural text extremely problematic. This brings to the surface the unwelcome fact that a great deal of black politics, constructed, addressed and developed directly in relation to questions of race and ethnicity, has been predicated on the assumption that the categories of gender and sexuality would stay the same and remain fixed and secured. What the new politics of representation does is to put that into question, crossing the questions of racism irrevocably with questions of sexuality. That is what is so disturbing, finally, to many of our settled political habits about *Passion of Remembrance*. This double fracturing entails a different kind of politics because, as we know, black radical politics has frequently been stabilised around particular conceptions of black masculinity, which are only now being put into question by black women and black gay men. At certain points, black politics has also been underpinned by a deep absence or more typically an evasive silence with reference to class.

Another element inscribed in the new politics of representation has to do with the question of ethnicity. I am familiar with all the dangers of "ethnicity" as a concept and have written myself about the fact that ethnicity, in the form of a culturally constructed sense of Englishness and a particularly closed, exclusive and regressive form of English national identity, is one of the core characteristics of British racism today (Hall 1978). I am also well aware that the politics of antiracism has often constructed itself in terms of a contestation of "multi-ethnicity" or "multi-culturalism." On the other hand, as the politics of representation around the black subject shifts, I think we will begin to see a renewed contestation over the meaning of the term "ethnicity" itself.

If the black subject and black experience are not stabilised by Nature or by some other essential guarantee, then it must be the case that they are constructed historically, culturally, politically—and the concept which refers to this is "ethnicity." The term "ethnicity" acknowledges the place of history, language and culture in the construction of subjectivity and identity, as well as the fact that all discourse is placed, positioned, situated, and all knowledge is contextual. Representation is possible only because enunciation is always produced within codes which have a history, a position within the discursive formations of a particular space and time. The displacement of the "centred" discourses of the West entails putting in question its universalist character and its transcendental claims to speak for everyone, while being itself everywhere and nowhere. The fact that this grounding of ethnicity in difference was deployed, in the discourse of racism, as a means of disavowing the realities of racism and repression does not mean that we can permit the term to be permanently colonized. That appropriation will have to be contested, the term disarticulated from its position in the discourse of "multi-culturalism" and transcoded, just as we previously had to recuperate the term "black," from its place in a system of negative equivalences. The new politics of representation therefore also sets in motion an ideological contestation around the term "ethnicity." But in order to pursue that movement further, we will have to retheorise the concept of difference.

It seems to me that, in the various practices and discourses of black cultural production, we are beginning to see constructions of just such a new conception of ethnicity: a new cultural politics which engages rather than suppresses *difference* and which depends, in part, on the cultural construction of new ethnic identities. Difference, like representation, is also a slippery, and therefore contested concept. There is the "difference" which makes a radical and unbridgeable separation: and there is a "difference" which is positional, conditional and conjunctural, closer to Derrida's notion of *différance*, though if we are concerned to maintain a politics it cannot be defined exclusively in terms of an infinite sliding of the signifier. We still have a great deal of work to do to *decouple* ethnicity, as it functions in the dominant discourse, from its equivalence with nationalism, imperialism, racism and the state, which are the points of attachment around which a distinctive British or, more accurately, English ethnicity have been constructed. Nevertheless, I think such a project is not only possible but necessary. Indeed, this decoupling of ethnicity from the violence of the state is implicit in some of the new forms of cultural practice that are going on in films like *Passion* and *Handsworth Songs*. We are beginning to think about how to represent a noncoercive and a more diverse conception of ethnicity, to set against the embattled, hegemonic conception of "Englishness" which, under Thatcherism, stabilizes so much of the dominant political and cultural discourses, and which, because it is hegemonic, does not represent itself as an ethnicity at all.

This marks a real shift in the point of contestation, since it is no longer only between antiracism and multiculturalism but *inside* the notion of ethnicity itself. What is involved is the splitting of the notion of ethnicity between, on the one hand, the dominant notion which connects it to nation and "race" and, on the other hand, what I think is the beginning of a positive conception of the ethnicity of the margins, of the periphery. That is to say, a recognition that we all speak from a particular place, out of a particular history, out of a particular experience, a particular culture, without being contained by that position as "ethnic artists" or film-makers. We are all, in that sense, *ethnically* located and our ethnic identities are crucial to our subjective sense of who we are. But this is also a recognition that this is not an ethnicity which is doomed to survive, as Englishness was, only by marginalising, dispossessing, displacing and forgetting other ethnicities. This precisely is the politics of ethnicity predicated on difference and diversity.

The final point which I think is entailed in this new politics of representation has to do with an awareness of the black experience as a *diaspora* experience, and the consequences which this carries for the process of unsettling, recombination, hybridisation and "cut-and-mix"—in short, the process of cultural *diaspora-isation* (to coin an ugly term) which it implies. In the case of the young black British films and film-makers under discussion, the diaspora experience is certainly profoundly fed and nourished by, for example, the emergence of Third World cinema; by the African experience; the connection with Afro-Caribbean experience; and the deep inheritance of complex systems of representation and aesthetic traditions from Asian and African culture. But, in spite of these rich cultural "roots," the new cultural politics is operating on new and quite distinct ground—specifically, contestation over what it means to be "British." The relation of this cultural politics to the past, to its different "roots," is profound, but complex. It cannot be simple or unmediated. It is (as a film like *Dreaming Rivers* reminds us) complexly mediated and transformed by memory, fantasy and desire. Or, as even an explicitly political film like *Handsworth Songs* clearly suggests, the relation is inter-textual—mediated through a variety of other "texts." There can, therefore, be no simple "return" or "recovery" of the ancestral past which is not re-experienced through the categories of the present: no base for creative enunciation in a simple reproduction of traditional forms which are not transformed by the technologies and the identities of the present. This is something that was signalled as early as a film like *Blacks Britannica* and as recently as Paul Gilroy's important book *There Ain't No Black in the Union Jack* (1988). Fifteen years ago we didn't care, or at least I didn't care, whether there was any black in the Union Jack. Now not only do we care, we must.

This last point suggests that we are also approaching what I would call the end of a certain critical innocence in black cultural politics. And here, it might be appropriate to refer, glancingly, to the debate between Salman Rushdie and myself in *The Guardian* some months ago (Rushdie 1987; Hall 1987). The debate was not about whether *Handsworth Songs* or *The Passion of Remembrance* were great films or not, because, in the light of what I have said, once you enter this particular problematic, the question of what good films are, which parts of them are good and why, is open to the politics of criticism. Once you abandon essential categories, there is no place to go apart from the politics of criticism and to enter the politics of criticism in black culture is to grow up, to leave the age of critical innocence.

It was not Salman Rushdie's particular judgement that I was contesting, so much as the mode in which he addressed them. He seemed to me to be addressing the films as if from the stable, well-established critical criteria of a *Guardian* reviewer. I was trying, perhaps unsuccessfully, to say that I thought this an inadequate basis for a political criticism and one which overlooked precisely the signs of innovation, and the constraints, under which these film-makers were operating. It is difficult to define what an alternative mode of address would be. I certainly didn't want Salman Rushdie to say he thought the films were good because they were black. But I also didn't want him to say that he thought they weren't good because "we creative artists all know what good films are," since I no longer believe we can resolve the questions of aesthetic value by the use of these transcendental, canonical cultural categories. I think there *is* another position, one which locates itself *inside* a continuous struggle and politics around black representation, but which then is able to open up a continuous critical discourse about themes, about the forms of representation, the subjects of representation, above all, the regimes of representation. I thought it was important, at that point, to intervene to try and get that mode of critical address right, in relation to the new black film-making.

It is extremely tricky, as I know, because as it happens, in intervening, I got the mode of address wrong too! I failed to communicate the fact that, in relation to his *Guardian* article, I thought Salman was hopelessly wrong about *Handsworth Songs*, which does not in any way diminish my judgement about the stature of *Midnight's Children*. I regret that I couldn't get it right, exactly, because the politics of criticism has to be able to get both things right.

Such a politics of criticism has to be able to say (just to give one example) why *My Beautiful Laundrette* is one of the most riveting and important films produced by a black writer in recent years and precisely for the reason that made it so controversial: its refusal to represent the black experience in Britain as monolithic, self-contained, sexually stabilised and always "right-on"—in a word, always and only "positive," or what Hanif Kureishi (1985) has called "cheering fictions":

> the writer as public relations officer, as hired liar. If there is to be a serious attempt to understand Britain today, with its mix of races and colours, its hysteria and despair, then, writing about it has to be complex. It can't apologise or idealise. It can't sentimentalise and it can't represent only one group as having a monopoly on virtue.

Laundrette is important particularly in terms of its control, of knowing what it is doing, as the text crosses those frontiers between gender, race, ethnicity, sexuality and class. *Sammy and Rosie* is also a bold and adventurous film, though in some ways less coherent, not so sure of where it is going, overdriven by an almost uncontrollable, cool anger. One needs to be able to offer that as a critical judgement and to argue it through, to have one's mind changed, without undermining one's essential commitment to the project of the politics of black representation.

NOTES

This essay was originally printed as "New Ethnicities," in *ICA Documents, 7, Black Film, British Cinema*, edited by Kobena Mercer (London: Institute of Contemporary Arts, 1988), 27–31.

1 The Yorkshire town of Dewesbury became the focus of national attention when white parents withdrew their children from a local school with predominantly Asian pupils, on the grounds that "English" culture was no longer taught on the curriculum. The contestation of multicultural education from the Right also underpinned the controversies around Bradford headmaster Ray Honeyford. See Gordon 1987.

REFERENCES

Bailey, David A., ed. 1986. "Black Experiences." *Ten.8* 22.
Gilroy, Paul. 1988. *There Ain't No Black in the Union Jack: The Cultural Politics of Race and Nation*. London: Hutchinson.
Gordon, Paul. 1987. "The New Right, Race and Education." *Race and Class* 29, no. 3 (Winter).
Hall, Stuart. 1978. "Racism and Reaction." In *Five Views on Multi-racial Britain*. London: Commission for Racial Equality.
Hall, Stuart. 1987. "Songs of *Handsworth* Praise." *Guardian*, 15 January.
Kureishi, Hanif. 1985. "Dirty Washing." *Time Out*, 14–20 November.
Mercer, Kobena. 1987. "Imaging the Black Man's Sex." In *Photography/Politics: Two*, edited by Patricia Holland, Jo Spence, and Simon Watney. London: Comedia.
Rushdie, Salman. 1987. "*Songs* Doesn't Know the Score." *Guardian*, 12 January.
Spivak, Gayatri C. 1987. *In Other Worlds: Essays in Cultural Politics*. London: Methuen.

CHAPTER 13

Cultural Identity and Diaspora

A new cinema of the Caribbean is emerging, joining the company of the other "Third Cinemas." It is related to, but different from, the vibrant film and other forms of visual representation of the Afro-Caribbean (and Asian) "blacks" of the diasporas of the West, the new postcolonial subjects. All these cultural practices and forms of representation have the black subject at their centre, putting the issue of cultural identity in question. Who is this emergent, new subject of the cinema? From where does he/she speak? Practices of representation always implicate the positions from which we speak or write—the positions of *enunciation*. What recent theories of enunciation suggest is that, though we speak, so to say, "in our own name," of ourselves and from our own experience, nevertheless who speaks, and the subject who is spoken of, are never identical, never exactly in the same place. Identity is not as transparent or unproblematic as we think. Perhaps instead of thinking of identity as an already accomplished fact, which the new cultural practices then represent, we should think, instead, of identity as a "production," which is never complete, always in process, and always constituted within, not outside, representation. This view problematises the very authority and authenticity to which the term "cultural identity" lays claim.

We seek, here, to open a dialogue, an investigation, on the subject of cultural identity and representation. Of course, the "I" who writes here must also be thought of as, itself, "enunciated." We all write and speak from a particular place and time, from a history and a culture—which is specific. What we say is always "in context," *positioned*. I was born into and spent my childhood and adolescence in a lower-middle-class family in Jamaica, I have lived all my adult life in England, in the shadow of the black diaspora—"in the belly of the beast." I write against the background of a lifetime's work in cultural studies. If the paper seems preoccupied with the diaspora experience and its narratives of displacement, it is worth remembering that all discourse is "placed," and the heart has its reasons.

There are at least two different ways of thinking about "cultural identity." The first position defines "cultural identity" in terms of one, shared culture, a sort of collective "one true self," hiding inside the many other, more superficial or artificially imposed "selves," which people with a shared history and ancestry hold in common. Within the terms of this definition, our cultural identities reflect the common historical experiences and shared cultural codes which provide us, as "one people," with stable, unchanging and continuous frames of reference and meaning, beneath the shifting divisions and vicissitudes of our actual history. This "oneness," underlying all the other, more superficial differences, is the truth, the essence, of "Caribbeanness," of the black experience. It is this identity which a Caribbean or black diaspora must discover, excavate, bring to light and express through cinematic representation.

Such a conception of cultural identity played a critical role in all the postcolonial struggles which have so profoundly reshaped our world. It lay at the centre of the vision of the poets of "Negritude," like Aimé Césaire and Léopold Senghor, and of the Pan-African political project, earlier in the century. It continues to be a very powerful and creative force in emergent forms of representation amongst hitherto marginalised peoples. In postcolonial societies, the rediscovery of this identity is often the object of what Frantz Fanon once called a "passionate research . . . directed by the secret hope of discovering beyond the misery of today, beyond self-contempt, resignation and abjuration, some very beautiful and splendid era whose existence rehabilitates us both in regard to ourselves and in regard to others." New forms of cultural practice in these societies address themselves to this project for the very good reason that, as Fanon puts it, in the recent past, "colonisation is not satisfied merely with holding a people in its grip and emptying the native's brain of all form and content. By a kind of perverted logic, it turns to the past of oppressed people, and distorts, disfigures and destroys it" (1963, 170).

The question which Fanon's observation poses is, What is the nature of this "profound research" which drives the new forms of visual and cinematic representation? Is it only a matter of unearthing that which the colonial experience buried and overlaid, bringing to light the hidden continuities it suppressed? Or is a quite different practice entailed—not the rediscovery but the *production* of identity? Not an identity grounded in the archaeology, but in the *retelling* of the past?

We should not, for a moment, underestimate or neglect the importance of the act of imaginative rediscovery which this conception of a rediscovered, essential identity entails. "Hidden histories" have played a critical role in the emergence of many of the most important social movements of our time—feminist, anticolonial and antiracist. The photographic work of a generation of Jamaican and Rastafarian artists, or of a visual artist like Armet Francis (a Jamaican-born photographer who has lived in Britain since the age of eight), is a testimony to the continuing creative power of this conception of identity within the emerging practices of representation. Francis's photographs of the peoples of the Black Triangle, taken in Africa, the Caribbean, the USA and the UK, attempt to reconstruct in visual terms "the underlying unity of the black people whom colonisation and slavery distributed across the African diaspora." His text is an act of imaginary reunification.

Crucially, such images offer a way of imposing an imaginary coherence on the experience of dispersal and fragmentation, which is the history of all enforced diasporas. They do this by representing or "figuring" Africa as the mother of these different civilisations. This Triangle is, after all, "centred" in Africa. Africa is the name of the missing term, the great aporia, which lies at the centre of our cultural identity and gives it a meaning which, until recently, it lacked. No one who looks at these textural images now, in the light of the history of transportation, slavery and emigration, can fail to understand how the rift of separation, the "loss of identity," which has been integral to the Caribbean experience only begins to be healed when these forgotten connections are once more set in place. Such texts restore an imaginary fullness or plenitude, to set against the broken rubric of our past. They are resources of resistance and identity, with which to confront the fragmented and pathological ways in which that experience has been reconstructed within the dominant regimes of cinematic and visual representation of the West.

There is, however, a second, related but different view of cultural identity. This second position recognises that, as well as the many points of similarity, there are also critical points of deep and significant *difference* which constitute "what we really are" or rather—since history has intervened—"what we have become." We cannot speak for very long, with any exactness, about "one experience, one identity," without acknowledging its other side—the ruptures and discontinuities which constitute, precisely, the Caribbean's "uniqueness." Cultural identity, in this second sense, is a matter of "becoming" as well as of "being." It belongs to the future as much as to the past. It is not something which already exists, transcending place, time, history and culture. Cultural identities come from somewhere, have histories. But, like everything which is historical, they undergo constant transformation. Far from being eternally fixed in some essentialised past, they are subject to the continuous "play" of history, culture and power. Far from being grounded in a mere "recovery" of the past, which is waiting to be found, and which, when found, will secure our sense of ourselves into eternity, identities are the names we give to the different ways we are positioned by, and position ourselves within, the narratives of the past.

It is only from this second position that we can properly understand the traumatic character of "the colonial experience." The ways in which black people, black experiences, were positioned and subject-ed in the dominant regimes of representation were the effects of a critical exercise of cultural power and normalisation. Not only, in Said's "Orientalist" sense, were we constructed as different and other within the categories of knowledge of the West by those regimes. They had the power to make us see and experience *ourselves* as "Other." Every regime of representation is a regime of power formed, as Foucault reminds us, by the fatal couplet "power/knowledge." But this kind of knowledge is internal, not external. It is one thing to position a subject or set of peoples as the Other of a dominant discourse. It is quite another thing to subject them to that "knowledge," not only as a matter of imposed will and domination, by the power of inner compulsion and subjective conformation to the norm. That is the lesson—the sombre majesty—of Fanon's insight into the colonising experience in *Black Skin, White Masks*.

This inner expropriation of cultural identity cripples and deforms. If its silences are not resisted, they produce, in Fanon's vivid phrase, "individuals without an anchor, without horizon, colourless, stateless, a race of angels" (1963, 176). Nevertheless, this idea of otherness as an inner compulsion changes our conception of "cultural identity." In this perspective, cultural identity is not a fixed essence at all, lying unchanged outside history and culture. It is not some universal and transcendental spirit inside us on which history has made no fundamental mark. It is not once-and-for-all. It is not a fixed origin to which we can make some final and absolute return. Of course, it is not a mere phantasm either. It is *something*—not a mere trick of the imagination. It has its histories—and histories have their real, material and symbolic effects. The past continues to speak to us. But it no longer addresses us as a simple, factual "past," since our relation to it, like the child's relation to the mother, is always-already "after the break." It is always constructed through memory, fantasy, narrative and myth. Cultural identities are the points of identification, the unstable points of identification or suture, which are made within the discourses of history and culture. Not an essence but a *positioning*. Hence, there is always a politics of identity, a politics of position, which has no absolute guarantee in an unproblematic, transcendental "law of origin."

This second view of cultural identity is much less familiar, and more unsettling. If identity does not proceed, in a straight, unbroken line, from some fixed origin, how are we to understand its formation? We might think of black Caribbean identities as "framed" by two axes or vectors, simultaneously operative: the vector of similarity and continuity; and the vector of difference and rupture. Caribbean identities always have to be thought of in terms of the dialogic relationship between these two axes. The one gives us some grounding in, some continuity with, the past. The second reminds us that what we share is precisely the experience of a profound discontinuity: the peoples dragged into slavery, transportation, colonisation, migration, came predominantly from Africa—and when that supply ended, it was temporarily refreshed by indentured labour from the Asian subcontinent. (This neglected fact explains why, when you visit Guyana or Trinidad, you see, symbolically inscribed in the faces of their peoples, the paradoxical "truth" of Christopher Columbus's mistake: you *can* find "Asia" by sailing west, if you know where to look!) In the history of the modern world, there are few more traumatic ruptures to match these enforced separations from Africa—already figured, in the European imaginary, as "the Dark Continent." But the slaves were also from different countries, tribal communities, villages, languages and gods. African religion, which has been so profoundly formative in Caribbean spiritual life, is precisely *different* from Christian monotheism in believing that God is so powerful that he can only be known through a proliferation of spiritual manifestations, present everywhere in the natural and social world. These gods live on, in an underground existence, in the hybridised religious universe of Haitian voodoo, Pocomania, Native Pentecostalism, Black baptism, Rastafarianism and the black Saints Latin American Catholicism. The paradox is that it was the uprooting of slavery and transportation and the insertion into the plantation economy (as well as the symbolic economy) of the Western world that "unified" these peoples across their differences, in the same moment as it cut them off from direct access to their past.

Difference, therefore, persists—in and alongside continuity. To return to the Caribbean after any long absence is to experience again the shock of the "doubleness" of similarity and difference. Visiting the French Caribbean for the first time, I also saw at once how different Martinique is from, say, Jamaica: and this is no mere difference of topography or climate. It is a profound difference of culture and history. And the difference *matters*. It positions Martiniquais and Jamaicans as *both* the same and different. Moreover, the boundaries of difference are continually repositioned in relation to different points of reference. Vis-à-vis the developed West, we are very much "the same." We belong to the marginal, the underdeveloped, the periphery, the "Other." We are at the outer edge, the "rim," of the metropolitan world—always "South" to someone else's *El Norte*.

At the same time we do not stand in the same relation of the "otherness" to the metropolitan centres. Each has negotiated its economic, political and cultural dependency differently. And this "difference," whether we like it or not, is already inscribed in our cultural identities. In turn, it is this negotiation of identity which makes us, vis-à-vis other Latin American people, with a very similar history, different—Caribbeans, *les Antilliennes* ("islanders" to their mainland). And yet, vis-à-vis one another, Jamaican, Haitian, Cuban, Guadeloupian, Barbadian, etc. . . .

How, then, to describe this play of "difference" within identity? The common history—transportation, slavery, colonisation—has been profoundly formative for all these societies, unifying us across our differences. But it does not constitute a common *origin*, since it was, metaphorically as well as literally, a translation. The inscription of difference is also specific and critical. I use the word "play" because the double meaning of the metaphor is important. It suggests, on the one hand, the instability, the permanent unsettlement, the lack of any final resolution. On the other hand, it reminds us that the place where this "doubleness" is most powerfully to be heard is "playing" within the varieties of Caribbean musics. This cultural "play" could not therefore be represented, cinematically, as a simple, binary opposition—"past/present," "them/us." Its complexity exceeds this binary structure of representation. At different places, times, in relation to different questions, the boundaries are re-sited. They become, not only what they have, at times, certainly been—mutually excluding categories—but also what they sometimes are, differential points along a sliding scale.

One trivial example is the way Martinique both *is* and *is not* "French." It is, of course, a *department* of France, and this is reflected in its standard and style of life. Fort de France is a much richer, more "fashionable" place than Kingston—which is not only visibly poorer, but itself at a point of transition between being "in fashion" in an Anglo-African and Afro-American way—for those who can afford to be in any sort of fashion at all. Yet, what is distinctively "Martiniquais" can only be described in terms of that special and peculiar supplement which the black and mulatto skin adds to the "refinement" and sophistication of a Parisian-derived *haute couture*: that is, a sophistication which, because it is black, is always transgressive.

To capture this sense of difference which is not pure "otherness," we need to deploy the play on words of a theorist like Jacques Derrida. Derrida uses the anomalous "a" in his way of writing "difference"—*différance*—as a marker which sets up a disturbance in our settled understanding or translation of the word/concept. It sets the word in motion to new meanings without erasing the *trace* of its other meanings. His sense of *différance*, as Christopher Norris puts it, thus

> remains suspended between the two French verbs "to differ" and "to defer" (postpone), both of which contribute to its textual force but neither of which can fully capture its meaning. Language depends on difference, as Saussure showed ... the structure of distinctive propositions which make up its basic economy. Where Derrida breaks new ground ... is in the extent to which "differ" shades into "defer" ... the idea that meaning is always deferred, perhaps to this point of an endless supplementarity, by the play of signification. (1982, 32)

This second sense of difference challenges the fixed binaries which stabilise meaning and representation and show how meaning is never finished or completed, but keeps on moving to encompass other, additional or supplementary meanings, which, as Norris puts it elsewhere, "disturb the classical economy of language and representation" (1987, 15). Without relations of difference, no representation could occur. But what is then constituted within representation is always open to being deferred, staggered, serialised.

Where, then, does identity come in to this infinite postponement of meaning? Derrida does not help us as much as he might here, though the notion of the "trace" goes some way towards it. This is where it sometimes seems as if Derrida has permitted his profound theoretical insights to be reappropriated by his disciples into a celebration of formal "playfulness," which evacuates them of their political meaning. For if signification depends upon the endless repositioning of its differential terms, meaning, in any specific instance, depends on the contingent and arbitrary stop—the necessary and temporary "break" in the infinite semiosis of language. This does not detract from the original insight. It only threatens to do so if we mistake this "cut" of identity—this *positioning*, which makes meaning possible—as a natural and permanent, rather than an arbitrary and contingent "ending"—whereas I understand every such position as "strategic" and arbitrary, in the sense that there is no permanent equivalence between the particular sentence we close, and its true meaning, as such. Meaning continues to unfold, so to speak, beyond the arbitrary closure which makes it, at any moment, possible. It is always either over- or underdetermined, either an excess or a supplement. There is always something "left over."

It is possible, with this conception of "difference," to rethink the positionings and repositionings of Caribbean cultural identities in relation to at least three "presences," to borrow Aimé Césaire's and Léopold Senghor's metaphor: *Présence Africaine, Présence Européenne*, and the third, most ambiguous, presence of all—the sliding term, *Présence Americaine*. Of course, I am collapsing, for the moment, the many other cultural "presences" which constitute the complexity of Caribbean identity (Indian, Chinese, Lebanese, etc.). I mean America, here, not in its "first-world" sense—the big cousin to the North whose "rim" we occupy, but in the second, broader sense: America, the "New World," *Terra Incognita*.

Présence Africaine is the site of the repressed. Apparently silenced beyond memory by the power of the experience of slavery, Africa was in fact present everywhere: in the everyday life and customs of the slave quarters, in the languages and patois of the plantations, in names and words, often disconnected from their taxonomies, in the secret syntactical structures through which other languages were spoken, in the stories and tales told to children, in religious practices and beliefs, in the spiritual life, the arts, crafts, musics and rhythms of slave and postemancipation society. Africa, the signified which could not be represented directly in slavery, remained and remains the unspoken, unspeakable "presence" in Caribbean culture. It is "hiding" behind every verbal inflection, every narrative twist of Caribbean cultural life. It is the secret code with which every Western text was "re-read." It is the ground-bass of every rhythm and bodily movement. *This* was—is—the "Africa" that "is alive and well in the diaspora" (Hall and Jefferson 1976).

When I was growing up in the 1940s and 1950s as a child in Kingston, I was surrounded by the signs, music and rhythms of this Africa of the diaspora, which only existed as a result of a long and discontinuous series of transformations. But, although almost everyone around me was some shade of brown or black (Africa "speaks"!), I never once heard a single person refer to themselves or to others as, in some way, or as having been at some time in the past, "African." It was only in the 1970s that this Afro-Caribbean identity became historically available to the great majority of Jamaican people, at home and abroad. In this historic moment, Jamaicans discovered themselves to be "black" just as, in the same moment, they discovered themselves to be the sons and daughters of "slavery."

This profound cultural discovery, however, was not, and could not be, made directly, without "mediation." It could only be made *through* the impact on popular life of the postcolonial revolution, the civil rights struggles, the culture of Rastafarianism and the music of reggae—the metaphors, the figures or signifiers of a new construction of "Jamaican-ness." These signified a "new" Africa of the New World, grounded in an "old" Africa:—a spiritual journey of discovery that led, in the Caribbean, to an indigenous cultural revolution; this is Africa, as we might say, necessarily "deferred"—as a spiritual, cultural and political metaphor.

It is the presence/absence of Africa, in this form, which has made it the privileged signifier of new conceptions of Caribbean identity. Everyone in the Caribbean, of whatever ethnic background, must sooner or later come to terms with this African presence. Black, brown, mulatto, white—all must look *Présence Africaine* in the face, speak its name. But whether it is, in this sense, an *origin* of our identities, unchanged by four hundred years of displacement, dismemberment, transportation, to which we could in any final or literal sense return, is more open to doubt. The original "Africa" is no longer there. It too has been transformed. History is, in that sense, irreversible. We must not collude with the West which, precisely, normalises and appropriates Africa by freezing it into some timeless zone of the primitive, unchanging past. Africa must at last be reckoned with by Caribbean people, but it cannot in any simple sense be merely recovered.

It belongs irrevocably, for us, to what Edward Said once called an "imaginative geography and history," which helps "the mind to intensify its own sense of itself by dramatising the difference between what is close to it and what is far away" (1985, 55). It "has acquired an imaginative or figurative value we can name and feel" (Said 1985, 55). Our belongingness to it constitutes what Benedict Anderson (1982) calls "an imagined community." To *this* "Africa," which is a necessary part of the Caribbean imaginary, we can't literally go home again.

The character of this displaced "homeward" journey—its length and complexity—comes across vividly, in a variety of texts. Tony Sewell's documentary archival photographs, *Garvey's Children: The Legacy of Marcus Garvey*, tells the story of a "return" to an African identity which went, necessarily, by the long route—through London and the United States. It "ends," not in Ethiopia, but with Garvey's statue in front of the St. Ann Parish Library in Jamaica: not with a traditional tribal chant but with the music of Burning Spear and Bob Marley's Redemption Song. This is our "long journey" home. Derek Bishton's courageous visual and written text *Black Heart Man*—the story of the journey of a *white* photographer "on the trail of the promised land"—starts in England, and goes through Shashemene, the place in Ethiopia to which many Jamaican people have found their way on their search for the Promised Land, and slavery; but it ends in Pinnacle, Jamaica, where the first Rastafarian settlement was established, and "beyond"—among the dispossessed of twentieth-century Kingston and the streets of Handsworth, where Bishton's voyage of discovery first began. These symbolic journeys are necessary for us all—and necessarily circular. This is the Africa we must return to—but "by another route": what Africa has *become* in the New World, what we have made of "Africa": "Africa"—as we retell it through politics, memory and desire.

What of the second, troubling, term in the identity equation—the European presence? For many of us, this is a matter not of too little but of too much. Where Africa was a case of the unspoken, Europe was a case of that which is endlessly speaking—and endlessly speaking *us*. The European presence interrupts the innocence of the whole discourse of "difference" in the Caribbean by introducing the question of power. "Europe" belongs irrevocably to the "play" of power, to the lines of force and consent, to the role of the *dominant*, in Caribbean culture. In terms of colonialism, underdevelopment, poverty and the racism of colour, the European presence is that which, in visual representation, has positioned the black subject within its dominant regimes of representation: the colonial discourse, the literatures of adventure and exploration, the romance of the exotic, the ethnographic and travelling eye, the tropical languages of tourism, travel brochure and Hollywood and the violent, pornographic languages of *ganja* and urban violence.

Because *Présence Européenne* is about exclusion, imposition and expropriation, we are often tempted to locate that power as wholly external to us—an extrinsic force, whose influence can be thrown off like the serpent sheds its skin. What Frantz Fanon reminds us, in *Black Skin, White Masks*, is how this power has become a constitutive element in our own identities:

"The movements, the attitudes, the glances of the other fixed me there, in the sense in which a chemical solution is fixed by a dye. I was indignant; I demanded an explanation. Nothing happened. I burst apart. Now the fragments have been put together by another self" (1986, 109). This "look," from—so to speak—the place of the Other, fixes us, not only in its violence, hostility and aggression, but in the ambivalence of its desire. This brings us face to face, not simply with the dominating European presence as the site or "scene" of integration where those other presences which it had actively disaggregated were recomposed—reframed, put together in a new way; but as the site of a profound splitting and doubling—what Homi Bhabha has called "the ambivalent identifications of the racist world ... the 'otherness' of the self inscribed in the perverse palimpsest of colonial identity" (1986, xv).

The dialogue of power and resistance, of refusal and recognition, with and against *Présence Européenne* is almost as complex as the "dialogue" with Africa. In terms of popular cultural life, it is nowhere to be found in its pure, pristine state. It is always-already fused, syncretised, with other cultural elements. It is always-already creolised—not lost beyond the Middle Passage, but ever-present: from the harmonics in our musics to the ground-bass of Africa, traversing and intersecting our lives at every point. How can we stage this dialogue so that, finally, we can place it, without terror or violence, rather than being forever placed by it? Can we ever recognise its irreversible influence, whilst resisting its imperialising eye? The enigma is impossible, so far, to resolve. It requires the most complex of cultural strategies. Think, for example, of the dialogue of every Caribbean filmmaker or writer, one way or another, with the dominant cinemas and literature of the West—the complex relationship of young black British filmmakers with the "avantgardes" of European and American filmmaking. Who could describe this tense and tortured dialogue as a "one-way trip"?

The Third, "New World" presence, is not so much power, as ground, place, territory. It is the juncture-point where the many cultural tributaries meet, the "empty" land (the European colonisers emptied it) where strangers from every other part of the globe collided. None of the people who now occupy the islands—black, brown, white, African, European, American, Spanish, French, East Indian, Chinese, Portuguese, Jew, Dutch—originally "belonged" there. It is the space where the creolisations and assimilations and syncretisms were negotiated. The New World is the third term—the primal scene—where the fateful/fatal encounter was staged between Africa and the West. It also has to be understood as the place of many, continuous displacements: of the original pre-Columbian inhabitants, the Arawaks, Caribs and Amerindians, permanently displaced from their homelands and decimated; of other peoples displaced in different ways from Africa, Asia and Europe; the displacements of slavery, colonisation and conquest. It stands for the endless ways in which Caribbean people have been destined to "migrate"; it is the signifier of migration itself, of travelling, voyaging and return as fate, as destiny; of the Antillean as the prototype of the modern or postmodern New World nomad, continually moving between centre and periphery. This preoccupation with movement and migration Caribbean cinema shares with many other "Third Cinemas," but it is one of our defining themes, and it is destined to cross the narrative of every film script or cinematic image.

Présence Americaine continues to have its silences, its suppressions. Peter Hulme (1987), in his essay "Islands of Enchantment," reminds us that the word "Jamaica" is the Hispanic form of the indigenous Arawak name—"land of wood and water"—which Columbus's renaming (Santiago) never replaced. The Arawak presence remains today a ghostly one, visible in the islands mainly in museums and archaeological sites, part of the barely knowable or usable "past." Hulme notes that it is not represented in the emblem of the Jamaican National Heritage Trust, for example, which chose instead the figure of Diego Pimienta, "an African who fought for his Spanish masters against the English invasion of the island in 1655"—a deferred, metonymic, sly and sliding representation of Jamaican identity if ever there was one! He recounts the story of how Prime Minister Edward Seaga tried to alter the Jamaican coat-of-arms, which consists of two Arawak figures holding a shield with five pineapples, surmounted by an alligator. "Can the crushed and extinct Arawaks represent the dauntless character of Jamaicans? Does the low-slung, near extinct crocodile, a cold-blooded reptile, symbolise the warm, soaring spirit of Jamaicans?" Prime Minister Seaga asked rhetorically (*Jamaica Hansard* 1983–84, quoted in Hulme 1987). There can be few political statements which so eloquently testify to the complexities entailed in the process of trying to represent a diverse people with a diverse history through a single, hegemonic "identity." Fortunately, Mr. Seaga's invitation to the Jamaican people, who are overwhelmingly of African descent, to start their "remembering" by first "forgetting" something else, got the comeuppance it so richly deserved.

The "New World" presence—America, *Terra Incognita*—is therefore itself the beginning of diaspora, of diversity, of hybridity and difference, what makes Afro-Caribbean people already people of a diaspora. I use this term here metaphorically, not literally: diaspora does not refer us to those scattered tribes whose identity can only be secured in relation to some sacred homeland to which they must at all costs return, even if it means pushing other people into the sea. This is the old, the imperialising, the hegemonising, form of "ethnicity." We have seen the fate of the people of Palestine at the hands of this backward-looking conception of diaspora—and the complicity of the West with it. The diaspora experience as I intend it here is defined, not by essence or purity, but by the recognition of a necessary heterogeneity and diversity; by a conception of "identity" which lives with and through, not despite, difference; by *hybridity*. Diaspora identities are those which are constantly producing and reproducing themselves anew, through transformation and difference. One can only think here of what is uniquely—"essentially"—Caribbean: precisely the mixes of colour, pigmentation, physiognomic type; the "blends" of tastes that is Caribbean cuisine; the aesthetics of the "crossovers," of "cut-and-mix," to borrow Dick Hebdige's telling phrase, which is the heart and soul of black music. Young black cultural practitioners and critics in Britain are increasingly coming to acknowledge and explore in their work this "diaspora aesthetic" and its formations in the postcolonial experience:

> Across a whole range of cultural forms there is a "syncretic" dynamic which critically appropriates elements from the master-codes of the dominant culture and "creolises" them, disarticulating given signs and re-articulating their symbolic meaning. The subversive force of this hybridising tendency is most apparent at the level of language itself where creoles, patois and black English decentre, destabilise and carnivalise the linguistic domination of "English"—the nation-language of master-discourse—through strategic inflections, re-accentuations and other performative moves in semantic, syntactic and lexical codes. (Mercer 1988, 57)

It is because this New World is constituted for us as place, a narrative of displacement, that it gives rise so profoundly to a certain imaginary plenitude, recreating the endless desire to return to "lost origins," to be one again with the mother, to go back to the beginning. Who can ever forget, when once seen rising up out of that blue-green Caribbean, those islands of enchantment? Who has not known, at this moment, the surge of an overwhelming nostalgia for lost origins, for "times past"? And yet, this "return to the beginning" is like the imaginary in Lacan—it can neither be fulfilled nor requited, and hence is the beginning of the symbolic, of representation, the infinitely renewable source of desire, memory, myth, search, discovery—in short, the reservoir of our cinematic narratives.

We have been trying, in a series of metaphors, to put in play a different sense of our relationship to the past, and thus a different way of thinking about cultural identity, which might constitute new points of recognition in the discourses of the emerging Caribbean cinema and black British cinema. We have been trying to theorise identity as constituted, not outside but within representation; and hence of cinema, not as a second-order mirror held up to reflect what already exists, but as that form of representation which is able to constitute us as new kinds of subjects, and thereby to enable us to discover places from which to speak. Communities, Benedict Anderson argues in *Imagined Communities*, are to be distinguished not by their falsity/genuineness, but by the style in which they are imagined (1982, 15). This is the vocation of modern black cinema: by allowing us to see and recognize the different parts and histories of ourselves, to construct those points of identification, those positionalities we call in retrospect our "cultural identities."

"We must not therefore be content with delving into the past of a people in order to find coherent elements which will counteract colonialism's attempts to falsify and harm. . . . A national culture is not a folklore, nor an abstract populism that believes it can discover a people's true nature. . . . A national culture is the whole body of efforts made by a people in the sphere of thought to describe, justify, and praise the action through which that people has created itself and keeps itself in existence" (Fanon 1963, 233).

NOTE

This essay appeared as "Cultural Identity and Diaspora," in *Identity: Community, Culture, Difference*, edited by Jonathan Rutherford (London: Lawrence and Wishart, 1990), 222–37; was first published as "Cultural Identity and Cinematic Representation," *Framework*, no. 36 (1989): 68–81; and is reproduced by kind permission of the editor, Jim Pines.

REFERENCES

Anderson, Benedict. 1982. *Imagined Communities: Reflections on the Origin and Spread of Nationalism*. London: Verso.
Bhabha, Homi. 1986. Foreword to Frantz Fanon, *Black Skin, White Masks*, translated by Charles Lam Markmann. London: Pluto.
Fanon, Frantz. 1963. *The Wretched of the Earth*. Translated by Constance Farrington. New York: Grove.

Fanon, Frantz. 1986. *Black Skin, White Masks*. Translated by Charles Lam Markmann. London: Pluto.
Hall, Stuart, and Tony Jefferson, eds. 1976. *Resistance through Rituals: Youth Subcultures in Post-war Britain*. London: Hutchinson.
Hulme, Peter. 1987. "Islands of Enchantment." *New Formations* 3 (Winter).
Mercer, Kobena. 1988. "Diaspora Culture and the Dialogic Imagination." In *Black Frames: Critical Perspectives on Black Independent Cinema*, edited by Mbye B. Cham and Claire Andrade-Watkins. Cambridge, MA: MIT Press.
Norris, Christopher. 1982. *Deconstruction: Theory and Practice*. New York: Methuen.
Norris, Christopher. 1987. *Derrida*. Cambridge, MA: Harvard University Press.
Said, Edward. 1985. *Orientalism*. Harmondsworth, UK: Penguin.

CHAPTER 14

C. L. R. James:
A Portrait

The life and work of C. L. R. James can be divided into four parts: the early years in Trinidad, the first years in England, the American sojourn and, finally, James's return to the Caribbean. During all four periods he was intensively active, both politically and creatively.

I will emphasize the political context in which James worked because I think that he has not been accorded his proper due. James was an extremely important political and intellectual figure who is only just beginning to be widely recognized for his achievements. His work has never been critically and theoretically engaged as it should be. Consequently, much writing on James is necessarily explanatory, descriptive and celebratory. However, major intellectual and political figures are not honored by simply celebration. Honor is accorded by taking his or her ideas seriously and debating them, extending them, quarreling with them and making them live again. Thus I will raise some interesting but not quite settled questions about James's intellectual and political work. It is not because I think less of him, but because I think so much of him, that I think he should be part of a much wider intellectual and political discourse. Paul Buhle's book *C. L. R. James: The Artist as Revolutionary* (1988) raises some of those themes, but there is much more to be done.

James was born in Trinidad in 1901; his father was a schoolmaster whose background was of the skilled lower middle class in a colonial British Caribbean society. His mother, an educated woman, had a profound influence upon James and introduced him to books. A great reader, she had a wide variety of books in the home, which was uncommon even among so-called educated people in the Caribbean. It is easy to find people in the Caribbean who are well off but have no tradition of reading. James was thus fortunate in having had early access to books. Some, and there are surprising ones among them, he still read in later years. He confessed to me that he read *Vanity Fair* every year.

Another fortunate event in James's life was that he attended Queen's Royal College, one of the large secondary schools for boys that were common in the Caribbean at the time. James received a scholarship, and it provided him with a local variant of an English education. Queen's Royal College was not quite an English public school, but it provided an academic education. Students took English examinations, played cricket and read an English curriculum. James learned the classics there and to read and speak French.

When James left Queen's Royal College he thought of himself as a writer. He was hired to teach at the school, and among his students was Eric Williams, later to be one of the first leaders of independent Trinidad. Williams was the founder of the Peoples National Movement (PNM), one of the major parties of Caribbean politics in the sixties. Before that, he wrote a major work on the Caribbean slave trade, *Capitalism and Slavery* (1944), a work responsible for a profound historical reevaluation of the nature of the antislavery movement. The thesis of *Capitalism and Slavery*, Williams's Ph.D. dissertation at Oxford, came from the germ of an idea that James had written on the back of an envelope. Much later in his life when Williams repudiated James, James reminded Williams that he had known him since Williams was a little boy.

By any measure, James was a bold, ambitious and wide-ranging young man in the colonial society of his native Trinidad. After being educated, he became involved gradually in the artistic and intellectual movements that were developing on the island. He joined with other young writers and began to write short stories. After a collection of the best short stories was sent to him that contained one of his, James began to take himself even more seriously as a writer and soon produced his first novel, *Minty Alley* (1936). The book, about popular life in Trinidad and partly autobiographical, focuses on a young black middle-class esthete in Port of Spain who comes to understand what Trinidadian life is like by listening to ordinary people instead of by writing books.

At the same time, James became involved in the early stages of the Trinidadian labor movement and the movement for national independence. One of the leading figures of the era was Arthur Cipriani, a Corsican. Cipriani's leadership reflected a peculiar feature of Caribbean society, which contains influences from almost everywhere else in the world. That is what is unique about the Caribbean, half of it belongs to everyone else. Thus the fact that a Corsican led a Trinidadian labor movement should not be surprising. Cipriani, who fought in World War I, protested the situation of black soldiers who returned from the war, and he became involved in organizing the Trinidad Working Men's Association. He developed Trinidad's first organized program for workmen's compensation and the limitation of working hours. James worked for this pioneer in the birth of the Trinidadian labor movement. He wrote for the newspaper Cipriani founded and eventually produced his biography. The book, *The Life of Captain Cipriani*, was produced in 1932, just before James left the Caribbean for England, where a portion of it was republished as *The Case for West-Indian Self Government* (1933). Thus James laid claim to the labor movement as a young intellectual in Port of Spain and to the whole development of West Indian nationalism in the interwar period.

Three things are noteworthy about the first phase of James's life. First, James's intellectual formation was through a colonial education. He was educated in a sort of mimicry of an English public school, but the school influenced James in such things as his understanding of cricket. Second, he became linked to the birth of the organized labor movement in the Caribbean. Third, he was part of a small but important and quite ambitious group of young black intellectuals in Port of Spain. It was quite remarkable to consider oneself a writer in Trinidad, a tiny island that had no publishing facilities and no large reading audience. James in particular was very ambitious, and his experiences would be translated into a new political project in the next period of his life.

This second period began with James's departure for Great Britain. He arrived in 1932, still very much committed to making his fortune as a writer. All West Indian writers of James's generation and the next would go to England to work. George Lamming, Sam Selvon and Wilson Harris all moved to the center of the metropolis; only later in the sixties was the Caribbean public large and organized enough for writers to remain there.

In England, James met another friend, Learie Constantine, the first outstanding black cricketer who made a significant impact on West Indian cricket. Constantine came to England with the West Indian touring team and was the first black cricketer to be employed in the English league cricket. Today, a Puerto Rican ball player comes to the United States and is hired by one of the major league clubs. Then, to be hired by the Lancashire Cricket Club was an equally important thing. Constantine was not only a great cricketer, but also an important figure in the early formation of a black consciousness movement in Britain.

Even more important for the second phase of James's development was the fact that it was Constantine who introduced him to Neville Cardus, the cricket correspondent for the *Manchester Guardian*. Cardus liked James and discovered that he had a phenomenal memory and knew the scores every touring team had made since about 1901. He got James a job as his substitute on the *Guardian*; when Cardus didn't want to go to matches, James went in his place. Through this connection with Constantine, and his early interest in cricket, James's writing aspirations led him in a new direction—sports writing.

During this period, James also began to develop the project of writing something else about the Caribbean, a history of the slave revolution in Haiti. As he worked on the project, James became involved with British Trotskyism. He read Marx first in the light of the Trotskyist movement. His first Marxist connections were with the political movement of the Trotskyist and neo-Trotskyist groups in England, and through them he encountered the popular literature of Leninist and Marxist texts, which were circulated for people's self-education. James first became involved with a Marxist party called the Independent Labour Party (ILP). The British Labour Party, the major social democratic party, had a different political character. The ILP was an independent leftist socialist party that had long debated the fledgling British Communist Party over whether or not the ILP would join with the Comintern. Eventually the Independent Labour Party decided not to join. Consequently, James's relationship to Marxism was from the first critical of Stalinism and the Comintern. He was never a Stalinist, but encountered Marxism in its non-Stalinist form. As a Trotskyist, he was an independent socialist.

What is James's critique of the forms of Stalinist organizations? Why did he think it important to have Marxist formations outside of the Comintern? This is the beginning of a long critique that belongs to James's "Trotskyism." I put the term in quotation marks because there are many forms of Trotskyism, and James's is just one. But his Trotskyism arose from this moment. It was a critique of the authoritarian forms of Stalinist rule and of the absence of democracy, a critique of a revolution that is not democratic in its form, which does not energize the popular consciousness, and in which the party has been substituted for the people. James was critical of the whole notion of a vanguard party that would accomplish the revolution for the people or tell or educate them about what they should think.

This early critique first took James to the ILP and through that to the smaller Trotskyist groups in British politics. In 1937 he published *World Revolution*, a critique of the history of the Comintern. In it, James examined the ways in which the popular energies of leftist movements throughout the world had been subordinated to the interest of the Soviet Union through the Comintern, and how the Comintern prevented such movements from growing. James also translated from the French a critical biography of Stalin by the important Trotskyist historian Boris Souvarine (1939).

To the interest in cricket and Trotskyism of James's second period must also be added Pan-Africanism, because James was also becoming involved in the revival of the movement in England. Pan-Africanism had a long history before this attempt at revival, a history particularly evident in the work of W. E. B. Du Bois and the Pan-African Congress, which from the early twentieth century was part of American history. Further, the revival was related to the Pan-Africanist elements in Garveyism and the formation of Marcus Garvey's Universal Negro Improvement Association. Consequently, in the 1920s the Pan-African movement shifted some of its activity to London, where James came into contact with it. One of his most intriguing contacts was through George Padmore, an old school friend from Trinidad. Before James came to England, Padmore, whose real name was Malcolm Nurse, left for the United States and joined the Communist Party. An intellectual, he was sent to the Soviet Union, was given a position in the Comintern in charge of African and Pan-African affairs, and was later sent back to the West. There he was to organize the black and African elements in the world revolution on behalf of the Comintern. James heard of George Padmore, met him and discovered that "Padmore" was actually his old friend Malcolm Nurse, snuggled away in a new historical role. In his casual way, James greeted Nurse in the following manner: Hey Malcolm, you are the great George Padmore. I heard that you are the great Comintern man and I am not a Comintern man. We are supposed to be antagonists. I did not know it was you. How are you?

Both this story and the case of James's friendship with Paul Robeson illustrate a striking feature of James's character. In this period, he had a classically Trotskyist way of differentiating among those people with whom he did not agree, a great political skill that Trotsky had honed. Trotskyists differentiated themselves, there was never just one Trotskyist group, there were at least four or five. James was good at making such distinctions, but he was also astonishingly good at collaborating with people with whom he did not agree. Thus, Robeson's ties to the American Communist Party did not prevent James from writing a play for Robeson, or from thinking well of him.

Malcolm Nurse, as an agent of the Comintern, had a view on the relationship of the black struggle to both the class struggle and the revolution, and although James did not agree with him, the men still spoke to each other. James and Padmore were influential in reviving the Pan-African movement in London. The movement began to grow through the League of Coloured Peoples and through the work of Garvey's first wife, Amy Ashwood Garvey, who was active in it. James and Padmore played important roles in the lives of young black African leaders who were studying in London during the 1930s. James met Kwame Nkrumah and Jomo Kenyatta, both of whom were heavily influenced by Pan-Africanism.

The movement was also punctuated by an important development in international affairs. This was the period of the Abyssinian war, in which Italy invaded Abyssinia (Ethiopia). The invasion spawned the League for the Protection of Ethiopia and *Toussaint L'ouverture* ([1936] 2013); the play that James wrote and Robeson performed was staged under the auspices of the League at a small theater in London.

The remarkable breadth of James's sympathies, as displayed in his friendships with Robeson and Padmore, was evident in another friendship related to the Abyssinian crisis and the larger Pan-African struggle. This was James's collaboration with Ras Makonnen, an important Guyanese who was involved in the league. Makonnen was suspicious of the whole Marxist, Trotskyist historical materialist baggage, but James held him in high regard and worked with him as an ally. The combination of a hard edge in James's political positions and the remarkable breadth of his human sympathies is arresting and unusual. People who hold clear political positions are frequently thought to be sectarian. James was not a classic revolutionary sectarian in that sense, however. He was able to collaborate with a wide range of people.

Completing this second phase of James's life was the publication of *The Black Jacobins* in 1938. The book is a major work of historical scholarship, with a grand majestical sweep. It was the first and most elaborate history of the major slave revolution in the Caribbean, that in Haiti. The work is well theorized and wonderfully narrated, with a sense of drama clearly linked to the play James had completed earlier. It can be compared to Trotsky's *History of the Russian Revolution* (1932). Along with a wonderfully dramatic sense of event, James demonstrates a Marxist understanding of the historical context and sweep of events. He went to France and was the first person to examine the historical records of the Haitian Revolution in the French archives. Consequently, his work contains a history of the Central African people from which slaves first came, as well as a history of the Atlantic slave trade. During this research James had an idea that he wrote on the back of an envelope, an idea upon which Eric Williams's dissertation was based. It was against this historical backdrop that the narrative of the eruption of the Haitian Revolution was allowed to unfold.

The Black Jacobins was also informed by James's understanding of the contemporary political scene. Toussaint L'Ouverture, the great leader of the Haitian Revolution, was motivated by the domination that defined the social position of slaves and also by the events of the French Revolution. Because of the latter influence, the black revolutionaries assumed the garb, indeed the uniforms, of the French Revolution and so became Jacobins. L'Ouverture himself was similar to Napoleon. The same thing happened to him that happened to Napoleon: he became seduced into not leading a democratic movement and instead became the charismatic leader of an autocratic one. "Bonapartism" is a Trotskyist concept for what happened to Stalin. L'Ouverture fell from a Bonapartist error and was replaced by Jean-Jacques Dessalines, who was unafraid to be a true political party apparatchik, that is, like Stalin. James reread the Haitian Revolution as a mass uprising in which the leader became trapped in bureaucracy and was slowly transformed into a self-effacing dictator who capitulated, contained and defused the popular revolution. *The Black Jacobins* is a wonderful book and a fitting conclusion to the second phase of James's life.

The third phase of James's life began when he met J. P. Cannon, a leading American Trotskyist, who invited him to come to the United States in 1938. Although James accepted the invitation thinking that he would be in the United States briefly, his sojourn marked a long and important period of his life. In America, he was partly involved in, and excited by, the Harlem Renaissance. He knew Richard Wright and was a friend of Carl Van Vechten. He was moved by the music, the film, the fiction and the popular culture of the era.

More important than such cultural interests was the fact that James was a leading figure in the Trotskyist movement. As a result, he quickly got involved and embroiled in the deep arguments of American Trotskyism. He also began to entertain serious reservations about how Trotskyism understood the relationship between the revolutionary movement and the black struggle. Although James did not want to privilege the black struggle, he did not think Trotskyism or any other Marxist movements, which often made the factor of race too incidental, were correct. James felt that questions of race were subsidiary to questions of class and politics and that to think of imperialism in terms of race is disastrous. But he also argued that to neglect race as incidental would be as grave as to make it the fundamental issue. And when Leon Trotsky invited James to come to Mexico in 1939, that was the issue they debated.

Trotsky compared the black struggle in America to a national struggle inside Eastern Europe; it was a subordinate struggle that, like that of the Poles, would be temporary. Trotsky further suggested that once the revolution had solved it, the black problem would cease. James disagreed, considering the question to be in need of more careful attention. Consequently, he felt that in America the black struggle must have a more pivotal, central role in the constitution of any revolutionary movement than Trotsky's position gave it. He failed to get satisfactory answers from Trotsky and remained unsatisfied by how the theoretical and conceptual relationship between the black struggle and the revolutionary struggle was posed and answered in Trotskyism.

After their meeting, James began to work his way out of organized Trotskyism, although he remained in touch with the movement over a long period and was in and out of the movement's many splits. In 1941, he formed his own tendency, which was called the Johnson–Forest tendency. James called himself "J. R. Johnson," and "Freddy Forest" was the name taken by the extremely intelligent Marxist theoretician Raya Dunayevskaya.

Dunayevskaya was extremely important to James, both in a personal and intellectual sense, because she was deeply and profoundly a Hegelian scholar. Through Dunayevskaya, James returned to some of the philosophical foundations of Marxism, and a form of Hegelian Marxism entered his political perspective. *Notes on Dialectics* ([1948] 1980) is one of his most complex and difficult theoretical works. This study of Hegel reinforced the differences and reservations James had developed concerning Trotskyism and culminated in an open break with Trotskyism, later articulated in *State Capitalism and World Revolution* ([1950] 1986). The book analyzes the degeneration of the revolution in Soviet society as a consequence of bureaucratic deformation. It contains a critique of the Trotskyist position on degeneration, breaks with the whole notion of the vanguard party and comes down on a particular side of a debate long popular in Trotskyism.

In the 1930s and 1940s any Trotskyist group could be divided in terms of its view of what produced the degeneration of the revolution in the Soviet Union. Was it a "degenerated workers' state"? This position claimed that the revolution was basically all right, but that the excrescences of the particular political forms were responsible for holding it back. Opposed to this view was the state capitalist position that these excrescences had created a deeply bureaucratic system that would require another revolution to overthrow it. In contrast to the degeneration thesis of orthodox Trotskyism, James argued that the Soviet Union was state capitalist. As a result, its internal dynamics must be understood in terms of the growth of a state and of a party bureaucracy that had become an instrument of capital accumulation rather than of workers' power. The "workers' state" had become the new class enemy. As such, it would have to be overthrown if it maintained this authoritarian substitution of itself in place of a more genuine, proletarian rule. The evolution of a post-Trotskyist position constituted the new political work of this period of James's life.

In addition to the post-Trotskyist analysis, this period was culturally productive. James embarked upon an analysis, which he never completed, of American popular culture. The summation of this work, *Mariners, Renegades and Castaways* (1953), was a book on Herman Melville, a text rather like *Black Jacobins* and structured in much the same way. The revolutionary force is symbolized by the tensions in social relations among the crew of the Pequod. This ship is the stage upon which the drama of Melville's *Moby-Dick* unfolds. The men down below are the masses; Ahab is a Stalinist figure in control at the top, trying to rule things; and Ishmael is a figure of James himself, an intellectual with a tendency to be pulled toward abstractions, to watch things from the side and to think about them in theoretical terms but not become involved. The whale's identity is unclear—perhaps nature, chaos, or history. It is an untameable force, energy that the crew tries to harness.

The figurative device that James was most interested in was that of the *Pequod* as microcosm of labor, the ship as a factory. Melville, James, argues, thought of whaling ships as factories and saw factory organization reproduced in how ships' crews worked. Ahab, for example, can also be seen as an entrepreneur, driving the ship forward from the top. Melville elaborately describes the clearly defined division of labor aboard the *Pequod*, that is, who hunted, who creamed off the oil, and other laborious details on how to extract the oil from whales. In all of this James saw how the relationships of production get hold of the forces of production. Hence my suggestion that the whale may be equated with nature; it is matter to be worked upon, harnessed, caught, held, drained and refined. James's view of the ship as a factory teaming with productive life is a fantastic metaphor. It is also a peculiar one, and a singular interpretation of Melville.

In 1953, James was asked to leave the United States because of his Trotskyist activities. He was imprisoned on Ellis Island and decided to fight the expulsion. As a part of his defense, he made a wonderfully Jamesian gesture: he attempted to present *Mariners, Renegades and Castaways* as testimony to the fact that he was a much better American than the immigration authorities. It was as though he was saying, "You do not understand your greatest artist, Melville, and I do. How can you expel me for un-American activities when I am telling you that next to Shakespeare, here is the greatest use of the English language? It is because you do not understand what your own author is telling you that you can expel me. You should welcome me—not throw me out." The remarkable gesture ended the third phase of James's life.

James was primarily in the Caribbean during the fourth and final phase of his life. He was invited back to the region in 1958 by Eric Williams, who led what was widely understood to be a clearly and skillfully articulated form of anti-imperialist politics through the People's National Movement. Williams was elected overwhelmingly to power and was believed to be the first true leader of an independent, nationalist Trinidadian movement. He astutely made James, his former mentor, the editor of the *Nation*, the PNM's newspaper. He also made James the secretary of the Caribbean Labour Party, which was to bring together all of the left-wing parties of the region. The party was an attempt to constitute a federal socialist movement, a strategic move on Williams's part. During this period James also visited Africa. Nkrumah, then in power in Ghana, regarded him as a mentor. From James's trip came *Nkrumah and the Ghana Revolution* (1977).

After James had worked on the *Nation* for about two years, he and Williams split. Among the causes of friction was a move against Williams, no one knows precisely why, which was made by the Americans. It appears to have involved the American Chaguaramas military base in Trinidad. The lease on the base had run out, and it was generally assumed that it would not be renewed. Williams had always preached about how the North, that is Great Britain and America, had exploited the Caribbean, and the need for regional territories to cut these links and regain independence. He did not throw the Chaguaramas treaty away in the early stages of the controversy, but gave the impression that when the renewal of the treaty came up, he would say enough is enough. In fact, whether or not he was being squeezed economically or in any other fashion, Williams decided to renew the Chaguaramas agreements. James, quite rightly, regarded that renewal as a major point of rupture and used his position on the *Nation* to criticize the decision. It became the source of a major conflict that was at the basis of the break. James was shocked and scandalized when he was repudiated and went on speaking out against Williams. Williams, in turn, brought politics to bear against James to silence him. That story is in a book called *Party Politics in the West Indies* (James 1962).

Something else happened in this period; James wrote a book on the importance of popular culture, a task that his return to the Caribbean allowed him time to do. The popular activity that he analyzed was the game of cricket, and the book is called *Beyond a Boundary* (1963). In this text he not only wrote about cricket, but he also redefined the game as one of the civilized ways in which the anti-imperialist struggle is played out through sports. James often remarked that the British said that the Empire was won on the playing fields of Eton and would be lost on the playing fields of Lord's Cricket Ground. Just as the British had trained themselves to create the Empire on the playing fields, so on the playing fields they would symbolically lose the Empire.

A second important theme is who would defeat the British on the playing fields. James suggested that it would be the emerging, strong West Indian cricket team and analyzed the social reasons for the team's new strength. It was strong because it had broken down existing team divisions between professionals and nonprofessionals. When the first West Indian touring teams went to England, the first five batsmen were always nonprofessional white West Indians. The blacks, who actually earned a living from playing the game, quite often did not live in the same areas as their white teammates. During the 1950s everyone on the West Indian team had equal status for the first time. They won the first test match after the war and defeated the British. The team included two bowlers, Sonny Ramadhin and A. Valentine, one from Trinidad and one from Jamaica, and three batsmen: Frank Worrell, Clyde Walcott and Everton Weeks. Out of the team's exploits came the first cricket calypsoes ever sung in Great Britain. They celebrated the defeat of the English and the wonderful performances of Ramadhin and Valentine.

James thus redefined cricket as the playing out of these popular forces. It was more than just the game. What made the West Indian team was not only that they were good at cricket; they were also able to draw on the popular ingenuity and energies of different people. James was sensitive to the unique skills that such players as Worrell or Weeks brought to the game. For him, the cricket team drew on the popular skills and energies of the whole region, and not just those of its upper classes. Thus, *Beyond a Boundary* had a profound and imaginative anti-imperialist message.

James was in love with the game of cricket in the most archetypal way. He thought that W. G. Grace, an English batsman, was a perfect master, epical in the sense that Aeschylus was to drama. And he felt that the traditional stories about cricket, for example, *Tom Brown's School Days*, were masterful. "C. L. R.," I once asked him, "some of your writings about cricket venerate English Victorian society, why?" He said, "To organize an effective cricket team is an act of collective mastery. It is an act of social organization. It doesn't matter who is doing it. Through cricket a society raises its capacity to organize its own life, and if you can use an individual like W. G. Grace, a figure of mastery over nature, that is fine. The ability to transform nature into an aesthetic is itself a human accomplishment irrespective of whether the individual is red, white, green or blue."

Thus James's investment in cricket was not just a symbolic replay of how the colonies defeated the metropolitan power. It was a much larger imaginative notion of the game as symbolic of how one talks of the energies of a whole people. He wrote in the same way about calypso, carnival and the leading singer in the Trinidadian carnival, Mighty Sparrow. Worrell was to West Indian cricket as Grace was to early cricket, as Shakespeare was to the Elizabethan period, as Melville was to American civilization and as Sparrow was to carnival. To James, what created the magnificence of any cultural or esthetic product is such a condensation of historical forces. It was the rise of a new class, a new conception of humanity that created the language from which Shakespeare wrote. It was the rise and formation of American civilization with all its contradictions that created the historical moment from which Melville wrote. It was the new drawing together of the energies of the Caribbean people that created the cricket team of the 1950s and allowed Worrell to play with grace. It was the popular energies of calypso music in the Caribbean that created Sparrow as an artist.

These are all instances of the relationship of the artist, the great forces of history and the historical moment. James steadfastly refused simply to read off cultural things against the economic base. His Hegelianism was a notion connective of historical movement, of whole classes and of esthetic production. He saw such things as one, as not separated into different practices, a notion of collective and creative totality. These were also James's politics. This complex, connective view enabled him to argue against attempts to create a revolutionary movement by making divisions between the black and the white sections of the revolutionary class, or by making divisions between the party and the masses. The movement would be made by the masses, or not made at all. Anything that does not trust the instincts and creative life of the masses would be a deformation, bureaucratic and Stalinist. Another reason why James was not a Stalinist is that he always trusted the masses' cultural and political creative energies. Shakespeare, for example, could only be a great writer because something connected him through the English language to those new energies that were being mobilized.

I once asked James about the three great moments in which he could see a single artist speaking on behalf of a whole historical revolutionary moment. He told me about the Acropolis, even though its architect is unknown. He told me about Shakespeare, and he told me about Picasso's *Guernica*. He said, "Look at Picasso. Look at *Guernica*. A wonderful painting. What is it about? It is about the Spanish people. It is about the energies of the Spanish revolution. When you look at *Guernica* you see the whole movement, the whole maelstrom of the Spanish revolution encapsulated in an esthetic form." James would take a postcard of *Guernica* to cricket matches, and during intervals when play stopped he would take it out and study it. When play resumed, he would put it away.

The end of the fourth period, 1962, was the end of James's active political life. He returned to live in London and was rediscovered in the United States in the 1960s and 1970s. In particular, *Radical America* discovered his importance, as did many black writers. Others who would study American slavery discovered the importance of James's work on the history of black revolts. The rediscovery gave him a late legitimation and recognition in the United States during his seventies. His nephew, Darcus Howe, is a leading black intellectual, the editor of one of the major black radical journals in Great Britain and one of the leading spokespersons for a black documentary television series, *Bandung File*. Darcus fixed up a flat for C. L. R. in Brixton, which was where he lived. Paul Buhle's book about him was published in 1988 in London, and James was present at the book's launch. Generally, he hardly moved from the flat. People visited him constantly, visits that reflected the many generations of black political and intellectual figures privileged to talk to James and to know him. Such novelists as George Lamming and Wilson Harris, or young intellectuals who either returned to the

Caribbean or remained active in black metropolitan politics all benefited from James's advice and wisdom. Whether or not they agreed with James at first, they were all influenced by him. James was eighty-eight when he died in May of 1989; he was buried in his native Trinidad.

NOTE

This essay first appeared as "C. L. R. James: A Portrait," in *C. L. R. James's Caribbean*, edited by Henry Paget and Paul Buhle (Durham, NC: Duke University Press, 1992), 3–16.

REFERENCES

Buhle, Paul. 1988. *C. L. R. James: The Artist as Revolutionary*. London: Verso.
James, C. L. R. 1932. *The Life of Captain Cipriani: An Account of British Government in the West Indies*. Nelson, Lancashire, UK: Cartmel and Co.
James, C. L. R. 1933. *The Case for West Indian Self-Government*. London: Hogarth.
James, C. L. R. 1936. *Minty Alley*. London: Secker and Warburg.
James, C. L. R. (1936) 2013. *Toussaint L'Ouverture: The Only Successful Slave Revolt in History*. Edited by Christian Høgsbjerg. Durham, NC: Duke University Press.
James, C. L. R. 1937. *World Revolution, 1917–1936: The Rise and Fall of the Communist International*. London: Secker and Warburg.
James, C. L. R. 1938. *The Black Jacobins: Toussaint L'Ouverture and the San Domingo Revolution*. London: Secker and Warburg.
James, C. L. R. (1948) 1980. *Notes on Dialectics: Hegel, Marx, Lenin*. London: Allison and Busby.
James, C. L. R. (1950) 1986. *State Capitalism and World Revolution*. In collaboration with Raya Dunayevskaya and Grace Lee. Chicago: Charles H. Kerr.
James, C. L. R. 1953. *Mariners, Renegades and Castaways: The Story of Herman Melville and the World We Live In*. New York.
James, C. L. R. 1962. *Party Politics in the West Indies*. Port of Spain: Inprint Caribbean.
James, C. L. R. 1963. *Beyond a Boundary*. London: Hutchinson.
James, C. L. R. 1977. *Nkrumah and the Ghana Revolution*. Westport, CT: Lawrence Hill.
Melville, Herman. 1851. *Moby-Dick; or, The Whale*. New York: Harper and Brothers.
Souvarine, Boris. 1939. *Stalin: A Critical Survey of Bolshevism*. Translated by C. L. R. James. New York: Longmans, Green and Co.
Trotsky, Leon. 1932. *History of the Russian Revolution*. Translated by Max Eastman. London: Gollancz.
Williams, Eric. 1944. *Capitalism and Slavery*. Chapel Hill: University of North Carolina Press.

CHAPTER 15

Calypso Kings

Since West Indians first began to settle in Britain in large numbers after the Second World War, a succession of black musics have transformed the British music scene. Ska, bluebeat and, of course, reggae were followed by rap, dancehall, "jungle," techno and house.

But the oldest of these musical forms is the calypso—the music and lyrics associated with the Trinidad Carnival—which, according to Lloyd Bradley, became "the official soundtrack of black Britain" in the 1950s and early 1960s. Calypso was the first popular music transported directly from the West Indies, and in the early days, migrants from the southern Caribbean would meet to listen nostalgically to the recording of that year's winning calypso or their favourite calypsonian, and relive memories of the street marching, the costume floats and steel-pan music that dominate Port of Spain in the four-day saturnalia leading up to the beginning of Lent.

However, shortly after the arrival of the first postwar contingent, calypso music about the migration experience also started to be composed and performed in Britain, about Britain. Now this nearly forgotten moment in the story of Britain's black diaspora can be recaptured in word and sound. The record label Honest John has salvaged twenty calypsos composed and recorded by calypsonians in and about London in the early 1950s and issued them as a new CD titled *London Is the Place for Me*.

The start of the postwar Caribbean diaspora is usually associated with the arrival of the rather dilapidated troopship, the SS *Empire Windrush*, which docked at Tilbury in June 1948. The ship had been sent to scour the Caribbean and bring back Second World War volunteers who had been given temporary home leave to visit their families before returning to Britain to be demobbed. Three hundred servicemen and women from throughout the islands gathered in Jamaica for the return trip, and since the ship's capacity was 600, the extra berths were offered to anyone who wanted to emigrate and could stump up the fare of £28. No papers or visas were required since these were the innocent days when all West Indians had right of entry as legitimate British passport holders. Among those who took up the option were two of the Caribbean's most famous and best-loved calypsonians, Lord Beginner and Lord Kitchener.

Aldwyn "Lord Kitchener" Roberts, a Trinidadian and former nightclub vocalist, had worked on several of the other islands before deciding—as he told Mike and Trevor Phillips, the authors of *Windrush: The Irresistible Rise of Multi-racial Britain* (1999)—that he had always wanted to visit England. Kitchener, a colourful presence on the voyage, helped to organise a concert to raise funds to pay the passage of a stowaway woman who had been discovered (there were many stowaways, some of whom dived overboard and swam to safety when the boat finally docked). As the ship neared land, Kitchener was overcome by "the wonderful feeling that I'm going to land on the mother country . . . touch the soil of the mother country," and was moved to compose the song that provides the title track of the collection, "London Is the Place for Me."

A week later, he visited a London dance club called the Paramount where, to his surprise, he discovered many of his fellow passengers already well in place, jiving and dancing. A month later, a band led by a twenty-two-year-old Guyanese trumpeter, Rannie Hart, started to play regularly in the saloon bar of the Queens Hotel in Brixton and with them, hoping to extend the popularity of calypso, was their star, Lord Kitchener. He went on to a highly successful career, playing at pubs, dance clubs, cellar bars and the semilegal "bottle parties" of the London and Manchester underground scenes until he returned permanently to Trinidad in 1962.

Confined for some time to small clubs and dancehalls, calypso really made its breakthrough in 1950, with the triumph of the West Indies cricket team at Lords. This was a symbolic victory, and a major reversal of fortunes. The great Trinidadian historian C. L. R. James, who wrote the best book ever written about cricket, *Beyond a Boundary* (1963), had long argued that true West Indian independence and the national consciousness it required would be impossible until the West Indies had taken on the colonisers at their sacred game and mastered it sufficiently to defeat them at home in open play: 1950 was that moment. The West Indian team included three of the world's finest batsmen, but the true heroes of the game and architects of victory were the spinners, Ramadhin and Valentine.

It is difficult to believe reports that there were only thirty or forty West Indians present at the ground, but however many there were, they made their presence felt by exuberant shouting, singing and the rattling of tin cans throughout the game, in ways that astonished the natives and transformed for ever the ethos of Test cricket. "Unnecessary" was the snotty opinion of the MCC diarist.

But the victory moved the calypsonian Lord Beginner, another *Windrush* survivor, to compose on the spot the calypso that became the anthem of the moment—"Cricket, Lovely Cricket," with its telling refrain, "With those little pals of mine / Ramadhin and Valentine"; while Kitchener himself led the march round the field and down into Piccadilly. People stared at this extraordinary sight out of windows—"I think it was the first time they'd ever seen such a thing in England," Kitchener observed. "And we're dancing Trinidad-style, like mas, and dance right down Piccadilly and . . . around Eros." The Caribbean ethos and style of celebration was the most commented upon aspect of the game and marks the moment when a distinctively new Caribbean spirit and rhythm first announced itself as an emergent element in the rapidly changing national culture.

In fact, calypso in Britain has an interesting prehistory. The oldest living calypsonian on the Honest John CD is Young Tiger, now 82, who was born in Trinidad, became a seaman on oil tankers sailing the seven seas, and finally disembarked in Glasgow in 1942. Though not musically trained, he played and sang a little and when he and a friend landed a job in the famous Minstrel Show, they were bitten by the showbiz bug. Singing and playing all sorts of music in the small London drinking clubs, he composed a Christmas Calypso in 1943, which became a seasonal favourite. Playing and singing with a rumba band at the swanky Orchid Room, Young Tiger adopted the calypsonian's practice of instant commentary on the rich and famous and composed a few verses on the spot when Prince Philip and party paid the club a visit. Reprimanded by management, Young Tiger was surprised when, the following night, royalty returned in force to hear the composition—which he had since thrown away. This royal connection may have prompted the composition of his Coronation Calypso in 1953.

After playing and touring with a number of successful groups, he recorded with Melodisc, the first British company to produce calypso records, a cover version of Single Man by the calypsonian Tiger—and thus inherited the title Young Tiger.

Though he had never had the ambition to be a professional musician, George "Young Tiger" Brown was "steeped in calypso" and greatly admired the calypsonian's gift as poet, raconteur and reporter. He left Trinidad before the steel bands that are now so closely associated with calypso music really took hold, though he remembers as a child hearing the pans being played in the backyards of Charlotte Street, Port of Spain, and the shango and "tambo-bambo" music (played on various lengths of bamboo) that were their precursors and the preferred instruments of popular music at the time.

It is difficult to separate the spirit of calypso from its context in the Trinidad Carnival. Preparing for Carnival is an all-year-round activity. As the Carnival season approaches, the clubs enter a period of feverish activity, designing and completing the construction of the elaborate costumes and astonishing headdresses that the bands will wear for the parade. Richly coloured fabrics, sequined plumes and feathers are suspended across wire, steel and fibreglass frames according to the year's theme. In the period leading up to the opening day—Jour Ouvert—the calypsonians compete in their respective tents, hoping their own compositions will win favour as the favourite for the Road March, and so lead the "jump-up," or joovay—the dancing and rhythmic shuffling through the streets to the accompaniment of drums, bottles and whistles with which the days of revelling climax. For a few days, the whole town gives itself up to pure bacchanal, known as "playing Ole Mas." The word "mas" has multiple derivations: "masking," the Christian "mass" (with which the days of revelling conclude on Ash Wednesday) and "masquerade."

Trinidad Carnival is a syncretic popular form, drawing on Christian tradition and pagan ritual, fused in the vortex of plantation society. It is now more than 200 years old. The French settlers (in Trinidad, and places of largely Catholic settlement, like Martinique and Haiti, which also have carnivals) brought their custom of grand pre-Easter balls in the plantation houses and parading masked through the streets. The slaves were also allowed a few days of revelling, often marching in the streets in rough costumes and crude disguises, in both imitation and ironic mimicry of their masters, to the accompaniment of much drumming, prancing and threatening stick-play. The authorities were constantly trying to ban this practice of ritualised popular resistance, without success.

The calypso, a topical song associated with Carnival, specially composed for the occasion, was much influenced by this carnivalesque tradition—a period of licensed expression, when for a time, the normal rules of everyday life are suspended, the world is turned upside down, and the people of "the below" are granted the freedom both to revel in public and to comment on and satirise the actions and behaviour of those in authority. The calypsonian is free to comment ironically on any aspect or event of everyday life, to expose the sexual and political scandals of the politicians and the rich, to recount gossip and to scandalise the powerful without fear of redress. Political commentary, the quirks, foibles, the petty dramas and the licentious stories of everyday street life are grist to the calypsonian's mill. The calypso is the repository of that year's distilled popular knowledge and wisdom—the informal "court" before which every powerful figure fears being ultimately judged.

The essence of the successful calypso lies in capturing the event or occasion in a vivid, piquant, creole idiom. The music has a driving, springy, forward-impelled, rolling two-beat, adaptable to the rhythmic movement of the road march. The lyrics, which are strung across and accented so as to insinuate themselves between the bass rhythm, are driven by the sinuous lilt of Trinidadian creole speech patterns. Unlike later black British music, which has been dominated by the prevalence of almost unintelligibly deep Jamaican patois, the calypso's rhymes depend on the Trinidadian accent, but the language is otherwise well-enunciated in Caribbean standard English. Kitchener reported that, when he first began to sing in a Brixton pub, the manager fired him because he said his customers couldn't understand what "Kitch" was saying. But before the mixed audience of the Sunset Club, when Kitchener began to sing, "Kitch come go to bed / I have a small comb to scratch your head," the punters understood the sexual references well enough, and those who didn't get it had its meaning explained to them by the Caribbean customers.

This carnivalesque tradition was finely adapted and retuned to the migrant experience in Britain. The tracks on the new CD cover an immensely wide variety of topics. There are calypsos composed about specific events, like the Coronation, the Test match victory at Lords, the Jamaican hurricane, the birth of Ghana, the West Indian Federation. Many more offer satirical but largely good-humoured commentary on bizarre aspects of daily life as the migrants first experience them: nosy English landladies; putting money in the geezer for hot water for a bath; English housewives; dogs; riding the underground; Lyons Corner Houses; the weather . . . Others range more broadly—mixed marriages (Beginner's "Mix Up Matrimony"), race and those who vainly try to pass as European (Kitchener's "You can't get away from the fact / If you ain't white you considered black") and, of course, sex (Kitch's scandalous Saxophone No. 2, with the complaint that his new girlfriend won't stop "blowing me saxophone").

These compositions represent a vibrant, piquantly observed and often hilarious running commentary on life for the newly arrived immigrant in the London of the 1950s. They crystallise the migrants' first response to the encounter with that strange object, "the English at home." They have to be seen as part and parcel of the experience that produced the West Indian novel, which emerged in London at about the same moment, with writers like V. S. Naipaul, George Lamming and Sam Selvon. Lamming has said that his generation (and, incidentally, mine) came as members of the individual islands and only in London discovered that they were "West Indian." C. L. R. James, writing about another famous Trinidadian calypsonian, Sparrow, observed that "he is in every way a genuinely West Indian artist . . . a living proof that there is a West Indian nation" (James [1960] 1977).

Much the same is true of the black British calypso, which began as a Trinidadian music and, in London, became the first signature music of the whole West Indian community. The calypsos of the 1950s therefore must be "read" and heard alongside books like *Lonely Londoners* (1956) by Sam Selvon (also a Trinidadian) as offering the most telling insights into the early days of the migrant experience. They are still overwhelmingly jaunty and positive in attitude—this is the music of a minority who have travelled to a strange or strangely familiar place in search of a better life and are determined to survive and prosper. The same confidence, grit and determination are evident in the press and magazine images of immigrant families arriving during the 1950s at London railway stations.

As I have written elsewhere, "Men, women and children already battened down against the freezing weather by the ubiquitous wearing of hats. People dressed up to the nines, for 'travelling,' and even more for 'arrival.' Wearing that expectant look—facing the camera, open and outward, into something they cannot yet see . . . a new life . . . 'Face the music, darling, and let's make a move'" (Hall 1991).

But the darker shadows are also already evident. Kitchener's "Sweet Jamaica" invites Jamaicans to reflect on their decision to leave home and family behind only to find themselves "crying with regret / No sort of employment can they get" and to think fondly of the ackee and saltfish they have left behind in the islands where the sun shines every day. As The Mighty Terror accurately observed, "No Carnival in Britain"—but, of course, there was to be one; and the Notting Hill Carnival, which survives despite the best-engineered efforts to close it down or dampen its insurgent spirit, remains one of the few homes for indigenous calypso left in Britain.

London Is the Place for Me is a witty and joyous testament to the creative power of popular culture and a document of more innocent times. It constitutes one of the best starting points for that rich, unfinished history of the black British diaspora and its intricate interweaving with British life that remains to be written.

NOTE

This essay first appeared as "Calypso Kings," *Guardian*, June 28, 2002.

REFERENCES

Hall, Stuart. 1991. "Reconstruction Work: Images of Postwar Black Settlement." In *Family Snaps: The Meanings of Domestic Photography*, edited by Jo Spence and Patricia Holland, 152–64. London: Virago.
James, C. L. R. (1960) 1977. "The Mighty Sparrow." In *The Future in the Present*, vol. 1 of *Selected Writings*, 191–201. London: Allison and Busby.
James, C. L. R. 1963. *Beyond a Boundary*. Port of Spain: Hutchinson.
Phillips, Mike, and Trevor Phillips. 1999. *Windrush: The Irresistible Rise of Multi-racial Britain*. New York: HarperCollins.
Selvon, Samuel. 1956. *The Lonely Londoners*. Harlow: Longmans.

PART III: CULTURAL AND MULTICULTURAL QUESTIONS

CHAPTER 16

Gramsci's Relevance for the Study of Race and Ethnicity

I.

The aim of this collection of essays is to facilitate "a more sophisticated examination of the hitherto poorly elucidated phenomenon of racism and to examine the adequacy of the theoretical formulations, paradigms and interpretive schemes in the social and human sciences . . . with respect to intolerance and racism and in relation to the complexity of problems they pose." This general rubric enables me to situate more precisely the kind of contribution which a study of Gramsci's work can make to the larger enterprise. In my view, Gramsci's work does *not* offer a *general* social science which can be applied to the analysis of social phenomena across a wide comparative range of historical societies. His potential contribution is more limited. It remains, for all that, of seminal importance. His work is, precisely, of a "sophisticating" kind. He works, broadly, within the Marxist paradigm. However, he has extensively revised, renovated, and sophisticated many aspects of that theoretical framework to make it more relevant to contemporary social relations in the twentieth century. His work therefore has a direct bearing on the question of the "adequacy" of existing social theories, since it is precisely in the direction of "complexifying existing theories and problems" that his most important theoretical contribution is to be found. These points require further clarification before a substantive résumé and assessment of Gramsci's theoretical contribution can be offered.

Gramsci was not a "general theorist." Indeed, he did not practice as an academic or scholarly theorist of any kind. From beginning to end, he was and remained a political intellectual and a socialist activist on the Italian political scene. His "theoretical" writing was developed out of this more organic engagement with his own society and times and was always intended to serve, not an abstract academic purpose, but the aim of "informing political practice." It is therefore essential not to mistake the level of application at which Gramsci's concepts operate. He saw himself as, principally, working within the broad parameters of historical materialism, as outlined by the tradition of Marxist scholarship defined by the work of Marx and Engels and, in the early decades of the twentieth century, by such figures as Lenin, Luxemburg, Trotsky, Labriola, Togliatti, etc. (I cite those names to indicate Gramsci's frame of reference within Marxist thought, not his precise position in relation to those particular figures—to establish the latter is a more complicated issue.) This means that his theoretical contribution has, always, to be *read* with the understanding that it is operating on, broadly, Marxist terrain. That is to say, Marxism provides the general limits within which Gramsci's developments, refinements, revisions, advances, further thoughts, new concepts, and original formulations all operate. However, Gramsci was never a "Marxist" in either a doctrinal, orthodox, or "religious" sense. He understood that the general framework of Marx's theory had to be constantly developed theoretically; applied to new historical conditions; related to developments in society which Marx and Engels could not possibly have foreseen; and expanded and refined by the addition of new concepts.

Gramsci's work thus represents neither a "footnote" to the already-completed edifice of orthodox Marxism nor a ritual evocation of orthodoxy which is circular in the sense of producing "truths" which are already well known. Gramsci practices a genuinely "open" Marxism, which develops many of the insights of Marxist theory in the direction of new questions and conditions. Above all, his work brings into play concepts which classical Marxism did not provide but without which Marxist theory *cannot* adequately explain the complex social phenomena which we encounter in the modern world. It is essential to understand these points if we are to situate Gramsci's work against the background of existing "theoretical formulations, paradigms and interpretive schemes in the social and human sciences."

Not only is Gramsci's work not a *general* work of social science, of the status of, say, the work of such "founding fathers" as Max Weber or Émile Durkheim; it also does not anywhere appear in that recognizable, general, synthesizing form. The main body of Gramsci's theoretical ideas are scattered throughout his occasional essays and polemical writing—he was an active and prolific political journalist—and, of course, in the great collection of *Prison Notebooks*, which Gramsci wrote without benefit of access to libraries or other reference books, either during his enforced leisure in Mussolini's prison after his arrest (1926–33) or after his release, but when he was already terminally ill (1933–37). This fragmentary body of writing, including the *Notebooks* (the *Quaderni del carcere*), is mainly to be found now in the Istituto Gramsci in Rome, where a definitive critical edition of his work is still in the course of completion for publication.[1]

Not only are the writings scattered; they are often fragmentary in form rather than sustained and "finished" pieces of writing. Gramsci was often writing—as in the *Prison Notebooks*—under the most unfavorable circumstances: for example, under the watchful eye of the prison censor and without any other books from which to refresh his memory. Given these circumstances, the *Notebooks* represent a remarkable intellectual feat. Nevertheless, the "costs" of his having to produce them in this way, of never being able to go back to them with time for critical reflection, were considerable. The *Notebooks* are what they say—*notes*—shorter or more extended but not woven into a sustained discourse or coherent text. Some of his most complex arguments are displaced from the main text into long footnotes. Some passages have been reformulated, but with little guidance as to which of the extant versions Gramsci regarded as the more "definitive" text.

As if these aspects of "fragmentariness" do not present us with formidable enough difficulties, Gramsci's work may appear fragmentary in another, even deeper sense. He was constantly using "theory" to illuminate concrete historical cases or political questions—or thinking large concepts in terms of their application to concrete and specific situations. Consequently, Gramsci's work often appears almost *too* concrete: too historically specific, too delimited in its references, too "descriptively" analytic, too time- and context-bound. His most illuminating ideas and formulations are typically of this conjunctural kind. To make more general use of them, they have to be delicately disinterred from their concrete and specific historical embeddedness and transplanted into new soil with considerable care and patience.

Some critics have assumed that Gramsci's concepts operate at this level of concreteness only because he did not have the time or inclination to raise them to a higher level of conceptual generality—the exalted level at which "theoretical ideas" are supposed to function. Thus both Althusser and

Poulantzas have proposed at different times "theorizing" Gramsci's insufficiently theorized texts. This view seems to me mistaken. Here, it is essential to understand, from the epistemological viewpoint, that concepts can operate at very different *levels of abstraction* and are often consciously intended to do so. The important point is not to "misread" one level of abstraction for another. We expose ourselves to serious error when we attempt to "read off" concepts which were designed to operate at a high level of abstraction as if they automatically produced the same theoretical effects when translated to another, more concrete, "lower" level of operation. In general, Gramsci's concepts were quite explicitly designed to operate at the lower levels of historical concreteness. He was not aiming "higher"—and missing his theoretical target! Rather, we have to understand this level of historico-concrete descriptiveness in terms of Gramsci's relation to Marxism.

Gramsci remained a "Marxist," as I have said, in the sense that he developed his ideas within the general framework of Marx's theory: that is, taking for granted concepts like "the capitalist mode of production," the "forces and relations of production," etc. These concepts were pitched by Marx at the most general level of abstraction. That is to say, they are concepts which enable us to grasp and understand the broad processes which organize and structure the capitalist mode of production when reduced to its bare essentials, and at *any* stage or moment of its historical development. The concepts are "epochal" in their range and reference. However, Gramsci understood that as soon as these concepts have to be applied to specific historical social formations, to particular societies at specific stages in the development of capitalism, the theorist is required to move from the level of "mode of production" to a lower, more concrete level of application. This "move" requires not simply more detailed historical specification, but—as Marx himself argued—the application of new concepts and further levels of determination in addition to those pertaining to simple exploitative relations between capital and labor, since the latter serve to specify "the capitalist mode" only at the highest level of reference. Marx himself, in his most elaborated methodological text (his "1857 Introduction" to the *Grundrisse*), envisaged the "production of the concrete in thought" as taking place through a succession of analytic approximations, each adding further levels of determination to the necessarily skeletal and abstract concepts formed at the highest level of analytic abstraction. Marx argued that we could only "think the concrete" through these successive levels of abstraction. That was because the concrete, in reality, consisted of "many determinations"—which, of course, the levels of abstraction we use to think about it with must approximate, in thought. (On these questions of Marxist epistemology, see Hall 1974.)

That is why, as Gramsci moves from the general terrain of Marx's mature concepts (as outlined, for example, in *Capital*) to specific historical conjunctures, he can still continue to "work within" their field of reference. But when he turns to discuss in detail, say, the *Italian* political situation in the 1930s, or changes in the complexity of the class democracies of "the West" after imperialism and the advent of mass democracy, or the specific differences between "eastern" and "western" social formations in Europe, or the type of politics capable of resisting the emerging forces of fascism, or the new forms of politics set in motion by developments in the modern capitalist state, he understands the necessity to adapt, develop, and *supplement* Marx's concepts with new and original ones. First, because Marx concentrated on developing his ideas at the highest level of application (as in *Capital*) rather than at the more concrete historical level (for example, there is no real analysis in Marx of the specific structures of the British nineteenth-century state, though there are many suggestive insights). Second, because the historical conditions for which Gramsci was writing were not the same as those in and for which Marx and Engels had written. (Gramsci had an acute sense of the historical conditions of theoretical production.) Third, because Gramsci felt the need for new conceptualizations at precisely the levels at which Marx's theoretical work was itself at its most sketchy and incomplete: that is, the levels of the analysis of specific historical conjunctures, or of the political and ideological aspects—the much-neglected dimensions of the analysis of social formations in classical Marxism.

These points help us, not simply to "place" Gramsci in relation to the Marxist tradition, but to make explicit the level at which Gramsci's work positively operates and the transformations this shift in the level of magnification required. It is to the generation of new concepts, ideas, and paradigms pertaining to the analysis of political and ideological aspects of social formations in the period after 1870, especially, that Gramsci's work most pertinently relates. Not that he *ever* forgot or neglected the critical element of the economic foundations of society and its relations. But he contributed relatively little by way of original formulations to *that* level of analysis. However, in the much-neglected areas of conjunctural analysis, politics, ideology and the state, the character of different types of political regimes, the importance of cultural and national-popular questions, and the role of civil society in the shifting balance of relations between different social forces in society—on *these* issues, Gramsci has an enormous amount to contribute. He is one of the first original "Marxist theorists" of the historical conditions which have come to dominate the second half of the twentieth century.

Nevertheless, in relation specifically to *racism*, his original contribution cannot be simply transferred wholesale from the existing context of his work. Gramsci did *not* write about race, ethnicity, or racism in their contemporary meanings or manifestations. Nor did he analyze in depth the colonial experience or imperialism, out of which so many of the characteristic "racist" experiences and relationships in the modern world have developed. His principal preoccupation was with his native Italy, and, behind that, the problems of socialist construction in western and eastern Europe, the failure of revolutions to occur in the developed capitalist societies of "the West," the threat posed by the rise of fascism in the interwar period, and the role of the party in the construction of hegemony. Superficially, all this might suggest that Gramsci belongs to that distinguished company of so-called "western Marxists" whom Perry Anderson identified, who, because of their preoccupations with more "advanced" societies, have little of relevance to say to the problems which have arisen largely in the non-European world, or in the relations of "uneven development" between the imperial nations of the capitalist "center" and the englobalized, colonized societies of the periphery.

To read Gramsci in *this* way would, in my opinion, be to commit the error of literalism (though, with qualifications, that is how Anderson reads him). Actually, though Gramsci does not write about racism and does not specifically address those problems, his *concepts* may still be useful to us in our attempt to think through the adequacy of existing social theory paradigms in these areas. Further, his own personal experience and formation, as well as his intellectual preoccupations, were not in fact quite so far removed from those questions as a first glance would superficially suggest.

Gramsci was born in Sardinia in 1891. Sardinia stood in a "colonial" relationship to the Italian mainland. His first contact with radical and socialist ideas was in the context of the growth of Sardinian nationalism, brutally repressed by troops from mainland Italy. Though, after his movement to Turin and his deep involvement with the Turin working-class movement, he abandoned his early "nationalism"; he never lost the concern, imparted to him in his early years, with peasant problems and the complex dialectic of class and regional factors. (For this and later, see Quintin Hoare and Geoffrey Nowell-Smith's excellent "Introduction" to *Prison Notebooks* [1971].) Gramsci was acutely aware of the great line of division which separated the industrializing and modernizing "North" of Italy from the peasant, underdeveloped, and dependent "South." He contributed extensively to the debate on what came to be known as "the Southern question." At the time of his arrival in Turin in 1911, Gramsci almost certainly subscribed to what was known as a "Southernist" position. He retained an interest throughout his life in those relations of dependency and unevenness which linked "North" and "South": and the complex relations between city and countryside, peasantry and proletariat, clientism and modernism, feudalized and industrial social structures. He was thoroughly aware of the degree to which the lines of separation dictated by class relationships were compounded by the cross-cutting relations of regional, cultural, and national difference; also, by differences in the tempos of regional or national historical development. When, in 1923, Gramsci, one of the founders of the Italian Communist Party, proposed *Unitá* as the title of the party's official newspaper, he gave as his reason "because . . . we must give special importance to the Southern question." In the years before and after the First World War, he immersed himself in every aspect of the political life of the Turin working class. This experience gave him an intimate, inside knowledge of one of the most advanced strata of the industrial "factory" proletarian class in Europe. He had an active and sustained career in relation to this advanced sector of the modern working class—first, as a political journalist on the staff of the Socialist Party weekly, *Il Grido del Popolo*; then during the wave of unrest in Turin (the so-called "Red Years"), the factory occupations and councils of labor; and finally, during his editorship of the journal *Ordine Nuovo* up to the founding of the Italian Communist Party. Nevertheless, he continued to reflect, throughout, on the strategies and forms of political action and organization which could *unite* concretely different kinds of struggle. He was preoccupied with the question of what basis could be found in the complex alliances of and relations between the different social strata for the foundation of a specifically *modern* Italian state. The preoccupation with the question of regional specificity, social alliances, and the social foundations of the state also directly links Gramsci's work with what we might think of today as "North/South," as well as "East/West," questions.

The early 1920s were taken up, for Gramsci, with the difficult problems of trying to conceptualize new forms of political "party" and with the question of distinguishing a path of development specific to Italian *national* conditions, in opposition to the hegemonising thrust of the Soviet-based Comintern. All this led ultimately to the major contribution which the Italian

Communist Party has made to the theorization of the conditions of "national specificity" in relation to the very different concrete historical developments of the different societies, East and West. In the later 1920s, however, Gramsci's preoccupations were largely framed by the context of the growing threat of fascism, up to his arrest and internment by Mussolini's forces in 1929.

So, though Gramsci did not write directly about the problems of racism, the preoccupying themes of his work provide deeper intellectual and theoretical lines of connection to many more of these contemporary issues than a quick glance at his writings would suggest.

II.

It is to these deeper connections, and to their fertilizing impact on the search for more adequate theorizations in the field, that we now turn. I will try to elucidate some of those core conceptions in Gramsci's work which point in that direction.

I begin with the issue which, in some ways, for the chronological student of Gramsci's work, comes more toward the end of his life: the question of his rigorous attack on all vestiges of "economism" and "reductionism" within classical Marxism. By "economism" I do not mean—as I hope I have already made clear—to neglect the powerful role which the economic foundations of a social order or the dominant economic relations of a society play in shaping and structuring the whole edifice of social life. I mean, rather, a specific theoretical approach which tends to read the economic foundations of society as the *only* determining structure. This approach tends to see all other dimensions of the social formation as simply mirroring "the economic" on another level of articulation, and as having no other determining or structuring force in their own right. The approach, to put it simply, reduces everything in a social formation to the economic level and conceptualizes all other types of social relations as directly and immediately "corresponding" to the economic. This collapses Marx's somewhat problematic formulation—the economic as "determining in the last instance"—to the reductionist principle that the economic determines, in an immediate way, in the first, middle, and last instances. In this sense, "economism" is a theoretical reductionism. It simplifies the structure of social formations, reducing their complexity of articulation, vertical and horizontal, to a single line of determination. It simplifies the very concept of "determination" (which in Marx is actually a very complex idea) to that of a mechanical function. It flattens all the mediations between the different levels of a society. It presents social formations—in Althusser's words—as a "simple expressive totality," in which every level of articulation corresponds to every other, and which is, from end to end, structurally transparent. I have no hesitation in saying that this represents a gigantic crudification and simplification of Marx's work—the kind of simplification and reductionism which once led him, in despair, to say that "if that is Marxism, then I am not a Marxist." Yet there certainly are pointers in this direction in some of Marx's work. It corresponds closely to the orthodox version of Marxism, which did become canonized at the time of the Second International, and which is often even today advanced as the pure doctrine of "classical Marxism." Such a conception of the social formation and of the relationships between its different levels of articulation—it should be clear—has little or no theoretical room left in it for ways of conceptualizing the political and ideological dimensions, let alone ways of conceptualizing other types of social differentiation such as social divisions and contradictions arising around race, ethnicity, nationality, and gender.

Gramsci, from the outset, set his face against this type of economism; and in his later years, he developed a sustained theoretical polemic against precisely its canonization within the classical Marxist tradition. Two examples from different strands in his work must suffice to illustrate this point. In his essay titled "The Modern Prince" Gramsci is discussing how to set about analyzing a particular historical conjuncture. He substitutes, for the reductionist approach which would "read off" political and ideological developments from their economic determinations, a far more complex and differentiated type of analysis. This is based, not on a "one-way determination," but on the analysis of "the relations of force" and aims to differentiate (rather than to collapse as identical) the "various moments or levels" in the development of such a conjuncture (*Prison Notebooks* [Gramsci 1971] 180–81, hereafter PN). He pinpoints this analytic task in terms of what he calls "the decisive passage from the structure to the spheres of the complex superstructures." In this way he sets himself decisively against any tendency to reduce the sphere of the political and ideological superstructures to the economic structure or "base." He understands this as the most critical site in the struggle against reductionism. "It is the problem of the relations between structure and superstructure which must be accurately posed if the forces which are active in the history of a particular period are to be correctly analysed and the relations between them determined" (PN 177). Economism, he adds, is an inadequate way, theoretically, of posing this critical set of relationships. It tends, among other things, to substitute an analysis based on "immediate class interests" (in the form of the question "Who profits directly from this?") for a fuller, more structured analysis of "economic class formations . . . with all their inherent relations" (PN 163). It may be ruled out, he suggests, "that *immediate* economic crises of themselves produce fundamental historical events" (my italics). Does this mean that the economic plays no part in the development of historical crises? Not at all. But its role is, rather, to "create a terrain more favourable to the dissemination of certain modes of thought, and certain ways of posing and resolving questions involving the entire subsequent development of national life" (PN 184). In short, until one has shown how "objective economic crises" actually develop, via the changing relations in the balance of social forces, into crises in the state and society, and germinate in the form of ethical-political struggles and formed political ideologies, influencing the conception of the world of the masses, one has not conducted a proper kind of analysis, rooted in the decisive and irreversible "passage" between structure and superstructure.

The sort of immediate infallibility which economic reductionism brings in its wake, Gramsci argues, "comes very cheap." It not only has no theoretical significance—it also has only minimal political implications or practical efficacy. "In general, it produces nothing but moralistic sermons and interminable questions of personality" (PN 166). It is a conception based on "the iron conviction that there exist objective laws of historical development similar in kind to natural law, together with a belief in a predetermined teleology like that of a religion." There is no alternative to this collapse—which, Gramsci argues, has been incorrectly identified with historical materialism—except "the concrete posing of the problem of hegemony."

It can be seen from the general thrust of the argument in this passage that many of Gramsci's key concepts (hegemony, for example) and characteristic approaches (the approach via the analysis of "relations of social forces," for example) were consciously understood by him as a barrier against the tendency to economic reductionism in some versions of Marxism. He coupled with his critique of "economism" the related tendencies to positivism, empiricism, "scientism," and objectivism within Marxism.

This comes through even more clearly in "The Problems of Marxism," a text explicitly written as a critique of the "vulgar materialism" implicit in Bukharin's *Theory of Historical Materialism: A Manual of Popular Sociology*. The latter was published in Moscow in 1921, went through many editions, and was often quoted as an example of "orthodox" Marxism (even though

Lenin observed about it that Bukharin was unfortunately "ignorant of the dialectic"). In "Critical Notes on an Attempt at Popular Sociology," which forms the second part of his essay "The Problems of Marxism," Gramsci offers a sustained assault on the epistemologies of economism, positivism, and the spurious search for scientific guarantees. They were founded, he argues, on the falsely positivistic model that the laws of society and human historical development can be modeled directly on what social scientists conceived (falsely, as we now know) as the "objectivity" of the laws governing the natural scientific world. Terms like "regularity," "necessity," "law," and "determination," he argues, are to be thought of not "as a derivation from natural science but rather as an elaboration of concepts born on the terrain of political economy." Thus "determined market" must *really* mean a "determined relation of social forces in a determined structure of the productive apparatus," this relationship being guaranteed (that is, rendered permanent) by a "determined political, moral and juridical superstructure." The movement in Gramsci's formulation from an analytically reduced positivistic formula to a richer, more complex conceptualization framed with social science is lucidly clear from that substitution. It lends weight to Gramsci's summarizing argument, that

> the claim presented as an essential postulate of historical materialism, that every fluctuation of politics and ideology can be presented and expounded as an immediate expression of the structure (i.e., the economic base), must be contested in theory as primitive infantilism, and combated in practice with the authentic testimony of Marx, the author of concrete, political and historical works. (PN 407)

This shift of direction, which Gramsci set himself to bring about within the terrain of Marxism, was quite self-consciously accomplished—and decisive for the whole thrust of his subsequent thought. Without this point of theoretical departure, Gramsci's complicated relationship to the tradition of Marxist scholarship cannot be properly defined.

If Gramsci renounced the simplicities of reductionism, how then did he set about a more adequate analysis of a social formation? Here we may be helped by a brief detour, provided that we move with caution. Althusser (who was profoundly influenced by Gramsci) and his coauthor of *Reading Capital* (Althusser and Balibar 1970) make a critical distinction between "mode of production," which refers to the basic forms of economic relations which characterize a society, but which is an analytic abstraction, since no society can function by its economy alone, and, on the other hand, what they call the "social formation." By this latter term they meant to invoke the idea that societies are necessarily complexly structured totalities, with different levels of articulation (the economic, the political, the ideological instances) in different combinations, each combination giving rise to a different configuration of social forces and hence to a different type of social development. The authors of *Reading Capital* tended to give as the distinguishing feature of a "social formation" the fact that, in it, more than one mode of production could be combined. But, though this is true, and can have important consequences (especially for postcolonial societies, which we take up later), it is not, in my view, the most important point of distinction between the two terms. In "social formations" one is dealing with complexly structured societies composed of economic, political, and ideological relations, where the different levels of articulation do not by any means simply correspond or "mirror" one another but which are—in Althusser's felicitous metaphor—"overdetermining" on and for one another (Althusser 1969). It is this complex structuring of the different levels of articulation, not simply the existence of more than one mode of production, which constitutes the difference between the concept of "mode of production" and the necessarily more concrete and historically specific notion of a "social formation."

Now this latter concept *is* the conception to which Gramsci addressed himself. This is what he meant by saying that the relationship between "structure" and "superstructures," or the "passage" of any organic historical movement right through the whole social formation, from economic "base" to the sphere of ethico-political relations, was at the heart of any nonreductionist or economistic type of analysis. To pose and resolve *that* question was to conduct an analysis, properly founded on an understanding of the complex relationships of overdetermination between the different social practices in any social formation.

It is this protocol which Gramsci pursued when, in "The Modern Prince," he outlined his characteristic way of "analyzing situations." The details are complex and cannot be filled out in all their subtlety here, but the bare outlines are worth setting out, if only for purposes of comparison with a more "economistic" or reductionist approach. He considered this "an elementary exposition of the science and art of politics—understood as a body of practical rules for research and of detailed observations useful for awakening an interest in effective reality and for stimulating more rigorous and more vigorous political insights"—a discussion, he added, which must be *strategic* in character.

First of all, he argued, one must understand the fundamental structure—the objective relations—within society or "the degree of development of the productive forces," for these set the most fundamental limits and conditions for the whole shape of historical development. From here arise some of the major lines of tendency which *might* be favorable to this or that line of development. The error of reductionism is then to translate these tendencies and constraints *immediately* into their absolutely determined political and ideological effects, or, alternatively, to abstract them into some "iron law of necessity." In fact, they structure and determine only in the sense that they define the terrain on which historical forces move—they define the horizon of possibilities. But they can, in neither the first nor the last instance, fully determine the content of political and economic struggles, much less objectively fix or guarantee the outcomes of such struggles.

The next move in the analysis is to distinguish "organic" historical movements, which are destined to penetrate deep into society and be relatively long lasting, from more "occasional, immediate, almost accidental movements." In this respect, Gramsci reminds us that a "crisis," if it is organic, can last for decades. It is not a static phenomenon but, rather, one marked by constant movement, polemics, contestations, etc., which represent the attempt by different sides to overcome or resolve the crisis and to do so in terms which favor their long-term hegemony. The theoretical danger, Gramsci argues, lies in "presenting causes as immediately operative which in fact only operate indirectly, or in asserting that the immediate causes are the only effective ones." The first leads to an excess of economism, the second to an excess of ideologism. (Gramsci was preoccupied, especially in moments of defeat, by the fatal oscillation between these two extremes, which in reality mirror one another in an inverted form.) Far from there being any "law-like" guarantee that some law of necessity will inevitably convert economic causes into immediate political effects, Gramsci insisted that the analysis only succeeds and is "true" if those underlying causes become a new reality. The substitution of the conditional tense for positivistic certainty is critical.

Next, Gramsci insisted on the fact that the length and complexity of crises cannot be mechanically predicted, but develop over longer historical periods; they move between periods of relative "stabilization" and periods of rapid and convulsive change. Consequently, *periodization* is a key aspect of the analysis. It parallels the earlier concern with historical specificity. "It is precisely the study of these 'intervals' of varying frequency which enables one to reconstruct the relations, on the one hand, between structure and superstructure, and on the other between the development of organic movement and conjunctural movement in the structure." There is nothing mechanical or prescriptive, for Gramsci, about this "study."

Having thus established the groundwork of a dynamic historical analytic framework, Gramsci turns to the analysis of the movements of historical forces—the "relations of force"—which constitute the actual terrain of political and social struggle and development. Here he introduces the critical notion that what we are looking for is *not* the absolute victory of this side over that, nor the total incorporation of one set of forces into another. Rather, the analysis is a relational matter—that is, a question to be resolved *relationally*, using the idea of "unstable balance" or "the continuous process of formation and superseding of unstable equilibria." The critical question is, are "relations of forces *favourable or unfavourable to this or that tendency*" (my italics)? This emphasis on "relations" and "unstable balance" reminds us that social forces which lose out in any particular historical period do not thereby disappear from the terrain of struggle, nor is struggle in such circumstances suspended. For example, the idea of the "absolute" and total victory of the bourgeoisie over the working class or the total incorporation of the working class into the bourgeois project is totally foreign to Gramsci's definition of hegemony—though the two are frequently confused in scholarly commentary. It is always the tendential balance in the relations of force which matters.

Gramsci then differentiates the "relations of force" into its different moments. He assumes no *necessary teleological evolution* between these moments. The first has to do with an assessment of the objective conditions which place and position the different social forces. The second relates to the political moment—the "degree of homogeneity, self-awareness and organization attained by the various social classes" (PN 181). The important thing here is that so-called "class unity" is never *assumed*, a priori. It is understood that classes, while sharing certain common conditions of existence, are also crosscut by conflicting interests, historically segmented and fragmented in this actual course of historical formation. Thus the "unity" of classes is necessarily complex and has to be *produced*—constructed, created—as a result of specific economic, political, and ideological practices. It can never be taken as automatic or "given." Coupled with this radical historicization of the automatic conception of classes lodged at the heart of fundamentalist Marxism, Gramsci elaborates further on Marx's distinction between "class in itself" and "class for itself." He notes the different stages through which class consciousness, organization, and unity can—under the right conditions—develop. There is the "economic corporate" stage, where professional or occupational groups recognize their basic common interests but are conscious of no wider class solidarities. Then there is the "class corporate" moment, where class solidarity of interests develops, but only in the economic field. Finally, there is the moment of "hegemony," which transcends the corporate limits of purely economic solidarity, encompasses the interests of other subordinate groups, and begins to "propagate itself throughout society," bringing about intellectual and moral as well as economic and political unity, and "posing also the questions around which the struggle rages . . . thus creating the hegemony of a fundamental social group over a series of subordinate groups." It is this process of the coordination of the interests of a dominant group with the general interests of other groups and the life of the state as a whole that constitutes the "hegemony" of a particular historical bloc (*PN* 182). It is only in such moments of "national popular" unity that the formation of what he calls a "collective will" becomes possible.

Gramsci reminds us, however, that even this extraordinary degree of organic unity does not *guarantee* the outcome of specific struggles, which can be won or lost on the outcome of the decisive tactical issue of the military and politico-military relations of force. He insists, however, that "politics must have priority over its military aspect, and only politics creates the possibility for manoeuvre and movement" (*PN* 232).

Three points about this formulation should be particularly noted. First, "hegemony" is a very particular, historically specific, and temporary "moment" in the life of a society. It is rare for this degree of unity to be achieved, enabling a society to set itself a quite new historical agenda, under the leadership of a specific formation or constellation of social forces. Such periods of "settlement" are unlikely to persist forever. There is nothing automatic about them. They have to be actively constructed and positively maintained. Crises mark the beginning of their disintegration. Second, we must take note of the multidimensional, multiarena character of hegemony. It cannot be constructed or sustained on *one* front of struggle alone (for example, the economic). It represents a degree of mastery over a whole series of different "positions" at once. Mastery is not simply imposed or dominative in character. Effectively, it results from winning a substantial degree of popular consent. It thus represents the installation of a profound measure of social and moral authority, not simply over its immediate supporters but across society as a whole. It is this "authority," and the range and diversity of sites on which "leadership" is exercised, which makes possible the "propagation," for a time, of an intellectual, moral, political, and economic collective will throughout society. Third, what "leads" in a period of hegemony is no longer described as a "ruling class" in the traditional language, but as a historic bloc. This has its critical reference to "class" as a determining level of analysis, but it does *not* translate whole classes directly onto the political-ideological stage as unified historical actors. The "leading elements" in a historic bloc may be only one fraction of the dominant economic class—for example, finance rather than industrial capital, national rather than international capital. Associated with it, within the "bloc," will be strata of the subaltern and dominated classes, who have been won over by specific concessions and compromises and who form part of the social constellation but in a subordinate role. The "winning over" of these sections is the result of the forging of "expansive, universalizing alliances" which cement the historic bloc under a particular leadership. Each hegemonic formation will thus have its own, specific social composition and configuration. This is a very different way of conceptualizing what is often referred to, loosely and inaccurately, as the "ruling class."

Gramsci was not, of course, the originator of the term "hegemony." Lenin used it in an analytic sense to refer to the leadership which the proletariat in Russia was required to establish over the peasantry in the struggles to found a socialist state. This in itself is of interest. One of the key questions posed for us by the study of developing societies, which have not passed through the "classic" path of development to capitalism which Marx took as his paradigm case in *Capital* (that is, the English example), is the balance of and relations between different social classes in the struggle for national and economic development; the relative insignificance of the industrial proletariat, narrowly defined, in societies characterized by a relatively low level of industrial development; and above all, the degree to which the peasant class is a leading element in the struggles which found the national state and even, in some cases (China is the outstanding example, but Cuba and Vietnam are also significant examples), the *leading* revolutionary class. It was in this sort of context that Gramsci first employed the term "hegemony." In his unfinished 1926 "Notes on the Southern Question," he argued that the proletariat in Italy could only become the "leading" class insofar as it "succeeds in creating a system of alliances which allows it to mobilize the majority of the working population against capitalism and the bourgeois state . . . [which] means to the extent that it succeeds in gaining the consent of the broad peasant masses."

In fact, this is already a theoretically complex and rich formulation. It implies that the actual social or political force which becomes decisive in a moment of organic crisis will not be composed of a single homogeneous class but will have a complex social composition. Second, it is implicit that its basis of unity will have to be, not an automatic one, given by its position in the mode of economic production, but, rather, a "system of alliances." Third, though such a political and social force has its roots in the fundamental class division of society, the actual forms of the political struggle will have a *wider* social character—dividing society not simply along "class versus class" lines but, rather, polarizing it along the broadest front of antagonism ("the majority of the working population"): for example, between *all* the popular classes, on the one side, and those representing the interests of capital and the power bloc grouped around the state, on the other. In fact, in national and ethnic struggles in the modern world, the actual field of struggle is often actually polarized precisely in this more complex and differentiated way. The difficulty is that it often continues to be described, theoretically, in terms which *reduce* the complexity of its actual social composition to the more simple, descriptive terms of a struggle between two apparently simple and homogeneous class blocs. Further, Gramsci's reconceptualization puts firmly on the agenda such critical strategic questions as the terms on which a class like the peasantry can be won for a national struggle, not on the basis of compulsion but on the basis of "winning their consent."

In the course of his later writings, Gramsci went on to expand the conception of hegemony even further, moving forward from this essentially "class alliance" way of conceptualizing it. First, "hegemony" becomes a general term, which can be applied to the strategies of *all* classes, applied analytically to the formation of all leading historical blocs, not to the strategy of the proletariat alone. In this way, he converts the concept into a more general analytic term. Its applicability in this more general way is obvious. The way, for example, in which in South Africa the state is sustained by the forging of alliances between white ruling-class interests and the interests of white workers against blacks, or the importance in South African politics of the attempts to "win the consent" of certain subaltern classes and groups—for example, the colored strata or "tribal" blacks—in the strategy of forging alliances against the mass of rural and industrial blacks, or the "mixed" class character of all the decolonizing struggles for national independence in developing, postcolonial societies—these and a host of other concrete historical situations are significantly clarified by the development of this concept.

The second development is the difference Gramsci comes to articulate between a class which "dominates" and a class which "leads." Domination and coercion can maintain the ascendancy of a particular class over a society. But its "reach" is limited. It has to rely consistently on coercive means, rather than the winning of consent. For that reason it is not capable of enlisting the positive participation of different parts of society in a historic project to transform the state or renovate society. "Leadership," on the other hand, has its "coercive" aspects too. But it is "led" by the winning of consent, the taking into account of subordinate interests, the attempt to make itself popular. For Gramsci there is no pure case of coercion/consent—only different combinations of the two dimensions. Hegemony is not exercised in the economic and administrative fields alone, but encompasses the critical domains of cultural, moral, ethical, and intellectual leadership. It is only under those conditions that some long-term historic "project"—for example, to modernize society, to raise the whole level of performance of society or transform the basis of national politics—can be effectively put on the historical agenda. It can be seen from this that the concept of "hegemony" is *expanded* in Gramsci by making strategic use of a number of distinctions: for example, those between domination and leadership, coercion and consent, economic and corporate, and moral and intellectual.

Underpinning this expansion is another distinction based on one of Gramsci's fundamental historical theses. This is the distinction between state and civil society. In his essay titled "State and Civil Society," Gramsci elaborated this distinction in several ways. First, he drew a distinction between two types of struggle—the "war of manoeuvre," where everything is condensed into one front and one moment of struggle, and there is a single, strategic breach in the "enemy's defenses," which, once made, enables the new forces "to rush in and obtain a definitive (strategic) victory." Second, there is the "war of position," which has to be conducted in a protracted way, across many different and varying fronts of struggle, where there is rarely a single breakthrough which wins the war once and for all—"in a flash," as Gramsci puts it (PN 233). What really counts in a war of position is not the enemy's "forward trenches" (to continue the military metaphor) but "the whole organizational and industrial system of the territory which lies to the rear of the army in the field"—that is, the whole structure of society, including the structures and institutions of civil society. Gramsci regarded "1917" as perhaps the last example of a successful "war of manoeuvre" strategy: it marked "a decisive turning-point in the history of the art and science of politics."

This was linked to a second distinction—between "East" and "West." These stand, for Gramsci, as metaphors for the distinction between eastern and western Europe, and between the model of the Russian Revolution and the forms of political struggle appropriate to the much more difficult terrain of the industrialized liberal democracies of "the West." Here, Gramsci addresses the critical issue, so long evaded by many Marxist scholars, of the failure of political conditions in "the West" to match or correspond with those which made 1917 in Russia possible—a central issue, since, despite these radical differences (and the consequent failure of proletarian revolutions of the classic type in "the West"), Marxists have continued to be obsessed by the "Winter Palace" model of revolution and politics. Gramsci is therefore drawing a critical analytic distinction between prerevolutionary Russia, with its long-delayed modernization, its swollen state apparatus and bureaucracy, and its relatively undeveloped civil society and low level of capitalist development, and, on the other hand, "the West," with its mass democratic forms, its complex civil society, the consolidation of the consent of the masses, through political democracy, into a more consensual basis for the state:

> In Russia the State was everything, civil society was primordial and gelatinous; in the West, there was a proper relation between State and civil society, and when the State trembled, a sturdy structure of civil society was at once revealed. The State was only an outer ditch, behind which there stood a powerful system of fortresses and earthworks: more or less numerous from one state to another.... This precisely necessitated an accurate reconnaissance of each individual country. (PN 237–38)

Gramsci is not merely pinpointing a difference of historical specificity. He is describing a historical *transition*. It is evident, as "State and Civil Society" makes clear, that he sees the "war of position" *replacing* the "war of manoeuvre" more and more as the conditions of "the West" become progressively more characteristic of the modern political field in one country after another. (Here, "the West" ceases to be a purely *geographical* identification and comes to stand for a new terrain of politics, created by the emerging forms of state and civil society and new, more complex relations between them.) In these more "advanced" societies, "where civil society has become a very complex structure ... resistant to the catastrophic 'incursions' of the immediate economic element, ... the superstructures of civil society are like the trench-systems of modern warfare." A different type of political strategy is appropriate to this novel terrain. "The war of manoeuvre [is] reduced to more of a tactical than a strategic function," and one passes over from "frontal attack" to a "war of position" which requires "unprecedented concentration of hegemony" and is "concentrated, difficult and requires exceptional qualities of patience and inventiveness" because, once won, it is "decisive definitively" (PN 238–39).

Gramsci bases this "transition from one form of politics to another" historically. It takes place in "the West" after 1870 and is identified with "the colonial expansion of Europe," the emergence of modern mass democracy, a complexification in the role and organization of the state, and an unprecedented elaboration in the structures and processes of "civil hegemony." What Gramsci is pointing to, here, is partly the diversification of social antagonisms, the "dispersal" of power, which occurs in societies where hegemony is not sustained exclusively through the enforced instrumentality of the state but, rather, is grounded in the relations and institutions of civil society. In such societies, the voluntary associations, relations, and institutions of civil society—schooling, the family, churches and religious life, cultural organizations, so-called private relations, gender, sexual and ethnic identities, etc.—become, in effect, "for the art of politics . . . the 'trenches' and the permanent fortifications of the front in the war of position: they render merely 'partial' the element of movement which before used to be 'the whole' of war" (PN 243).

Underlying all this is therefore a deeper labor of theoretical redefinition. Gramsci in effect is progressively transforming the limited definition of the state, characteristic of some versions of Marxism, as essentially reducible to the coercive instrument of the ruling class, stamped with an exclusive class character which can only be transformed by being "smashed" with a single blow. He comes gradually to emphasize, not only the complexity of the formation of modern civil society, but also the parallel development in complexity of the formation of the modern state. The state is no longer conceived as simply an administrative and coercive apparatus—it is also "educative and formative." It is the point from which hegemony over society as a whole is ultimately exercised (though it is not the only place where hegemony is constructed). It is the point of condensation—not because all forms of coercive domination necessarily radiate outward from its apparatuses but because, in its contradictory structure, it *condenses* a variety of different relations and practices into a definite "system of rules." It is, for this reason, the site for conforming (that is, bringing into line) or "adapting the civilization and the morality of the broadest masses to the necessities of the continuous development of the economic apparatus of production."

Every state, he therefore argues, "is ethical in as much as one of its most important functions is to raise the great mass of the population to a particular cultural and moral level (or type) which corresponds to the needs of the productive forces for development, and hence to the interests of the ruling class" (PN 258). Notice here how Gramsci foregrounds *new* dimensions of power and politics, new areas of antagonism and struggle—the ethical, the cultural, the moral. How, also, he ultimately returns to more "traditional" questions—"needs of the productive forces for development," "interests of the ruling class": but not immediately or reductively. They can only be approached *indirectly*, through a series of necessary displacements and "relays": that is, via the irreversible "passage from the structure to the sphere of the complex superstructures."

It is within this framework that Gramsci elaborates his new conception of the state. The modern state exercises moral and educative leadership—it "plans, urges, incites, solicits, punishes." It is where the bloc of social forces which dominates over it not only justifies and maintains its domination but wins by leadership and authority the active consent of those over whom it rules. Thus it plays a pivotal role in the construction of hegemony. In this reading, it becomes, not a *thing* to be seized, overthrown, or "smashed" with a single blow, but a complex *formation* in modern societies which must become the focus of a number of different strategies and struggles because it is an arena of different social contestations.

It should now be clearer how these distinctions and developments in Gramsci's thinking all feed back into and enrich the basic concept of "hegemony." Gramsci's actual formulations about the state and civil society vary from place to place in his work and have caused some confusion (Anderson 1977). But there is little question about the underlying thrust of his thought on this question. This points irrevocably to the increasing complexity of the interrelationships in modern societies *between* state and civil society. Taken together, they form a complex "system" which has to be the object of a many-sided type of political strategy, conducted on several different fronts at once. The use of such a concept of the state totally transforms, for example, much of the literature about the so-called "postcolonial state," which has often assumed a simple, dominative, or instrumental model of state power.

In this context, Gramsci's "East"/"West" distinction must not be taken too literally. Many so-called "developing" societies already have complex democratic political regimes (that is, in Gramsci's terms, they belong to the "West"). In others, the state has absorbed into itself some of the wider, educative, and "leadership" roles and functions which, in the industrialized Western liberal democracies, are located in civil society. The point is therefore not to apply Gramsci's distinction literally or mechanically but to use his insights to unravel the changing complexities in state/civil society relationships in the modern world and the decisive shift in the predominant character of strategic political struggles—essentially, the encompassing of civil society as well as the state as integral arenas of struggles—which this historic transformation has brought about. An enlarged conception of the state, he argues at one point (stretching the definitions somewhat), must encompass "political society and civil society" or "hegemony protected by the armour of coercion" (PN 263). He pays particular attention to how these distinctions are differently articulated in different societies—for example, within the "separation of powers" characteristic of liberal parliamentary democratic states as contrasted with the collapsed spheres of fascist states. At another point, he insists on the ethical and cultural functions of the state—raising "the great mass of the population to a particular cultural and moral level," and to the "educative functions of such critical institutions as the school (a 'positive educative function') and the courts ('a repressive and negative educative function')." These emphases bring a range of new institutions and arenas of struggle into the traditional conceptualization of the state and politics. It constitutes them as specific and strategic centers of struggle. The effect is to multiply and proliferate the various fronts of politics and to differentiate the different kinds of social antagonisms. The different fronts of struggle are the various sites of political and social antagonism, and constitute the objects of modern politics when it is understood in the form of a "war of position." The traditional emphases, in which differentiated types of struggle, for example, around schooling, cultural or sexual politics, and institutions of civil society like the family, traditional social organizations, ethnic and cultural institutions, and the like, are *all* subordinated and reduced to an industrial struggle, condensed around the workplace, and a simple choice between trade-union and insurrectionary or parliamentary forms of politics, is here systematically challenged and decisively overthrown. The impact on the very conception of politics itself is little short of electrifying.

Of the many other interesting topics and themes from Gramsci's work which we could consider, I choose, finally, the seminal work on ideology, culture, the role of the intellectual, and the character of what he calls the "national-popular." Gramsci adopts what, at first, may seem a fairly traditional definition of ideology, a "conception of the world, any philosophy, which becomes a cultural movement, a 'religion,' a 'faith,' that has produced a form of practical activity or will in which a philosophy is contained as an implicit theoretical 'premise.'" "One might say," he adds, "ideology ... on condition that the word is used in its best sense of a conception of the world that is implicitly manifest in art, in law, in economic activity and in all manifestations of individual and collective life." This is followed by an attempt clearly to formulate the problem ideology addresses in terms of its social function: "The problem is that of preserving the ideological unity of the entire social bloc which that ideology serves to cement and unify" (*PN* 328). This definition is not as simple as it looks, for it assumes the essential link between the philosophical nucleus or premise at the center of any distinctive ideology or conception of the world and the necessary elaboration of that conception into practical and popular forms of consciousness, affecting the broad masses of society, in the shape of a cultural movement, political tendency, faith, or religion. Gramsci is *never* only concerned with the philosophical core of an ideology; he always addresses *organic* ideologies, which are organic because they touch practical, everyday common sense and they "organize human masses and create the terrain on which men move, acquire consciousness of their position, struggle, etc."

This is the basis of Gramsci's critical distinction between "philosophy" and "common sense." Ideology consists of two distinct "floors." The coherence of an ideology often depends on its specialized philosophical elaboration. But this formal coherence cannot guarantee its organic historical effectivity. That can only be found when and where philosophical currents enter into, modify, and transform the practical, everyday consciousness or popular thought of the masses. The latter is what he calls "common sense." "Common sense" is not coherent: it is usually "disjointed and episodic," fragmentary and contradictory. Into it the traces and "stratified deposits" of more coherent philosophical systems have sedimented over time without leaving any clear inventory. It represents itself as the "traditional wisdom or truth of the ages," but in fact, it is deeply a product of history, "part of the historical process." Why, then, is common sense so important? Because it is the terrain of conceptions and categories on which the practical consciousness of the masses of the people is actually formed. It is the already-formed and "taken-for-granted" terrain on which more coherent ideologies and philosophies must contend for mastery; the ground which new conceptions of the world must take into account, contest, and transform if they are to shape the conceptions of the world of the masses and in that way become historically effective:

Every philosophical current leaves behind a sediment of "common sense"; this is the document of its historical effectiveness. Common sense is not rigid and immobile but is continually transforming itself, enriching itself with scientific ideas and with philosophical opinions which have entered ordinary life. Common sense creates the folklore of the future, that is as a relatively rigid phase of popular knowledge at a given place and time. (PN 362n5)

It is this concern with the structures of *popular thought* which distinguishes Gramsci's treatment of ideology. Thus, he insists that everyone is a philosopher or an intellectual insofar as he or she thinks, since all thought, action, and language is reflexive, contains a conscious line of moral conduct, and thus sustains a particular conception of the world (though not everyone has the specialized function of "the intellectual").

In addition, a class will always have its spontaneous, vivid but not coherent or philosophically elaborated, instinctive understanding of its basic conditions of life and the nature of the constraints and forms of exploitation to which it is commonly subjected. Gramsci described the latter as its "good sense." But it always requires a further work of political education and cultural politics to renovate and clarify these constructions of popular thought—"common sense"—into a more coherent political theory or philosophical current. This "raising of popular thought" is part and parcel of the process by which a collective will is constructed, and requires extensive work of intellectual organization—an essential part of any hegemonic political strategy. Popular beliefs, the culture of a people, Gramsci argues, are not arenas of struggle which can be left to look after themselves. They "are themselves material forces" (PN 165).

It thus requires an extensive cultural and ideological struggle to bring about or effect the intellectual and ethical unity which is essential to the forging of hegemony: a struggle which takes the form of "a struggle of political hegemonies and of opposing directions, first in the ethical field and then in that of politics proper" (PN 333). This bears very directly on the type of social struggles we identify with national, anticolonial, and antiracist movements. In his application of these ideas, Gramsci is never simplistically "progressive" in his approach. For example, he recognizes, in the Italian case, the absence of a genuine popular national culture which could easily provide the groundwork for the formation of a popular collective will. Much of his work on culture, popular literature, and religion explores the potential terrain and tendencies in Italian life and society which might provide the basis of such a development. He documents, for example, in Italy, the extensive degree to which popular Catholicism can make and has made itself a genuinely "popular force," giving it a unique importance in forming the traditional conceptions of the popular classes. He attributes this, in part, to Catholicism's scrupulous attention to the organization of ideas—especially to ensuring the relationship between philosophical thought or doctrine and popular life or common sense. Gramsci refuses all notions that ideas move and ideologies develop spontaneously and without direction. Like every other sphere of civil life, religion requires organization: it possesses its specific sites of development, specific processes of transformation, specific practices of struggle. "The relation between common sense and the upper level of philosophy," he asserts, "is assured by 'politics'" (PN 331). Major agencies in this process are, of course, the cultural, educational, and religious institutions; the family and voluntary associations; but also political parties, which are also centers of ideological and cultural formation. The principal agents are intellectuals who have a specialized responsibility for the circulation and development of culture and ideology and who either align themselves with the existing dispositions of social and intellectual forces ("traditional" intellectuals) or align themselves with the emerging popular forces and seek to elaborate new currents of ideas ("organic" intellectuals). Gramsci is eloquent about the critical function, in the Italian case, of traditional intellectuals who have been aligned with classical, scholarly, or clerical enterprises and the relative weakness of the more emergent intellectual strata.

Gramsci's thinking on this question encompasses novel and radical ways of conceptualizing the *subjects* of ideology, which have become the object of considerable contemporary theorizing. He altogether refuses any idea of a pregiven unified ideological subject—for example, the proletarian with its "correct" revolutionary thoughts or blacks with their already-guaranteed current antiracist consciousness. He recognizes the "plurality" of selves or identities of which the so-called "subject" of thought and ideas is composed. He argues that this multifaceted nature of consciousness is not an individual but a collective phenomenon, a consequence of the relationship between "the self" and the ideological discourses which compose the cultural terrain of a society. "The personality is strangely composite," he observes. It contains "Stone Age elements and principles of a more advanced science, prejudices from all past phases of history . . . and intuitions of a future philosophy" (PN 324). Gramsci draws attention to the contradiction in consciousness between the conception of the world which manifests itself, however fleetingly, in action and those conceptions which are affirmed verbally or in thought. This complex, fragmentary, and contradictory conception of consciousness is a considerable advance over the explanation by way of "false consciousness" more traditional to Marxist theorizing but which is an explanation that depends on self-deception and which he rightly treats as inadequate. The implicit attack which Gramsci advances on the traditional conception of the "given" and unified ideological class subject, which lies at the center of so much traditional Marxist theorizing in this area, matches in importance Gramsci's effective dismantling of the state, on which I commented earlier.

In recognizing that questions of ideology are always collective and social, not individual, Gramsci explicitly acknowledges the necessary complexity and interdiscursive character of the ideological field. There is never any one, single, unified, and coherent "dominant ideology" which pervades everything. Gramsci in this sense does not subscribe to what Nicholas Abercrombie et al. (1980) call "the dominant ideology thesis." His is not a conception of the incorporation of one group totally into the ideology of another, and their inclusion of Gramsci in this category of thinkers seems to me deeply misleading. There coexist many systems and currents of philosophical thought. The object of analysis is therefore not the single stream of "dominant ideas" into which everything and everyone has been absorbed, but rather the analysis of ideology as a differentiated terrain, of the different discursive currents, their points of juncture and break, and the relations of power between them: in short, an ideological complex, ensemble, or discursive *formation*. The question is "how these ideological currents are diffused and why in the process of diffusion they fracture along certain lines and in certain directions."

I believe it is a clear deduction from this line of argument that, though the ideological field is always, for Gramsci, articulated to different social and political positions, its shape and structure do *not* precisely mirror, match, or "echo" the class structure of society. Nor can they be reduced to their economic content or function. Ideas, he argues, "have a centre of formation, of irradiation, of dissemination, of persuasion" (PN 192). Nor are they "spontaneously born" in each individual brain. They are not psychologistic or moralistic in character "but structural and epistemological." They are sustained and transformed in their materiality within the institutions of civil society and the state. Consequently, ideologies are not transformed or changed by replacing one, whole, already-formed conception of the world with another, so much as by "renovating and making critical an already existing activity."

The multi-accentual, interdiscursive character of the field of ideology is explicitly acknowledged by Gramsci when, for example, he describes how an old conception of the world is gradually displaced by another mode of thought and is internally reworked and transformed:

> What matters is the criticism to which such an ideological complex is subjected. . . . This makes possible a process of differentiation and change in the relative weight that the elements of the old ideologies used to possess . . . what was previously secondary and subordinate . . . becomes the nucleus of a new ideological and theoretical complex. The old collective will dissolve into its contradictory elements since the subordinate ones develop socially.

This is an altogether more original and generative way of perceiving the actual process of ideological struggle. It also conceives of culture as the historically shaped terrain on which all "new" philosophical and theoretical currents work and with which they must come to terms. He draws attention to the given and determinate character of that terrain, and the complexity of the processes of deconstruction and reconstruction by which old alignments are dismantled and new alignments can be effected between elements in different discourses and between social forces and ideas. It conceives ideological change not in terms of substitution or imposition but rather in terms of the articulation and the disarticulation of ideas.

III.

It remains, now, to sketch some of the ways in which this Gramscian perspective could potentially be used to transform and rework some of the existing theories and paradigms in the analysis of racism and related social phenomena. Again, I emphasize that this is *not* a question of the immediate transfer of Gramsci's particular ideas to these questions. Rather, it is a matter of bringing a distinctive theoretical *perspective* to bear on the seminal theoretical and analytic problems which define the field.

First, I would underline the emphasis on historical specificity. No doubt there are certain general features to racism. But even more significant are the ways in which these general features are modified and transformed by the historical specificity of the contexts and environments in which they become active. In the analysis of particular historical forms of racism, we would do well to operate at a more concrete, historicized level of abstraction (that is, not racism in general but racisms). Even within the limited case that I know best (that is, Britain), I would say that the differences between British racism in its "high" imperial period and the racism which characterizes the British social formation now, in a period of relative economic decline, when the issue is confronted, not in the colonial setting, but as part of the indigenous labor force and regime of accumulation within the domestic economy, are greater and more significant than the similarities. It is often little more than a gestural stance which persuades us to the misleading view that because racism is everywhere a deeply antihuman and antisocial practice, it is therefore everywhere *the same*—either in its forms, its relations to other structures and processes, or its effects. Gramsci does, I believe, help us to interrupt decisively this homogenization.

Second, and related, I would draw attention to the emphasis, stemming from the historical experience of Italy, which led Gramsci to give considerable weight to *national* characteristics, as an important level of determination, and to *regional* unevenness. There is no homogenous "law of development" which impacts evenly throughout every facet of a social formation. We need to understand better the tensions and contradictions generated by the uneven tempos and directions of historical development. Racism and racist practices and structures frequently occur in some but not all sectors of the social formation; their impact is penetrative but uneven, and their very unevenness of impact may help to deepen and exacerbate these contradictory sectoral antagonisms.

Third, I would underline the nonreductive approach to questions concerning the interrelationship between class and race. This has proved to be one of the most complex and difficult theoretical problems to address, and it has frequently led to the adoption of one or another extreme position. Either one "privileges" the underlying class relationships, emphasizing that all ethnically and racially differentiated labor forces are subject to the same exploitative relationships within capital, or one emphasizes the centrality of ethnic and racial categories and divisions at the expense of the fundamental class structuring of society. Though these two extremes appear to be the polar opposites of one another, in fact, they are inverse, mirror images of each other, in the sense that *both* feel required to produce a single and exclusive determining principle of articulation—class *or* race—even if they disagree as to which should be accorded the privileged sign. I believe the fact that Gramsci adopts a nonreductive approach to questions of class, coupled with his understanding of the profoundly historical shaping to any specific social formation, does help to point the way toward a nonreductionist approach to the race/class question.

This is enriched by Gramsci's attention to what we might call the culturally specific quality of class formations in any historically specific society. He never makes the mistake of believing that, because the general law of value has the tendency to homogenize labor power across the capitalist epoch, therefore, in any concrete society, this homogenization can be assumed to exist. Indeed, I believe Gramsci's whole approach leads us to question the validity of this general law in its traditional form, since, precisely, it has encouraged us to neglect the ways in which the law of value, operating on a global as opposed to a merely domestic scale, operates through and *because* of the culturally specific character of labor power rather than—as the classical theory would have us believe—by systematically eroding those distinctions as an inevitable part of a worldwide, epochal historical tendency. Certainly, whenever we depart from the "Eurocentric" model of capitalist development (and even within that model), what we actually find is the many ways in which capital can preserve, adapt to its fundamental trajectory, and harness and exploit these particularistic qualities of labor power, building them into its regimes. The ethnic and racial structuration of the labor force, like its gendered composition, may provide an inhibition to the rationalistically conceived "global" tendencies of capitalist development. And yet, these distinctions have been maintained, and indeed *developed and refined*, in the global expansion of the capitalist mode. They have provided the means for differentiated forms of exploitation of the different sectors of a fractured labor force. In that context, their economic, political, and social effects have been profound. We would get much further along the road to understanding how the regime of capital can function *through* differentiation and difference, rather than through similarity and identity, if we took more seriously this question of the cultural, social, national, ethnic, and gendered composition of historically different and specific forms of labor. Gramsci, though he is not a general theorist of the capitalist mode, does point us unalterably in that direction.

Moreover, his analysis does also point to the way different modes of production can be *combined* within the same social formation, leading not only to regional specificity and unevenness but to differential modes of incorporating so-called "backward" sectors within the social regime of capital (for example, southern Italy within the Italian formation; the "Mediterranean" South within the more advanced "northern" sectors of industrial Europe; the "peasant" economies of the hinterland in Asian and Latin American societies on the path to dependent capitalist development; "colonial" enclaves within the development of metropolitan capitalist regimes; historically, slave societies as an integral aspect of primitive capitalist development of the metropolitan powers; "migrant" labor forces within domestic labor markets; "Bantustans" within so-called sophisticated capitalist economies, etc.). Theoretically, what needs to be noticed is the persistent way in which *these* specific, differentiated forms of "incorporation" have consistently been associated with the appearance of racist, ethnically segmentary, and other similar social features.

Fourth, there is the question of the nonhomogeneous character of the "class subject." Approaches which privilege the class, as opposed to the racial, structuring of working classes or peasantries are often predicated on the assumption that because the mode of exploitation vis-à-vis capital is the same, the "class subject" of any such exploitative mode must be not only economically but politically and ideologically unified. As I have just argued, there is now good reason for qualifying the sense in which the operation of modes of exploitation toward different sectors of the labor force *are* "the same." In any case, Gramsci's approach, which differentiates the conditional process, the different "moments," and the contingent character of the passage from "class in itself" to "class for itself," or from the "economic-corporate" to the "hegemonic" moments of social development, does radically and decisively problematize such simple notions of unity. Even the "hegemonic" moment is no longer conceptualized as a moment of *simple* unity, but as a process of unification (never totally achieved), founded on strategic alliances between different sectors, not on their pregiven identity. Its character is given by the founding assumption that there is no automatic identity or correspondence between economic, political, and ideological practices. This begins to explain how ethnic and racial difference can be constructed as a set of economic, political, or ideological antagonisms *within* a class which is subject to roughly similar forms of exploitation with respect to ownership of and expropriation from the "means of production." The latter, which has come to provide something of a magical talisman, differentiating the Marxist definition of class from more pluralistic stratification models and definitions, has by now long outlived its theoretical utility when it comes to explaining the actual and concrete historical *dynamic* within and between different sectors and segments within classes.

Fifth, I have already referred to the lack of assumed correspondence in the Gramscian model between economic, political, and ideological dimensions. But here I would pull out for specific emphasis the *political* consequences of this noncorrespondence. This has the theoretical effect of forcing us to abandon schematic constructions of how classes *should*, ideally and abstractly, behave politically in place of the concrete study of how they actually *do* behave, in real historical conditions. It has frequently been a consequence of the old correspondence model that the analysis of classes and other related social forces *as* political forces, and the study of the terrain of politics itself, has become a rather automatic, schematic, and residual activity. If, of course, there is "correspondence," plus the "primacy" of the economic over other determining factors, then why spend time analyzing the terrain of politics when it only reflects, in a displaced and subordinate way, the determinations of the economic "in the last instance"? Gramsci certainly would not entertain that kind of reductionism for a moment. He knows he is analyzing structurally complex, not simple and transparent, formations. He knows that politics has its own "relatively autonomous" forms, tempos, and trajectories, which need to be studied in their own right, with their own distinctive concepts, and with attention to their real and retroactive effects. Moreover, Gramsci has put certain key concepts into play which help to differentiate this region, theoretically, of which such concepts as hegemony, historical bloc, "party" in its wider sense, passive revolution, transformism, traditional and organic intellectuals, and strategic alliance constitute only the beginnings of a distinctive and original range. It remains to be demonstrated how the study of politics in racially structured or dominated situations could be positively illuminated by the rigorous application of these newly formulated concepts.

Sixth, a similar argument could be mounted with respect to the state. In relation to racial and ethnic class struggles, the state has been consistently defined in an exclusively coercive, dominative, and conspiratorial manner. Again, Gramsci breaks irrevocably with all three. His domination/direction distinction coupled with the "educative" role of the state, its "ideological" character, its position in the construction of hegemonic strategies—however crude in their original formulation—could transform the study, both of the state in relation to racist practices and the related phenomenon of the "postcolonial state." Gramsci's subtle use of the state/civil society distinction—even when it fluctuates in his own work—is an extremely flexible theoretical tool, and may lead analysts to pay much more serious attention to those institutions and processes in so-called "civil society" in racially structured social formations than they have been encouraged to do in the past. Schooling, cultural organizations, family and sexual life, the patterns and modes of civil association, churches and religions, communal or organizational forms, ethnically specific institutions, and many other such sites play an absolutely vital role in giving, sustaining, and reproducing different societies in a racially structured form. In any Gramscian-inflected analysis, they would cease to be relegated to a superficial place in the analysis.

Seventh, following the same line of thought, one might note the centrality which Gramsci's analysis always gives to the *cultural* factor in social development. By culture, here, I mean the actual, grounded terrain of practices, representations, languages, and customs of any specific historical society. I also mean the contradictory forms of "common sense" which have taken root in and helped to shape popular life. I would also include that whole distinctive range of questions which Gramsci lumped together under the title "the national-popular." Gramsci understands that these constitute a crucial site for the construction of a popular hegemony. They are a key stake as objects of political and ideological struggle and practice. They constitute a national resource for change as well as a potential barrier to the development of a new collective will. For example, Gramsci perfectly well understood how popular Catholicism had constituted, under specific Italian conditions, a formidable alternative to the development of a secular and progressive "national-popular" culture, how in Italy it would have to be engaged, not simply wished aside. He likewise understood, as many others did not, the role which fascism played in Italy in "hegemonizing" the backward character of the national-popular culture in Italy and refashioning it into a reactionary national formation, with a genuine popular basis and support. Transferred to other comparable situations, where race and ethnicity have always carried powerful cultural, national-popular connotations, Gramsci's emphasis should prove immensely enlightening.

Finally, I would cite Gramsci's work in the ideological field. It is clear that "racism," if not exclusively an ideological phenomenon, has critical ideological dimensions. Hence, the relative crudity and reductionism of materialist theories of ideology have proved a considerable stumbling block in the necessary work of analysis in this area. Especially, the analysis has been foreshortened by a homogeneous, noncontradictory conception of consciousness and of ideology, which has left most commentators virtually undefended when obliged to account, say, for the purchase of racist ideologies within the working class or within related institutions like trade unions, which, in the abstract, ought to be dedicated to antiracist positions. The phenomenon of "working-class racism," though by no means the *only* kind requiring explanation, has proved extraordinarily resistant to analysis.

Gramsci's whole approach to the question of the formation and transformation of the ideological field of popular consciousness, and its processes of formation, decisively undercuts this problem. He shows that subordinated ideologies are necessarily and inevitably contradictory: "Stone Age elements and principles of a more advanced science, prejudices from all past phases of history . . . and intuitions of a future philosophy." He shows how the so-called "self" which underpins these ideological formations is not a unified but a contradictory subject and a social construction. He thus helps us to understand one of the most common, least explained features of "racism": the "subjection" of the victims of racism to the mystifications of the very racist ideologies which imprison and define them. He shows how different, often contradictory elements can be woven into and integrated within different ideological discourses but, also, the nature and value of ideological struggle which seeks to transform popular ideas and the "common sense" of the masses. All this has the most profound importance for the analysis of racist ideologies and for the centrality, within that, of ideological struggle.

In all these different ways—and no doubt in other ways which I have not had time to develop here—Gramsci proves, on closer inspection, and *despite* his apparently "Eurocentric" position, to be one of the most theoretically fruitful, as well as one of the least known and least understood, sources of new ideas, paradigms, and perspectives in the contemporary studies of racially structured social phenomena.

NOTES

This essay first appeared as "Gramsci's Relevance for the Study of Race and Ethnicity," *Journal of Communication Inquiry* 10, no. 2 (1986): 5–27. This essay was originally delivered to the colloquium titled "Theoretical Perspectives in the Analysis of Racism and Ethnicity" organized in 1985 by the Division of Human Rights and Peace, UNESCO, Paris. The original title was "Gramsci's Relevance to the Analysis of Racism and Ethnicity."

1 Some volumes of the planned eight-volume critical edition of the collected works have already been published, at the time of writing, as *Scriti* by Einaudi in Turin. A number of collections of his work, under various headings, exist in English, including the excellent *Selections from the Prison Notebooks,* edited by Quintin Hoare and Geoffrey Nowell-Smith (London: Lawrence and Wishart, 1971); *Selections from Political Writings, 1910–1920,* edited by Quintin Hoare (London: Lawrence and Wishart, 1977); and *Selections from Political Writings, 1921–1926,* edited by Quintin Hoare (London: Lawrence and Wishart, 1978); and the more

recent *Selections from Cultural Writings*, edited by David Forgacs and Geoffrey Nowell-Smith (London: Lawrence and Wishart, 1985). The references and quotations in this essay are all from the English translations cited above.

REFERENCES

Abercrombie, Nicholas, Stephen Hill, and Bryan S. Turner. 1980. *The Dominant Ideology Thesis*. London: Allen and Unwin.

Althusser, Louis. 1969. *For Marx*. Harmondsworth, UK: Penguin.

Althusser, Louis, and Étienne Balibar. 1970. *Reading Capital*. London: New Left Books, 1970.

Anderson, Perry. 1977. "The Antinomies of Antonio Gramsci." *New Left Review*, no. 100.

Gramsci, Antonio. 1971. *Selections from the Prison Notebooks*. Edited by Quintin Hoare and Geoffrey Nowell-Smith. London: Lawrence and Wishart.

Gramsci, Antonio. 1977. *Selections from Political Writings, 1910–1920*. Edited by Quintin Hoare. London: Lawrence and Wishart.

Gramsci, Antonio. 1978. *Selections from Political Writings, 1921–1926*. Edited by Quintin Hoare. London: Lawrence and Wishart.

Gramsci, Antonio. 1985. *Selections from Cultural Writings*. Edited by David Forgacs and Geoffrey Nowell-Smith. London: Lawrence and Wishart.

Hall, Stuart. 1974. "Marx's Notes on Method: A Reading of the *1857 Introduction* to the *Grundrisse*." *Working Papers in Cultural Studies* 6. Birmingham: Centre for Contemporary Cultural Studies, University of Birmingham.

Hoare, Quintin, and Geoffrey Nowell-Smith. 1971. Introduction to *Selections from the Prison Notebooks*, by Antonio Gramsci, xviii–xcvi. London: Lawrence and Wishart.

CHAPTER 17

Subjects in History:
Making Diasporic Identities

I am the only participant from another part of the "black diaspora," and, as a consequence, what we in England know as the "burden of representation" lies particularly heavy on my shoulders. As a consequence of that burden, it seems to me incumbent in some ways to try to add to an ongoing discussion; my function, it seems to me, is partly to bring to bear on the discussion a perspective that adds a transnational, global, "diasporic dimension" to what is inevitably U.S. terrain. I'm going to do so, in part, by referring to a number of points that have already arisen in the debate simply to bring to bear on them some experiences, some similar and parallel lines of approach and political work elsewhere in the "black Atlantic."

I don't want to get into details, into particular aspects of ideological analysis, or cultural production, although I'm going to draw some examples from cultural production. Instead, I want to outline something more general; I want to express some views about the place of cultural politics in the present racial conjuncture, about how it is shifting and changing, and about the problems thrown up in our attempts to theorize and define adequate strategies for dealing with the place of cultural politics. That is what is required by the moment the conference itself addressed, and to do so I want to return to that conference's "electric opening," which I'll never forget, not to rerun the West-Steinberg conversation,[1] but partly to explain the reason for my own brief intervention in that debate in order to spell out the grounds on which I made it. To those of you who weren't there, I simply said, "Please remember that questions of culture are not superstructural to the problems of economic and political change; they are constitutive of them!"

What does it mean to take seriously, in our present conjuncture, the thought that cultural politics and questions of culture, of discourse, and of metaphor are absolutely deadly political questions? That is my purpose. I want to persuade you that that is so. And that we ought to sort of preach on this occasion, no, not only to give up the bad habits of smoking and drinking and whoring and gambling, but to give up certain forms of political essentialism and the way in which it makes you sleep well at night.

There are two basic reasons at this point why I wanted to suggest to you why questions of culture and representation, of cultural productions, and of aesthetics, politics, and power are of absolute centrality. There are many other reasons, but I can't deal with them now. I want to deal with two particular reasons because they are central to how we need to conceptualize the question of race itself. You see, if indeed, as we mouth the mantra, race is indeed a sociohistorical concept, not a transhistorical discourse grounded in biology, then it must function not through the truth of the "biological referent" but as a discursive logic. That is to say, as a logic in which, of course, the biological trace still functions even when it's silent, but now, not as the truth, but as the guarantor of the truth. That is a question of discursive power. Not a question of what is true but what is *made* to be true. Such is the way in which racial discourses operate. To use a familiar Foucault phrase, it is a "regime of truth." I want to insist that its logic is discursive in this sense, that racial discourses produce, mark and fix the infinite differences and diversities of human beings through a rigid binary coding. That logic establishes a chain of correspondences both between the physical and the cultural, between intellectual and cognitive characteristics; it gives legibility to a social system in which it operates; it allows us to decipher different signifiers from the racial fixing of the signifier "race"; and through that reading it organizes, regulates, and gives meaning to social practices through the distribution of symbolic and material resources between different groups and the establishment of racial hierarchy.

To say that is to say that race is a discourse, that it operates through the movement of the signifiers, and yet, at the same time, to say that the whole historical organization of human social practices through the binary coding of race is dependent on the meanings that it is able to give to the relationships of power and representation between human societies.

The second reason culture is absolutely central to our concerns, in my view, is that it constitutes the terrain for producing identity, for producing the constitution of social subjects. It is one of the social conditions of existence for setting subjects in place in historical relations, setting them in place, in position. They are unable to speak, or to act in one way or another, until they have been positioned by the work that culture does, and in that way, as subjects they function by taking up the discourses of the present and the past.

It is that taking up of positions that I call "identities." You see the consequence of turning the paradigm around that way: the political question (for there is always a political question, at any rate, in the way I pose the issue) is not "How do we effectively mobilize those identities which are already formed?" so that we could put them on the train and get them onto the stage at the right moment, in the right spot—an act the Left has historically been trying to do for about four hundred years—but something really quite different and much deeper.

How can we organize these huge, randomly varied, and diverse things we call human subjects into positions where they can recognize one another for long enough to act together, and thus to take up a position that one of these days they might live out and act through as an identity? Identity is at the end, not the beginning, of the paradigm. Identity is what is at stake in political organization. It isn't that the subjects are there and we just can't get to them. It is that they don't know yet that they are subjects of a possible discourse. And that always in every political struggle, since every political struggle is always open, it is possible either to win their identification or to lose it.

Indeed, for those of you who have been in politics for as long as I have, usually it is possible both to win and to lose it, and then to win it again and to lose it again, in an infinitely recurring struggle. That is the open-ended, contingent nature of political struggle, and just as a warning to intellectuals, there isn't any final theoretical solution, any grand deconstructive scheme which we can pull out of the air, which we can ensure will tell us that the subjects are going to stay like that, that the subjects are in place and the moment is going to come. And then the intellectuals can go home and get on with their business. It isn't like that. Remember: identifications, not identities. Once you've got identification you can decide which identities are working *this* week.

I speak of the process of identification, of feeling yourself through the contingent, antagonistic, and conflicting sentiments of which human beings are made up. Identification means that you are called in a certain way, interpolated in a certain way: "you, this time, in this space, for this purpose, by this barricade with these folks." That's what is at stake in political struggle. And you can't ahead of time either know that or know how to recognize that, or know how to imagine the collectivity that all those folks together might make. For how else would you know them? They weren't there before, or they weren't gathered together in the proper place. You can only come as you were, come together because somehow you can represent yourself and begin to share an imagined community of some kind with others which without representation and culture you could not express to anybody else.

The idea that somehow, out of some space, a politics of antiracism will arise without our giving thought as to how the subjects of it are to be formed is, to my mind, unintelligible. So then the questions that arise are, how and what kind? What are the natures of the cultural, social, and political identities that can and cannot be formed in these processes so as to conduct a political struggle, a cultural and social struggle that has the possibility of affecting something in the world? I want to insist that that is an open question, because I think at some level it remains more difficult than we think to take on the implications of what I've just been trying to say. Because when that rigid binary, racial logic is being used against us, we certainly know what's wrong with it. But when it seems to be working for us, we find that it's extremely difficult to give it up. We just can't let go of it in good moments, it makes us feel together; we can't imagine what a politics would be like if it wasn't there. How would you mobilize, what would you say to people, on what basis would you appeal to them, under what banner would you get them together? The whole thing begins to disintegrate, polarize, pluralize, get away from us, and we find ourselves confused by it. So, unfortunately, I think, people who know in their hearts that if you say race is not biological, that it is historical, cultural, and political, know you must follow the logic of that provision in terms of the alternative strategies you try to develop. Then, just at one minute to midnight, you're not beyond reaching for the final guarantee, and the whole biological fix actually slips back into place. Therefore, I want to explore what I think are the difficulties of what I'm going to call the end of the essentialized black subject, the end of an essentialist conception of the black experience.

One of the problems that confront a politics of this kind is that it effects some of our most central cultural and political concepts and images. Take the notion of tradition, for example. It is almost impossible to think of a cultural community as shared cultural meanings which exist over any period of time, which persist and have persisted over any period of time, which has managed to survive against all the odds, without thinking of the element of tradition that has enabled that community to hold together. Nevertheless, I think one of the implications of what I've just been saying is, indeed, that the question of tradition itself has to be conceptually rephrased.

Let me (walking dangerous waters, I know) talk about civil rights. Could one imagine the civil rights struggle of the sixties without the long traditions of black struggle that historically go back at least as far as the beginning of slavery? And yet, is there anybody here who wouldn't want to describe the civil rights movement as a movement that produced new black subjects? But new black subjects—now, what is that "new" then in the light of the tradition? Would it have happened without that tradition? Absolutely not. Where would traditions of struggle, where would the accumulated knowledge, where would the expectivity of human values that kept people going in dark days, where would that have come from if there hadn't been languages and historical traditions of one kind or another that sustained them across time? That sustained human beings in their lives of struggle across time—and yet the particular way that black people occupied that identity, lived that identity, and struggled around it, produced something which had never been seen before.

This is not the game you know, of trading "your victimage is bigger than mine," "my heroism is bigger than yours"—you don't have to say it's greater than what has happened before. That's not my argument; but my argument is that it was, and is, significantly different. And what was different about it was a particular reworking of that tradition under the force of the present conjuncture, not of a tradition which is simply a transmission belt that takes you from the past teleologically marching through to the future. A reworking that precisely delivers the much more complex idea that is a phrase you know well, "the changing same." That reworking transmits the capacity to be both the same and different, both located in a tradition and yet not constrained by it. Able to think freely on the basis of the particular ground. That reworking is almost musical and it has to be. What else is any successful blues, any successful jazz standard, or any gospel song but the given ground and the performance that translates it? But you couldn't listen to it if all there was was just the same damn thing once over again. It has to be that process of reworking the elements of a tradition, of taking forward what has been left, or engaging what is new, and of trying to put together a new kind of configuration. If you don't believe me because you think civil rights belongs to you, let me tell you that it didn't simply belong to you and it didn't simply produce some new black subjects here, it produced a lot of new black subjects elsewhere.

In the place where I came from in Jamaica, the conjuncture of the civil rights movement and the black consciousness movement of decolonization, the naming—the possibility at last to name the unspeakable fact of slavery and the imaginative, metaphorical connection with Africa—made Jamaica, where I was born, a black country for the first time in the 1960s. I don't mean it was the first time any black people were there. I mean black as a political category. I mean black as a culture. I mean black as a sociohistorical fact. It was the first time that I ever called myself that. I had called myself thousands of things before, but until that historical moment, it had been a word that I would never have applied to my own identity. So, if your own identities don't change, believe me, mine certainly have. They keep going on and on, and not only that, I most recognize them when other people say something different. In the sixties, after having been in England for ten years over that period when Afro-Caribbeans came to Britain for the first time, I went home and my mother said to me, "I hope they don't think you're one of those immigrants over there." I had never called myself an immigrant in all my life, and suddenly I said, "That's what I am." After all, I've gone to the people's place, I'm going to stay whether they like it or not, I intend to get a job if they're going to give me one. What am I but an immigrant? My life, far from the unfolding of this great identity I always knew about, this fabric endlessly unfolding but not changing toward some particular end, changes drastically, and when I get to the end, I can't say "There you are, you've always been like that, God help me, always been like that." No, the transformations have made me something different. Because historically, to say suddenly that you know we are black people, and to name the names, meant that the cultural terrain on which those names worked and struggled was thereby transformed. Cultural change is constitutive of political change and moral awareness of human consciousness.

And I want to say a word about political history as a way of passing on to another element and its complexity. In the 1970s, the signifier "black" was adopted as a political category of struggle, both by Afro-Caribbean migrants and by migrants from the Asian continent. People who manifestly were not, in any of the significant ways in which the term "race" had ever been used, the same race called themselves by the racial signifier. They said, "Since the British can't tell the difference between us, we must be the same." We might as well call one another by the same name. That's what identity is; it always has a constitutive outside. Those people didn't know about a "constitutive outside," but they knew one when they got it. Since they were manifestly not white, they were black. They called themselves black. They organized under that *political* roof.

It was a very important moment politically in Britain. It isn't the moment that we're in now. That significance has gone. It is partly dissolved into a variety of new, more ethnically specific signifiers. People now call themselves not only Asians, but Indians, Bangladeshis, Pakistanis, and indeed, South Indians. Things have moved into a new kind of ethnicized politics of difference. And that has presented certain profound difficulties of political organization when the signifier "black" has disappeared.

Still, I want to speak about this moment that I've just mentioned. What is this moment of the pluralization of cultural difference? Sometimes it is a racialized kind, sometimes an ethnicized kind—which is in my view increasingly characteristic of social antagonisms on a world scale. These antagonisms are a product of huge, planned, and unplanned world migrations—the greatest and most constitutive cultural fact of the late modern world, the planned and unplanned, forced and unforced movements of peoples, taking up hundreds of years later after that first forced migration of slavery with which modernity began. Here we are in late modernity, and what is happening is exactly the same kind of proliferation of movement as peoples. They are torn apart by poverty, by drought, by civil war, by the international arms trade, and they are moving, moving, moving from their settled homes to somewhere else.

Let me put that in cultural terms. They're moving like we have done before into the narratives, through which they will have to tell their history of migration, loss, displacement, redefining themselves, of home, of another home, of the question of where is home, of all of the images and metaphors of a perpetually unsettled people. That is the modern fact that is transforming this society; it is transforming Europe, Western European society. It is a world-historical fact of astonishing proportions and partly because it goes by different names—now refugees, now economic migrants, etc. And partly because it happens in this completely unplanned late-modern way, where people just calculate for themselves that the only thing to do is to buy a one-way plane ticket and get on a plane for paradise or, you know, the South Bronx, or wherever paradise is these days, in that way trying to resolve what is the global maldistribution of material and symbolic goods.

One of the consequences of that fact, within different national societies, has been to pluralize and complicate the terrain of social struggle. For what you find in each society is the integration of different forms of racialized and ethnicized difference, marked in different ways with very different and discrete histories. Nevertheless, it is part of the long history of the dialectics of "othering": these are all others of one kind or another, those that weren't othered through slavery were othered through colonialism or othered through imperialism. And some were othered through all three. Each of these people cling to the particular homes and identities that were formed through those histories. But what is most dramatic about them is that they are now convened in the very center of modernity, in the very "hotbed" of the modern, and what we find then as a consequence is that what the modern itself now means is precisely this conflict, this struggle, this complicated and differentiated line of struggle, between those who have had to move, and go on moving to survive, who have constantly been "the racialized other" of some system of supremacy, and on the other hand, the cultural nationalist racism that is the backlash against this multicultural drift, which is evolving in every society of the advanced, modern, Western industrial world.

I won't at this stage try to tell you what it means to us to see active fascism in the streets of London, to see the fascist right in alliance with a respectable center, to hear what we've heard before said about blacks, now said about North Africans, now said between peoples who call themselves European, who are hastily cobbling together in these societies that are hybridized and mongrelized to their roots. I couldn't find a "pure folk" anywhere. One would have to go into the museum to dig up the pure Bosnian-Serbian folk. Haul him out, mount him, etc.

Nevertheless, cobbling is a kind of defense against the modern world, a defense against living with difference, this retreat into the bunker of cultural and racist nationalism. I call it by that name, because although in its many respectable forms it doesn't recognize itself as such, this racism exists as a defense of "Englishness," of "Britishness," and of "Americanness." How could anybody object to Americans, or some Americans, defending a certain kind of "Americanness"? Who could argue against the possible claim that American children might not speak the "American language" first in American schools, and what is racist about that, what could possibly be racist about that?

I told a story recently in the Du Bois Lectures at Harvard, of a very close friend of Mrs. Thatcher's, Lord Tebit, who has devised a simple kind of handy test for deciding who culturally belongs to whom and who does not (call it "the Tebit test"). It is a very simple one. It's a question of whether or not the migrant families cheer the Pakistanis and the West Indians when they come touring for cricket. You have only to go to the cricket match and pavilion, and look around when the West Indians get to six hundred or whatever it is, and the "black stands," the ones closest to the oval, start to jump up and down, you know you can identify them. Because clearly their hearts cannot be in the right place. On the other hand, it is a very serious business indeed, this question of reconstructing a "little Englandism," reconstructing a little Americanism, through the struggles that are sometimes called "the culture wars."

Don't fool yourself that this is some superstructural, marginal question. At the center of this is the question of who can belong, who has access to the transmission belt through which Britishness, Englishness, is carried and can be inculcated. And who doesn't belong. And whether or not they have yet arrived at the moment when the lines are going to be drawn in blood and fire. Symbolic lines are being drawn, and what we know about culture is that once the symbolic difference exists, that is the line around which power coheres. Power uses difference as a way of marking off who does and who does not belong.

That is the shape of a new kind of cultural difference that impacts and sits atop another older kind: the politics of cultural difference. Today people sometimes say, "Of course, politics is a very confusing game, because there aren't those old stabilized identities around which we used to mobilize, and there aren't exactly those old kinds of struggles that we used to know how to fight." It is not, I warn you, because things are going through a little postmodern shake, and then they're going to settle down; then we're going to go back to the stabilized, well-organized, clearly demarcated frontiers of the past. We are in a new political conjuncture not without racism, not a conjuncture without difference; it is not a conjuncture without poverty and deprivation and marginalization on a world scale. But it is one in which the marking of difference, the careful and overlatticed marking of finely drawn distinction, can't be easily convened under a single political roof and fought in a simple battle. It is a much more differentiated, sophisticated, positional kind of struggle that has to be developed, to be conducted, if we are serious about refusing its human cost.

Sometimes the term "diaspora" is used as a way of conjuring up a kind of imagined community that would cut across the configurations of cultural nationalism. And I'm not only very much in favor of that, having contributed in some way to giving the term "liftoff." But let me warn you and warn myself that after all diaspora, too, has been the site of some of the most closed narratives of identity known to human beings. It is a word that has lodged there for a people who are not going to change, who sat on top of a sacred text and erected the barriers, and who then wanted to make the return exactly to the place where they came from. And who have gone back and sat on the head of all the other people who were there, too. If you open yourself to the politics of cultural difference, there is no safety in terminology. Words can always be transcoded against you, identity can turn against you, race can turn against you, difference can turn against you, diaspora can turn against you because that is the nature of the discursive.

I am trying to persuade you that the word is the medium in which power works. Don't clutch onto the word, but do clutch onto certain ideas about it. The diaspora is a place where traditions operate but are not closed, where the black experience is historically and culturally distinctive but is not the same as it was before. We are to move from one end of the diaspora to another and be ready to move from differently translated worlds, each with its own inflection, places where the law is almost certainly the law of syncretism, of taking in influences, of translating what has been given, of disarticulating and rearticulating, of creolization. And here I give my last injunction: to give up smoking and give up the idea, the commitment to the politically pure. The future belongs to the impure. The future belongs to those who are ready to take in a bit of the other, as well as being what they themselves are. After all, it is because their history and ours is so deeply and profoundly and inextricably intertwined that racism exists. For otherwise, how could they keep us apart?

NOTES

This essay first appeared as "Subjects in History: Making Diasporic Identities," in *The House That Race Built*, edited by Wahneema Lubiano (New York: Vintage, 1998), 289–300.

1 During the discussion following on Steinberg's critique of Cornel West's ideas about the "underclass," and after a few additional criticisms leveled from the floor, I stood up to intervene in order to address what I saw as an unhelpful reduction of culture to the conditions of the economic.

CHAPTER 18

Why Fanon?

Why Fanon? Why, after so many years of relative neglect, is his name once again beginning to excite such intense intellectual debate and controversy? Why is this happening at this particular moment, at this conjuncture? And why is it around the text *Black Skin, White Masks* (Fanon 1986) that the renewed "search for Fanon" is being conducted? This essay addresses these questions as they were posed in the context of the ICA's *Mirage: Enigmas of Race, Difference and Desire*, a programme of film, installation, performance and visual art works by contemporary black artists who acknowledge some debt of influence, usually indirect, to Fanon's work. It is written in the spirit of the title of the conference which took place during the season: "Working with Fanon."

Why, of the many figures whose emblematic presence could have triggered off such a profusion of discursive and figural production, does the incitation turn out to be Frantz Fanon? Though at one time his name would have been widely known and recognised—usually as the signifier of a certain brand of incendiary Third World–ism—he is now virtually unknown, even amongst those young, practising, black writers and artists whose work appears, unwittingly, to betray the "trace" of his presence. Of course, events do not obey any singular, unfolding, teleology of causality or time. But I cannot help feeling that the re-call of Fanon, now, in this moment, here, in this way, has something of the overdetermined "return of the repressed" about it—a timeliness constituted from many directions at once, as well as a certain "un-timeliness."

Rather than trying to recapture the "true" Fanon, we must try to engage the after-life of Frantz Fanon—that which Jacques Derrida would call, following his recent essay on Marx, his "spectral effect" (was *that* the *Mirage* of the title?) in ways that do not simply restore the past in a cycle of the eternal return, but which will bring the enigma of Fanon, as Benjamin (1973, 247) said of history, flashing up before us at a moment of danger. "The colonial man who writes for his people" that is, of course, colonial man and woman, an elision in Fanon which is as characteristic as it is un-timely, "ought to *use* the past with the intention of opening up the future," Fanon observed; "an invitation to an action and a basis of hope" (Fanon 1966, 69). What action, what hope is proposed to us here? And why, of all his writings, is the subject of these aspirations *Black Skin, White Masks*?

For many years it was the essay on national liberation movements in *The Wretched of the Earth*, with its invitation to the violent, self-cleansing, self-remaking anticolonial struggle, which constituted, for many, the "invitation to an action"—and for others, the nightmare spectre of black barbarism stalking the streets. "They want to take our place" is the fantasy which best seems to describe the latter response—which is how Fanon himself described the white colonial settler's "paranoid fantasy of primordial dispossession" when confronted by the black man (Bhabha 1986, xv). This contest over "which text of Fanon's?" as a way of trying to annex his political legacy after the event is far from concluded. In his sceptical but accomplished *tour d'horizon* of recent writing on Fanon, "Critical Fanonism," Henry Louis Gates (1991), who is basically sympathetic to much in the postcolonial and poststructuralist enterprise, nevertheless takes some delight in exposing how varied, even internally contradictory, the recent "readings" of Fanon as a global theorist have been. On the other hand, in an essay entitled "The Appropriation of Fanon," which savages the whole "revisionist" expropriation of Fanon, Cedric Robinson (1993) argues that to privilege *Black Skin, White Masks* over *The Wretched of the Earth* is a motivated political strategy which, perversely, reads Fanon backwards from his "immersion in the revolutionary consciousness of the Algerian peasantry" to the "petit-bourgeois stink" of the former text.

It cannot be just by pure chance that it is *Black Skin, White Masks*, with its psychoanalytically inspired exploration of the unconscious mechanisms of racism and colonialism, its attention to the role of projective fantasy, its opening up of the dislocated subjective complexity of the "deceptively obvious 'fact of blackness'" and its attention to the dialectic of identity, otherness and desire, which provides the privileged ground of Fanon's "return" and of the contestation over him. Kobena Mercer (1994), in his introductory essay to the *Mirage* catalogue, "Busy in the Ruins of Wretched Phantasia," reminds us—as if we are likely to forget—that, because every reading is also a re-reading, it is bound to be political. He offers us one condition of existence for Fanon's untimely "return": "Whereas earlier generations privileged the Marxist themes of Fanon's later work . . . at the height of the optimism of the postwar social movements, the fading fortunes of the independent left during the 1980s provided the backdrop to renewed interest in *Black Skin, White Masks*, Fanon's first and most explicitly psychoanalytic text." Although there is much to this argument, it is worth recalling how, both during his lifetime and since, almost as much rhetorical energy has gone into proving how far "Fanonism" deviated from anything like a classical Marxism. The struggle to colonise Fanon's work has been an ongoing process from the moment of his death, and the identification of Fanon's writing in terms of its "Marxist themes" in the '60s and '70s was, itself, already the product of a re-reading. As another contributory factor, Mercer cites the many-layered, discursive structure of *Black Skin, White Masks*, "whose authorial eye constantly oscillates between multiple points of view," and whose voice, we should add, draws on multiple registers, "autobiographical, clinical, sociological, poetical, philosophical, political." I will come back to the dubious proposition of some final symptomatic breaks between Fanon's early and late work, as well as to the question of how we are to re-read the multivocality of *Black Skin, White Masks*.

The view, boldly stated by Fanon in his introduction to *Black Skin, White Masks*—that "only a psychoanalytic interpretation of the black problem can lay bare the anomalies of affect that are responsible for the structure of the complex" that is racism and colonialism—is what constitutes the novelty of this text (Fanon 1986, 12). But it also makes absurd the claim that "Fanon was a political activist rather than a theorist," which those who would recuperate Fanon to some earlier, more "revolutionary" manifestation find so seductive. Incidentally, the idea that it is only "politics," and not also "theory," which is at issue in these contentious readings and re-readings of Fanon is, of course, something that it suits the recuperators to have us believe, but it is not a proposition which can be seriously sustained. The problem is that Fanon's 1952 text anticipates poststructuralism in a startling way, even if the addition of the phrase "effective disalienation of the black man entails immediate recognition of social and economic realities" inflects his anachronistically prescient observation in an unexpected direction. The dependency complex, he says, "is the outcome of a double process, primarily economic . . .

subsequently the internalization—or, better, the epidermalization—of this inferiority" (Fanon 1986, 13). A wonderful word, *epidermalization*: literally, the inscription of race on the skin. This armature of "race" provides the black subject with that which elsewhere Fanon calls an alternative "corporeal schema." But, as he always insists, this schema is cultural and discursive, not genetic or physiological: "Below the corporeal schema I had sketched a historico-racial schema . . . woven . . . out of a thousand details, anecdotes, stories" (Fanon 1986, 111).

Another deep source of the contemporary appeal of *Black Skin, White Masks* is the association it establishes between racism and what has come to be called the scopic drive—the eroticisation of the pleasure in looking and the primary place given in Fanon's text to the "look" from the place of the "Other" (see Freud 1977). It is the exercise of power through the dialectic of the "look"—race in the field of vision, to paraphrase Jacqueline Rose—which *fixes* the Negro from the outside (Fanon's word, which I will use in this context) by the fantasmatic binary of absolute difference (see Rose 1986): "sealed into that crushing objecthood" (Fanon 1986, 109); "overdetermined from without" (Fanon 1986, 116). Not only is Fanon's Negro caught, transfixed, emptied and exploded in the fetishistic and stereotypical dialectics of the "look" from the place of the Other; but he/she *becomes*—has no other self than—this *self-as-Othered*. This is the black man *as* his [sic] alienated self-image; or as Homi Bhabha puts it, "not Self and Other but the 'Otherness' of the Self inscribed in the perverse palimpsest of colonial identity." It is this "bizarre figure of desire" which, as Bhabha (1986, xiv) rightly observes, "compels Fanon to put the psychoanalytic question to the historic condition of colonial man."

There can be little doubt that, as Gates (1991, 458) suggested, "Fanon's current fascination for us has something to do with the convergence of the problematic of colonialism with that of subject-formation." This bringing to bear of the poststructuralist and psychoanalytic engines of contemporary theory on the primordial—and primordially resistant—structure of racism and the historic colonial relation excites in us a disjunctive frisson of stimulation and pleasure which is only, in part, cognitive (the *jouissance* of theory having long been underestimated). Nevertheless, the familiarity of these concepts, now, may lead us to underestimate the novelty and originality of Fanon's insights at the time of writing. The grain of his text runs incontrovertibly towards the recognition that an account of racism which has no purchase on the inner landscape and the unconscious mechanisms of its effects is, at best, only half the story. The simplistic counterposing of

Black Skin, White Masks to *The Wretched of the Earth*, with the implication that, in the passage from one to the other Fanon somehow "graduated" from childish petit-bourgeois things to greater "maturity," does not explain why *The Wretched of the Earth* ends, in the chapter on "Colonial War and Mental Disorders," with a series of psychiatric case studies, presented in a language which clearly echoes the paradigm first sketched in *Black Skin, White Masks*. "Because it is a systematic negation of the other person and a furious determination to deny the other person all attributes of humanity, colonialism forces the people it dominates to ask themselves the question constantly: 'In reality, who am I?'" Fanon adds, pointedly, "Perhaps these notes on psychiatry will be found ill-timed and singularly out of place in such a book; but we can do nothing about that" (Fanon 1966, 203). Nuff said.

In *Black Skin, White Masks*, this fixing of the Negro by the fantasmatic binaries of fear and desire which have governed the representation of the black figure in colonial discourse and which, Fanon argues, lie at the heart of the psychic reality of racism, is profoundly and mordantly explored. Indeed, the operation is unmasked in such a penetrating way that, in effect, we are tempted to read Fanon's text as more simple and straightforward than it is. Since the text so remorselessly returns to the binary oppositions *black/white, coloniser/colonised*, I wonder how many of his readers unconsciously slip into reading him as if binaries are the exclusive focus of his tale? As if the real title of his book was "Black Skin, White Skin"? Ignoring the fact that, though his subject is, of course, framed throughout by the dichotomous and manichean structure of racism as a binary system of representation and power, it is the split or divided self, the two sides within the *same* figure—the colonial Negro—which centrally preoccupies him.

The central figure of the book is the colonial Negro, especially the Antillean, who is obliged, in the scenarios of the colonial relation, to have a relationship to self, to give a performance of self, which is scripted by the coloniser, producing in him the internally divided condition of "absolute depersonalization" (Fanon 1970, 63). The mechanisms of this substitution are very precisely described. The bodily or corporeal schema, which Fanon says is "a definitive structuring of self and the world," necessary to any sense of self because it "creates a real dialectic between my body and the world," is fragmented and shattered (Fanon 1986, 111). Such a scopic *gestalt*, which Jacques Lacan, for example, suggested is of great formative importance for the constitution of the subject, cannot be formed (see Lacan 1977). In its place, Fanon suggests, there arises the "historico-racial schema," which *weaves him* "out of a thousand details, anecdotes, stories"—"battered down by tom-toms, cannibalism, intellectual deficiency, fetishism, racial defects, slave ships, and above all: 'Sho' good eatin'" (Fanon 1986, 112). "Now the fragments have been put together again by another self" (Fanon 1986, 109).

There are, Fanon insists, "two camps: the white and the black" (Fanon 1986, 10). But, he adds, "Overnight, the Negro has been given two frames of reference within which he has to place himself.... For not only must the black man be black; he must be black in relation to the white man" (Fanon 1986, 110). The problem which preoccupies Fanon, then, is not the *existence* of the white man in colonialism, but the fact that the black man can only exist in relation to himself through the alienating presence of the white "Other." As Homi Bhabha correctly observes, this is "not a neat division" but "a doubling, dissembling image of being in at least two places at once" (Bhabha 1986, xvi). The subject to which Fanon addresses himself is historically specific. It is not racism as a general phenomenon but racism in the colonial relation which he dissects. His task was to unpack its inner landscapes—and to consider the conditions for the production of a new kind of subject and the decolonisation of the mind as the necessary subjective conditions for the decolonisation of the world: "I propose nothing short of the liberation of the man of color *from himself*" (Fanon 1986, 10, emphasis added). It is the opening up of this radical aperture at the centre of Fanon's text which constitutes its novelty, its originality, its "timeliness."

Today, the question for us is how to read, how to interpret, the problem he posed, the answers which his text proposes, and the invitation to action and to hope which it prefigured.

One response has been to occupy the structure of Fanon's argument, turning the mechanisms which he identifies against themselves. This takes the question of "the look" seriously, goes to the heart of the representational process itself, which Fanon—against the objectivist grain of the history of the analysis of racism—gave so central and constitutive a role. By the practices of trans-coding and re-signing, he attempted to contest, to disturb, to unsettle, and to re-inscribe the look "other-wise." Of course, for those who believe that history is a "process without a subject," this attempt to constitute forms of subjectivity and representation in some different register from that of the colonial relation may appear to be of little serious consequence: mere scribbling in the margins. Perhaps the short history of postcolonial Algeria, in which that so-called objective entity, "the Algerian peasantry," has been powerfully inscribed in several different and contradictory positions in the postindependence narratives, from "revolutionary vanguard" to "faithful multitude," may make them pause for thought. For those who take these questions of representation and subjectivity as *constitutive* of the politics of decolonisation, especially amongst the young cultural practitioners and visual artists of the African diaspora, Fanon's work has had an enormous, unpredicted and unpredictable influence in recent years—evidence of which is to be seen everywhere in the work exhibited, screened and performed in *Mirage*. The principal counterstrategy here has been to bring to the surface—into representation—that which has sustained the regimes of representation unacknowledged: to subvert the structures of "othering" in language and representation, image, sound and discourse, and thus to turn the mechanisms of fixed racial signification against themselves, in order to begin to constitute new subjectivities, new positions of enunciation and identification, without which the most "revolutionary" moments of national liberation quickly slide into their postcolonial reverse gear (Algeria being one of the most troubling and heart-wrenching instances).

From this practice of resignification—this new politics of the black signifier—has flowed both the amazing volume, but more significantly, the astonishing formal diversity, of much recent black art work. Again and again, this practice has taken the form of working *on the black body itself*: driving the suppressed violence of racism so deep into itself that it reveals the transgressive lineage of the suppressed desire on which it feeds; putting together what we may think of as new "corporeal schemas"; that which Fanon (1986, 109) himself describes as having been fixed "as a chemical solution is fixed by a dye," dismembered "fragments... put together again by another self." Often, this process consists of the artist taking his or her own body as the "canvas," light-sensitive "frame" or "screen," so that the work of translation and re-appropriation is literally a kind of "re-writing of the self on the body," a re-epidermalisation, an *auto-graphy*. Elsewhere, I have called this reworking of the abjected black body through desire the production of a new "black narcissus" (S. Hall 2017).

The field of visual representation is foregrounded here because of the constitutive role of "the look" as a site of power-knowledge, of the sexualisation of the gaze, and its fantasmatic fetishisation of the body and the skin as signifiers of racial difference. However, the body in Fanon's text is both a privileged and an ambivalent site of strategic intervention. "O my body, make of me always a man who questions!" (Fanon 1986, 232). In the "epidermalization" of the racial look, Fanon tells us, exclusion and abjection are imprinted on the body through the functioning of these signifiers as an objective taxonomy—a "taxidermy"—of radicalised difference; a specular matrix of intelligibility.

To that which W. E. B. Du Bois (1966) once referred in terms of "hair, skin and bone," after Fanon, we would have to add genitals.[1] We know that the fetishistic and stereotypical excess required to secure these markers of racial difference in a stable equivalence with the black body, far from being genetically secured, is a "form of intelligibility" which racism shares with other regimes of difference and othering with which it has many features in common—especially, of course, gender and sexuality (Butler 1993). It is therefore sometimes tempting to believe that these are indeed the "evidence" rather than the *markers* of difference. We mis-take their function as signifiers for their biological fact and thus read "race" as the product of a genetic or biological schema rather than as a *discursive regime*.

Many visual practices influenced by poststructuralist and psychoanalytic ideas seem to have managed to evade a foundational materialism, only to allow "the body" to make a surreptitious return as a sort of "token" of the material, a terminal signifier, which brings the discursive slide, the infinite semiosis of meaning around "race," to an abrupt halt. Sometimes, even in Foucault, who has taught us so much about its contingency (and even more in the Foucauldeans), "the body" seems to be invoked in the place where once stood those great transcendental signifiers, God, His Majesty and The Economy: becoming the last refuge, the *objet petit a*, of a misplaced materiality.

It is important that this work of returning to the enigmatic site of "the black body" in the representation of radicalised difference should not be mistaken for a return to a dehistoricised, transcendental, biologically fixed, essentialised conception of racial identity. The binary "Manicheism delirium [sic]" of racialised discourse to which Fanon so effectively draws attention is not given by nature (Fanon 1986, 183). It involves an arbitrary discursive operation, a suturing. Arbitrary, because "race" is a sliding signifier with equivalencies outside discourse that cannot be fixed. "Racism's very rigidity ... is the clue to its complexity. Its capacity to punctuate the universe into two great opposite masks ... the complexes of feelings and attitudes ... that are always refusing to be so neatly stabilised and fixed. ... All that symbolic and narrative energy ... is directed to securing us 'over here' and them 'over there,' to fix each in its appointed species place" (S. Hall 1992). "Race" is not a genetic but a social category. Racism is not a biological but a discursive regime. The so-called bodily insignia—black skin, thick lips, curly hair, penises "as big as cathedrals" and the rest—which appear to function as foundational are not only constituted through and through in fantasy, but are really signifying elements in the discourse of racism. Even in racist discourses, where the evidence of racial difference appears to be figured so *obviously* on the surface of the body, so plain for all to see ("Look! A Negro! . . . Mama, see the Negro! I'm frightened!" [Fanon 1986, 112]), they are capable of carrying their negative connotations *only* because they function, in fact, as the signifiers of a deeper code—the genetic—*which cannot be seen* but which, it is believed, has the power of a science to fix and stabilise racial difference. It is not the status of racist discourse as "scientific" but the fact that its elements function *discursively* which enables it to have "real effects." They can only carry meaning because they signify, through a process of displacement, further along the chain of equivalencies—*metonymically* (black skin—big penis—small brain—poor and backward—it's all in the genes—end the poverty programme—send them home!). That is, because their arrangement within a discursive chain enables physiological signs to function as signifiers, to stand for and be "read" further up the chain; socially, psychically, cognitively, politically, culturally, civilisationally . . . (for an elaboration of the discursive character of racism, see S. Hall 2017).

Fanon certainly knew that, in the system of radicalised exclusion and abjection sustained by the look from the place of the Other, the bodily schema is constituted, not given, and culturally and historically shaped ("Below . . . I had sketched a historico-racial schema" [Fanon 1986, 111]). Thus, any notion that the return to the site of the body represents a recovery of some essential ground or foundation that will restore the essential black subject is not only mistaken but has taken a message from Fanon's work which he explicitly precludes. These are indeed, to paraphrase Judith Butler, "bodies that matter": they count, not because they can produce the truth, but because they signify within what Judith Butler in another context calls the regulatory norm, the regulative "ideal" of the racial matrix. How could the black body function foundationally when, as Fanon shows, it is so manifestly constructed in narrative ("there were legends, stories, history, and above all, historicity"), through desire, in fantasy, through the exorbitant play of "lack" and "excess"? This is surely the lesson we should take from Fanon's long and uneasy dialogue with the Negritude movement.

This body of visual work, then, assumes that "the look" can be subverted, displaced, resisted. But can it be refused, destroyed, abandoned? Can the split—black skin/white masks—which threatens to destroy the black subject from within be healed? Is the subject not *inevitably* a site of splitting? And if so, what then is the status of the "universal, unified subject," beyond Negritude, towards which Fanon is gesturing in that highly resonant but ambiguous formulation at the close of his text: "The Negro is not. Any more than the white man" (Fanon 1986, 231)?

Homi K. Bhabha's foreword to the 1986 edition of *Black Skin, White Masks* has become the *locus classicus* of many aspects of this debate, reminding us that "Remembering Fanon," as his text is called, remains a difficult and inevitably contested practice. In "Critical Fanonism," Henry Louis Gates (1991), borrowing a phrase from Benita Parry (1987), critiques Bhabha's reading for its "premature post-structuralism." Both writers mean his attempt to produce Fanon as a sort of Lacanian *avant la lettre*, as if Fanon would have taken Lacan's position on the split in the subject, and treated "the Other" as the necessary source of division which arises in all so-called unified identities, and not "as a fixed phenomenological point opposed to the self."[2] Has Bhabha, then, been fishing around in that black box—Fanon's text—for all the world like a magician or a conjurer, drawing forth at the appropriate moment, to everyone's astonishment, the figure of the proverbial Lacanian rabbit?

In fact his critics, in their haste, do not always acknowledge how clearly Bhabha marks out the points in his text at which his interpretation departs from and goes beyond his Fanonian brief: "In his more analytic mode Fanon can impede the exploration of these ambivalent, uncertain questions of colonial desire. . . . At times Fanon attempts too close a correspondence between the *mise-en-scène* of unconscious fantasy and the phantoms of racist fear and hate that stalk the colonial scene" (Bhabha 1986, xix); "Fanon's sociodiagnostic psychiatry tends to explain away the ambivalent turns and returns of the subject of colonial desire" (Bhabha 1986, xx); "Fanon must sometimes be reminded that the disavowal of the Other always exacerbates the 'edge' of identification, reveals that dangerous place where identity and aggressivity are twinned" (Bhabha 1986, xxii). Bhabha acknowledges that, again and again, Fanon falls back too hastily onto Sartrean and Hegelian ground, is too driven by the demand for "more insurgent answers, more immediate identifications," too hungry for an "existential humanism." Bhabha's real argument is, I believe, more complex. It is that Fanon constantly and implicitly poses issues and raises questions in ways which cannot be adequately addressed within the conceptual framework into which he seeks often to resolve them; and that a more satisfactory and complex "logic" is often implicitly threaded through the interstices of his text, which he does not always follow through but which we can discover by reading him "against the grain." In short, Bhabha produces a *symptomatic reading* of Fanon's text. The question for us, then, is whether we should limit such a "symptomatic reading." With what authority, but more significantly, with what effects, do we actively appropriate Fanon's work against the textual grain?

We should be clear that what is entailed here is not a matter of restoring the "true meaning" of the text or of fixing it once and for all in that fantasmagorical territory known as "what Fanon really meant." But it may be also important, in an archaeological or genealogical sense, to retrace the turns he actually took, to grasp the matrix of intelligibility within which he came to say what he did (and not say what he was unable to) and to confront its implications. For these conceptual moves and shifts had, for him then and for us now, real political consequences.

Let us put it simplistically. I think it is impossible to read *Black Skin, White Masks* without acknowledging that it is also—and not just by chance—the product of at least three interrelated but unfinished dialogues, to which Fanon kept returning throughout his life and work. First, there is Fanon's dialogue with traditional French colonial psychiatry (a much more elaborated formation than anything comparable in British colonialism, about which Françoise Verges writes elsewhere in this volume with great insight) and, within that, with psychoanalysis, Freud and the French Freudians. For, if this text is "where Lacan makes his interruption into colonial discourse theory," as Gates (1991) asserts, it is also where Fanon "reads" Lacan in the light of his own preoccupations. In the long footnote on the "mirror phase," it is Fanon's *appropriation* of Lacan which strikes us most vividly (Fanon 1986, 161). First, the "Other" in this transaction is *raced*: "The real Other for the white man is and will continue to be the black man. And conversely." It is difficult not to agree that he writes here as if "the real Other" is indeed "a fixed phenomenological point." Secondly, the split in the subject which the "mirror phase" engenders, and which, for Lacan, is a *general* mechanism of misrecognition which provides the conditions of existence of all identification, is relocated by Fanon *in the specificities of the colonial relation*: "In the Antilles, perception always occurs at the level of the imaginary.... For the Antillean the mirror hallucination is always neutral [i.e., colourless]."

This divergence is critical. On the one hand, it reminds us, as a startling discovery, how racially neutral, how strikingly *un-raced*, Lacan's discourse is, and how rarely this unmarked whiteness of his language has received comment. On the other hand, it clearly marks Fanon's distance from the logic of

Lacan's position. For Lacan, as Bhabha remarks, "identity is never an *a priori* nor a finished product; it is only ever the problematic process of access to an image of totality" (Bhabha 1986, xviii). To this we might necessarily add that, for Lacan, identity also operates "at the level of the imaginary." Fanon follows Lacan in substituting the psychoanalytic concept of "identification" for the Hegelian concept of "recognition." This is a procedure which marks their common lineage in the French reception of Hegel, via the highly influential post-Heideggerean reading of *The Phenomenology* provided by Kojève (1969). But, for Fanon, the blockage which detotalises the Hegelian "recognition" of the One by the Other in the exchange of the *racialised* look, arises from the historically specific, specular structure of racism, not from the general mechanism of self-identification. The political implications of this deviation are highly significant. For the whole thrust of Bhabha's text— accepting a politics of subversion which lives with ambivalence, without trying to transcend or sublate it (*Aufhebung*)—is the *political* consequence of a Lacanian theoretical position, where ambivalence is a necessary part of the script, whereas Fanon's theoretical position—that this radicalisation of the "mirror stage" is a "pathological" condition, forced on the black subject by colonialism—has the political question of *how to end this alienation* inscribed in it. Fanon cannot, politically, "live with this ambivalence," since it is the ambivalence that is killing him!

So, is the mechanism of misrecognition which, according to Lacan, is the condition for the formation of subjectivity in the dialectics of desire "from the place of the Other" (implying a permanent "lack" of fullness for the self) part of a *general ontology*, or is it historically specific to the colonial relation? Fanon's answer, at least, seems clear. "There is of course the moment of 'being for others' of which Hegel speaks, but every ontology is made unattainable in a colonized and civilized society. . . . Ontology . . . does not permit us to understand the being of the black man. For not only must the black man be black; he must be black in relation to the white man. Some critics remind us that this proposition has a converse. I say this is false" (Fanon 1986, 109–10).

In fact, the strategy of Fanon's text is to engage with certain positions which have been advanced as part of a general ontology, and then to show how this fails to operate or to explain the specific predicament of the black colonial subject. What we have to confront, then, is not some mere textual or theoretical squabble between the different ways in which the Lacanian "look from the place of the Other" is inscribed in Fanon's text and Bhabha's re-reading of it, which we can resolve by some brutal and arbitrary act of political judgement. It is a much deeper, more serious, more politically and theoretically resonant problem than that. It points to the as yet deeply unresolved question in so-called "postcolonial studies" as to how to reconcile—or at least hold in a proper balance—in its paradigm of explanation and reading, *both* Fanon's spectacular demonstration of the power of the racial binary to *fix*, and Bhabha's equally important and theoretically productive argument that all binary systems of power are nevertheless, *at the same time*, often if not always, troubled and subverted by ambivalence and disavowal. Our dilemma is how to *think together* the overwhelming power of the binary, which persists despite everything in all racially inflected systems of power and representation (and certainly survives their endless theoretical deconstruction); *and simultaneously* the ambivalences, the openings, the slippages which the suturing of racial discourse can never totally close up. In my view, this is inadequately resolved by subscribing to *either* position on its own. We remain between "Bhabha's moment of discursive ambivalence and Fanon's moment of fixity" (B. Hall 1995).

Where did Fanon get this version of the dialectic of desire and recognition which, in a sense, he grafts on to Lacan? How did he get so deep into the Lacanian "look," and yet so profoundly misconstrue it? These are important questions, not least because it is precisely their double register—the absence of a final resolution between them—which constitutes the excitement of Fanon's work for so many contemporary black visual artists. This question brings us to the second overlapping but unconcluded dialogue, which Homi Bhabha's account tends to underplay for obvious reasons: the dialogue of Fanon with Sartre, or, more accurately, through Sartre to the ghost of Hegel, especially the master/slave dialectic outlined in *The Phenomenology*. The master/slave trope governs a great deal of Fanon's thinking in *Black Skin, White Masks*, as it did much of French intellectual thought at this time. It was in reference to the master/slave trope that Lacan said "at every turn, I take my bearings" and it is this metaphor which opens the dialogue of otherness and desire in Fanon's text: man can be for himself only when he is a "being-for-the-Other" (see Forrester 1988, 222). It speaks especially to Fanon's concerns, not only because of its historical relevance in the master/slave form (elsewhere, it had been translated as bondsman/serf), but also because of the centrality which Hegel's account gives to the "life-and-death struggle" which is the final phase of the slave's struggle for recognition. For Fanon, it is the fundamental inequality, the lack of all reciprocity inscribed in the positions of master and slave, when read in the colonial relation, which opens the necessity for the slave's struggle to the death—a theme which comes to dominate Fanon's later work.

However, here again, Fanon explicitly marks his difference from a general Hegelian ontology (Fanon 1986, 220n8). At the foundation of the Hegelian dialectic, he argues, "Man is human only to the extent to which he tries to impose his existence on another man in order to be recognized by him" (Fanon 1986, 216). There must be "an absolute reciprocity... '*they recognize themselves as mutually recognizing each other*'" (Fanon 1986, 217). When this is resisted, it awakens the "desire for recognition" and it is this which makes the slave willing to undertake a savage struggle, even to the death, since it is "solely by risking life that freedom is obtained" (Fanon 1986, 218). However, for Fanon, the Negro "slave" has never struggled to the death with the master, or staked his life. He has been *given* freedom, which is, in reality, nothing but the freedom to "assume the attitude of the master," to sit at his table. "Let's be nice to niggers" (Fanon 1986, 220). Once again, then, the colonial relation has interposed a specificity which *deflects* the Hegelian master/slave dialectic (just as, earlier, it inflected the Lacanian "mirror phase") in a new direction.

In Hegel, Fanon argues, the master imposes a "slavish work" on the slave. But in turning from the master towards work, the slave "raises himself above his own given nature," creating himself objectively—"voluntarily and consciously, or, better, actively or freely" (Kojève 1969, 229). However, Fanon says, in the colonial relation, the master does *not* want recognition, only work. And the slave does not abandon the master, but turns *to* him, abandoning the object. The Negro is therefore less independent in the struggle for recognition than the Hegelian slave, because he "wants to be like the Master." He is denied recognition, *and constructs his own being-for-himself through that denial.*

There is, however, another twist. The description of the look in the chapter titled "The Fact of Blackness" not only appropriates the Hegelian trope for Fanon's own purpose. It has also been further refracted through the existential universe of Sartre's re-reading of Hegel in *Being and Nothingness*. In Sartre, the "look from the place of the Other" is more appropriative and possessive than the narcissistic form it assumes in Lacan. It steals the self from its in-itself. It empties the subject, a metaphor which seems only a whisper away from Lacan's "lack" but is in fact light-years away, lodged as it is in a Sartrean universe of existential scarcity. As Sartre wrote in *Being and Nothingness* (1969), "If we start with the first revelation of the Other as a look, we must recognize that we experience our inapprehensible being-for-others in the form of a possession. I am possessed by the Other. The Other's look fashions my body in its nakedness.... By virtue of consciousness the Other is for me simultaneously the one who has stolen my body from me and the one who causes there to be a being which is my being."

I believe we can see the complex "trace" of the master/slave trope in a number of unexpected places in Fanon's text. I have noted the pervasive masculinist focus of *Black Skin, White Masks*. It is the question of the black *man's* desire—"What does the black man want?"—which, as Kobena Mercer points out, triggers the text. The chapters "The Woman of Color and the White Man" and "The Man of Color and the White Woman" which deal with the white woman's so-called pathological desire to sleep with black men, and with the neurotic meaning, as Fanon interprets it, of the black man's desire for white women, though containing some important insights into the way projective sexual fantasies become racialised as they become gendered and racialised fantasies become "genitalised" (rather than simply "sexualised"), are nevertheless extremely problematic. The absence of any proper discussion of how the general dialectics of the racialised look applies, and how it may be differentiated between black men and women, is even more troubling. The way Fanon deals with the black woman when she unexpectedly surfaces in his text registers as shocking, but not unsurprising: "Those who grant our conclusions on the psychosexuality of the white woman may ask what we have to say about the woman of colour. I know nothing about her" (1986, 179–80).

Equally troubling are the passages on homosexuality (dissected at length in Kobena Mercer's essay elsewhere in this collection). It is in the context of the passage in which Fanon both acknowledges and disavows that there is any homosexuality in Martinique that he makes the astonishing remark about the "absence of the Oedipus complex in the Antilles" (Fanon 1986, 180n44). The debate as to whether the Oedipus complex is culturally relative is a long-running saga. There may well be cultures where it can be shown to take another form or even not exist at all (although, far from freeing us from some Eurocentric tyranny, this usually throws us back to an essentialist biological notion of how sexual difference is constituted). But I am afraid the Caribbean is the *least* promising scenario in which to try to prove the absence of the Oedipal drama. With its son-fixated mothers and mother-fixated sons, its complex paternities common to all slave societies of "real" black fathers and "symbolic" white ones, along with its deeply troubled, assertively heterosexual and often homophobic black masculinities, the Caribbean "lives out" the loss of social power by substituting an aggressively phallocentred "black manhood." The absence of women and the mother in Fanon's text leads one to wonder whether, figuratively, he didn't *replace* the triadic structure of the Oedipal scenario with the binary coupling of the master/slave trope. This ambiguous "primal scene" was beautifully transposed during *Mirage* into a different, more complex and less homophobic register in *Bear*, Steve McQueen's 1993 film of two black men locked in a playful wrestle.

Do all these Hegelian and Sartrean convolutions matter? There are some critics who believe that the status of Fanon as a black hero and icon is damaged by the suggestion that he might have learned anything or—worse— actually been in dialogue with the themes of European philosophy. This kind of essentialism is worse than useless if we are to think seriously about Fanon. It reveals how little such critics understand Fanon's deep implication in French culture and philosophy as a result of his French colonial upbringing, formation and education in Martinique: how much of the tortured thinking-through of the complicities of the colonial relation which was part of the impulse behind *Black Skin, White Masks* was autobiographical in inspiration. These critics forget that Fanon, like many other bright young colonial intellectuals, went to study in France; became locked in a deep internal argument with the various currents of thought which he found there; and went to North Africa as a salaried member of the French colonial psychiatric service (see Vergès 1996). They do not understand that, in Martinique, for many intellectuals, to be anticolonial and opposed to the old white indigenous plantocracy was to be *for* French Republican ideology, with its rallying cry of liberty, equality and fraternity. Fanon may have travelled far from all that, but it is not clear that he ever left it all behind. The career of someone like his compatriot Aimé Césaire is incomprehensible without understanding the complexity of the relations which constituted French colonialism for black intellectuals in the Antilles.

The Hegelian-Sartrean convolutions matter in another respect. It is only in the light of Hegel's "life-and-death struggle" that we can understand the shadow of death which lengthens over Fanon's later work: that which he called "the savage struggle" and "the convolutions of death" is that which opens up the "possibility of the impossibility." It is death, Hegel's "absolute lord," that makes possible the restoration of the black man's self-constituting activity, "in-itself-for-itself" (Fanon 1986, 218). This can be seen in Fanon's commitment-to-the-death to the Algerian struggle as well as *The Wretched of the Earth*, with its in-the-shadow-of-death urgency (it was written when Fanon already knew he was dying of leukemia) and its invocation of the necessity of violence in the revolutionary struggle for freedom.

This brings us to the third dialogue, which is Fanon's debate with Negritude, or the idea of black culture as a positive source of identification, and the question of cultural nationalism and race as an autonomous force. Fanon returns to this subject matter in *Black Skin, White Masks* in relation to Césaire, but more significantly in relation to Sartre's famous "Black Orpheus" preface to Senghor's *Presence Africaine* anthology of African writing. The underlying issue had to do with Fanon's complex relation, on the one hand, to Sartre's "humanist universalism," which saw Negritude as a necessary transitional stage of consciousness, and on the other hand Fanon's unresolved oscillations in relation to nationalism. He was critical of nationalism as the privileged form of Third World struggle; yet he was a passionate supporter of the national cultural movement in the wider revolutionary struggle in Africa. This made Fanon, in Neil Lazarus's terms (1987), not a "nationalist" but a *nationalitarian*. The question touches an issue of continuing controversy in postcolonial Africa and elsewhere which is probably more significant now in the wake of the crisis of the postindependence state than it was for Fanon at the time of writing, an issue whose surface was barely scratched by the ICA conference's focus on *Black Skin, White Masks*.

It was in relation to the Negritude question (which is far too convoluted to attempt to disentangle here) that Fanon (1970) wrote some of his most vitriolic phrases on the "illusion of black culture"—and where, incidentally, one can find one of his most ambiguous and startling uses of the word "mirage," which was the title of the ICA's project: "With his eyes on Africa, the West Indian . . . discovered himself to be a transplanted son of slaves; he felt the vibration of Africa in the depth of his body and aspired only to one thing: to plunge into the great 'black hole.' It thus seems that the West Indian, after the great white error, is now living in the great black mirage." This was by no means his last or most definitive comment on the issue, but it is a pretty decisive one—and deeply paradoxical, as is so much of Fanon in relation to any simple cultural-nationalist appropriation of his legacy. The passages of severe criticism levelled at Césaire and Negritude in *Black Skin, White Masks* are countered elsewhere by a more sympathetic treatment. The supreme confidence with which Sartre "placed" Senghor's collection as "transitional" in relation to a universal humanism did not rest easily in Fanon's mind. He never resolved the tensions between these two claims.

I find myself in agreement, on this point at least, with Benita Parry's recent (1994) insistence on Fanon's "persistent instabilities," on the unresolved arguments and the incomplete oscillations which make *Black Skin, White*

Masks fundamentally an *open text*, and hence a text we are obliged to go on working *on*, working *with*. In particular, I am pulled back to Fanon's many voices as the sign of the multivocality of the dialogue going on in his head, which came to no settled conclusions. Parry proposes that *Black Skin, White Masks* is Fanon's "learning process," a kind of journey of self-education and self-transformation without the solace of an arrival.

I agree, then, with the reasons which Homi K. Bhabha advances for the importance of *Black Skin, White Masks* at this conjuncture. He characterises Fanon's text as a "jagged testimony of colonial dislocations" which in the end "refuses the ambition of any total theory of colonial oppression." In my reading of the text, Fanon *is* more consistently drawn to "the question of political oppression" in a specifically colonial historical context as "the violation of a human 'essence'" than Bhabha suggests. This refrain is textually insistent, central to his evolving political vision, less a "lapse into . . . a lament in his more existential moment" than Bhabha allows. But I also agree with Bhabha about Fanon's insistence on exploring the question "What does the black man want?" to its depths. This question, as enigmatic and unconsciously charged as Freud's "What does woman want?," nevertheless pushes us to that dangerous point, beyond the limit, where "cultural alienation bears down on the ambivalence of psychic identification" (Bhabha 1986, xi). This is a place many "right-on" critics are determined to avoid. Fanon's insistence on thinking this dangerous moment in terms of fantasy and the desire-for-the-Other transforms our notion of politics and of political demands. The question is, what are we to do with the "uncertain dark" which Bhabha suggests is always the accompaniment to the emergence of truly radical thought?

Does "working with Fanon" require that we undertake a symptomatic re-reading of *Black Skin, White Masks*, re-sighting through the aporias in his text a conceptual scheme which is somehow struggling towards enunciation; a "going beyond" of the text to that absent-presence which it implicates but cannot name? Or should we acknowledge that he did not name it because, though uncannily closer to it in more ways than many of his followers and subsequent critics have understood, he is also more distant? Racism is never, for Fanon, simply something which the Other does to Us. His thinking about it, though finally unresolved, is shaped by an appropriation of some ideas that significantly depart from and in some respects explicitly contradict the place from which we tend to read him today. This requires us to live with a much more radically incomplete Fanon; a Fanon who is somehow more "Other" to us than we would like him, who is bound to unsettle us from whichever direction we read him. This also requires us to engage with the uncomfortable truth that just as "truly radical thought never dawns without casting an uncertain dark," so there is no "life" without its after-life.

NOTES

This essay is from "The After-Life of Frantz Fanon: Why Fanon? Why Now? Why *Black Skin, White Masks?*" in *The Fact of Blackness: Frantz Fanon and Visual Representation*, edited by Alan Read (London: Institute of Contemporary Arts; Seattle: Bay Press, 1996), 12–37.

1 Fanon quotes Michel Cournot as saying that "four Negroes with their penises exposed would fill a cathedral" (Fanon 1986, 169).
2 This is rather in the way that Althusser and Balibar in *Reading Capital* (1970) used structural concepts to "re-read" Marx in his partially theorised state, to produce— hey, presto!—the fully structuralist Marx.

REFERENCES

Althusser, Louis, and Étienne Balibar. 1970. *Reading Capital*. London: New Left Books.
Benjamin, Walter. 1973. "Thesis on the Philosophy of History." In *Illuminations*, translated by Hannah Arendt. London: Fontana.
Bhabha, Homi K. 1986. "Remembering Fanon." Foreword to *Black Skin, White Masks*, by Frantz Fanon. London: Pluto.
Butler, Judith. 1993. *Bodies That Matter: On the Discursive Limits of Sex*. London: Routledge.
Du Bois, W. E. B. 1966. "The Conservation of Races." In *Negro Social and Political Thought*, edited by Howard Brotz. New York: Basic Books.
Fanon, Frantz. 1966. *The Wretched of the Earth*. New York: Grove.
Fanon, Frantz. 1970. *Towards the African Revolution*. Harmondsworth, UK: Penguin.
Fanon, Frantz. 1986. *Black Skin, White Masks*. London: Pluto.
Forrester, J., ed. 1988. *The Seminars of Jacques Lacan, 1*. Cambridge: Cambridge University Press.
Freud, Sigmund. 1977. *On Sexuality*. Pelican Freud Library, vol. 7. Harmondsworth, UK: Penguin.
Gates, Henry Louis. 1991. "Critical Fanonism." *Critical Inquiry* 17, no. 3 (Spring).
Hall, B. 1995. "Reading the Mulatta." Unpublished ms., University of York.
Hall, Stuart. 1992. "Race, Culture and Communication." *Rethinking Marxism* 5, no. 1 (Spring).
Hall, Stuart. 2017. "Race—the Sliding Signifier." In *The Fateful Triangle: Race, Ethnicity, Nation*, edited by Kobena Mercer. Cambridge, MA: Harvard University Press.
Kojève, Alexandre. 1969. *Introduction to the Reading of Hegel*. New York: Basic Books.
Lacan, Jacques. 1977. *Four Fundamental Concepts of Psychoanalysis*. London: Hogarth.

Lazarus, Neil. 1987. "Disavowing Decolonisation." *Research in African Literatures* 24, no. 4 (Winter).

Mercer, Kobena. 1994. "Busy in the Ruins of Wretched Phantasia." In *Mirage: Enigmas of Race, Difference and Desire*. London: ICA/inIVA.

Parry, Benita. 1987. "Problems in Current Theories of Colonial Discourse." *Literary Review* 6 (Winter).

Parry, Benita. 1994. "Signs of the Times." *Third Text* 28/29 (Autumn/Winter).

Robinson, Cedric. 1993. "The Appropriation of Frantz Fanon." *Race and Class* 35, no. 1 (July/September).

Rose, Jacqueline. 1986. *Sexuality in the Field of Vision*. London: Verso.

Sartre, Jean-Paul. 1969. *Being and Nothingness*. New York: Citadel.

Vergès, Françoise. 1996. "Chains of Madness, Chains of Colonialism: Fanon and Freedom." In *The Fact of Blackness: Frantz Fanon and Visual Representation*, edited by Alan Read. Seattle: Bay Press.

CHAPTER 19

Race, the Floating Signifier:
What More Is There to Say about "Race"?

I want, at what you might think a rather late stage in the game, to return to the question of what we might mean by saying that race is a discursive construct, that it is a sliding signifier. Statements of this kind have acquired a certain status in advanced critical circles these days, but it's very clear that critics and theorists don't always mean the same thing or draw the same inference from the statement when they make it. What's more, the idea that race might be described as a signifier is not one which, in my experience, has penetrated very deeply into or done very effectively the work of unhinging and dislodging what I would call common-sense assumptions and everyday ways of talking about race, and of making sense about race in our society today. I'm really talking in part about that great untidy, dirty world in which race matters, outside of the academy as well as what light we may throw on it from inside.

More seriously, the dislocating effects on the world, of political mobilization around issues of race and racism, the dislocating effects on the strategies of antiracist politics and education of thinking of race as a signifier, have not been adequately charted or assessed. Well, you may not be persuaded by the story yet, but that's my excuse for returning at this late date to a topic about which I know many people feel that all that can usefully be said about race has already been said.

What do I mean by a floating signifier? Well, to put it crudely, race is one of those major concepts which organize the great classificatory systems of difference, which operate in human societies. And to say that race is a discursive category recognizes that all attempts to ground this concept scientifically, to locate differences between the races, on what one might call scientific, biological, or genetic grounds, have been largely shown to be untenable. We must therefore, it is said, substitute a sociohistorical or cultural definition of race for the biological one. As the philosopher Anthony Appiah once put it succinctly in his now renowned and elegantly argued contribution in a book which I think many of you will know, it's the Critical Inquiry book called *"Race," Writing and Difference* edited by Henry Louis Gates (Gates and Appiah 1992). He argues that "it is time, as it were, that the biological concept of race was sunk without trace." As we know, human genetic variability between different populations, normally assigned a racial category, is not significantly greater than it is within those populations.

And what W. E. B. Du Bois, who is a great African American thinker and writer on these questions, a figure not necessarily known in the United Kingdom as well as he should be, who wrote a wonderfully moving text called *The Souls of Black Folk* (1903). What Du Bois argues in his essay called "The Conservation of Races" (1897) concerns what he called "the differences of color, hair, and bone." He observed, and I quote, that (races) though they may "transcend scientific definition" are "clearly defined to the eye of the historian and the sociologist" (this is a good thing, because there's a lot of things sociologists don't see). Du Bois thought that racial difference was something they might just make out. Such things are, on the whole, poorly correlated with genetic difference and on the other hand, impossible to correlate significantly with the cultural, intellectual, or the cognitive characteristics of people—quite apart from being subject to extraordinary variation within any one family, let alone within any one so-called family of races.

The Survival of Biological Thinking

I want to note four things at once about this general position. First, it represents the by now common and conventional wisdom among leading scientists in the field. Second, that fact has never prevented intense scholarly activity being devoted by a minority of committed academics to attempting to prove a correlation between racially defined genetic characteristics and cultural performance. In other words, we are not dealing with a field in which, as it were, the scientifically and rationally established fact prevents scientists from continuing to try to prove the opposite.

Thirdly, I observe that though the radicalized implications of this continuing scientific work into, for example, race and intelligence are vociferously refused and condemned by large numbers of people, certainly by most liberal professionals and especially by Black groups of all kinds, in fact a great deal of what is said by such groups, amongst themselves, is predicated precisely on some such assumption, i.e., that some social, political or cultural phenomenon, like the rightness of a political line, or the merits of a literary and musical production, or the correctness of an attitude or belief, can be traced to and explained by and especially fixed and guaranteed in its truth by the racial character of the person involved. I deduce from this intense scholarly activity the awkward lesson that diametrically opposed political positions can often be derived from the same philosophical argument; that though the genetic explanation of social and cultural behavior is often denounced as racist, the genetic, biological, and physiological definitions of race are alive and well in the common-sense discourse of us all; that the biological, physiological, or genetic definition, having been shown out the front door, tends to sidle around the veranda and climb back in through the window. This is the paradoxical finding which I want to explore and address in what follows. Why should this be so?

The Badge of Race

In an article in *Crisis* of August 1911, we find Du Bois moving decisively towards writing, and I quote, "of civilizations where we can now speak of races," adding that "even the physical characteristics including skin color are to no small extent the direct result of a physical and social environment. In addition to being too indefinite and too elusive," he says, "to serve the basis for any origin, classification, or division of human groups." Now on the basis of this recognition in *Dusk of Dawn* (1940), Du Bois abandons the scientific definition of race in favor of the fact that he's writing about Africans, that Africans and people of African descent have what he calls a common racial ancestry, because—it's important to note this—"they have a common history, have suffered a common disaster, and have one long memory of disaster." Because color, though of little meaning in itself, is really important, Du Bois argues, "as a badge for the social heritage of slavery, the dissemination and the insult of that experience."

A badge, a token, a sign: here indeed is the idea, hinted at in the title of my talk, that race is a signifier, and that racialized behavior and difference needs to be understood as a discursive, not necessarily as a genetic or biological fact.

Race as a Language, a "Floating Signifier"

I don't want to deviate here with a long theoretical disquisition about the terms that I'm using, to bore you to tears, I simply want to remind you that the model being proposed here is closer to that of how a language works than of how our biology or our physiologies work. That race is more like a language, than it is like the way in which we are biologically constituted. You may think that's an absurd and ridiculous thing to say; you may even now be surreptitiously glancing around the room, just to make sure that you know your visual appearances are in full working order. I assure you they are: people do look rather peculiar; some of them are brown, some of them are quite black, some of you are pretty brown, some of you are really disgustingly pink in the current light. But, there's nothing wrong with your appearances, but I want to insist to you that nevertheless, the argument that I want to make to you is that *race works like a language*. And signifiers refer to the systems and concepts of the classification of a culture, to its practices for *making meaning*. And those things gain their meaning, not because of what they contain in their essence, but in the shifting relations of difference, which they establish with other concepts and ideas in a signifying field. Their meaning, because it is relational, and not essential, can never be finally fixed, but is subject to the constant process of redefinition and appropriation: to the losing of old meanings, and appropriation and collection and contracting of new ones, to the endless process of being constantly resignified, made to mean something different in different cultures, in different historical formations at different moments of time.

The meaning of a signifier can never be finally or transhistorically fixed. That is, it is always, or there is always, a certain sliding of meaning, always a margin not yet encapsulated in language and meaning, always something about race left unsaid. Always someone—a constitutive outside—whose very existence the identity of race depends on, and which is absolutely destined to return from its expelled and abjected position outside the signifying field to trouble the dreams of those who are comfortable inside.

But What about the Reality of Racial Discrimination and Violence?

I address this point directly because I believe this is exactly where the more skeptical amongst you may be beginning to think, "All right, you might say perhaps race is not after all a matter of genetic factors, of biology, of physiological characteristics, of the morphology of the body, not a matter of color, hair, and bone, that chilling threesome that Du Bois frequently quotes." But you may say, "Can you seriously be claiming that it is simply a signifier, an empty sign, that it is not fixed in its inner nature, that it cannot be secured in its meaning, that it floats in a sea of relational differences—is that the argument that you're advancing?" And "Isn't it not only wrong, but a trivial, and"—I hear the word being rustled in the audience—"an *idealist* approach to the brute facts of human history, which after all have disfigured the lives, and crippled and constrained the potentialities of literally millions of the world's dispossessed? After all, why don't we use the evidence of our eyes? If race was such a complicated thing, why would it be so manifestly obvious everywhere we look?" I have to say it again because I can feel the sense of relief that after skirting around through these various discursive structures we have come to know after all what we all know about race. It's reality. You can see its effects, you can see it in the faces of the people around you, you can see people pulling the skirts aside as people from another racial group come into the room. You can see the operation of racial discrimination in institutions and so on. What is the need of all this scholarly hullabaloo about race, when you can just turn to its reality?

What trail through history is more literally marked by blood and violence, by the genocide of the Middle Passage, by the horrors of plantation servitude, and the hanging tree? A signifier, a discourse, yes, that is my argument.

Two Positions: The Realist and the Textual

Since we are concerned here not with abstract theoretical critique but with an attempt to unlock the secrets of the functioning in modern history of racial systems of classification, let me turn to this question of how indeed one sees this functioning around the troubling question of the gross physical differences of color, bone, and hair, which constitute the material substratum, the absolute final common denominator of racial classifying systems. When all the other refinements have been wiped away, there seems to be a sort of irreducible, ineradicable minimum there, the differences, which are palpable among people, which we call race. Where on earth do they come from, if they are simply, as I want to claim, discursive?

Broadly speaking, as I understand it there are really three options here. First, we can hold that the differences of a physiological kind or nature really do provide the basis for classifying human races into families, and once they can be proved to do so, they can adequately be represented in our systems of thought and language. That's a kind of realist position, it really is there, and all we have to do is reflect what is out there in the world, adequately in the systems of language and knowledge which we use to conduct investigations into its effects.

Well, a second possibility is to hold what is sometimes called the purely textual or linguistic position. Race here, is autonomous of any system reference. It can only be tested, not against the actual world of human diversity, but within the play of the text, within the play of the differences that we construct in our own language.

A Third Position: The Discursive

But there is a third position, the third position is the one to which I subscribe. It's often the third position I subscribe to, as it turns out (I don't know what you want to make of that, but there it is). The third position is that there are probably differences of all sorts in the world, that difference is a kind of anomalous existence out there, a kind of random series of all sorts of things in what you call the world. There's no reason to deny this reality or this diversity. I think it's sometimes, not always, what Foucault means when he talks about the extradiscursive (I don't want to stir up the Foucauldians there)—it's only when these differences have been organized within language, within discourse, within systems of meaning, that the differences can be said to acquire meaning and become a factor in human culture and regulate conduct. That is the nature of what I'm calling the discursive concept of race. It's not that nothing exists of differences, but that what matters are the systems we use to make sense, to make human societies intelligible. The system we bring to those differences, how we organize those differences into systems of meaning, with which, as it were, we could find the world intelligible. And this has nothing to do with denying that, as I say, the audience test—if you looked around, you'd find we did after all look somewhat different from one another.

I think these are discursive systems because the interplay between the representation of racial difference, the writing of power, and the production of knowledge, is crucial to the way in which they are generated, and the way in which they function. I use the word "discursive" here to mark the transition theoretically from the more formal understanding of difference to an understanding of how ideas and knowledges of difference organize human practice between individuals.

Religion: A First Go at Racial Classification

Racial classifying systems themselves have a history, and their modern history seems to emerge where peoples of very different kinds first encounter and have to make sense of peoples of another culture who are significantly different from them, and we can date when that historical encounter occurred (I don't want to talk about that at the moment).

When the Old World first encountered the New, the peoples of the New World, they put to them a question; it's the famous question that Sepulveda put to Las Casas when the subject was debated within the Catholic Church: "What is the nature of the peoples that we have found in the New World?" Now, they didn't say what I think the religious amongst you would like to hear them say, "Well, these are, are they not, men like us, and our brothers? Are they not women like us, and our sisters?" No, they didn't say that, that took a very, very long time to come—about two or three hundred years before the abolitionist movement thought of putting a question like that. No, what they said is, "Are these true men?" That is to say, do they belong even to the same species as we do, or are they born of another creation? And here for centuries it was not science, but religion, religion standing as the signifier of knowledge and truth. Where the human science is, and then science itself was later destined to stand, would ground the truth of human difference and diversity in some fact which was controllable, which could put *them* over there, and *us* over here; *them* in the boats and *us* on top of the civilization that we had conquered and so on.

Sleeping Easier: The Cultural Function of Knowledge

It is that act of organizing people through their differences into different social groups, which is the act of social and human classification, that is what is being sought—first in a religious discourse, then in an anthropological discourse, and finally in a scientific discourse. Here, each of these knowledges is functioning not as the provision of the truth, but as what makes men and women sleep well in their beds at night. They're kind of soothers—they're knowledge soothers, they're tucking the soothers into the mouth; first you pop in the religious one, and you hope to find that after all, when after all is said and done, God actually created two kinds of men, he had two goes at it—one weekend and then another weekend, and they were over there and we were over here and its only long afterwards that we happen to stumble across one another. But there's no thought that we both came from the same place. That soother doesn't work so you take that out. You pop in another one: an anthropological one that would say, "Well they're sort of really like us, that's because we all really come from monkeys, but some of them are much closer to monkeys than we are." Although that may not be an absolute difference, it is enough to found differences in university departments, in publishing, etc. And then finally, when that anthropology itself finally gives up, along comes James Clifford, and he gives us knowledge of what anthropology can do: sort out the sheep from the goats. Then science comes along and says, "I can do it, I can do it." Higher genetics, you can't see genetics, it's a wonderful, internal system, we have the clue to it, we can look at it in the laboratory—but human beings can't see it. What they see are the *effects* of the genetic code operating. So it's a wonderfully secret code that only a small number of people have at their disposal, which can do exactly what religion didn't manage to do, and anthropology didn't quite bring off. It can tell you why these people do not belong in the same camp, why they are very different from one another, why they really are a different species. And wouldn't it be good to know that instead of trying to work out whether the ones who are your friends are closer to you than the ones who are not, all that complicated map of alliances, etc., which constitute human relations—wouldn't it be good if you just had something simple to say? I'll just pop into the lab and I'll tell you whether they are or not. And that's what it'll do.

Fixing Difference: The Cultural Function of Science

Science has a function, a cultural function in our society. Let me pause before I get carried away. I'm not suggesting that there's nothing to science; that's not my business today, and talking about the function which science performs within human cultural systems, I'm talking about the *cultural* function of science, and I'm saying that the *cultural* functions of science, in the languages and discourses of racism, have been to provide precisely that guarantee and certainty of absolute difference which no other systems of knowledge up until that point have been able to provide. And that is why the scientific trace remains such a remarkably powerful instrument in human thinking, not only in the academy but everywhere in people's ordinary common-sense discourse. For centuries, the struggle was to establish a binary distinction between two kinds of people. But once you get to the Enlightenment, which says or recognizes everybody is one species, then you have to begin to find a way which marks the difference *inside* the species; not two species, but how, why, one bit of the species is different—more barbarous, more backwards, more civilized—than another part. And you get into a different marking of difference, the difference that is marked *inside* the system. You know, I mean, listen to the way in which Edmund Burke once wrote to Robertson in 1877: "We need no longer go to history," he said, "to trace the knowledge of human nature in all its stages and periods. Why? Because now the great map of mankind is on a road all at once and there's no state or gradation of barbarism and no mode of refinement which we do not have at the same instant under our view" (as quoted by Meek 1976, 173). That is the panoptic glance of the Enlightenment—everything, all of human creation, is now, as it were, under the eye of science. And within that, can be marked, the differences that very much matter. And what are they? "The very different civility of Europe and of China. The barbarism of Tartary and of Arabia; and the savage state of North America and New Zealand."

The point I'm making is it is not science as such, but whatever is in the discourse of a culture, which grounds the truth about human diversity, which unlocks the secret of the relations between nature and culture. Which unties the puzzling fact of the human difference which matters. And what matters is not that they contain the scientific truth about difference, but that they function foundationally in the discourse of racial difference. They fix and secure what else otherwise cannot be fixed or secured. They warrant and guarantee the truth of differences, which they discursively construct.

Nature = Culture

The relationship here, then, is that culture is made to follow on from nature, to lean on it for its justification. Nature and culture here operate as metaphors for one another. They operate metonymically. It is the function of the discourse and race as a signifier, to make these two systems—nature and culture—correspond with one another, in such a way that it is possible to read off the one against the other. So that once you know where the person fits in the classification of natural human races, you can infer from that what they're likely to think, what they're likely to feel, what they're likely to produce, the aesthetic quality of their productions, and so on. It is constituting a system of equivalencies between nature and culture, which is the function of race as a signifier.

In my view, as a discursive system, the biological trace is required so long as this essentializing, naturalizing function, this way of taking racial difference out of history, out of culture, and locating it beyond the reach of change, so long as that function is part of what racial systems are about.

Seeing Is Believing

However, this is not the only reason why biological reasoning, while functioning, as it were, as if it's largely untrue but still somehow hangs around in the conversation which we conduct around race. That's not the only reason why that is so. What Du Bois had started with was precisely the grosser physical differences of color, hair, and bone. There remain anomalous fractural populations that transcend scientific definition. They are, when we come down to it, providing the foundation for the languages of race that we speak every day. The stubborn gross physical facts, of color, hair, or bone. Now, the central fact about these gross physical differences is not that they are based on genetic differences, but they are clearly visible to the eye. They are what, palpably, to the untutored, unscientific eye, makes race a thing which we continue to talk about. They are, in a sense, beyond dispute. They are brute, physical biological facts about human vision that appear in the field of vision. Where seeing is believing.

In *Black Skin, White Masks* (1967), Frantz Fanon was transfixed by the inscription of racial difference on the surface of the black body itself. What he called the dark and unarguable evidence of his own blackness. "I am a slave," he said, "not of an idea that others have of me, but of my own appearance, I am fixed by it." For what indeed, of course, what can people be transfixed by other than by that which is so powerfully and evidently concretely undeniable there?—a racial difference which writes itself indelibly on the script of the body.

Genetics: Making Sense of Difference

What gives rise to these evident and visible signs of racial difference? Fuzzy hair, big noses, thick lips, large behinds. And as the French writer Michel Cournot once delicately put it, "penises as big as cathedrals." What gives rise to all that is of course the genetic code. I mean it's not just that those things are there because nobody ever conducted the experiment and tried to actually sort out a palpable group of people who contain some of these differences, you know, carefully and discreetly into two opposing groups. It simply cannot be done. Just simply can't be done. You get some people over there and a few people over there, and then they are all those wishy-washy things in the middle that keep slipping and sliding from inside to outside. It's just not quite possible to actually fix it. So, actually, though race is something that you can plainly see, what fixes it is because we all know, we scientific folk, what is behind these is the genetic code which regrettably you cannot see but from which you can infer the fact that some have large behinds, and some people have fuzzy hair, and some people have big noses and some people for all I know have penises as big as a cathedral. But you can't set about organizing the population, you know, if I say drop your pants and if I tell you whether you are this or that, because the thing is just too anomalous for that. But you can be sure that genetically some code has actually given—at the level of the surface, of appearances—these differences. We poor mortals have to work with this confusing surface of appearances because we can't get access to the genetic code.

Reading the Body

Well, this is quite true, but what I am afraid that you're saying, what you're telling me, is that actually, these things which you can see are also signifiers! You are reading them as signs of a code that you can't see. You assume that it is the genetic code creating these gross differences of color, hair, and bone. And only because of that can you use it as a way of distinguishing between one group of people and another. If I were to say, "It happened by chance," that is not the answer we are looking for. We are looking for the fact that you can read the body as a text. It is a text. Now my friends, you know, I know you will say, "If you hit me, cut me, I'll bleed. You run over me in the street, as is frequently the case in front of the New Cross entrance. You know, I will be flattened." It may be, but insofar as what we are talking about is the system for classifying difference, the body is a text. And we are all readers of it. And we go around, looking at this text, inspecting it like literary critics. Closer and closer for those very fine differences, these are such small differences, and then when that does work, we start to run like a true structuralist, we start to run the combinations. Well, if I perm, you know, not so big nose, with rather fuzzy hair, and a sort of largish behind and goodness knows what, I might sort of come out. We are readers of race, that's what we are doing, we are readers of social difference. And the body is here, which you know is sighted as if it is what terminates the argument when you say race is a signifier: "No it is not! See the folks out there, they are different! You can tell they are different." Well, that very obviousness, the very obviousness of the visibility of race is what persuades me that it functions because it is signifying something. It is a text, which we can read.

Why We Have to Move beyond "Reality"

Now this notion that even the genetic code is only imprinted on us through the body rather than on the body, that you can't stop at the surface of the black body itself, as if that, well, I was going to say, as if that brought the argument to a close. But that is exactly why the body is invoked in the discourse in that way. In the hope that it will bring the argument to a close, that if you invoke reality itself—if you say, "The blackest person in the room step this way"—somehow pointing to him or her will destroy all my argument. Just look there. That is exactly the function of invoking the body as if it is the ultimate transcendental signifier—as if this is the marker beyond which all arguments will stop, all language will cease, all discourse will fall away before this reality. I think we can't turn to the reality of race because the reality of race itself is what is standing in the way of our understanding, in a profound way. What the meaning is of saying that race is cultural system.

Analyzing the Stories of the Body

I said that in Fanon's book *Black Skin, White Masks* he's entranced and obsessed by the trauma of his own appearance and what it means. He is driven wild by the fact that he is caught, caught and locked in this body which the other, the white other, knows just by looking at him. The other can see through him just by reading the text of the black body. He's obsessed by that fact. And yet, as I am sure you know, when it came to it, the power and importance of *Black Skin, White Masks* is that Fanon understood that beneath what he called the bodily and corporeal schema was another schema. It's a schema composed of the stories and the anecdotes, and the metaphors, and the images, which is really what constructs the relationship between the body and its social and cultural space. Those stories, not the fact itself. The fact itself is just that trap of the surface which allows us to rest with what is obvious. It's so manifestly there. The trap in racism is precisely to allow what is manifestly there, what offers it to us as a symptom of appearance, to stand in the place of what is in fact one of the most profound and deeply complex of the cultural systems. It allows us to make a distinction between inside and outside, between us and them, between who belongs and who doesn't belong. That apparently simple, obvious and banal fact requires the invocation of whole territories of knowledge in order to produce it as a simple, obvious, visible fact. In this way, race is more like sexual difference. Racial difference is more like sexual difference than it is like the other systems of difference precisely because anatomy, physiology, appears to wind the question up and what we know about and have learned gradually about sexual difference, that is to say the profundity of the depth that lies behind the making of that distinction, is what we need now to begin to learn about the languages of race which we speak.

Why Does It Matter? Battling Racism

Though race cannot perform the function it was asked to do by providing the truth and fixing that truth beyond the shadow of a doubt, it is difficult to get rid of because it is so difficult in the languages of race to do without some kind of foundational guarantee. The point I am making here, about the necessity of a foundational guarantee, is not a theoretical argument, or not a theoretical argument only. It is a political argument, because so much of the politics both of race and of antirace are founded on the notion that somehow, somewhere, biology or genetics or physiology or color or something other than human history and culture will guarantee the truth and authenticity of the things we believe and want to do. It is the search for that guarantee—as much in the politics of antiracism, as in the politics of racism—which makes us, which addicts us, to the preservation of the biological trait. It is hard to give up because in the end, we don't know what it is like to try to conduct a politics, especially a politics of antiracism, without a guarantee. We don't know what it is like to conduct politics without a guarantee. We want somehow to be told something which tells us that the contingent, open-ended, usually wrong political choices we make can, in the end, be read off against some other more scientific theoretical template which, if we only had hold of the beginning, would have told us what was right and what was not. We need the guarantee we need to have in the sleep of reason, that which says, "Yes, do it," because it not only feels like and looks like, and *is* the right thing as far as your calculations can take it, but in the end it will be right, there is something which will make it right. That is because the people holding it, after all, these are the people you know, these are good people, how in the name of people come together around this common form of identification, how could they be wrong? But the truth is that, like all ordinary human beings, they could. We could all be wrong. And often are. Quite usually are in fact and in our politics almost always are, you might say. The one thing we are not is guaranteed in the truth of what we do. Indeed, I believe that without that kind of guarantee we would need to begin again, begin again in another space, begin again from a different set of presuppositions to try to ask ourselves what might it be in human identification, in human practice, in the building of human alliances, which without the guarantee, without the certainty of religion or science or anthropology or genetics or biology or the appearance of your eyes, without any guarantees at all, might enable us to conduct an ethically responsible human discourse and practice about race in our society. What might it be like to conduct that, without having at our backs just a touch of a certainty that even if we look as if we were wrong, if we only had access to the code, something would have told us in the beginning what we should do.

And this is an uncomfortable truth. It's an uncomfortable truth, of course, for those who would have liked to invoke the biological or genetic trace as a way of stopping the argument. But it is also a very difficult truth to come to terms with amongst those people who feel, as it were, the reality of race gives a kind of guarantee or underpinning to their political argument and their aesthetic judgments and their social and cultural beliefs. Once you enter the politics of the end of the biological definition of race, you are plunged headlong into the only world we have. The maelstrom of a continuously contingent unguaranteed political argument, debate, and practice. A critical politics against racism, which is always a politics of criticism.

NOTE

"Race, the Floating Signifier" is a transcript of the film *Race: The Floating Signifier*, directed by Sut Jhally (Northampton, MA: Media Education Foundation, 1997).

REFERENCES

Du Bois, W. E. B. 1897. "The Conservation of Races." American Negro Academy Occasional Papers, no. 2. Washington, DC: American Negro Academy.
Du Bois, W. E. B. 1903. *The Souls of Black Folk*. Chicago: A. C. McClurg and Co.
Du Bois, W. E. B. 1911. "Races." *Crisis* 2, no. 4 (August): 157–58.
Du Bois, W. E. B. 1940. *Dusk of Dawn: An Essay toward an Autobiography of a Race Concept*. New York: Harcourt, Brace and Co.

Fanon, Franz. 1967. *Black Skin, White Masks*. Translated by Charles Lam Markmann. New York: Grove.

Gates, Henry Lewis, and Kwame Anthony Appiah, eds. 1992. *"Race," Writing, and Difference*. Chicago: University of Chicago Press.

Meek, R. 1976. *Social Science and the Ignoble Savage*. Cambridge: Cambridge University Press.

CHAPTER 20

"In but Not of Europe":
Europe and Its Myths

Europe is literally an invention of the Third World.
—Frantz Fanon, *The Wretched of the Earth*

Where does Europe begin and end? Has it always existed, and if not, when did it start? What is the "new" Europe's relation to its past? Which parts of Europe belong to "the idea of Europe" and which do not? Is Europe the product of a universal idea, whose contemporary existence can be adequately captured in terms of some earlier figure or trope? Or is it only now emerging in response to forces which are radically, constitutively, novel—the withering of the nation-state, the new global economy, the reconfigurations of global power, the challenge of a super-power American hegemony? What role does the imaginary or myth have to play in this process?

My title is drawn from some observations by C. L. R. James, one of the leading Caribbean-born intellectuals of his and of any generation, who lived for many years in Europe and North America, and who was the author of that still unsurpassed history of the slave revolution in Santo Domingo (Haiti) in the 1790s, *The Black Jacobins* (1980). James's life and work could be seen as personifying many of the contradictions of the encounter between Europe and its others. He was born in Trinidad, but left it as a young man for England in the early years of the twentieth century to become the first black cricket correspondent for the *Manchester Guardian*. He wrote a wonderful autobiographical memoir entitled *Beyond a Boundary*. James was "schooled," like all of us colonials in the years before independence, in the classics of English and European literature. He told me with great pride that he read Thackeray's *Vanity Fair* once every year, and spoke French well enough to research his history of the Haitian Revolution from the original sources in the Bibliotheque National. A Marxist and a passionate anti-Stalinist, he wrote a treatise on Hegel and the dialectic, and interviewed Trotsky in exile in Mexico on "the Negro Question" (and then broke with Trotskyism because of the unsatisfactory nature of the old man's replies). He was active in the Pan-African movement in England between the wars, a close friend of Jomo Kenyatta's and Francis Nkrumah's, and mentor of Trinidad's Prime Minister Eric Williams (an outline for whose groundbreaking study *Capitalism and Slavery* [Williams 1944] James is alleged to have sketched on the back of an envelope). Active in left circles in the US in the 1940s, James wrote an unfinished masterpiece, *American Civilisation* (the closest parallel is Gramsci's brilliantly prophetic essay "Americanism and Fordism"); and when he was finally deported for "un-American activities," he offered as his defence his reading of *Moby-Dick*—he thought it *"the* great American novel." He identified the great climacterics of European history—Greek drama, the frescoes of Michelangelo, the language of Shakespeare, Hegel and Marx, the ideas of the French Revolution, the music of Beethoven, Lenin and the Russian Revolution—as the privileged moments of human creativity (see, *inter alia*, James 1978, 1980, 1993, 1994).

Yet when asked what his attitude was towards Europe, C. L. R. James replied that he was "in but not of it." "Those people," he added "who are in western civilisation, who have grown up in it but yet are not completely a part [of it], have a unique insight ... something special to contribute" (James 1984). Georg Simmel said something similar about the figure of "the stranger." I don't know about a "unique insight," or a "special contribution"; but I do know, as someone formed through and through in a relationship in colonial dependence, subalternity and "otherness" to Europe, that "in but not of it" most accurately captures the ambivalences that haunt my own identifications. Much of this ambivalence is situational: I confess to feeling most aggressively "European" in America, most aware that I can never really be "European" when actually in Europe....

I want to stay with James's ambivalent formulation because it says so much about the difficulties in finding a "figure" for Europe. The Jamaican anthropologist David Scott (2004) argues that James represented Toussaint L'Ouverture, the slave leader of the San Dominican revolution, as ultimately a tragic figure. Not because of his tactical mistakes, but because of the historical space in which he was obliged to operate. Toussaint abhorred the savage and humiliating plantation regime imposed by French colonists on the African slaves, and was drawn to the flame of resistance when it flared up in the slave villages. But his concept of "freedom," as James shows, was also deeply shaped by his reading of the radical Enlightenment *philosophes*, and the ideas of the French Revolution itself. As a "Black Jacobin," Toussaint looked to revolutionary France for the gift of emancipation. He was destined to be disappointed. *Les amis des noirs* at first emancipated only the "coloureds." Abolition was then reluctantly extended to all slaves, but when Napoleon came to power he revoked the edict and restored slavery. It was only many decades later that slavery was eventually abolished in the French empire.

According to David Scott, Toussaint's conception of the political future "depended upon the horizon established by the categories liberty, fraternity, equality"—ideas which constituted the framework of his mind. Trapped in the horizon—the "problem-space"—of these ideas, he was confronted by an impossible choice, for he could neither return to slavery nor conceive of San Domingue without France. Slavery and the Haitian Revolution thus constituted the *limit-case* of the great European idea of the Universal Rights of Man. "Freedom" for black slaves represented an unsurpassable frontier—the constitutive outside—to the so-called "universality" of the European conception of "liberty, equality, fraternity." Scott argues that the "problem-space" within which Toussaint had to think the question of freedom, and the conditions he lived—which harnessed the "backward" brutalities of plantation slavery to the "advanced" European economy—condemned him to be a "modern" figure but of a modernity he could only live as *fate*. In Scott's felicitous phrase, Toussaint was a "conscript of modernity." I believe all of us who, in C. L. R. James's terms, are "in but not of Europe"—who live our intimacy with Europe, as well as its impossibility as "fate"—are in that sense Europe's conscripts.

Inevitably, therefore, we conscripts view the rising demand to find a "figure" for the new Europe—a myth which encapsulates and condenses "the idea of Europe," which shows that the new configuration had its foundation in a classical idea of great antiquity—very differently from those who see it from inside. From within, Europe has always represented itself as somehow autochthonous—producing itself, by itself, from within itself; whereas we have always been obliged to ask, "How does Europe imagine its 'unity'? How can it be imagined, in relation to its 'others'? What does Europe look like from its liminal edge, from what Ernesto Laclau or Judith Butler would call its 'constitutive outside'?" (see, *inter alia*, Laclau and Mouffe 1985; Butler 1993).

For Laclau and Butler, all identities are ultimately an effect of power, since their inner homogeneity—what gives their members the sense that they belong together because they are all "the same"—is the effect of symbolically excluding difference. Identities are thus constructed *through* difference: they are what they are because of all the things they are not, because of what they *lack*. But insofar as identities depend on what they are *not*, they implicitly affirm the importance of what is outside them—which often then returns to trouble and unsettle them from the inside. Nothing could be more true of Europe, which has constantly, at different times, in different ways, and in relation to different "others," tried to establish what it is—its identity—by symbolically marking its difference from "them." Each time, far from producing a stable and settled entity, Europe has had to re-imagine or re-present itself differently. We are at another such moment now.

Of course I understand what is driving the search for "the myths of Europe"—that idea, figure or image which might impose a unifying vision, a common framework of intelligibility, on highly diverse societies, whose histories have dramatically diverged over the centuries; a story, perhaps, which could lend depth and texture to the relative cultural "thinness" which the emerging spectre of the "new Europe," or the European Union, presents (not to speak of its potentially fissiparous cultural diversity). It is an imaginative project to try to examine Europe from the point of view of a history of its imaginary. However, disconcertingly, the search for Europe's myth could also turn out to be an exercise in the production of yet another version of Europe's foundational story. After all, isn't this what foundational myths are for? They provide a magical starting point. They suggest that the present can be imagined as just another episode in a long-running story that has been unfolding since time immemorial, and which was already foreshadowed and foretold—and thus legitimated—in its origins. There is a possibility that current efforts to rework the myth of Europe's foundations, and the search for some newly defined "origin," will license Europe, once again, to disavow its historic instability and its deep interconnections with other histories, and to somehow seamlessly reconnect the mythical past with Europe's disrupted recent present and future. We must beware lest—as all such foundational myths attempt to do—it binds the disconcerting discontinuities, brutal ruptures, grim inequalities and unforeseen contingencies of Europe's real history into the *telos* of a consoling circular narrative whose end is already foreshadowed by its beginning.

Benedict Anderson (1983) calls such efforts at narrativisation the construction of an "imagined community." Imagined, he argues, because its members can never know or meet their fellow-members, so that the latter exist for them, principally, in the way each must "live" the image of their community—what he calls their "deep, horizontal comradeship"—*in the mind*. So nations—and supranational communities—if they are to hang together, and construct a sense of belongingness amongst their members—cannot simply be political, economic or geographical entities; they also depend on how they are represented and imagined: they exist within, not outside, representation, the imaginary. Stories, symbols, images, rituals, monuments, historic events, typical landscapes, and above all *myths*, told and retold, lend significance to our humdrum existence by connecting our banal, everyday, lives with a larger, more poetic, destiny which predates and will outlive us. As Homi Bhabha (1990) observed, communities, "like narratives, lose their origins in the myths of time and only fully realise their horizons in the mind's eye." Myths, Lévi-Strauss (1966) once remarked, are "good to think with." But he also took care to remind us that the "solutions" they seem to offer are often "magical" ones.

The Europa Myth

The Europa myth is an attractive starting point. It is drawn from the ur-European myth reservoir of classical Greece, the wellspring of the European imaginary. The beautiful Phoenician maiden succumbs on the beach to the seductions of Zeus in the shape of the horned and garlanded white bull, and rides off on his back into the sunset, only later—much later—presumably when she has sown her wild oats, conceding to a respectable union and domestic married bliss with Astrios. This lunar goddess, with the wide, round face and big eyes of the moon, whose abduction was the proximate cause of the founding of Thebes, symbolises—we are told—the continuous movement westwards: the migratory drift from Asia, Egypt and the eastern Mediterranean, the diffusion of the alphabet and writing, the spread of agriculture into the fertile western European plain. Her very name derives from a Semitic root meaning "western." She is indeed a prophetic figure for Europe: richly suggestive but difficult to decode. If she represents Europe, why is she from "elsewhere"? If this is "an allegory of love," what has it to tell us about the European conception of the relation between love and seduction, sexual desire and marriage? And who or what, pray, is the bull?—deceptively white, but with a definite aura about him of "otherness," of sexual power, male compulsion and patriarchal possessiveness: something "dark" and dangerous, who comes lumbering out of the European collective unconscious and steals Europa away to Crete.

Europa is a recurring figure in European art and mythology, as the beautiful book by Luisa Passerini, *Il mito d'Europa* (2002), demonstrates. The many, varied ways she has been embodied down through the centuries—differently figured and bearing very different meanings—is a testimony to the versatility of the great myths, their multiple possibilities to carry and construct meaning, and to the imaginative capacities of mankind. The tracing of these rich and variegated symbolic patterns, and unlocking of the very different interpretive *schemas* and narratives within which Europa and the bull have been "figured," is a major contribution to European scholarship. But in our enthusiasm for interpretation we must also be alert not only to meaning but also to function, to the *politics* of the enterprise, and to what Roland Barthes in "Myth Today" (1972) called its "meta-meanings." Myth, Barthes reminded us, is "de-politicised speech." It does its work by a process of naturalisation re-presenting History as Nature, which is another way of translating real time into mythic time.

Is there something almost too predictable and overdetermined about the return to the figure of Europa? After all, it is by common consent many centuries after the era of classical Greece before anything vaguely resembling Europe or a "European identity" begins to make itself felt. There was no such visible continent formation, identity or destiny until the late middle ages, and the period just prior to the moment when Europe finally overtook the hitherto superior civilisations of Asia, after about 1450 (Mann 1988); before that it was only what Michael Mann described as "a multiple ancephalous federation" with no head or centre but a number of largely localised, cross-cutting interaction networks and overlapping powers. And even at that time its identification was "primarily Christian, for its name was Christendom more often than it was Europe" (Mann 1988). Greek culture has, of course, retrospectively become crucial to Europe's identity, because of the richness of its civilisation, the greatness of its achievements in art, literature, philosophy and culture, and its massive subsequent influence on every branch of European thought. Its mythological stories are therefore bound to be a particularly privileged and suggestive source for reimagining Europe today. But this was not the only mythological system on offer—the Norse and the Celtic also have some claim on the European imaginary. Its centring in Greek classical mythology was in fact a process, not a product of Nature; accomplished, in part, by steadily detaching Greek culture from its roots in

Asia and Egypt, and relocating it firmly in Europe—an aspect of that "Aryanization" of Greek civilisation which Martin Bernal (among other scholars) has written about in his riveting study *Black Athena* (Bernal 1991).

Privileging Greek mythology as a way of fixing Europe's origin has the effect of effacing a profound truth about the emerging Europe—namely "the steady western drift of the leading edge of power . . . to the west and north." Contrary to what the naturalisation of Greek mythological sources might suggest, European identity was created as much "by the fusion of the Germanic barbarians and the northwestern parts of the Roman Empire" as it was by the Greeks; and it partly emerged from the stimulus provided by "the blocking presence of Islam to the south and east" and of the Huns, Mongols and Tartar tribes of the steppes (Mann 1988). The real avenues of expansion lay in this westward movement—promoting agricultural innovation and navigational development linked to the rise of trade and science, and crowned eventually by Europe's break-out from its geographical and mental confinement at the end of the fifteenth century. John Roberts (1985) noted that the word "European" seems to appear for the first time in an eighth-century reference to Charles Martel's victory over Islamic forces at Tours. Others, like Peter Hulme (1986), speak of "the consolidation of an ideological identity through the testing of Europe's eastern frontiers prior to the adventure of Atlantic exploration." Hulme argues that Pius III's identification of Europe with Christendom in 1458 could be considered a symbolic end to the process; this offered that overarching canopy of normative and moral regulation that no other system provided. It is not surprising, therefore, that the point when we can most confidently say that a European identity exists coincides with the defeat and expulsion of the Muslims from Spain by a militant and purified Catholic monarchy; the expulsion and forced conversion of the Jews; and the launching of the great "experiment" of conquest and exploration down the African coast and into the great unknown across the Green Sea of Darkness. As the Great Mariner, Christopher Columbus, put it: "In this present year, 1492, after Your Highnesses have brought to an end the war against the Moors . . . after having driven the Jews out of your realm, Your Highnesses commanded me to set out with a sufficient armada to the said countries of India" (quoted in Cohen 1969).

Some readings of the myth of Europa and the Bull argue that the myth *does* acknowledge Europe's wider, non-European roots. The fact that Europa is herself from Asia Minor, and not in any proper sense "European," but is taken to Europe by the bull, is cited as evidence that myths can sometimes speak more "truthfully" than they appear to know. Michael Rice's work suggests that the Europa and the bull myth is almost certainly part of—and indeed a probably very late addition to—the cult of the bull, which belongs to a much wider and more ancient arc of religious cults and practices stretching from Asia Minor, through the Levant, the Arabian peninsula and the Gulf, and arriving only quite late in the day in Crete (Rice 1998). Other readings suggest that, because Europa is a progenitor of the Minotaur, whom Minos, her offspring, confines below earth in the Labyrinth in the Palace at Knossos in Crete, the myth is also able to encompass the fact that Europe produced its own "monstrosities." According to this interpretive procedure, then, in the end, the myth can and does say *everything*. The problem with this approach is that these are *not* the ways in which the myth of Europa and the bull is actually being deployed today. This figure is certainly *not* being used to remind contemporaries that much of what now think of as Europe's achievements were originally external to Europe, and had non-European, Asian, African and Islamic roots. It is not being summoned up as a way of reminding us how deeply intertwined in the history of Europe are the values of "civilisation" and "barbarism." To the contrary, Europa and the Bull is being deployed foundationally—as a way of inviting us to reimagine the new Europe as somehow beginning with, and continuous with, that *old* Europe celebrated in classical Greek mythology. It is therefore not enough to allow each new reading to lie alongside all the others, untransformed. The meanings they carry point in very different directions, and those differences are precisely what makes them a significant site, not of celebration but of *contestation*—because it matters profoundly for the future which meaning about the past of Europe is being affirmed. Myth analysis is not enough. There is also the necessary work of *deconstruction*.

In making this deconstructive move, are there alternative mythological sources we should attend to? One, more raucous, less literary and finely wrought, source might be those rich medieval mythological and legendary systems which imaginarily peopled the outer perimeters of the European heartland. Their purpose was to establish, symbolically, the dividing line between "them" and "us." This corpus of popular and scholarly legend mapped Europe's shifting internal borders, and began the process—still vigorously alive—of marking out the continent into its different zones, distinguishing between the "real" European home and the rest, charting the always porous, always moving frontiers between civilisation and barbarism, and trying to fix the limit of Europe's internal "others." We can only gesture at its bewildering multiplicity: the "wild men" and "wild women," and the "wild" armies of the night, who emerged from the borders; the progeny of Homer's Cyclops and the wandering bands of Graeco-Roman tradition, who were thought to haunt the woods and wildernesses surrounding the plains and cities and the outer edges of settlement, with their matted hair and naked, hirsute bodies. These figures, suspended halfway between fear and fantasy, dream and speculation, mapped out Europe's liminal edge; they were markers of the ever-shifting boundaries between Europe's inside and outside. Then there was the vast literature devoted to classifying the "monstrous races of Mankind," from Hesiod to Pliny's *Natural History*, a repertory of exotic marvels. Herodotus helped to construct early prototypes of western Man, against whom the monsters, hybrids, hermaphrodites and anthropophagi of the classical periphery could be measured and placed: "Greece is the domain of measure, while the extremities of the earth are the domain of extreme riches and the extremely bizarre." Into this simmering brew were fed the speculative geographies and legendary tall tales of the mysterious East, from Marco Polo's, Mandeville's and other travellers' tall tales, with their enticing accounts of Cathay's vast wealth, splendid cities and royal courts. And across all of these categories one could trace the itinerant pathway of that epitome of the internal Other—the wandering Jew.

The gaze which Europe first turned on the "New World" was therefore not an "empty" one. In some ways it was full to overflowing: shaped by a thousand legendary encounters, peopled by tribes of misshaped monstrosities, loaded down with the detritus of classical learning and the romance of travellers' tales. These discourses about Europe's internal others helped form the template through which the New World took shape in the European mind. The conquistadors did not always find what they were looking for. But they tried to assimilate what they saw into the epistemic framework through which they looked. The New World was produced within the specular gaze of the West, within the conventions of European looking. "Otherness" was from the beginning an invention of European ways of seeing and representing difference. It has been reinventing "the Rest" ever since. For Todorov in his *The Conquest of America: The Question of the Other* (1999), America marks the start of Europe's attempt to assimilate the "other," to deprive it of its radical alterity, while at the same time fixing it in its difference. Though it was by no means the only space in which the European "gaze" was developed and refined (the interiors of Africa, Asia and the Pacific were still to come), the New World constituted a formative episode in Europe's great adventure with, and negotiation of, difference.

The Return of the Myth

All, you might say, a very long time ago. And yet these matters, like most mythic structures, have a way of making a fateful return. The lowering of barriers within Europe, the coming together around the "lingua franca" of a common market in goods, capital and ideas, the incorporation of a "wider Europe" which the modern "myth" of the Euro is supposed to symbolise, each continues to display its reverse side. What is "open" within is increasingly barred without. "Our common European home" is still more of a "home" to some Europeans than it is to others, as the Poles, Bulgarians, Kosovans, Albanians and others from the former Soviet republics, clamouring for entry at the gates of "Europe," testify. Then there are the suppressed histories. Moderate, liberal, democratic, tolerant, free-market, constitutional Europe may be a way of requiting for that other Europe, the one we can hardly remember—the Europe of the camps. But it has not prevented the horrendous spectacle of "ethnic cleansing" from recurring at its very heart. Is there a myth which can help us to encompass in a single narrative the obscenity that was Auschwitz or the Warsaw Ghetto, and the obscenity that is Ramallah or the Jenin refugee camp today? Where is the myth that can reconnect the one to the other? By what historical equation did it come about that the destruction of European Jewry—a cataclysmic event as endemic within European history and culture as Plato or the siege of Troy—came to be a burden expiated by the native inhabitants of the West Bank? Can we explain within what mythic logic the latter could be said in any way to redeem the former? It remains to be seen whether Europe, against the background of its troubled, divided past, has something significantly different to say about the vale of tears that is the Gaza today, or whether it is content to be His Master's Voice (the US) writ small.

Consider the myth of the Promised Land. This myth provided consolation for generations of Jews that their suffering in the pogroms and massacres that marked their experience of antisemitism in the European diaspora was not in vain, and would one day lead on to something better. Seventeenth-century English Puritans crossed the Atlantic to a new and inhospitable land in search of it. Black slaves in the New World seized on this myth, which they read in English in the Bible, and appropriated it as a way of metaphorically speaking their profound desire to be led out of slavery and into Freedom. The fact that they "translated" it from the sacred text of a religion and a language that had served as instruments of their servitude did not undermine the power of the hope of redemption embedded in the narrative. Rastafarians who wanted to say that they were still enslaved "in Babylon" reused the myth of the Promised Land in the same way—to connote the dream of liberation—in the Caribbean and the twentieth-century black diasporas (Hall 1999). Does this varied but persistent lineage guarantee the myth's liberatory meaning? Not at all. For when the myth is transferred to the Middle East, and used literally to divide and appropriate a land that was once shared, we find that one person's "Promised Land" can easily become another's historical nightmare. The myth of the Promised Land has underpinned the founding of a religious state to which only Jews can belong, and legitimated the illegal occupation of land and the driving into exile by Israel of thousands of Palestinians whose ancestors had occupied the land alongside Jews for centuries. Israel may exist because of the myth of the Promised Land. But Palestinians are dying because of it. The idea, then, that any and all versions of a myth which provide a "charter for action" are valid is, in the light of this experience, ethically and politically indefensible.

Meanwhile, as what Edward Luttwalk calls "turbo-capitalism" unleashes its forces across the globe, tens of thousands who can no longer survive at the margins of the system are loosed from their moorings and sent drifting across the world: Spinoza's "multitudes." Could Europe be a home for some of the homeless and hopeless, too? Or, as it lowers its frontiers within, is it proving only too effective at raising them, fortress-like, to face the new, straggling armies of the night? Thousands of those who have been nightly hurling themselves at passing Euro-star trains at the mouth to the Channel Tunnel are from that "other" Europe on whose difference "the idea of Europe" has always depended. Perhaps we have had enough of myths. Perhaps Europe has had one myth too many.

Of course, as Europeans keep saying, it couldn't happen here. If by this they mean that we can all sleep safe in our European beds until the jackboots appear on the streets again, then perhaps we have secured for Europe a gentle and liberal future. But what if this time around the storm troopers wear Armani suits? Today, in the face of current European political trends, when asked for "a figure for Europe," I cannot help thinking of Paul Klee's image—not his Europa, with its beautifully enigmatic exclamation point, but his Angel of Progress, clanking towards Armageddon, with its face resolutely turned to the past: and of the myopic Walter Benjamin, peering through glasses as thick as marble, trying to make sense of it all and—failing to do so—taking his own life at some dark, lonely, forsaken European frontier checkpoint.

NOTE

This originally appeared as "In but Not of Europe: Europe and Its Myths," *Soundings*, no. 22 (Winter 2002/2003): 57–69.

REFERENCES

Anderson, Benedict. 1983. *Imagined Communities: Reflections on the Origin and Spread of Nationalism*. London: Verso.
Barthes, Roland. 1972. "Myth Today." In *Mythologies*. London: Cape.
Bernal, Martin. 1991. *Black Athena*. London: Free Association Books.
Bhabha, Homi, ed. 1990. *Nations and Narration*. London: Routledge.
Butler, Judith. 1993. *Bodies That Matter*. London: Routledge.
Cohen, J. M. 1969. *The Four Voyages of Christopher Columbus*. London: Cresset Library.
Fanon, Frantz. 1963. *The Wretched of the Earth*. New York: Grove.
Hall, Stuart. 1999. "Thinking the Diaspora." *Small Axe* 6 (September).
Hulme, Peter. 1986. *Colonial Encounters: Europe and the Native Caribbean*. London: Methuen.
James, C. L. R. 1978. *Mariners, Renegades and Castaways: The Story of Herman Melville and the World We Live In*. Detroit: Bewick.
James, C. L. R. 1980. *The Black Jacobins: Toussaint L'Ouverture and the San Domingo Revolution*. London: Allison and Busby.
James, C. L. R. 1984. "African and Afro-Caribbeans: A Personal View." *Ten.8* 16.
James, C. L. R. 1993. *American Civilisation*. Oxford: Blackwell.
James, C. L. R. 1994. *Beyond a Boundary*. London: Serpent's Tail.
Laclau, Ernesto, and Chantal Mouffe. 1985. *Hegemony and Socialist Strategy*. London: Verso.
Lévi-Strauss, Claude. 1966. *The Savage Mind*. London: Weidenfeld and Nicolson.
Luttwalk, Edward. 1999. *Turbo-Capitalism: Winners and Losers in the Global Economy*. New York: HarperCollins.
Mann, Michael. 1988. "European Development: Approaching a Historical Explanation." In *Europe and the Rise of Capitalism*, edited by J. Baechler, J. Hall, and M. Mann. Oxford: Blackwell.
Passerini, Luisa. 2002. *Il mito d'Europa*. Florence, Italy: Giunti.
Rice, Michael. 1998. *The Power of the Bull*. London: Routledge.
Roberts, John. 1985. *The Triumph of the West*. London: BBC.
Scott, David. 2004. *Conscripts of Modernity: The Tragedy of Colonial Enlightenment*. Durham, NC: Duke University Press.
Todorov, Tzvetan. 1999. *The Conquest of America: The Question of the Other*. Norman: Oklahoma University Press.
Williams, Eric. 1944. *Capitalism and Slavery*. Chapel Hill: University of North Carolina Press.

CHAPTER 21

Cosmopolitan Promises, Multicultural Realities

These reflections take as their focus the contemporary "global/multicultural" city, which has emerged in recent years as a new type of urban configuration. They are written largely in reference to the UK and, more particularly though not exclusively, to London. The global/multicultural pattern is not absolutely novel: it has been grafted on to well-established historical forms of the city. However, the social and spatial configurations of London and other metropolitan cities have been significantly reshaped or "translated" in recent years by many forces, two of which—globalization and migration—are foregrounded here. In the course of my argument, I will expand on why the two terms "global" and "multicultural," which often seem to point in different directions and to different realities, are so closely juxtaposed in my account; and I will discuss the relationship between the processes of globalization and migration that underpin them. My particular concern is with the new social and spatial divisions in the city which are emerging as a consequence of the interdependence between new forms of globalization and new patterns of migration, and the distinctive tensions and conflicts to which they give rise.

Cities are the product—the material and spatial expression—of their times. In the nineteenth and twentieth centuries, the great English cities were motors of industrial production and centres of world trade, commerce and finance. Some were also integrated into the networks of imperial power and colonial trade as monuments to the imperial life of the nation. Later, cities became the sites for a modernist aesthetics of corporate power, a development more evident in New York and elsewhere in the US, as the axis of world power shifted westwards, than in Europe. Western cities are no longer like this, though their transformations are slow, complicated and highly uneven.

Many forces have been at work in bringing about change, but I draw attention here to three. The first is the uneven transition from an industrial to a postindustrial economy and society. Cities today not only embody this shift towards the service and information economy, but vividly represent the dislocations which have inevitably accompanied this process of deindustrialization. The second is globalization. Of course, globalization has taken many forms in history. A kind of globalization has been in progress since Europe broke out of its confines towards the end of the fifteenth century, and began to construct the beginnings of a world market and to explore, conquer, subdue by trade and naval power and ultimately to colonize much of the rest of the globe. But the globalization I have in mind here is that represented by the new forms of the "global" economy, based on the multinational capitalist corporation and augmented financial flows, which began to emerge in the mid-1970s. The third factor is migration. Migration is often understood as subsidiary to—a mere unintended consequence of—a more general "globalization" process. However, I want to explore more fully the intricate, but also disjunctive, relations between the new forms of globalization and the new patterns of migration. What concerns me especially is how the ethnic, social and cultural diversity that results necessarily from migration is changing the face of the modern urban landscape and reconfiguring the social divisions and conflicts characteristic of so-called "global" cities.

The worldwide movement of peoples across the globe is, in its scale, composition, direction and diversity, a phenomenon of world significance. There are more people "on the move" across the globe than at any time in modern history—whether driven by persistent poverty, underdevelopment, hunger and unemployment, by the modern pandemics of disease and ill health, ecological devastation and environmental disaster, or by civil war, ethnic cleansing, religious or tribal conflict. The cities of the developed world exercise a magnetic pull over this human tide, thereby reversing the historic flows associated with the imperial cities of recent centuries. We need to understand better than we do the far-reaching consequences of this global movement, its connection with emerging configurations of economic and geopolitical power, the new patterns of conflict it sets in play, and their implications for the wider pursuit of equality and social justice.

The great African American civil rights leader W. E. B. Du Bois once prophesied that the key problem of the twentieth century would be "the problem of the colour line." Events in recent years have led one to wonder whether, looking back with hindsight at the twenty-first century, historians may not be tempted to say that its problem was the much-denied but manifest "clash of civilizations," in which "the colour line" continues to play a significant (though transformed) role, and of which world migration is one major symptom. One question that the "clash of civilizations" raises is what I have called elsewhere "the multicultural question" (see Hall 2000). This arises with particular salience when the "clash" occurs within the metropolises of the developed world.

The multicultural question runs something like this: What are the chances that we can construct in our cities shared, diverse, just, more inclusive and egalitarian forms of common life, guaranteeing the full rights of democratic citizenship and participation to all on the basis of equality, whilst respecting the differences that inevitably come about when peoples of different religions, cultures, histories, languages and traditions are obliged to live together in the same shared space? Can they do so without falling apart—socially, spatially, politically—into warring and embattled enclaves, or, alternatively, without those in power engaging in punitive "missionary" campaigns to obliterate difference and make everyone become more like them? How can shared, reciprocal forms of life emerge, given the glaring disparities of power, recognition and material and symbolic resources between the different elements?

These issues have to be addressed both in terms of what cities are or are becoming, and of how they are imagined and represented. Though these two facets relate to different domains of practice, I do not propose to make any sharp distinction between them. Like Benedict Anderson's "imagined communities," cities are always both socially, economically and culturally constituted and, at the same time, configured in the imaginary through the regimes of representation. That cities are also spatially constituted, and that disposition in and across space is both a fact of social organization (the urban economy) and a regime of representation (architecture and planning), make cities a critical zone of mediation between these two aspects. It goes without saying that how cities are imagined has real effects upon how they are lived, and vice versa. Their spatial character gives the city a particular visible intelligibility, allowing it to be "read." Indeed, the city itself may be conceived in some respects as a "machinery of representation," because of its nearly unique role in materializing social relationships in space. It sets in motion a complex reciprocity in the sphere of the urban between "being" and "seeing," living and looking, of which Baudelaire and Walter Benjamin, theorists of the *flâneur*, were conceptual pioneers.

Cities have always been divided. They are divided by class and wealth, by rights to and over property, by occupation and use, by lifestyle and culture, by race and nationality, ethnicity and religion, and by gender and sexuality. The template of these social divisions can be read into the differentiated zones of the city's cartography. The well-off and the rich, the propertied and the corporate, the entrepreneurial and the middle classes, the professionals and the clericals, the artisans and the poor, the underclasses and the outcast, have always occupied different areas of the city. The boundaries between these spaces, however, have never been entrenched. They merge and overlap at their invisible borders, shift and change across time. Often, boundaries are more informally than formally marked and maintained. The various zones, however distinctive to those who know how to "read" on the run, are never uniform in look or homogeneous in social composition. Differences edge, slide and blur into one another. They overlay one another, creating a complex, overlapping matrix or palimpsest effect. These juxtapositions and overlaps may be multiplying: this is one of the dimensions along which the contemporary city is said to be changing most quickly. However, intangible as these boundaries often are and maintained as they are by complex cultural and social codes legible only to those who practise them on a daily basis in the banal routines of everyday life, they tend nevertheless to divide the city into distinct, though not tightly bounded or impenetrable, clusters.

On the other hand, cities also bring elements together and establish relations of interchange and exchange between them. They connect different life-worlds and temporalities, the space-time combinations that Bakhtin calls "chronotopes." They function as spatial magnets for different, converging streams of human activity. That is why cities have a very long history as centres of trade, as markets and thus as sites of cultural exchange and social complexity. This is the basis of their often unplanned "cosmopolitanism." The points of convergence, as well as the routes and passages through and across them, are as significant as the spatially defined and socially maintained differences. Cities both divide and connect. They condense difference. Inevitably, they are caught in a double rhythm of involvement and exclusion, proximity and separation, fixity and fluidity.

This aspect has been considerably intensified—but also modified—in the new "global" conditions. The question for us is how these complex impulses of homogeneity and diversity are working out and how the cartography of the contemporary city is being gradually reconfigured under the impact of globalization and migration. Here the metaphor of the palimpsest is particularly apposite: one layer is to be seen superimposed on another, in which the lines of definition of an older pattern persist and continue to invade the surface even as another, more recent patina overlays it. In significant ways, the old, hierarchical ordering of urban space seems to have disappeared for good (see Sassen 1996). As Bridge and Watson put it:

> Global cities are a result of transactions that fragment space, such that we can no longer talk about global cities as whole cities—instead, what we have [are] bits of cities that are highly globalized and bits juxtaposed that are completely cut out [from the globalizing process.] . . . In this sense, some parts of cities can have more in common with parts of other global cities in the same region than with the part of the city [most closely] juxtaposed. This valorization and devalorization of space goes hand in hand, and in many places is becoming more and more extreme.
>
> Urban centres nevertheless concentrate enormous power and potential global control. . . . The devalued sectors which rest largely on the labour of women [and] immigrants . . . represent a terrain where battles are fought on many fronts and in many sites and these battles lack clear boundaries. (2002, 255)

Some of the forces driving these changes are undoubtedly related to the new forms of globalization that emerged in the mid-1970s. They reflect the new division of labour to have occurred as a result of the general decline of manufacturing in the developed West and its transnationalization to other, less developed parts of the globe, with which corporate and financial centres in the West can remain connected through "space-time condensations" which the new technologies of finance and communication make possible (Harvey 1989). This is a division of labour more appropriate to the new service- and information-led economy. These forces for change are associated with the dominance of the transnational corporation, the renewed power of finance capital, the pace of global investment flows, currency switching and the spread of a global consumer culture and media disseminating, largely from the West, images of "the Good Life." These are the engines of the now hegemonic deregulating, free-market, privatizing, neoliberal economic regime known appropriately in another context as "the Washington Consensus" and to which, incidentally, New Labour in the UK is a paid-up, loyal, junior signatory. These forces constitute and define the true, substantial meaning and content of that deceptive term "the global."

They, in turn, have been integrated within a planetary strategy designed to open up the world, especially the developing "South," to the twin gods of the neoliberal revolution—free markets and liberal democracy—which, in Fukuyama's terms (1992), have brought all history to an end within a single planetary system or world order. This is now the governing world system, rooted economically in the free play of deregulated market forces, global capitalist penetration, the privatization of public goods, the monopoly of scarce or valuable resources, the dismantling of welfare and health programmes and the lure of "free trade" between profoundly unequal partners on a fundamentally skewed playing field.

The decolonization that occurred at the end of World War II, often hailed as "setting the colonial world free," was in fact marked by three broad stages redefining relations between the developed West and the rest. In the first phase, fundamental relations of neocolonial dependency were established between the developed and underdeveloped worlds in the context of the Cold War. In this phase, the difficult problems of establishing independent postcolonial states on the basis of autonomous economies were redefined as and subordinated to the struggle between the two rival camps: the Cold War was fought out largely by proxy on postcolonial terrain. In the second phase, "structural adjustment" regimes were imposed by the West on the developing world, via international organizations coupled with massive indebtedness through the banking system. More recently, with the collapse of the Soviet empire and the rise of the US to single superpower hegemony, an unholy alliance of global corporate forces, collusive indigenous elites and legal and illegal armies on the loose has been able to treat the world's poor and the societies of the South as open marketplaces, repositories of scarce resources and reservoirs of cheap labour. These are open to those corporate global agents best positioned to exploit them under the canopy of a form of "global governance" provided by international agencies such as the IMF, the World Bank and the WTO, whose disasters are mopped up by UN humanitarian, NGO, charitable and foreign-aid programmes.

If earlier phases of globalization worked through conquest, trade, mercantile and naval supremacy, direct colonization, imperial investment and mandated rule—all of which left their indelible imprint on the cities of the metropole in former times—the new system operates through a double repertoire: routinely, "at a distance," through market forces and geopolitical and global economic management; but also, at moments of crisis, through strategic military intervention in distant places. One of the principal unintended consequences of this "new world order," though it is in no sense reducible to an economic logic, has been to secure the conditions for the "free" reproduction of global inequalities. The world has, of course, been riveted by the military, strategic and geopolitical consequences of these processes, especially in terms of the US-led role in the Middle East, the oil-rich Gulf states, Afghanistan and Iraq. The role of covert US-inspired intervention—which has been a constant feature of the geopolitical system since the end of World War II—has, in the new situation of single-power dominance, become a matter of overt and systematic strategy based on overwhelming military and economic power. The civilian disaster of September 11, 2001, no doubt concentrated minds and hardened hearts, and the "war" on a generalized Terror has drawn many states—some of them reluctantly—into the orbit of a new "humanitarian interventionism." But few have tried to connect the hatreds and resentments which drive the fundamentalist assault on Western power and values with the massive planetary imbalances in life chances between the world's rich and marginalized poor which are driven by the new neoliberal "world system."

Hardt and Negri, in the widely discussed volume which names the emerging new world order as an imperial one, argue that the "informal networks of Empire" are no longer directly related to the power of nation-states (Hardt and Negri 2000). This has a certain validity: the new system is essentially transnational. But in the interests of underlining the radical novelty of the present, and too eager to underline the self-sustaining and systemic character of globalization, the authors overplay this aspect in describing it as "a system without a centre." In the radical terms in which they advance the argument, this claim is both true and not true. Even in a transnational system, large Western nation-states remain key players, though more and more often as partners in larger regional groupings or "coalitions." It is also true that they are able to operate less and less independently of the global system which sustains them, because their role in this system is the stake on which their power increasingly depends. In the developing world, it could be said that it is the failure to establish strong, independent nation-states that has been the problem, and that where such states have been successful—as, for example, in South-East Asia—strong states and independent national state policies have been the secret of their success.

The post-9/11 situation suggests, on the contrary, that the so-called new world order is one in which the US, the only remaining superpower, has an overwhelming influence. It does so less as an old-style colonizing nation—at which, if the disaster that is Iraq currently is any measure, it is hopelessly incompetent—and more as a global nation-state: the nodal power-centre of a wide-ranging global, geopolitical, economic, military and strategic network which is nevertheless deeply imprinted with American cultural values and national interests. The US is thus an exceptional case: it is a rich and powerful nation-state and also the leading "market state" (Bobbitt 2002), with a massive internal market, productive economy, advanced technology, land and raw materials; but it is also a state whose planetary power nevertheless depends on its transnational character and global economic, cultural, geopolitical and military reach. This is the nature of the "new imperialism" which is reshaping the globe.

All this has consequences for global/multicultural cities, which are linked to this new world-system of power through corporate global economic networks, rather than in their earlier function as the city bases of giant industrial firms, as centres of imperial investment, national greatness and colonial rule. Their characteristic new skyline is now increasingly dominated by the corporate headquarters of globally dispersed transnational companies, surrounded by their ancillary and supportive outsourced dependencies in financial services, marketing, banking, investment, advertising, design and information technologies. The urban architecture which mirrors this shift is most paradigmatically to be found in Canary Wharf–style corporate "towers" of glass and steel, functionally exposed transparent cubes or architect-inspired cucumber-shaped pods now dominating financial centres and urban skylines around the globe: the corporate "canyons" of the City of London around Bishopsgate and Liverpool Street rather than the porticoed splendour of the Natural History and Science Museums, the Victoria and Albert, Imperial College and Royal Albert Hall, those monuments to Victorian and Edwardian imperial grandeur, with their South Kensington satellite of trendy streets, neo-Georgian townhouses and the great department-store shopping emporia.

Since the mid-1970s, the forces we have been identifying have, with rapidly increasing intensity, intervened across the world to influence the strategies and steer the social, political and economic outcomes of "development" in a neoliberal, free-market, deregulative, open-investment, free-trade, "trickle-down" direction. They have radically rewritten the domestic political agenda of former developed welfare states, bringing to an end the historic compromise between capital and labour that defined the social-democratic character of the immediate postwar settlement, and driving these societies towards what Philip Bobbitt calls the "market-state model" and all major political parties and governments towards the centre-right ground of what has been called a "one-party politics." These are the lines of force that bind together the domestic and international political agendas of "caring" neoconservatism in the US and New Labour's hybrid version of modernizing Third Way neoliberalism (see Hall 2003). They connect the so-called "reform agenda" in the UK domestically with the new doctrine of "humanitarian interventionism" and pre-emptive strike in the geopolitical and strategic arena. This new world order must be made safe globally for liberal democracy and the free market economy—defended where necessary by "shock and awe," or "measured force," as Mao Tse Tung and President George W. Bush would, in their different ways, put it.

Meanwhile, the promises designed to make the poor complicit with their global fate—rising living standards, a more equal distribution of goods and life chances, an opportunity to compete on equal terms with the developed world, a fairer share of the world's wealth—have comprehensively failed to be delivered. Both the trickle-down theory of wealth redistribution and the manifestly utopian nonsense about a "new win-win global economy" have proved themselves to be the waste material of yesterday's common sense so far as large sections of the "developing" world are concerned. The product of the upswing in the economic cycle has vanished into thin air as the cycle turns down and the war clouds gather. Those at home and their allies in the new states who profited from the massive inflation in shareholder value largely escaped the downturn unscathed, although a few, such as Enron, were caught out before they could find cover.

The poor of the world, however, did not escape. The gaping difference in the distribution of economic, social, cultural resources across the world has remorselessly widened. The UN-Habitat Report, commenting on the unprecedented rising rate of urbanization, recently reported that the global urban population increased by thirty-six percent in the 1990s and that there are 550 million urban slum dwellers in Asia, 187 million in Africa and 128 million in Latin America and the Caribbean. The new megalopolises of the developing world, with their New York–style financial city centres floating like glittering glass islands in a veritable ocean of poverty-stricken and drug-ridden *favelas*, are the urban markers of this process. Even the thirty richest countries in the world account for another 54 million urban poor. Globalization, *The Guardian* reported on 10 October 2003,

> has partly caused and greatly exacerbated the perilous social and physical condition of slum dwellers. . . . The new insecurities that globalization

has caused are legion, with barely any benefits going to the poor. . . . Dominant "neo-liberal" economic doctrines . . . have explicitly demanded an increase in inequality, including the reduction of all government welfare spending, the privatization of everything that the state controlled, the reform of regulation and the removal of planning restrictions.

The rapidly growing disparities between the haves and the have-nots, which is glaringly obvious at the global level, are being reproduced within the richest societies of the developed world. Following the long period of levelling incomes and wealth after World War II—the era of redistributive welfare states—these inequalities began to rise exponentially after 1980. The gap between rich and poor in the UK is wider now than when New Labour took power in 1997. The richest one percent of Americans own more than forty percent of the nation's wealth. Even in the UK, the comparable figure is as much as eighteen percent, and the top twenty percent are richer than the bottom twenty-nine percent by a ratio of 9.6 to one; in the US, it is by a ratio of eleven to one (*The Guardian*, 5 November 2003). Meanwhile, millions in the US are still without any form of health insurance and more than 3 million children remain below current restrictive definitions of the poverty line in Britain, even in a period when child poverty has been one of the areas targeted for reform.

At the same time, the powers seeking to impose permanently adverse terms of trade on the poor countries of the South through free-trade open investment regimes, and defending the right of transnational corporations (energy, pharmaceutical, biotechnology and agribusiness interests especially) to buy up basic public utilities, patent the genetic sequences of natural products, subsidize and dump cheap commodities, drive out indigenous producers and pay day-labourers below subsistence wages, have come together to design a new World Trade Organization round, which the vigorous but belated opposition of some developing societies only temporarily delayed at the Cancun WTO meeting in 2003. No Western economy has been known successfully to develop, with benefits for the majority of its population, under the conditions such a regime would impose. The delay, however, is only temporary. The major economic powers are determined to return to this privatizing free-trade agenda.

Reliance on market forces as the sole driver of global economic and social development has brought in its train other insuperable problems that have an indirect impact on social life: ecological and environmental disaster, the disruption of the fragile balance of indigenous economies, disease epidemics, the massive exploitation of rural low-wage labour, the destruction of peasant farming and of subsistence agriculture and the collapse of world commodity prices. The result has been rapid and unsustainable urbanization and—coupled with collapsing postcolonial state regimes, civil unrest and the militarization of ethnic conflict—the phenomenon of mass migration. These global disasters form the invisible infrastructure of the changing cartography of globalization/migration and are powerful contributors to the only too visible crisis of the metropolitan city.

Migration is increasingly the joker in the globalization pack, the subterranean circuit connecting the crisis of one part of the global system with the growth rates and living standards of the other. The logic of globalization says that every element of growth must be free to move fluidly across every regulative boundary, including that of the nation-state: capital, investment, commodities, technologies, currencies, profits, cultural messages and images all flow. Ideologically, barriers must be thrown over, the circuits kept open. In fact, the reality is something different: all the major proponents of free trade and open investment borders manage, in practice, to impose their own selective preferential regimes where it is in their national interest to do so. However, when the model is working perfectly, only one commodity—labour—is required to stay still or to be strictly controlled in its movement. Otherwise, how can transnational corporations take "competitive advantage" of the cheap labour, low wage conditions, tax breaks and favourable investment regimes offered by developing societies? Suppose thousands of workers in Bangladesh, Indonesia, the Republic of the Congo or Guatemala were free to desert their one-dollar-a-day jobs and turn up as high-waged labour in the high-tech economies of the cities of the American west coast? The fact that, in the UK, small numbers of highly trained and scarce workers (such as computer technicians and nurses) and untrained, unemployed seasonal labourers willing to work in shocking conditions at below minimum wage levels (such as fruit pickers, kitchen porters and building labourers) are encouraged to migrate in selective and controlled numbers—in keeping with the uncertain rhythms of the labour market—does not undermine the general model.

Nevertheless, and in spite of the logic of the system, there has been an unprecedented explosion in the largely unplanned movement of peoples across the globe. Whether fleeing the consequences of mass poverty, malnutrition and unemployment in search of better economic or personal opportunities, or displaced by political violence, regime change, persecution, religious conflict, ethnic cleansing or civil war, those people stigmatized as "economic migrants," refugees and asylum-seekers now constitute the homeless multitudes of the modern metropolitan city. Seeking by whatever means—legal or illegal—to escape the consequences of globalization and the new world order, they move along unchartered routes, secrete themselves in the most inhospitable interstices, mortgage their worldly goods to the human traffickers, seal life-threatening contracts with gang-masters and pimps and exploit their lateral family connections in order to subvert the physical barriers, legal constraints and immigration regimes that metropolitan powers are vigorously putting in place. These are the overspill of the global system, the world's surplus populations, the *sans-papiers* of the modern metropolis, who slip across borders at the dead of night or stow away in the backs of lorries or under trains and silently disappear into the hidden depths of the city. This is the human face of the new globalization "from below." The global cities of the developed world are the sluice-gates of this new tidal movement.

In earlier phases, the problems of religious, social and cultural difference were largely kept at a safe distance from the metropolitan homelands of imperial systems. Metropolitan liberals, long distanced from the day-to-day management of slave and plantation regimes or mining outposts in the tropics, could indulge themselves with the thought that, when finally the full benefits of the slave trade had been extracted, Britain had vigorously pursued the ships on the high seas still engaged in that nefarious traffic. On this slippery foundation a great deal of national self-congratulation has been constructed. Today, the new kinds of differences whose deep, underlying causes we have sketched intrude directly into the heart of the Western metropolitan city, disturb, challenge and undermine the social and political space of its urban centres, disrupt its long-settled class equilibrium and subvert its relatively homogenous cultural character. They challenge the idea that the nation-state is the sole source and effective guardian of human rights or a universally democratic conception of citizenship. They project the vexed issue of global poverty, social and religious pluralism and cultural difference into the largely settled monocultural spaces of the Western metropolis. This produces an epistemic rupture and a new social problematic—that of the postcolonial paradigm.

The global city has been significantly transformed by these forces. They have had massive effects upon the spatial, social and cultural reconfiguring of cities, as the old industrial city's material ecology declines and social strata whose interrelationships were forged in the crucible of industrialization, mass production, democratization and imperial hegemony change in orientation, composition and lifestyle. Manufacturing in Britain is now in general decline and large-scale industrial production no longer dominates city centres, governs their economies or defines the character and tempo of their social life as they once did. These are now often urban areas of extensive social deprivation and economic dislocation, endemic unemployment, and environmental degradation as well as sites of a widespread social despair and hopelessness leading to the defensive mobilization of difference—and thus of ethnic tension, intraclass hostility, racial conflict, social alienation and civil unrest.

In the wake of civil disturbances between white residents and Muslim youths in northern British industrial towns and cities such as Bradford, Oldham and Burnley in 2001, Kundani observed that in such places in earlier times, "the textile industry was the common thread binding the White and Asian working class into a single social fabric. But with its collapse, each community was forced to turn inwards on to itself" (2001). This has been compounded by the long drift towards ethnic segregation in neighbourhood housing and in schools, a breakdown in communication between groups, the rivalry over scarce urban regeneration funding and poor local services, highlighted in Herman Ouseley's report on social fragmentation in Bradford (2001). It has also been deepened by the fear of difference and change, the hatred stimulated by racism, the growth in Islamophobia and a general failure of political leadership. Asian community leaders are often out of touch with the younger generations. The White working class, part of Labour's heartlands, feel progressively detached from New Labour's modernizing project and, lacking progressive political leadership that would place local defensiveness in a broader context, are open to the seductions of racially activist minority parties such as the National Front and the British National Party.

Professor Ash Amin, summarizing extensive recent urban research, identifies two types of neighbourhood as typical of these degraded urban spaces:

> The first are run down inner urban areas in which the conflict is between an old White working class lamenting the loss of a golden and ethnically homogenous past and non-White immigrants claiming a right of place, often against one another.... The second type consists of "White flight" suburbs and estates dominated by an aspirant working class or inward-looking middle class repelled by what it sees as the replacement of a homely White nation by another land of "foreign" people and cultures. Here frightened families, White youths, and nationalist/Fascist activists disturbed by the fear (rarely the experience) of Asian and Black contamination

terrorize a few immigrants and asylum seekers who happen to settle there. (2002b)

Both types of neighbourhood can be found in the new global/multicultural city. The former is the state of play in many so-called inner-city areas. The latter is more typical of the outer London suburbs such as Eltham into which Stephen Lawrence and his friend inadvisedly strayed looking for a bus home on the night when he was murdered by five white youths. In between, there are many mixed neighbourhoods up and down the country that seem relatively settled after years of patient negotiation, but which are nevertheless, in a subterranean and invisible way, "riddled with prejudice and conflict between their varied ethnic groups" (Amin 2002b).

No longer "the workshops of the world," English cities have become the service centres, the financial and speculative investment engines and consumer retail hubs of the global economy. One after another, large cities—Leeds, Manchester, Bristol, Birmingham, Liverpool and Newcastle as well, of course, as parts of London—have been revamped into transparent atrium-bedecked cosmopolises dominated by the corporate glass HQs of globally orientated enterprises. Surrounding the city bases of investment banking, entertainment, consumer retail, technology and other corporate global giants are the sprawling satellites of outsourced service industries, both the "producer services" (finance and investment, personnel, marketing, PR, advertising and media consultants, computer and design workshops) that provide the critical circuitry that knits the global economy together, and the consumer services that nourish the appropriate cultural tastes and lifestyles of its inhabitants.

The suited executives—those well-groomed, toned and limousined corporate "heroes" whose well-fleshed faces adorn the business pages of the quality newspapers and magazines—are either a new global entrepreneurial class or, alternatively, the remnants of an old stuffy one who have undergone a makeover. They are as at home in New York, Los Angeles, Hong Kong, Moscow, Kuala Lumpur, Tokyo or Beijing as they are in Bishop's Avenue in London, in their country homes in Hampshire, or on their temporarily beached yachts at San Tropez. The gap between senior directors and CEOs has narrowed, since both have the same deep commitment to "the business" and the "bottom line," an overriding investment in the nurturing of "shareholder value," exorbitant six- or seven-figure salaries, reinforced by astronomical annual bonuses, generous share-option deals, private medical cover, and copper-bottomed retirement and pension schemes. Individually, their fortunes seem to rise and fall with surprising regularity, scandal and failure crowning meteoric rise as night follows day. But, as a class, they are installed as the permanent executive officers of the new global capitalism.

Many wealthier executives now live well outside the city or in its increasingly gated enclaves and *pied-à-terres*. They too are more cosmopolitan in orientation. They travel constantly for work and pleasure. They remain in touch, through the circuits of instant communication, with mobile transnational elites elsewhere as they glide in comfort and style across the globe. In contrast with their predecessors, they know much more about business and finance, marketing and PR, management buyouts and branding than they know about producing, building or making anything. They too are at home anywhere, and the more so since "elsewhere" is increasingly like "here," only more so. They are focused on profit margins and share values, on restructuring core businesses and absorbing other companies by merger and takeover. They are remorselessly attuned—and without a shadow of embarrassment—to salary settlements unrelated to any calculable performance achievements, guaranteeing the steady supply of staggering amounts of money for skiing holidays and private school fees. Their wives are fully occupied ferrying the younger children in 4-by-4s, people carriers or SUVs (Sports Utility Vehicles) to select and selective private schools, those launchpads to success. Fitzjohns Avenue in northwest London (or what the fancy estate agents call "Hampstead borders"), where there must be twelve or fifteen private primary schools and nurseries within a half-mile stretch of traffic-crammed road, is notorious with taxi drivers. For the school run brings an army of jeeps, with their ranch-like bumpers, some parked in driveways, others perched on the banksides, others still blithely reversing into oncoming traffic.

In terms of lifestyle, this new global executive class increasingly blends into and makes common cause with the new rich—the self-made tycoons, the celebrities, and the new "flashocracy"—for whom key sites in the city function as stage, playground, and photo-opportunity. They are "flash, fast, fun, feckless, and fantastically frivolous," as the editor of *Tatler*, Geordie Greig—who should know—describes them (*The Observer*, 6 June 2004). Powered by a Veblenesque resurgence of conspicuous consumption, the nouveaux riches are also attached to global rather than national itineraries, agendas and hot spots: film festivals, fashion house openings, award ceremonies, opening nights, race meets and so on. Rapidly trading tweed for bling, they are experts in visualizing for the rest new forms of urban style and status: not "status" as an alternative to "class," as in the old Marx vs.

Weber dialogue, but status as the cultural signifier of new riches, as the materialization of social success. They, too, are beginning to impose their tastes, ideas and lifestyles on the global city.

The "creatives" who service this corporate and celebrity world are very different in background and in attitudes to the older professional and managerial middle classes. They are more individualistic, consumer-oriented, culturally savvy, lifestyle focused, entrepreneurial and hedonistic. More often they are on fast-track mobility or aspirational escalators from lower in the social order. Here, rather than higher up the urban pecking order, the leading edge of the rising Asian and Afro-Caribbean new middle classes are beginning to carve out an elegant niche. The places they aspire to live in, the lifestyles they covet and the kinds of leisure pursuits and entertainment they invest in are very different to older, more puritan tastes. Far from moving to the suburbs for a quiet life in respectable surroundings (later on in life they may, of course, buy a renovated barn or two in the country for weekends), they are the advance party of the new urban living—the agents of the "gentrification" of older working-class residential areas and of industrial small-manufacturing dockland or storage areas of the city, whose abandoned warehouses, refashioned into loft spaces and city-centre "pads," they are rapidly colonizing. Good food, art galleries, smart cafes and health clubs are the necessary accompaniments to this lifestyle. These are the pioneers of an intense, designer-shaped, global consumerism, the avid readers of upmarket style magazines and celebrity supplements and the cultural happy few exquisitely attuned to every minor shift or wobble in global postmodern taste and design.

At the other end of the scale are the poor areas that surround this vibrant "global" centre. Some until very recently were "the inner city." But as city centres are increasingly trendified and colonized for urban nightlife and clubbing, their older inhabitants have increasingly been pushed to migrate towards the outer ring. In London, this means Harlesden, Cricklewood, Wembley, Southall, Tottenham, Haringey and Tower Hamlets: *White Teeth* or *Brick Lane* territory. These are areas of mixed residency in which the new multiculturalism is being tested in myriad everyday encounters. Here the better housing is highly sought after by professionals harried by ferociously rising house prices and land values. But these are typically areas of high and multiple disadvantage, with poor schools, forbidding estates, rundown or boarded-up high streets, high crime and drug rates and drab terraces. They are often dilapidated, poorly serviced and grim in terms of the conditions of life they offer. Increasingly, these are the colonized areas of immigrant settlement, whether by the first (Afro-Caribbean), second (Asian subcontinent: Indian, Pakistani and Bangladeshi), third (West African, Turkish and Greek Cypriot), fourth (North African: Somali, Sudanese, Moroccan, Algerian, etc.), fifth (Bosnian, Albanian and Kosovan), sixth (Afghan, Iraqi and Middle Eastern) or seventh (post-Soviet East European) migrant waves.

In these areas, white residents—who now feel threatened by change, abandoned by modernizing and multicultural political agendas, and neglected because they lack the entrepreneurial and "creative" skills which the new service economy demands—meet the "ethnic minority communities," whether in their young posse, trapped-and-deprived, veiled and turbaned or in their aspirational, socially and occupationally mobile manifestations. Corner grocery shops, greengrocers, market stalls, record shops, newsagents, minicab firms, small under-the-bridge mechanics and car-repair yards, cafes and fast-food late-night outlets are the small "motors" of the local high-street economy of these city enclaves. The inner city, as the urbanists remind us, is a servicing-oriented economy too, a place of markets, exchange, the vigorous trading of goods and services and the exploitation of niches—though at a much more depressed, small-scale and marginal level than those described above.

Occasionally, there are small sweatshops. These are patriarchal havens where migrant owners oversee a workforce composed largely of migrant female labour working at marginal rates of pay to produce designer "versions," imitation branded goods and fake fashion items for the street stalls. Family and female labour are the working backbone of these communities. Some (especially black women and educated second-generation Asians), by dint of enormous struggle and further education or training achieved at considerable personal and financial cost, manage to find a niche in the wider economy or are drawn into local government and the health and welfare services. If the men have steady work outside shop and home, it is often in transport. The more recent arrivals are overwhelmingly illegals: so-called economic migrants and asylum-seekers working at below minimum wages, washing up in cafes or on building sites, or brutally dragooned into the sex trade. Here, economic survival and family stability are tenuous, difficult accomplishments, and survival strategies, whether legal or illegal, are at a premium. "Hustling," within or at the margins of the law, is the name of the game.

Some of these areas continue to function as "transition zones" in which different groups interact and in which a sort of multicultural diversity is, here and there, beginning to appear on the ground. You see black and white groups at street corners, mixed-race couples in the local clubs and pubs, Asian shopkeepers and greengrocers who have become familiar local figures, the acceptance of a multiethnic, multicultural reality as the normal form of "the local." As the Parekh Report titled *The Future of Multi-ethnic Britain* observed:

> Post-migration communities are distinct cultural formations but they are not cut off from the rest of British society.... These communities are not and have never aspired to be separate enclaves. They are not permanently locked into unchanging traditions, but interact at every level with mainstream social life, constantly adapting and diversifying their inherited beliefs and values in the light of the migrant experience. (Parekh 2000, 27)

Les Back has charted how, in some largely black areas of South London and elsewhere, a certain genuine cultural syncretism is emerging among young people in which music and urban street-style are critical zones of interchange, not only cementing a "new ethnic" urban lifestyle among black and Asian youth, but drawing in a section of white "wannabes"—Estuary/patois fluent, garage or drum-and-bass music aficionados (Back 1996). In many ways, these longer-standing communities, which have negotiated a sort of truce with the dominant society that enables them to operate effectively while remaining in touch with community habits and values, are also part of an emerging transnational trend and belong to global urban formations. This is globalization from below. The syncretic forms of Black and Asian urban culture, especially, are integrated into informal and largely invisible city-to-city global cultural "flows" in music, fashion and street-style as well as drugs, from Kingston to Brixton and Harlesden to Queens and Brooklyn in New York to Manchester, to the Compton district in Los Angeles, to Atlanta and on to the Berlin, Stockholm and Warsaw club scenes.

However, other patterns exist and may be becoming stronger. Professor Amin is certainly right to warn that "inter-ethnic understanding is not guaranteed by cultural hybridization" (2002a). In some areas, the minority ethnic and "host" communities live relatively separate lives, with everyday public exchanges conducted in a spirit of live and let live. In still other localities, not very far away from these, the local populations—young and old—have fallen apart into a silent but sullen separateness, a hostile and mutual defensiveness. Here, an embattled "little Englandism" has won vital sympathetic space within white urban working-class culture, and those perceived as outsiders on a number of criteria, of which skin colour is only one, really are at risk.

This is especially true of recently arrived "asylums." Since the moral panic about the politicization of Islam, 9/11 and the "war on terror," Islamophobia is everywhere close to the surface, and young Muslim men and women are particularly vulnerable.

It is clear that as we try, however roughly and impressionistically, to map the connections between the changing social and spatial configurations of the city and the new and emerging forces of globalization, a more complex picture of the "global city" emerges. It is a city of more multiple and overlapping spaces, with complex patterns of interaction and the distribution of activities, resources and attitudes. Diverse practices are to be found coexisting in the same urban spaces. However, divisions have also become more intense and entrenched. The reality is and for a long time has been that multiculturalism and racism proceed hand in hand. Indeed, in some ways these tendencies are becoming deeper, more entrenched and wider in scope. But they do not mark the face of the city in such clear ways. The global city is more one of an intricate network of differences, any of which can at any time be activated as a potentially explosive line of division. In the global/multicultural city, as Bridge and Watson argue, "differences and identities are constituted in multiple and complex ways in multiple spaces of the city and shift and change, producing different city spaces and new boundaries and borders" (2002).

The history of postwar racism, as it relates to migration, has not been seriously studied. Popular and public attitudes in the early postwar years—migration in the shadow of decolonization and the "end of empire"—were deeply implicated in the legacies of slavery, indenture and colonization: they were still, broadly speaking, routed through the imperial connection. This involved the subordination of colonized economies to the advantage of the metropole—a fact visible in "imperial" cities such as Bristol, Cardiff and Liverpool—and was also reflected in the symbolic role the imperial idea played in the construction of British identity as a master and governing "race." This civilizational superiority became deeply woven into—and remains an active trace within—a postimperial consciousness. It was very much to the fore in the early confrontations between native and migrant people. However, as the tides of migration broadened and settlement became more permanent and extensive, a profound shift occurred. To the degraded repertoires of race and colour were added other dimensions of racialized otherness more to do with cultural differences—historical, religious, linguistic, enshrined in custom, dress, familial practices and values and so on—in the racialized system which came to be known as "the new racism." Since then, racialization of difference has increasingly drawn on these two repertoires, biogenetic and cultural (Hall 2000). Recently, migration flows into the UK, driven in connection with new developments in globalization, have broadened even further into multiple and diverse streams. Far from easing the associated tensions, a more complex overlapping system of civilizational differences has come into play alongside the older racialized repertoires, producing what Wieviorka and others call "differential racism": a racism of racialized differences complexly articulated in relation to, but also between, different groups.

What promise, then, do these new urban patterns and formations hold out for a just and progressive resolution to the questions of social justice, equality and diversity? The prospects are not optimistic. A kind of "cosmopolitanism" does exist in the new elite spaces and formations of the global/multicultural city, because these spaces are now extensively connected with and orientated towards the wider world and its networks and agencies. However, this kind of cosmopolitan outlook has strict limits. Its principal effect is to reproduce within the city the divisions which globalization in its contemporary forms assumes in the wider world. Although the term "globalization" has benefited greatly from its positive associations with an earlier version of "internationalism," it has very little to do with distributing the wealth and resources of the planet to humanity in general in a more universal and egalitarian manner. Globalization is planetary in its scope, global in its operations. It creates and depends upon greater interdependence between different parts of the globe. But it and the elites it has created form a system rooted in power relations, driven by the imperatives and interests of the developed Western world and grounded in the massive disparities of wealth and power between the world's rich and poor, the most critical dimension of which remains that between the West and its subalterns, and the Rest. Its principal effects are, largely, to exploit and reproduce these divisions and differences within the global city. Despite its implied promise of a better future for all, globalization is thus a highly contradictory system. For, as a sort of excess effect of the system or an unintended consequence, globalization "from below" is also the site of a proliferation of differences which refuse to be corralled into a single unitary formation. This contradiction between the drive to political, economic and cultural homogenization and the subaltern proliferation of difference across the globe is deeply unresolved by globalization in its contemporary form.

Of course, everybody is now being progressively drawn into the net of global investment, consumption and technology. In this sense, a planetary cultural homogenization is making deep inroads. The new urban elites, and the parts of the city connected with them, have been pulled into its orbit. But resources, opportunities and life chances are not being levelled or equalized across the globe or within the city just because the system no longer has any real or effective "outside." The workers producing runner beans in East Africa for Western supermarkets are part and parcel of a global system of production, but that has no effect in equalizing their miserable rates of pay. The logging companies driving through the Amazonian forests may be dragging indigenous people into the web of globalization, but in the process they are also destroying the livelihoods and ecologies of those very people and laying waste to planetary resources.

For a time, at the other end of the scale, a sort of "practical" multiculturalism seemed to offer a viable alternative. This was globalization from below—against the grain and logic of, and often in the very teeth of, globalization from above—though, as we have shown, still clearly articulated to its effects. Cosmopolitan in any simple sense it was not, for it was rooted in the significance and persistence of differences that refused to be homogenized into a planetary cultural consumerism, Western style. But it seemed for a time as if these were genuine differences which safeguarded the historical routes, memories, trajectories and traditions that had sustained people and their ways of life through the terrible vicissitudes and dislocations of migration. These differences needed not to be subscribed to in a rigid, essentialist, doctrinal or fundamentalist way and could, in the right circumstances, begin to be "traded" and translated into broader, more inclusive patterns, as people with different histories who had come to the Western metropolis by different routes learned to live with and negotiate the terms on which they could occupy the same spaces as one another. The hope was that this might eventually give rise to forms of "vernacular cosmopolitanism."

However, the more globalization is harnessed to global systems of economic, military and geopolitical power, the more it has become, in its dominant form, an integrated, expansionist and missionary system. It obliges everyone to come into line with it and thus aims, by assimilation or forced conformity, to universalize itself; it makes its claims to universality come "true" by ensuring that it is universal (or global) in its real operations and effects. Interventions in foreign places around the globe are no longer made just to safeguard Western interests but in the name of "Western values," in

President Bush's terms, and in order to bring "freedom" to mankind and to liberate the world by making it "just like us." (A more detailed account of this development in the US—and of its effect on policing and justice in American cities—is offered by Williams 2006.) In the UK in recent months, in the context of the "war on terror," the adventure in Iraq, and rising new immigration numbers, multiculturalism, which for a time was official government doctrine, has been undermined and subverted as an ideal by spokespersons in and near to New Labour. It is being quietly buried. As the barriers to migration across Europe have become more entrenched, the pursuit of illegal immigrants more vigorous, and the policing of borders more systematic, so a widespread assimilationism not seen in the UK since the 1970s is rising to the surface and becoming de rigueur. Often it seems to proceed—paradoxically—under the cover of the call for social cohesion. Naturally, the enemies of this global universalism throughout the world have become more entrenched in their differences, and are now being represented as antithetical to "modernity" (or Western-dominated globalization), primordial, essentialist, untranslatable and fundamentalist.

The global/multicultural city is being spatially and socially reconfigured by these processes and forces and, at the same time, becoming one of the critical sites where these contradictory tendencies, conflicts and trajectories are being worked through. The city cannot resolve the wider contradictions of the globalization movement it reflects and embodies. But it will continue to be a sensitive recording template of the panoptic recomposition of power that is taking place as "the global" continues to make its decisive mark.

NOTE

This essay first appeared as "Cosmopolitan Promises, Multicultural Realities," in *Divided Cities: The Oxford Amnesty Lectures, 2003*, edited by Richard Scholar (Oxford: Oxford University Press, 2006), 20–49.

REFERENCES

Amin, Ash. 2002a. "The Economic Base of Contemporary Cities." In *A Companion to the City*, edited by Gary Bridge and Sophie Watson. Oxford: Blackwell.
Amin, Ash. 2002b. *Ethnicity and the Multicultural City*. London: Economic and Social Research Council.
Back, Les. 1996. *New Ethnicities and Urban Culture*. London: UCL Press.
Bobbitt, Philip. 2002. *The Shield of Achilles*. Harmondsworth, UK: Penguin.

Bridge, Gary, and Sophie Watson. 2002. "City Economies." In *A Companion to the City*, edited by Bridge and Watson. Oxford: Blackwell.

Fukuyama, Francis. 1992. *The End of History and the Last Man*. Harmondsworth, UK: Penguin.

Hall, Stuart. 2000. "The Multicultural Question." In *Un/settled Multiculturalisms*, edited by Barnor Hesse. London: Zed Books.

Hall, Stuart. 2003. "Labour's Double Shuffle." *Soundings* 24.

Hardt, Michael, and Antonio Negri. 2000. *Empire*. Cambridge, MA: Harvard University Press.

Harvey, David. 1989. *The Condition of Postmodernity*. Oxford: Blackwell.

Kundani, A. 2001. "From Oldham to Bradford: The Violence of the Violated." *Race and Class* 43.

Ouseley, Herman. 2001. *Community Pride not Prejudice*. Report to Bradford City Council.

Parekh, Bhikhu, ed. 2000. *The Parekh Report: The Future of Multi-ethnic Britain*. London: Profile Books.

Sassen, Saskia. 1996. *The Global City*. Princeton, NJ: Princeton University Press.

Williams, Patricia. 2006. "Theatres of War." In *Divided Cities*, edited by Richard Scholar. Oxford Amnesty Lectures. Oxford: Oxford University Press.

CHAPTER 22

The Multicultural Question

Chairman, ladies and gentlemen, former colleagues, friends, political editor of *The Daily Mail*, and other assorted folks, I am very pleased indeed to be at the Open University again, and especially so under these auspices. As perhaps some of you do know, but I think many of you may not, the Pavis Centre was the consequence of a bequest from a former Open University student who had studied especially with the Faculty of Social Sciences here, who took courses in sociology and who, at his untimely death, left a generous bequest to start this programme of research in the social sciences, of which the annual lecture and its publications are a part. It is not very often that such an unusual bequest is made to an institution like this by a student, and I just wanted to start by acknowledging the enormous generosity of that act.

I have chosen the title "The Multicultural Question." I have to confess that it is a very large and circumscribing one and it has been especially in the focus of my attention since I joined the Runnymede Trust's Commission on the Future of Multi-ethnic Britain two years ago, whose report appeared last Wednesday amidst a maelstrom from which I have not yet fully recovered. It is such a wide and all-embracing topic and theme that I can't possibly do it anything like overall justice in the one lecture. In fact, the truth is that I have been giving a lecture variously titled "The Multicultural Question," of which this, I think, is the fifth or sixth version, and each has looked at rather different aspects of the problem. So I hope you won't limit questions and discussions to precisely what I say; if you want to ask questions outside of that [topic], please feel free to do so and if I don't know anything about it, I hope I have the courage to say so.

My proposition is that we need to take the multicultural question seriously; that is to say, that its disruptive potential as a topic of discussion, debate, and research has not yet been exhausted. This proposition may appear to you as an untimely anachronism. Surely you are entitled to think, "We have had that one already," and so indeed in some ways we have. Over the years the term "multiculturalism" has come to reference a diffuse, indeed maddeningly spongy and imprecise, discursive field: a train of false trails and misleading universalities. Its references are a wild variety of political strategies. Thus conservative multiculturalism assimilates difference into the customs of the majority. Liberal multiculturalism subordinates difference to the claims of a universal citizenship. Pluralist multiculturalism corrals difference within a communally segmented social order. Commercial multiculturalism exploits and consumes difference in the spectacle of the exotic "other." Corporate multiculturalism manages difference in the interests of the centre.

Multiculturalism accordingly has a multitude of different enemies. Conservatives oppose it by citing the cultural integrity and purity of the nation, and we saw some of that last week.[1] Liberals oppose it for reasons of personal autonomy and individual liberty. The Left often contests it on the grounds that it privileges culture over economics and divides the united front against injustice and exploitation. Modernizers affirm against its pluralist particularism the universal values of Western cosmopolitanism. It has in recent months been subject to a far-reaching new assault. In a wide-ranging critique,[2] the journalist Yasmin Alibai-Brown has argued that multiculturalism no longer offers a shared narrative of who we are today; doesn't speak to young people or capture their aspirations, identities and the way that they feel about the world. We need, she says, collectively to reimagine ourselves and our society, preparing ourselves for a very different world from that which multiculturalism was created to serve. This sense that the debate is entering a radically new phase is, I find, quite widespread and is captured in the title of Alibai-Brown's recent book *After Multiculturalism*. More radically, one of the greatest contemporary social theorists, Pierre Bourdieu, and his colleague, Loïc Wacquant, have recently argued that multiculturalism is an issue peculiar to American society and its universities and has been imposed, in apparently dehistoricized form, upon the whole planet: a sort of American academic imperialism. Slavoj Žižek, for whom no twist in the Christian Hegelian dialectic can be the last, insists that multiculturalism is a new racism; indeed, is the cultural logic of multinational capital. With this final turn, which is simultaneously apocalyptic, reductive and banal, the wheel appears to have come full circle.

But I should say at this point that multiculturalism is not in fact my precise concern. The term refers to a variety of strategies for dealing with the cultural diversity and social heterogeneity of modern societies. The problem, it's been said, is that the "-ism" in "multiculturalism" converts it into a single political doctrine which reduces it, fixing it into a cemented condition. It thus assimilates the heterogeneous character of multicultural conditions to a pat and pedestrian doctrine. Well, my purpose is to return us to those underlying conditions and the problems which they pose, both of practice and of theorization. The multicultural question is, in my mind, the question of how we are to envisage the futures of those many different societies now composed of peoples from very different histories, backgrounds, cultures, contexts, experiences and positions in the ranking order of the world. Societies where difference refuses to disappear. That is to say, where an unspoken social and cultural homogeneity cannot be assumed to provide an implicit consensual horizon of action, practice, policy or interpretation, but where nevertheless there is a determination to build a common and, if possible, a just life together. So the question, to reduce it, is: How is this commonness in difference to be imagined and constructed? One important difference between a focus on multiculturalism and a focus on the multicultural question is that, whereas multiculturalism is addressed principally at ethnic and racial minority people and communities, the multicultural question, in my view, concerns the nature of society as a whole, and thus addresses the changed conditions of everyone.

This question, which I have tried to define in this simple way, entails focusing on a collection or set of issues around the question of difference. The major factor which undercuts both the claims of some overarching set of universal values and the claims of self-sufficient separate and distinct communities, is the force which has been unleashed in the world at an increased or exaggerated pace, which appears to undermine and unsettle all of the existing totalities. We might term this "the play of difference." The play of difference can be traced at the local, the national and the global level and exists at a plurality of different sites within society. At the local level we may think of the so-called ethnic minority communities in this country. The term "community" is here, as we know, a deeply ambiguous one. The model is an idealized representation of the face-to-face relationships which are sometimes said to characterize the one-class village (if you can find such a thing), one which connotes a homogenous group or homogenous groups, with strong binding, overlapping internal ties and clearly marked external boundaries. It is immediately obvious how, for the so-called ethnic minority communities, the divergence between the model and the practice exists. There are, of course, densely overlapping, intersecting variables, such as residence; location; shared place and cultural background of origin; shared relative social and economic deprivation; similarity of position in the social structure in terms of access to goods, wealth and opportunities, real and symbolic. There are these many overlapping and intersecting variables which, I suppose, provide that element of reality to the notion of a shared community. But the term "community," in this context, also reflects certain shared self-understandings by people who are in it: a strong sense of group identity; the binding ties of common language, religious practices, history, social customs and customary types of relationship, especially those maintained in familial and domestic settings. Here we may think of some of the Afro-Caribbean communities of Brixton or Tottenham or Moss Side or Handsworth or Toxteth, or the Asian communities of Southall, Tower Hamlets or Bradford or Balsall Heath or Chapeltown.[3] Now, on the other hand, these overlapping densities have refused, steadfastly refused, to be consolidated into permanently separate social spheres. None of these so-called communities is a racially or ethnically segregated "ghetto." Both Asian and Afro-Caribbean communities are internally highly differentiated and becoming more so, along class, gender and nationality lines, social attitudes and lifestyles, and especially generational dimensions. These are not inert social variables, they positively and actually inflect contemporary positions, internal relationships and future orientations.

All these communities are in fact racially mixed, with substantial white populations with which the minority population share many critical life conditions. All are multiply embedded in and implicated by relationships with the rest of so-called mainstream society. So-called traditional ways of life, while remaining important in terms of self-definition and identity, consistently operate alongside extensive daily interaction with all spheres of mainstream social life, so far as this is permitted. Contrary to the stereotypes, these are not communities immersed in something called immutable "Tradition," with a capital "T." Traditions here are being constantly revised and transformed in relation to the migration experience. And I want to say that this includes religious tradition. Traditions are increasingly variable, without ever completely disappearing. They are variable from group to group, from person to person—indeed, within persons. There is considerable variation now, both of commitment and of practice, between different nationalities and linguistic groups, and different class positions; and the class positions of the so-called ethnic minorities are diversifying at a very fast rate, within different religious faiths across locations throughout society, between men and women and across generations. Some maintain cultural and religious practices in an intensified form. That is to say, they become more of what they originally were, as the influences on them from the outside deepen. Some others express continuing allegiance in the abstract alongside what is now known, in research, to be the visible decline in actual practice, especially amongst the younger generation. Many women, for example, both defend the right of their parents to honour and practice the traditions of their original culture whilst strongly opposing the view that their own rights in education, marriage, relationships, careers should be policed by communal norms or patriarchally enforced. Every family—I am quoting Bhikhu Parekh—"has become a terrain of subdued and explosive struggles." Just like normal folks.

On the wider societal level we are aware of the increasingly mixed visible and actual presence of the dissemination of difference, while being simultaneously struck by the depth of involvement in every social sphere and by the fact that this dissemination is itself socially structured and shaped. Now, this explosive and unsettled combination is, in fact, closer to the true character of so-called multicultural diversity—which, for good or ill, has come to be recognized in many places in British social life and political discourse. It would, in my view, be a fundamental, category mistake, either to imagine or to develop policies which imply that this distinctively diasporic mix is either, on the one hand, just a superficial disguise for the continuation of an original cultural inheritance; or, on the other hand, the sign of some slow inevitable transition to full assimilation. Neither of those things in its pure form, in my view, is what is happening and I don't think they are likely to happen either. They represent, rather, a novel and (for social scientists, who like things to stay in boxes that they can measure and count) an unsettling configuration: what we may call, despite the fact of its obvious oxymoron, *cosmopolitan communities*. They have had a massive pluralizing impact on British public and social life, transforming the face of one British city after another—unevenly, of course—into multicultural metropolises. None of them, even should they wish, can, or indeed try very hard, to preserve themselves inviolate from the pressures to interact and adapt. None of them are about to disappear into an assimilated invisibility. They are all communities in translation.

Something of the same kind is visible at what, with many caveats, we may call "the national level," in quotation marks. This is one of the many points where a disturbing truth, which seems to arise at the margins of society, somehow floods the mainstream, changing all perceptions as it goes. The most obvious aspect is simply the way the ethnically and culturally homogeneous culture of the British mainstream has, as is true of most developed societies of North America, Europe and the Pacific, been pluralized by the unstoppable, often illegal, tide of forced or impelled or so-called free migration. Migration is the dark side, or one of the dark sides, the unacknowledged underbelly, of globalization, where everything moves—capital, goods, élites, images, currencies—and only people and labour are supposed to stay put. However, I would argue that migration is only one of the many factors which are massively pluralizing and diversifying British society, unsettling and unstitching its many historical settlements and undoing its so-called cultural homogeneity. . . . It's true that migration is one of the causes of this, but in my view, it is just one of the factors (though of course it happens to be the factor which is usually selected out in order to define the cause of why, unfortunately, everything doesn't seem to stand still and be recognizable anymore).

To describe this diversification of British society and culture in detail is quite beyond the scope of this paper. I have to content myself by identifying some of its principal causes: relative decline over a long period of Britain's position economically and militarily on the international stage; the so-called profound end of empire which was for so long deeply intertwined with the national identity, its sense of itself and its image of its own greatness; the growth or intensification of national and regional sentiment within the so-called nation—alongside the recognition that it never was a single nation, has always been a multi-nation—leading to the currently stalled process of devolution; the enormous social upheaval consequent on the decline of the old industrial economy and all the values, occupations, communities of interest and experience associated with it; and the fragmenting consequences of the internally uneven and contradictory so-called new economy; the relative erosion everywhere in Britain, as in many other places, of what one might think of as the sovereignty of action associated with the nation-state as a political form—with the so-called national economy as a strongly bounded one with national policy, where policies of redistribution, taxation, and so on, can be made with reference, as it were, to one's own population; national cultures and the corresponding growth of influence or salience of below-the-state and above-the-state (especially of supraregional and global) forces and influences. And above all, what can't be detailed at this stage—the massive forms of pluralization, which have overtaken one sphere or another in recent years. This is widely believed to be something which happened, so to speak, towards the end of the twentieth century. Until then the dominant definition of the national culture suggests that Britain really was something like a tight little island unified by a sort of floating spirit or gas, called Britishness, which was evenly distributed across the land, from the Outer Hebrides to the White Cliffs of Dover and from the Wash to Omagh. Recently, Gerald Howarth, Conservative MP, said the report that we had produced was "an insult by the 6 percent to the 94 percent." And I note that the 94 percent is supposed to be homogeneously welded into an absolute unity on these questions, and that its distinction from the 6 percent could, in fact, be defined without the use of the concepts "race" or ethnicity. Now, it would, of course, be silly even in this setting to deny that long historical stability of settlement since the wave of invasions: a more or less common language—some would say less rather than more—but a more or less common language and a sort of shared framework of governance (but the Scots won't stand to attention immediately). These things have created what one can loosely call, in very uneven ways, common solidarities and reciprocal ties. However, again without being able to argue it in detail, I would suggest that so-called British society has always been much more diverse, much more internally divided and contradictorily related to itself than it was ever represented in the dominant historical myth.

Britain is, of course, a political unit, but it is also an imagined community. In the only time in which with approval I quote Enoch Powell: "The life of nations like that of men [not women], is lived largely in the imagination." (And what an imagination it was!) That is, it depends on how it is represented and imagined. It is through the national culture—which is not a sort of thing, but a system of social representation rather than a primordial being—and its forms of representation that so-called identifications with national identity (identity means identification, or requires it) can be made. That is to say, won, and sometimes accordingly, lost. The liberal view of a so-called civic nationalism in which no cultural particularism is permitted to override the secular universal forms of citizenship in public is, in retrospect, quite inadequate. It needs to be radically supplemented by the recognition that the said Britain is not just a political unit but is also an imagined community. That

Britishness, like all national discourses, is deeply embedded in the dense integument of a complex tissue of cultural meanings, symbols and images, selectively woven together in a dominant national narrative. It is this alone which fills Britishness, which is otherwise an empty signifier, with specific social content. The dominant version of the national story has, in my view, systematically overplayed the unity and homogeneity of the nation. It has systematically underrepresented the deep differences of nation, region, locality, class, gender and language which have persisted throughout. The fact is that national discourses like this don't reflect a unity which is already there, they constitute a sort of unity built out of the many differences with which it is confronted. Its many complicated and conflicting strands are reduced to a simple unfolding story of essential, enduring, unified and triumphal unity. For example, almost every one of the totemic items which constitute the great majority of English or British achievements—most of them, indeed, are English, as you will see—that great majority in which we might list the sovereignty of parliament, free speech (or at least the ability to report on parliament), the extensions of the franchise, the ending of slavery, the end of child labour, the right to combine to defend working conditions, the National Health Service, the welfare state: every one of them was a product of a ferocious struggle between one sort of English person and another. Only retrospectively, after the real dust had cleared, were they rewoven into the seamlessly unfolding story of an ascendant Englishness, which effortlessly is then elided into Britishness.

When *The Daily Mail* was on, in its six pages, about rubbishing our report, they commissioned Paul Johnson to write a historical essay called "In Praise of Being British." This was headed by a photograph of outstanding British figures. I note that it contained no black or Asian people. Big surprise! *[Laughter.]* That it had nobody who was born after Queen Victoria; that the only Scots were Charles I and James I; that Charles I's representation was coupled with that of Cromwell's so that both the sovereignty of divine right and sovereignty of parliament are both equally and in the same moment things of which we British should be proud. As Norman Davies once remarked, "England is assumed to be fixed and eternal, and the English sometimes seem unaware that anything fundamental has changed since 1066."

Finally, let us turn to the question of difference at the global level. Culturally, globalization's dominant tendency is towards cultural homogenization. This is not a complete explanation of course, but that seems to be what most people would feel is the overall push which globalization has made in the cultural sphere across the world. The thing we need to remind ourselves of is that it also has extensive differentiating effects both within and between different societies. From this perspective, globalization—whether one thinks that it is going to change everything or that it is simply an updated and modernized form of a system which we have had for a long time; whatever is your perspective—globalization has to be seen, not as a natural and inevitable process, whose imperatives, like fate, cannot be resisted or inflected, only obeyed. That is to say, it is not as Anthony Giddens represents it to Tony Blair. Rather, it is a hegemonizing process in the proper Gramscian sense; that is, it is of course structured in dominance, it has some main driving, overall tendencies, but it cannot control and simultaneously saturate everything within its orbit. Indeed, it produces, as one of its unintended effects, subaltern formations and emergent counter-tendencies which still remain fragmented and dispersed, but which it cannot simply integrate and must try instead to hegemonize—that is to say, to harness into its wider purposes. It is a system for conforming difference rather than a synonym for the obliteration of all differences, and this argument is absolutely critical if we are to take account of where and how its limits occur, of where resistances and counter-strategies are likely to develop.

Alongside globalization's homogenizing tendencies there is what I want to call the *subaltern proliferation of difference*. It is a paradox that, culturally, on the one hand, things appear to look more alike—a sort of Americanization of global culture, for example—while at the same time there is a subordinate proliferation of apparent differences; that is to say, the vertical of American cultural, economic and technological power seems constantly to be crosscut and slightly offset by lateral connections, producing the sense of a world composed of many local differences with which the global vertical is obliged to reckon (although these local differences do not instantly cohere into an alternative to globalization or an image of what the world might be). In this model the classic Enlightenment binary, which has recurred in this area so often between traditionalism and modernity, is displaced by what I want to call a series of vernacular modernities. Consider, for example, the way the effort to saturate India and China with a staple diet of Western television was forced into—well, not its opposite, that's too optimistic—into a tactical retreat. It could only advance through the indigenization of local television industries, and their very indigenization, though of course linked to the technology and the global imperatives of the large media corporations, genuinely complicates the range of images which can be offered locally and sets in motion the development of an indigenous industry rooted in different cultural traditions. Some see this as just a slower version of Westernization, others see it as the way in which peoples in these areas do indeed try to enter modernity—that is to say, to acquire the fruits of its technologies—and yet want to do so on their own terms.

In the global context the struggle here—between local and global interests—is not in any sense finally resolved, it is not even fully defined. In a completely different context the French philosopher Derrida has used the concept of *différance* rather than of difference, and he calls *différance* the plain movement that produces these effects of difference. The important thing about the notion of *différance* is that this is not a binary, either/or form of difference between what is absolutely the same and what is absolutely other or different, but is "a weave of similarities and differences which refuse to separate into fixed binary oppositions." *Différance* characterizes a system where every concept or meaning is inscribed in a chain or a system within which it refers to the others, to other concepts and meanings by means of the systematic play of differences. Meaning in that sense here has no origin or final destination, cannot be finally fixed, is always in process, in translation, being defined positionally along a spectrum. Its political value cannot be essentialized; that is to say, it can't be snatched out of the play of similarity and differences which are constantly constructing it, it can only be defined in relation to all the other forces which are trying, as it were, to define the cultural sphere at that moment.

Now, it is absolutely true and realistic to acknowledge that the strategies of *différance* are not yet able to inaugurate totally different forms of life or to preserve older forms of life wholly intact. They operate best in what Homi Bhabha has called "the borderline time of minorities." The interesting thing is that more and more of us mainstream folks operate in the borderline time of minorities. However, the important thing about *différance* is that it prevents any system at all from stabilizing itself as a fully sutured and finished totality. It arises, rather, in the gaps which constitute political sites of resistance, of change and intervention, of translation.

Within these interstices lies the possibility of what I called earlier a disseminated set of vernacular modernities—and you understand what I mean now by talking about societies which have not refused modernity, but which do not believe that modernity must always come packaged in the forms in which it is offered to them. Culturally, strategies of this order cannot frontally stem the tide of Westernizing techno-modernity. However, it is my understanding that they continue to deflect and translate its imperatives from below, and, in doing so, they constitute what I want to call *a new kind of localism*—a localism which is not self-sufficiently particular but which arises, so to speak, *within* (without being simply a reflection of) the global.

This localism is no mere residue of the past that is going to pass away. It is something rather new: it is globalization's accompanying shadow. It is what is always left aside in globalization's rather panoramic sweep. It returns to trouble and disturb what appeared to be globalization's cultural settlements. It is what a philosopher would call globalization's "constitutive outside." That is to say, there is no identity which doesn't leave something outside. Indeed, to know what a thing is, is to know what it is not, so every identity has a constitutive outside which it has not included, or does not yet include. It is here that we find what we might call the return of the particular and the specific, of the specifically different at the centre of globalization's so-called panoptic aspiration to closure. The local, in this sense, has no stable transhistorical character: it is not always traditional practices or patriarchal forms of power or what everybody has done since the beginning of time. It resists this sweep with what one might call different conjunctural times. It doesn't have a fixed political inscription: sometimes it is progressive, sometimes it is emergent, sometimes it is critical, sometimes it is revolutionary. It doesn't have a fixed political character to which you can, as it were, attach a set of political baggage. It emerges at many sites—although one of the most significant is the planned and unplanned free and compelled migration which has brought the margins to the centre. And the fact is that, even at the heart of modernity's project, we do all continue to live in different time schemes: personal time, family time, work time, social time, nonsocial time, the time of Europe, the time beyond Europe. We occupy more than one of these chronotopes.

I HAVE BEEN TRYING—in an inevitably grossly summarizing, generalizing way—to describe the persistent dissemination of difference, at different levels, in different ways across the world. It variously affects those levels and I want to insist on the unevenness and unfinished character of its effects. In the final section, then, what I want to do is examine briefly just two implications for political theory and social practice which this dissemination of difference carries for societies which are trying to live its fate.

The first concern is the tension between difference and equality. The projects for social justice, for an end to racial violence and discrimination;

the projects for greater social equality and the guarantee of civic and social rights to everyone as an intrinsic aspect of citizenship—all of these projects have customarily been underpinned by a commitment to equality. We should notice at once—given the frequency with which it is invoked—how deep are the ambiguities around this idea. Liberal theorists who support a universal citizenship founded on civic nationalism and individual autonomy believe difference, in any real sense, has no place in the public domain at all. It should be reserved for the private sphere. And they feel that it is possible these days, although I think it's heroic of them, to separate neatly what is now public from what is now private. However, the equality which they advance—the equality of opportunity, the equality to compete, the equality of so-called level playing fields (and if I hear that term "joined-up government"[4] once more!—it belongs to the lexicon of language which should really be ditched) . . . that is the kind of equality which they have in mind, the equality of the level playing field where we all begin from the same place. And, of course, given our various talents etc. we are all going to end up in a different place, but that's the game. This is, of course, a negative version of equality, it is drawn from the repertoire of classical liberalism—no matter how long ago that was—its commitment to end the constraints to enter social competition, which otherwise should recognize no wider, social or collective commitments. Universal as this liberal discourse now appears to have become, it has never on its own been able to bring social justice to particular groups at risk; or to recognize the persistent strength of collective inequalities; or even to acknowledge that, as human beings, we are dialogically constructed—that is to say, we depend intrinsically on other people and on the "other"—and that we are not simply national, calculative atoms but are also always embedded in a variety of particular relationships and forms of life which have real rights, claims and needs of their own.

Racism is one such particularism which has stubbornly refused to yield in response to the negative version of right, justice or the "good life," and this is because differences which racism constructs operate at a deeper level than the formal play of citizenship, equality and individual autonomy. This is compounded by the fact that racism, far from having, as it were, one strand, has in the contemporary world radically expanded its forms.

To the biological racism of skin colour or antisemitism we must now add the proliferating forms of racism of cultural difference, of ethnic violence and cleansing, and of religious bigotry which the end of the Cold War and the ethnicization of conflict in its wake has brought into existence. This means that what we might, in our cynical wisdom, define as the old antiracist agenda of racial justice and social equality, not only remains in force but has been compulsorily intensified. Its need now is greater than it was before and this is because the problem of resisting racial oppression, injustice and violence is compounded by the new need in multicultural societies, not negatively to stop disadvantage, but *positively* to advance a recognition of diversity as a basis of social being and as a positive goal of social action of government practice, of diversity as a political objective. The fact is that multicultural drift, which is the condition we have been experiencing, can coexist with racism. There is no intrinsic opposition, no necessary opposition, between multiculturalism and racism: both can flourish. In the moment of the celebration of the arrival of the *Windrush* when Britain congratulated itself on having become, having crossed the line to, a multicultural society, the Stephen Lawrence inquiry opened.[5] Does one cancel out the other? Not at all, both exist, both are real, both are to be found in a society.

Quite apart from this society being unified by some 94 percent consensus among its mainstream majority, I would say that, as a rough guess, on the multicultural question it's divided into three parts. One group simply couldn't understand modern life without it. They are mainly young and they live in the cities. They just wouldn't understand modern urban metropolitan existence in which people were ethnically and culturally homogeneous: they're with it. Another group sees that it has happened, thinks that you probably can't do anything much about it. They have mainly moved out of the urban centres and they think that, as long as they don't go down to the South-East or to any big cities, multiculturalism will leave them alone and certainly will not propose to their daughters. The third group are militantly hostile to multiculturalism. It undermines everything about their being, especially it underwrites the degree to which they are not part of so-called mainstream liberal society. And a minority of those are perfectly prepared to stick knives into multiculturalism, or to throw it into the Thames or to set it alight if they pass it on the streets. Now, that is the real situation produced by multicultural drift. It is not some kind of consensual, homogeneous unity from end to end that this is a "great thing" and so we don't need to think about it anymore.

The new claims which arise, then, from this situation, especially among the ethnic minorities, are, in my view, for a genuinely universal racial justice, for equal outcomes to the major social and economic processes and also—also—for the recognition of difference. That is to say, for both a politics of equality and a politics of recognition.

Now, how to combine the claims of equality, justice and the recognition of difference in such a way that none of these factors trumps or neutralizes the other is, of course, an extremely difficult question, both in theory and in practice, and my argument here can only be a starting point to try to persuade you that that is really the political task with which the multicultural question confronts us. This is indeed increasingly a double demand—you might think of it as an impossible demand—in which the proliferation of difference within an increasingly interdependent world puts diversity on the agenda of equality without displacing it. Let us note how profoundly any attempt to bring together in the same sphere, of policy or debate or negotiation, both equality and difference, disrupts and dislocates our inherited political vocabularies. I would say that it signals nothing short of the emergence of a transformed political logic.

Of course, in making the move towards greater cultural diversity at the heart of modernity we must have a care lest we simply reverse into new forms of ethnic closure. We have to remember that so-called ethnicity (in the singular), and its naturalized relationship to community, is another term which is operating under a kind of erasure: it doesn't quite mean, any longer, what it claims to represent. We all locate ourselves in cultural vocabularies: without them we are incapable of speaking intelligibly at all as cultural subjects. We all come from and speak from somewhere, we all have different routes into modernity, we are all "located"—and, in that sense, even the most modern bears the traces of a cultural identity and cannot be without it. However, cosmopolitan critics are quite right to remind us that, in late modernity, we tend to draw on the fragmented traces and repertoires of several cultural and ethical languages. It's not a denial of culture to insist that the social world does not divide up neatly into distinct particular cultures, one to every community, nor that what everyone needs is just one of those entities, a single coherent culture, to give shape and meaning to life. We often operate, indeed, with a far too simplistic conception of belongingness. Sometimes we are most spoken by our attachments when we struggle to be free of them, when we quarrel with them, when we criticize them or, indeed, dissent radically from them. Like parental relationships, cultural traditions shape us both when they nurture and sustain us and when we have to break with them in order to survive. And beyond, although we don't always recognize it, there are always the attachments we have to those who share our world with us but who are necessarily different from us. The pure assertion of difference is only ultimately viable in rigidly segregated societies; that is to say, its ultimate logic is that of apartheid.

Well, after this long detour, must personal liberty, individual choice, liberal citizenship in the end trump every particularity in modern society? Is it stronger, bigger, more inclusive than any other identity which is, as it were, vying for recognition? That's what liberalism claims. I would argue not necessarily so. The right, for example, to live one's life from within—not as it is imposed or dictated simply from outside, but from within, to give it a kind of authenticity from within—this is at the heart of the modern conception of individuality. Well, it was, of course, honed and developed within the Western liberal tradition. And it has had, in its most contemporary forms, many very negative social consequences. But one needs to recognize that this sense of the need and the right for all peoples to live their life from within, of the forms of life in which they are placed, is no longer a value which is restricted to the West—in part because the very forms of life in which it developed are no longer exclusively Western. It has become a cosmopolitan value and, in the form, for example, of the discourse of human rights (although there are problems about that discourse), it is as pertinent to Third World workers struggling at the periphery of the global system, or to the women in the developing world up against patriarchal conceptions of a woman's role, or to political dissenters subject to the threat of torture—it is as relevant to them as it is to Western consumers in the so-called weightless economy. (Though after the "oil thing" it doesn't look quite as weightless as it did *[laughter]*!)[6]

In that sense, paradoxically, cultural belongingness is something of which everybody partakes, everybody is particular in this way. It's what Marx once called a concrete universal. By definition, a multicultural society must always involve practices and debates between more than one group. There has, therefore, to be some framework in which serious conflicts of outlook, belief and interests can be negotiated, and this can't be simply the framework of one group writ large or universalized—which was precisely the problem with Eurocentric assimilation. The specific and particular difference of a group or community cannot be asserted absolutely without regard to the wider context provided by all the others to whom particularity acquires a relative value. Philosophically, the logic of *différance* means that meaning and identity are always constituted in relation to an "other." A particular identity cannot be defined only by its positive content. All identity terms depend on marking their limits; that is to say, defining what they are in relation to what they are not. As Ernesto Laclau has argued, I cannot assert a different identity without distinguishing from a context and in the process I make the distinction and the context part of the term itself. I am asserting the existence in reality of the context in order to define why a particular term is different from that. Every identity is founded on an exclusion and is in that sense necessarily an effective power. There must be something which is external to an identity and that outside is constituted by all the other terms of the system whose absence or lack is constitutive of its presence. I am a subject precisely because I cannot be an absolute consciousness because something constitutively alien to the so-called self confronts me at every moment of social life. Every particular identity then in this sense is radically insufficient in terms of its others and this means that the universal is part of my identity insofar as I am formed, very much, by the lack of those others to whom I'm obliged to relate. The problem is that this argument seems to provide an alibi for the surreptitious return, by the back door, of the good old liberal universalism.

Finally, when we can't run and where we don't have energy—the energy for struggling with these complicated questions of difference—we reach into the tool bag of universal values in the hope that that will provide some resting place which will resolve our difficulties. The [cadres] remind us that European imperialist expulsion had to present itself in terms of a universal civilizing function, and the resistances of other cultures had to be presented as part of particularity and particularism. And that is true, indeed, of Enlightenment reason. You know, Enlightenment is not successful in the sense of an effective, unstinted march of reason to its logical conclusion. It's a much more dirty, mixed Foucauldian kind of power game and has a lot to do with those who win being able to define themselves as the universal self. In this paradigm—the classic liberal and Western cosmopolitan one—universalism is opposed at every point to difference. However, if, as I have tried to argue, this "other" is in fact part of the difference we are researching, then any generalized claim or conversation which includes the "other" doesn't come from outer space where universal values exist—timeless universal values throbbing away there since the birth of the cosmos—they must arise from *within* some particular culture or set of organizations. The universal only emerges out of the particular, not as some underlying principle which explains the particular, but as an incomplete horizon which stitches your particular together with mine. That's what generalizes and makes insufficient my view of the world because I have to take yours into being. That is to say, universality is the very process of negotiating with that which is different from yourself. Why is this process incomplete? Because it can't be filled with a specific and unchanging historical content. It will be redefined whenever a particular culture or identity, in taking account of those others who are different from itself, has to acknowledge its own radical insufficiency, is obliged to expand the horizon within which the demands of all can be met and within which the difficulties—and there are enormous difficulties between conflicting forms of life—have to be negotiated. Its content cannot be known in advance. Laclau argues it is a horizon to action.

The fact is that the particular and the universal, the claims of difference and equality cannot be recognized by some theoretical sleight of hand. There is no simple answer lying out there for us, as it were, to pluck out of existing political vocabularies. This is the dilemma, this is the conundrum, this is the problem, this is the multicultural question. At the very heart of the multicultural reconfigurative impact on all societies it requires us to think beyond the traditional boundaries of existing political discourses and their existing, ready-made solutions. It suggests, rather, that we have to put our minds seriously, not to reiterating the sterile arguments between liberals and communitarians and others, but to some new and novel way of finding the space for difference and identity to commune and communicate together, drawing on the same terrain and drawing together what have, in political theory until very recently, been considered incommensurable: liberty and equality with difference, the good and the right.

Questions, Comments and Discussion

> GRAHAME THOMPSON: *Stuart, a term which I was thinking about whilst you were talking, which didn't enter your vocabulary or lexicon, was "toleration." And I just wondered why. Is it because it is thoroughly compromised, in your view, by being one of the classic virtues of liberalism? Or is there some other reason? I ask because it seems to me quite an attractive possibility would be to think about toleration in the context in which you are talking. I mean here toleration as, in a sense, the cultivation of a studied indifference towards difference. That kind of way of thinking about toleration seems to me to be a potentially attractive sort of project in the context you are talking about. But my general question is: What happened to the concept of toleration in your talk?*
> STUART HALL: Yes, it's a very good question. It isn't that I think it's not relevant, particularly in the sense in which you describe it. I guess it would be closer to my position to say that it is one of many compromised terms because of the condescension that has come to figure in

toleration: "Yes, OK, you can stay around if you have to, and I agree not to be bothered by you." But that's not quite the same thing as a kind of dialogue between equals, between cultures that recognize themselves as both having a weight in defining what the space that they are going to coexist in will be like. But that is not because I don't think that that cultivation of an indifference to difference in this binary form isn't a very important element. Standing in this traditional place, I couldn't use the term "community," I couldn't use "racism," and "toleration" is one of these many words which are under erasure in our society. That is to say, they carry history and a certain baggage, which is now unusable in its own place. On the other hand, you can't think the future without them. So every time you were to speak you have first to undertake the process of deconstruction: "I don't mean that and I don't mean that." I think "toleration" must belong in the mix, but I don't find it as easy to reincorporate in its transformed form because it seems to carry, I suppose from the point of view of the excluded . . . I don't know why the excluded always feel that "toleration" does not express an equality of relationship, an equality of recognition, so to speak, but that is why I avoid it. But insofar as we are talking about negotiation, negotiation has to be framed by willingness to engage with those with whom we radically disagree and therefore you have to tolerate the tension and the frisson which all those conversations are bound to entail.

QUESTION: *I just want to ask you, Stuart: in a world that to many of us seems to be becoming very destabilized and deconstructed—and that often undermines a lot of the principles that we hold dear—do you still believe that there is really a possibility that diversity and equality can come about? I have a grave doubt about that possibility but maybe you feel optimistic about it.*

STUART HALL: Optimism of the intellect, pessimism of the will. That it is increasingly difficult is undeniable. And also that the difficulties now operate on such a large scale; you know, when one talks about global forces, it seems almost they occupy the full stage, as it were, of one's awareness. It's impossible to think one's way around them, except by, you know, sporadic action which doesn't seem to entail very much, and so on. So I understand people who feel pessimistic about that. I am just not constitutionally constructed that way. I suppose that is because I have never believed in snatching some simple good alternative out of the mess. I think we are always, always working on the mess.

We are working for the good side of the mess or on the bad side. So I am not surprised that things feel as if they are not going very well. I just think that is the way life is. If you are really trying to, in as complex and interdependent a world as ours, read some of the marginalized or more marginal values and virtues back into the middle, that will not be an easy prospect. It will not be an easy matter, it must entail struggle, organization and also, even more troubling really, some critical reinspection of the ethical and political baggage we carry with us, which is the most difficult part. It is not going to be constructed out of what we always thought because it cannot be constructed out of the world as we always thought it existed, because it is changing in front of our very eyes.

Now, of course, people can read change in such a way as to say, "The whole idea is completely irrelevant," and I don't say that; but I do say that, unless—which is why I sort of began the talk with what might just seem to you a fairly simple, straightforward description of things we all know—you go back to the difficult description of the world you have in front of you, as it is, in all its contradictoriness, only then do you get an ethic or political ethic which is grounded, which is situated, which is relevant. And only then can you begin to say, "Who might be drawn to this rather than the existing way of thinking about things?" So it's a tempered, qualified optimism, it isn't continuously transformative, it isn't triumphalist. We have not yet got to the end of history. History is always an open horizon, it doesn't open immediately to freedom and total change, but it can never be closed, or it's not history. It has to have contingent possibilities not yet taken account of in the existing dominant organizations, practices, corporations, structures of power, and so on. Something is left behind that is the constituent outside and you have to work from the constituent outside to understand the structure that presents itself as finished. This is the age in which we have talked about history coming to an end. People in the West have really been so hubristic as to define for the rest of the world that history has ended. Well, at the moment I think we have to say it hasn't.

JOHN CLARKE: *I wanted to ask a question which connects with what you just said, but goes back to your description of the three [attitudes to multiculturalism], the with it, the in retreat and the in denial. My question is [about] what the politics of movement across those three parts might be. In particular, is there a politics of re-engaging the exurban in retreat,* "don't-really-quite-want-to-know-about-this" group, which remobilizes them in a positive direction? Or, if it is partly generational—I don't even know quite how to phrase the last part of the question—do I just wait for them to die maybe? [Laughter.]

STUART HALL: That's the hopeful view of university promotions, for example *[laughter]*. Death cannot be long in coming. No, I suppose the most important thing to say is that it is probably a differentiated strategy. That's the first thing. The second thing is that it is probably a combination of shorter-term measures which do try to make those advances that have been made real and [to] deepen them and make them stick, and at the same time carrying the news that this can be done in such a way that is not so deeply alienating and undermining [of] people's sense of themselves and the sense of history that they had to give up. I think one wants both things. Paradoxically, as far as those who appear to be most hostile to it, I honestly think that, though we can trade with them, at least we understand why that is their response. We understand why it is. They are people who don't have any other set of ways of belonging to society, except a kind of imaginary Englishness—and this multiculturalism takes even that away from them.

Have you ever stopped to think—apart from the horrendous nature of their crime—of those five white boys who allegedly murdered Stephen Lawrence? They don't have a steady job to share amongst them. They don't have an O Level to share amongst them. They feel betrayed even by the fact that they are now a target for the police, because they thought at least there must be space for skinhead rogues in the police force. But if the police force is going to modernize and liberalize itself, where on earth do they go? It is not [the men acquitted of the murder] I am talking about specifically, but those conditions of marginalization and exclusion which make the message about "race" and the message about multiculturalism and the message about declining England and having to change our story of ourselves etc., profoundly undermining. They are asking the question: "Where on earth do you expect us to stand?" Now, I have to acknowledge that it's a tall order to require those of us who are trying to make this society more just and equal to spare a thought for those who are ready to stick pins into us. But actually, unless the strategies we undertake are going to do something to undermine the conditions which sustain that kind of powerlessness and hopelessness, there will always be such an active minority which are seeking to reverse any advance. So it's not easy, but I sort of know where I go there. I find it more difficult to know what I say to older middle- and lower-middle-class people who moved out of the cities because they don't like change. It's not because they don't like blacks; they don't like change of any kind. They want to live in a country which they falsely believe is the place of continuity and stability. And they would say: "Well, I don't have the problem: it's not here, you don't see black people in my village." I can't see my way to the end of my life without reconsidering anything profound about how I have understood my life, society, the nation, the culture to which I belong and feel at home in.

Again, they are not impossible to address. I think one of the most remarkable things about the Stephen Lawrence inquiry—not about the murder, about the inquiry—is that it actually did reach many of those people who don't face the problem every day, they don't live in the inner cities, they don't see it every day, [they are] not part of urban life. But they did say: "This is a respectable boy with an academic future with Christian parents who are trying to bring him up as well as they could—[he] could be my son except that he is black—it can't happen, things like that can't happen." I thought there was a moment there, in this society, when really, if the opportunity had been taken, a large number of those people could have been converted to feel that some aspect of antiracist policy is really their concern and does not belong to the South-East or somewhere else, but I don't think the opportunity was taken at that point and in that way. So, all of these are stubborn resistances to any of the difficult things I was trying to outline, but they are not immovable. But I think you do have to think more strategically about the way in which the question is presented to very different audiences. Just as there is a temptation on the conservative side to sort of homogenize Britain—94 percent of everybody thinking the same—so there is, rather, a tendency on the part of antiracists to . . . think that everybody is [either] antiracist or racist, and that is not so. We don't ourselves have a sufficiently differentiated picture of what the society is in order to understand these longer questions of educative refashioning.

A QUESTION FROM MEXICO CITY, RELAYED FROM THE INTERNET CHAT ROOM SET UP FOR THE LECTURE: *What part do media—both noninteractive media like TV or film and interactive media like the internet—play in this multicultural narrative?*

STUART HALL: Well, that's a very big question. But I would say, first of all, about the more mainstream media, when I said that I thought the discourse of the nation is always, in fact, a system of cultural representations, it's a question of how Britain and its history and its relationships are represented. Well, you can see instantly that media, in a very broad sense in which I would include literature—because in the English setting, at any rate, literature is a major carrier of images of Englishness, a major, profound carrier of images of Englishness—the media generally play a very clear, very important role in reproducing a certain definition of what it is to be British, what British history is, and so on. I think that it is also true of the education system, incidentally, of which I didn't have an opportunity to say anything very much. And in terms of the education system in Britain, if I can just make that point, I think that if you're concerned with addressing the population as a whole, the absence of history in the National Curriculum—that is to say, the absence for even the so-called native populations of any profound way of understanding the formation of this society and how complex and diffuse it has been—that is a crucial battle we have lost. And I do not see it being repaired in the so-called citizenship education which is about to come into existence. It hardly acknowledges the diversity of Britishness.

But just to return to the question. The media do not simply reproduce one story. It would be wrong to say that they do. We have to talk about the overwhelming weight of what seems to be constantly taken for granted, the kind of background assumptions made whenever you say, "The British people think," "Everybody thinks," "Everybody supports." What everyone? Which everybody? And for how long everybody? That's where it seems to me indirectly the media consolidate the notion that there is a kind of consensus in spite of the superficial apparent diversity of modern society. That is really [what constitutes] the core meanings and core values of the national identity. Now, the interactive media are very different, significantly different. And their differences have to do with the extraordinary way in which they are able to open access to relatively small communities—relatively weak societies and marginalized communities—to a so-called global public. Of course, it's not a global public which includes everybody. It is not speaking to that great mass of people out there that Murdoch's News Corporation is able to speak to, but it is carrying out a kind of niche communication. In that sense it is a very flexible form of communication because it has to ask itself who in the global arena would be interested in the problems of, I don't know, the indigenous peoples in the Amazon. Nobody is interested? Well, that is not true, not true, and [the interactive media] create forms of lateral communication which are relatively uncontrollable.

In fact, to tell you the truth, I am surprised by how uncontrollable the media authorities have allowed them to be. It may be because, technologically, they are not easy to control at all. But this does leave a certain room for so-called minority cultures not to be dominated by their relative size and relative marginality in terms of world importance, but to communicate outwards. And it does make the possibility to have people generalizing their own particular problems and struggles to those who might support them in a wider terrain. Questions of the environment always arise locally and they are always transnational, translocal in their implications because they always have implications for what people very far removed from you can do, or need to do. So they have this combination of the local to the global which doesn't pass through the usual filtering channels of a national media, of regional news, which is only to the back end of the evening news. It is able to jump over those and to begin to speak to people everywhere. So small groups are everywhere and this is a very important new development, and I think that people in England will certainly have imprinted in their minds the picture of the road haulers with their mobile phones co-ordinating a major stoppage which brought the country to a halt. This is a reminder that technology has no intrinsic political content but can be deployed in a variety of useful and nefarious purposes. But that doesn't matter—it simply means understanding what the potentiality is of no longer being restricted to those carefully segmented relationships between local, regional, national and global media, but of bypassing and condensing some of those connections and channels.

QUESTION: *I am another member of the Spanish-speaking community. This multicultural question you have addressed—what implications may [it] have for an institution like the Open University, for its growing teaching in a global, online, electronically connected multicultural environment? And perhaps related to that, how could an Open University protect itself from the temptation to give in to merely exporting, through commercially driven practices, [a] UK-centric curriculum worldwide?*

STUART HALL: And will I put my head into the noose? Well, in terms of its impact in broader terms, in terms of curriculum and so on, it seems to me that there are two factors, two ways in which it impinges on the OU's [Open University's] practice, and they are simple to identify. One is to begin to understand, really to understand, and begin to reflect, not just by the odd qualifying sentence at the end of paragraphs, the real increasing diversity of the British population which is itself a major audience. So already the question of diversity begins at home, it begins at home. And I think the OU is better than many other universities in terms of this. If you were to do—it would be really interesting to do a sort of inventory of major courses in the OU and ask yourself at each point who is the "who" that is being described. Who is the "us," who is the implied "us," who is the implied "them" that is being talked about, and what are the strategies of writing and of discourse and presentation? Because we are sensitive to the external environment, we have begun to incorporate those wobbles from the mainstream, but still, by and large, feel ourselves required to address the society as if it is more homogeneous than we really know it is. So that's the first way.

And the second is that, participating in global educational environments and networks, as undoubtedly we must, I think . . . it would be a fundamental error to, as it were, try to solve the problem of a declining audience at home, if that is so, with filling it out by sporadic audiences across the world because that gives a vagueness of address. After a while you get so cosmopolitan that you don't know who is talking about what to whom and for what. You can make yourself generally intelligible to a large number of people, but education, the educational discourse or conversation, requires a more focused interaction than that, and so I think that would be bad. On the other hand, we are inevitably, the OU is in that wider network and insofar as it's in that wider network it has to understand, but I think it can't, to the same extent at the moment, feel as responsible for the way in which it speaks to audiences unless they can begin to be defined more clearly. So I think there is sometimes a sort of weak open-ended way in which the global is invoked, partly as a kind of response to local problems and difficulties and partly as a kind of fashion word. You know, "we are going global."

The truth is, if you really understood the global—hardly anybody goes global in that generalized way—nobody does. It belongs to another era. Going global is not to go the same [way as] everybody, which is what I think that people mean. Going global is to understand how many languages one has to speak in order really to be in connection with people in different situations. It's that pluralization of language which makes it more difficult, not easier, to operate at the global level. It's not because we shouldn't, but it's because it is really difficult to do that and maintain the function of education. That is to say, the function of education, which I still archaically regard as a very specific discourse, different from other kinds of discourse, not just chatting, not just selling people something . . . a different kind, very distinctive kind of discourse in which people who are not necessarily located in an equal relationship come to build a relationship of mutual understanding and trust because of what is carried in the way in which people discourse with one another. A fundamental recognition of their commonness, with a careful attention to the responsibilities of teaching and learning, which are related but different. And if you have a sense of what is distinctive about an educational institution, which is not the same as [a supermarket], you can't operate in the global market as if you were [a supermarket], you do have to have a more situated approach. To which particular audiences would it be relevant for this institution saying this kind of thing really to try to teach on the broadest framework? And that is a really difficult question and involves, I think, a lot of actual analysis of what the so-called globe is really like.

NOTES

This text is based on a transcript of an October 19, 2000, Pavis Lecture given by Hall at the Walton Hall Campus, Open University, Milton Keynes. A different version of the text was published as an essay in *Un/Settled Multiculturalisms: Diasporas, Entanglements, Transruptions*, edited by Barnor Hesse (London: Zed Books, 2000), 209–41. All of the following endnotes have been supplied by the editor.

1 Professor Hall is referring here to media coverage of the Runnymede Trust report of the Commission on the Future of Multi-ethnic Britain (2000). This also lies behind his reference to the political editor of the *Daily Mail*, an ultraconservative national daily newspaper, which was particularly scathing in its coverage of the report.
2 As this paper originated as a lecture, references have not been provided.
3 For the benefit of readers unfamiliar with English geography, Balsall Heath and Handsworth are in Birmingham, Moss Side in Manchester, Chapeltown in Leeds, Toxteth in Liverpool. All the other named places are in London (apart, of course, from Bradford, which is a city in the north of England).

4 "Joined-up government" was a term widely used by UK policymakers in the late 1990s and early 2000s to refer to attempts to coordinate the different branches of government.
5 Stephen Lawrence was a black British teenager murdered in southeast London in 1993. The trial of five men accused of his murder collapsed in 1996. After a long campaign by his parents and by antiracist activists, an inquiry was launched by the Labour administration in 1998 into police failures in the light of the murder. The resulting Macpherson Report (1999) identified institutional racism within the London Metropolitan Police. The case highlighted the continuing presence of racism in Britain, and failures on the part of institutions, such as the police, with regard to black and Asian British communities.
6 Professor Hall is referring here to a series of protests that had just taken place in the UK concerning the high price of diesel and petrol. Protesting lorry drivers blockaded ports and managed to cut off supplies to fuel retailers, bringing about a week of "crisis" for the Labour government.

INDEX

Abercrombie, Nicholas, 320
Abrams, Mark, 35–36
Absolute Beginners (MacInnes), 37–40
abstraction, 195, 202, 234–35, 280, 298–99, 321
Abyssinian war, 277. *See also* Ethiopia
adolescence and adolescents, 23, 26–29, 32, 48, 258; black teenagers, 45, 49; *The Teenage Consumer* (Abrams), 35; teenagers, 28, 35–45; working-class teenagers, 31, 44. *See also* young people
Afghanistan, 392, 402
Africa and Africans, 138, 153, 161–69, 173–75, 179–83, 185–88, 189–93, 259, 261, 264–68, 276, 355, 361; African continent, 170; African cultural heritage, 140, 145, 164, 166, 168, 170, 174, 180, 190, 253; African diaspora, 162, 164, 259, 345; African languages, 166; African Orthodox Church, 182; African Reform Church, 184; African religions, 167, 175–76, 261; African tribes, 142, 190; African-based music, 168–69, 190; Ashanti region, 164; "Back to Africa" movements, 181–82, 185; Central African people, 278; enslavement of Africans, 145, 147, 164–66, 170–71, 174, 376 (*see also* slaves and slavery); freedom fighters in, 110; Ghana, 281, 290; independent nations in, 182–83; Old Rhodesia, 110; portrayal in the media, 111; West African kingdoms, 163–69. *See also* North Africa; Pan-African movement; South Africa; West Africa
Afro-Caribbeans and the Afro-Caribbean experience, 161–62, 191, 253, 257, 268, 334, 401–2; Afro-Caribbean communities, 412; Afro-Caribbean identity, 265
Afro-Christianity, 168, 175–77, 180; Native Baptists, 175–78; Native Pentecostalism, 261. *See also* religion
Afropessimism, 11
agriculture, 150, 213–14, 218, 235, 237, 378, 380; small farming class in Jamaica, 178; subsistence, 155, 238, 396. *See also* plantations
Algeria, 340, 344, 345, 354, 402
Alibai-Brown, Yasmin, 410

Althusser, Louis, 140, 158, 219–28, 231–32, 303–6, 357n2; Althusserians, 228; Althusser's concept of determination, 222; and Gramsci, 297; *Reading Capital*, 224, 357n2

America and Americans, 58, 68, 107, 165, 169, 264, 276–81, 283, 382, 383; African Americans, 9, 266, 360, 388; American Indians, 148, 268; Americanization of global culture, 393, 417; Americanness, 336; American Revolution, 175; Chaguaramas military base, 281–82; children in, 336; cities in, 387, 396, 407; civil rights movement in, 8, 11, 62; Communist Party in, 277; filmmaking in, 267; and Fordism, 375; Garvey and, 182, 266; income inequality in, 395; James and, 278–81, 284, 375; "little Americanism," 337; migration into, 237–38, 274, 276; multiculturalism and, 410; pluralism in, 138; popular culture in, 280; religion in, 177; schools in, 336; slavery in, 210, 284; as superpower, 391–95, 407; teenage consumers in, 36; Trotskyism in, 278

American Communist Party, 277
Amnesty International, 16
Anderson, Benedict, 265, 270, 377, 388
Anderson, Perry, 300
Anderton, James, 93
anticolonialism. *See* decolonization; independence struggles
antifascism, 14, 113
Antilles, 262, 268, 343, 349, 353–54. *See also* Caribbean, the; West Indies
Anti-Nazi League, 72, 113, 120. *See also* National Front; Nazis
antiracism and antiracists, 7–8, 124, 250–53, 259, 319, 429; antiracist struggle, 5, 97–99, 103, 111–20, 318, 371, 421; Hall as antiracist activist, 12–17, 97; politics of, 246, 332, 371. *See also* racism

antisemitism, 383, 420; anti-Jewish jokes, 111. *See also* Jews
Appiah, Kwame Anthony, 360
Arabia and Arabs, 170, 367, 381
Arawak peoples, 163, 268
art, 23, 27, 31, 33, 171, 264, 312, 317, 379; art schools, 40; Black Arts movement, 16; European, 379. *See also* artists
articulation, 5, 63, 100, 125, 134, 146–47, 162, 214, 216–27, 229, 232–33, 235, 237–38, 240, 250, 302–3, 306, 322; articulated hierarchy, 223, 225; and disarticulation, 233; double, 174; triple, 152
artists, 16, 254, 259, 272, 281–85, 339, 345; black, 17, 351; ethnic, 253–54. *See also* art
Asia, 45, 128, 261, 268, 334, 378–80, 382, 394, 402; Asia Minor, 380–81
Asians and Asian communities, 51, 60, 64, 73, 108, 112–13, 253, 257, 323, 335, 381, 398, 412, 416; educated second-generation, 401–3; Asian working class, 64, 398; Asian youth, 64, 255n1, 403
Aufhebung, 350
authoritarianism, 1, 7, 15, 64, 67, 77–78, 84, 175; authoritarian populism, 79, 83

Babylon, 161, 183, 186, 384
"Back to Africa" movements, 181–82, 185
bad faith, 72, 115, 119
Bakhtin, Mikhail, 389
Balibar, Étienne, 219, 221–22, 225, 357n2
Banaji, Janius, 213, 217
Bangladesh and Bangladeshis, 335, 396, 402
Bantu peoples, 201, 203; "Bantustans," 227, 324
Baptist War, 177
Baran, Paul, 196
Barbados, 136, 150–51
barbarism, 109, 367, 381

436 | INDEX

Barthes, Roland, 379
Baudelaire, Charles, 389
BBC, 98, 114, 117
Beckford, George, 158
Bedward, Alexander, 181
Beechey, Veronica, 213–14
Benjamin, Walter, 340, 384, 389
Berger-Hamerschlag, Margareta, 23, 27–29, 33
Bernal, Martin, 380
Bethel, Andrew, 99
Bettelheim, Charles, 215
Beyond a Boundary (James), 282–83, 287, 374
Bhabha, Homi, 267, 342, 344, 348–51, 356, 378, 418
Bible, 129, 176–77, 183, 383; Book of Revelation, 183; Old Testament, 185–86
biology, 31, 330, 362; biological conceptions of race, 197; genetics, 366, 368, 371–72
Birmingham, 19n17, 58, 90, 399, 433n3
Black Arts movement, 16
Black Athena (Bernal), 380
Black Jacobins (James), 277–78, 280, 374
"Black Orpheus" (Sartre), 355
Black Power movement, 2
blacks and black existence, 12, 15–16, 51–56, 60–61, 70, 72, 77, 110–12, 114–15, 149–50, 152–53, 163, 170–76, 182–83, 188–94, 240–41, 246–49, 252–60, 332–38, 402, 429; black activism, 62, 64, 72, 120, 190, 277, 279, 333; black artists, 247–48; contemporary, 339; black athletes, 110, 274; black body, 345–47, 368, 370; black Caribbean identities, 261; black communities, 14–15, 17, 51, 53, 73, 75–76, 102, 112, 135; black consciousness, 53–54; black counterculture, 76; black crime, 64; black culture, 13, 189, 246–54, 355; black diaspora, 258, 286, 329; black intellectuals, 1, 274, 354; "Black Jesus" (Garvey), 182; black middle class, 53, 157; black migration, 10, 12, 51, 57–62, 128, 238; black nationalism, 182, 188; blackness, 7, 10, 187, 352, 368; black population, 62–64, 68, 74, 90–91, 128, 131–32, 134, 168; black religion, 175, 177, 183 (*see also* Afro-Christianity; religion); black representation, 254–55; black revolts, 7, 278, 284; black soldiers, 274; black subject, 247, 248–52, 257, 266, 333, 342, 347; black women, 251, 402; black workers, 58, 60, 70, 128, 145, 157, 200, 207, 209, 235–39; black youth, 64, 75, 90, 112, 188, 191; *See also* race; racism; slaves and slavery
Blacks Britannica (film), 254
Black Skin, White Masks (Fanon), 260, 266, 339, 340–43, 348–49, 351, 353, 350–56, 368
Blair, Tony, 3, 417; government of, 16. *See also* New Labour
Bobbitt, Philip, 393
Bogle, Paul, 8, 178
Bonapartism, 278
Bosnian-Serbian people, 336, 402
Bourdieu, Pierre, 410
Bradford, 58, 255n1, 398, 412, 433n3
Bradley, Lloyd, 286
Braithwaite, E. R., 23–29, 33
Braithwaite, Lloyd, 149
Brathwaite, Edward (Kamau), 3, 12, 150–51, 166, 168–70, 176
Breitbart News Network, 19n20
Bridge, Gary, 390, 404
Bristol, 15, 73, 112, 399, 404
Britain and the United Kingdom, 5–10, 12–13, 16–19, 42–54, 74, 78–79, 90–91, 103, 111, 127, 131–34, 235–36, 259, 274, 281–88, 360, 386, 390–97, 403–5, 414–16, 431–33; Black Arts in, 3; black experience in, 55, 70, 72, 255, 286; British cities, 71, 192, 413 (*see also* Birmingham; Bradford; Bristol; Leeds;

Britain and the United Kingdom (cont.) Liverpool; London; Manchester); British imperialism, 7, 58, 107, 151, 163, 349; British media's portrayal of race, 103–13 (*see also* BBC; television); Britishness, 69, 322, 336–37, 415–16, 430; British West Indies, 148, 170, 245; culture of, 106, 247; economy of, 64, 78, 128; history of, 3, 52, 129, 430; industry in, 57, 60, 127–28; as multicultural society, 11; music scene in, 286; police in, 68, 92 (*see also* Metropolitan Police; police and policing); politics in, 10, 132; racism in, 9, 56–70, 251, 322; socialism in, 11; Trotskyism in, 275; working class in, 103. *See also* England

British National Party, 398

broadcasters and broadcasting, 51–55, 98, 106, 114. *See also* BBC; media; television

Buhle, Paul, 272, 284

Bukharin, Nikolai, 211, 304–5

Burke, Edmund, 367

Burning Spear, 266

Bush, George W., 394, 407

Butler, Judith, 347, 376–77

Cabral, Amilcar, 162

calypso, 283, 286–91; Calypso Kings, 286–87, 289, 291–92; Hall's essay on, 13; indigenous calypso, 292

Campaign Against Racism in the Media (CARM), 98–100, 106, 114–17

Campaign for Nuclear Disarmament (CND), 3

Cannon, J. P., 278

capital, 101, 200, 208–9, 213–14, 216–17, 219, 223, 227, 229, 231, 237–40, 298–99, 310–11, 322–24, 412; accumulation of, 212, 216, 229, 280; industrial, 215, 310; international, 310; mercantile, 214

Capital (Marx), 157, 207, 215, 217, 223, 299, 310

capitalism, 2, 5, 8, 88, 104, 199–203, 204–5, 209–19, 223, 226–27, 237–40, 245, 273, 298, 310, 323; capitalist development, 201–2, 205–6, 210–11, 227, 236, 313, 323–24; capitalist relations, 200, 205, 212–15; capitalist social formations, 200, 207, 230–31; class relations in, 134, 178, 202–3, 209; global capitalist market, 212; industrial, 237; market relations in, 205; mode of production in, 200, 206–9, 213, 218, 298; modern, 84, 239, 299–300; and plantation slavery, 213–14; Western, 230

Carchedi, Guglielmo, 208

Cardus, Neville, 275

Caribbean, the, 3–5, 17, 57–58, 128, 131, 136–58, 163, 175, 201, 257–68, 272–75, 281–83, 287–90, 353; Caribbean Artists Movement, 6; Caribbean cinema, 257, 268, 270; Caribbean cuisine, 269; Caribbean diaspora, 8, 286; Caribbean slave societies, 144–46, 235, 273; Caribbean social/class structures, 144, 151, 154, 157, 217, 238; French and British Antilles, 148, 170, 262; indigenous peoples, 163, 268; migration to, 9. *See also* Carnival; music; plantations; religion; West Indies; individual Caribbean nations

Caribbean Labour Party, 277, 281

Caribs and Arawaks, 163, 268

Carnival, 283, 286, 289–90

Catholic Church, 289, 365; popular Catholicism, 319, 326

Césaire, Aimé, 258, 264, 354, 355

Chaguaramas military base, 281–82

children, 45; child poverty, 395; television for, 54; working-class, 27–28. *See also* young people

China and Chinese people, 138, 148, 264, 267, 310, 367, 417

Christianity, 166–68, 170, 176, 261, 289, 379; Afro-Christianity in the Carib-

bean, 175–78, 180–81, 261, 289; Christian missions and missionaries, 168, 175–77; Old Testament, 185–86. *See also* religion; individual churches
Christmas, 131, 168–69; Christmas Calypso, 288
Church of England, 166
cinema, 33, 35, 36, 257–59, 269–70; Caribbean, 257, 268, 270; Hollywood, 33, 108, 266; modern black, 270; "Third Cinemas," 257, 268. *See also* films
Cipriani, Arthur, 273–74
cities, 46–47, 55, 71–72, 90–91, 179, 184, 382, 421, 429; global, 386–91, 396–98, 400–401, 404–8; inner, 60–61, 68, 399, 401–2, 429; suburbs and white flight, 46, 398, 401
civil liberties, 10, 79–80, 95–96, 120
civil rights struggles, 11, 72, 265, 333, 388
civil war, 157, 335, 387, 396
Clammer, John, 218–19
Clarke, John, 427
class, 31, 43–44, 61–62, 69–70, 81–86, 103, 125–30, 136–41, 147–49, 151–59, 172, 187, 200–209, 214–16, 232–34, 237–41, 301, 308–12, 320–25, 413; alliances, 156, 218–19, 228–30, 309; in Caribbean society, 136–59; conflict, 13, 25, 69, 86–87, 105, 200–205, 208, 228, 230–333, 237–41, 277; and color, 136–37, 178; dominant, 88, 231, 233, 240–41; lower, 143, 156, 186; peasant, 148, 310; slave-owning, 151, 171–73. *See also* Marxism: concepts of class in; middle classes; ruling class; working class
Clifford, James, 366
clubs, social, 26, 36, 40, 47–48, 287–89, 403
Cochrane, Kelso, 13
Cohen, Stan, 66
Cold War, 11, 391, 420
colonialism, 59, 178, 219, 240, 266, 270, 288, 336, 340–44, 349–52, 354, 393; colonial dependence, 375; colonial desire, 348; colonial oppression, 356; colonial trade, 386; colonies, 9–10, 58, 62, 147–51, 177–80, 283; colonization, 108, 165–66, 191, 199, 201, 258–59, 261–62, 268, 387, 391, 404; French, 354. *See also* imperialism
color. *See* race; skin color
Columbus, Christopher, 261, 268, 380
Comintern, 275–77
commodities, 32, 36, 207, 213–15, 227, 237, 396
Communist Manifesto, The (Marx and Engels), 210, 215
Communist Party, 275–76, 302; US, 277
communists, 7, 10; black American, 185
communities, imagined, 265, 270, 332, 337, 376–78, 388, 415
concentration camps, 39; ethnic cleansing, 383
Conservative Party (UK), 16, 88
Constantine, Learie, 274–75
consumption, 35, 223, 400, 406
Coordinating Committee against Racial Discrimination (Birmingham), 19n17
Coronation Calypso, 288
cosmopolitanism, 389, 405–6
creole society, 137, 141, 148, 153, 163, 165, 174, 178–79, 269; creole idiom, 166, 290; creolization, 16, 141, 145, 147, 267, 338; in Jamaica, 179. *See also* calypso; Caribbean, the; Jamaica and Jamaicans; Trinidad
cricket, 48, 273–76, 282–83, 336; "Cricket, Lovely Cricket" (song), 288; cricket calypsoes, 282, 288; English league cricket, 274; James and, 274–75, 282–83; and Tebit test, 336; West Indian team, 282–83, 287–88
crime, 34, 61, 74, 89, 112; criminalization, 90–91; criminal justice system, 4; high, 401; hooliganism, 61. *See also* "law and order" policies; police and policing

Crown, British, 88; Crown colony period, 148, 151
Cuba, 185, 310, 262; Cuban Revolution, 198
cults, 5, 175, 177, 183, 186; millenarian, 183. *See also* religion
culture, 153, 163, 179, 191, 246–49, 370, 416; cultural difference, 196, 246, 335, 337–38, 397, 404, 420; cultural homogenization, 405, 416; cultural identity, 179, 249, 257–62, 264, 270, 422; cultural pluralism, 136, 141, 143, 153, 158; cultural politics, 247, 252–53, 318, 329–30; cultural revolution, 62, 265; cultural theory, 2, 248; ideology as a cultural movement, 316–17; popular, 32, 108–9, 278, 282, 326. *See also* identification
Curtin, Philip D., 163, 166

Daily Mail, 66, 409, 416, 433n1
dance, 39, 48, 168–70, 174, 191, 288; dancehalls, 286–87; Jonkunnu dance, 168; Trinidad-style, 288
Davies, Norman, 416
Day, Robin, 98, 114
decolonization, 2, 10, 11, 143, 151, 153–55, 188, 259, 282, 318, 354, 391, 404; in Algeria, 344–45; in Jamaica, 179, 187, 333; and liberation struggles, 7, 8, 53, 163, 340, 384. *See also* independence struggles
deconstruction, 16, 117–18, 321, 351, 381, 426
deindustrialization, 16, 75, 387
democracy, 77, 92, 97; democratic society, 32, 84–85, 388; democratization, 116, 397; parliamentary, 226–27
Derrida, Jacques, 252, 263, 340, 418
Dessalines, Jean-Jacques, 278
dialectics, 13, 172, 229, 279, 300, 335, 340, 342–43, 350–53, 375; Marxian dialectic, 220; master/slave dialectic, 352

diaspora, 257–70, 337–38; "African," 161–64, 181–83, 259, 263–65, 345; Afro-Caribbean, 8, 257–63, 286, 292; black, 286, 292, 329, 384; "diaspora aesthetic," 269; diasporic culture and identities, 253, 269; European, 383
différance, 252, 263, 418, 423
difference. *See* culture: cultural difference; race: racial difference
discipline, 1, 17, 24, 30, 44, 47–48, 67, 76, 78–79, 86, 130, 165, 167; disciplinary society, 73, 78, 88, 94, 95. *See also* "law and order" policies; police and policing
discourses and discursive systems, 83–84, 101, 115, 248, 250, 258, 330–31, 345–46, 363–64, 366–67, 370, 423, 430, 432–33; discursive structures, 232, 252, 320, 341, 363–64; racial, 330, 346, 351; religious, 365
discrimination, racial, 11–13, 362–63. *See also* racism
Dobb, Maurice, 206
Du Bois, W. E. B., 276, 346, 360–61, 363, 368, 388; Du Bois Lectures, 336
Dummett, Michael, 14
Dunayevskaya, Raya, 279
Dupré, Georges, 218
Durkheim, Émile, 296

economic anthropologists, 218
economic historians, 156, 206
economics, 76, 407, 410; economic relations, 5, 125–30, 196–203, 205, 212, 215–16, 223–26, 230–31, 303, 305; free market economy, 394; high-tech economy, 396; peasant economy, 323; postindustrial economy, 387. *See also* capitalism; Marxism; neoliberalism
economism, 103, 127, 229–30, 233, 302–7; economistic monism, 233
education, 4, 11, 16, 44, 53, 67, 149, 152, 155, 178, 354, 359, 430; academic, 273;

in America, 336; colonial, 274; English public school, 272–74; function of, 433; grammar schools, 27, 30; Hall's work as a secondary school teacher, 43; multicultural, 6, 255n1; primary schools, 26; private schools, 400; school-leavers, 25; schools, 23–34, 37, 45–49, 98–99, 123, 197, 211, 219, 222, 398, 400–401; secondary modern schools, 24–25, 31–32; second-class educational stream, 29; teaching profession, 24–25

Egypt, 187, 378, 380

Eighteenth Brumaire of Louis Bonaparte, The (Marx), 157

Elizabeth I, Queen, 56; Elizabethan period, 107, 283

Elkins, Stanley, 169–70

Emancipation, 176–78, 182, 376

Engels, Friedrich, 226, 296, 299

Engerman, Stanley, 213

England, 34, 47–48, 53, 56–59, 176–77, 183, 247, 272, 274–76, 282, 287–88, 329, 334, 374–75, 431, 433n3; Church of England, 166; cities in, 56, 58, 177, 191, 247, 255n1, 399 (*see also* Birmingham; Bradford; Bristol; Leeds; Liverpool; London; Manchester); class-cultural differentiation in, 139; English culture and ethnicity, 57–58, 252, 255; English language, 166, 168, 281, 284; English literature, 108, 375; Englishness, 251, 253, 336–37, 416, 428–30; in decline, 428; industrialization in, 154; invasion of Jamaica, 268; "little Englandism," 337, 403; media's portrayal of race, 103–16 (*see also* BBC; television); and "plural society" concept, 138; policing in, 96 (*see also* Metropolitan Police; police and policing); public schools in, 273–74; "Young Englanders," 12, 42–50. *See also* Britain and the United Kingdom; London

Enlightenment, 366–67, 376, 417, 424

entertainment, 35, 54, 109–11, 191, 399, 401

essentialism, 354, 220, 353, 406–7

Ethiopia, 183–84, 186, 266; Abyssinian war, 277. *See also* Haile Selassie I, Emperor

ethnic cleansing, 383; concentration camps, 39

ethnicity, 152, 253, 422; ethnic backgrounds, 141, 149, 201, 265; ethnic cleansing, 383; ethnic groups, 6, 76, 101, 124, 137, 140–41, 158, 201, 215, 238, 241, 399; ethnic identities, 145, 246, 252–53, 314; ethnic minorities, 140, 311, 402, 411–13, 421; ethnicization, 420; vs. race, 250, 251–53; in South African society, 200–202. *See also* race; skin color

Europe, 152–53, 162, 165–70, 180, 212, 226, 266–68, 291, 299, 301, 336, 367, 374–84, 387, 407, 414, 419; colonial past of, 7, 10, 163, 107, 144, 267n, 424; common market in, 377, 383; current political trends in, 6, 384; during slave trade, 219; Eastern, 279, 300; Eurocentrism and the Eurocentric model, 207, 248, 323, 327, 353, 423; Europa myth, 378–82; European culture, 107, 145, 153, 165, 178–79; European diaspora, 383; European identity, 379–80; European imaginary, 261, 378–79; European thought and attitudes, 3, 170, 354, 379; industrial, 323; Jewry of, 383; missionaries from, 176; myths of, 378–82, 383–84; postcolonial crisis of, 7; religion in, 168; Western, 34, 230, 313, 335

exploitation, 32, 204, 210, 213, 298

false consciousness, 156, 201, 231, 320

Fanon, Frantz, 3, 10, 207, 250, 258, 260, 266, 339–56, 370; "Critical Fanonism" (Gates), 340, 348; Fanonism, 341; and Lacan, 349. *See also Black Skin, White Masks*

fantasy, 5, 33, 340, 348; racialized, 353
fascism, 113, 232, 299–300, 302, 326; fascist states, 316
fetishization, 247, 251, 342, 345–46
feudalism, 154, 212, 213, 218, 222, 230
fiction. *See* literature
films, 16, 107, 108, 249–50, 253–55, 257, 268, 278, 339, 354, 429; filmmakers, 4, 253–54, 267; film festivals, 400. *See also* cinema
floating signifier, race as, 2, 359–60, 362–63, 371–73
Fogel, Robert, 213
folklore, 250, 270, 318
Foster-Carter, Aidan, 218, 219
Foucault, Michel, 260, 330, 346, 364; Foucauldian views, 424
France, 62, 72, 157, 218; archives in, 278; and colonialism, 267, 354, 376; "economic anthropology" tradition in, 218; Fanon and, 354; French Caribbean, 148, 170, 262–63, 289; French Guiana, 148; French language, 30–31, 263, 273; French Revolution, 173, 278, 375–76; French theorists, 119, 349–51, 354, 418; Marx on French society, 157; right to strike in, 87
Francis, Armet, 259. *See also* photography
Frank, Andre Gunder, 196, 198, 211–14
free market. *See* laissez-faire; markets: free
Freud, Sigmund, 349, 356
Fukuyama, Francis, 391
Furnivall, John Sydenham, 138, 197, 200
Furtado, Celso, 211

gangs, 34, 44, 397
ganja, 184, 185, 188, 266
Gardner, Carl, 99, 116–17
Garnett, Alf, 111
Garvey, Amy Ashwood, 277
Garvey, Marcus, 8, 182–83, 266, 276, 277; Garveyism, 15, 182–83, 276

Garvey's Children (Sewell), 266
Gates, Henry Louis, 340, 348, 349, 360
gender, 9, 15, 101, 250–51, 255, 303, 314, 346, 389, 412, 416
genetics, 366, 368, 371–72. *See also* biology
Genovese, Eugene, 170–71, 173, 213
Gilroy, Paul, 254
globalization, 6, 9, 16, 386–87, 390–92, 394, 396–97, 399–400, 403–7, 414, 416–17, 419; and cities, 386, 393, 399, 407; and culture, 417; "global governance," 391–92; and migration, 396, 407; "new world order," 391–92, 394, 397. *See also* neoliberalism
Godelier, Maurice, 218
Gold Coast, 164
Gramsci, Antonio, 17, 63, 102, 117, 142, 154, 228–33, 236, 249, 295–328, 375, 417; Gramsci's definition of hegemony, 308; Gramsci's treatment of ideology, 318; Hall's Gramscian vocabulary, 8; Istituto Gramsci, 297; key concepts of, 304; *Prison Notebooks* (Gramsci), 297, 300, 327n1; relevance of, 297–325; "war of position" vs. "war of maneuver," 117, 228, 229, 312–14, 316
Greece, 283–84, 402; Greek drama, 375; Greek myths, 378–82
Greig, Geordie, 400
Grenada, 136–37
Grundrisse (Marx), 210, 222, 298
Guardian newspaper (*Manchester Guardian*), 104, 254, 275, 374, 394–95
Guyana, 136–37, 140–41, 148, 261, 277

Haile Selassie I, Emperor, 183–84, 186. *See also* Ras Tafari movement
Haiti, 170, 177, 261–62, 275, 277, 289, 374; Haitian Revolution, 172–73, 278, 375–76
Hall, Stuart, 1–18, 425–32; Caribbean origins of, 1, 258; interest in urban

environments, 16; on optimism vs. pessimism, 426–27; at Oxford, 18n11; political pedagogy of, 17; as a secondary school teacher, 43
Handsworth, 10, 70, 266, 412, 433n3
Handsworth Songs (film), 253–55
Hardt, Michael, 392
Harlem Renaissance, 278
Harris, Wilson, 274, 284
Hebdige, Dick, 188, 192, 269
Hegel, G. W. F., 220, 224, 279, 283, 348, 350–52, 354, 375; French reception of, 350; Hegelian idealism, 220; Hegelian Marxism, 279; master/slave dialectic, 352
hegemony, 63, 142–43, 151, 154, 163, 177, 228–31, 236, 240, 304, 307–18, 324–26, 390; American, 374; construction of, 233, 269, 300, 315; hegemonic conceptions of identity, 246, 253, 268; superpower, 391
Henry, Margaret, 99, 116–17
Hindess, Barry, 213, 217, 222
Hindu marriage, 140–42
Hirst, Paul, 213, 217, 222
historical materialism, 296, 304–5
historicity, 140, 225, 228, 347
Hoare, Quintin, 300, 327n1
Hoggart, Richard, 12
Hollywood, 33, 108, 266
homogenization and homogeneity, 308, 322–23, 390, 412, 416; ethnic, 141; inner, 377; national, 8
Honest John (record label), 286, 288
housing, 11, 46, 52, 55, 127, 205, 401; housing market, 206
Howe, Darcus, 284
Hulme, Peter, 268, 380

ICA (Institute for Contemporary Arts), 339, 355
identification, 331, 345, 371–72, 415; class, 144, 208; cultural, 261, 270; Fanon and, 348–50, 355–56; and ideologies, 101; racial, 53, 144, 249–51, 355. *See also* culture: cultural identity
ideological state apparatuses, 67, 102–3, 231–32, 314
ideology, 100–104, 115–20, 248, 216–18; Althusser on, 231–32, 306; and class, 156, 187, 208–9, 239–40; "folk-ideology," 171; French Republican, 354; Gramsci on, 228–33, 236, 299, 305–7, 316–21, 326–27; Hall on, 5, 6; ideological discourses, 106, 115–17, 232, 241, 319, 327; ideological formations, 130, 241, 327; ideological structures, 200, 206, 214, 217, 225, 303; ideological struggle, 97, 100, 102–3, 241, 318, 321, 326–27; nationalist, 154–55; and race, 123–24, 129–30, 132, 134, 237; of repressive policing, 73, 77; racist, 62, 63, 66–70, 105–6, 114–15, 126
"Ideology and Ideological State Apparatuses" (Althusser), 231
Imagined Communities (B. Anderson), 270
IMF (International Monetary Fund), 391
immigration and immigrants, 10, 42–50, 54–57, 61–64, 98, 106, 114, 127, 205, 291, 334, 390, 397–99, 401, 407; immigrant youth, 12, 42–50; immigration authorities, 132, 281. *See also* migration
imperialism, 103, 107–8, 216, 230, 240, 250, 252, 279, 299–300, 336; anti-imperialism and "end of empire," 7, 59, 182, 198, 281–83, 404, 414; British, 52, 57–59, 133, 236, 282, 322; in the Caribbean, 9, 163; French, 376; ignorance about, 8; imperial cities, 386–87, 393, 404; imperial hegemony, 163, 236, 397; imperial subjects, 7, 10; imperialist chain, 58, 211–12; in the late nineteenth century, 78, 236; new, 392–93; old-style, 133; and policing, 15. *See also* colonialism

independence struggles, 188–89; in the Caribbean, 173, 186, 273, 281, 287; in southern Africa, 8, 311. *See also* decolonization
Independent Labour Party, 275
India and Indians, 109, 203, 264, 267, 402; British Raj period, 58, 107; East Indian communities in the Caribbean, 138, 140–41, 148, 151; East Indian migrants in Britain, 25, 42, 45–46, 57, 335; globalization and, 417; Indian and Pakistani Workers' Associations, 11
indigenous peoples, 406, 431
indigenous racism, 5, 9, 58–59, 66, 128, 133, 236
individualism, 67, 100
industrialization, 154, 301, 397; industrialized Western democracies, 313, 316; Industrial Revolution, 58
inner cities, 60–61, 68, 399, 401–2, 429. *See also* cities
intelligentsia, 155, 188
interpellations and interpellative structures, 232, 239, 241
Iraq, 392–93, 402, 407
Islam, 380–81, 404; Islamophobia, 398, 404
Israel, 39, 384; Israelites, 187, 189
It Ain't Half Racist, Mum (CARM program), 98–99, 106, 114
Italy, 62, 87, 230–31, 277, 296, 299–301, 310, 319, 322–23, 326; Istituto Gramsci, 297; modern Italian state, 301; and Mussolini, 228, 297, 302; southern, 131, 301

Jamaica and Jamaicans, 8, 136–37, 161, 184–92, 218, 265–66, 333–34; Afro-Christianity in, 168–69, 175–77, 180–83; British invasion of, 163; class mobility in, 150–51; and creolization, 141, 148; Hall and, 1, 258, 262, 333–34; Jamaican artists, 259; Jamaican coat-of-arms, 268; Jamaican culture, 13, 163–65; Jamaican dialect, 166, 290; Jamaican identity, 189, 265, 268; Jamaican music, 191; Jamaican society, 138, 178–79, 185–87, 189–91; media portrayals of, 110; migration from, 287–88, 291–92; modern, 186–92; Morant Bay Rebellion, 177–78; old white plantocracy in, 154; origin of name, 268; Pentecostalism in, 181; politics in, 188; respectable vs. lower-class, 179–80, 185, 188–89; during slavery, 107, 163–66, 168–78; "two Jamaicas," 163, 179–80, 183, 189–90; unemployment in, 191. *See also* calypso; Kingston; Ras Tafari movement; reggae
Jamaican National Heritage Trust, 268
Jamaican Slave Society, 158
James, C. L. R., 3, 173, 272–85, 287, 291, 374–76; *Beyond a Boundary*, 282–83, 287, 374; *The Black Jacobins*, 277–78, 280, 374; *The Case for West-Indian Self Government*, 274; and cricket, 274–75, 282–83; and Dunayevskaya, 279; in England, 274–78; *The Life of Captain Cipriani*, 274; *Mariners, Renegades and Castaways*, 280–81; on Melville, 280–81; *Minty Alley*, 273; and Nkrumah, 281; *Notes on Dialectics*, 279; *Party Politics in the West Indies*, 282; politics of, 275–80, 284, 375; and Robeson, 276, 277; *State Capitalism and World Revolution*, 279; *Toussaint Louverture*, 277; in Trinidad, 272–74, 281–85; and Trotsky, 276, 279, 375; in the United States, 278–81
Jardine, James, 89, 94, 113–14
jazz, 39, 333
Jehovah's Witnesses, 181
Jews, 39, 111, 138, 267, 380–84; anti-Jewish jokes, 111
Jim Crow (US), 237
John Canoe (Jonkunnu), 168
Johnson, Linton Kwesi, 8
Johnson, Paul, 416
Johnson-Forest tendency, 279

jokes: racist and anti-Jewish, 111–12, 133
Jones, Claudia, 13
Jonkunnu dance, 168
justice, 2, 5–7, 9, 12, 40, 48, 91, 195, 224, 409, 420, 422; racial, 421; reparative, 10; social, 40, 76, 387, 405, 419–20

Kenyatta, Jomo, 277, 375
Kingston, 180–84, 186–89, 191, 263–64, 266, 403. See also Jamaica and Jamaicans
Kitch. See Lord Kitchener
Kojève, Alexandre, 350
Kristeva, Julia, 119
Kuper, Adam, 136
Kuper, Leo, 138, 156, 200
Kureishi, Hanif, 255. See also *My Beautiful Laundrette*; *Sammy and Rosie Get Laid*

labor, 110, 127–32, 144, 146, 239, 280, 298, 301, 314, 323–24; female, 402; forced (unfree), 147–49, 164–66, 173, 200, 203, 206, 207, 209, 227; free (wage), 80, 177, 201, 205, 210, 213; globalization and, 390–95; immigrant, 192; indentured, 261; labor institutions, 201–2; labor market, 30, 202, 205, 208–9, 396; labor movement, 62, 69, 72, 77, 103, 119, 274; labor relations legislation, 87; labor socialism, 103; labor-power, 58, 205, 207, 213, 216, 222, 226–27, 237–38; migrant, 130–31, 201–2; organized, 86–88, 90; reserve army of, 15, 238; surplus, 128, 208; white, 207, 209. See also workers; working class
Labour Party (UK), 6, 11, 71, 77, 275. See also New Labour
Lacan, Jacques, 269, 343, 348–52
Laclau, Ernesto, 102, 212–13, 215, 232–33, 376–77, 423, 425
laissez-faire: "laissez-faire period" in British immigration politics, 60; laissez-faire social market, 80. See also markets: free
Lamming, George, 3, 13, 274, 284, 291
LaRose, John, 3
Latin America and Latin Americans, 198, 212–13, 217, 226, 323, 262; Central America, 238
law: common, 87; natural, 304; rule of, 91, 95
"law and order" policies, 63, 73, 78–79, 89, 93–96
Lawrence, Stephen, 399, 434n5; official inquiry regarding his murder, 421, 428–29
League of Coloured Peoples, 277
Leeds, 399, 433n3
Left, the, 57; and antiracist groups, 99
Lenin, Vladimir, 102, 119, 211, 221, 226, 232, 296, 305, 310, 375; Leninist texts, 275
Lévi-Strauss, Claude, 378
Lewis, Monk, 167
liberalism, 68, 108, 420, 425
liberties, 24, 410, 423; defined, 83. See also rights
literature, 4, 30–31, 107–8, 200, 219, 266–67, 275, 315, 318, 379, 382, 430; children's, 108, 283; *Moby-Dick* as "*the* great American novel," 375; nineteenth-century fiction, 108; Shakespeare, 281, 283–84, 375; short stories, 273
Liverpool, 16, 71, 399, 404, 433n3
London, 14–15, 18–19, 23, 123, 276–77, 284, 291, 393, 400, 403, 407; Afro-Caribbean communities in, 412; Brixton, 61, 71, 73, 75, 284, 287, 290, 403, 412; fiction set in, 4, 291–92; police and Special Patrol Group in, 10, 74, 80, 90–92, 434n5; Pan-African movement in, 277; suburbs of, 399; underground scenes in, 287. See also Britain and the United Kingdom; England; Metropolitan Police; Notting Hill

Lonely Londoners (Selvon), 291–92
Long, Edward, 107, 171
Lord Beginner, 287–88. *See also* calypso
Lord Kitchener ("Kitch"; Aldwyn Roberts), 287–88, 290–91. *See also* calypso
Louverture, Toussaint, 173, 277–78, 375–76
Luttwalk, Edward, 384

MacInnes, Colin, 4, 13, 23, 37–40, 150
Manchester, 74, 90, 399, 403, 433n3; *Manchester Guardian*, 275, 374; textile workers in, 213
Manley, Norman, 8
Mann, Michael, 379–80
Mapplethorpe, Robert, 251
marginalization, 211, 246–47, 253, 337, 428; marginalised peoples, 258
Mark, Robert, 74, 80, 89, 91, 96
markets, 35, 58, 80, 83, 205, 207, 212, 389, 402; free, 73, 100, 179, 391; global, 433; labor, 324
Marley, Bob, 13, 191, 266
Maroons, 148, 173, 184
Martinique, 136, 263, 289, 353–54
Marx, Karl, 146, 154, 158, 201–2, 205–27, 233–34, 296, 298–99, 302–5, 308, 310, 357; *Capital* (Marx), 157, 207, 215, 217, 223, 299, 310; *The Eighteenth Brumaire of Louis Bonaparte*, 157; and Fanon, 207; Marxian analyses, 14, 157, 204–6, 208; method of, 217, 223; and Weber, 207
Marxism, 2–4, 105, 188, 200, 207–8, 222, 233, 245, 275–79, 298, 303–5, 313–14, 357; black, 188; classical, 204, 208, 210–11, 215, 220, 296, 299, 302–4, 320, 341; concepts of class in, 156, 204, 207, 324; Fanon and, 341; fundamentalist, 308; Hegelian, 279; James and, 275, 277–79, 375; Marxist analysis, 156–57, 206, 209, 214; Marxist epistemology, 299; Marxist movements, 188, 279;

Marxist paradigm, 208, 211; Marxist scholars, 196, 296, 305, 313; Marxist texts, 202, 275; Marxist theorists, 206, 228, 230, 300; nonreductionist, 228; structuralist, 219, 222, 228, 357n2; Western, 300. *See also Capital*; *The Communist Manifesto*; Gramsci, Antonio; Trotsky, Leon
masculinity, 101, 250; black, 251
masses, 134, 162, 186, 280, 284, 289, 304, 311, 313, 317, 327; mass democracy, 32, 299
master/slave dialectic, 172, 351
McNee, David, 74, 93, 113
McQueen, Steve (filmmaker), 354
media, 4, 8, 16, 51–55, 65, 82–83, 90, 93, 97–100, 102–6, 118, 120, 132, 141, 390, 429–31, 433n1; broadcasters and broadcasting, 51–55, 98, 106, 114; global, 431; mass, 51–52, 63–64, 66, 79, 81, 98; media consultants, 399; new, 108; racism and, 100, 103–16; traditional, 116; white, 51, 53, 55. *See also* BBC; Campaign Against Racism in the Media; television
Meillassoux, Claude, 218
Melodisc, 289
Melville, Herman, 283; James's work on, 280–81, 375
Mercer, Kobena, 269, 341, 353
Merseyside, England, 75, 80
Metropolitan Police (London), 10, 80, 92, 434n5
middle classes, 155, 187–89, 203, 272, 389, 398, 401; Jamaican, 164; middle-class people, 51, 53, 119, 139, 150, 152, 179, 190, 401
Middle East, 381–84, 392, 402; Palestinians, 384
Middle Passage, 163–64, 267, 363
Midnight's Children (Rushdie), 255
Mighty Sparrow, the, 283
Mighty Terror, the, 292

migration, 43, 184, 261, 268, 386–87, 390, 396, 404–7, 414, 419; migrant labor system, 130–31, 202; migrants, 7, 47, 286, 290–91, 334–36, 397, 402, 412; new patterns of, 386–87; postwar, 236. *See also* immigration and immigrants

millenarianism, 180, 182, 185. *See also* religion

Moby-Dick (Melville), 375

Modern Jazz Quartet, 36, 38

modernity, 335–36, 376, 407, 417–18, 422

modes of production, 102, 154, 157, 205, 212, 214–16, 221–22, 225, 229, 298, 305–6; precapitalist, 214, 217, 219

moral panics, 8, 56, 61, 66–67, 404

Morant Bay Rebellion, 177–78

multiculturalism, 5–6, 251–253, 293, 336, 386–407, 410–11, 413, 421–29; debates about, 3, 16, 388–89, 409–33; multiethnic Britain, 16, 70, 287, 292, 403–9, 433

music, 168, 190–91, 286, 289, 403; black British, 290–91; drumming, 109, 167–69, 174, 180, 289; jazz, 39, 333; reggae, 15, 76, 191, 192, 265, 286; ska, 190–91, 286; steel-pan, 286, 289; tambo-bambo, 289. *See also* calypso

Mussolini, Benito, 228, 297, 302

My Beautiful Laundrette (film), 250, 255

myth, 261, 269, 374, 415; regarding Europe, 376–84; Greek, 378–82; popular, 82

Naipaul, V. S., 13, 291

Nanny, 8

Napoleon, 278, 376

National Council for Civil Liberties (NCCL), 10, 14, 80, 96, 112, 120

National Front, 14, 70, 112–13, 116, 134, 398. *See also* Anti-Nazi League

nationalism, 2, 7, 9, 103, 154, 178, 182, 187–88, 232, 252, 270, 300; cultural, 337, 355; romantic, 14

Native Baptists, 175–78

Nazis, 10, 169. *See also* Anti-Nazi League; National Front

Negri, Antonio, 392

Negritude, 258, 347–48, 355

neocolonialism, 219; and dependency, 187, 391

neoliberalism, 9, 16, 390, 392; trickle-down theory, 394. *See also* capitalism; globalization

New Labour, 390, 394–95, 398, 407. *See also* Blair, Tony; Labour Party; neoliberalism

New York, 110, 387, 394, 399, 403

Nixon, Richard, 63

Nkrumah, Kwame, 277, 281, 375

Norris, Christopher, 263

North Africa, 131, 336, 354, 402

Notting Hill, 13, 23, 28, 38–39, 43, 50, 60–62; Notting Hill Carnival, 292

Nowell-Smith, Geoffrey, 300

Nurse, Malcolm, 276–77

O'Callaghan, Marion, 3, 18n6

obeah, 167, 175, 180

Open University, 409, 431–32

orientalism, 250, 260

others, racialized, 43, 63, 336; "otherness," 46, 250–51, 260, 262–63, 267, 340, 342, 351, 375, 378, 382, 404

Padmore, George (Malcolm Nurse), 276–77

Pakistanis, 25, 42, 46, 48, 54, 335–36, 402; Pakistani Workers' Associations, 11

Palmer, Leslie, 13

Pan-African movement, 258, 276–77, 375. *See also* Africa and Africans

Parekh, Bhikhu, 413

Parekh Report, 403

Parry, Benita, 348, 355, 356

Passerini, Luisa, 379

patois, 180, 264, 269, 290, 403

Peach, Blair, 14, 113

peasantry, 150, 155, 211, 230, 301, 310–11, 324
petty-bourgeoisie, 61, 69, 102, 340
Philip, Prince, 288
photography, 38–39, 259, 291
Picasso, Pablo, 284
plantations, 147–55, 158, 177–78, 213–14, 261; overseers on, 171; owners of, 147, 163–65, 180, 354; servitude on, 173, 235, 363, 397. *See also* slaves and slavery
pluralism, 136–43, 153, 202, 242, 249, 410; Caribbean, 4; religious, 397; sociological, 225, 233
police and policing, 6, 8–11, 14–16, 47, 52, 64, 71–77, 86–96, 102, 110–14, 130, 184–85, 407, 428; Metropolitan Police (London), 10, 80, 92, 434n5; Special Patrol Group, 14, 64, 90–92; Police Federation, 71, 80, 94–95, 113; police powers, 11, 90, 93; police racism and harassment, 14, 74–75, 112; Police Superintendents' Association, 94; Southall police riot, 10, 14, 64, 73, 75, 92, 112–13, 120, 401, 412. *See also* "law and order" policies; riots
politics, 2, 52, 55, 63, 66, 76, 128, 290; anti-imperialist, 281; antiracist, 7, 14, 135, 359; black, 8, 249, 251, 285; cultural, 247, 252–53, 318, 329–30; of cultural difference, 337–38; and ideology, 198, 305 (*see also* ideology); and the political elite, 151, 157, 190; and political power, 17, 64, 133, 138, 140, 150, 201, 203; and political struggle, 72, 100, 120, 198, 239, 311, 313, 331–32; and political theory, 318, 419, 425; racial, 12, 134, 113; sexual, 316
populism, 62, 66, 69, 232, 270; populist demonology, 82; populist politics, 7, 10, 13–15, 77, 79, 83, 93
Port of Spain, Trinidad, 273–74, 286, 289, 380

postcolonialism, 11, 209, 258, 340, 345; postcolonial psychopolitics, 5; postcolonial societies, 13, 315, 325, 344, 397
postmodernism, 248, 337
poststructuralism, 248, 340–42, 346
postwar period, 34, 40, 56, 58, 68, 76, 78, 127, 286; in Britain, 12, 56–70, 238
Poulantzas, Nicos, 228, 232, 298
poverty, 15, 40, 52, 68, 158, 187, 266, 335, 337, 347, 387; global, 397; urban, 64
Powell, Enoch, 3, 12, 15, 52, 54, 63, 65, 114, 132, 415; Powellism, 14, 63–64, 114, 116, 132
Prison Notebooks (Gramsci), 297, 300, 327n1
profits, 83, 88, 396, 400
proletariat, 301, 310–11, 319; industrial, 230, 310; plantation, 178–79; rural, 156, 177
psychiatry, 343, 349
psychoanalysis and psychoanalytic concepts, 248, 341–42, 346, 349, 350, 357. *See also* Fanon, Frantz; Freud, Sigmund; Lacan, Jacques; Vergès, Françoise
psychology, 30, 236; psychosexuality, 353
Puerto Rico, 170, 274

race, 1–2, 47, 56–57, 59–61, 63–70, 128–36, 195–225, 234–42, 249–51, 279, 330, 357–65, 367–73; biological and sociological conceptions of, 197; and British media, 51–55, 103–12; in Caribbean society, 136–59; as a floating signifier, 2, 359–60, 362–63, 371–73; Gramsci's work and, 297–325; and ideology, 123–25, 129–30, 132, 134, 237; languages of, 368, 371; politics of, 7, 61, 132, 134; race/color issues, 137–38, 149, 151–53; race relations, 12, 42–43, 53, 62, 106, 125, 132, 135, 199, 239; race riots in Notting Hill, 60–61; race warfare, 15, 112, 201; racial difference, 126, 152, 206,

324, 345–47, 360, 364, 367–68, 371; racial hierarchy and classifying systems, 6–7, 10–11, 217, 330, 363, 365; racialized minorities, 6, 336, 404. *See also* blacks and black existence; ethnicity; racism; skin color

racism, 23, 54, 60–70, 73–75, 97–99, 103–6, 111–17, 124–28, 133–35, 216, 234–37, 239–42, 247–52, 267, 321–22, 325–27, 340–48; anti-Irish, 129; biological, 420–21; cultural, 247, 336; Hall and, 1–6, 9, 11–12, 15; and ideology, 62, 63, 66–70, 105–6, 114–15, 120, 126, 245; indigenous, 5, 9, 58–59, 66, 128, 133, 236; institutional, 10; juridical, 235; and nationalism, 336; new, 404–5, 411; police, 14, 91; polite, 192; racist jokes and slogans, 110–12, 120; and slavery, 164; systemic, 8, 63, 73; trade union, 134; unconscious, 106; working-class, 17, 134, 326. *See also* antiracism; Campaign Against Racism in the Media; race

Ramadhin, Sonny, 282, 288

Ras Tafari (Rastafari) movement, 73, 161, 183–93, 261, 265–66, 384; and politics, 188; Rastafarian art and artists, 190, 259; Rasta language, 186; Rasta symbols, 188; street rastafarianism, 76

Rawick, George, 172–74, 176

Reading Capital (Althusser et al.,), 219, 305–6, 357n2

rebellion, 8, 45, 165, 171–78, 191

reductionism, 225, 241, 302, 303, 306; economic, 197, 199, 217, 220, 304

reggae, 15, 76, 191, 192, 265, 286

religion, 162, 175, 181, 46, 48, 140, 167–68, 314, 325, 384, 413; evangelical, 168, 177–78, 182; millenarianism, 180, 182, 185; missionaries in Caribbean, 166–68, 175–77; obeah, 167, 175, 180; preachers, 180–84; religious bigotry, 420; religious cults, 167, 381; religious fervour, 176–78; Revivalism, 177, 180–81, 183. *See also* Afro-Christianity; Christianity; individual churches

representation, 3, 103, 105, 109, 151, 231, 326, 332, 378, 388, 411, 415; "burden of," 248, 329; cultural, 430; economic, 84; political, 81, 83, 86, 227, 239–40; race and, 5, 241, 247–48, 250–55, 257–60, 262–70, 343–51, 364

reserve army of labor, 15, 60, 130, 238

resistance, cultures of, 161–62, 172, 174, 192, 241

Revival Zion, 181

revolutions and revolutionary struggles, 279, 284, 345, 354–55; in France, 376; revolutionary consciousness, 340–41

Rex, John, 200–211, 214, 216

Rey, Pierre-Philippe, 218–19

rights, 6, 57, 72, 76, 79–86, 88, 92, 94, 97, 112–13, 203, 247, 255, 376, 388–89, 420; civil, 86, 96, 163, 333; property, 146; workers,' 87, 89–90

riots, 12–13, 15, 21, 71–77, 91, 112–13, 184. *See also* crime; violence

Roberts, Aldwyn. *See* Lord Kitchener

Roberts, John, 380

Robeson, Paul, 276, 277

Robinson, Cedric, 340

Rose, Jacqueline, 342

Rude Boys, 188, 191

ruling class, 69, 103–4, 176, 178, 186, 228–31, 310, 314–15

Runnymede Trust, 16, 90, 409, 433n1

Rushdie, Salman, 254–55

Russia, 221, 310, 313; Russian Revolution, 277, 285, 313, 375

Salkey, Andrew, 3, 13

Sambo stereotype, 108, 110, 163, 170–74, 180. *See also* stereotypes and stereotyping

Sammy and Rosie Get Laid (film), 250, 255

INDEX | 449

Sartre, Jean-Paul, 348, 351–52, 354–55
Saussure, Ferdinand de, 222, 263
schools. *See* education
science, 30, 158, 304–6, 312, 347, 365–67, 380; cultural function of, 366; science museums, 393
Scott, David, 375, 376
Seaga, Edward, 268
secondary modern schools, 24–25, 31–32. *See also* education
Selvon, Sam, 274, 291
Senghor, Léopold Sédar, 258, 264, 355
sex and sexuality, 9, 27, 39, 44, 129–30, 250–51, 255, 291, 346, 357–58, 389
sexism, 129, 134
Shakespeare, William, 281, 283–84, 375
Shyllon, Folarin, 12
Simmel, Georg, 375
Sivanandan, A., 60
ska, 190–91, 286
skin color, 38, 46, 48, 49, 75, 136–39, 142–44, 147, 149–53, 155–57, 163, 178, 239, 241, 255, 266, 269, 353, 376, 403–4, 420; and class, 137; the color line, 388; epidermalization, 342, 345; "mulattos," 107, 163, 263, 265. *See also* blacks and black existence; ethnicity; race; racism
slaves and slavery, 144–49, 163–78, 181, 187, 189, 192, 213–15, 235–37, 240, 259–66, 278, 333–36, 351–52, 355, 375–76; folk culture of, 166, 175, 179, 190; housing, 145, 264, 376; history of, 107, 172, 236; slave labor, 173, 237; plantations, 144–47, 163–65, 167, 180, 201, 213–14, 235, 376; rebellions, 170–76; revolution, 275, 277, 374–75; society, 144–47, 163–79, 324, 353; stereotypes, 108, 110; suicide, 168; slave trade, 56, 58, 107, 144, 163–64, 176, 213–14, 219, 397; slave owners, 133, 165, 167–68, 170–71, 213–14
Smith, Michael G., 138, 141, 147, 156, 197, 200–201

smoking, 184, 185, 188, 330, 338; ganja, 184
social class. *See* class
social conflict, 80, 86–87, 200–201
social formations, 59, 100, 125, 219–22, 224–33, 235–37, 239–40, 299, 302–6, 322–23; agricultural, 218; capitalist, 199–202, 205–7, 214; postcolonial, 209–10; racially structured, 195–97, 215, 233, 325
social mobility, 144, 149, 152
social science, 123, 125, 127, 197–98, 296, 305, 409, 413. *See also* sociology and sociologists
Socialist Party, 301
sociology and sociologists, 12, 72, 127, 185, 200, 242, 360, 409. *See also* social science
Souls of Black Folk, The (Du Bois), 360
South Africa, 5, 40, 69, 152, 196, 199–209, 215–16, 218, 227, 311; Cape Coloureds, 203
"South African Society in Comparative Perspective" (Rex), 200
Soviet Union, 34, 276, 279, 280, 301, 383, 391
Spain and Spanish people, 163, 268, 284, 380, 431
Spinoza, Baruch, 222, 384
Spivak, Gayatri, 250
sports, 275, 282. *See also* cricket
Stalin, Joseph, 276, 278; Stalinism, 275, 280, 284
state, 65, 67, 74, 78–81, 84, 86, 89, 105, 228–30, 252–53, 311–16, 320, 325, 392–93; state capitalism, 279
status, cultural/class, 27, 31, 149–50, 152–53, 202; migrant, 131
Steed, Maggie, 99
stereotypes and stereotyping, 4, 49, 52, 107–8, 170–71, 112, 173, 412; Sambo stereotype, 108, 110, 163, 170–74, 180; sexual, 99; stereotyped black villains, 54

stratification, social, 136–39, 143, 147, 149–52, 155, 200, 204, 206, 210, 301, 397; stratification matrix, 152
structuralism, 223, 369; structuralist linguistics, 222; structuralist Marx, 357n2
subalternity, 310, 375, 405
sugar, 58, 154–55; sugar plantations, 144, 148, 179
superstructures, 229, 231, 304, 306, 308, 313
Suriname, 136–37, 148
"Sweet Jamaica" (song), 291
syncretism, cultural, 153, 162, 403

Tebit test, 336
Teddy Boys (Teds), 36–38, 62, 66
teenagers. *See* adolescence and adolescents
television, 4, 36–39, 52–54, 71, 105–18, 417, 429; children's, 54; editors and journalists, 88, 104; racism on, 116; Thames Television Schools, 99. *See also* BBC; media
Terray, Emmanuel, 218
Thatcher, Margaret, 14, 71, 74, 101, 103, 336; cabinet of, 16; Thatcherism, 6, 103, 116, 247, 253
There Ain't No Black in the Union Jack (Gilroy), 254
Third World, 110, 188, 253, 339, 355, 374, 423
tobacco, 35–36
trade, free, 391, 396
trade unions, 11, 14, 73, 87, 141, 151, 163, 316, 326; racism in, 134
traditionalism, 79, 83, 93, 94, 417
transnationalization, 329, 390, 392, 403, 431. *See also* globalization
trauma, 5, 34, 186, 370
Trinidad, 13, 136–37, 140, 148, 150–51, 261, 272–74, 276, 281–82, 285, 287–91, 374–75; carnival in, 283; creole speech patterns in, 290; labor movement in, 273–74; music in, 291; nationalist movement in, 281
Trotsky, Leon, 276–79, 296; in England, 275; in Mexico, 279, 375; Trotskyism, 72, 113, 275–81, 375

Underground Railroad, 173
unemployment, 64–65, 75, 103, 130–31, 387, 396, 398
UNESCO, 4, 18n6, 158, 162
unions. *See* trade unions
United Kingdom. *See* Britain and the United Kingdom; England
United Nations, 211, 391
United States. *See* America and Americans
Universal Negro Improvement Association, 182, 276. *See also* Garvey, Marcus
universalism, 407, 424; humanist, 355
universities, 2, 40–41, 410, 432
University of Birmingham, 87

Valentine, A., 282, 288
Van Vechten, Carl, 278
Vanity Fair (Thackeray), 273, 375
Vergès, Françoise, 349
Victoria, Queen, 393, 416
Vietnam, 310; Vietnam War, 62
violence, 28, 72, 89–90, 185, 187, 201; cool, 37; ethnic, 420; racial, 419; suppressed, 345; teenage, 61; unconscious, 76; urban, 38, 266. *See also* crime; "law and order" policies; police and policing; riots
visual art. *See* art; artists; photography
vulgar materialism, 220, 304

Wacquant, Loïc, 410
wages and wage labor, 73, 101, 103, 202, 218; minimum wage, 396, 402
Walcott, Clyde, 282
Walvin, James, 12, 56
"war on terror," 404, 407

Weber, Max, 204–6, 296; and Marx, 207, 401
Weeks, Everton, 282, 283
welfare, 46, 53, 131, 391, 402; "scroungers," 64, 81–83; welfare state, 29, 37, 64, 80–84, 393, 416
West, Cornel, 338n1
West, the, 184, 262, 299–300, 313–14, 336, 405; Western civilization, 375, 406, 410; Westerners, 423, 424; Westernization, 418
West Africa, 163–67, 183, 189, 259, 402; returning to, 183; postcolonial, 355; as source of enslaved Jamaicans, 164
West Indies, 45, 145–46, 148, 282; West Indians, 23, 25, 28, 40, 42–43, 46, 48, 51, 274, 282–83, 286–88, 291, 336, 355. *See also* Caribbean, the; Jamaica and Jamaicans
whites, 43, 47, 49, 97, 99, 101, 103, 105–20, 131, 135, 178, 183–84, 188, 200, 209, 255, 266, 282, 402, 412, 428; white bias, 145, 155, 179; colonizers, 150–51, 165–67, 340; white creole elites, 136–37; immigrants, 238–39; indentured labor, 144, 235; missionaries, 175, 177; oppressors, 110, 147–51, 165, 182, 184, 186; planter class, 151, 154; pride, 8; White Power skinheads, 14; women, 149, 353; working class, 60–62, 73, 202, 208–9, 236, 240, 311, 398; youths, 13, 47, 61, 75–76, 398–99. *See also* plantations; race; racism
Williams, Eric, 177, 213, 273, 278, 281–82, 375
Williams, Raymond, 53
Wilson, Harold, 11
Windrush, ss *Empire*, 286–88, 292, 421; *Windrush* generation, 11
Wolpe, Harold, 200, 207–9, 215–18

women, 43, 382; black slave, 147; women's suffrage, 81
workers, 58, 88–90, 101, 202, 213, 280, 396, 406; black migrant, 127; skilled, 147. *See also* labor
working class, 62, 64–69, 73, 77, 103, 105, 134, 200, 209, 236–37, 239, 308, 324, 326; districts, 68, 401; families, 46, 53; modern, 300–301; semi-skilled, 51; urban, 87; working-class youth, 8, 27–28, 31, 120. *See also* labor; workers
World Bank, 391
world economy, 154, 199, 211–15, 235, 387. *See also* globalization
World War I, 274, 301
World War II: global change after, 391–92, 395; migration from Caribbean after, 11, 286–87. *See also* postwar period
Worrell, Frank, 282, 283
Wretched of the Earth, The (Fanon), 340, 343, 354
Wright, Richard, 278
WTO (World Trade Organization), 391, 395
Wynter, Sylvia, 3

young people, 14–15, 23–40, 42–49, 61–66, 188, 403, 410; black youths, 47, 49, 65, 113; and British schools, 23–33; clubs for, 23, 26, 32, 45; and crime/violence, 27–28, 34, 39; Muslim, 398, 404; spending by, 35–37; working-class, 8, 27–28, 31; youth culture, 12, 35–37, 44; young Englanders, 12, 42–50
Young Tiger (George Brown), 288–89. *See also* calypso

Žižek, Slavoj, 410

PLACE OF FIRST PUBLICATION

Chapter 1: "Absolute Beginnings: Reflections on the Secondary Modern Generation." *Universities and Left Review*, no. 7 (Autumn 1959): 16–25.

Chapter 2: *The Young Englanders*. London: National Committee of Commonwealth Immigrants, 1967.

Chapter 3: "Black Men, White Media." *Savacou* 9/10 (1974): 97–101.

Chapter 4: "Race and 'Moral Panics' in Postwar Britain." Public lecture, British Sociological Association, London, May 2, 1978. In BBC, *Five Views of Multi-racial Britain*, 23–35. London: Commission for Racial Equality, 1978.

Chapter 5: "Summer in the City." *New Socialist* (September/October 1981): 4–7.

Chapter 6: *Drifting into a Law and Order Society: The 1979 Cobden Trust Human Rights Day Lecture*. London: Cobden Trust, 1980.

Chapter 7: "The Whites of Their Eyes: Racist Ideologies and the Media." In *Silver Linings: Some Strategies for the Eighties*, edited by George Bridges and Rosalind Brunt, 28–52. London: Lawrence and Wishart, 1981.

Chapter 8: "Teaching Race." *Multiracial Education* 9, no. 1 (1980): 3–14.

Chapter 9: "Pluralism, Race and Class in Caribbean Society." In *Race and Class in Post-colonial Society: A Study of Ethnic Group Relations in the English-Speaking Caribbean, Bolivia, Chile and Mexico*, 150–84. Paris: UNESCO, 1977.

Chapter 10: "'Africa' Is Alive and Well in the Diaspora: Cultures of Resistance: Slavery, Religious Revival and Political Cultism in Jamaica.'" Paper presented at UNESCO

Seminar on Social Structure, Revolutionary Change and Culture in Southern Africa, Maputo, Mozambique, July 1976.

Chapter 11: "Race, Articulation and Societies Structured in Dominance." In *Sociological Theories: Race and Colonialism*, 305–45. Paris: UNESCO, 1980.

Chapter 12: "New Ethnicities." In *ICA Documents, 7, Black Film, British Cinema*, edited by Kobena Mercer, 27–31. London: Institute of Contemporary Arts, 1988.

Chapter 13: "Cultural Identity and Diaspora." In *Identity: Community, Culture, Difference*, edited by Jonathan Rutherford, 222–37. London: Lawrence and Wishart, 1990. First published as "Cultural Identity and Cinematic Representation," *Framework*, no. 36 (1989): 68–81.

Chapter 14: "C. L. R. James: A Portrait." In *C. L. R. James's Caribbean*, edited by Henry Paget and Paul Buhle, 3–16. Durham, NC: Duke University Press, 1992.

Chapter 15: "Calypso Kings." *Guardian*, June 28, 2002.

Chapter 16: "Gramsci's Relevance for the Study of Race and Ethnicity." *Journal of Communication Inquiry* 10, no. 2 (1986): 5–27.

Chapter 17: "Subjects in History: Making Diasporic Identities." In *The House That Race Built*, edited by Wahneema Lubiano, 289–300. New York: Vintage, 1998.

Chapter 18: From "The After-Life of Frantz Fanon: Why Fanon? Why Now? Why *Black Skin, White Masks*?" In *The Fact of Blackness: Frantz Fanon and Visual Representation*, edited by Alan Read, 12–37. London: Institute of Contemporary Arts; Seattle: Bay Press, 1996.

Chapter 19: "Race, the Floating Signifier." Transcript of the film *Race: The Floating Signifier*, directed by Sut Jhally. Northampton, MA: Media Education Foundation, 1997.

Chapter 20: "In but Not of Europe: Europe and Its Myths." *Soundings*, no. 22 (Winter 2002/2003): 57–69.

Chapter 21: "Cosmopolitan Promises, Multicultural Realities." In *Divided Cities: The Oxford Amnesty Lectures, 2003*, edited by Richard Scholar, 20–49. Oxford: Oxford University Press, 2006.

Chapter 22: "The Multicultural Question." This text is based on a transcript of an October 19, 2000, Pavis Lecture given by Hall at the Walton Hall Campus, Open University, Milton Keynes. A different version of the text was published as an essay in *Un/Settled Multiculturalisms: Diasporas, Entanglements, Transruptions*, edited by Barnor Hesse, 209–41. London: Zed Books, 2000.